D0985204

PENGUIN CLASSICS

CAPTAIN AMERICA

Born Jacob Kurtzberg in 1917 to Jewish-Austrian parents on New York's Lower East Side, JACK KIRBY came of age at the birth of the American comic book industry. Horrified by the rise of Nazism, Kirby co-created the patriotic hero Captain America with Joe Simon in 1940. Cap's exploits on the comic book page entertained millions of American readers at home and inspired US troops fighting the enemy abroad. Kirby's partnership with Simon continued throughout the 1940s and early '50s; together, they produced comics in every popular genre, from Western to romance. In 1958, Kirby began his equally fruitful collaboration with writer-editor Stan Lee, and in 1961 the two men co-created the foundational text of the modern Marvel Universe: *The Fantastic Four*. Over the next decade, Kirby and Lee would introduce a mind-boggling array of new characters—including the Avengers, the Hulk, Thor, Iron Man, the Silver Surfer, and the X-Men. Kirby's groundbreaking work with Lee formed the foundation of the Marvel Universe. In the early 1970s, Kirby moved to DC Comics, where he created his interconnected Fourth World series, as well as freestanding titles such as *The Demon*. He returned to Marvel in 1975, writing and illustrating The Black Panther and Captain America, and introducing series such as Devil Dinosaur, and the Eternals. Kirby died in 1994. Today, he is generally regarded as one of the most important and influential creators in the history of American comics. His work has inspired multiple generations of writers, artists, designers, and filmmakers, who continue to explore his vast universe of concepts and characters. He was an inaugural inductee into the Eisner Hall of Fame in 1987.

While sharing a studio with Jack Kirby, artist JOE SIMON co-created Captain America, a stirring symbol of American idealism and pride during the war-torn 1940s. Simon and Kirby would go on to form one of the most productive partnerships of the early American comic book industry. The two men co-created comics in every genre—crime, war, horror, science fiction, Western, humor, and romance—for numerous different publishers between 1940 and 1954. Noted characters and series included the Sandman and the Newsboy Legion for DC Comics, Young Romance for Crestwood, and Boys' Ranch for Harvey. Simon also wrote two autobiographies— *The Comic Book Makers* (1990), coauthored with his son, Jim Simon, and *Joe Simon: My Life in Comics* (2011)—essential reading for any historian of comic book history and culture.

Writer-editor STAN LEE (1922–2018) and artist Jack Kirby made comic book history in 1961 with *The Fantastic Four* #1. The success of its new style inspired Lee and his many collaborators to develop a number of new super heroes, including, with Jack Kirby, the Incredible Hulk and the X-Men; with Steve Ditko, the Amazing Spider-Man and Doctor Strange; and with Bill Everett, Daredevil. Lee oversaw the adventures of these creations for more than a decade before handing over the editorial reins at Marvel to others and focusing on developing Marvel's properties in other media. For the remainder of his long life, he continued to serve as a creative figurehead at Marvel and as an ambassador for the comics medium as a whole. In his final years, Lee's signature cameo appearances in Marvel's films established him as one of the world's most famous faces.

JIM STERANKO rocked the comic book world in the late 1960s with a revolutionary approach to design and narrative, influenced by the contemporary worlds of both commercial and fine art. Steranko produced very little comics work after the 1970s, but his illustrations would grace the covers of numerous science fiction and fantasy novels, as well as film posters and record album sleeves. He has also produced character designs for a number of filmmakers, including George Lucas, Steven Spielberg, and Francis Ford Coppola. His two-volume *History of Comics* was one of the first modern works of comics scholarship, and his film industry magazine *Prevue* enjoyed an impressive twenty-five-year run. Steranko was inducted into the Eisner Hall of Fame in 2006.

JOHN ROMITA SR. was born in Brooklyn in 1930 and attended Manhattan's School of Industrial Art before entering the comic book industry in 1949. He drew many comics for Marvel (then known as Timely or Atlas) during the early 1950s before moving to DC Comics in 1958, where he established a reputation as a master of romance comics. In 1965 he returned to Marvel, inking Don Heck's pencils on an issue of the Avengers. After a short stint penciling *Daredevil*, Romita Sr. was tapped by Stan Lee to take over *The Amazing Spider-Man* when original artist Steve Ditko left the book. Romita Sr. brought a new emotional warmth to the series, while his slick, clean craftsmanship took the title to even greater commercial heights. His renditions of the title character, as well as supporting cast members such as Gwen Stacy and Mary Jane Watson, were considered definitive by a generation of fans. In the 1970s, Stan Lee appointed Romita Sr. as art director for the company; while in this position, he helped design numerous characters (including the Punisher, Wolverine, and Luke Cage). He was inducted into the Eisner Hall of Fame in 2002.

GENE LUEN YANG is a MacArthur "genius," the fifth National Ambassador for Young People's Literature, and the author of the half-million-copy *New York Times*–bestselling graphic novel and National Book Award Finalist *American Born Chinese*. He lives in San Jose, California.

BEN SAUNDERS is a professor of English at the University of Oregon. He is the author of *Desiring Donne: Poetry, Sexuality, Interpretation* and *Do the Gods Wear Capes?: Spirituality, Fantasy, and Superheroes*, as well as numerous critical essays on subjects ranging from the writings of Shakespeare to the recordings of Little Richard. He has also curated several museum exhibitions of comics art, including the record-breaking multimedia touring show *Marvel: Universe of Super Heroes*—a retrospective exploring the artistic and cultural impact of Marvel Comics from 1939 to the present.

CAPTAIN AMERICA

Debuting in 1941—almost a year before the events of Pearl Harbor—
Captain America was initially conceived by Joe Simon and Jack
Kirby as a pop-culture argument for US intervention in the European war against fascism. His fortunes faded with the end of that
conflict, but in the 1960s, Stan Lee teamed up with Kirby to bring
Cap back. This collection includes his very first appearances from
1941 alongside key examples of his first solo stories of the 1960s, in
which the newly resurrected hero of World War II struggles to find
his place in a new and unfamiliar world. As the contents reveal, the
transformation of this American icon marks a parallel transformation in the nation itself.

The Penguin Classics Marvel Collection presents these influential comics in a scholarly context for the first time. The detailed introduction offers insight into the social and political significance of
Captain America both as a character and as a national symbol, while
an extended critical apparatus and appendixes shed further light on
his creative development. This volume features a new foreword by
Gene Luen Yang.

PENGUIN CLASSICS
MARVEL COLLECTION

It is impossible to imagine American popular culture without Marvel Comics. For decades, Marvel has published groundbreaking visual narratives that sustain attention on multiple levels: as explorations of the relationship between power and responsibility; as metaphors for the experience of difference and otherness; as meditations on the pain of adolescence and the fluid nature of identity; as examinations of the meaning, and limits, of patriotism; as ironic juxtapositions of the cosmic and the quotidian; as resources for the understanding of political and social history; and as high-water marks in the artistic tradition of American cartooning.

These carefully curated collections present the foundational tales and characters of the Marvel Universe as Penguin Classics. Scholarly introductions and supplemental materials provide essential context for the modern reader, while forewords by contemporary authors speak to the enduring significance of Spider-Man, the Fantastic Four, the X-Men, and many other iconic creations. The Penguin Classics Marvel Collection serves as a testament to Marvel's transformative and timeless influence on an entire genre of fantasy.

JACK KIRBY, JOE SIMON,
STAN LEE, JIM STERANKO,
AND JOHN ROMITA SR.

Captain America

Foreword by
GENE LUEN YANG

Edited with an Introduction by
BEN SAUNDERS

Series Editor
BEN SAUNDERS

PENGUIN BOOKS

PENGUIN BOOKS

An imprint of Penguin Random House LLC
penguinrandomhouse.com

© 2022 MARVEL

Series introduction, volume introduction, critical synopses, appendixes, and compilation
copyright © 2022 by Ben Saunders
Foreword copyright © 2022 by Gene Luen Yang

ISBN 9780143135746 (hardcover)
ISBN 9780143135753 (paperback)

Printed in China
1 3 5 7 9 10 8 6 4 2

Set in Sabon LT Pro

Contents

CAPTAIN AMERICA

Series Introduction

If you were suddenly gifted with powers that set you apart from ordinary humanity, what would you do?

For the first generation of comic book super heroes, launched in the late 1930s, the answer was obvious: You used your special abilities for the benefit of others. You became a "champion for the helpless and oppressed" and waged an "unceasing battle against evil and injustice."[1]

It was a fantasy predicated on the effortless fusion of moral certainty with aggressive action, the national appetite for which only increased after America's entry into the Second World War in 1941. More than seven hundred super-powered do-gooders debuted in the boom years of 1938–1945.[2] Collectively, they helped to transform the comic book business from a vestigial limb of print culture into a muscular arm of the modern entertainment industry.[3] With the social tensions and abiding inequalities of US culture temporarily obscured by the Nazi threat, super heroes even came to emblematize the (sometimes contradictory) principles of individualism, democracy, and consumerism: the American way.[4]

After the war, comics remained big business—the genres of romance, Western, crime, horror, and humor all thrived—but audiences turned decisively away from super heroes.[5] Indeed, by the summer of 1953, the costumed crime-fighter appeared on the verge of extinction. Of the hundreds of characters that had once crowded the newsstands, only five still had their own titles: Quality Comics' Plastic Man and DC Comics' Superman, Superboy, Batman, and Wonder Woman.[6] Old-fashioned products of a simpler time, they were ripe targets for satire.[7] There were sporadic attempts to revive the craze, of course—most notably in 1954, when a wave of national hysteria over the putative effects of crime and horror comics on younger readers led several publishers to seek more parent-friendly alternatives. The companies of Ajax, Atlas, Charlton, Harvey, Magazine Enterprises, Prize, and Sterling all tried out a few super hero books in an effort to recapture a small portion of the market that they once had dominated. Significantly, all failed.[8]

No single factor can definitively explain this shift in popular taste, but clearly times had changed. Against the background of the wasteful and inconclusive war in Korea, the vicious theater of McCarthyism, and the ugly response to the first stirrings of the civil rights movement in Montgomery, Alabama, the moral simplicity of the super hero fantasy looked naïve at best and reactionary at worst. Clearly, if super heroes were going to be revived successfully, they would have to be reinvented.

The process began at DC Comics, the only American comic book publisher to have a real stake in the genre at the time, with the return of the Flash in mid-1956.[9] Writer Bob Kanigher revised the concept (which dated back to 1940), adding a self-reflexive element; his hero, Barry Allen, had a nostalgic fondness for old Flash comics. Kanigher thereby acknowledged and incorporated DC's earlier Flash stories while simultaneously placing them at an ironic distance—making his own tale seem more authentic and contemporary. The summer of 1959 saw a similar modernization of the Green Lantern. The origin story of the first Lantern, from almost twenty years prior, has been a messy Orientalist hodgepodge; the new version drew on science fiction tropes more suited to the age of the space race. In late 1959, these revitalized heroes joined forces with Superman, Batman, and Wonder Woman to form a team: the Justice League of America.

The strong sales of the JLA made other publishers sit up and take notice. Among them was Martin Goodman, the owner of the company not yet known as Marvel.[10] Goodman had enjoyed plenty of success with super hero comics in the 1940s and owned the rights to such former hits as Captain America, the Human Torch—somewhat misnamed, as he was actually a flame-powered android—and Namor the Sub-Mariner. (A true original, the Sub-Mariner was perhaps the only super-powered character of the first generation to regard ordinary humanity with open hostility.) But Goodman had canceled all his super hero books in 1949 to pursue more popular trends.[11] Now, at the dawn of the '60s, half the titles in his comics division were romances or "teen humor" titles, while the other half was divided among war, Western, and "monster" books—anthologies that served up a different B-movie-style menace month after month—without a single super hero in the bunch.

Goodman decided that he needed a super team of his own on the shelves, fast, and assigned the job to a writer-editor named Stanley Lieber, better known today as Stan Lee. A cousin of Goodman's wife, Lee had joined the company in 1939 at the age of seventeen, rising to oversee Goodman's entire line. He'd grown up in the comic book industry, knew all its formulas and limitations, and longed to transcend them—but by his own account, he was starting to wonder if he ever would. When Goodman told him to create a copycat Justice League, Lee turned for help to Jack Kirby, a veteran artist who had co-created Captain America (among many other super heroes) with Joe Simon back in the 1940s. The result of their collaboration would be far more than a knockoff of the latest trend, however. Drawing inspiration from multiple sources, the two men managed to blend a whole new pop-cultural cocktail: a transformative take on the super hero. The comic was called The Fantastic Four, and in its pages, Lee and Kirby would also map out the basic contours of the Marvel Universe.

The Fantastic Four focused on a super team that was also a family. This simple choice immediately brought a new level of emotional dynamism to the super hero genre. The members of the Four loved one another fiercely, but like all families (and unlike the super friends of the JLA), they also bickered and fought. They were distinct individuals, with their own virtues and, more important, their own flaws. Lee and Kirby also added a previously unexplored dimension of tragedy to the generic mix with the character of the Thing—who was crippled with self-loathing after his transformation into a hideous behemoth. At the same time, Lee and Kirby took the potential for self-reflexivity that Kanigher had glimpsed in his revival of the Flash to even greater heights: playing with conventions, occasionally breaking the fourth wall, and cleverly insulating themselves against the charge of naivete with a protective layer of irony. The result was surprisingly tonally complex—a self-conscious mixture of comedy and drama for which there really was no precedent in super hero comics.[12]

The Fantastic Four was the first bona fide hit that Goodman's company had enjoyed in a while. Galvanized by success, Lee and Kirby co-created several more of their new breed of super heroes between late 1961 and late 1963—introducing the characters of Ant-Man, the Incredible Hulk, the Mighty Thor, Iron Man, Sergeant Nick Fury, and the X-Men in that short span. (It should be noted that Lee's brother, Larry Lieber, wrote the first scripts for Ant-Man, Thor, and Iron Man after receiving short synopses from Lee. Similarly, artist Don Heck drew the first Iron Man story after receiving a character design from Kirby.) Lee and Kirby also somehow found time to unite several of these new characters in a title called The Avengers (launched in July 1963 on the same day as the X-Men), and to bring back a war-traumatized version of Captain America in the fourth issue. All the while, they continued to create new stories and characters every month in the pages of the Fantastic Four. As if that were not enough, working in collaboration with artist Steve Ditko, Lee co-created and launched Spider-Man and Doctor Strange during the same period.[13]

It was an astounding burst of creativity over the course of which Goodman's company forged a new brand identity: Marvel Comics. Developing and extending the formula of the Fantastic Four, Marvel's new characters were "Super Heroes with Super Problems."[14] At times they struggled to do the right thing—and frequently they did not seem to know whether to regard their powers as a blessing or as a curse. Nor were they necessarily regarded with respect and admiration in their communities, but were just as likely to be regarded as criminals or monsters. Suddenly, it was no longer quite so obvious how you were supposed to respond if you were granted powers beyond those of ordinary humanity—or how ordinary humanity would respond to you.

Marvel's reinvention of the super hero comic book did not end with these changes, however. As the overseer of all of Marvel's titles, Lee also decided to locate the new characters in the same story-world. Events in one comic could thus be referenced in another, and characters could cross over from title to title—giving the impression that every comic in the line was part of one huge story. This development of what we might call "lateral continuity" across different titles was matched with more extended forms of linear continuity within the individual series. The dominant mode of comic book narrative at the time, even in the most enduring franchise, was that of the self-contained episode—so that it hardly mattered in what order one read, say, the Batman comics published in any given year. Now Lee, Kirby, and Ditko began to experiment with long-running subplots, such as the arc of Reed and Sue's romance in the Fantastic Four, or the mystery of the Green Goblin's identity in the Amazing Spider-Man—storylines that were developed over months and even years, in the manner of a soap opera.

These ever more elaborate forms of continuity rewarded the most-devoted readers—something that Lee was quick to recognize and embrace as one of several tools he would employ to fan the flames of Marvel fandom. Indeed, Lee's skillful fostering of fan culture was every bit as important to the success of the company as was his work as a writer. He began to address the growing readership in a distinctive editorial voice, combining the hyperbole of a carnival barker with the hipster flippancy of a rock and roll DJ, and cultivating a (largely fictitious) image of a carefree office space—the "Marvel Bullpen"—in which "Jolly" Jack Kirby and "Sturdy" Steve Ditko and the rest of the gang assembled the machinery of the "Marvel Revolution." (In fact, Ditko had his own office space, while Kirby generally worked at home.)

As the public face of Marvel, Lee was brilliant: compellingly persuasive with regard not only to his faith in Marvel's products but also to the potential of comics as an aesthetic form. Long after he had ceased to create comics, he remained a great ambassador for Marvel and for the medium as a whole. But among the many hundreds of journalists with whom Lee spoke over the years, few actually understood the process whereby Marvel Comics were produced. Frequently, he was treated as the sole author of the franchise, rather than a key member of a creative organization. These misunderstandings would later become a source of bitterness between Lee and several of his closest artistic partners—particularly Jack Kirby and Steve Ditko, who continued to labor in relative obscurity throughout the 1970s and '80s, while Lee became that most unlikely of things: a comic book celebrity.

But the true origins of Marvel Comics were fundamentally collaborative, as Lee himself acknowledged to an audience of fans at the San Diego Comic-Con in 1975:

> The way we worked, for those of you who don't know, is not the way they work at other companies, where the writer writes the script, and it's given to an artist, and the artist draws it, and that's the end of it. With us, it's a marriage of talents. The artist and writer will discuss the plots together, then the artist goes off to his little nook where he works, and he—without benefit of script—only with this vague, ridiculous plot that he's discussed—goes and draws the whole story all by himself. . . . Then, when the writer has to put in the copy, just imagine how much easier it is to look at a drawing and suit the dialogue perfectly to the expression of the character's face—to what the drawing represents—than to try and write perfect dialogue when you're looking at a blank sheet of paper, trying to imagine what the drawing will be like. . . .
>
> The artists are great storytellers themselves. They know which sequence to enlarge upon, which to cut short. . . . They'd put in characters I knew nothing about. . . . The competition still hasn't learned [that] this technique gives our stories a certain freshness, a spirit, that I think is Marvel.[15]

This way of working eventually became known as the "Marvel Method," and as these comments make clear, Lee liked it precisely because it gave artists such as Kirby and Ditko more control than the traditional "full script" method, where the details of page breakdowns and dialogue were decided by the writer beforehand. As Lee also acknowledges here, he was happy to place a very significant amount of storytelling responsibility in the artists' hands—to the point that they would add numerous elements that he had not anticipated and "knew nothing about." In addition, Lee felt that this profoundly collaborative creative process was essential to the "spirit" of Marvel and helped to set the company apart from the competition.

But understanding the Marvel Method is only the first step in appreciating the extent to which artistic labor was broadly distributed at Marvel in the 1960s. There was certainly room for key creators such as Lee, Kirby, and Ditko to place their distinctive, individual stamp upon the work, but they made their comics within a factory system where many vital tasks were dispersed across multiple hands. Their astonishing rate of productivity would not otherwise have been possible. Besides Lee's regular reliance on his brother, Larry, for scripting assistance, for example, we have to consider the fact that Kirby almost never inked his own work; his penciled pages were "embellished" (as the process was sometimes called) by numerous different artists, including Dick Ayers, Vince Colletta, Paul Reinmann, George Roussos, Joe Sinnott, and Chic Stone. Consequently, when we look at a page by Kirby, it is actually almost never by him alone. (This does not diminish Kirby's status as one of the most significant comic book creators of the past century, but it does make the task of thinking critically about his achievement that much more complex.) Lettering and coloring were also separate but highly skilled jobs—the former task generally handled at Marvel in the early days by Artie Simek or Sam Rosen, while Stan Goldberg and Marie Severin were responsible for the latter. Marvel's cultural ascendance over the course of the '60s was then further abetted by a number of talented creators who continued to develop the properties that Lee, Lieber, Kirby, Ditko, and Heck had launched—John Buscema, Gene Colan, John Romita Sr., Jim Steranko, Herb Trimpe, and Roy Thomas chief among them.[16]

To summarize their collective achievements in a single sentence:

together, these creators expanded the emotional and aesthetic horizons of an entire genre of fantasy in ways that continue to reverberate across the popular culture of the twenty-first century. The works that they produced were long ago accorded "classic" status by comic book fans and industry professionals alike—and as the primary source material for the Marvel Cinematic Universe, their influence has only grown, registering now on a global scale. And moreover—as teachers and scholars in numerous disciplines are now beginning to realize—these classic super hero stories can sustain intellectual scrutiny on multiple levels: as explorations of the relationship between power and responsibility; as intriguing metaphors for the experience of racial difference; as meditations on the pain of adolescence; as examinations of the meaning, and limits, of patriotism; as reflections on the joys and challenges of family life; as experiments in the juxtaposition of the cosmic and the quotidian; as the artistic working through of a variety of forms of trauma; as unexpected resources for the understanding of our political and social history; as revealing representations of our shifting attitudes toward various categories of identity; and as high aesthetic watermarks in the semiotically rich tradition of American cartooning. As such, these comics not only continue to give pleasure to readers everywhere but also merit our deepest critical engagement—something that this Marvel Penguin Classics series is designed to foster.

BEN SAUNDERS

Foreword

Back when I was in high school, new comic books came out every Friday. After the last bell, my friend Jason and I would pick up my little brother and drive to our neighborhood comic bookstore. My brother was in the seventh grade.

What high school junior wants to hang out with a seventh grader? We took him with us to keep him from snitching.

My immigrant parents didn't approve of me wasting money on frivolities like comic books. I'd earned the money myself by working at our local department store, but that didn't matter. In the Chinese way of thinking, my money was my parents' money until I got married.

Every Friday afternoon, Jason and I would pull into the driveway of my house. My brother would come out with Fruit Roll-Up stuck between his braces and climb into the backseat of my Dodge Aspen. I would tell him to stay quiet. He didn't always listen.

Jason's favorite comic book series was The Punisher. Mine was The Incredible Hulk. We both also bought Uncanny X-Men even though neither of us really understood the storylines. In the late '80s, nothing was cooler than Uncanny X-Men.

My little brother was the only one who collected Captain America.

Captain America: the hero with no fancy guns, no gamma-ray rage, no adamantium claws. The hero who wears little wings on the sides of his head, whose only weapon is a glorified Frisbee. The hero who dresses like an American flag. You can't get much cornier than that.

No doubt about it, Cap was a dork through and through. And that made his fans dorks, too, including my little brother.

I made fun of my brother's Captain America comics, but I still read them. When you're a true comic book fan, you read every comic book in the house, no exceptions.

The strangest thing about those stories was that everyone in the Marvel Universe seemed oblivious to Captain America's dorkiness. Heroes way cooler than Cap—heroes with high-tech armor, heroes who were actual gods—would defer to him. They listened when he spoke. They executed his plans. Did they not notice that this dude walked around with a giant letter *A* plastered to his forehead?

At some point, I came across the cover of *Captain America Comics #1*. This was Cap's debut, first published in 1940. It was written by Joe Simon and drawn by Jack Kirby, both children of immigrants. Like me.

On the cover, Captain America punches Adolf Hitler in the mouth. It's an arresting image. The United States wouldn't enter World War II until a year later, in December 1941, so Cap was battling Nazis before almost any of his countrymen.

When I was a college freshman, Marvel published *The Adventures of Captain America: Sentinel of Liberty* by writer Fabian Nicieza and artist Kevin Maguire. I wasn't living at home anymore, so I couldn't rely on my brother to buy it. I had to buy it myself. In the story, we learn that Cap is the son of immigrants from Ireland.

An immigrants' kid punched Hitler in the mouth while cosplaying the American flag.

That might be even cooler than Uncanny X-Men.

As I'm writing this, American social media is raging over a controversy about the flag and a shoe. Just before Independence Day 2019, Nike, the nation's largest shoe company, announced a shoe design featuring America's first flag, the one with thirteen stars arranged in a circle, popularly known as the Betsy Ross flag. Former San Francisco 49ers quarterback Colin Kaepernick, a Nike-sponsored athlete, expressed to the company's leadership that he found the Betsy Ross flag offensive because of its connection to slavery. Nike canceled the shoe.

Now folks on social media are arguing about whether or not Nike made the right call. Some are buying Nike shoes to show support. Others are burning them in protest. Some are calling Kaepernick an ingrate. Others are calling him a revolutionary.

I have never been a revolutionary. Even so, the more American history I read, the more I understand Kaepernick's position. It is impossible to deny the role white supremacy played in our nation's founding. For some Americans, the symbols of the time—including the flag of the time—are painful reminders of that fact.

But here's the thing. The Betsy Ross flag is no longer America's official flag. If American history were a comic book, the Betsy Ross flag would only be the first panel. And as every comic book fan knows, you can't do much with a single panel. You can't have a story because your characters can't change in the space of one panel. They can't even move.

And that is why the Betsy Ross flag—or at least, the Betsy Ross flag on its own—does not represent the America that I believe in. My America has a story. Its characters change. My America constantly searches out the best path forward and course corrects when necessary. The greatness of my America is not in its memories, but in its vision for the future.

The America that I believe in is a nation on the move.

And perhaps my America is most accurately represented by a flag on the move, a flag that runs across battlefields and cityscapes and even the surface of the moon. A flag that defends the downtrodden, leads coalitions, and relentlessly pushes toward a more perfect justice. A flag that fights for a country where anyone, no matter the origins of their family, can proudly wear red, white, and blue.

A flag that is a hero.

My little brother isn't so little anymore. He's now a husband, a father, and a doctor. He still has a longbox of comics tucked away somewhere in his home, and in that longbox is a run of Captain America from the '80s, every single issue of which I've read.

Maybe my brother saw the truth about Cap even as a seventh grader. Maybe he isn't such a dork after all.

These days, reading the news often leaves me feeling hopeless. Our nation's rifts seem to grow ever wider and ever deeper.

Reading the stories in this volume, however, reminds me that America doesn't stay still. Change is woven into the very fabric of who we are. Today's evils shall pass so long as we're willing to take up our shields and forge ahead.

Captain America—the hero who is a flag on the move—has set his sights on the future.

He invites us to do the same.

GENE LUEN YANG

Volume Introduction

There is more than one America. The identity of the nation is plural and multivalent. It is the product of a long and sometimes violent history of negotiations between apparent oppositions—native and immigrant, rural and urban, idealism and pragmatism—and of the ongoing, painful, inadequate but still desperately necessary attempt to mediate the differences of gender and race. And because there is more than one America, it should come as no surprise that there is more than one Captain America, too.

Across the entire canon of Marvel Comics, the roster of those who have at different times borne the name and rank of "Captain America" actually runs into double figures. This list includes several people of color and at least five women.[1] These various Captains also express a range of political opinions, from the relatively conservative John Walker to the more progressive Sam Wilson.[2] But as the stories in this collection demonstrate, the capacity for plurality is apparent even in the supposedly singular case of Steve Rogers—the original Captain America—who was so radically reimagined between World War II and the early 1960s that he became almost an entirely different character.

Joe Simon and Jack Kirby first created Cap in late 1940 to fight Hitler and the Nazis.[3] Indeed, according to Simon's recollections, this was a case where the villains preceded the hero:

Adolf Hitler and his Gestapo bully-boys were real . . . [and] hated by more than half of the world. What a natural foil he [Hitler] was, with his comical moustache, the ridiculous cowlick, his swaggering, goose-stepping minions eager to jump out of a plane if their mad little leader ordered it . . . All that was left to do was devise a long underwear hero to stand up to him.[4]

Simon makes it sound simple. But calling out Hitler on the cover of a comic book was not without risk. America had not yet entered the war; the attack on Pearl Harbor was still almost twelve months off. As Jewish Americans, Simon and Kirby were acutely aware of the murderous threat Hitler represented, but others were uncertain about the prospect of entering the European conflict—and some were openly sympathetic to the Nazi cause. For example, in 1939, the German American Bund organized a Nazi rally at Madison Square Garden that attracted over twenty thousand attendees. The Bund's national headquarters was located on Manhattan's East 85th Street, just a short cab ride from the tiny one-room office on West 45th where Simon and Kirby worked.

In this tense political atmosphere, comic book publishers avoided making obvious references to the European war. Even overtly patriotic super heroes such as MLJ's The Shield fought robots or generic soldiers without identifying insignia on the covers of their books.[5] *Captain America Comics* #1 was therefore doubly historic not only for introducing Cap to the world, but also for placing a recognizable caricature of Adolf Hitler on the cover of an American comic book for the first time.[6] The result was as memorable in its own way as the iconic depiction of Superman lifting a car over his head from *Action Comics* #1.

Looking at the cover of *Captain America Comics* #1 today, we can see how the anti-isolationist message of the central image—Cap punching Hitler squarely in the face—is reinforced by other carefully placed details. These include a set of documents labeled "Sabotage Plans for USA" floating to the left of the reeling Führer, and a high-tech television screen showing the destruction of a US munitions factory, located immediately below the masthead. Taken together, these elements combine to make a relatively subtle visual argument. Against those who might oppose entering the war on the grounds that it was not America's place to serve as an international police force, Simon and Kirby imply that it is not a question of "intervention," but a matter of self-defense.

The content of the comic book leans into this argument by focusing not on the European theater but on so-called fifth columnists, determined to undermine the USA from the inside. Thus, the first pages depict a "wave of sabotage and treason [that] paralyzes the vital defense industries" of the nation. (No such attacks actually occurred during World War II, but memories of the Black Tom explosion in World War I made the threat seem real, and the specter of "the enemy within" was much evoked by anti-isolationists.) We then cut to a scene at the White House featuring President Roosevelt, his top military advisers, and FBI chief J. Edgar Hoover—thinly disguised as "J. Arthur Grover." The conversation concerns the danger of spies and saboteurs, and the overall effect is to suggest that such fears are informed, wise, and patriotic. The same message is hammered home in the subsequent pages, sometimes in ways that may surprise modern readers. For example, when the Red Skull makes his debut in the final story in the book, he is not actually a German, as in contemporary film and comic book continuity, but an American citizen—a businessman who hopes to enrich himself by abetting Hitler's conquest of the nation. At this point in history, even the villain who would become Cap's archnemesis originates from inside the US borders.

Simon and Kirby add to the fearful atmosphere by dressing up these prewar warnings in the tropes of gothic fiction: the old curio shop that hides the magical laboratory in which Cap is born; the hideous crone who becomes a beautiful woman; the "freak show" vaudeville act of Sando and Omar; and, of course, the death's head visage of the Red Skull himself. The book also featured an advertisement encouraging readers "to join Captain America's Sentinels of Liberty and help fight spies and traitors to the U.S.A."—an offer that implicitly invited the youngest members of the audience to cast themselves as real-life versions of Bucky Barnes, Cap's youthful sidekick, by aiding the hero in his efforts to defend America's shores. For ten cents, members received a badge and membership card (now among the rarest Marvel collectibles), and the promise of certificates of merit for "the best patriotic deed of the month."

While hardly government approved, it all added up to a tremendously effective piece of popular propaganda—and was immediately recognized as such by Nazi sympathizers, who wrote hate mail and made threatening phone calls to the publisher's office.[7] But among the target audience, the response was overwhelmingly positive. *Captain America Comics* #1 was a smash hit that established the creative team of Simon and Kirby as stars of their profession.[8]

Joe Simon (1913–2011) first entered the fledging comic book industry in 1939. He met Jack Kirby (1917–1994) shortly thereafter, and the two men swiftly formed a creative partnership. Both were capable writer-artists who regularly exchanged roles as part of their process.[9] They collaborated on numerous projects for a variety of publishers—including the lightning-powered Blue Bolt for Novelty Press and the dimension-traveling Vision for Martin Goodman's Timely Comics (the future Marvel)—before striking gold with Captain America, also for Timely.

Goodman had previously purchased most of his comic book content from an independent "packager" of strips and stories, Lloyd Jacquet's Funnies Inc. But in the wake of Captain America's success, the publisher decided to produce more work in-house. He hired Simon to be Timely's first official editor and brought on Kirby as a staff artist. At around the same time, he also gave a job to his wife's cousin—a seventeen-year-old high school graduate by the name of Stanley Martin Lieber—putting him to work as Simon and Kirby's assistant. Lieber's primary roles, according to Simon, were "to erase the penciled drawings from the pages after they had been inked, a chore that was always drudgery for the artist," and to fetch coffee and supplies when needed.[10] But the energetic teenager was soon asking for more responsibilities.

In those days, comics always included a couple of pages of prose fiction in order to meet USPS requirements for second-class mailing privileges, thereby allowing publishers to save money on subscription rates. Simon decided that since "nobody read" these text stories, it could do no harm to let the young gofer write them.[11] Lieber jumped at the chance, but also adopted a pen name to protect his future reputation as a serious novelist. So it was that *Captain America Comics* #3 (May 1941) contained the first published story to appear under the byline of Stan Lee.

Simon and Kirby left Timely in the fall of 1941 after a dispute with Goodman.[12] It's remarkable to realize that the USA still had not entered the war when they handed in the artwork for *Captain America Comics* #10, their last work together on the character. Production of the title now fell primarily to the artistic team of Al Avison and Syd Shores, under the general oversight of Lee—suddenly promoted at the tender age of eighteen to the position of editor for Goodman's comic book line.[13] Sales were not harmed by Simon and Kirby's abrupt departure, but rather buoyed by the surge of patriotic feeling that followed the attacks on Pearl Harbor. The propagandist aspects of the book ratcheted upward accordingly. For contemporary readers, stories from this era can be startling, not only for the savage caricatures of the enemy, but also for Cap's own casual brutality; he killed foes by the dozen, with guns, explosives, poison, his fists, and even his shield.

With the end of the war, Steve Rogers became a more conventional super hero—taking on a job as a teacher, while continuing to fight homegrown menaces as Cap. But as media scholar J. Richard Stevens perceptively writes, stories about "Captain America as mere crime-fighter robbed the character of the brashness that had stirred up interest in the first place, or that brashness seemed inappropriate when employed against his fellow countrymen."[14] Sales fell, and Lee found himself chasing trends in an effort to keep the once popular title alive. For example, when Simon and Kirby scored a surprise hit in 1947 with Young Romance at Prize Comics, starting a whole new craze for romance comics, Lee responded by replacing Bucky with a crime-fighting romantic partner for Cap named Golden Girl. Then, as crime, science fiction, and horror comics became more popular, Captain America Comics also began to include stories in those genres. Cap's own role was increasingly diminished, to the point where he some-times served as a mere narrator in his own comic. But despite these measures, sales continued to sink. Toward the end of 1949, the series was renamed Captain America's Weird Tales; the last issue was (as the title implies) a horror anthology, and despite the persistence of his name on the cover, Captain America appeared nowhere in its pages.

Readers would have to wait till 1953 for a new Captain America story, when Goodman directed Lee to revive him—along with the other two most successful Timely heroes of the war era, the Human Torch and the Sub-Mariner.[15] This go-around, Cap's enemies would not be fascists, but communists. (See Appendix One.) Aside from this act of ideological rebranding, however, the stories of Cap the Cold Warrior were essentially no different in their conception and execu-tion from those of Cap the World War II Hero. Steve Rogers found himself promoted from high school teacher to college professor (with Bucky now one of his students), but his character did not otherwise evolve, and his adventures were paced and plotted much like the mayhem-filled tales of his wartime heyday—filled with fifth colum-nists and Asian stereotypes all meeting their doom at Cap's gaunt-leted hands. But the formula that had sold millions in the early 1940s did not fare so well in the early 1950s, and Captain America . . . Com-mie Smasher was canceled after just three issues.

According to John Romita Sr., the artist for this title, Lee later came to feel that the political chauvinism of these stories had contrib-uted to their commercial failure.[16] Comics scholar Bradford Wright has also suggested that "comic book makers overestimated the size of the audience prepared to accept such naïve presentations of the Cold War."[17] But given that there were plenty of Americans who regarded the "Red Menace" as at least equivalent to the Nazi threat, the sim-plistic ideology of these comics was surely only part of the problem. The year 1953 was also the commercial nadir of the comic book super hero more generally; even sales of Superman comics were down from the prior decade (despite the unequaled publicity afforded by a suc-cessful weekly television show), and most costumed crime-fighters had disappeared from the stands altogether. The cancellation of

Commie Smasher Cap therefore probably owed less to his Cold War politics and more to the fact that tastes in popular entertainment had changed, while (ideological targets notwithstanding) the Captain America concept had not.

The middle 1950s were tough on the comic book industry. The rise of the rival medium of television, changes in the system of newsstand distribution, and a widespread moral panic about the relationship between comic books and juvenile delinquency all combined in a perfect storm that blew away more than a dozen publishers.[18] Since leaving Captain America behind in 1941, Simon and Kirby had enjoyed a great run as one of the most successful freelance teams in comics, but were now forced by the shrinking market to dissolve their partnership and seek work independently. It was in these difficult times that Kirby found himself once more inquiring for opportunities at the office of publisher Martin Goodman.

Kirby could not have known that he was about to embark on one of the great second acts in American pop-culture history. But Stan Lee knew that fate had dealt him a good hand when Kirby showed up at his door. The two men began to collaborate regularly, initially churning out monster tales for Goodman's mystery books. Their big breakthrough came in 1961, when they invented a new kind of super hero team in the pages of The Fantastic Four. (See "Series Introduction" for more on this foundational moment in Marvel history.) The book was a hit, and Lee and Kirby went on to co-create several more superpowered characters, including the Hulk, Ant-Man, Iron Man, Thor, and the X-Men over just two short years. With Kirby being one of the original creators of Captain America, and Lee having cut his teeth as a writer on Cap's wartime books, it was perhaps inevitable that they would start thinking about reviving him, too, for what Lee was now calling the "Marvel Universe." But Lee had already seen one Captain America relaunch fail and wanted reassurance that there was an audience for the character's return. Consequently, he and Kirby teased the idea in *Strange Tales* #114 (November 1963), whose cover seemed to depict Cap ("from out of the Golden Age of comics") locked in battle with the Human Torch—although in the interior story it turns out not to be Cap at all, but a rather dull villain named the Acrobat, in disguise. "This story was really a test," Lee admitted in a direct address to the readers in the final panel, "to see if you too would like Captain America to return! As usual your letters will give us the answer!"[19]

Clearly, responses were positive enough for Lee and Kirby to take another chance on the formerly bestselling hero of World War II. But the problem of how to manage Cap's return this time around was, if anything, trickier than it had been in 1953. By now he had been gone from the newsstands for almost a decade—an eternity in the annals of mid-twentieth-century comic book culture—during which time the speed of change in American society had only accelerated. The period of his absence had borne witness to the first Soviet victories in the space race, the first deaths of US soldiers in Vietnam, the first stirrings of the civil rights movement, the birth of rock and roll—and, more recently, the drama of the Cuban Missile Crisis (the closest the world has ever come to a nuclear conflict) and the shocking assassination of America's youngest elected president. Against this background, the events of World War II seemed further away than ever, and it was clear that if World War III broke out it would not be won by foot soldiers—not even superhuman ones. Captain America not only was tied by his comic book origin to a moment in real-world history that felt increasingly distant, but also represented a warrior ideal that seemed to have no place in the era of the atomic bomb. How would he fit in a newly conceived comic book fantasy world populated by radioactive monsters, misunderstood hero-misfits, and the occasional Norse god?

Lee and Kirby's answer to this question was brilliantly self-reflexive. They turned the artistic challenge of reviving a World War II hero in the 1960s into a theme of their narrative—making their problem Cap's problem, too, and transforming it into an additional source of drama. Rather than try to explain what Captain America might have been up to for the past ten years, they proceeded as if his previously published postwar adventures had never happened. He did not muster out to take a job as a schoolteacher; there was no romance with Golden Girl; he did not fight communism in Korea. (In later plotlines, another man, William Burnside, is said to have taken on the Captain America identity in the 1950s—thereby restoring Captain America the Commie Smasher to the canon while still maintaining distance between that version of the character and the primary figure of Steve Rogers.)[20] Instead, they decided, he had been frozen alive in the last months of the war and so had no knowledge of all that had happened in the intervening years. Thus, when accidentally discovered and revived in *The Avengers* #4, he became quite literally a man from another time. (See Appendix Two.) As such, he is suitably impressed on arriving in New York City by the new buildings, cars, and other technological achievements of the past two decades. ("I wonder if the youngsters of today, who've grown up with it, realize what a truly wonderful thing television is," he muses.) But he also expresses confusion about his role in this unfamiliar world. ("I don't belong in this age—in this year—no place for me here.")[21]

Besides these feelings of alienation, Lee and Kirby's Captain America is immediately and profoundly marked by the experience of traumatic loss. His first words upon returning to life are a cry of warning: "Bucky! Look out!" But the warning comes twenty years too late. As we soon learn, Bucky was killed on his final mission with Cap. (Modern movie audiences take Bucky's return for granted; but one of the most remarkable things about the comic book version of the character is that in the wake of his apparent demise in 1945, as established in 1964, he remained dead for decades of real-world time. It would be more than forty years before Ed Brubaker and Steve Epting decisively resurrected Bucky Barnes as the Winter Soldier in 2005—a lengthy period that is itself indicative of the foundational role played by Bucky's traumatic loss in Captain America's 1960s reinvention.)[22] With this move, Lee and Kirby established Bucky as functionally equivalent to Peter Parker's Uncle Ben: a paradoxical absent-presence around which the hero's subjectivity and motivations could be shaped. From the outset, however, Bucky had a tendency to manifest in both surrogate and spectral forms, even while remaining literally dead; for example, just a few pages later in *The Avengers* #4, the emotionally exhausted Steve Rogers mistakes the teenaged Rick Jones for his former sidekick, leading the younger man to question Rogers's sanity. ("Look, fella—after we find the Avengers, I am sure they can recommend a real nice head shrinker for you.")[23] Haunted, confused, and prone to distressing flashbacks, Captain America is clearly exhibiting symptoms of what we would now call PTSD, although that terminology and concept had yet to enter popular consciousness.[24]

With Cap's 1960s revival, then, Lee and Kirby added a quality of psychological complexity and a depth of suffering to his character that had been entirely absent in prior storylines (and, indeed, would have been antithetical to his original purpose as a work of popular propaganda). Having established his status as a temporal misfit, however, the problem of how to depict the new adventures of this time-warped and traumatized hero remained. Cap swiftly seemed at home in the pages of The Avengers—a team that was defined, after all, by the relative incongruity of the various members, and where his troubles would not be the sole focus of attention. But fans wanted to see more of the "Star-Spangled Avenger," as he was now termed. Lee and Kirby quickly obliged, creating a half-book-length solo strip for Tales to Astonish (the other half of each issue being taken up with the adventures of Iron Man), and it is these solo adventures of the revived 1960s Captain America that take up the majority of this collection.

The opening pages of Lee and Kirby's first solo Captain America story emphasize the hero's feelings of isolation and ongoing grief for Bucky; but then the tale takes a turn, becoming an extended, elaborately choreographed fight scene designed to showcase Kirby's talent for physical action. The violence is slapstick rather than realistic: at one point Cap evades his attackers by sliding across the room on a drinks trolley, and at another he employs his shield in the manner of a matador's cape—sequences that recall the movies of Harold Lloyd and Buster Keaton, and anticipate the comedic acrobatics of Jackie Chan. The humorous tone is sustained to the final page, with the depiction of Cap's unconscious attackers casually strewn about the wrecked living room of the Avengers' mansion, one even dangling from the chandelier. Lee and Kirby's next three stories (not included in this collection) repeat the same basic formula in different settings, with diminishing returns—suggesting that the two creators weren't yet sure what to do with the character outside of a team environment.

With *Tales to Astonish* #63, however, they returned the hero to World War II, when his purpose was clearer, and began working their way through the stories in *Captain America Comics* #1—starting with the origin, continuing with the tale of the vaudeville-saboteurs Sando and Omar, and on to the first appearance of the Red Skull. Like modern remakes of Hollywood classics, these stories compare fascinatingly with Simon and Kirby's originals not only with regard to what they retain but what they leave out. FDR, for example, is still a recognizable presence in the new origin story, but Hoover (a less well-regarded figure by the mid-1960s) is gone. Gradual shifts in attitudes toward gender are also apparent in the representation of Agent Thirteen, who here displaces the World War II figure of Betsy Ross. And after retelling the first Red Skull story, Lee and Kirby embarked on a substantial revision of that character, providing him with a detailed origin story in which Hitler serves as the Skull's personal mentor in the arts of evil.

It is also instructive to compare the representation of lethal violence across the two eras. Simon and Kirby's Captain America could be ruthless—a quality that intensified after the events of Pearl Harbor and was retained during the brief Commie Smasher era—but Lee and Kirby's Cap prefers to subdue rather than slay his enemies, even in a wartime setting. Lee and Kirby themselves don't always seem in agreement with regard to the murderous capacities of Cap's enemies, however; on page 6 of "The Fantastic Origin of the Red Skull," the visual narrative strongly implies that the Skull guns a man down in cold blood on Hitler's orders, while Lee's dialogue contrives to make the outcome seem less brutal. Overall, however, both creators work to suggest that there is a qualitative difference between the violence employed by the hero and that of his enemies—which is itself suggestive of larger transformations in America's own self-image between the war and the 1960s, particularly with regard to the public appetite for the political use of deadly force.[25]

With the conclusion of the Red Skull story arc, Kirby temporarily scaled back his contribution to providing layouts for other artists to finish, allowing him to devote more energy to other Marvel titles. Within a couple more issues, the series reverted back to workmanlike action stories (not included here) set in the contemporary 1960s, although the menaces (Nazi-designed "sleeper" robots) continued to originate in the past. However, "30 Minutes to Live!" from *Tales of Suspense* #75 saw a new focus on Captain America's emotional life; the two-page sequence of ruminative introspection constituted the most sustained exploration of Cap's loneliness and isolation since his reintroduction in *The Avengers* #4 almost three years earlier. This sequence concludes with the introduction of the (as yet unnamed) Sharon Carter, who would soon become a primary love interest. But despite this effort to give modern Cap something new to think about, the traumas of the past still seemed to cling to him; even his attraction to Sharon turns out to be rooted in his wartime experiences, as "If a Hostage Should Die!" makes clear. As the months went by, more aspects of the past seemed to infiltrate the present. For example, Kirby's return to full pencils with *Tales of Suspense* #78 saw the first meeting since the war between Cap and Nick Fury—a former World War II sergeant, now the head of S.H.I.E.L.D.—and also the return of the Red Skull in his first modern-era storyline.

Having acknowledged the depth of the hero's emotional wounds, and dangled the prospect of a healing romance before him, the most striking advances of the series over the next few years were visual. Kirby had been developing a more experimental style in his work on The Fantastic Four and The Mighty Thor, moving further away from conventional representational standards of form and proportion in favor of expressionistic exaggeration and overwhelming spectacle. As his style altered, he started to incorporate increasingly baroque design elements in those books—wildly extravagant costumes, elaborate technological wonders, interstellar visions crackling with dark energy— producing comics that looked like nothing else on the stands. Although Cap's limited power set and World War II origins might initially have seemed to preclude the inclusion of these elements, the Red Skull's acquisition of the Cosmic Cube—a device of seemingly infinite, matter-warping power—allowed Kirby to indulge his growing penchant for visual flamboyance on this strip, too. Lee responded by upping the rhetorical ante; both Cap and the Skull joust verbally with a new grandiloquence, even as they trade punches.

These elements of baroque spectacle were elevated still further when Kirby was paired with Joe Sinnott—perhaps his greatest inker—in the storyline that introduces the menace known as M.O.D.O.K. (*Tales of Suspense* #92–94). Consider, for example, the first page of the episode entitled "Into the Jaws . . . of A.I.M.!" which depicts a dramatically foreshortened Captain America floating toward the reader wearing a device that looks like a cross between a submarine and a space suit—appropriately enough, since Kirby's underwater landscape, with its swirling background of blots and circles, looks as otherworldly as it does oceanic. Almost every page of this story features some striking visual effect or elaborated technological element, as Kirby continued to reject naturalistic illusionism in favor of dynamic, elaborated forms and abstract artifice—such as the lines of radiating force that seem to emanate from everywhere in the final action sequences.

For the next year or so, Lee and Kirby stuck to the formula they had now established for modern Cap storylines. Steve Rogers would periodically experience bouts of survivor guilt over Bucky's loss, while Captain America would battle enemies such as the Red Skull (again) and Batroc (again) and even an artificial version of himself, grown in a lab in Mao's China. (These stories are not included here.) No matter how well executed, however, the cycle inevitably started to seem repetitious, and Kirby wanted to move on to other projects. After one final retelling of the origin story—in which Steve Rogers's motivations are more fleshed out than in any prior version—Lee handed the book to one of the most admired new artists of the period: Jim Steranko.

Steranko began his career heavily influenced by Kirby, but rapidly developed his own original style—combining Kirby's exaggeratedly dynamic approach to anatomy, perspective, and technology with a very different narrative technique that attempted to mimic the effects of cinematic pacing in the motionless medium of the comics page. He also took a postmodernist's delight in referring to other artistic traditions—both commercial and fine—alternately making allusions to the psychedelic designs of contemporary rock posters and to the surrealistic masterworks of Salvador Dalí, for example. Before working on Captain America, Steranko had successfully transformed Marvel's Nick Fury, Agent of S.H.I.E.L.D. series from a second-tier strip into a fan favorite that owed more to the glamour and sophistication of the recent James Bond movies starring Sean Connery than the old war stories that had first introduced Fury to the world. Lee clearly hoped that Steranko would bring a fresh feel to Captain America's adventures, too. (See Appendix Three for Steranko's personal account of his approach to the series.)

But while Steranko's Captain America certainly *looked* contemporary—that is, very late-1960s—the slick visuals disguised an essentially nostalgic approach to the character and concept. Steranko attempted to move the series forward by looking backward: first, by restoring Cap's secret identity (renounced some issues earlier); second, by "resurrecting" Bucky in the form of Rick Jones, in an effort to heal Cap's feelings of survivor guilt; third, by setting Cap against Hydra, a neo-fascist organization imported from Steranko's Nick Fury comics, thereby giving Cap a new overarching enemy and purpose; and, most important, by punctuating his narrative with dramatic poster-style images and double-page spreads emphasizing Captain America's emblematic, figurative status as "freedom's most fearless champion" over the inner life of the character. Having managed all this in just three exquisitely designed issues, Steranko declared his mission accomplished and promptly quit the book.

Aside from sticking with the restored secret identity, however, Lee would subsequently ignore almost all of the suggestions sketched out in Steranko's blueprint. Cap started questioning his place in the world again in the first pages of the following issue; and just three months later, Lee replaced Steranko's substitute-Bucky with a new companion called the Falcon—Marvel's first African American super hero.[26] This resonant choice signals Lee's recognition that American society was continuing to evolve, and that Captain America needed to evolve with it, if he hoped to survive. The letters pages of the comic also reflected a growing awareness on the part of the readership that Captain America could not stand above the fray of contemporary politics, but needed to negotiate that complex territory if he hoped to remain relevant. (See, for example, Albert Rodriquez's letter from *Captain America* #110, included in this volume.)[27] Indeed, in the decades that followed, Captain America's creators would go on to explore competing ideas about American values with ever-increasing self-consciousness—often by emphasizing the estranged condition of the hero within the very culture he was supposed to represent.[28]

Steranko's work therefore stands at the conclusion of this collection of "classic" Captain America stories from the 1960s as the last serious effort to revive the World War II formula that first established the character as a national icon—the last attempt to present Captain America as an uncomplicated symbol of the American fighting spirit, without qualms or misgivings, and mercifully free of psychological trauma. The fact that this emblematic approach was almost immediately abandoned again after Steranko's departure reflects less upon the artist than it does upon the historical transformation of American society in the years since the war. In the end, Lee and Kirby's endlessly self-questioning "man out of time" was simply more suited to the task of expressing America's increasingly complicated self-image. It is a testament to the power of their vision that Captain America remains a compelling vehicle for the pop-cultural exploration of America's multivalent national identity, even in the twenty-first century.

BEN SAUNDERS

Captain America

CAPTAIN AMERICA COMICS #1,

MARCH 1941

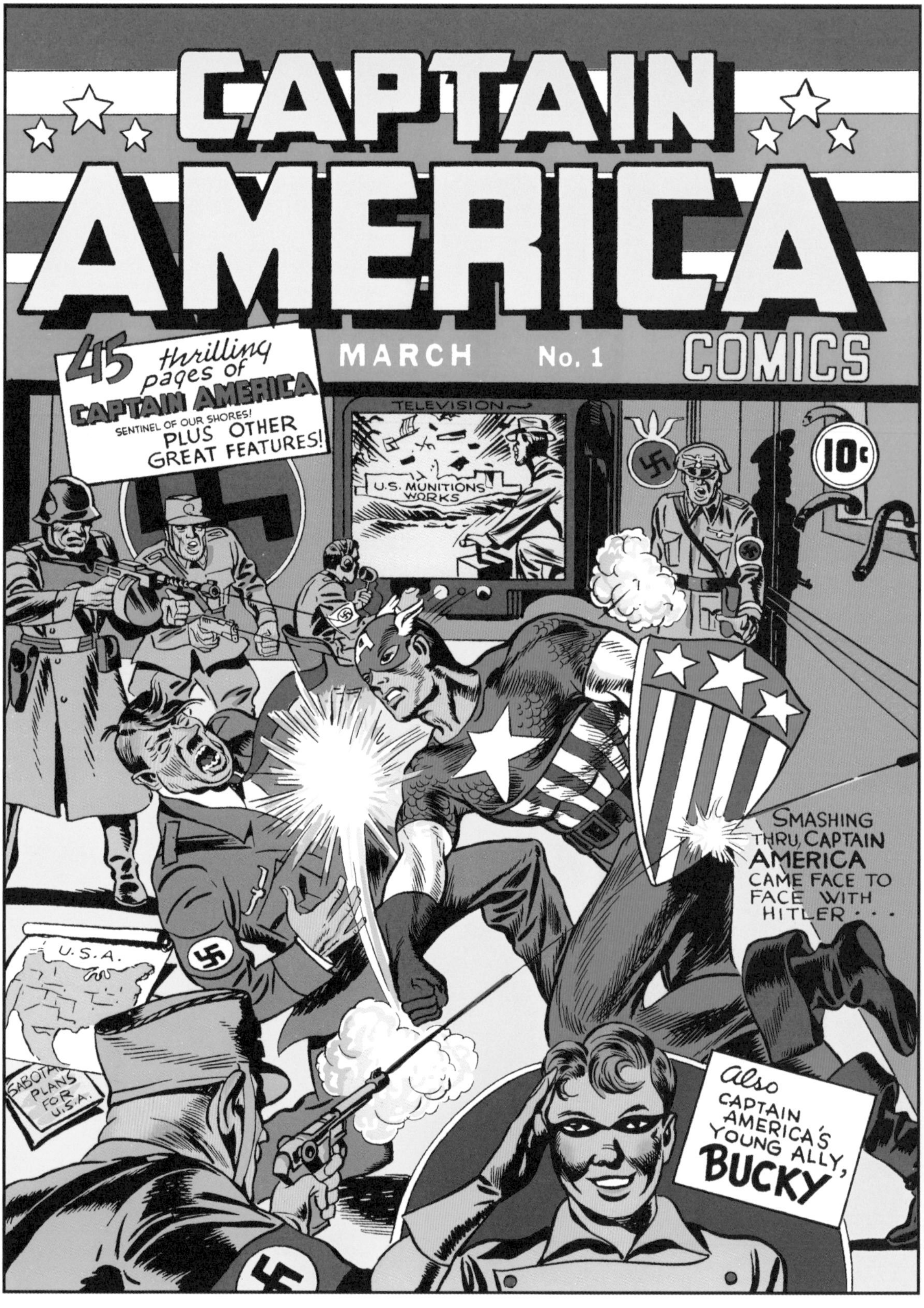
CAPTAIN AMERICA
COMICS
45 thrilling pages of CAPTAIN AMERICA SENTINEL OF OUR SHORES! PLUS OTHER GREAT FEATURES!
MARCH
No. 1
10¢
TELEVISION
U.S. MUNITIONS WORKS
SMASHING THRU, CAPTAIN AMERICA CAME FACE TO FACE WITH HITLER . . .
U.S.A.
PLANS FOR U.S.A.
Also CAPTAIN AMERICA'S YOUNG ALLY, BUCKY

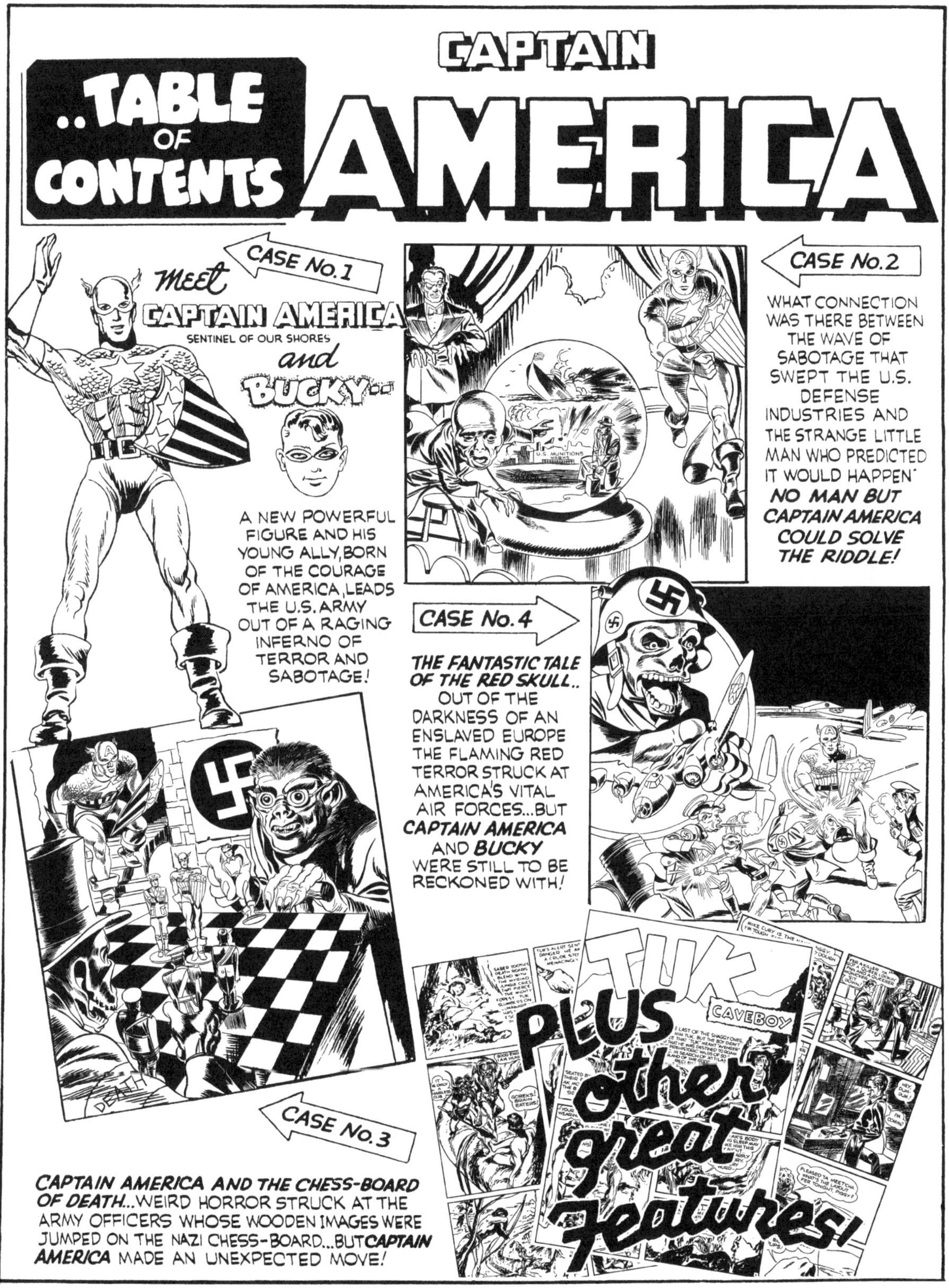

..TABLE OF CONTENTS
CAPTAIN AMERICA
CASE No.1
Meet CAPTAIN AMERICA SENTINEL OF OUR SHORES and BUCKY..
A NEW POWERFUL FIGURE AND HIS YOUNG ALLY, BORN OF THE COURAGE OF AMERICA, LEADS THE U.S. ARMY OUT OF A RAGING INFERNO OF TERROR AND SABOTAGE!
U.S. MUNITIONS WORKS
CASE No.2
WHAT CONNECTION WAS THERE BETWEEN THE WAVE OF SABOTAGE THAT SWEPT THE U.S. DEFENSE INDUSTRIES AND THE STRANGE LITTLE MAN WHO PREDICTED IT WOULD HAPPEN? NO MAN BUT CAPTAIN AMERICA COULD SOLVE THE RIDDLE!
CASE No.4
THE FANTASTIC TALE OF THE RED SKULL.. OUT OF THE DARKNESS OF AN ENSLAVED EUROPE THE FLAMING RED TERROR STRUCK AT AMERICA'S VITAL AIR FORCES...BUT CAPTAIN AMERICA AND BUCKY WERE STILL TO BE RECKONED WITH!
DEATH
CASE No.3
CAPTAIN AMERICA AND THE CHESS-BOARD OF DEATH...WEIRD HORROR STRUCK AT THE ARMY OFFICERS WHOSE WOODEN IMAGES WERE JUMPED ON THE NAZI CHESS-BOARD...BUT CAPTAIN AMERICA MADE AN UNEXPECTED MOVE!
TUK
CAVEBOY
PLUS other great features!

CAPTAIN AMERICA COMICS published monthly by Timely Publications, Meriden, Conn. Entered as second class matter at the Post Office, Meriden, Conn. Entire contents copyright 1940 by Timely Publications, 330 W. 42nd St., New York, N.Y. Vol. 2, No. 1, March 1941 issue. Yearly subscription $1.00. Printed in the U.S.A.

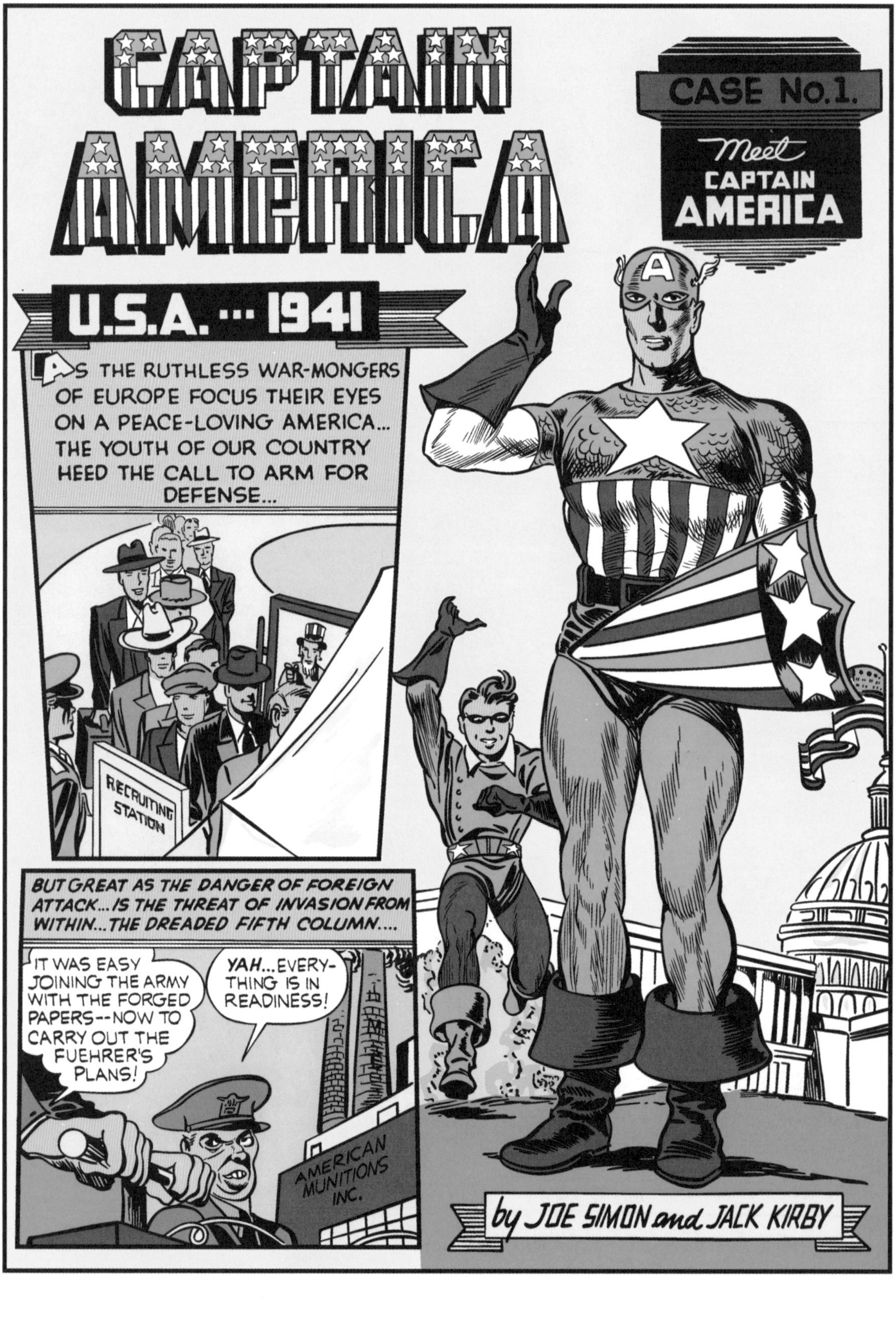
CAPTAIN AMERICA
CASE No.1.
Meet CAPTAIN AMERICA
U.S.A. ... 1941
AS THE RUTHLESS WAR-MONGERS OF EUROPE FOCUS THEIR EYES ON A PEACE-LOVING AMERICA... THE YOUTH OF OUR COUNTRY HEED THE CALL TO ARM FOR DEFENSE...
RECRUITING STATION
BUT GREAT AS THE DANGER OF FOREIGN ATTACK... IS THE THREAT OF INVASION FROM WITHIN... THE DREADED FIFTH COLUMN....
IT WAS EASY JOINING THE ARMY WITH THE FORGED PAPERS--NOW TO CARRY OUT THE FUEHRER'S PLANS!
YAH... EVERYTHING IS IN READINESS!
AMERICAN MUNITIONS INC.
by JOE SIMON and JACK KIRBY

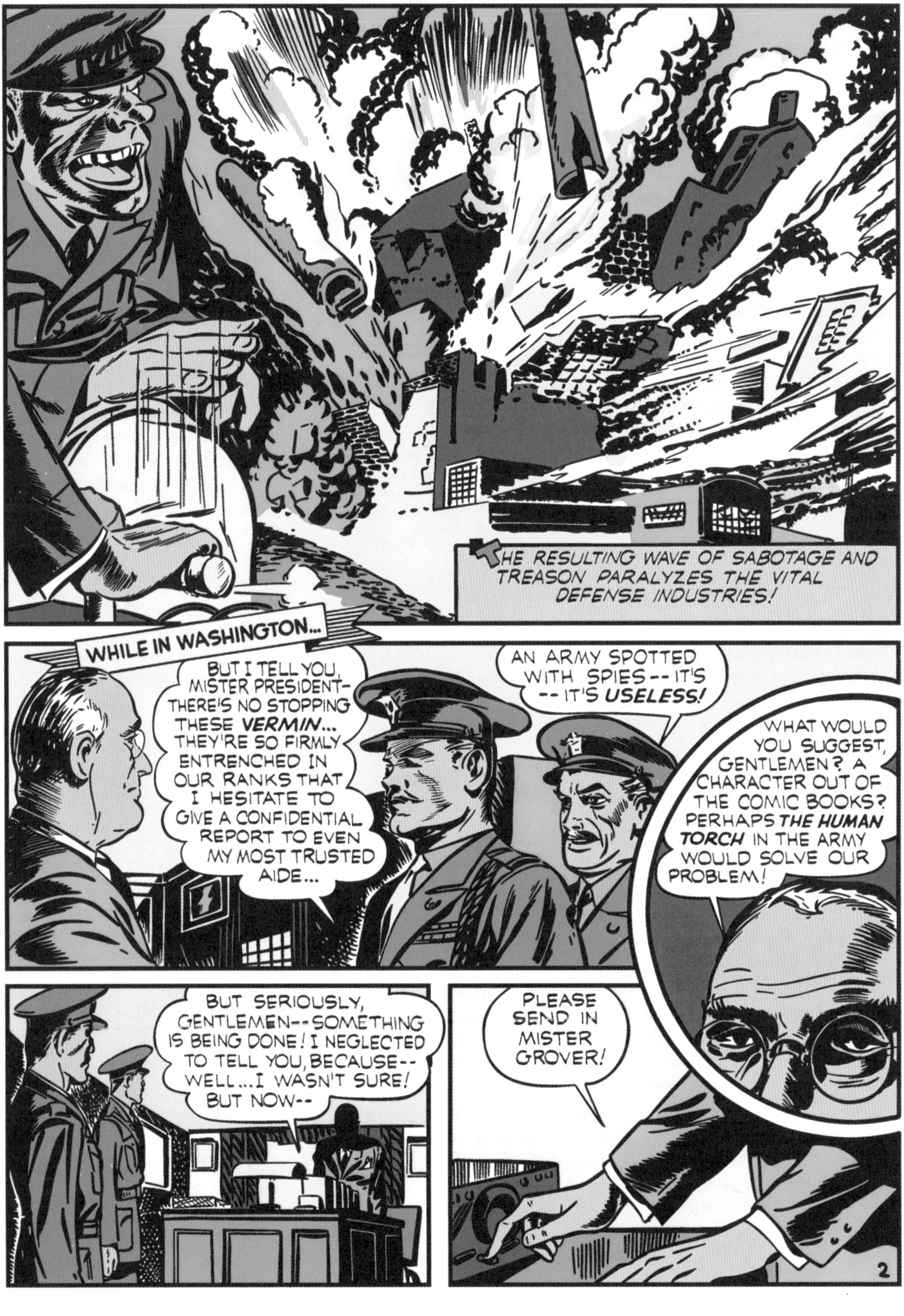
THE RESULTING WAVE OF SABOTAGE AND TREASON PARALYZES THE VITAL DEFENSE INDUSTRIES!
WHILE IN WASHINGTON...
BUT I TELL YOU, MISTER PRESIDENT-- THERE'S NO STOPPING THESE VERMIN... THEY'RE SO FIRMLY ENTRENCHED IN OUR RANKS THAT I HESITATE TO GIVE A CONFIDENTIAL REPORT TO EVEN MY MOST TRUSTED AIDE...
AN ARMY SPOTTED WITH SPIES -- IT'S -- IT'S USELESS!
WHAT WOULD YOU SUGGEST, GENTLEMEN? A CHARACTER OUT OF THE COMIC BOOKS? PERHAPS THE HUMAN TORCH IN THE ARMY WOULD SOLVE OUR PROBLEM!
BUT SERIOUSLY, GENTLEMEN--SOMETHING IS BEING DONE! I NEGLECTED TO TELL YOU, BECAUSE-- WELL... I WASN'T SURE! BUT NOW--
PLEASE SEND IN MISTER GROVER!
2

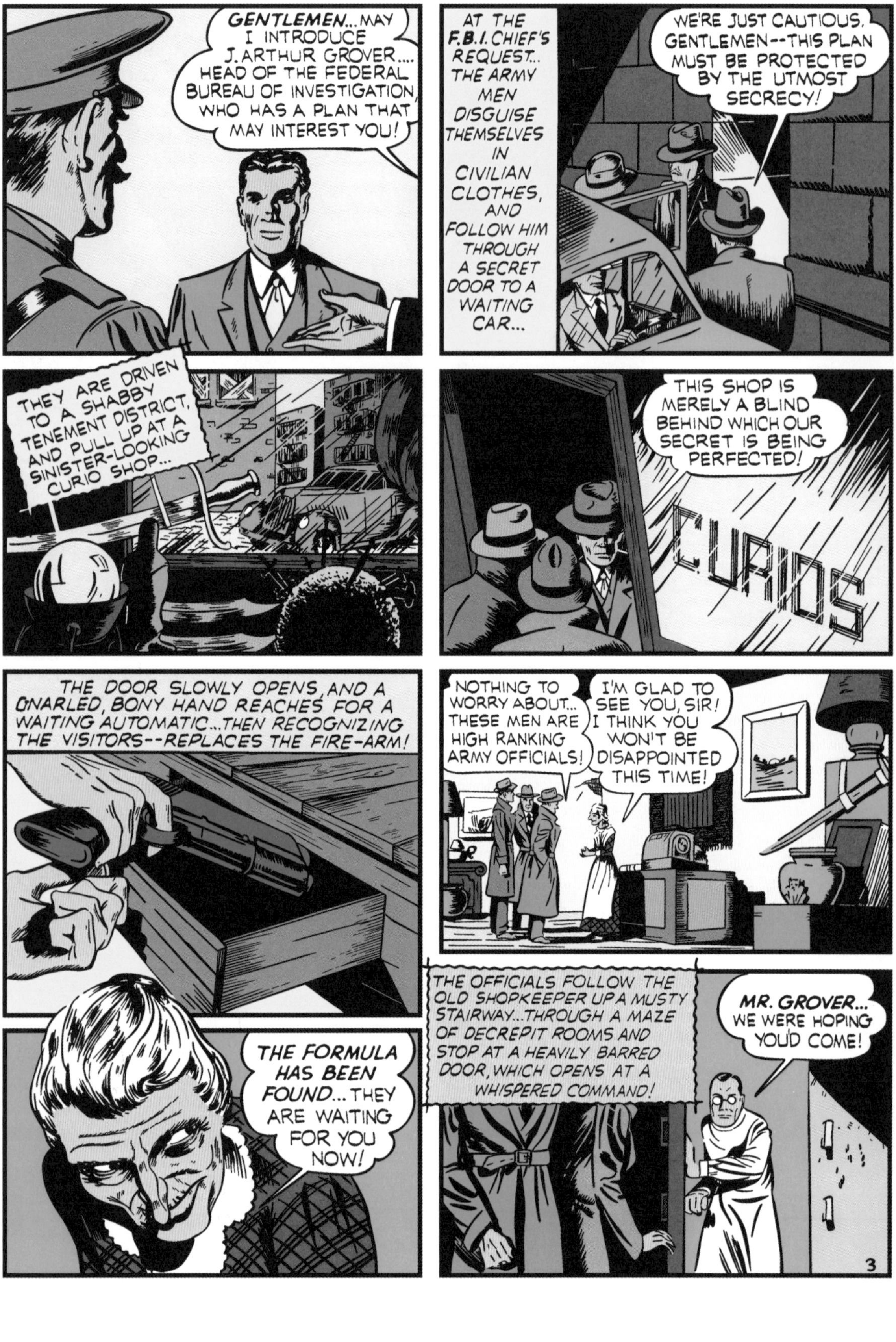
GENTLEMEN... MAY I INTRODUCE J. ARTHUR GROVER.... HEAD OF THE FEDERAL BUREAU OF INVESTIGATION, WHO HAS A PLAN THAT MAY INTEREST YOU!
AT THE F.B.I. CHIEF'S REQUEST... THE ARMY MEN DISGUISE THEMSELVES IN CIVILIAN CLOTHES, AND FOLLOW HIM THROUGH A SECRET DOOR TO A WAITING CAR...
WE'RE JUST CAUTIOUS, GENTLEMEN--THIS PLAN MUST BE PROTECTED BY THE UTMOST SECRECY!
THEY ARE DRIVEN TO A SHABBY TENEMENT DISTRICT, AND PULL UP AT A SINISTER-LOOKING CURIO SHOP...
THIS SHOP IS MERELY A BLIND BEHIND WHICH OUR SECRET IS BEING PERFECTED!
CURIOS
THE DOOR SLOWLY OPENS, AND A GNARLED, BONY HAND REACHES FOR A WAITING AUTOMATIC...THEN RECOGNIZING THE VISITORS--REPLACES THE FIRE-ARM!
NOTHING TO WORRY ABOUT... THESE MEN ARE HIGH RANKING ARMY OFFICIALS!
I'M GLAD TO SEE YOU, SIR! I THINK YOU WON'T BE DISAPPOINTED THIS TIME!
THE FORMULA HAS BEEN FOUND... THEY ARE WAITING FOR YOU NOW!
THE OFFICIALS FOLLOW THE OLD SHOPKEEPER UP A MUSTY STAIRWAY...THROUGH A MAZE OF DECREPIT ROOMS AND STOP AT A HEAVILY BARRED DOOR, WHICH OPENS AT A WHISPERED COMMAND!
MR. GROVER... WE WERE HOPING YOU'D COME!
3

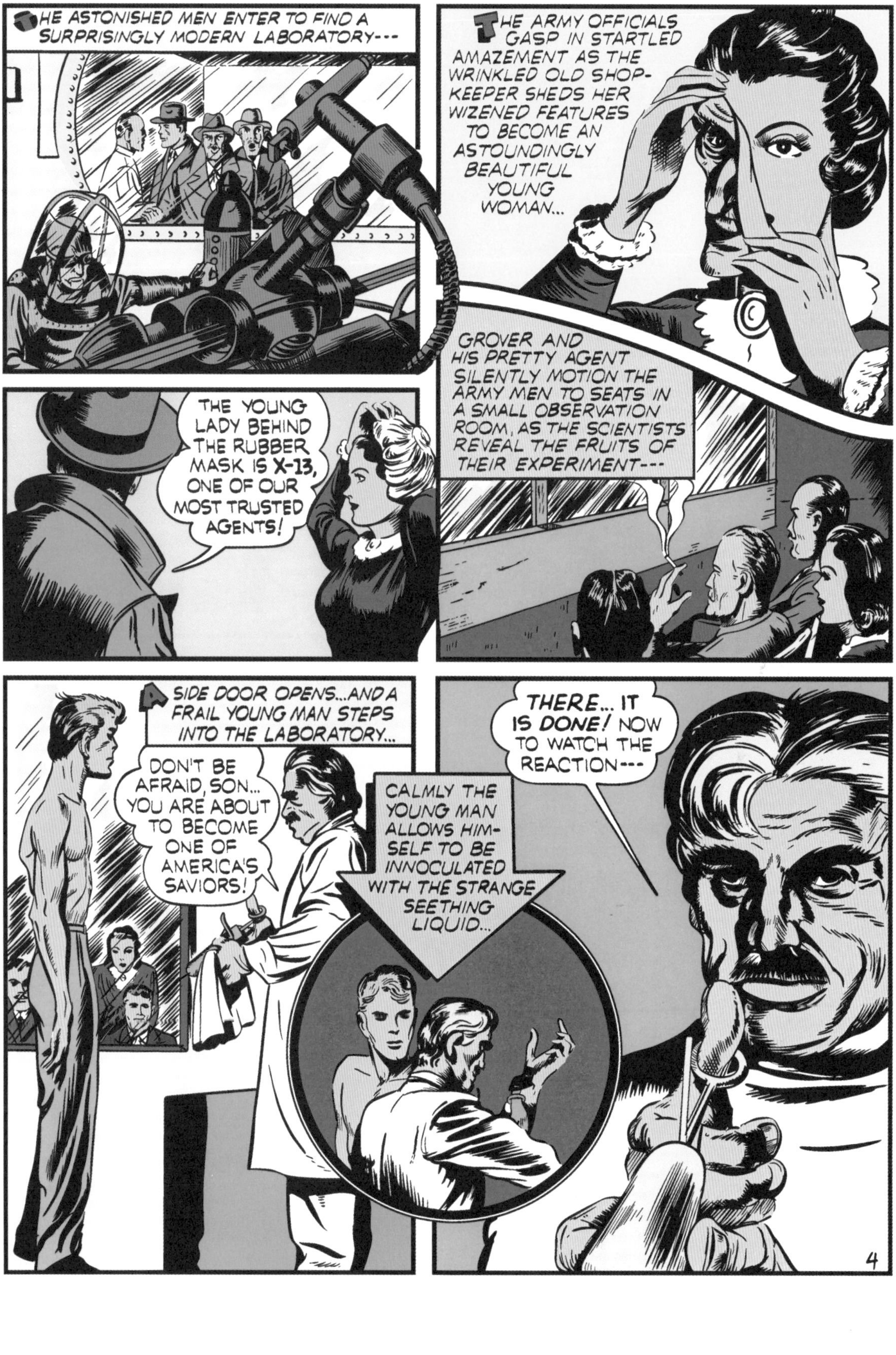
THE ASTONISHED MEN ENTER TO FIND A SURPRISINGLY MODERN LABORATORY---
THE ARMY OFFICIALS GASP IN STARTLED AMAZEMENT AS THE WRINKLED OLD SHOP-KEEPER SHEDS HER WIZENED FEATURES TO BECOME AN ASTOUNDINGLY BEAUTIFUL YOUNG WOMAN...
THE YOUNG LADY BEHIND THE RUBBER MASK IS X-13, ONE OF OUR MOST TRUSTED AGENTS!
GROVER AND HIS PRETTY AGENT SILENTLY MOTION THE ARMY MEN TO SEATS IN A SMALL OBSERVATION ROOM, AS THE SCIENTISTS REVEAL THE FRUITS OF THEIR EXPERIMENT---
A SIDE DOOR OPENS...AND A FRAIL YOUNG MAN STEPS INTO THE LABORATORY...
DON'T BE AFRAID, SON... YOU ARE ABOUT TO BECOME ONE OF AMERICA'S SAVIORS!
CALMLY THE YOUNG MAN ALLOWS HIM-SELF TO BE INNOCULATED WITH THE STRANGE SEETHING LIQUID...
THERE... IT IS DONE! NOW TO WATCH THE REACTION---
4

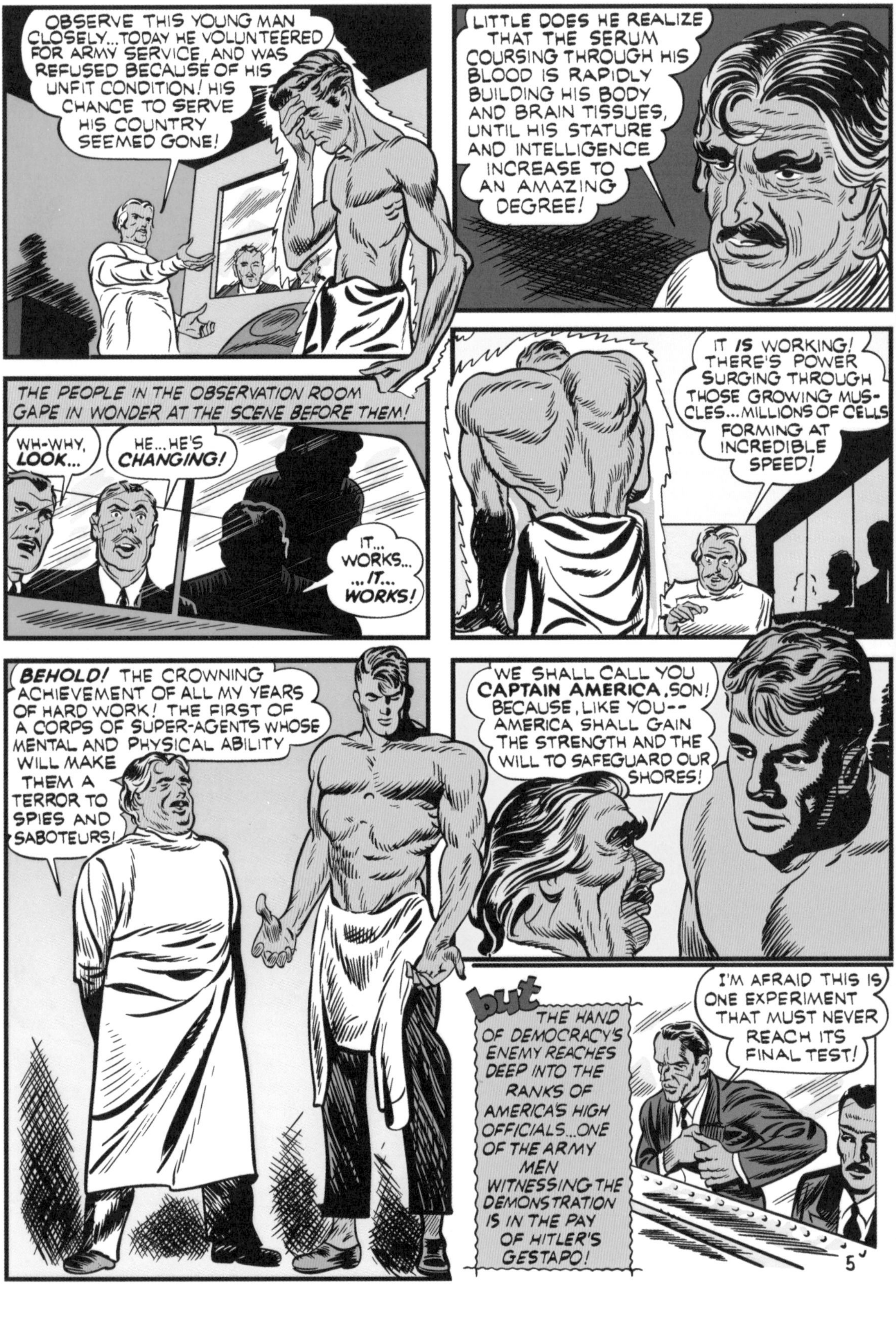
OBSERVE THIS YOUNG MAN CLOSELY...TODAY HE VOLUNTEERED FOR ARMY SERVICE, AND WAS REFUSED BECAUSE OF HIS UNFIT CONDITION! HIS CHANCE TO SERVE HIS COUNTRY SEEMED GONE!
LITTLE DOES HE REALIZE THAT THE SERUM COURSING THROUGH HIS BLOOD IS RAPIDLY BUILDING HIS BODY AND BRAIN TISSUES, UNTIL HIS STATURE AND INTELLIGENCE INCREASE TO AN AMAZING DEGREE!
THE PEOPLE IN THE OBSERVATION ROOM GAPE IN WONDER AT THE SCENE BEFORE THEM!
WH-WHY, LOOK...
HE...HE'S CHANGING!
IT... WORKS... ...IT... WORKS!
IT IS WORKING! THERE'S POWER SURGING THROUGH THOSE GROWING MUS-CLES...MILLIONS OF CELLS FORMING AT INCREDIBLE SPEED!
BEHOLD! THE CROWNING ACHIEVEMENT OF ALL MY YEARS OF HARD WORK! THE FIRST OF A CORPS OF SUPER-AGENTS WHOSE MENTAL AND PHYSICAL ABILITY WILL MAKE THEM A TERROR TO SPIES AND SABOTEURS!
WE SHALL CALL YOU CAPTAIN AMERICA, SON! BECAUSE, LIKE YOU-- AMERICA SHALL GAIN THE STRENGTH AND THE WILL TO SAFEGUARD OUR SHORES!
but THE HAND OF DEMOCRACY'S ENEMY REACHES DEEP INTO THE RANKS OF AMERICA'S HIGH OFFICIALS...ONE OF THE ARMY MEN WITNESSING THE DEMONSTRATION IS IN THE PAY OF HITLER'S GESTAPO!
I'M AFRAID THIS IS ONE EXPERIMENT THAT MUST NEVER REACH ITS FINAL TEST!
5

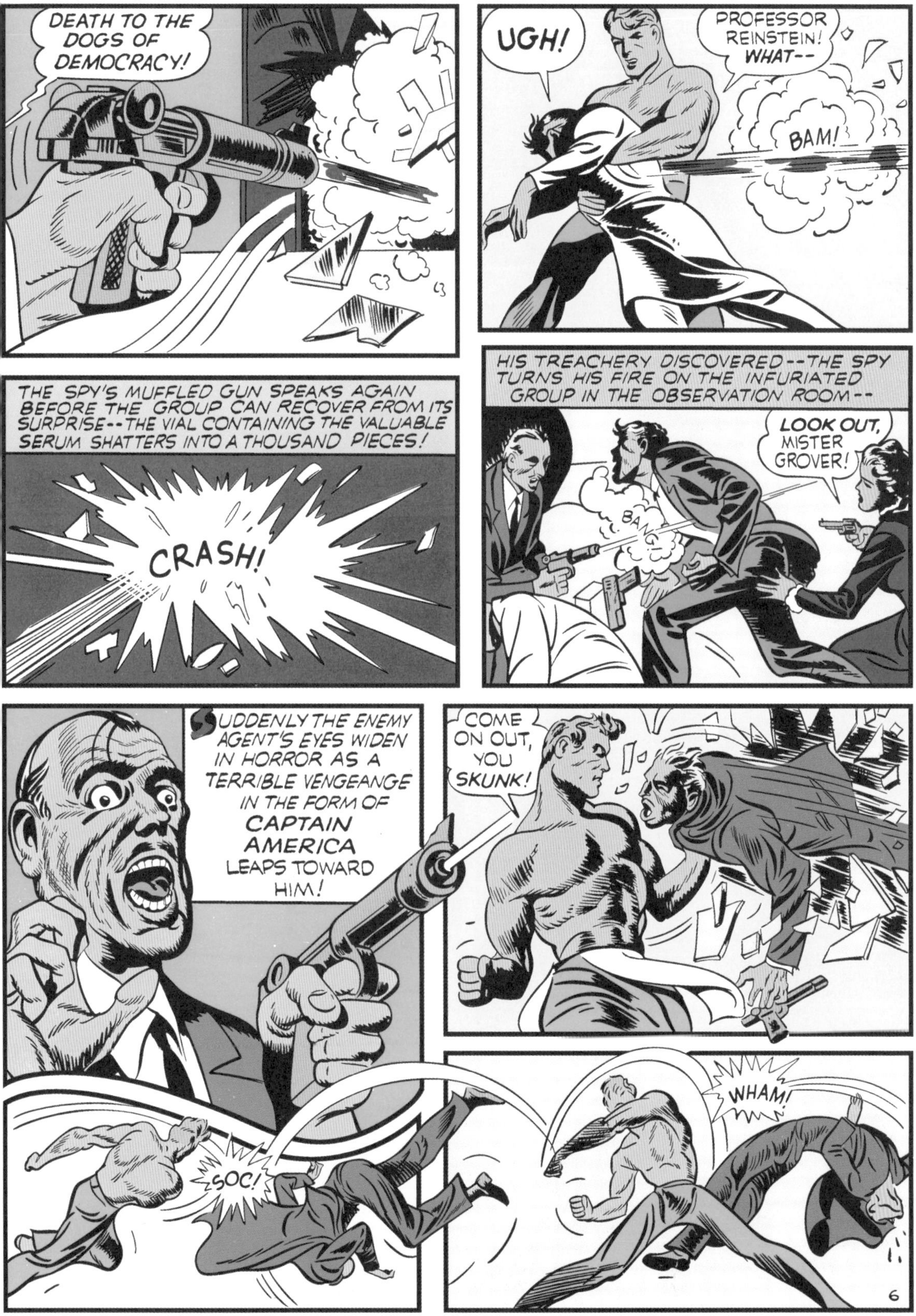
DEATH TO THE DOGS OF DEMOCRACY!
UGH!
PROFESSOR REINSTEIN! WHAT--
BAM!
THE SPY'S MUFFLED GUN SPEAKS AGAIN BEFORE THE GROUP CAN RECOVER FROM ITS SURPRISE--THE VIAL CONTAINING THE VALUABLE SERUM SHATTERS INTO A THOUSAND PIECES!
CRASH!
HIS TREACHERY DISCOVERED--THE SPY TURNS HIS FIRE ON THE INFURIATED GROUP IN THE OBSERVATION ROOM--
LOOK OUT, MISTER GROVER!
BANG!
SUDDENLY THE ENEMY AGENT'S EYES WIDEN IN HORROR AS A TERRIBLE VENGEANCE IN THE FORM OF CAPTAIN AMERICA LEAPS TOWARD HIM!
COME ON OUT, YOU SKUNK!
SOC!
WHAM!
6

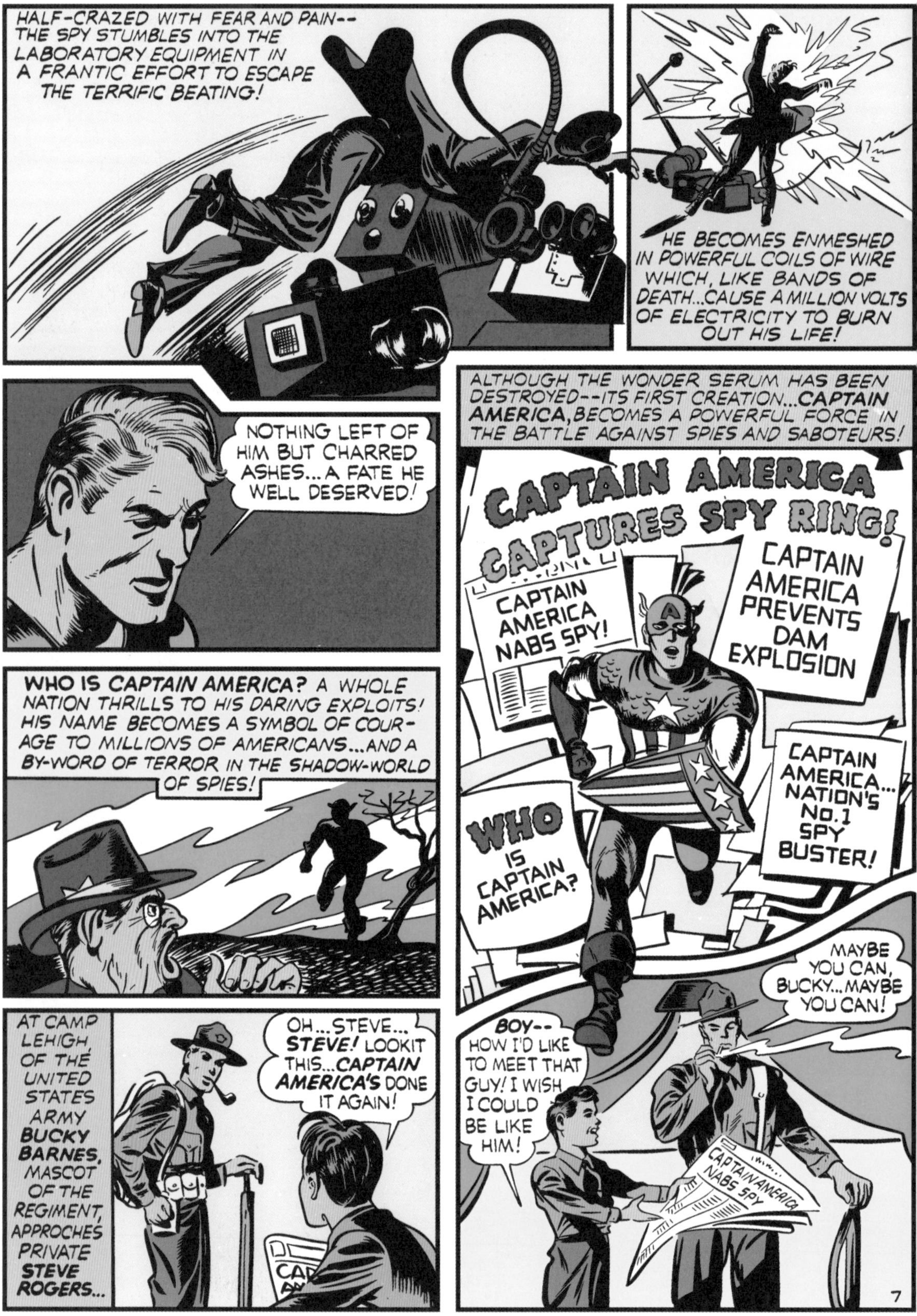
HALF-CRAZED WITH FEAR AND PAIN-- THE SPY STUMBLES INTO THE LABORATORY EQUIPMENT IN A FRANTIC EFFORT TO ESCAPE THE TERRIFIC BEATING!
HE BECOMES ENMESHED IN POWERFUL COILS OF WIRE WHICH, LIKE BANDS OF DEATH...CAUSE A MILLION VOLTS OF ELECTRICITY TO BURN OUT HIS LIFE!
NOTHING LEFT OF HIM BUT CHARRED ASHES...A FATE HE WELL DESERVED!
WHO IS CAPTAIN AMERICA? A WHOLE NATION THRILLS TO HIS DARING EXPLOITS! HIS NAME BECOMES A SYMBOL OF COURAGE TO MILLIONS OF AMERICANS...AND A BY-WORD OF TERROR IN THE SHADOW-WORLD OF SPIES!
AT CAMP LEHIGH, OF THE UNITED STATES ARMY BUCKY BARNES, MASCOT OF THE REGIMENT, APPROCHES PRIVATE STEVE ROGERS...
OH...STEVE... STEVE! LOOKIT THIS...CAPTAIN AMERICA'S DONE IT AGAIN!
ALTHOUGH THE WONDER SERUM HAS BEEN DESTROYED--ITS FIRST CREATION...CAPTAIN AMERICA, BECOMES A POWERFUL FORCE IN THE BATTLE AGAINST SPIES AND SABOTEURS!
CAPTAIN AMERICA CAPTURES SPY RING!
CAPTAIN AMERICA NABS SPY!
CAPTAIN AMERICA PREVENTS DAM EXPLOSION
CAPTAIN AMERICA... NATION'S No.1 SPY BUSTER!
WHO IS CAPTAIN AMERICA?
BOY-- HOW I'D LIKE TO MEET THAT GUY! I WISH I COULD BE LIKE HIM!
MAYBE YOU CAN, BUCKY...MAYBE YOU CAN!
CAPTAIN AMERICA NABS SPY
7

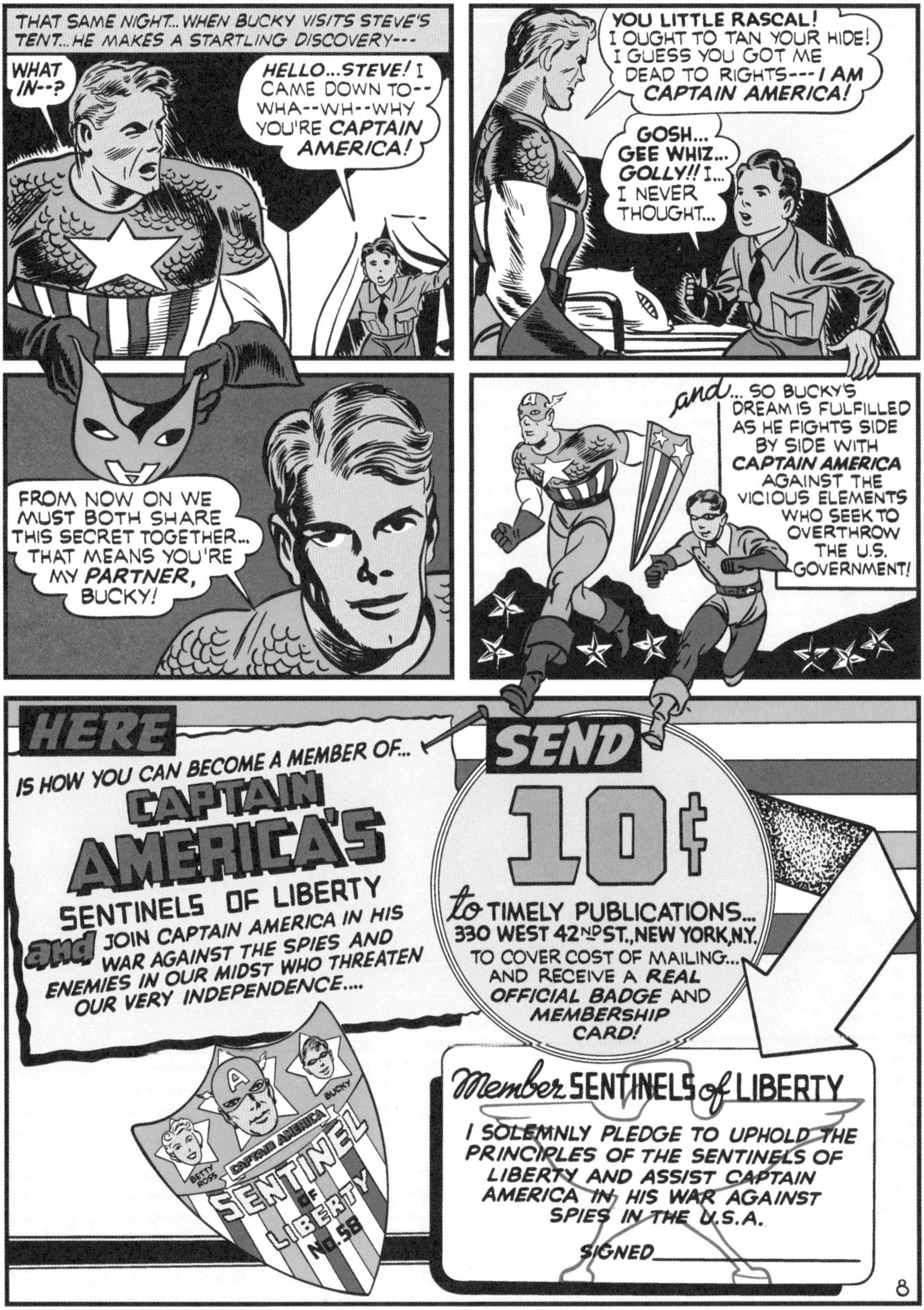
THAT SAME NIGHT... WHEN BUCKY VISITS STEVE'S TENT... HE MAKES A STARTLING DISCOVERY---
WHAT IN--?
HELLO...STEVE! I CAME DOWN TO-- WHA--WH--WHY YOU'RE CAPTAIN AMERICA!
YOU LITTLE RASCAL! I OUGHT TO TAN YOUR HIDE! I GUESS YOU GOT ME DEAD TO RIGHTS--- I AM CAPTAIN AMERICA!
GOSH... GEE WHIZ... GOLLY!! I... I NEVER THOUGHT...
FROM NOW ON WE MUST BOTH SHARE THIS SECRET TOGETHER... THAT MEANS YOU'RE MY PARTNER, BUCKY!
and... SO BUCKY'S DREAM IS FULFILLED AS HE FIGHTS SIDE BY SIDE WITH CAPTAIN AMERICA AGAINST THE VICIOUS ELEMENTS WHO SEEK TO OVERTHROW THE U.S. GOVERNMENT!
HERE IS HOW YOU CAN BECOME A MEMBER OF... CAPTAIN AMERICA'S SENTINELS OF LIBERTY and JOIN CAPTAIN AMERICA IN HIS WAR AGAINST THE SPIES AND ENEMIES IN OUR MIDST WHO THREATEN OUR VERY INDEPENDENCE....
SEND 10¢ to TIMELY PUBLICATIONS... 330 WEST 42ND ST., NEW YORK, N.Y. TO COVER COST OF MAILING... AND RECEIVE A REAL OFFICIAL BADGE AND MEMBERSHIP CARD!
BETTY ROSS
CAPTAIN AMERICA
BUCKY
SENTINEL OF LIBERTY
NO. 58
Member SENTINELS of LIBERTY
I SOLEMNLY PLEDGE TO UPHOLD THE PRINCIPLES OF THE SENTINELS OF LIBERTY AND ASSIST CAPTAIN AMERICA IN HIS WAR AGAINST SPIES IN THE U.S.A.
SIGNED___________
8

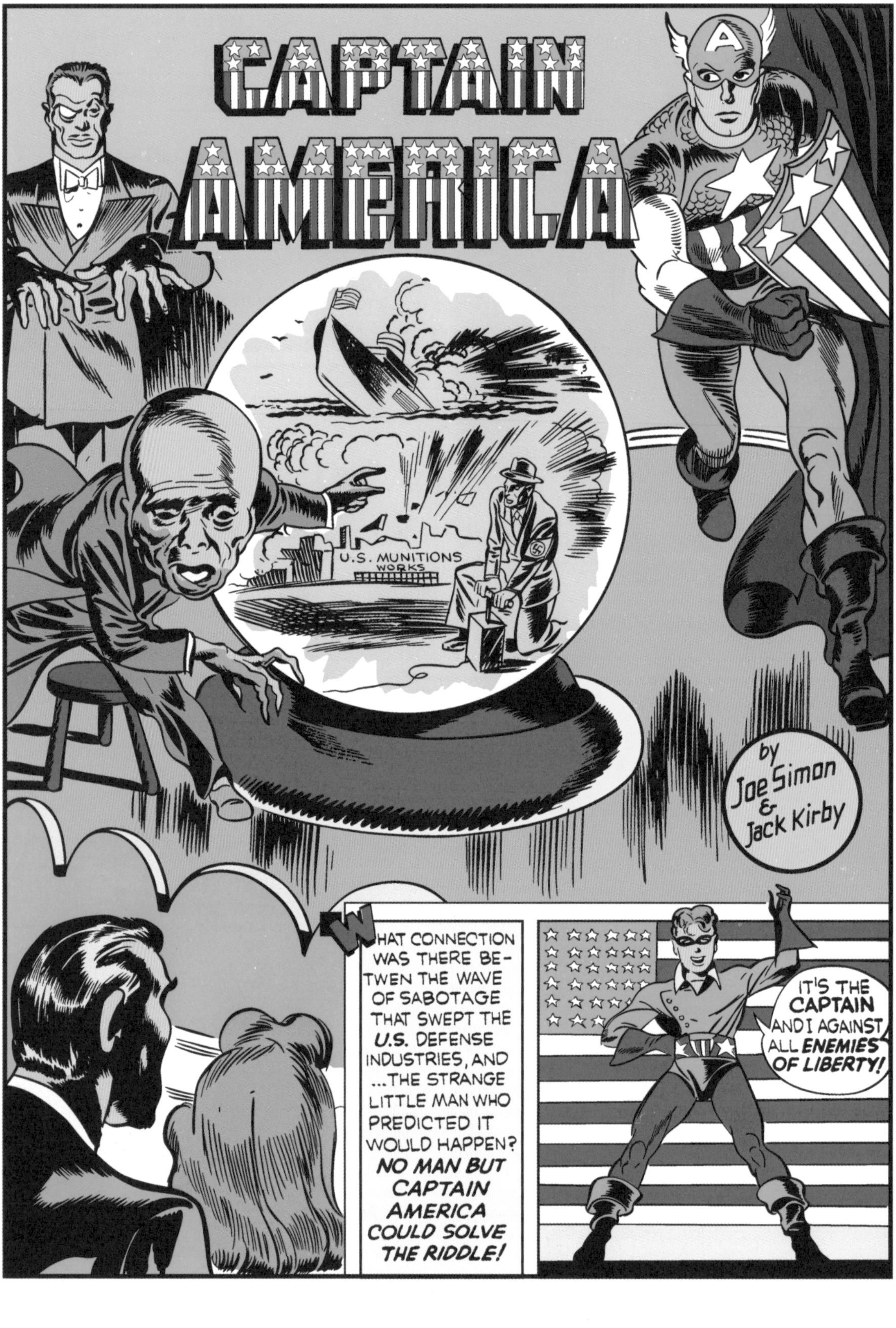
CAPTAIN AMERICA
U.S. MUNITIONS WORKS
by Joe Simon & Jack Kirby
WHAT CONNECTION WAS THERE BE- TWEN THE WAVE OF SABOTAGE THAT SWEPT THE U.S. DEFENSE INDUSTRIES, AND ...THE STRANGE LITTLE MAN WHO PREDICTED IT WOULD HAPPEN? NO MAN BUT CAPTAIN AMERICA COULD SOLVE THE RIDDLE!
IT'S THE CAPTAIN AND I AGAINST ALL ENEMIES OF LIBERTY!

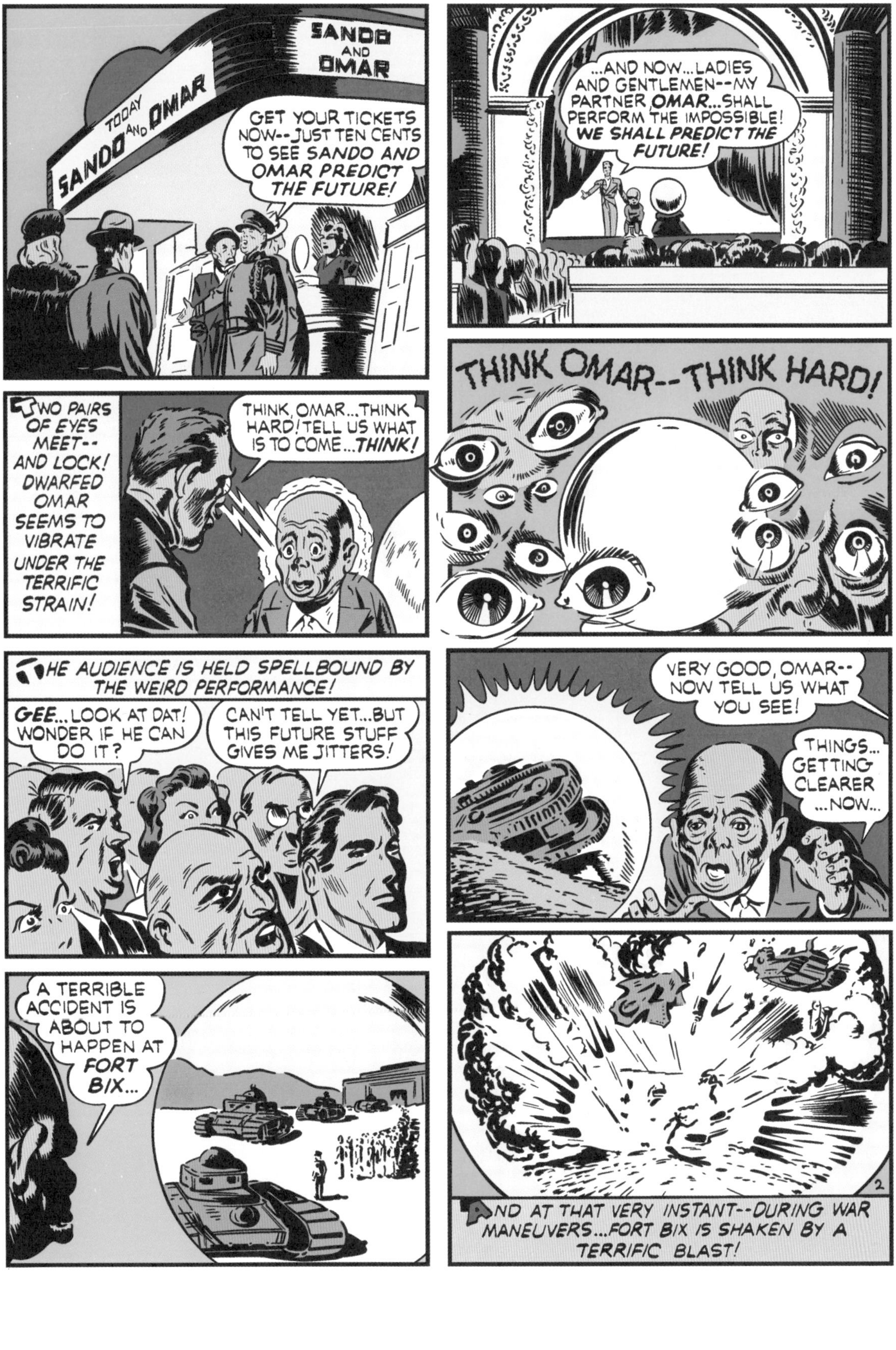
SANDO AND OMAR
TODAY SANDO AND OMAR
GET YOUR TICKETS NOW--JUST TEN CENTS TO SEE SANDO AND OMAR PREDICT THE FUTURE!
...AND NOW...LADIES AND GENTLEMEN--MY PARTNER OMAR...SHALL PERFORM THE IMPOSSIBLE! WE SHALL PREDICT THE FUTURE!
TWO PAIRS OF EYES MEET--AND LOCK! DWARFED OMAR SEEMS TO VIBRATE UNDER THE TERRIFIC STRAIN!
THINK, OMAR...THINK HARD! TELL US WHAT IS TO COME...THINK!
THINK OMAR--THINK HARD!
THE AUDIENCE IS HELD SPELLBOUND BY THE WEIRD PERFORMANCE!
GEE...LOOK AT DAT! WONDER IF HE CAN DO IT?
CAN'T TELL YET...BUT THIS FUTURE STUFF GIVES ME JITTERS!
VERY GOOD, OMAR--NOW TELL US WHAT YOU SEE!
THINGS... GETTING CLEARER ...NOW...
A TERRIBLE ACCIDENT IS ABOUT TO HAPPEN AT FORT BIX...
2
AND AT THAT VERY INSTANT--DURING WAR MANEUVERS...FORT BIX IS SHAKEN BY A TERRIFIC BLAST!

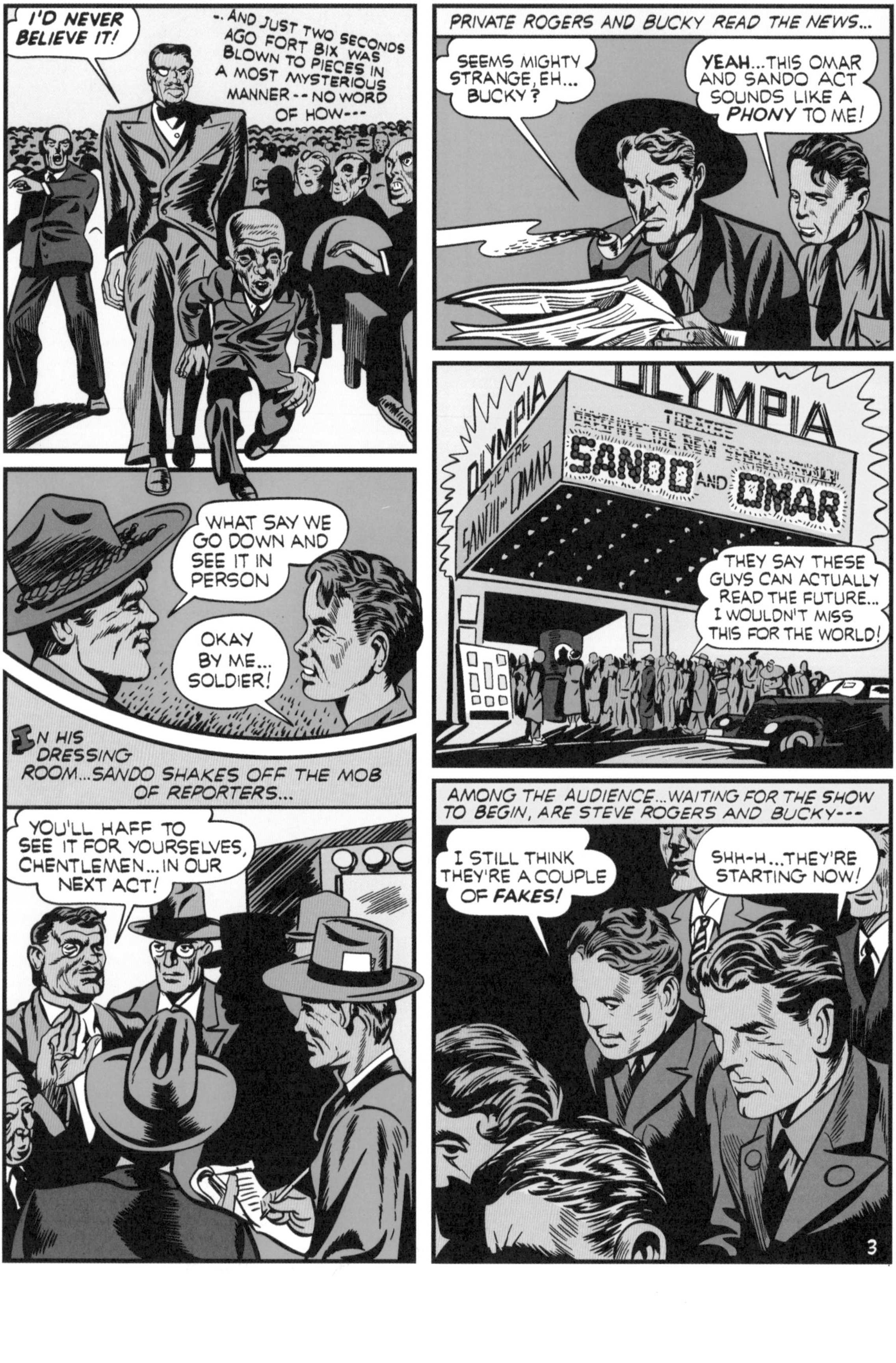
I'D NEVER BELIEVE IT!
-- AND JUST TWO SECONDS AGO FORT BIX WAS BLOWN TO PIECES IN A MOST MYSTERIOUS MANNER -- NO WORD OF HOW---
PRIVATE ROGERS AND BUCKY READ THE NEWS...
SEEMS MIGHTY STRANGE, EH... BUCKY?
YEAH... THIS OMAR AND SANDO ACT SOUNDS LIKE A PHONY TO ME!
WHAT SAY WE GO DOWN AND SEE IT IN PERSON
OKAY BY ME... SOLDIER!
OLYMPIA
THEATRE
SANDO AND OMAR
OLYMPIA THEATRE SANDO AND OMAR
THEY SAY THESE GUYS CAN ACTUALLY READ THE FUTURE... I WOULDN'T MISS THIS FOR THE WORLD!
IN HIS DRESSING ROOM... SANDO SHAKES OFF THE MOB OF REPORTERS...
YOU'LL HAFF TO SEE IT FOR YOURSELVES, CHENTLEMEN... IN OUR NEXT ACT!
AMONG THE AUDIENCE... WAITING FOR THE SHOW TO BEGIN, ARE STEVE ROGERS AND BUCKY---
I STILL THINK THEY'RE A COUPLE OF FAKES!
SHH-H... THEY'RE STARTING NOW!
3

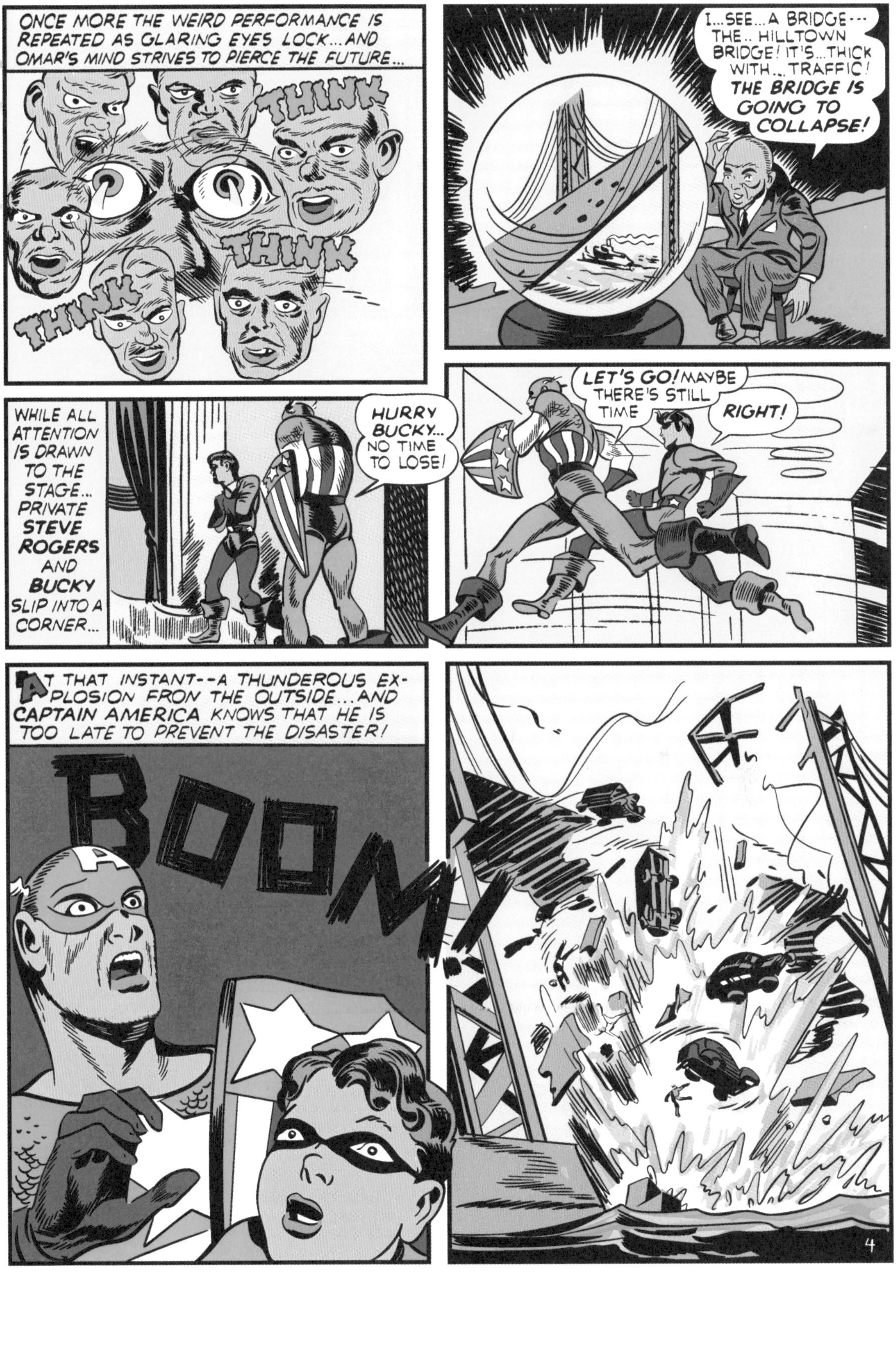
ONCE MORE THE WEIRD PERFORMANCE IS REPEATED AS GLARING EYES LOCK...AND OMAR'S MIND STRIVES TO PIERCE THE FUTURE...
THINK
THINK
THINK
I...SEE...A BRIDGE--- THE.. HILLTOWN BRIDGE! IT'S...THICK WITH...TRAFFIC! THE BRIDGE IS GOING TO COLLAPSE!
WHILE ALL ATTENTION IS DRAWN TO THE STAGE... PRIVATE STEVE ROGERS AND BUCKY SLIP INTO A CORNER...
HURRY BUCKY... NO TIME TO LOSE!
LET'S GO! MAYBE THERE'S STILL TIME
RIGHT!
AT THAT INSTANT--A THUNDEROUS EXPLOSION FROM THE OUTSIDE...AND CAPTAIN AMERICA KNOWS THAT HE IS TOO LATE TO PREVENT THE DISASTER!
BOOM!
4

THE THEATRE BUZZES WITH EXCITEMENT AS *CAPTAIN AMERICA* AND *BUCKY* TURN BACK TO FIND SANDO AND OMAR!

GANGWAY!

LET'S SEE WHAT OMAR HAS TO SAY TO *CAPTAIN AMERICA!*

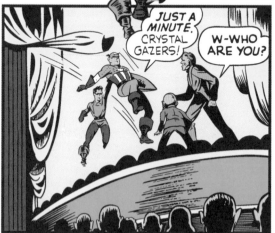

JUST A MINUTE, CRYSTAL GAZERS!

W-WHO ARE YOU?

I'LL ASK THE QUESTIONS, MISTER... HOW DID YOU KNOW THE BRIDGE WAS GOING TO TOPPLE?.... *SPEAK UP!*

SUDDENLY OMAR MAKES A QUICK DASH FOR THE DOOR---

COME BACK HERE, YOU RUNT!

A WOMAN'S SHRILL CRY FOR HELP CAUSES *CAPTAIN AMERICA* TO WHIRL ABOUT

THAT SCREAM CAME FROM SANDO'S DRESSING ROOM!

SORRY, SANDO! BUT I CAN'T LET YOU GET AWAY!

SOCK!

THAT'S FUNNY... THE ROOM IS QUIET AND DARK!

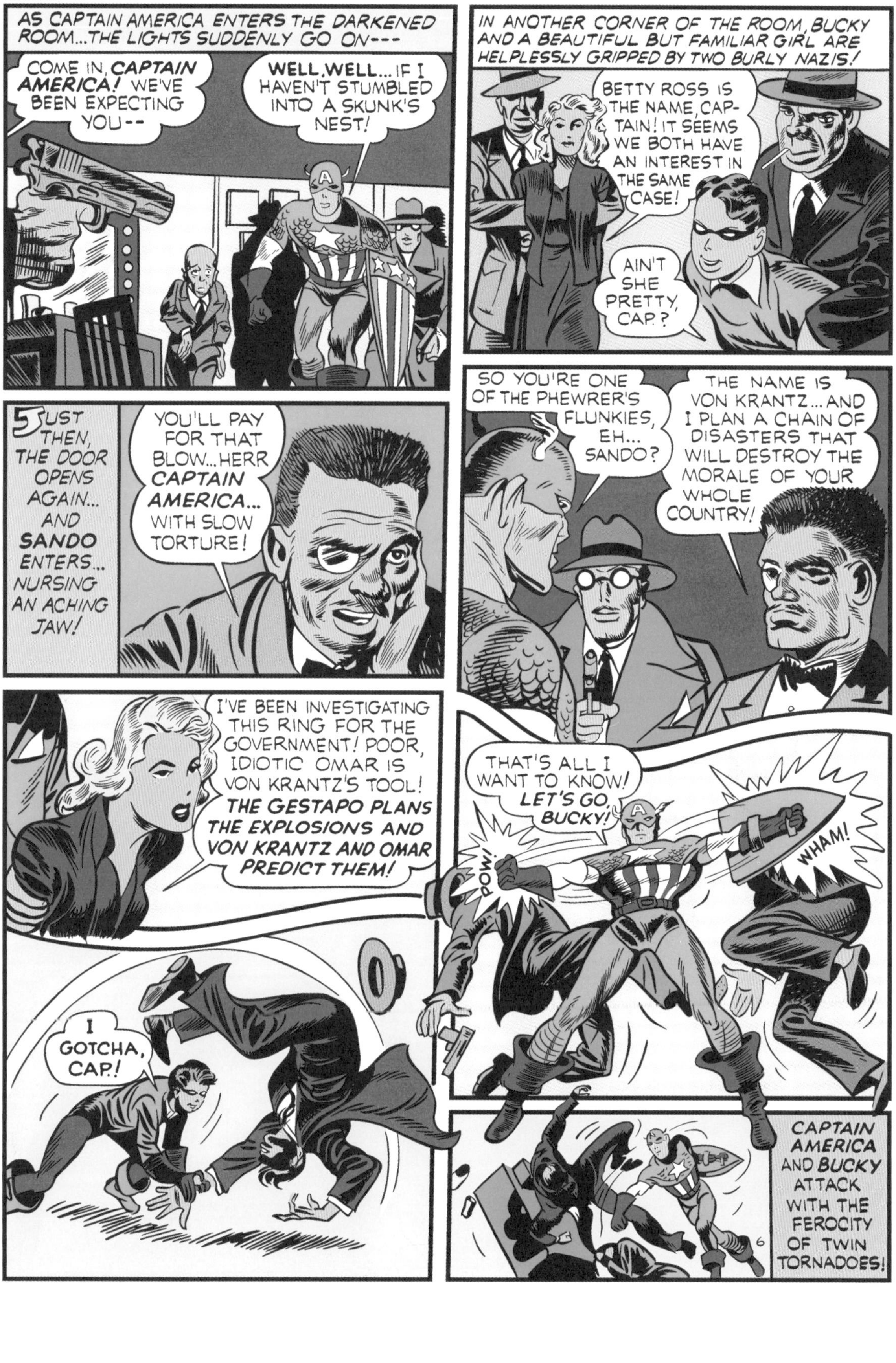
AS CAPTAIN AMERICA ENTERS THE DARKENED ROOM...THE LIGHTS SUDDENLY GO ON---
COME IN, **CAPTAIN AMERICA!** WE'VE BEEN EXPECTING YOU--
WELL, WELL... IF I HAVEN'T STUMBLED INTO A SKUNK'S NEST!
IN ANOTHER CORNER OF THE ROOM, BUCKY AND A BEAUTIFUL BUT FAMILIAR GIRL ARE HELPLESSLY GRIPPED BY TWO BURLY NAZIS!
BETTY ROSS IS THE NAME, CAPTAIN! IT SEEMS WE BOTH HAVE AN INTEREST IN THE SAME CASE!
AIN'T SHE PRETTY, CAP.?
JUST THEN, THE DOOR OPENS AGAIN... AND **SANDO** ENTERS... NURSING AN ACHING JAW!
YOU'LL PAY FOR THAT BLOW...HERR **CAPTAIN AMERICA...** WITH SLOW TORTURE!
SO YOU'RE ONE OF THE PHEWRER'S FLUNKIES, EH... SANDO?
THE NAME IS VON KRANTZ...AND I PLAN A CHAIN OF DISASTERS THAT WILL DESTROY THE MORALE OF YOUR WHOLE COUNTRY!
I'VE BEEN INVESTIGATING THIS RING FOR THE GOVERNMENT! POOR, IDIOTIC OMAR IS VON KRANTZ'S TOOL! **THE GESTAPO PLANS THE EXPLOSIONS AND VON KRANTZ AND OMAR PREDICT THEM!**
I GOTCHA, CAP.!
THAT'S ALL I WANT TO KNOW! **LET'S GO, BUCKY!**
POW!
WHAM!
CAPTAIN AMERICA AND BUCKY ATTACK WITH THE FEROCITY OF TWIN TORNADOES!

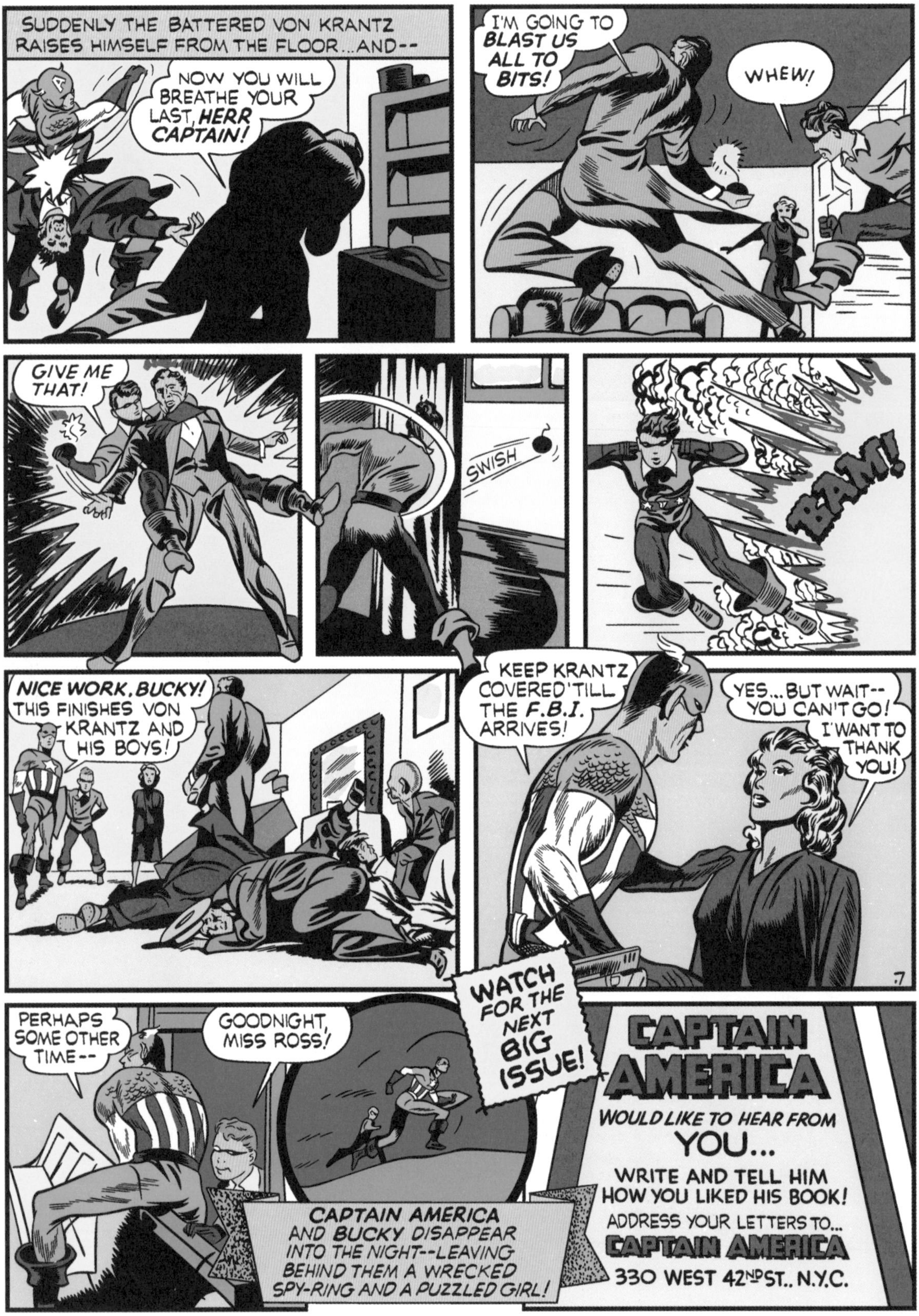
SUDDENLY THE BATTERED VON KRANTZ RAISES HIMSELF FROM THE FLOOR...AND--
NOW YOU WILL BREATHE YOUR LAST, HERR CAPTAIN!
I'M GOING TO BLAST US ALL TO BITS!
WHEW!
GIVE ME THAT!
SWISH
BAM!
NICE WORK, BUCKY! THIS FINISHES VON KRANTZ AND HIS BOYS!
KEEP KRANTZ COVERED 'TILL THE F.B.I. ARRIVES!
YES... BUT WAIT-- YOU CAN'T GO! I WANT TO THANK YOU!
7
PERHAPS SOME OTHER TIME--
GOODNIGHT, MISS ROSS!
WATCH FOR THE NEXT BIG ISSUE!
CAPTAIN AMERICA AND BUCKY DISAPPEAR INTO THE NIGHT--LEAVING BEHIND THEM A WRECKED SPY-RING AND A PUZZLED GIRL!
CAPTAIN AMERICA WOULD LIKE TO HEAR FROM YOU...
WRITE AND TELL HIM HOW YOU LIKED HIS BOOK!
ADDRESS YOUR LETTERS TO... CAPTAIN AMERICA
330 WEST 42ND ST., N.Y.C.

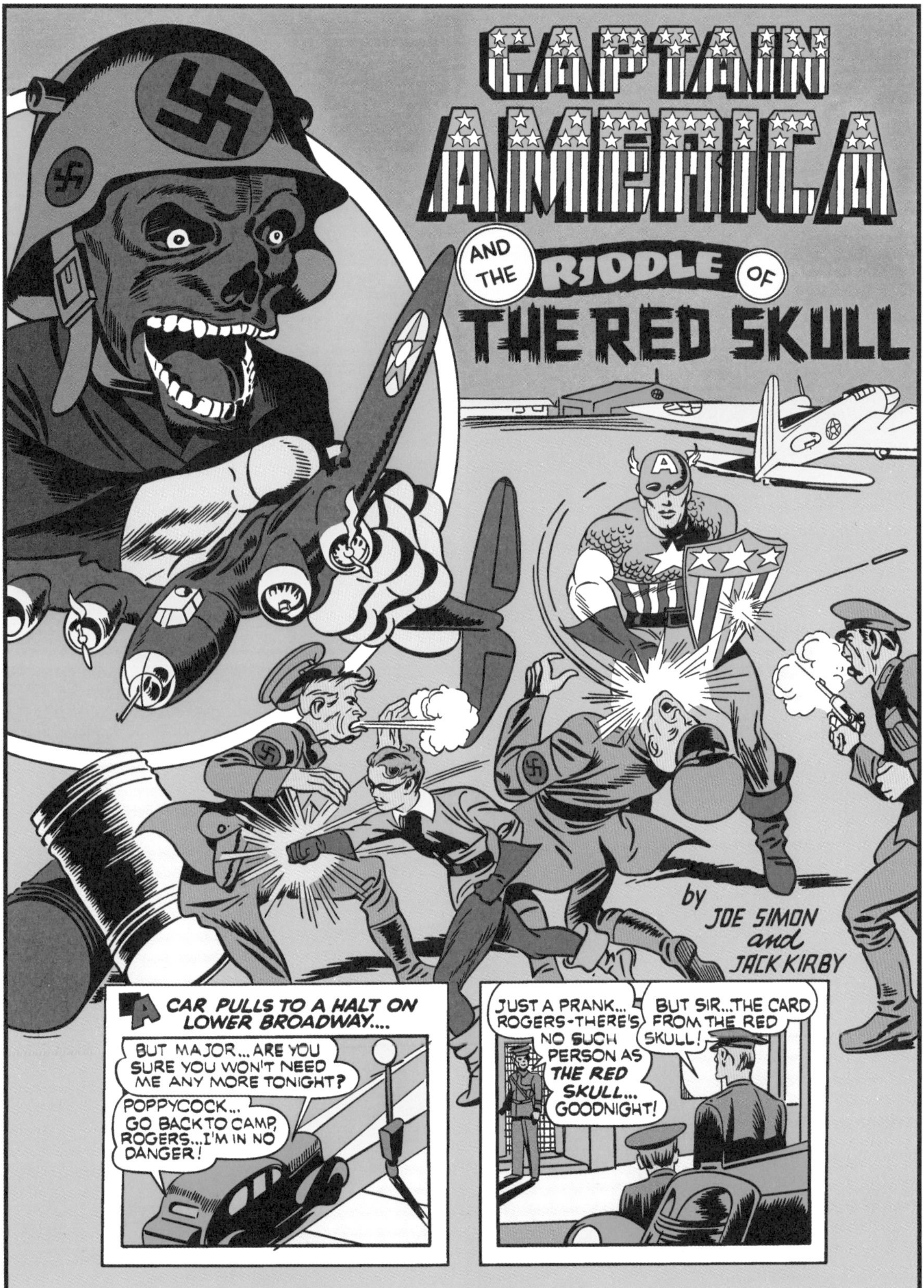

CAPTAIN AMERICA
AND THE RIDDLE OF THE RED SKULL
by JOE SIMON and JACK KIRBY
A CAR PULLS TO A HALT ON LOWER BROADWAY....
BUT MAJOR... ARE YOU SURE YOU WON'T NEED ME ANY MORE TONIGHT?
POPPYCOCK... GO BACK TO CAMP, ROGERS... I'M IN NO DANGER!
JUST A PRANK... ROGERS-THERE'S NO SUCH PERSON AS THE RED SKULL... GOODNIGHT!
BUT SIR... THE CARD FROM THE RED SKULL!

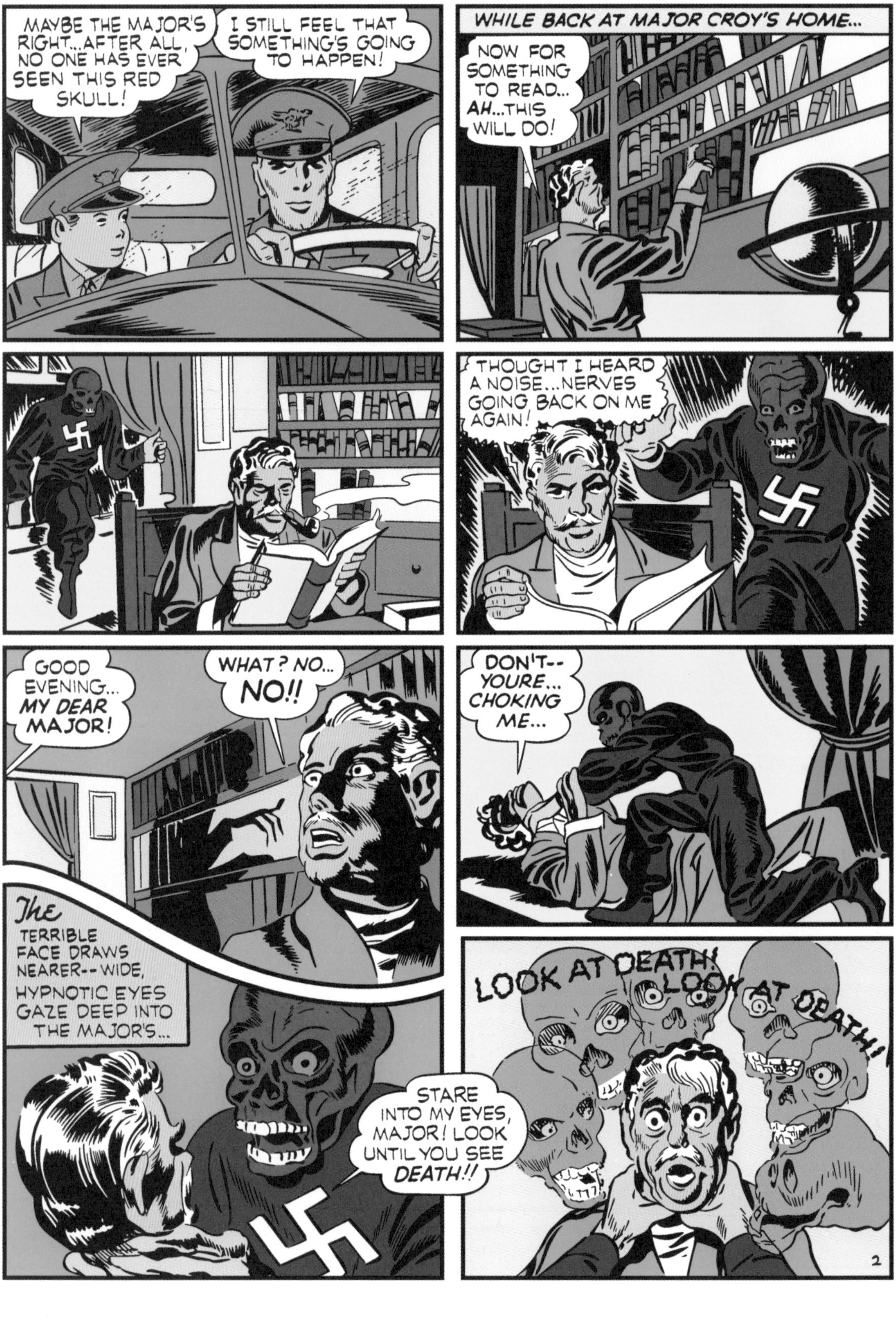
MAYBE THE MAJOR'S RIGHT...AFTER ALL, NO ONE HAS EVER SEEN THIS RED SKULL!
I STILL FEEL THAT SOMETHING'S GOING TO HAPPEN!
WHILE BACK AT MAJOR CROY'S HOME...
NOW FOR SOMETHING TO READ... AH...THIS WILL DO!
THOUGHT I HEARD A NOISE...NERVES GOING BACK ON ME AGAIN!
GOOD EVENING... MY DEAR MAJOR!
WHAT? NO... NO!!
The TERRIBLE FACE DRAWS NEARER--WIDE, HYPNOTIC EYES GAZE DEEP INTO THE MAJOR'S...
STARE INTO MY EYES, MAJOR! LOOK UNTIL YOU SEE DEATH!!
DON'T-- YOURE... CHOKING ME...
LOOK AT DEATH! LOOK AT DEATH!
2

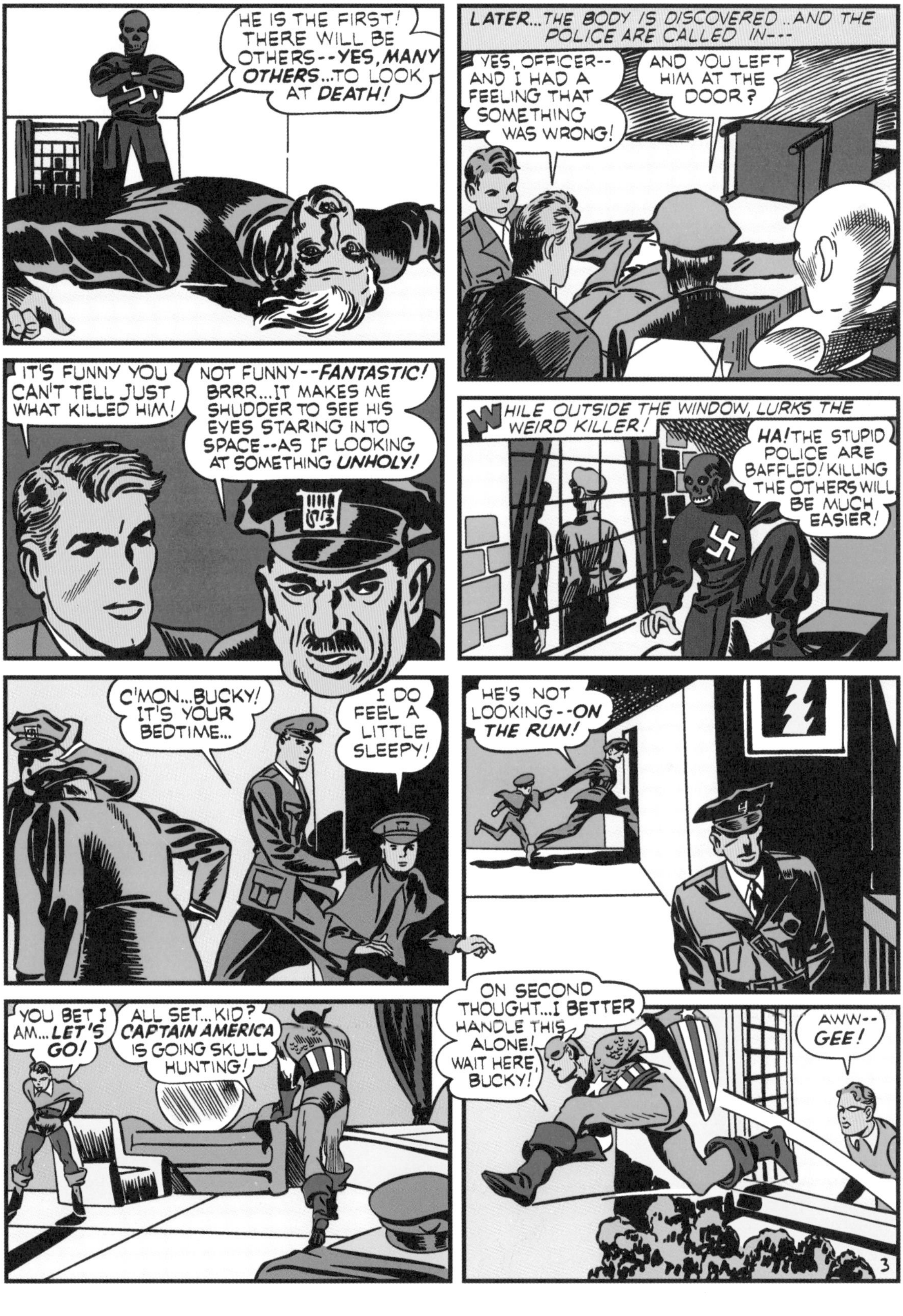
HE IS THE FIRST! THERE WILL BE OTHERS--YES, MANY OTHERS...TO LOOK AT DEATH!
LATER...THE BODY IS DISCOVERED..AND THE POLICE ARE CALLED IN---
YES, OFFICER--AND I HAD A FEELING THAT SOMETHING WAS WRONG!
AND YOU LEFT HIM AT THE DOOR?
IT'S FUNNY YOU CAN'T TELL JUST WHAT KILLED HIM!
NOT FUNNY--FANTASTIC! BRRR...IT MAKES ME SHUDDER TO SEE HIS EYES STARING INTO SPACE--AS IF LOOKING AT SOMETHING UNHOLY!
WHILE OUTSIDE THE WINDOW, LURKS THE WEIRD KILLER!
HA! THE STUPID POLICE ARE BAFFLED! KILLING THE OTHERS WILL BE MUCH EASIER!
C'MON...BUCKY! IT'S YOUR BEDTIME...
I DO FEEL A LITTLE SLEEPY!
HE'S NOT LOOKING--ON THE RUN!
YOU BET I AM...LET'S GO!
ALL SET...KID? CAPTAIN AMERICA IS GOING SKULL HUNTING!
ON SECOND THOUGHT...I BETTER HANDLE THIS ALONE! WAIT HERE, BUCKY!
AWW--GEE!
3

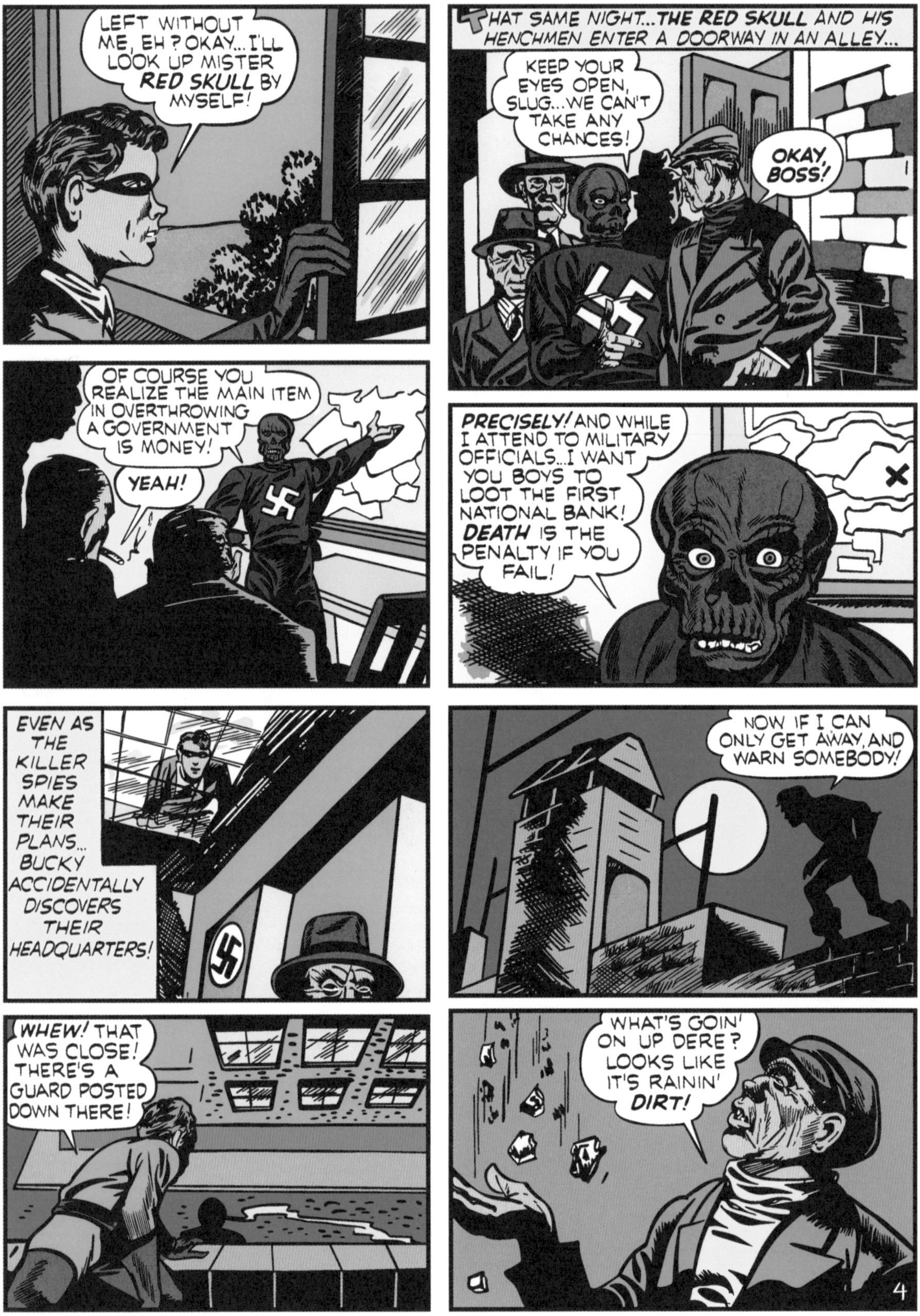
LEFT WITHOUT ME, EH ? OKAY... I'LL LOOK UP MISTER RED SKULL BY MYSELF!
THAT SAME NIGHT... THE RED SKULL AND HIS HENCHMEN ENTER A DOORWAY IN AN ALLEY...
KEEP YOUR EYES OPEN, SLUG... WE CAN'T TAKE ANY CHANCES!
OKAY, BOSS!
OF COURSE YOU REALIZE THE MAIN ITEM IN OVERTHROWING A GOVERNMENT IS MONEY!
YEAH!
PRECISELY! AND WHILE I ATTEND TO MILITARY OFFICIALS... I WANT YOU BOYS TO LOOT THE FIRST NATIONAL BANK! DEATH IS THE PENALTY IF YOU FAIL!
EVEN AS THE KILLER SPIES MAKE THEIR PLANS... BUCKY ACCIDENTALLY DISCOVERS THEIR HEADQUARTERS!
NOW IF I CAN ONLY GET AWAY, AND WARN SOMEBODY!
WHEW! THAT WAS CLOSE! THERE'S A GUARD POSTED DOWN THERE!
WHAT'S GOIN' ON UP DERE ? LOOKS LIKE IT'S RAININ' DIRT!
4

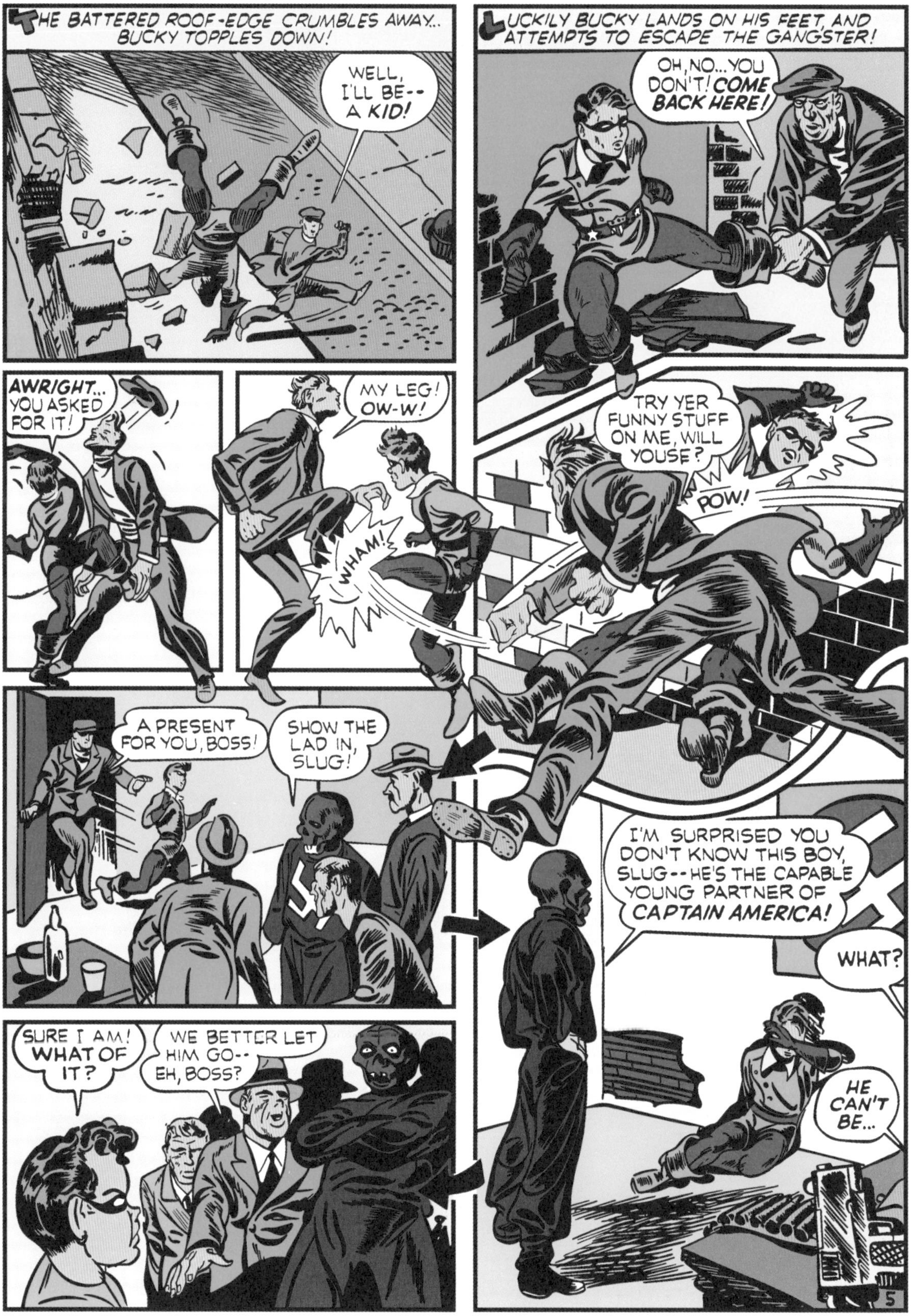
THE BATTERED ROOF-EDGE CRUMBLES AWAY.. BUCKY TOPPLES DOWN!
WELL, I'LL BE-- A KID!
LUCKILY BUCKY LANDS ON HIS FEET, AND ATTEMPTS TO ESCAPE THE GANGSTER!
OH, NO...YOU DON'T! COME BACK HERE!
TRY YER FUNNY STUFF ON ME, WILL YOUSE?
POW!
AWRIGHT... YOU ASKED FOR IT!
MY LEG! OW-W!
WHAM!
A PRESENT FOR YOU, BOSS!
SHOW THE LAD IN, SLUG!
I'M SURPRISED YOU DON'T KNOW THIS BOY, SLUG--HE'S THE CAPABLE YOUNG PARTNER OF CAPTAIN AMERICA!
WHAT?
HE CAN'T BE...
SURE I AM! WHAT OF IT?
WE BETTER LET HIM GO-- EH, BOSS?
5

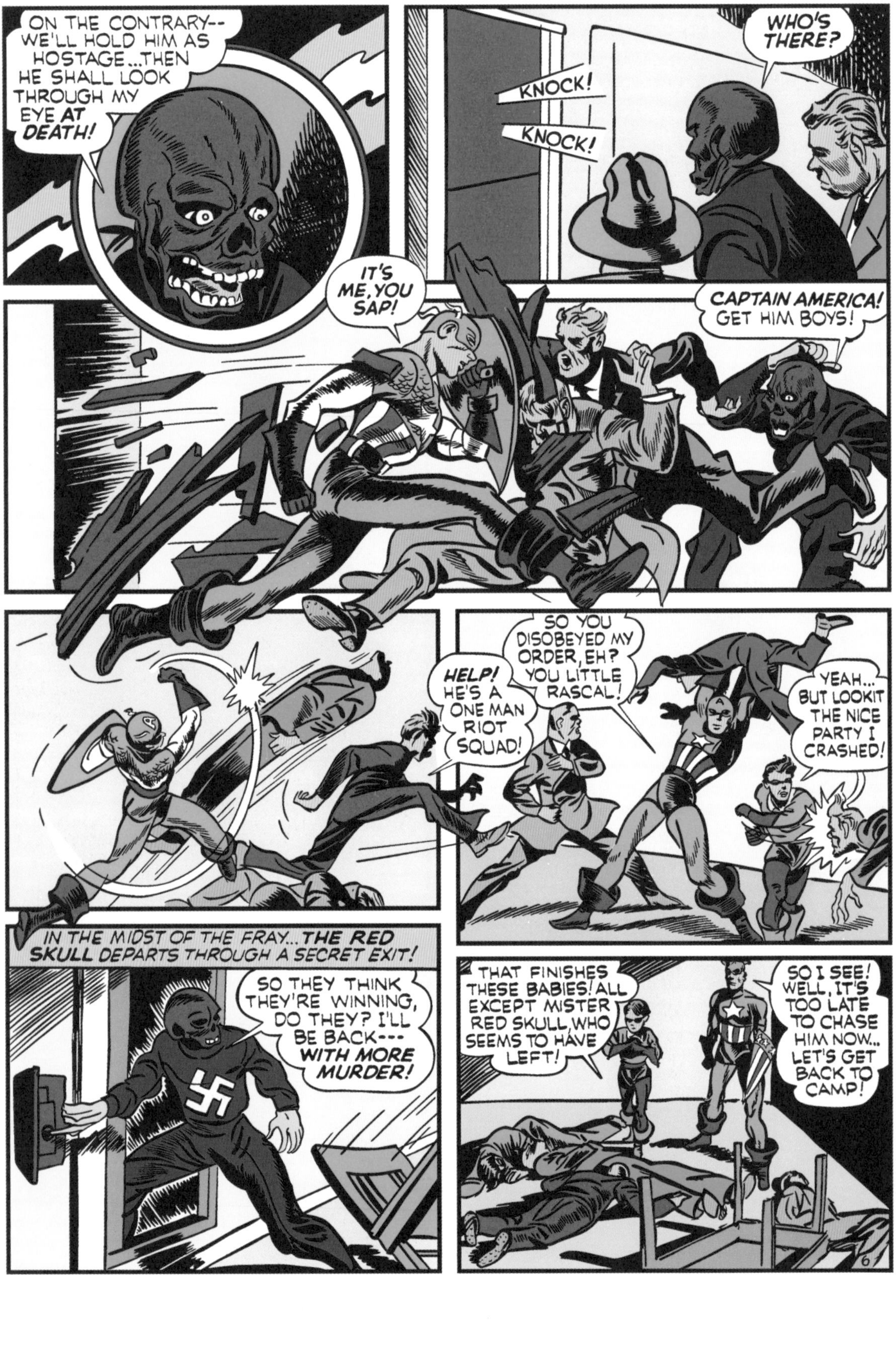
ON THE CONTRARY-- WE'LL HOLD HIM AS HOSTAGE...THEN HE SHALL LOOK THROUGH MY EYE **AT DEATH!**
KNOCK!
KNOCK!
WHO'S THERE?
IT'S ME, YOU SAP!
CAPTAIN AMERICA! GET HIM BOYS!
HELP! HE'S A ONE MAN RIOT SQUAD!
SO YOU DISOBEYED MY ORDER, EH? YOU LITTLE RASCAL!
YEAH... BUT LOOKIT THE NICE PARTY I CRASHED!
IN THE MIDST OF THE FRAY... **THE RED SKULL** DEPARTS THROUGH A SECRET EXIT!
SO THEY THINK THEY'RE WINNING, DO THEY? I'LL BE BACK--- **WITH MORE MURDER!**
THAT FINISHES THESE BABIES! ALL EXCEPT MISTER RED SKULL, WHO SEEMS TO HAVE LEFT!
SO I SEE! WELL, IT'S TOO LATE TO CHASE HIM NOW... LET'S GET BACK TO CAMP!
6

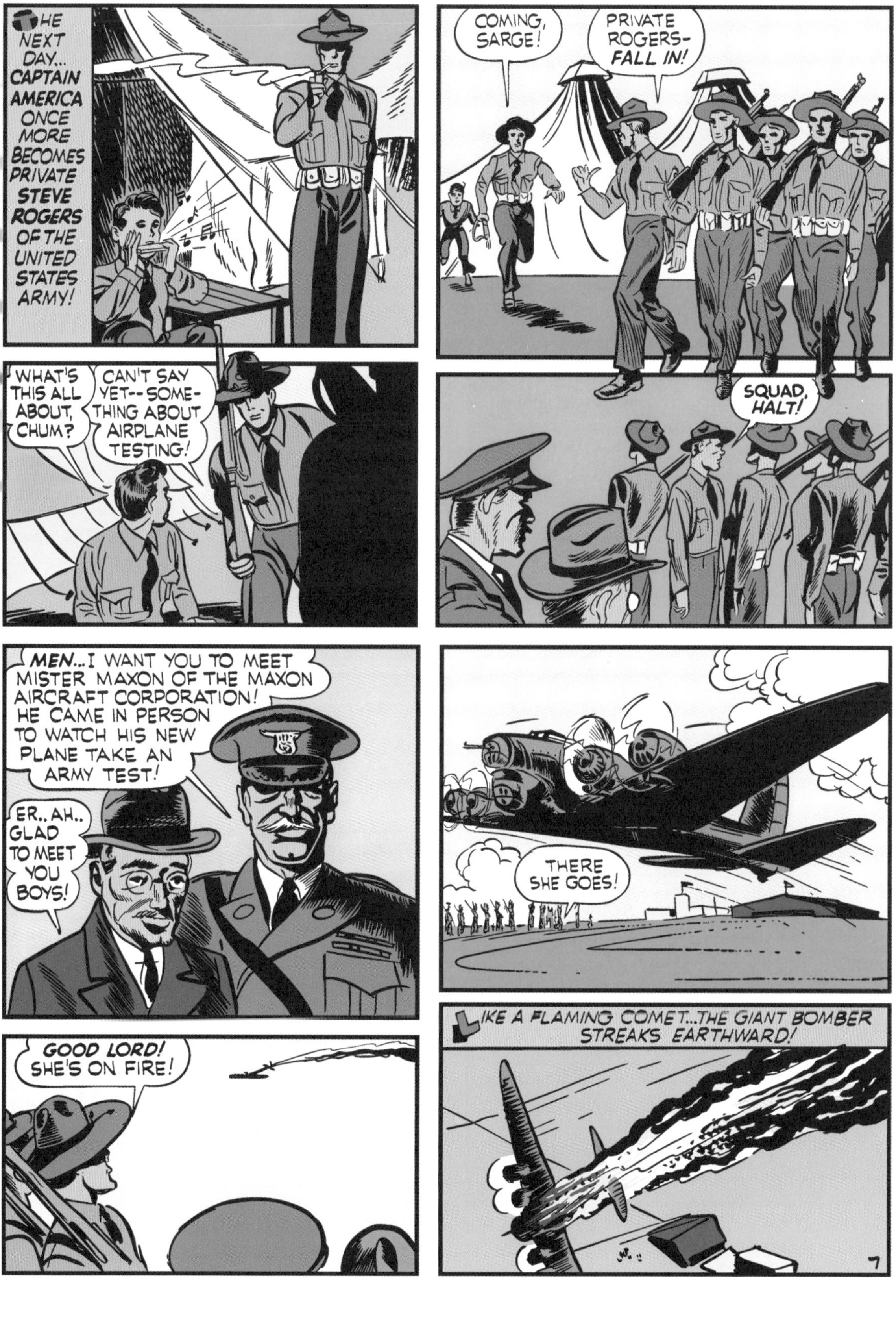
THE NEXT DAY... CAPTAIN AMERICA ONCE MORE BECOMES PRIVATE STEVE ROGERS OF THE UNITED STATES ARMY!
COMING, SARGE!
PRIVATE ROGERS- FALL IN!
WHAT'S THIS ALL ABOUT, CHUM?
CAN'T SAY YET-- SOMETHING ABOUT AIRPLANE TESTING!
SQUAD, HALT!
MEN...I WANT YOU TO MEET MISTER MAXON OF THE MAXON AIRCRAFT CORPORATION! HE CAME IN PERSON TO WATCH HIS NEW PLANE TAKE AN ARMY TEST!
ER..AH.. GLAD TO MEET YOU BOYS!
THERE SHE GOES!
GOOD LORD! SHE'S ON FIRE!
LIKE A FLAMING COMET...THE GIANT BOMBER STREAKS EARTHWARD!
7

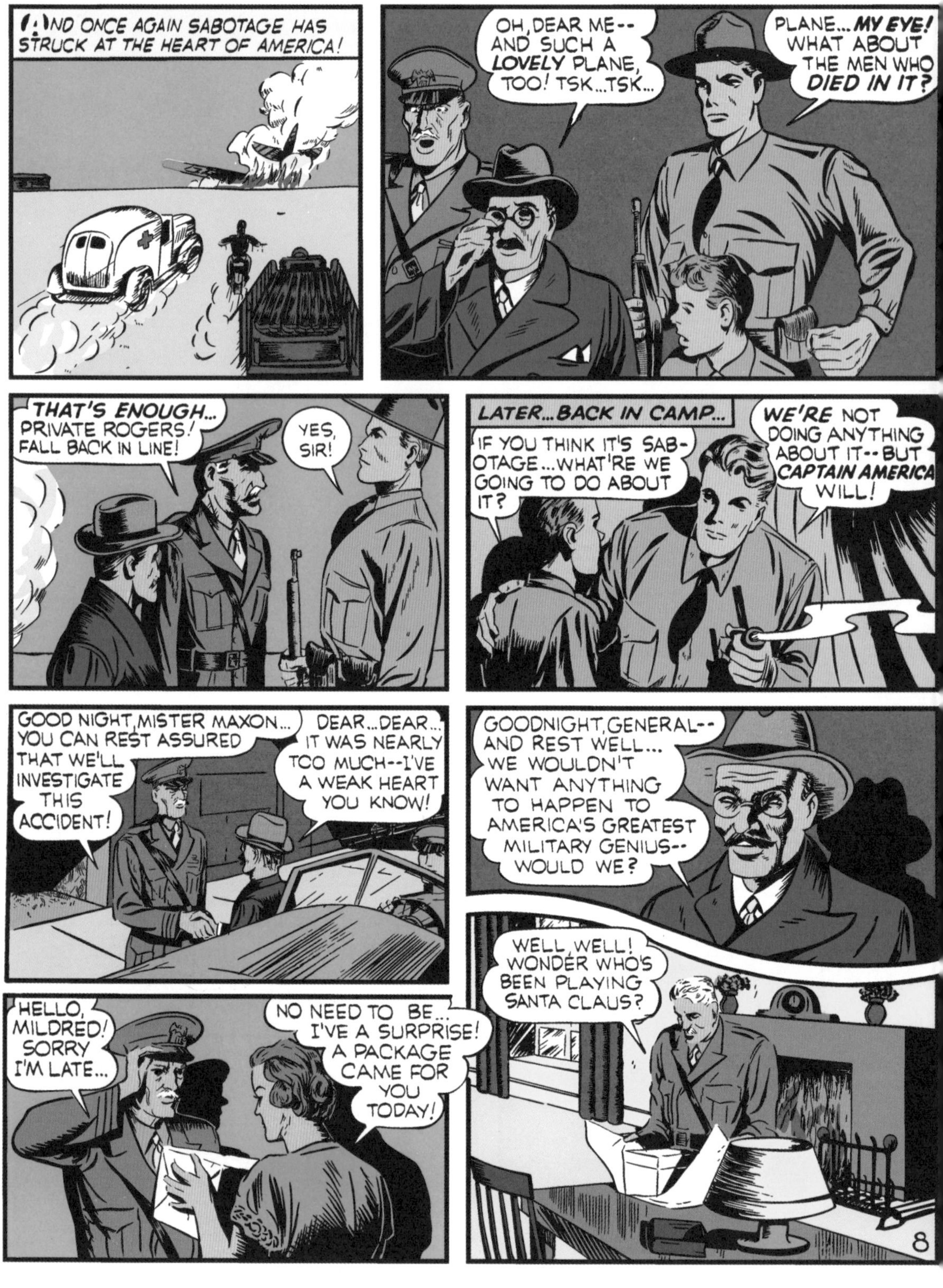
AND ONCE AGAIN SABOTAGE HAS STRUCK AT THE HEART OF AMERICA!
OH, DEAR ME-- AND SUCH A LOVELY PLANE, TOO! TSK...TSK...
PLANE... MY EYE! WHAT ABOUT THE MEN WHO DIED IN IT?
THAT'S ENOUGH... PRIVATE ROGERS! FALL BACK IN LINE!
YES, SIR!
LATER...BACK IN CAMP...
IF YOU THINK IT'S SABOTAGE...WHAT'RE WE GOING TO DO ABOUT IT?
WE'RE NOT DOING ANYTHING ABOUT IT-- BUT CAPTAIN AMERICA WILL!
GOOD NIGHT, MISTER MAXON... YOU CAN REST ASSURED THAT WE'LL INVESTIGATE THIS ACCIDENT!
DEAR...DEAR... IT WAS NEARLY TOO MUCH--I'VE A WEAK HEART YOU KNOW!
GOODNIGHT, GENERAL-- AND REST WELL... WE WOULDN'T WANT ANYTHING TO HAPPEN TO AMERICA'S GREATEST MILITARY GENIUS-- WOULD WE?
HELLO, MILDRED! SORRY I'M LATE...
NO NEED TO BE... I'VE A SURPRISE! A PACKAGE CAME FOR YOU TODAY!
WELL, WELL! WONDER WHO'S BEEN PLAYING SANTA CLAUS?
8

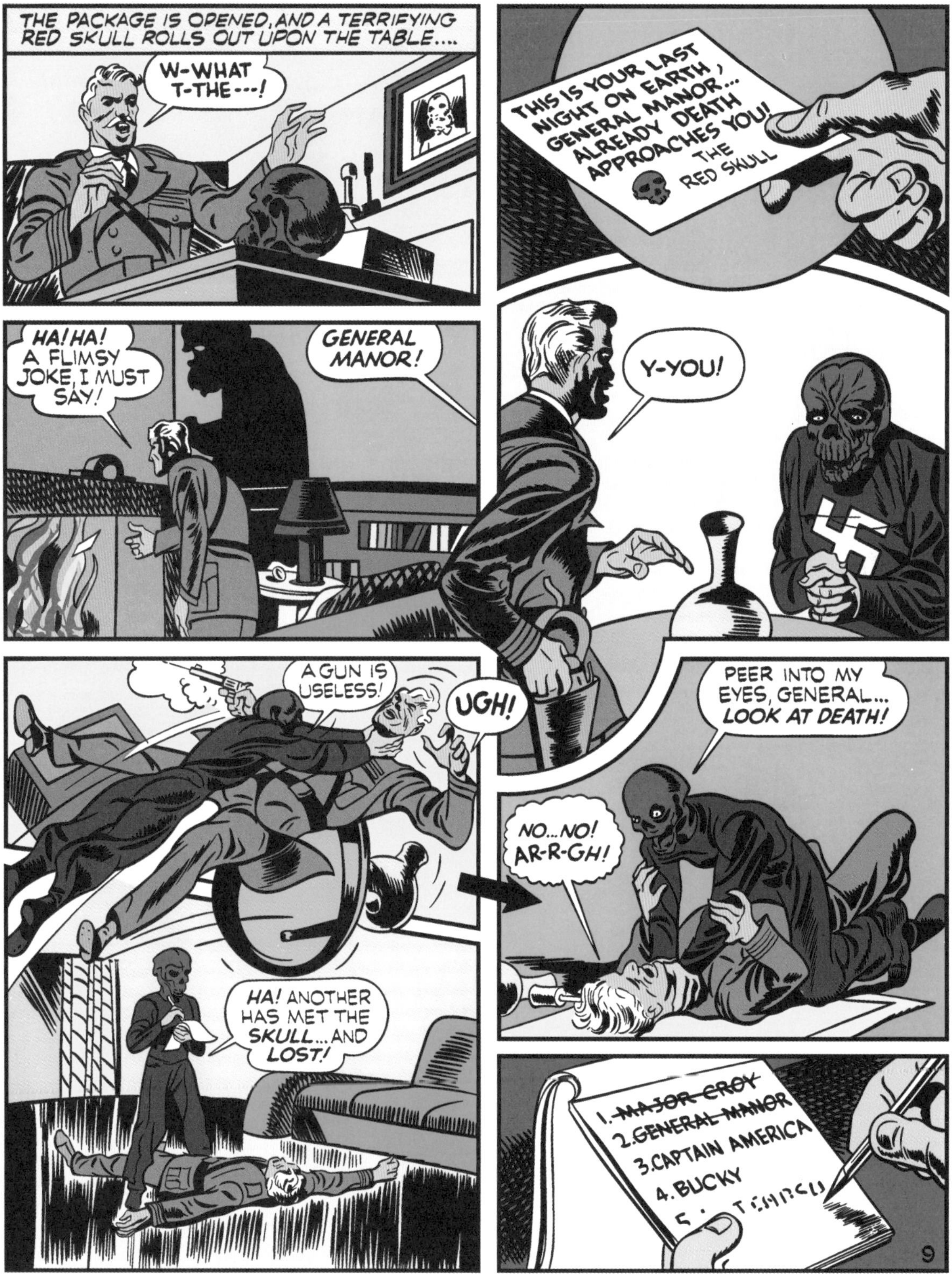
THE PACKAGE IS OPENED, AND A TERRIFYING RED SKULL ROLLS OUT UPON THE TABLE....
W-WHAT T-THE---!
THIS IS YOUR LAST NIGHT ON EARTH, GENERAL MANOR... ALREADY DEATH APPROACHES YOU! THE RED SKULL
HA! HA! A FLIMSY JOKE, I MUST SAY!
GENERAL MANOR!
Y-YOU!
A GUN IS USELESS!
UGH!
HA! ANOTHER HAS MET THE SKULL... AND LOST!
PEER INTO MY EYES, GENERAL... LOOK AT DEATH!
NO...NO! AR-R-GH!
1. ~~MAJOR CROY~~
2. ~~GENERAL MANOR~~
3. CAPTAIN AMERICA
4. BUCKY
9

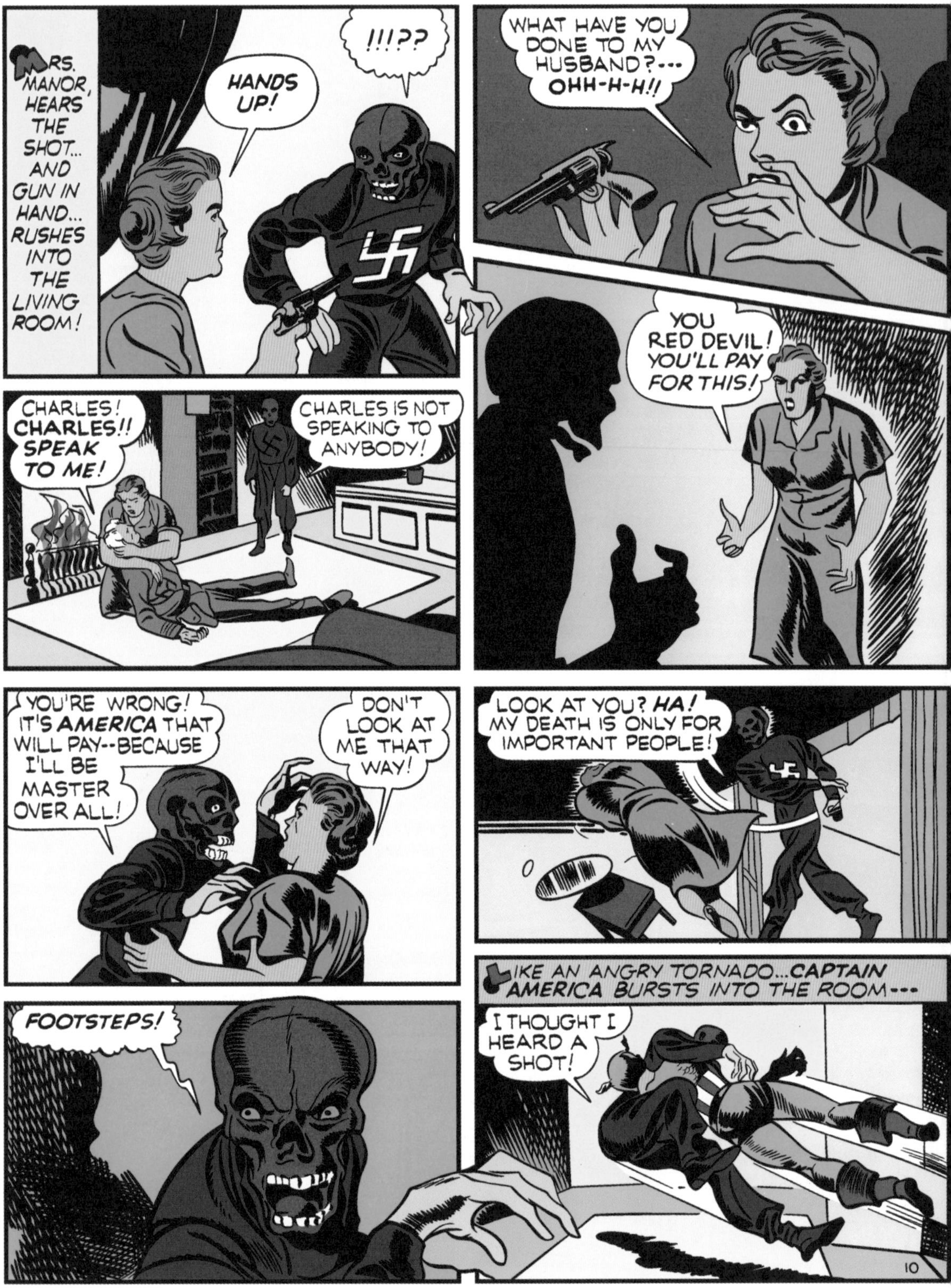
MRS. MANOR, HEARS THE SHOT... AND GUN IN HAND... RUSHES INTO THE LIVING ROOM!
HANDS UP!
!!!??
WHAT HAVE YOU DONE TO MY HUSBAND?--- OHH-H-H!!
CHARLES! CHARLES!! SPEAK TO ME!
CHARLES IS NOT SPEAKING TO ANYBODY!
YOU RED DEVIL! YOU'LL PAY FOR THIS!
YOU'RE WRONG! IT'S AMERICA THAT WILL PAY--BECAUSE I'LL BE MASTER OVER ALL!
DON'T LOOK AT ME THAT WAY!
LOOK AT YOU? HA! MY DEATH IS ONLY FOR IMPORTANT PEOPLE!
FOOTSTEPS!
LIKE AN ANGRY TORNADO...CAPTAIN AMERICA BURSTS INTO THE ROOM---
I THOUGHT I HEARD A SHOT!
10

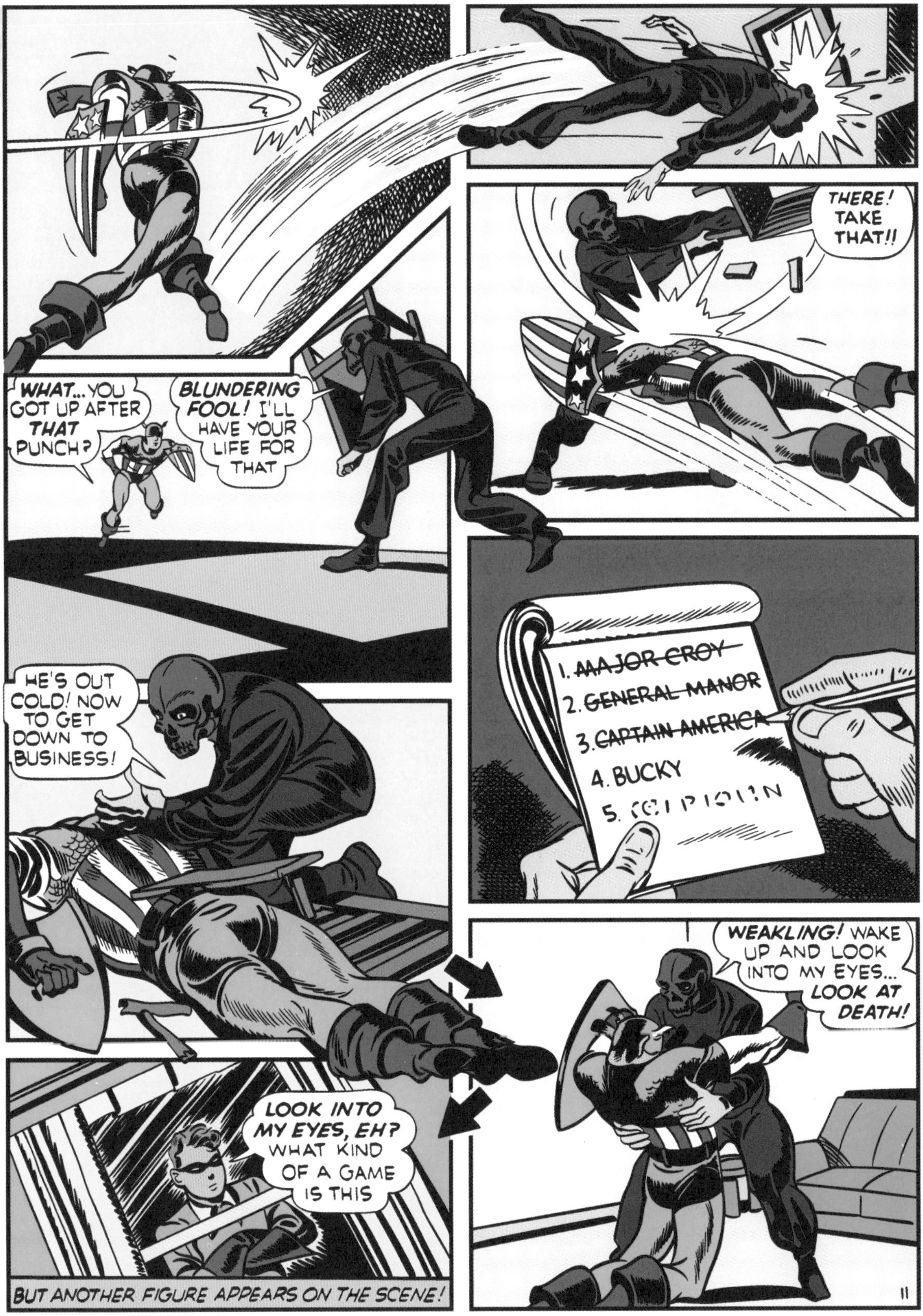
WHAT... YOU GOT UP AFTER THAT PUNCH?
BLUNDERING FOOL! I'LL HAVE YOUR LIFE FOR THAT
THERE! TAKE THAT!!
HE'S OUT COLD! NOW TO GET DOWN TO BUSINESS!
1. MAJOR CROY
2. GENERAL MANOR
3. CAPTAIN AMERICA
4. BUCKY
5.
WEAKLING! WAKE UP AND LOOK INTO MY EYES... LOOK AT DEATH!
LOOK INTO MY EYES, EH? WHAT KIND OF A GAME IS THIS
BUT ANOTHER FIGURE APPEARS ON THE SCENE!
11

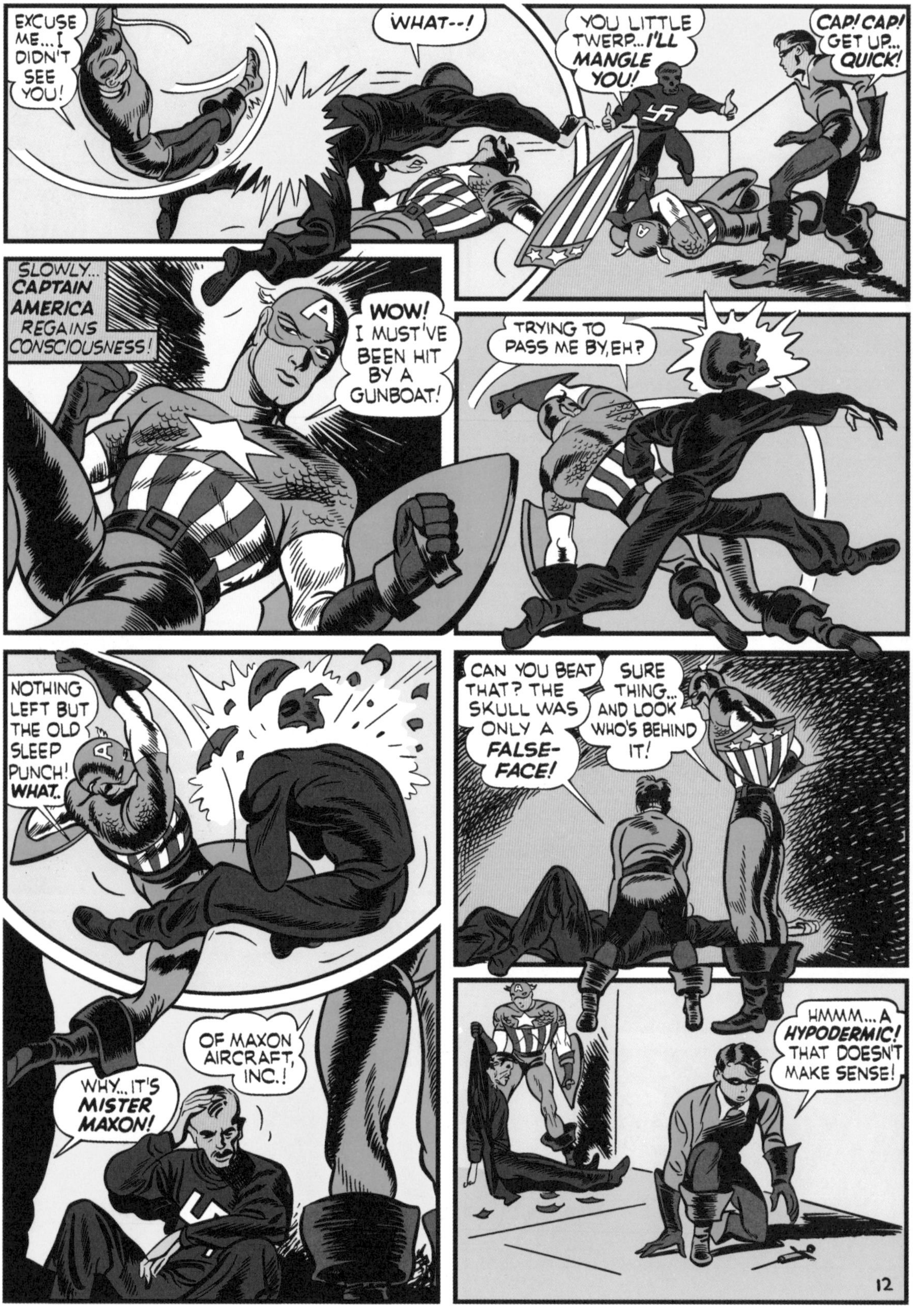
EXCUSE ME...I DIDN'T SEE YOU!
WHAT--!
YOU LITTLE TWERP...I'LL MANGLE YOU!
CAP! CAP! GET UP... QUICK!
SLOWLY... CAPTAIN AMERICA REGAINS CONSCIOUSNESS!
WOW! I MUST'VE BEEN HIT BY A GUNBOAT!
TRYING TO PASS ME BY, EH?
NOTHING LEFT BUT THE OLD SLEEP PUNCH! WHAT..
WHY...IT'S MISTER MAXON!
OF MAXON AIRCRAFT, INC.!
CAN YOU BEAT THAT? THE SKULL WAS ONLY A FALSE-FACE!
SURE THING... AND LOOK WHO'S BEHIND IT!
HMMM...A HYPODERMIC! THAT DOESN'T MAKE SENSE!
12

IT MAKES PLENTY OF SENSE, BUCKY--THIS IS MISTER RED SKULL'S *LOOK OF DEATH!*

I DON'T GET IT!

SO WHAT?

YOUR PLAN WAS TO SCARE YOUR VICTIMS OUT OF THEIR WITS, AND THEN INJECT THIS POISON INTO THEM, MAKING BELIEVE YOU KILLED THEM WITH YOUR *EYES!*

JUST A KILLER AT HEART...EH? SKULL--ER-- *MAXON?* THAT WRECKED PLANE WAS YOUR FAULT TOO! IT'LL TAKE MORE THAN *YOU* TO LICK THIS COUNTRY!

THE KILLER ATTEMPTS TO GET HIS DEATH WEAPON--

I'M NOT FINISHED-- JUST WATCH!

NO, YOU DON'T!

SORRY, YOU CAN'T HAVE THAT--IT'S STATE'S EVIDENCE!

THE FOOL! HE ROLLED OVER ON THE HYPO!

UGH!

BUT YOU SAW IT ALL--WHY DIDN'T YOU STOP HIM FROM KILLING HIMSELF?

I'M NOT TALKING, BUCKY!

13

HELLO FEDERAL BUREAU OF INVESTIGATION? THIS IS *CAPTAIN AMERICA!* I'M PHONING FROM GENERAL MANOR'S HOME...YES...HE'S *DEAD*...YES... SO IS HIS KILLER, *THE RED SKULL!* HE COMMITTED SUICIDE!

OUR WORK IS DONE...COME ON, BUCKY!

LATER...THE G-MEN INSPECT THE BODY OF *GEORGE MAXON...ALIAS THE RED SKULL!*

IT'S MAXON, ALRIGHT! BUT WHY SHOULD THE HEAD OF AN AIRPLANE CORPORATION RESORT TO THIS SPY STUFF!

WHAT'S THAT PIECE OF PAPER STICKING OUT OF HIS SIDE POCKET?

HMMM--I THINK THIS LETTER WILL EXPLAIN THE REASON FOR MAXON'S TERRORISTIC ACTIVITIES!

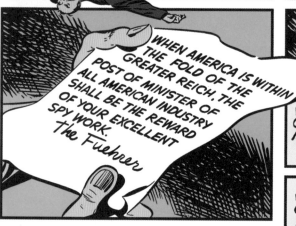

WHEN AMERICA IS WITHIN THE FOLD OF THE GREATER REICH, THE POST OF MINISTER OF ALL AMERICAN INDUSTRY SHALL BE THE REWARD OF YOUR EXCELLENT SPY WORK.
The Fuehrer

...AND SO ENDS THE BLOODY CAREER OF *GEORGE MAXON...ALIAS THE RED SKULL!*

BACK IN CAMP... PRIVATE *STEVE ROGERS* AND *BUCKY* RELAX IN THEIR TENT!

BUT THE WORK OF *CAPTAIN AMERICA* IS NEVER DONE AS THEY PLUNGE INTO NEW EXPLOITS AGAINST AMERICA'S ENEMIES!

WATCH FOR THE NEXT ISSUE! 14

TALES OF SUSPENSE #59,

NOVEMBER 1964,

"CAPTAIN AMERICA"

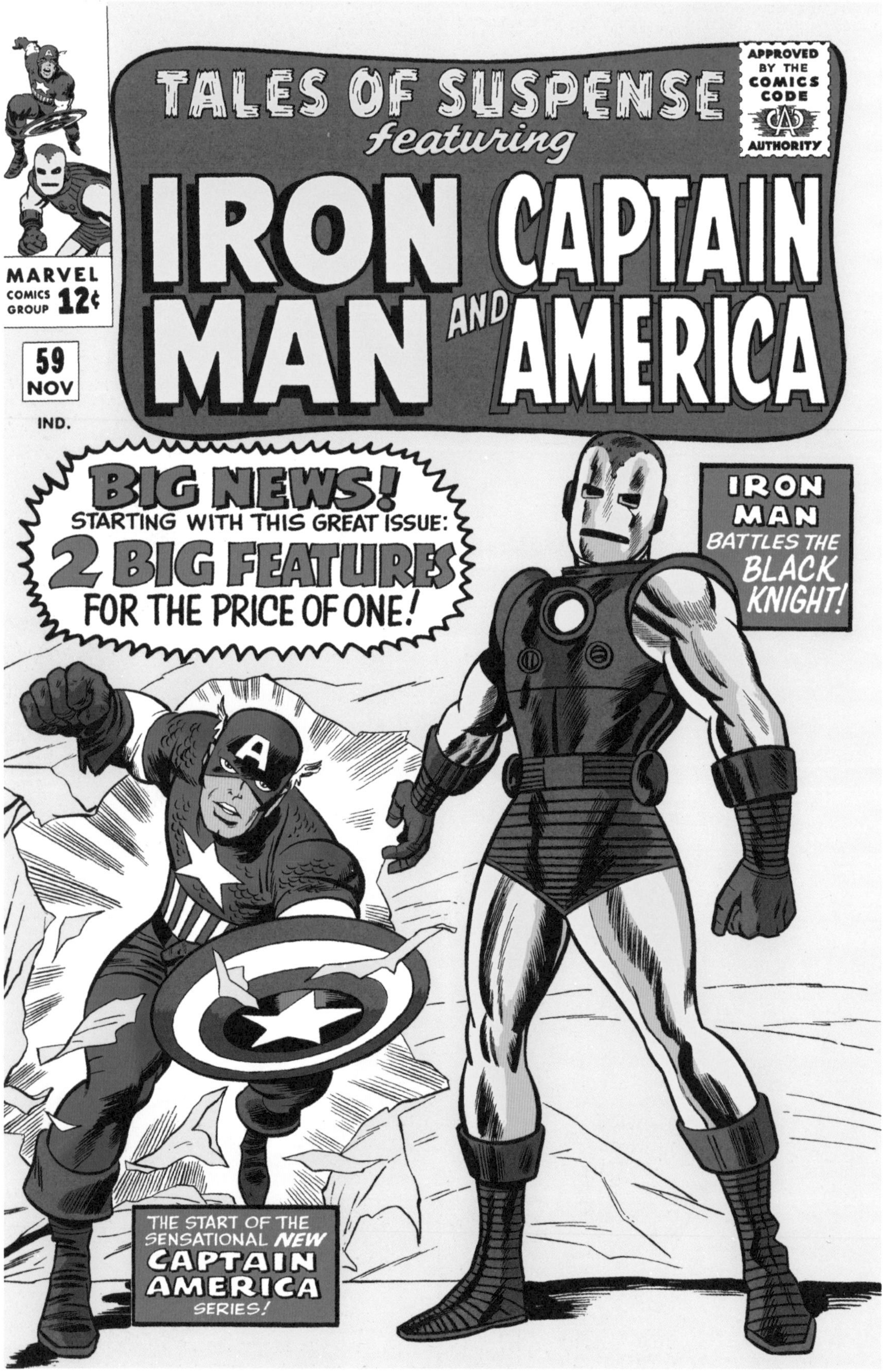
TALES OF SUSPENSE featuring
APPROVED BY THE COMICS CODE AUTHORITY
IRON MAN AND CAPTAIN AMERICA
MARVEL COMICS GROUP 12¢
59 NOV
IND.
BIG NEWS! STARTING WITH THIS GREAT ISSUE: 2 BIG FEATURES FOR THE PRICE OF ONE!
IRON MAN BATTLES THE BLACK KNIGHT!
THE START OF THE SENSATIONAL NEW CAPTAIN AMERICA SERIES!

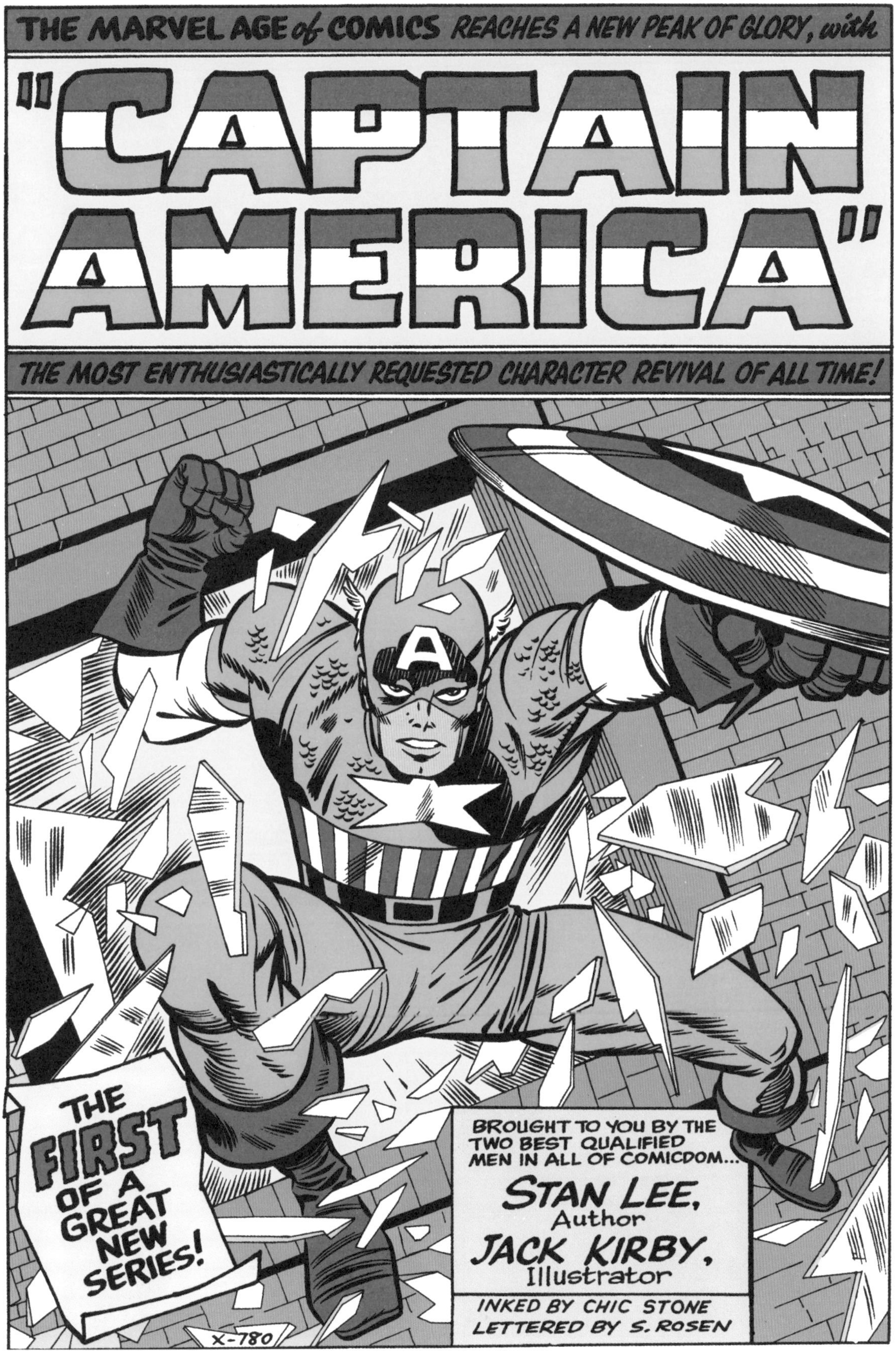
THE MARVEL AGE of COMICS REACHES A NEW PEAK OF GLORY, with
"CAPTAIN AMERICA"
THE MOST ENTHUSIASTICALLY REQUESTED CHARACTER REVIVAL OF ALL TIME!
THE FIRST OF A GREAT NEW SERIES!
BROUGHT TO YOU BY THE TWO BEST QUALIFIED MEN IN ALL OF COMICDOM...
STAN LEE, Author
JACK KIRBY, Illustrator
INKED BY CHIC STONE
LETTERED BY S. ROSEN
X-780

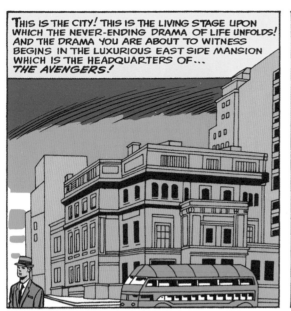

THIS IS THE CITY! THIS IS THE LIVING STAGE UPON WHICH THE NEVER-ENDING DRAMA OF LIFE UNFOLDS! AND THE DRAMA YOU ARE ABOUT TO WITNESS BEGINS IN THE LUXURIOUS EAST SIDE MANSION WHICH IS THE HEADQUARTERS OF... *THE AVENGERS!*

ACTUALLY, IT WAS ONCE THE RESIDENCE OF MULTI-MILLIONAIRE ANTHONY STARK, BUT HE DONATED IT TO THE WORLD'S MIGHTIEST FIGHTING TEAM AS A PUBLIC SERVICE...

BEFORE I LEAVE FOR THE EVENING, SIR, I THOUGHT YOU MIGHT LIKE SOME FRESHLY BREWED COFFEE!

WHENEVER POSSIBLE, THE AVENGERS LEAVE ONE OF THEIR MEMBERS AT THE MANSION IN THE EVENT THAT SOME EMERGENCY SHOULD OCCUR! TONIGHT, THE DUTY ASSIGNMENT HAS FALLEN TO THE MAN KNOWN AS... *CAPTAIN AMERICA!*

THANK YOU, JARVIS! I WON'T REQUIRE ANYTHING ELSE!

IT WAS CERTAINLY GENEROUS OF STARK TO PROVIDE US WITH A *BUTLER*, IN ADDITION TO THE MANSION ITSELF!

NOT EVEN THE AVENGERS THEM-SELVES SUSPECT THAT TONY STARK IS REALLY *IRON MAN*, ONE OF THEIR OWN MIGHTY MEMBERS!

FINALLY, THE BUTLER DEPARTS, LEAVING THE BROODING COSTUMED ADVENTURER ALONE WITH HIS THOUGHTS...

THESE TOURS OF DUTY CAN BE MIGHTY LONELY, ESPECIALLY TO A MAN WHO THRIVES ON ACTION!

PERHAPS I CAN MAKE TIME PASS MORE QUICKLY BY LOOKING THROUGH THIS OLD SCRAPBOOK ALBUM OF MINE!

BUT, CAPTAIN AMERICA IS DUE FOR MORE ACTION THAN HE SUSPECTS! FOR, NOT FAR AWAY, A MEETING IS TAKING PLACE WHICH IS SOON TO SHATTER THE QUIET OF THE STALWART AVENGER'S EVENING...

BUT HOW CAN A MOB LIKE *US* MANAGE TO PUT ANYTHING OVER ON THE *AVENGERS*, BOSS?

JUST HOLD THAT CHAIN TIGHT, AND I'LL *SHOW* YA...!

2.

SEE? EVEN A *CHAIN* CAN BE BUSTED IF YOU FIND THE *WEAKEST LINK!*

I *STILL* DON'T GET IT, BULL! WHAT'S THAT GOT TO DO WITH THE *AVENGERS?*

USE YOUR *HEAD,* STUPID! THEY ALL HAVE *SUPER POW-ERS,* AIN'T THEY? ALL EXCEPT ONE OF 'EM... *CAPTAIN AMERICA!*

HE'S NOTHIN' BUT A *GLORIFIED ACROBAT!* WE CAN HANDLE HIM *EASY!* SO, WE JUST HAVETA WAIT TILL WE CAN CATCH HIM AT STARK'S JOINT *ALONE!*

SECONDS LATER...

HERE'S THE BUTLER LIKE YA WANTED, BULL!

WHAT'S THE *MEANING* OF THIS? WHY WAS I BROUGHT HERE?

SHUDDUP! JUST TELL ME ONE THING ...WHO'S MINDIN' THE STORE TONIGHT AT AVENGERS' H.Q.?

IT'S NO *SECRET!* *CAPTAIN AMERICA* IS STATIONED THERE TONIGHT! WHY DIDN'T YOU JUST *PHONE?*

THIS IS *IT,* BOYS! GRAB YOUR HARDWARE! WE'LL POLISH CAP-TAIN AMERICA OFF, AND GRAB ALL THE AVENGERS' SECRET PLANS WE CAN FIND! THEY'LL BE WORTH A *FORTUNE!*

LET THE BUTLER GO! WE DON'T NEED 'IM ANY MORE!

WE'LL ATTACK THAT COSTUMED CLOWN LIKE A *TEAM*... JUST LIKE THE *AVENGERS* THEMSELVES!

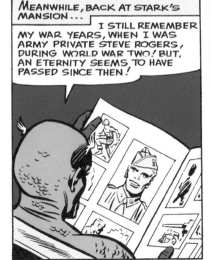

MEANWHILE, BACK AT STARK'S MANSION...

I STILL REMEMBER MY WAR YEARS, WHEN I WAS ARMY PRIVATE STEVE ROGERS, DURING WORLD WAR TWO! BUT, AN ETERNITY SEEMS TO HAVE PASSED SINCE THEN!

THEN, SUDDENLY, CAP SEES A PHOTO OF...

BUCKY! MY TEEN-AGE SIDEKICK!

I SHOULD HAVE KNOWN BETTER THAN TO LOOK AT THE ALBUM...TO REVIVE OLD MEMORIES!

IT'S NO GOOD! IT'S OVER NOW! OVER AND DONE WITH! BUCKY IS DEAD... THERE'LL NEVER BE ANOTHER LIKE HIM!

3.

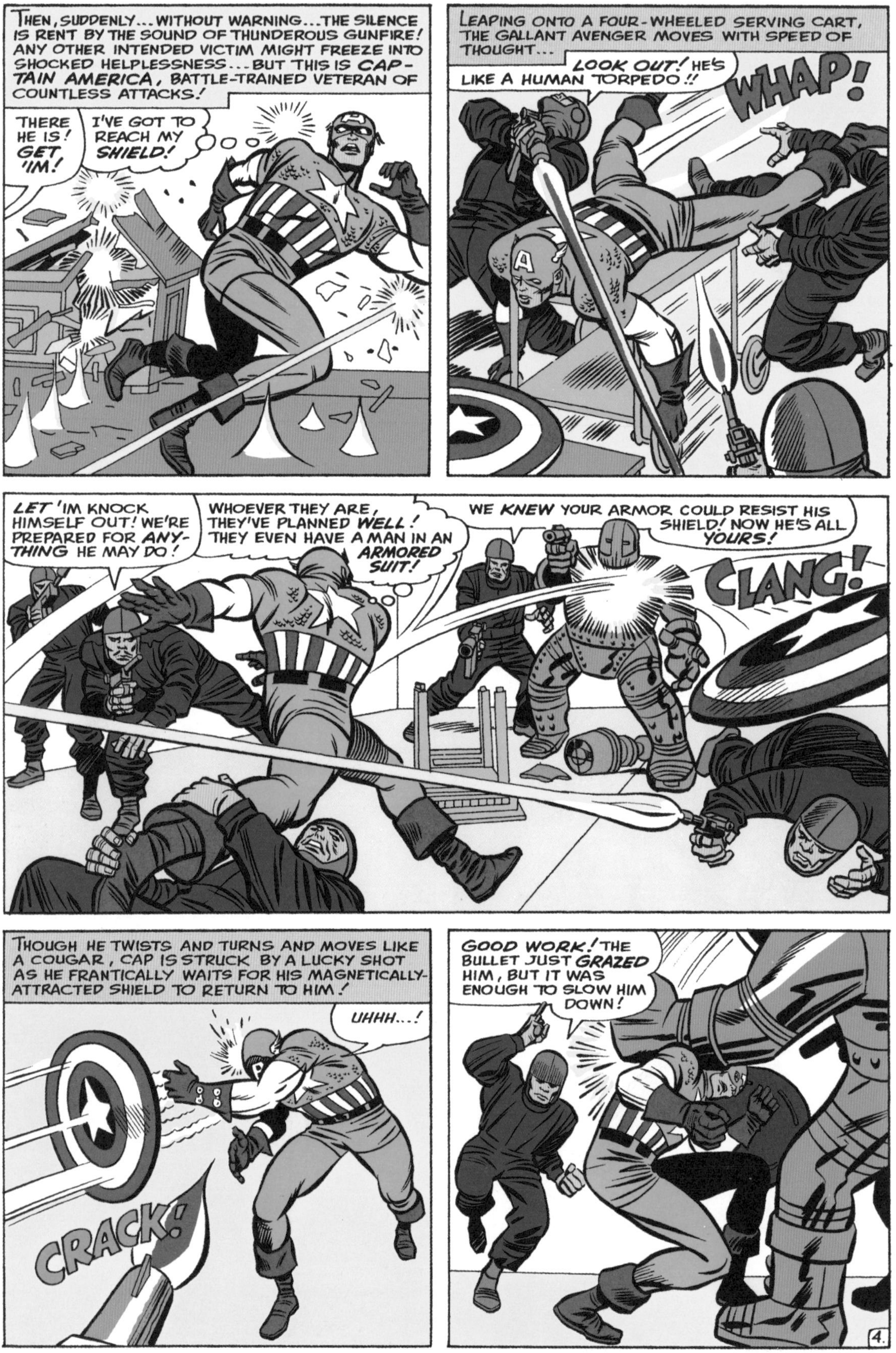
THEN, SUDDENLY... WITHOUT WARNING... THE SILENCE IS RENT BY THE SOUND OF THUNDEROUS GUNFIRE! ANY OTHER INTENDED VICTIM MIGHT FREEZE INTO SHOCKED HELPLESSNESS... BUT THIS IS CAPTAIN AMERICA, BATTLE-TRAINED VETERAN OF COUNTLESS ATTACKS!
THERE HE IS! GET 'IM!
I'VE GOT TO REACH MY SHIELD!
LEAPING ONTO A FOUR-WHEELED SERVING CART, THE GALLANT AVENGER MOVES WITH SPEED OF THOUGHT...
LOOK OUT! HE'S LIKE A HUMAN TORPEDO!!
WHAP!
LET 'IM KNOCK HIMSELF OUT! WE'RE PREPARED FOR ANYTHING HE MAY DO!
WHOEVER THEY ARE, THEY'VE PLANNED WELL! THEY EVEN HAVE A MAN IN AN ARMORED SUIT!
WE KNEW YOUR ARMOR COULD RESIST HIS SHIELD! NOW HE'S ALL YOURS!
CLANG!
THOUGH HE TWISTS AND TURNS AND MOVES LIKE A COUGAR, CAP IS STRUCK BY A LUCKY SHOT AS HE FRANTICALLY WAITS FOR HIS MAGNETICALLY-ATTRACTED SHIELD TO RETURN TO HIM!
UHHH...!
CRACK!
GOOD WORK! THE BULLET JUST GRAZED HIM, BUT IT WAS ENOUGH TO SLOW HIM DOWN!
4.

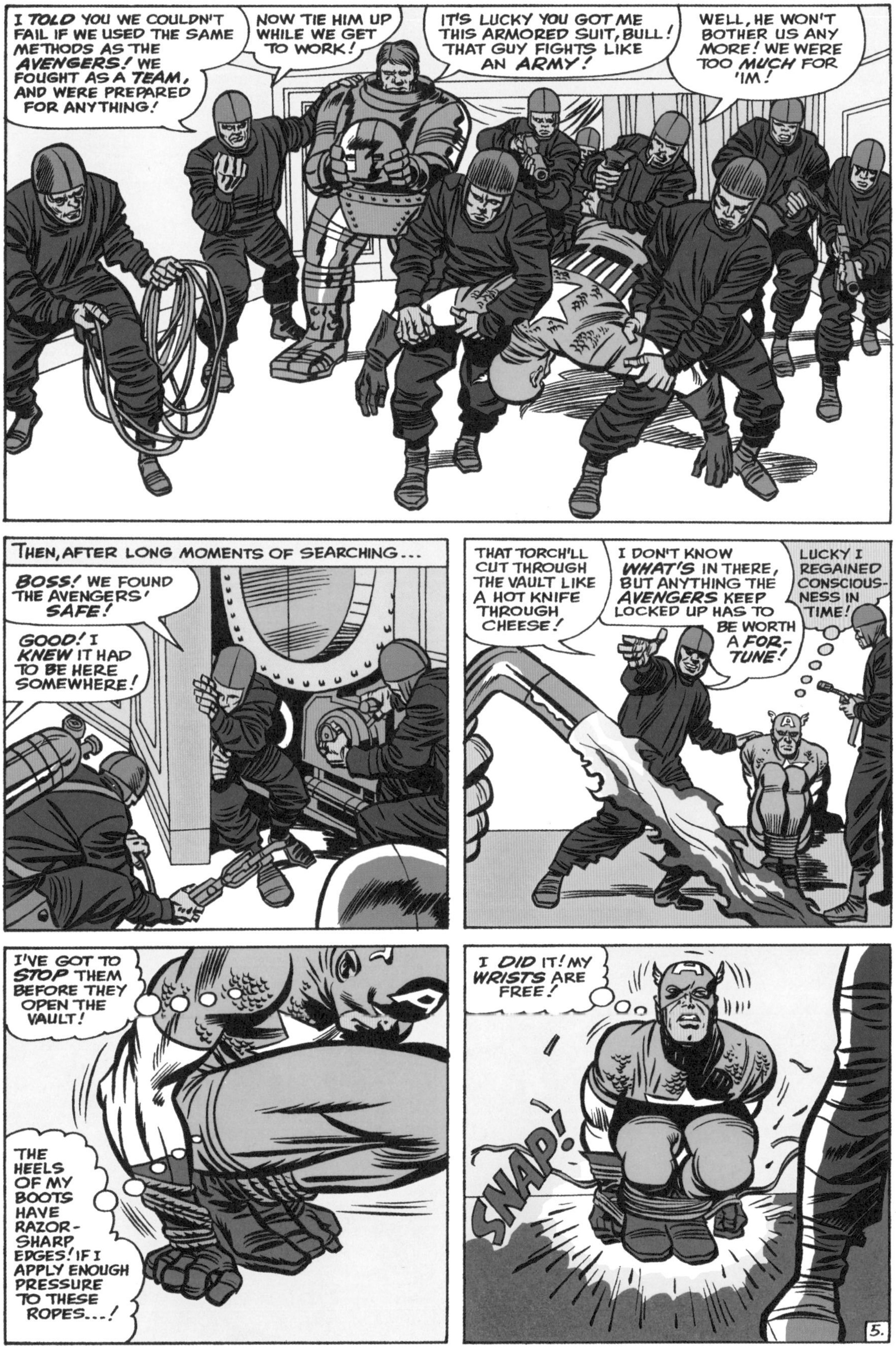
I TOLD YOU WE COULDN'T FAIL IF WE USED THE SAME METHODS AS THE AVENGERS! WE FOUGHT AS A TEAM, AND WERE PREPARED FOR ANYTHING!
NOW TIE HIM UP WHILE WE GET TO WORK!
IT'S LUCKY YOU GOT ME THIS ARMORED SUIT, BULL! THAT GUY FIGHTS LIKE AN ARMY!
WELL, HE WON'T BOTHER US ANY MORE! WE WERE TOO MUCH FOR 'IM!
THEN, AFTER LONG MOMENTS OF SEARCHING...
BOSS! WE FOUND THE AVENGERS' SAFE!
GOOD! I KNEW IT HAD TO BE HERE SOMEWHERE!
THAT TORCH'LL CUT THROUGH THE VAULT LIKE A HOT KNIFE THROUGH CHEESE!
I DON'T KNOW WHAT'S IN THERE, BUT ANYTHING THE AVENGERS KEEP LOCKED UP HAS TO BE WORTH A FOR-TUNE!
LUCKY I REGAINED CONSCIOUS-NESS IN TIME!
I'VE GOT TO STOP THEM BEFORE THEY OPEN THE VAULT!
THE HEELS OF MY BOOTS HAVE RAZOR-SHARP EDGES! IF I APPLY ENOUGH PRESSURE TO THESE ROPES...!
I DID IT! MY WRISTS ARE FREE!
SNAP!
5.

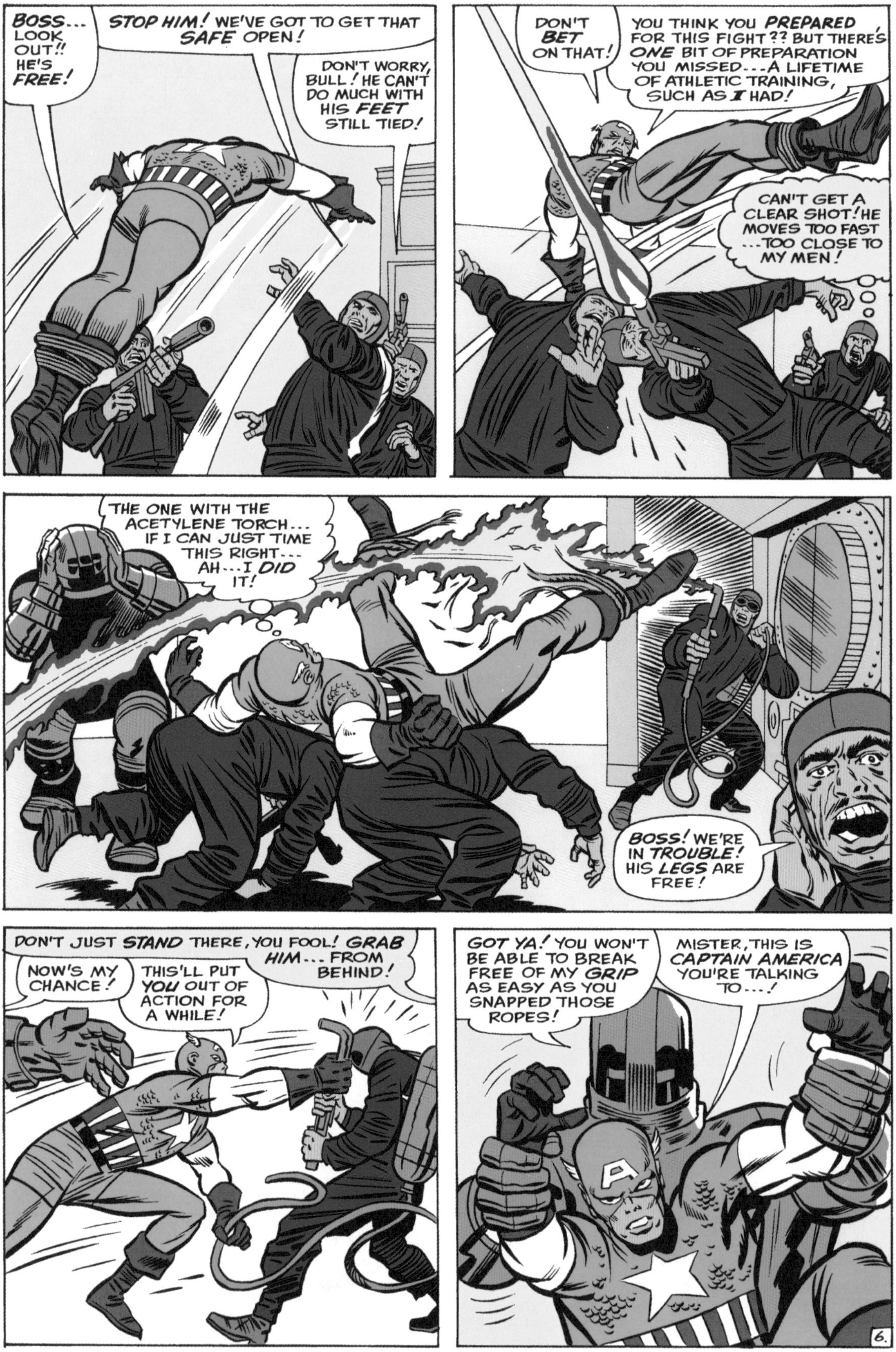
BOSS... LOOK OUT!! HE'S FREE!
STOP HIM! WE'VE GOT TO GET THAT SAFE OPEN!
DON'T WORRY, BULL! HE CAN'T DO MUCH WITH HIS FEET STILL TIED!
DON'T BET ON THAT!
YOU THINK YOU PREPARED FOR THIS FIGHT?? BUT THERE'S ONE BIT OF PREPARATION YOU MISSED...A LIFETIME OF ATHLETIC TRAINING, SUCH AS I HAD!
CAN'T GET A CLEAR SHOT! HE MOVES TOO FAST ...TOO CLOSE TO MY MEN!
THE ONE WITH THE ACETYLENE TORCH... IF I CAN JUST TIME THIS RIGHT--- AH...I DID IT!
BOSS! WE'RE IN TROUBLE! HIS LEGS ARE FREE!
DON'T JUST STAND THERE, YOU FOOL! GRAB HIM... FROM BEHIND!
NOW'S MY CHANCE!
THIS'LL PUT YOU OUT OF ACTION FOR A WHILE!
GOT YA! YOU WON'T BE ABLE TO BREAK FREE OF MY GRIP AS EASY AS YOU SNAPPED THOSE ROPES!
MISTER, THIS IS CAPTAIN AMERICA YOU'RE TALKING TO...!
6.

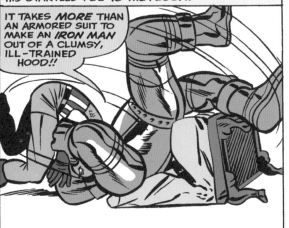

MOVING WITH THE EASY CAT-LIKE GRACE OF A TRAINED JUDO MASTER, CAP SUDDENLY SHIFTS HIS WEIGHT, THROWING HIS HEAVIER, SLOWER OPPONENT OFF BALANCE! AND THEN, APPLYING JUST THE RIGHT AMOUNT OF LEVERAGE, HE HURLS HIS STARTLED FOE TO THE FLOOR!

IT TAKES *MORE* THAN AN ARMORED SUIT TO MAKE AN *IRON MAN* OUT OF A CLUMSY, ILL-TRAINED HOOD!!

THEN, REMOVING THE MOBSTER'S HELMET IN ONE SWIFT MOTION, CAP SENDS HIM TO DREAM-LAND WITH ONE WELL-PLACED BLOW!

I'LL HAVE TO CUT THIS SHORT NOW! IT SOUNDS AS THOUGH THE *REST* OF YOUR LITTLE GANG WANTS TO GET IN ON THE ACTION!!

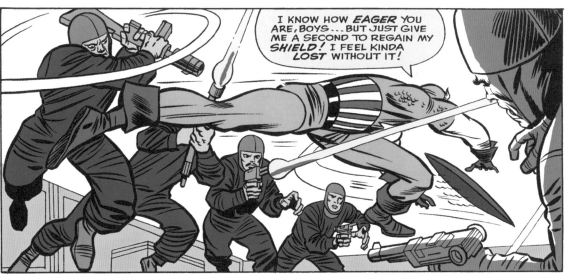

I KNOW HOW *EAGER* YOU ARE, BOYS... BUT JUST GIVE ME A SECOND TO REGAIN MY *SHIELD*! I FEEL KINDA *LOST* WITHOUT IT!

OKAY... THANKS FOR WAITING!

AND NOW, I'LL TRY TO MAKE UP FOR LOST TIME! HOW'S *THIS* FOR A STARTER?!!

PILE ON!! HE CAN'T BEAT US *ALL*!

NO? I'M BEGINNIN' TO *WONDER*!

BAH! MISSED HIM!

HE SHIFTED HIS WEIGHT AGAIN! HE'S GONNA *TRY* SOME-THIN'...!

7.

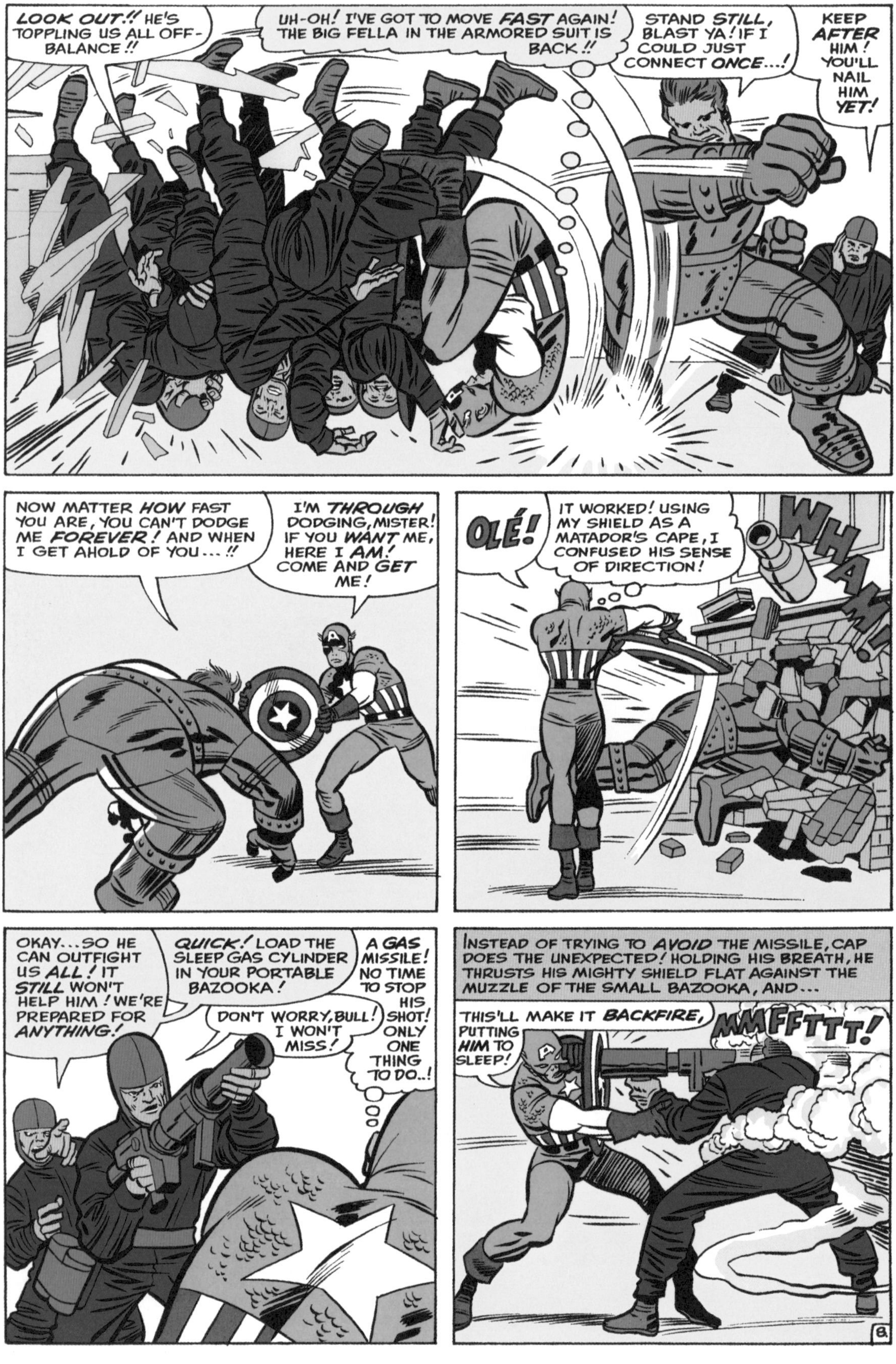
LOOK OUT!! HE'S TOPPLING US ALL OFF-BALANCE!!
UH-OH! I'VE GOT TO MOVE FAST AGAIN! THE BIG FELLA IN THE ARMORED SUIT IS BACK!!
STAND STILL, BLAST YA! IF I COULD JUST CONNECT ONCE...!
KEEP AFTER HIM! YOU'LL NAIL HIM YET!
NOW MATTER HOW FAST YOU ARE, YOU CAN'T DODGE ME FOREVER! AND WHEN I GET AHOLD OF YOU...!!
I'M THROUGH DODGING, MISTER! IF YOU WANT ME, HERE I AM! COME AND GET ME!
OLÉ!
IT WORKED! USING MY SHIELD AS A MATADOR'S CAPE, I CONFUSED HIS SENSE OF DIRECTION!
WHAM!
OKAY...SO HE CAN OUTFIGHT US ALL! IT STILL WON'T HELP HIM! WE'RE PREPARED FOR ANYTHING!
QUICK! LOAD THE SLEEP GAS CYLINDER IN YOUR PORTABLE BAZOOKA!
DON'T WORRY, BULL! I WON'T MISS!
A GAS MISSILE! NO TIME TO STOP HIS SHOT! ONLY ONE THING TO DO..!
INSTEAD OF TRYING TO AVOID THE MISSILE, CAP DOES THE UNEXPECTED! HOLDING HIS BREATH, HE THRUSTS HIS MIGHTY SHIELD FLAT AGAINST THE MUZZLE OF THE SMALL BAZOOKA, AND...
THIS'LL MAKE IT BACKFIRE, PUTTING HIM TO SLEEP!
MMFFTTTT!
8.

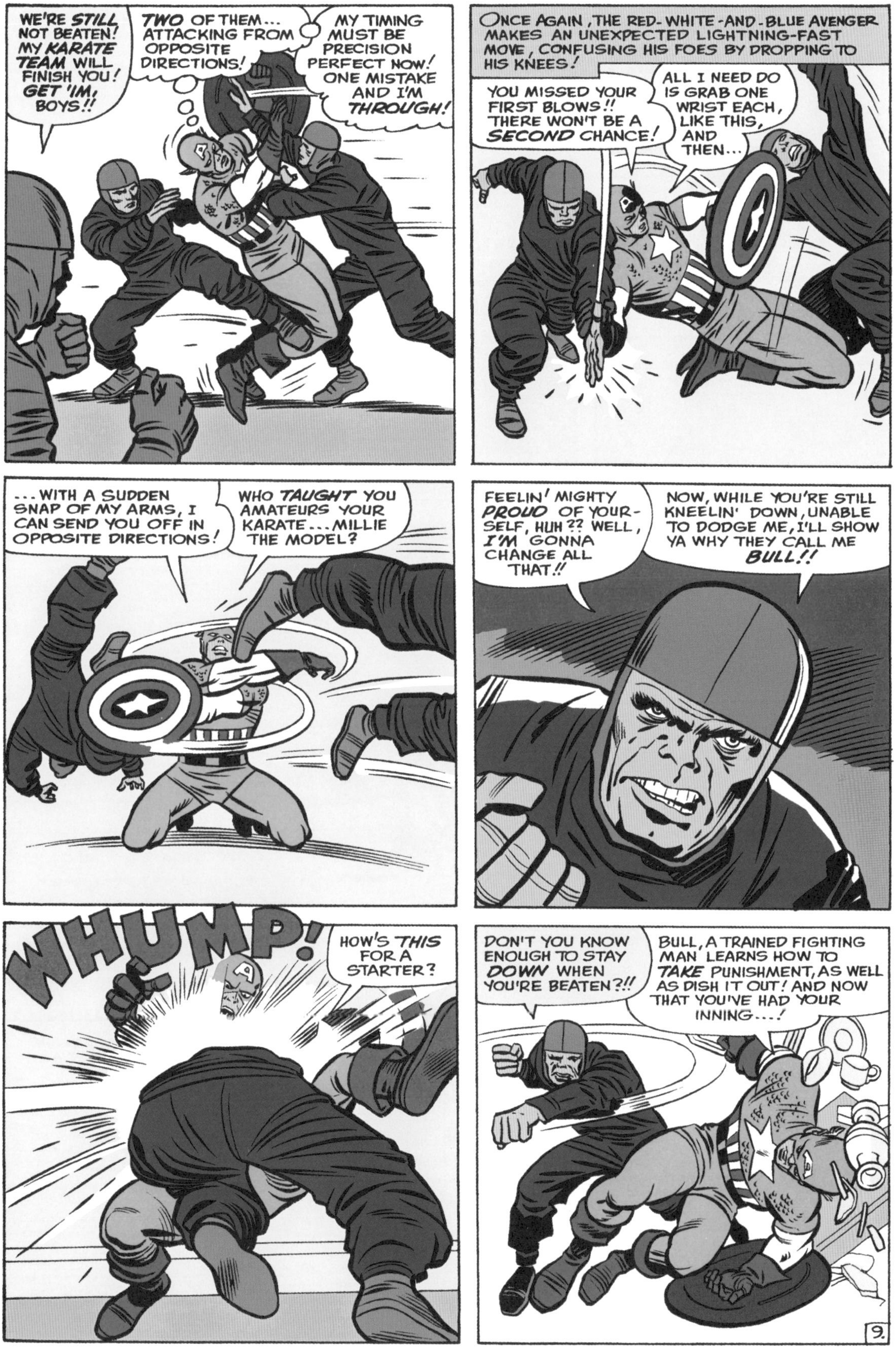

WE'RE STILL NOT BEATEN! MY KARATE TEAM WILL FINISH YOU! GET 'IM, BOYS!!
TWO OF THEM... ATTACKING FROM OPPOSITE DIRECTIONS!
MY TIMING MUST BE PRECISION PERFECT NOW! ONE MISTAKE AND I'M THROUGH!
ONCE AGAIN, THE RED-WHITE-AND-BLUE AVENGER MAKES AN UNEXPECTED LIGHTNING-FAST MOVE, CONFUSING HIS FOES BY DROPPING TO HIS KNEES!
YOU MISSED YOUR FIRST BLOWS!! THERE WON'T BE A SECOND CHANCE!
ALL I NEED DO IS GRAB ONE WRIST EACH, LIKE THIS, AND THEN...
...WITH A SUDDEN SNAP OF MY ARMS, I CAN SEND YOU OFF IN OPPOSITE DIRECTIONS!
WHO TAUGHT YOU AMATEURS YOUR KARATE... MILLIE THE MODEL?
FEELIN' MIGHTY PROUD OF YOURSELF, HUH?? WELL, I'M GONNA CHANGE ALL THAT!!
NOW, WHILE YOU'RE STILL KNEELIN' DOWN, UNABLE TO DODGE ME, I'LL SHOW YA WHY THEY CALL ME BULL!!
WHUMP!
HOW'S THIS FOR A STARTER?
DON'T YOU KNOW ENOUGH TO STAY DOWN WHEN YOU'RE BEATEN?!!
BULL, A TRAINED FIGHTING MAN LEARNS HOW TO TAKE PUNISHMENT, AS WELL AS DISH IT OUT! AND NOW THAT YOU'VE HAD YOUR INNING...!
9.

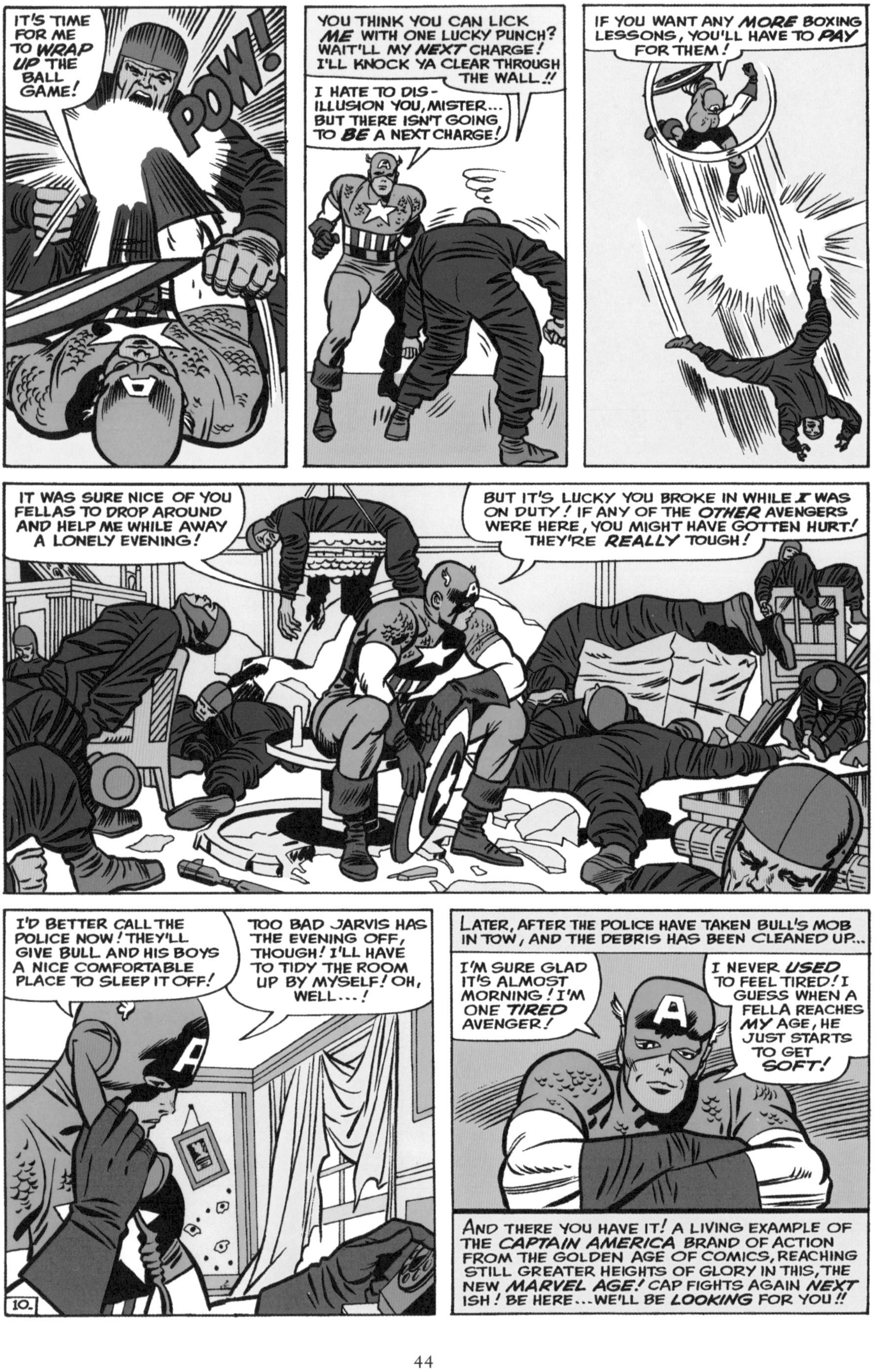
IT'S TIME FOR ME TO *WRAP UP* THE BALL GAME!
POW!
YOU THINK YOU CAN LICK *ME* WITH ONE LUCKY PUNCH? WAIT'LL MY *NEXT* CHARGE! I'LL KNOCK YA CLEAR THROUGH THE WALL!!
I HATE TO DIS-ILLUSION YOU, MISTER... BUT THERE ISN'T GOING TO *BE* A NEXT CHARGE!
IF YOU WANT ANY *MORE* BOXING LESSONS, YOU'LL HAVE TO *PAY* FOR THEM!
IT WAS SURE NICE OF YOU FELLAS TO DROP AROUND AND HELP ME WHILE AWAY A LONELY EVENING!
BUT IT'S LUCKY YOU BROKE IN WHILE *I* WAS ON DUTY! IF ANY OF THE *OTHER* AVENGERS WERE HERE, YOU MIGHT HAVE GOTTEN HURT! THEY'RE *REALLY* TOUGH!
I'D BETTER CALL THE POLICE NOW! THEY'LL GIVE BULL AND HIS BOYS A NICE COMFORTABLE PLACE TO SLEEP IT OFF!
TOO BAD JARVIS HAS THE EVENING OFF, THOUGH! I'LL HAVE TO TIDY THE ROOM UP BY MYSELF! OH, WELL...!
10.
LATER, AFTER THE POLICE HAVE TAKEN BULL'S MOB IN TOW, AND THE DEBRIS HAS BEEN CLEANED UP...
I'M SURE GLAD IT'S ALMOST MORNING! I'M ONE *TIRED* AVENGER!
I NEVER *USED* TO FEEL TIRED! I GUESS WHEN A FELLA REACHES *MY* AGE, HE JUST STARTS TO GET *SOFT*!
AND THERE YOU HAVE IT! A LIVING EXAMPLE OF THE *CAPTAIN AMERICA* BRAND OF ACTION FROM THE GOLDEN AGE OF COMICS, REACHING STILL GREATER HEIGHTS OF GLORY IN THIS, THE NEW *MARVEL AGE*! CAP FIGHTS AGAIN *NEXT* ISH! BE HERE... WE'LL BE *LOOKING* FOR YOU!!

TALES OF SUSPENSE #63,
MARCH 1965,
"THE ORIGIN OF CAPTAIN
AMERICA!"

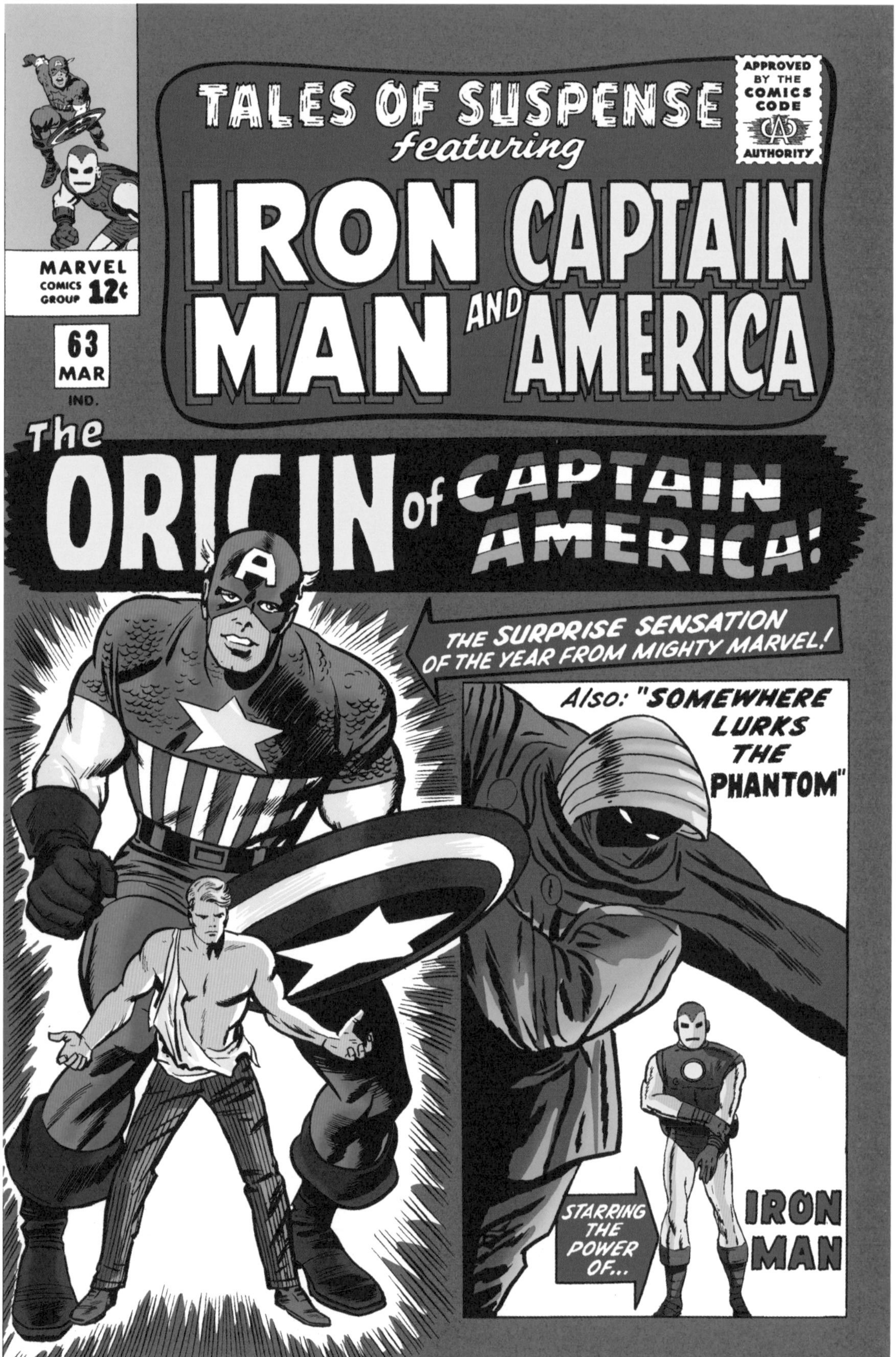
MARVEL COMICS GROUP 12¢
63 MAR
IND.
APPROVED BY THE COMICS CODE AUTHORITY
TALES OF SUSPENSE
featuring
IRON MAN AND CAPTAIN AMERICA
The ORIGIN of CAPTAIN AMERICA!
THE SURPRISE SENSATION OF THE YEAR FROM MIGHTY MARVEL!
Also: "SOMEWHERE LURKS THE PHANTOM"
STARRING THE POWER OF...
IRON MAN

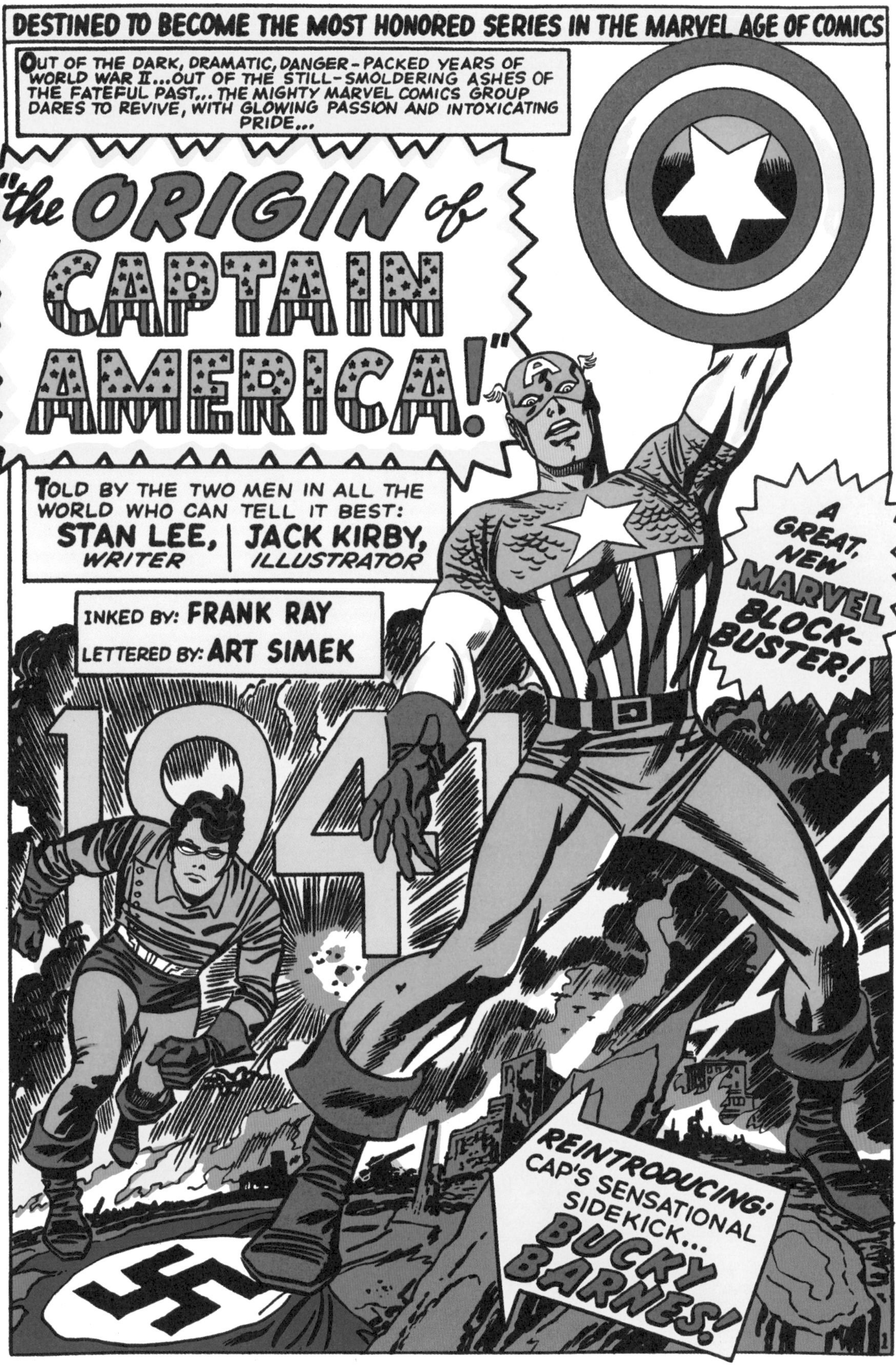
DESTINED TO BECOME THE MOST HONORED SERIES IN THE MARVEL AGE OF COMICS
OUT OF THE DARK, DRAMATIC, DANGER-PACKED YEARS OF WORLD WAR II...OUT OF THE STILL-SMOLDERING ASHES OF THE FATEFUL PAST... THE MIGHTY MARVEL COMICS GROUP DARES TO REVIVE, WITH GLOWING PASSION AND INTOXICATING PRIDE...
"the ORIGIN of CAPTAIN AMERICA!"
TOLD BY THE TWO MEN IN ALL THE WORLD WHO CAN TELL IT BEST: STAN LEE, WRITER | JACK KIRBY, ILLUSTRATOR
INKED BY: FRANK RAY
LETTERED BY: ART SIMEK
A GREAT, NEW MARVEL BLOCK-BUSTER!
1941
REINTRODUCING: CAP'S SENSATIONAL SIDEKICK... BUCKY BARNES!
1

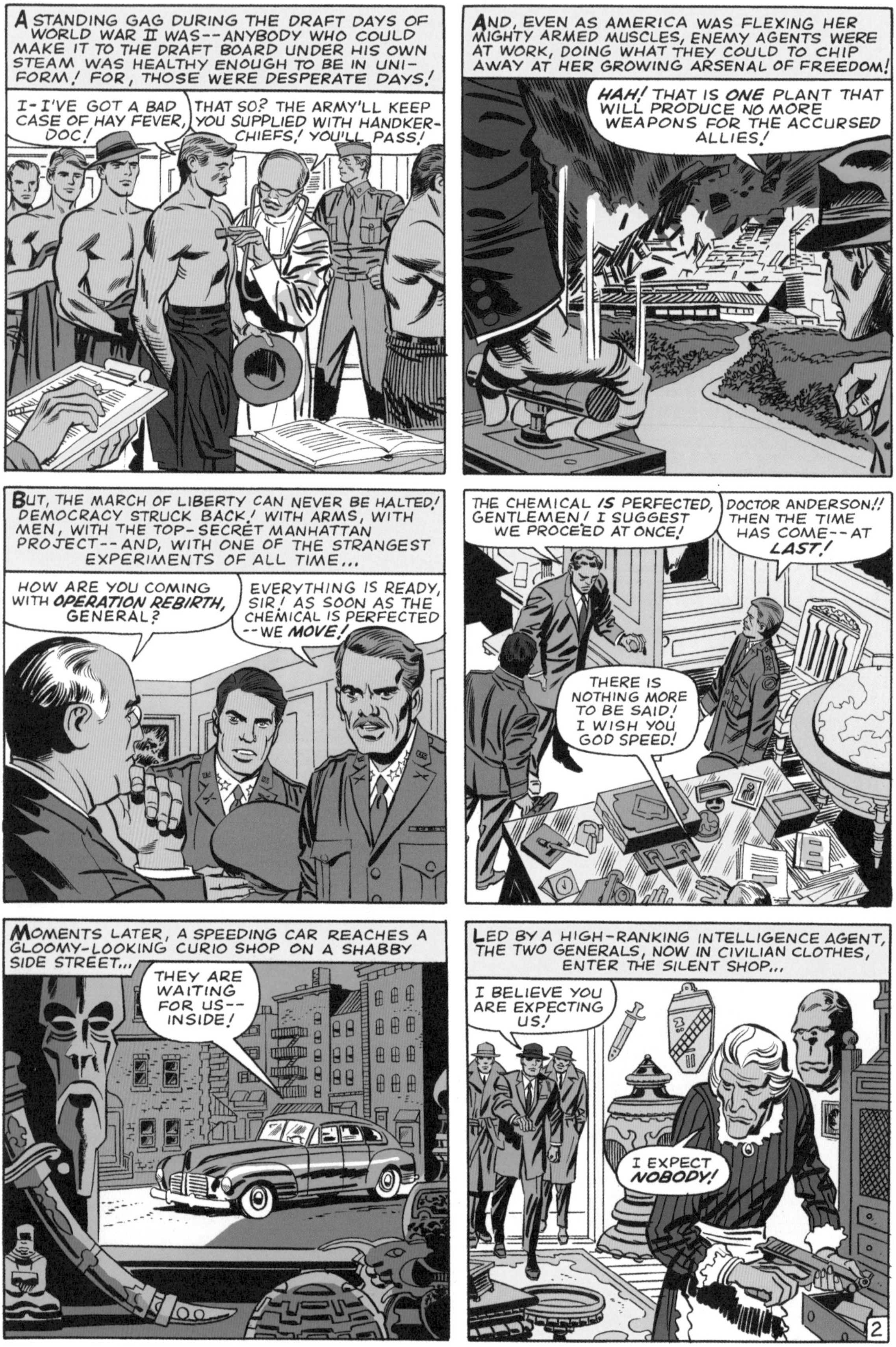
A STANDING GAG DURING THE DRAFT DAYS OF WORLD WAR II WAS--ANYBODY WHO COULD MAKE IT TO THE DRAFT BOARD UNDER HIS OWN STEAM WAS HEALTHY ENOUGH TO BE IN UNIFORM! FOR, THOSE WERE DESPERATE DAYS!
I-I'VE GOT A BAD CASE OF HAY FEVER, DOC!
THAT SO? THE ARMY'LL KEEP YOU SUPPLIED WITH HANDKERCHIEFS! YOU'LL PASS!
AND, EVEN AS AMERICA WAS FLEXING HER MIGHTY ARMED MUSCLES, ENEMY AGENTS WERE AT WORK, DOING WHAT THEY COULD TO CHIP AWAY AT HER GROWING ARSENAL OF FREEDOM!
HAH! THAT IS ONE PLANT THAT WILL PRODUCE NO MORE WEAPONS FOR THE ACCURSED ALLIES!
BUT, THE MARCH OF LIBERTY CAN NEVER BE HALTED! DEMOCRACY STRUCK BACK! WITH ARMS, WITH MEN, WITH THE TOP-SECRET MANHATTAN PROJECT--AND, WITH ONE OF THE STRANGEST EXPERIMENTS OF ALL TIME...
HOW ARE YOU COMING WITH OPERATION REBIRTH, GENERAL?
EVERYTHING IS READY, SIR! AS SOON AS THE CHEMICAL IS PERFECTED --WE MOVE!
THE CHEMICAL IS PERFECTED, GENTLEMEN! I SUGGEST WE PROCEED AT ONCE!
DOCTOR ANDERSON!! THEN THE TIME HAS COME--AT LAST!
THERE IS NOTHING MORE TO BE SAID! I WISH YOU GOD SPEED!
MOMENTS LATER, A SPEEDING CAR REACHES A GLOOMY-LOOKING CURIO SHOP ON A SHABBY SIDE STREET...
THEY ARE WAITING FOR US--INSIDE!
LED BY A HIGH-RANKING INTELLIGENCE AGENT, THE TWO GENERALS, NOW IN CIVILIAN CLOTHES, ENTER THE SILENT SHOP...
I BELIEVE YOU ARE EXPECTING US!
I EXPECT NOBODY!
2

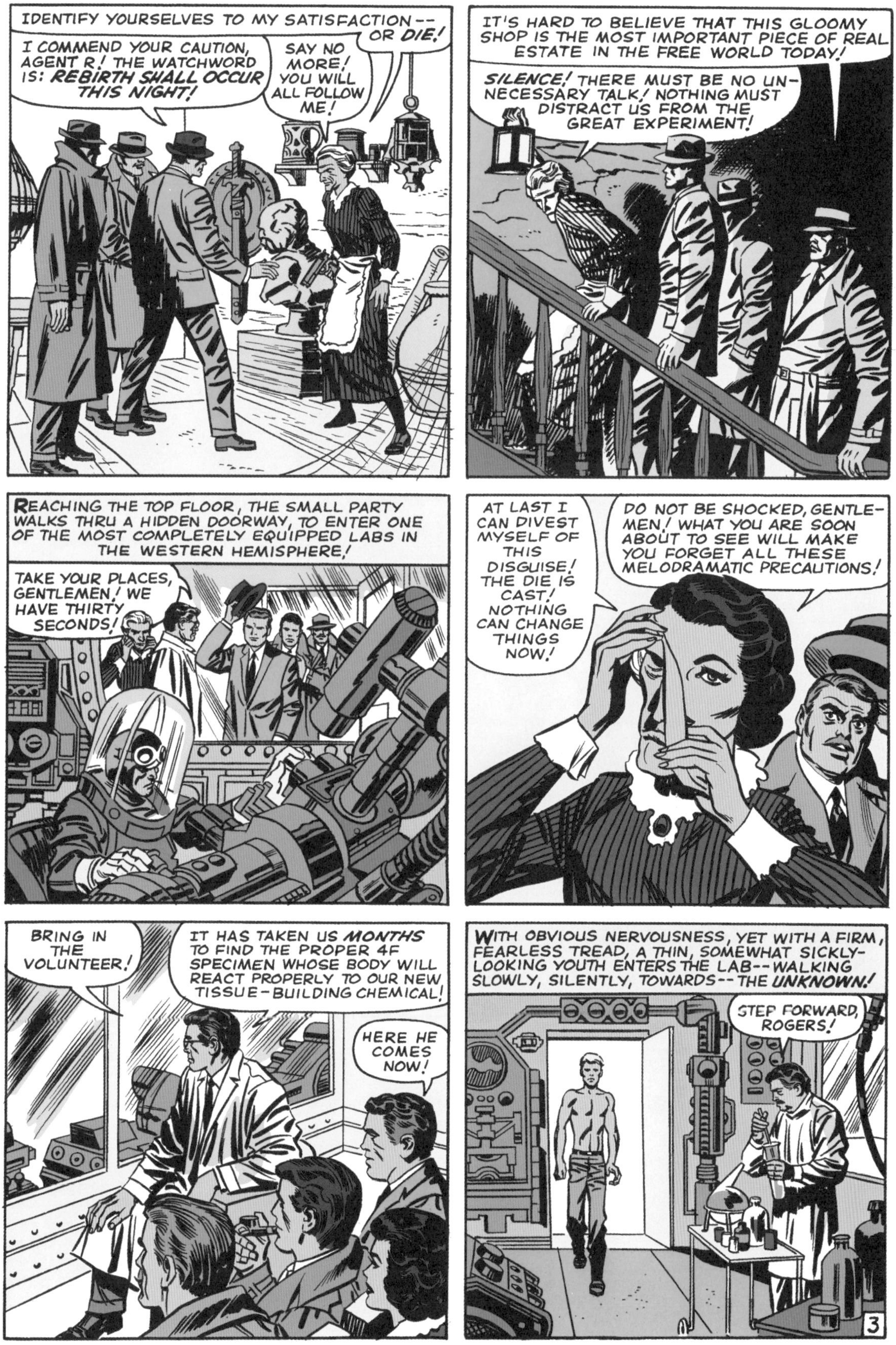
IDENTIFY YOURSELVES TO MY SATISFACTION -- OR DIE!
I COMMEND YOUR CAUTION, AGENT R! THE WATCHWORD IS: REBIRTH SHALL OCCUR THIS NIGHT!
SAY NO MORE! YOU WILL ALL FOLLOW ME!
IT'S HARD TO BELIEVE THAT THIS GLOOMY SHOP IS THE MOST IMPORTANT PIECE OF REAL ESTATE IN THE FREE WORLD TODAY!
SILENCE! THERE MUST BE NO UNNECESSARY TALK! NOTHING MUST DISTRACT US FROM THE GREAT EXPERIMENT!
REACHING THE TOP FLOOR, THE SMALL PARTY WALKS THRU A HIDDEN DOORWAY, TO ENTER ONE OF THE MOST COMPLETELY EQUIPPED LABS IN THE WESTERN HEMISPHERE!
TAKE YOUR PLACES, GENTLEMEN! WE HAVE THIRTY SECONDS!
AT LAST I CAN DIVEST MYSELF OF THIS DISGUISE! THE DIE IS CAST! NOTHING CAN CHANGE THINGS NOW!
DO NOT BE SHOCKED, GENTLEMEN! WHAT YOU ARE SOON ABOUT TO SEE WILL MAKE YOU FORGET ALL THESE MELODRAMATIC PRECAUTIONS!
BRING IN THE VOLUNTEER!
IT HAS TAKEN US MONTHS TO FIND THE PROPER 4F SPECIMEN WHOSE BODY WILL REACT PROPERLY TO OUR NEW TISSUE-BUILDING CHEMICAL!
HERE HE COMES NOW!
WITH OBVIOUS NERVOUSNESS, YET WITH A FIRM, FEARLESS TREAD, A THIN, SOMEWHAT SICKLY-LOOKING YOUTH ENTERS THE LAB--WALKING SLOWLY, SILENTLY, TOWARDS-- THE UNKNOWN!
STEP FORWARD, ROGERS!
3

STEVE ROGERS! TOO PUNY, TOO SICKLY, TO BE ACCEPTED BY THE ARMY! STEVE ROGERS! CHOSEN FROM HUNDREDS OF SIMILAR VOLUNTEERS BECAUSE OF HIS COURAGE, HIS INTELLIGENCE, AND HIS WILLINGNESS TO RISK DEATH FOR HIS COUNTRY IF THE EXPERIMENT SHOULD FAIL!

YOU MUST DRINK THIS QUICKLY, BEFORE THE CHEMICALS LOSE THEIR POTENCY! GOOD LUCK, MY BOY!

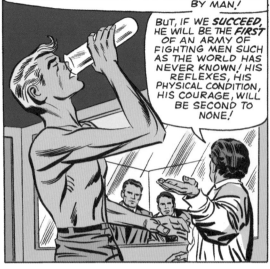

IF WE HAVE ERRED, ROGERS WILL BE DEAD WITHIN SECONDS! FOR, HE IS DRINKING THE STRONGEST CHEMICAL POTION EVER CREATED BY MAN!

BUT, IF WE SUCCEED, HE WILL BE THE FIRST OF AN ARMY OF FIGHTING MEN SUCH AS THE WORLD HAS NEVER KNOWN! HIS REFLEXES, HIS PHYSICAL CONDITION, HIS COURAGE, WILL BE SECOND TO NONE!

THIS EXPERIMENT HAS BEEN SO WELL-GUARDED, THAT ONLY DR. ERSKINE KNOWS THE FORMULA-- AND HE HAS COMMITTED IT TO MEMORY! THERE ARE NO WRITTEN NOTES FOR ENEMY AGENTS TO STEAL....!

BUT, IF WE'RE SUCCESSFUL, WE'LL PRODUCE THE POTION IN QUANTITY, GIVING IT TO ALL OUR FIGHTING MEN!

LOOK! SOMETHING IS HAPPENING TO ROGERS! HE--HE'S CHANGING RIGHT BEFORE OUR EYES!

EVERYTHING IS SPINNING AROUND--! BLACKING OUT! MUST HANG ON--HANG ON--!

IT'S WORKING! DON'T GIVE UP, SON! HOLD ON! THIS IS THE MOMENT OF CRISIS! YOU MUST SURVIVE IT!

AND THEN, IT IS OVER! THE CRISIS HAS PASSED! AND THE LAND OF THE FREE HAS A NEW CHAMPION, A NEW DEFENDER, BORN IN AN HOUR OF NEED--- DESTINED TO BE A LIVING SYMBOL OF THE GLORY THAT IS AMERICA!

BUT, DESPITE THE UNPRECEDENTED SECURITY MEASURES --DESPITE EVERY PRECAUTION-- THE DREAD SPECTRE OF NAZISM APPEARS AT THAT TRIUMPHANT INSTANT, IN THE FORM OF A DESPERATE, MURDEROUS GESTAPO SPY...

YOU, AND YOUR ACCURSED EXPERIMENT, SHALL DIE WITHIN THIS ROOM! HEIL HITLER!

4

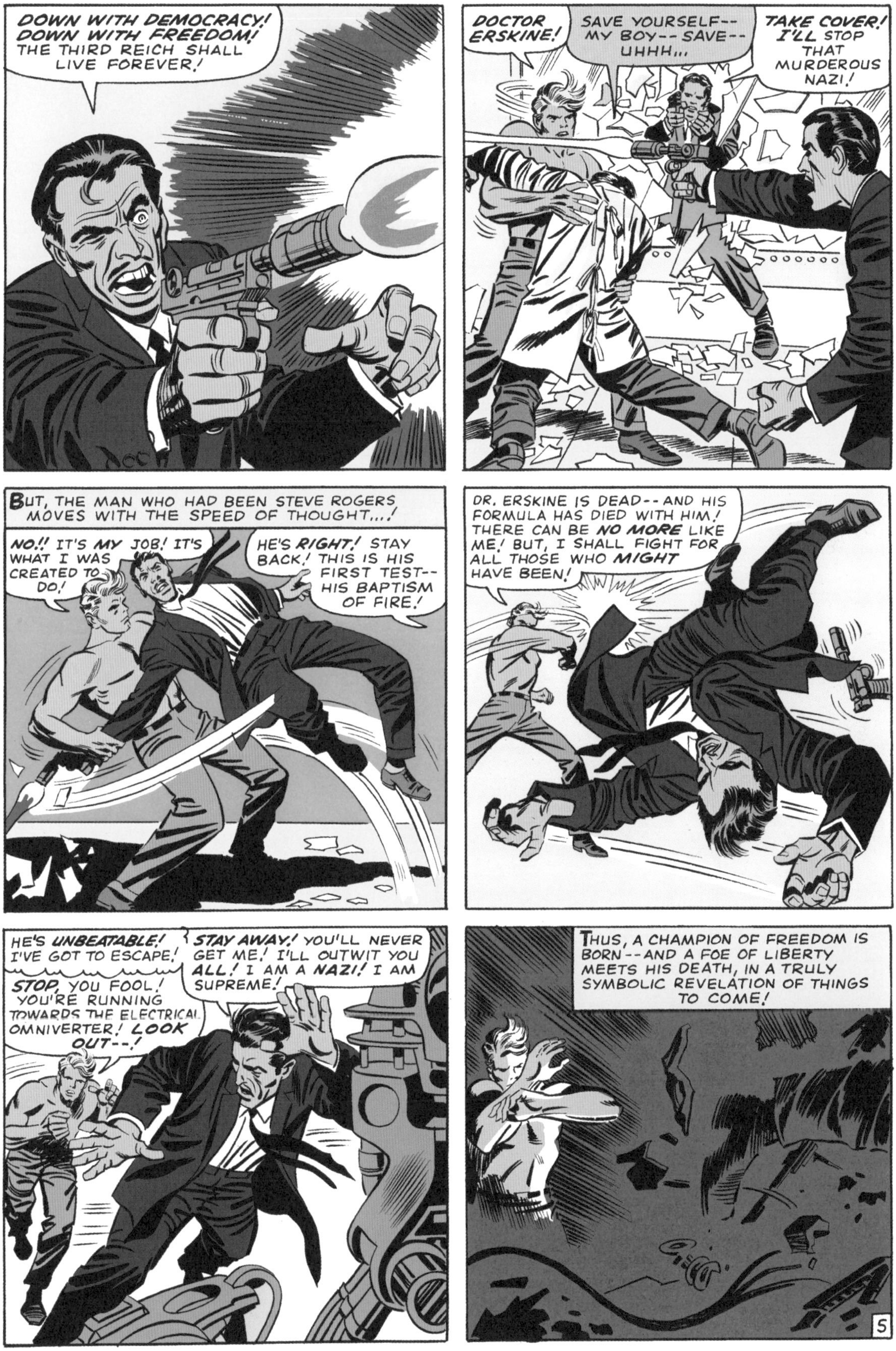
DOWN WITH DEMOCRACY! DOWN WITH FREEDOM! THE THIRD REICH SHALL LIVE FOREVER!
DOCTOR ERSKINE!
SAVE YOURSELF-- MY BOY-- SAVE-- UHHH...
TAKE COVER! I'LL STOP THAT MURDEROUS NAZI!
BUT, THE MAN WHO HAD BEEN STEVE ROGERS MOVES WITH THE SPEED OF THOUGHT...!
NO!! IT'S MY JOB! IT'S WHAT I WAS CREATED TO DO!
HE'S RIGHT! STAY BACK! THIS IS HIS FIRST TEST-- HIS BAPTISM OF FIRE!
DR. ERSKINE IS DEAD-- AND HIS FORMULA HAS DIED WITH HIM! THERE CAN BE NO MORE LIKE ME! BUT, I SHALL FIGHT FOR ALL THOSE WHO MIGHT HAVE BEEN!
HE'S UNBEATABLE! I'VE GOT TO ESCAPE!
STAY AWAY! YOU'LL NEVER GET ME! I'LL OUTWIT YOU ALL! I AM A NAZI! I AM SUPREME!
STOP, YOU FOOL! YOU'RE RUNNING TOWARDS THE ELECTRICAL OMNIVERTER! LOOK OUT--!
THUS, A CHAMPION OF FREEDOM IS BORN-- AND A FOE OF LIBERTY MEETS HIS DEATH, IN A TRULY SYMBOLIC REVELATION OF THINGS TO COME!
5

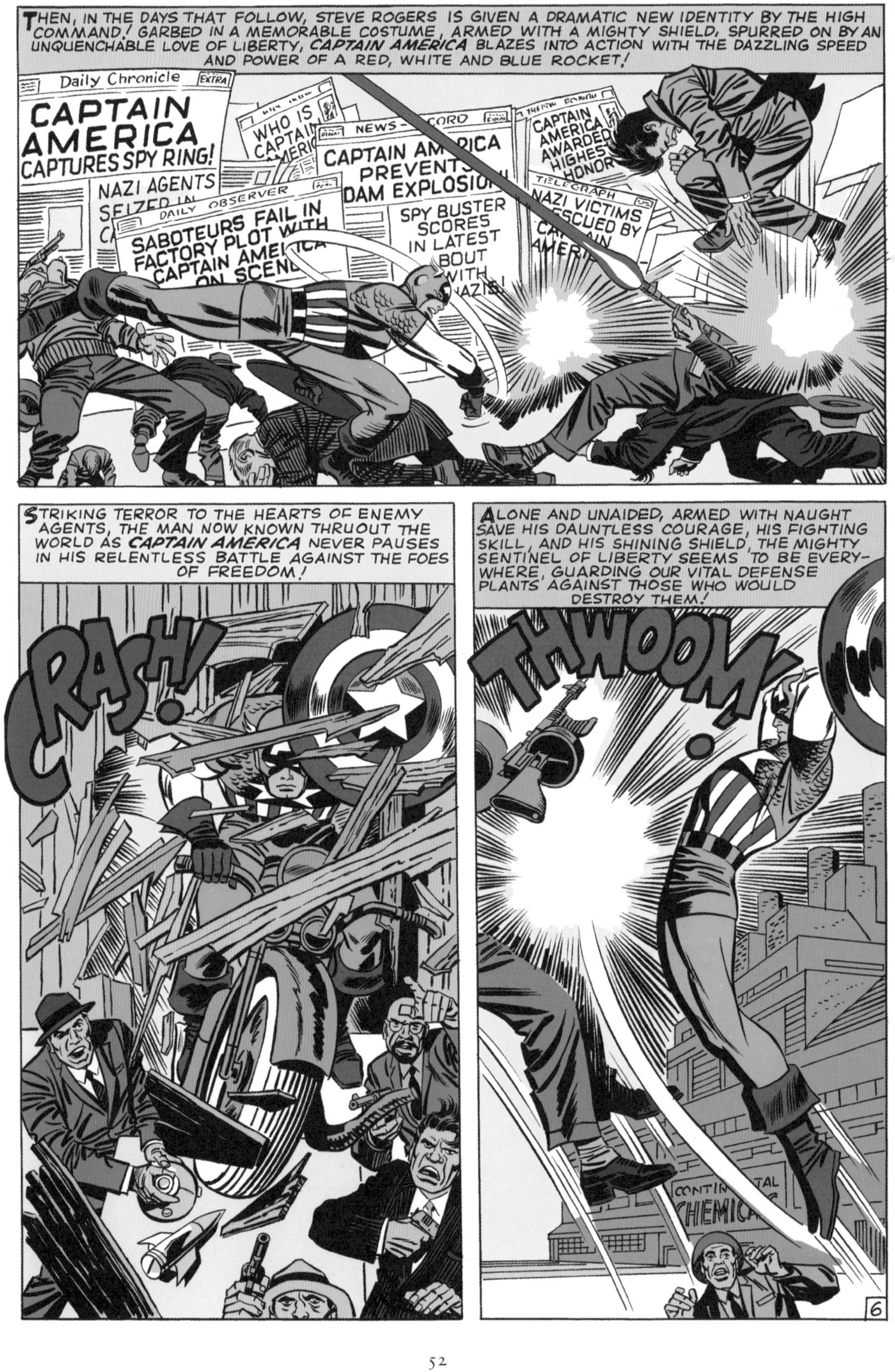
THEN, IN THE DAYS THAT FOLLOW, STEVE ROGERS IS GIVEN A DRAMATIC NEW IDENTITY BY THE HIGH COMMAND! GARBED IN A MEMORABLE COSTUME, ARMED WITH A MIGHTY SHIELD, SPURRED ON BY AN UNQUENCHABLE LOVE OF LIBERTY, CAPTAIN AMERICA BLAZES INTO ACTION WITH THE DAZZLING SPEED AND POWER OF A RED, WHITE AND BLUE ROCKET!
Daily Chronicle EXTRA
CAPTAIN AMERICA CAPTURES SPY RING!
NAZI AGENTS
WHO IS
CAPTAIN AMERICA
DAILY OBSERVER
SABOTEURS FAIL IN FACTORY PLOT WITH
PREVENTS
SPY BUSTER SCORES IN LATEST BOUT
CAPTAIN AMERICA AWARDED
TELEGRAPH
NAZI VICTIMS
STRIKING TERROR TO THE HEARTS OF ENEMY AGENTS, THE MAN NOW KNOWN THRUOUT THE WORLD AS CAPTAIN AMERICA NEVER PAUSES IN HIS RELENTLESS BATTLE AGAINST THE FOES OF FREEDOM!
CRASH!
ALONE AND UNAIDED, ARMED WITH NAUGHT SAVE HIS DAUNTLESS COURAGE, HIS FIGHTING SKILL, AND HIS SHINING SHIELD, THE MIGHTY SENTINEL OF LIBERTY SEEMS TO BE EVERY-WHERE, GUARDING OUR VITAL DEFENSE PLANTS AGAINST THOSE WHO WOULD DESTROY THEM!
THWOOM!
6

AND, WHILE A GRATEFUL NATION PONDERS CAPTAIN AMERICA'S TRUE IDENTITY, THE VALIANT DEFENDER CONCEALS IT BENEATH THE UNIFORM OF AN ARMY PRIVATE!

YOU BUMBLING MEATHEAD! IS *THAT* THE ONLY POSITION YOU KNOW.??

WHA—WHAT OTHER POSITION DO YOU *WANT*, SARGE?

I'LL DO THE TALKIN', ROGERS! YOU JUST *SNAP* TO IT!

PARAAAADE *REST!*

OWWW! NOT ON MY *FOOT*, YOU BLASTED IDJIT!

UH OH! POOR PRIVATE ROGERS IS IN HOT WATER WITH THE SARGE AGAIN!

THUNK!

YOU CLUMSY KNUCKLEHEAD! IF YOU DON'T GET ON THE BALL I'LL MAKE YOU THINK YOU WERE *BORN* ON K.P.!

DID I DO SOMETHING *WRONG*, SARGE?

ROGERS

WHAT'S THE *USE*??! I WONDER HOW MUCH THE GERMANS ARE *PAYIN'* ROGERS TO STAY ON *OUR* SIDE?!!

THE SARGE IS A RIGHT GUY! I HATE RIDIN' HIM, BUT IT'S THE WAY I'VE *GOT* TO PLAY IT, TO KEEP SUSPICION OFF ME!

BETTER STAY OUT OF HIS WAY FOR A WHILE, STEVE!

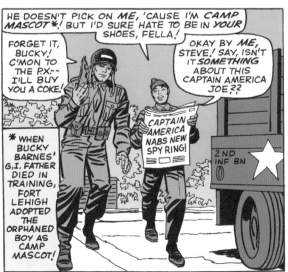

HE DOESN'T PICK ON *ME*, 'CAUSE I'M *CAMP MASCOT**! BUT I'D SURE HATE TO BE IN *YOUR* SHOES, FELLA!

FORGET IT, BUCKY! C'MON TO THE PX-- I'LL BUY YOU A COKE!

OKAY BY *ME*, STEVE! SAY, ISN'T IT *SOMETHING* ABOUT THIS CAPTAIN AMERICA JOE??

* WHEN BUCKY BARNES' G.I. FATHER DIED IN TRAINING, FORT LEHIGH ADOPTED THE ORPHANED BOY AS CAMP MASCOT!

CAPTAIN AMERICA NABS NEW SPY RING!

2ND INF BN

WHO *NEEDS* 'IM, BUCKY? YOU'VE GOT *ME*, HAVEN'T YOU?

BOY! WOULDN'T IT BE GREAT TO HAVE A GUY LIKE HIM AROUND *HERE*?!!

WOTTA GUY! YOU'RE ALWAYS CLOWNIN', STEVE!

POST-COURIER
CAPTAIN AMERICA NABS NEW SPY

POST-COURIER

7

53

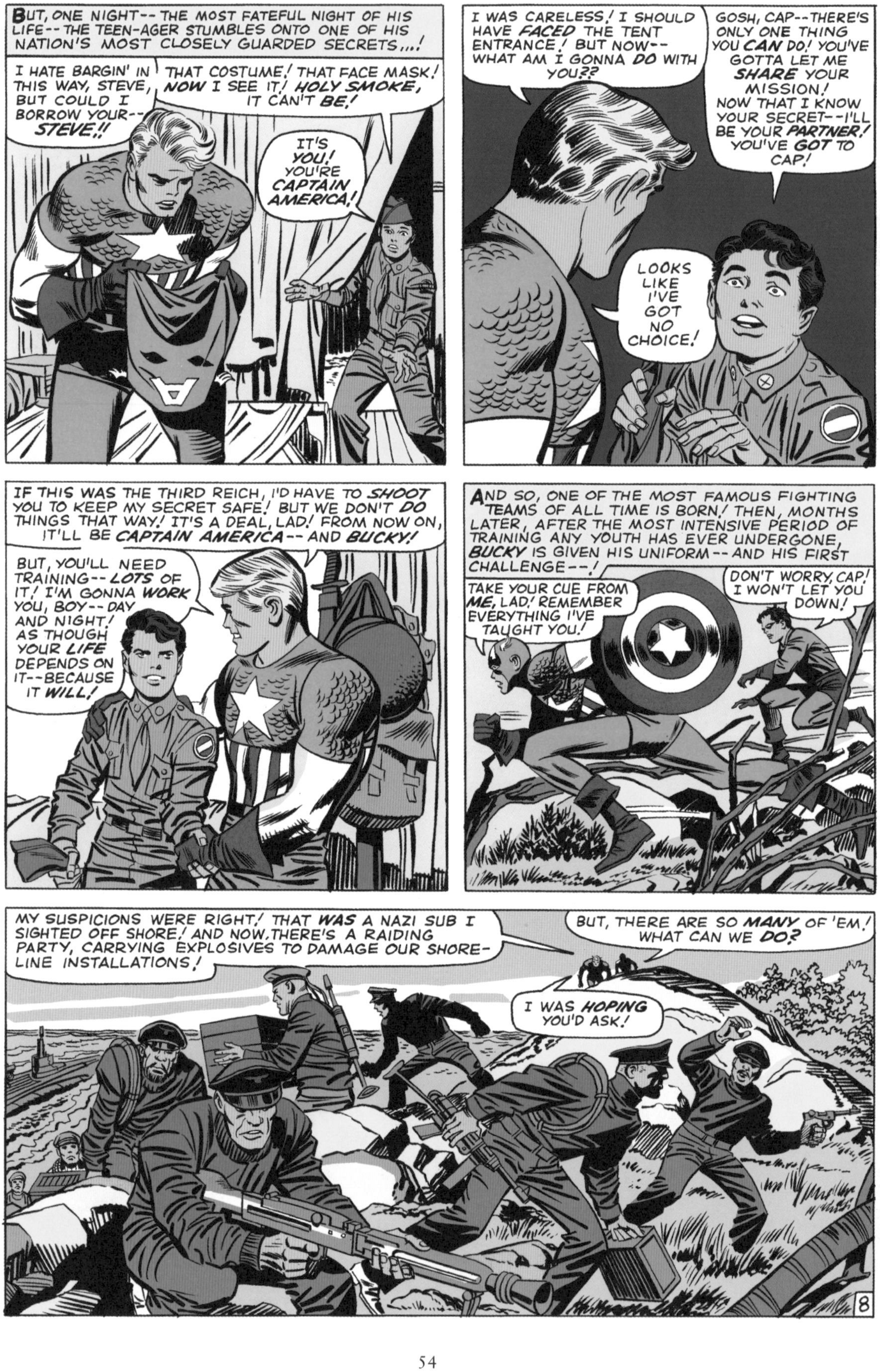
BUT, ONE NIGHT-- THE MOST FATEFUL NIGHT OF HIS LIFE-- THE TEEN-AGER STUMBLES ONTO ONE OF HIS NATION'S MOST CLOSELY GUARDED SECRETS...!
I HATE BARGIN' IN THIS WAY, STEVE, BUT COULD I BORROW YOUR-- STEVE!!
THAT COSTUME! THAT FACE MASK! NOW I SEE IT! HOLY SMOKE, IT CAN'T BE!
IT'S YOU! YOU'RE CAPTAIN AMERICA!
I WAS CARELESS! I SHOULD HAVE FACED THE TENT ENTRANCE! BUT NOW-- WHAT AM I GONNA DO WITH YOU??
GOSH, CAP--THERE'S ONLY ONE THING YOU CAN DO! YOU'VE GOTTA LET ME SHARE YOUR MISSION! NOW THAT I KNOW YOUR SECRET--I'LL BE YOUR PARTNER! YOU'VE GOT TO CAP!
LOOKS LIKE I'VE GOT NO CHOICE!
IF THIS WAS THE THIRD REICH, I'D HAVE TO SHOOT YOU TO KEEP MY SECRET SAFE! BUT WE DON'T DO THINGS THAT WAY! IT'S A DEAL, LAD! FROM NOW ON, IT'LL BE CAPTAIN AMERICA -- AND BUCKY!
BUT, YOU'LL NEED TRAINING-- LOTS OF IT! I'M GONNA WORK YOU, BOY-- DAY AND NIGHT! AS THOUGH YOUR LIFE DEPENDS ON IT--BECAUSE IT WILL!
AND SO, ONE OF THE MOST FAMOUS FIGHTING TEAMS OF ALL TIME IS BORN! THEN, MONTHS LATER, AFTER THE MOST INTENSIVE PERIOD OF TRAINING ANY YOUTH HAS EVER UNDERGONE, BUCKY IS GIVEN HIS UNIFORM -- AND HIS FIRST CHALLENGE--!
TAKE YOUR CUE FROM ME, LAD! REMEMBER EVERYTHING I'VE TAUGHT YOU!
DON'T WORRY, CAP! I WON'T LET YOU DOWN!
MY SUSPICIONS WERE RIGHT! THAT WAS A NAZI SUB I SIGHTED OFF SHORE! AND NOW, THERE'S A RAIDING PARTY, CARRYING EXPLOSIVES TO DAMAGE OUR SHORE-LINE INSTALLATIONS!
BUT, THERE ARE SO MANY OF 'EM! WHAT CAN WE DO?
I WAS HOPING YOU'D ASK!
8

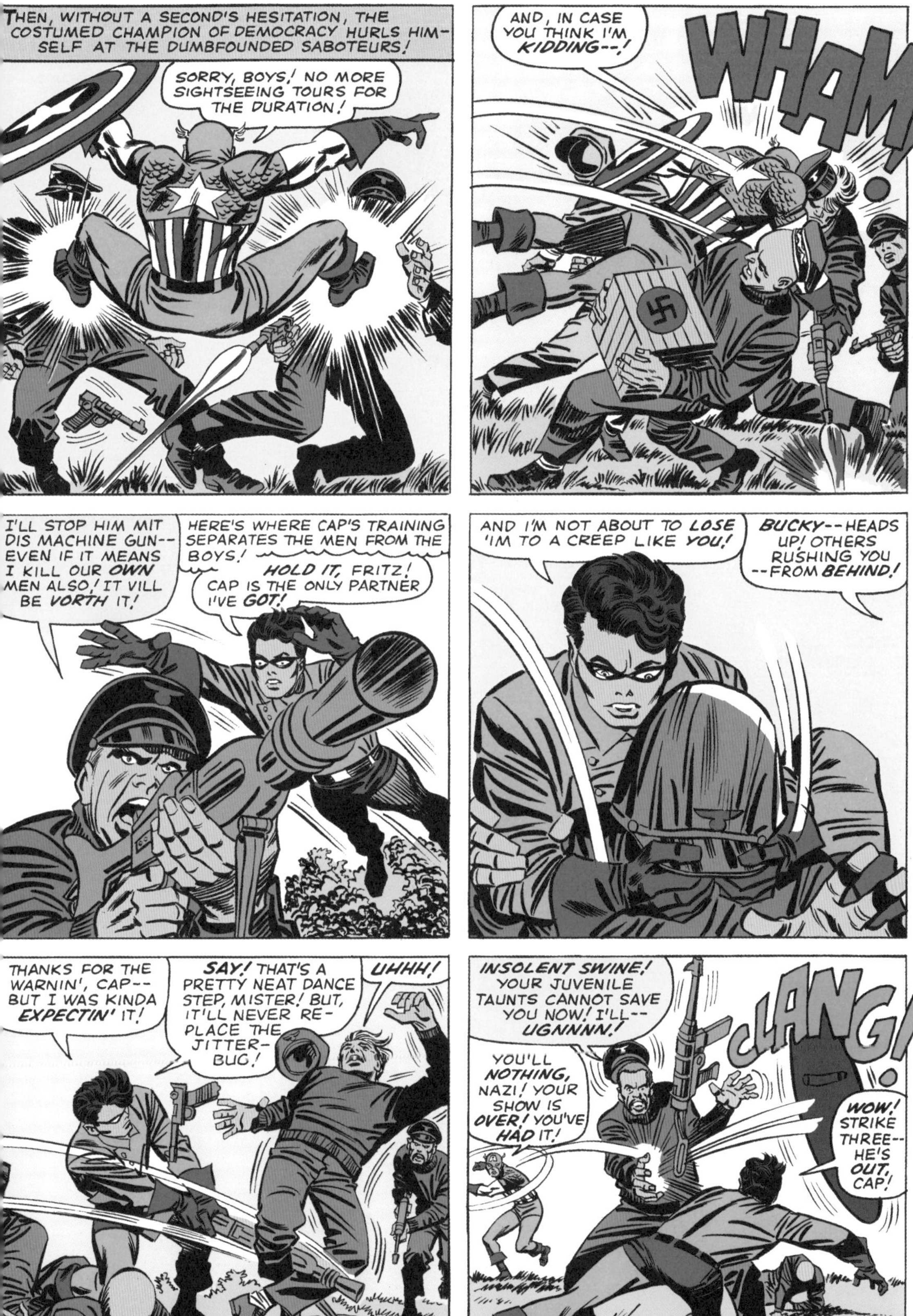
THEN, WITHOUT A SECOND'S HESITATION, THE COSTUMED CHAMPION OF DEMOCRACY HURLS HIMSELF AT THE DUMBFOUNDED SABOTEURS!
SORRY, BOYS! NO MORE SIGHTSEEING TOURS FOR THE DURATION!
AND, IN CASE YOU THINK I'M KIDDING--!
WHAM!
I'LL STOP HIM MIT DIS MACHINE GUN-- EVEN IF IT MEANS I KILL OUR OWN MEN ALSO! IT VILL BE VORTH IT!
HERE'S WHERE CAP'S TRAINING SEPARATES THE MEN FROM THE BOYS!
HOLD IT, FRITZ! CAP IS THE ONLY PARTNER I'VE GOT!
AND I'M NOT ABOUT TO LOSE 'IM TO A CREEP LIKE YOU!
BUCKY--HEADS UP! OTHERS RUSHING YOU --FROM BEHIND!
THANKS FOR THE WARNIN', CAP-- BUT I WAS KINDA EXPECTIN' IT!
SAY! THAT'S A PRETTY NEAT DANCE STEP, MISTER! BUT, IT'LL NEVER REPLACE THE JITTERBUG!
UHHH!
INSOLENT SWINE! YOUR JUVENILE TAUNTS CANNOT SAVE YOU NOW! I'LL-- UGNNNN!
CLANG!
YOU'LL NOTHING, NAZI! YOUR SHOW IS OVER! YOU'VE HAD IT!
WOW! STRIKE THREE-- HE'S OUT, CAP!
9

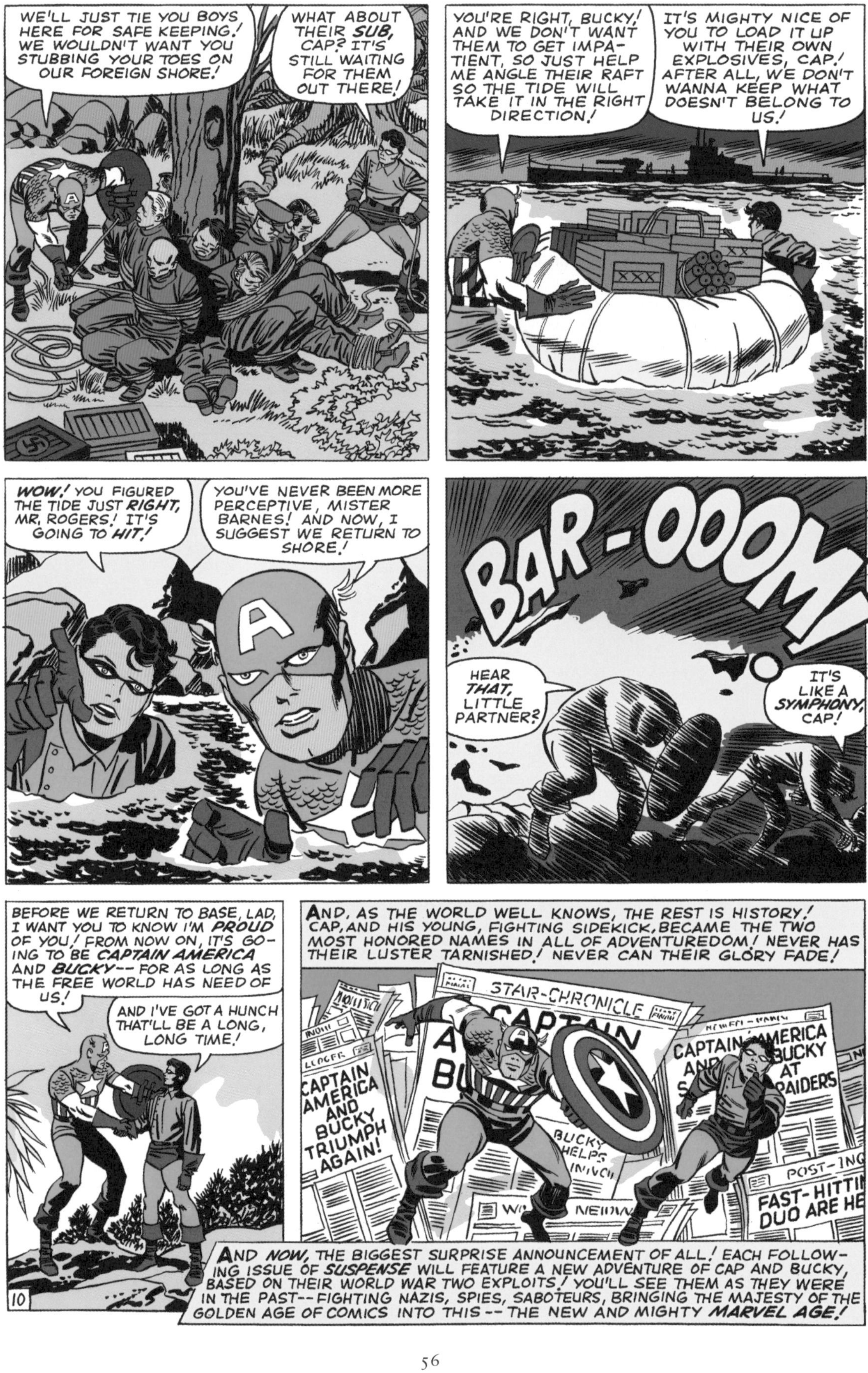
WE'LL JUST TIE YOU BOYS HERE FOR SAFE KEEPING! WE WOULDN'T WANT YOU STUBBING YOUR TOES ON OUR FOREIGN SHORE!
WHAT ABOUT THEIR SUB, CAP? IT'S STILL WAITING FOR THEM OUT THERE!
YOU'RE RIGHT, BUCKY! AND WE DON'T WANT THEM TO GET IMPATIENT, SO JUST HELP ME ANGLE THEIR RAFT SO THE TIDE WILL TAKE IT IN THE RIGHT DIRECTION!
IT'S MIGHTY NICE OF YOU TO LOAD IT UP WITH THEIR OWN EXPLOSIVES, CAP! AFTER ALL, WE DON'T WANNA KEEP WHAT DOESN'T BELONG TO US!
WOW! YOU FIGURED THE TIDE JUST RIGHT, MR. ROGERS! IT'S GOING TO HIT!
YOU'VE NEVER BEEN MORE PERCEPTIVE, MISTER BARNES! AND NOW, I SUGGEST WE RETURN TO SHORE!
BAR-OOOM!
HEAR THAT, LITTLE PARTNER?
IT'S LIKE A SYMPHONY, CAP!
BEFORE WE RETURN TO BASE, LAD, I WANT YOU TO KNOW I'M PROUD OF YOU! FROM NOW ON, IT'S GOING TO BE CAPTAIN AMERICA AND BUCKY-- FOR AS LONG AS THE FREE WORLD HAS NEED OF US!
AND I'VE GOT A HUNCH THAT'LL BE A LONG, LONG TIME!
10
AND, AS THE WORLD WELL KNOWS, THE REST IS HISTORY! CAP, AND HIS YOUNG, FIGHTING SIDEKICK, BECAME THE TWO MOST HONORED NAMES IN ALL OF ADVENTUREDOM! NEVER HAS THEIR LUSTER TARNISHED! NEVER CAN THEIR GLORY FADE!
STAR-CHRONICLE
CAPTAIN AMERICA AND BUCKY TRIUMPH AGAIN!
AND NOW, THE BIGGEST SURPRISE ANNOUNCEMENT OF ALL! EACH FOLLOWING ISSUE OF SUSPENSE WILL FEATURE A NEW ADVENTURE OF CAP AND BUCKY, BASED ON THEIR WORLD WAR TWO EXPLOITS! YOU'LL SEE THEM AS THEY WERE IN THE PAST--FIGHTING NAZIS, SPIES, SABOTEURS, BRINGING THE MAJESTY OF THE GOLDEN AGE OF COMICS INTO THIS -- THE NEW AND MIGHTY MARVEL AGE!

Mails of SUSPENSE

SEND YOUR LETTERS TO: THE MARVEL COMICS GROUP, SECOND FLOOR 625 MADISON AVE., NEW YORK, N. Y. 10022

We ask you—we beg you—keep your letters short! It's the only way we'll have time to read them!

Dear Stan and Don and Jack,

Now that you have double features in most of your mags, don't wreck the covers for these great stories by splitting them (as you tried on ASTONISH #60 and #61 and recent SUSPENSE issues). Why not try this alternate —one ish have Cap plastered on the cover and have Iron Man's head floating around somewhere reminding you that he's there too. Next ish do the plastering with Iron Man and knock Cap's head off to do the floating. (If I should come home sometime and find two oddly garbed guys waiting for me, ready to knock my brains around, I'll know why!) Give Cap and Shell-head their own mags, or we won't face front when you tell us to!

Joe Adams, 13807 Kornblum Ave.
Hawthorne, Calif.

You can't scare us, Joey boy! We can strike back by not reading your letters!

Dear Stan and Don and Jack,

I've been looking over your new letters pages and I think the titles are crummy. The worst of all is Iron Man's and Captain America's "Mails of Suspense." If the golden gladiator found out about this, Tony Stark would be writing instead of good ol' Stan. Why not give out another no-prize for best new title. I would call it "Scraps of Iron" —do you agree my title is better?

Richard Wilkee, 192 Elk St.
Buffalo 10, N. Y.

Well, let's say it's *different*, anyway! We won't know which is better till the rest of the fans have their say, Dick! Until we get the word from our rabid readers, we don't know nothin'!

Dear Stan and Don and Jack,

I think you're going to lose a fan of TALES OF SUSPENSE if you take out "Tales of the Watcher." He's better than Captain America. How about leaving him in?

Ira Friedman, 1903 Avenue U
Brooklyn 29, N. Y.

Nobody knocked themselves out telling us how great the Watcher was when we co-featured him! But, now that he's gone, we get a few letters a week like Ira's! (They're probably all from Ira!) Anyway, if you're still with us, what do *you* think?

Dear Stan and Don,

I've just read IRON MAN #57 for the umpteenth time. Though many will consider Hawkeye a terrific villain, I think that you have given him a bum steer. After all, he isn't really evil like the rest of your arch-foes. Hawkeye just wanted to be another costumed hero. Then, the cops misinterpreted his actions and dubbed him a crook. He fell into bad company (the Black Widow) and that was that. The next scene was his battling Iron Man. Now it's not that I want to ruin your plans for further Hawkeye vs. Iron Man battles, but I think that he would make a much better hero than villain. The bow and arrow has been used since the early 1940's and it's still in use. Hawkeye is much more colorful than any new character I've seen! I think Hawkeye should revert back to his first idea—that of being a costumed hero.

George Hagenauer, 10204 St. Lawrence
Chicago, Ill. 60628

Good thinking, Georgie! But, let's wait and see. Somehow, we suspect that you haven't heard the last of Hawkeye!

Dear Stan and Don and Jack,

Issue #59 was the first TALES OF SUSPENSE I had read. Captain America is what made me put my 12¢ down, and it was well worth it. His story had more hand-to-hand combat than any other tale ever written. To me the story was a success because Captain America proved that he is greater than the Fantastic Four when it comes to pure fighting power. It proved that he is more of a fighting man than the entire Avengers team. He has more

agility than Daredevil and is a far greater acrobat than Spider-Man. Give Captain America his own magazine. He deserves it! As for Iron Man, he's nothing compared with Cap. If issue #59 is a sell-out, Captain America is the reason—not Iron Man.

Richard Dickson, 150 E. Washington Ave.
Atlantic Highlands, N. J.

You might be right, Dick, but if you're ever in the neighborhood of Tony Stark's factory, we suggest you don't linger too long!

SPECIAL ANNOUNCEMENTS SECTION:

—Boy! If you enjoyed Cap's origin as much as we did, then you flipped, too! But, you aint seen nothin' yet! In the issues to come, we've got the most off-beat cloak-and-dagger World War II yarns ever told, gathered from Cap's great Golden Age of Comics days! But, you know us! They're not gonna be faded reprints! No sir! They'll be all-new, all specially prepared, all greater than ever! Well, so much for the soft sell!

—Y'know, it's a funny thing—we never can be sure what'll make a strip take off and soar to new heights of popularity. Iron-Man has been a steady favorite for years, but lately, for no special reason that we can figure out, more and more fans are "discovering" him, and those who've always read him are finding his tales more thrilling than ever. We're not aware that we've changed him lately, but we won't look a gift horse in the mouth! Perhaps it's the fact that darlin' Dick Ayers is now inking Don's pencilling. Maybe that was just the touch needed! Anyway, thanks for your ever-increasing support, Marvelites!

—We hope you're all proudly wearing your M.M.M.S. membership pins all over the place! And, for those of you callous enough not to have joined yet, what are you waiting for? We don't want any of our readers to be outcasts! (Aw, we're only kidding! You don't have to join if you don't want to!— Just don't ever talk to us again!)

—Well, next ish will be the same as this one, only better— if we can arrange it! So try to be with us for SUSPENSE #64, huh? (And, if you want a feeling of nostalgia, wait till you see the two whacky Golden Age foes Cap will be fighting then! It's the type of yarn you'd have written yourself, if you weren't so busy pasting your M.M.M.S. stickers all over town!) Be good to each other, and face *front!*

THE MIGHTY MARVEL CHECKLIST
A Line-Up Of Some Of The Marvel-ous Mags On Sale Right Now:

FANTASTIC FOUR #36: At last! Mighty Marvel has created a NEW F.F.! Don't miss the surprise sensation of the season when the FANTASTIC FOUR battles the dazzling, dangerous, daringly different FRIGHTFUL FOUR!

SPIDER-MAN #22: This seems to be Marvel's year for evil teams! Spidey reaches new heights of greatness as he goes into single-handed action against the deadly CLOWN, and his MASTERS OF MENACE!

AVENGERS #13: The Avengers have been almost all over, but never have they entered a place with the menace and mystery of "The Castle of Count Nefaria!" It's got that Bela Lugosi-ish flavor!

DAREDEVIL #6: And still another team of villains! But this one has a different gimmick! See why D.D. has become a winner in such a short time as you thrill to "The Fellowship Of Fear!"

THOR #113: It had to happen! At last the mighty Thor tells Jane his true identity! But, little does he dream it may cost him his life—especially with the grotesque Grey Gargoyle appearing from nowhere!

STRANGE TALES #130: Certain to be a sensation! The Torch and the Thing see the Beatles! Dr. Strange is defeated by the dread Dormammu! And, we introduce an exciting new artist!

ASTONISH #65: Another fabulous surprise! Wait till you see the NEW Giant-Man! New artist, new costume, but the same Marvel magic! And then you'll follow the incredible Hulk on a thundering rampage behind the iron curtain!

SGT. FURY #15: The Howlers find a new mascot on one of their most dangerous missions! If you appreciate the best, don't miss "Too Small To Fight, Too Young To Die!" in the war magazine for people who hate war magazines!

TALES OF SUSPENSE #64,

APRIL 1965,

"AMONG US, WRECKERS DWELL!"

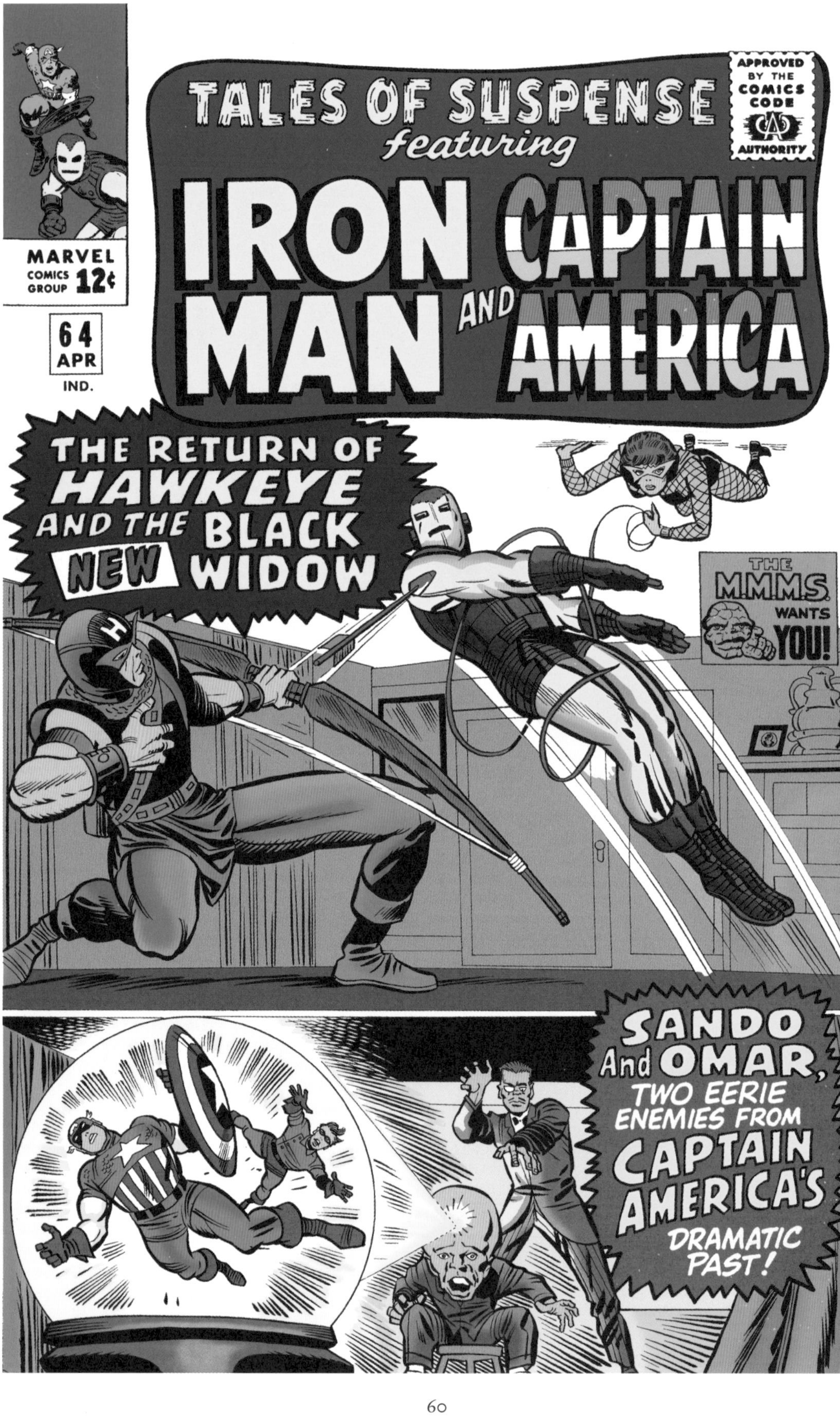
MARVEL COMICS GROUP 12¢
64 APR
IND.
APPROVED BY THE COMICS CODE AUTHORITY
TALES OF SUSPENSE featuring
IRON MAN AND CAPTAIN AMERICA
THE RETURN OF HAWKEYE AND THE NEW BLACK WIDOW
THE M.M.M.S. WANTS YOU!
SANDO And OMAR, TWO EERIE ENEMIES FROM CAPTAIN AMERICA'S DRAMATIC PAST!

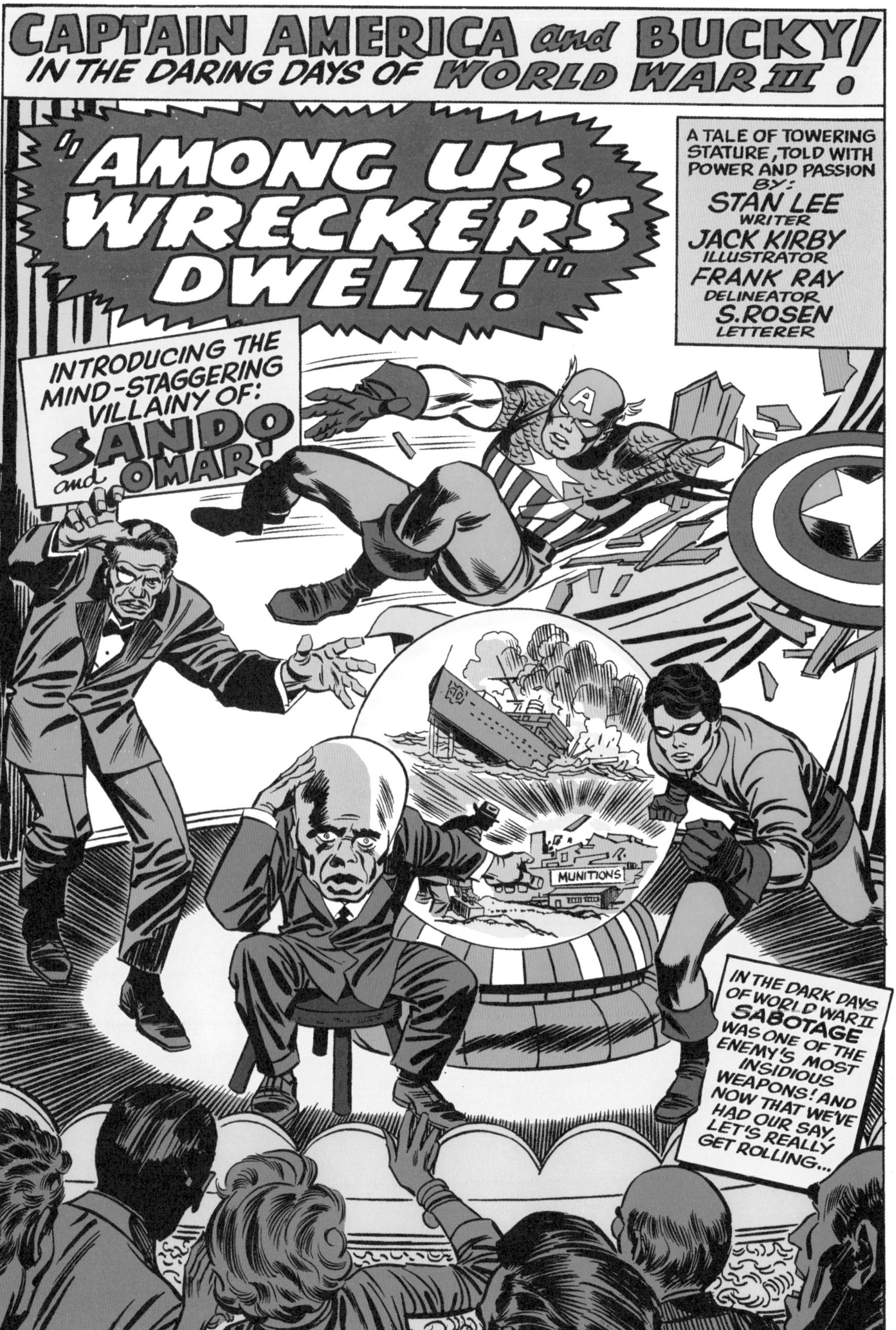
CAPTAIN AMERICA and BUCKY!
IN THE DARING DAYS OF WORLD WAR II!
"AMONG US, WRECKER'S DWELL!"
A TALE OF TOWERING STATURE, TOLD WITH POWER AND PASSION BY: STAN LEE WRITER JACK KIRBY ILLUSTRATOR FRANK RAY DELINEATOR S.ROSEN LETTERER
INTRODUCING THE MIND-STAGGERING VILLAINY OF: SANDO and OMAR!
MUNITIONS
IN THE DARK DAYS OF WORLD WAR II SABOTAGE WAS ONE OF THE ENEMY'S MOST INSIDIOUS WEAPONS! AND NOW THAT WE'VE HAD OUR SAY, LET'S REALLY GET ROLLING...
1

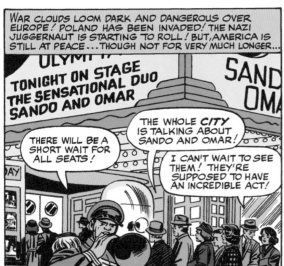

WAR CLOUDS LOOM DARK AND DANGEROUS OVER EUROPE! POLAND HAS BEEN INVADED! THE NAZI JUGGERNAUT IS STARTING TO ROLL! BUT, AMERICA IS STILL AT PEACE...THOUGH NOT FOR VERY MUCH LONGER...

TONIGHT ON STAGE THE SENSATIONAL DUO SANDO AND OMAR

THERE WILL BE A SHORT WAIT FOR ALL SEATS!

THE WHOLE *CITY* IS TALKING ABOUT SANDO AND OMAR!

I CAN'T WAIT TO SEE THEM! THEY'RE SUPPOSED TO HAVE AN INCREDIBLE ACT!

AND, ON THE STAGE INSIDE...

I MUST REQUEST *ABSOLUTE SILENCE* FROM THE AUDIENCE AS I CAUSE THE MYSTERIOUS *OMAR* TO GO INTO A HYPNOTIC TRANCE!

THEN WHEN I HAVE ESTABLISHED COMPLETE CONTROL OVER HIS BRAIN, YOU WILL SEE HIS AMAZING *MENTAL PREDICTIONS* PROJECTED UPON OUR CRYSTAL BALL!

AND NOW TO *BEGIN*...!

OMAR! YOU ARE MY SLAVE! I, *SANDO*, AM YOUR MASTER! I AM MASTER OF YOUR MIND! I AM MASTER OF YOUR THOUGHTS! AM I *NOT*, OMAR??

YOU..ARE.. THE..MASTER, SANDO!

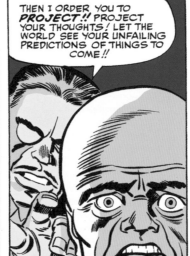

THEN I ORDER YOU TO *PROJECT!!* PROJECT YOUR THOUGHTS! LET THE WORLD SEE YOUR UNFAILING PREDICTIONS OF THINGS TO COME!!

FOR *YOU* HAVE THE POWER TO GAZE INTO THE FUTURE! AND *I* HAVE THE POWER TO REVEAL YOUR THOUGHTS IN THE MYSTIC CRYSTAL BALL! *PROJECT*, OMAR...*PROJECT!*

SLOWLY, UNBELIEVABLY, A *SCENE* BEGINS TO FORM WITHIN THE GIANT CRYSTAL! THE IMAGE OF A COLUMN OF U.S. WAR TANKS, ON MANEUVERS AT FORT LEHIGH...

BUT, AN INSTANT LATER, THE STARTLED AUDIENCE IN THE SILENT THEATRE SEES...

WHOOOOM!

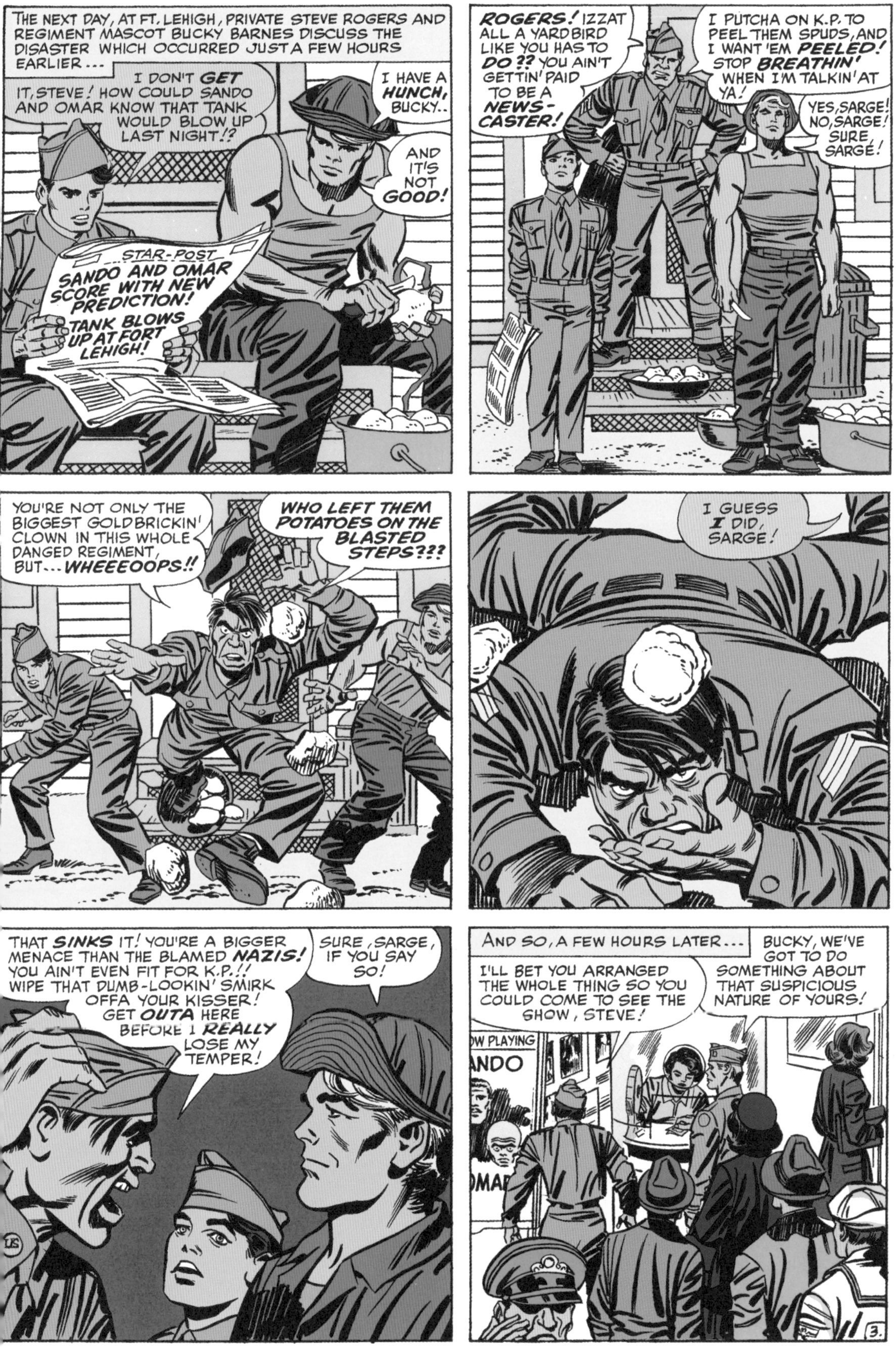
THE NEXT DAY, AT FT. LEHIGH, PRIVATE STEVE ROGERS AND REGIMENT MASCOT BUCKY BARNES DISCUSS THE DISASTER WHICH OCCURRED JUST A FEW HOURS EARLIER...
I DON'T GET IT, STEVE! HOW COULD SANDO AND OMAR KNOW THAT TANK WOULD BLOW UP LAST NIGHT!?
I HAVE A HUNCH, BUCKY..
AND IT'S NOT GOOD!
STAR-POST
SANDO AND OMAR SCORE WITH NEW PREDICTION!
TANK BLOWS UP AT FORT LEHIGH!
ROGERS! IZZAT ALL A YARDBIRD LIKE YOU HAS TO DO?? YOU AIN'T GETTIN' PAID TO BE A NEWS-CASTER!
I PUTCHA ON K.P. TO PEEL THEM SPUDS, AND I WANT 'EM PEELED! STOP BREATHIN' WHEN I'M TALKIN' AT YA!
YES, SARGE! NO, SARGE! SURE, SARGE!
YOU'RE NOT ONLY THE BIGGEST GOLDBRICKIN' CLOWN IN THIS WHOLE DANGED REGIMENT, BUT... WHEEEOOPS!!
WHO LEFT THEM POTATOES ON THE BLASTED STEPS???
I GUESS I DID, SARGE!
THAT SINKS IT! YOU'RE A BIGGER MENACE THAN THE BLAMED NAZIS! YOU AIN'T EVEN FIT FOR K.P.!! WIPE THAT DUMB-LOOKIN' SMIRK OFFA YOUR KISSER! GET OUTA HERE BEFORE I REALLY LOSE MY TEMPER!
SURE, SARGE, IF YOU SAY SO!
AND SO, A FEW HOURS LATER...
I'LL BET YOU ARRANGED THE WHOLE THING SO YOU COULD COME TO SEE THE SHOW, STEVE!
BUCKY, WE'VE GOT TO DO SOMETHING ABOUT THAT SUSPICIOUS NATURE OF YOURS!
OW PLAYING
ANDO
OMAR
3.

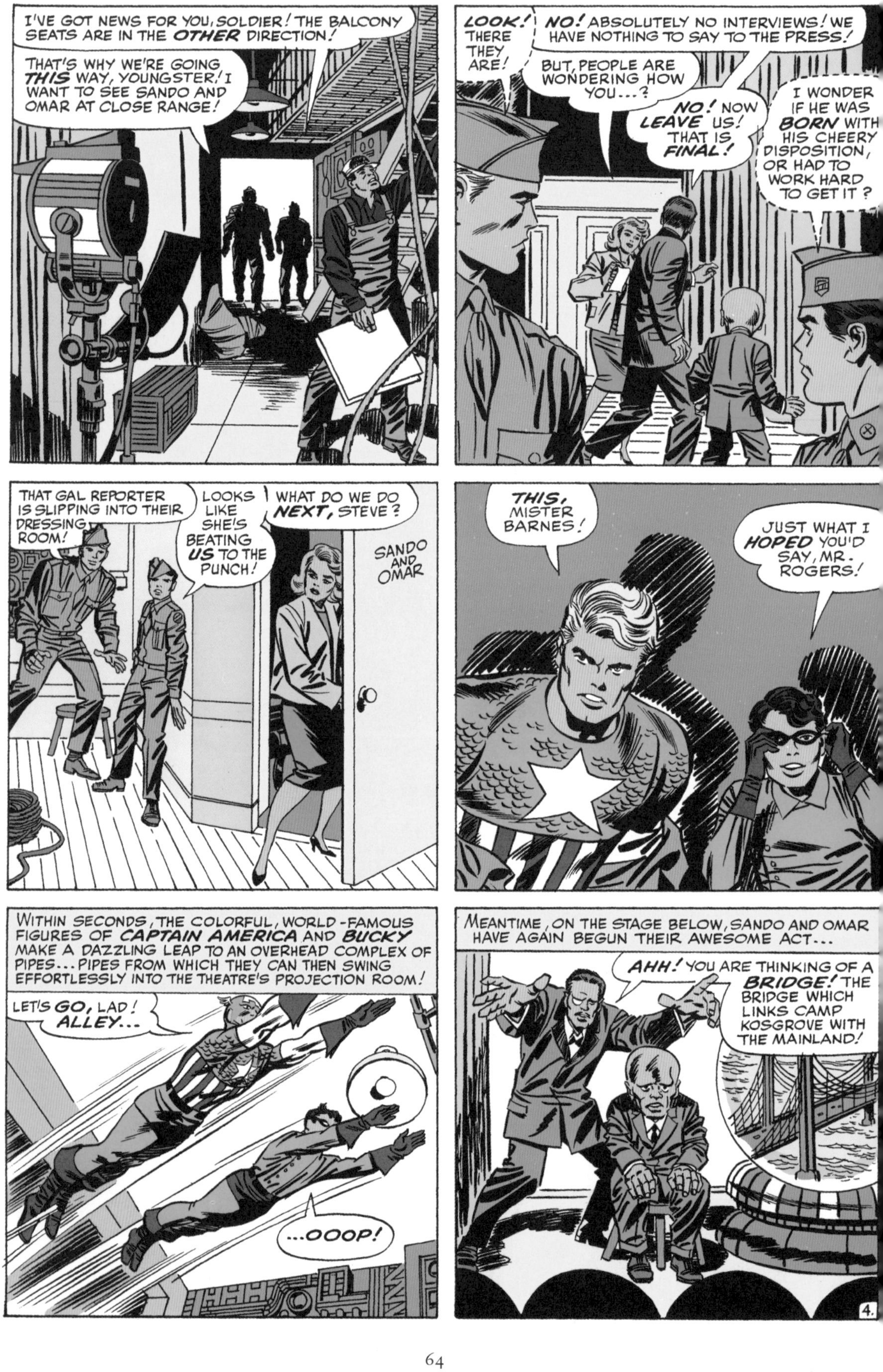
I'VE GOT NEWS FOR YOU, SOLDIER! THE BALCONY SEATS ARE IN THE OTHER DIRECTION!
THAT'S WHY WE'RE GOING THIS WAY, YOUNGSTER! I WANT TO SEE SANDO AND OMAR AT CLOSE RANGE!
LOOK! THERE THEY ARE!
NO! ABSOLUTELY NO INTERVIEWS! WE HAVE NOTHING TO SAY TO THE PRESS!
BUT, PEOPLE ARE WONDERING HOW YOU...?
NO! NOW LEAVE US! THAT IS FINAL!
I WONDER IF HE WAS BORN WITH HIS CHEERY DISPOSITION, OR HAD TO WORK HARD TO GET IT?
THAT GAL REPORTER IS SLIPPING INTO THEIR DRESSING ROOM!
LOOKS LIKE SHE'S BEATING US TO THE PUNCH!
WHAT DO WE DO NEXT, STEVE?
SANDO AND OMAR
THIS, MISTER BARNES!
JUST WHAT I HOPED YOU'D SAY, MR. ROGERS!
WITHIN SECONDS, THE COLORFUL, WORLD-FAMOUS FIGURES OF CAPTAIN AMERICA AND BUCKY MAKE A DAZZLING LEAP TO AN OVERHEAD COMPLEX OF PIPES... PIPES FROM WHICH THEY CAN THEN SWING EFFORTLESSLY INTO THE THEATRE'S PROJECTION ROOM!
LET'S GO, LAD! ALLEY...
...OOOP!
MEANTIME, ON THE STAGE BELOW, SANDO AND OMAR HAVE AGAIN BEGUN THEIR AWESOME ACT...
AHH! YOU ARE THINKING OF A BRIDGE! THE BRIDGE WHICH LINKS CAMP KOSGROVE WITH THE MAINLAND!
4.

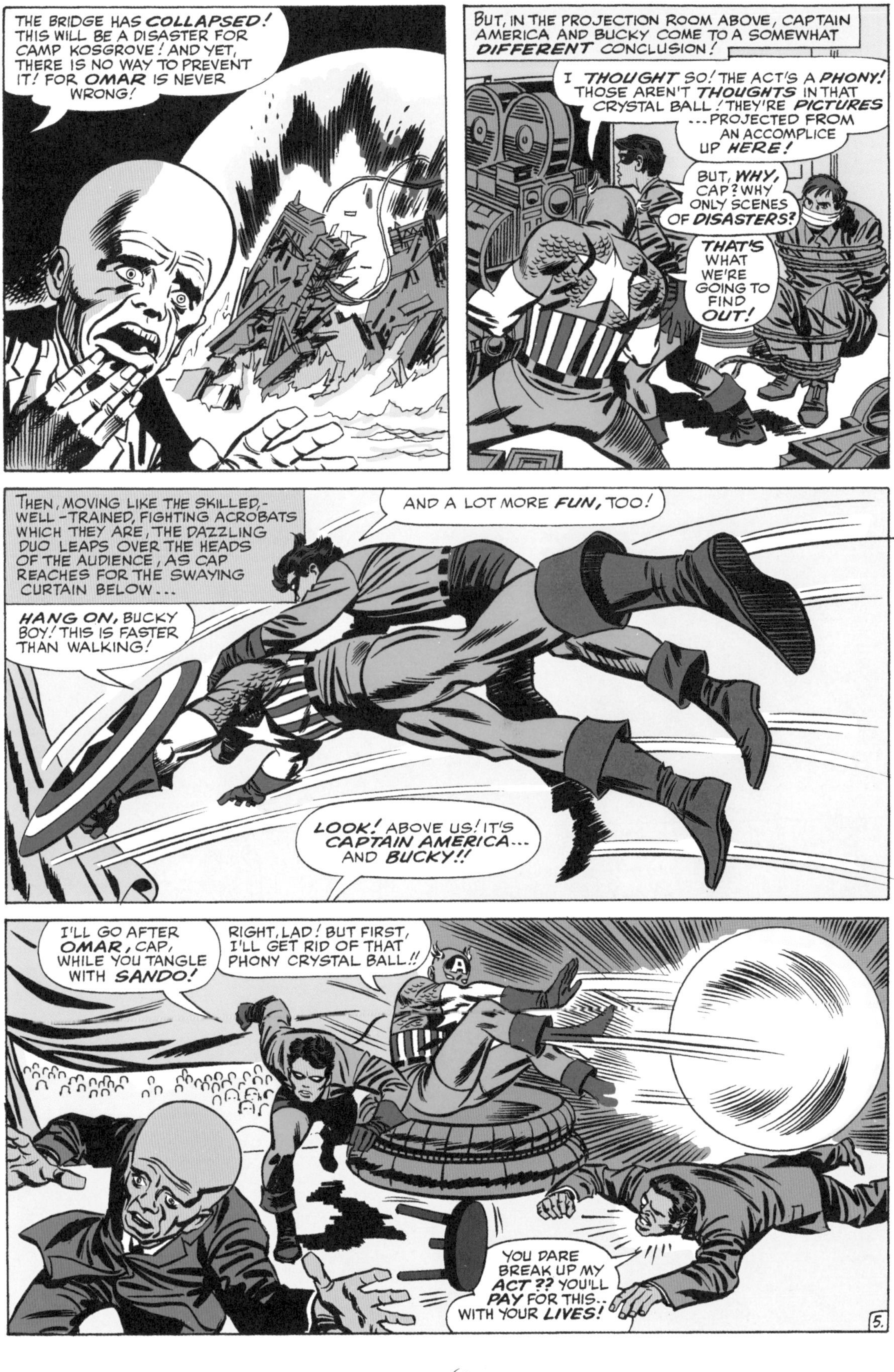
THE BRIDGE HAS COLLAPSED! THIS WILL BE A DISASTER FOR CAMP KOSGROVE! AND YET, THERE IS NO WAY TO PREVENT IT! FOR OMAR IS NEVER WRONG!
BUT, IN THE PROJECTION ROOM ABOVE, CAPTAIN AMERICA AND BUCKY COME TO A SOMEWHAT DIFFERENT CONCLUSION!
I THOUGHT SO! THE ACT'S A PHONY! THOSE AREN'T THOUGHTS IN THAT CRYSTAL BALL! THEY'RE PICTURES --- PROJECTED FROM AN ACCOMPLICE UP HERE!
BUT, WHY, CAP? WHY ONLY SCENES OF DISASTERS?
THAT'S WHAT WE'RE GOING TO FIND OUT!
THEN, MOVING LIKE THE SKILLED, WELL-TRAINED, FIGHTING ACROBATS WHICH THEY ARE, THE DAZZLING DUO LEAPS OVER THE HEADS OF THE AUDIENCE, AS CAP REACHES FOR THE SWAYING CURTAIN BELOW...
AND A LOT MORE FUN, TOO!
HANG ON, BUCKY BOY! THIS IS FASTER THAN WALKING!
LOOK! ABOVE US! IT'S CAPTAIN AMERICA... AND BUCKY!!
I'LL GO AFTER OMAR, CAP, WHILE YOU TANGLE WITH SANDO!
RIGHT, LAD! BUT FIRST, I'LL GET RID OF THAT PHONY CRYSTAL BALL!!
YOU DARE BREAK UP MY ACT?? YOU'LL PAY FOR THIS.. WITH YOUR LIVES!
5.

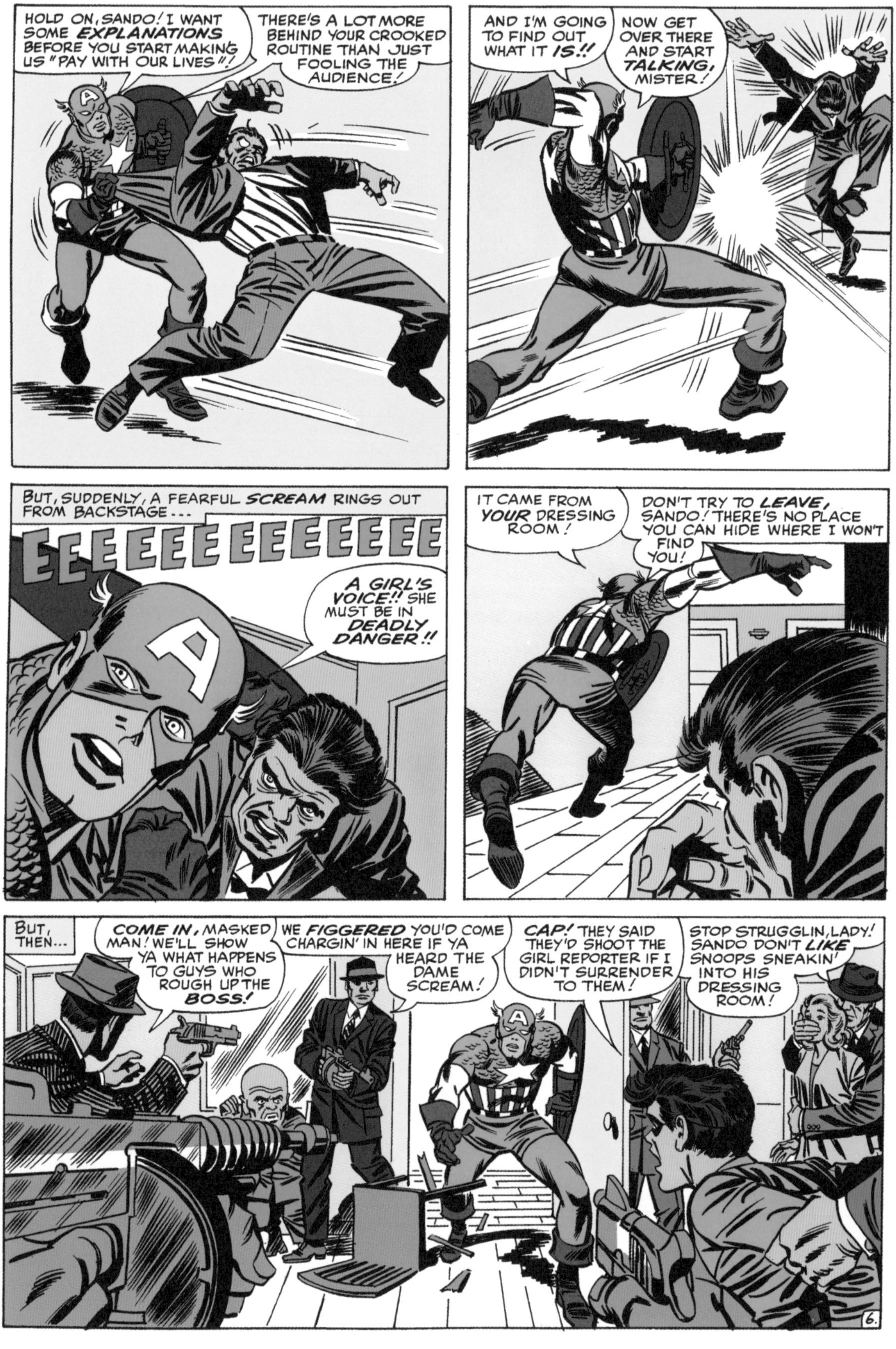
HOLD ON, SANDO! I WANT SOME EXPLANATIONS BEFORE YOU START MAKING US "PAY WITH OUR LIVES"!
THERE'S A LOT MORE BEHIND YOUR CROOKED ROUTINE THAN JUST FOOLING THE AUDIENCE!
AND I'M GOING TO FIND OUT WHAT IT IS!!
NOW GET OVER THERE AND START TALKING, MISTER!
BUT, SUDDENLY, A FEARFUL SCREAM RINGS OUT FROM BACKSTAGE...
EEEEEEEEEEEEE
A GIRL'S VOICE!! SHE MUST BE IN DEADLY DANGER!!
IT CAME FROM YOUR DRESSING ROOM!
DON'T TRY TO LEAVE, SANDO! THERE'S NO PLACE YOU CAN HIDE WHERE I WON'T FIND YOU!
BUT, THEN...
COME IN, MASKED MAN! WE'LL SHOW YA WHAT HAPPENS TO GUYS WHO ROUGH UP THE BOSS!
WE FIGGERED YOU'D COME CHARGIN' IN HERE IF YA HEARD THE DAME SCREAM!
CAP! THEY SAID THEY'D SHOOT THE GIRL REPORTER IF I DIDN'T SURRENDER TO THEM!
STOP STRUGGLIN, LADY! SANDO DON'T LIKE SNOOPS SNEAKIN' INTO HIS DRESSING ROOM!
6.

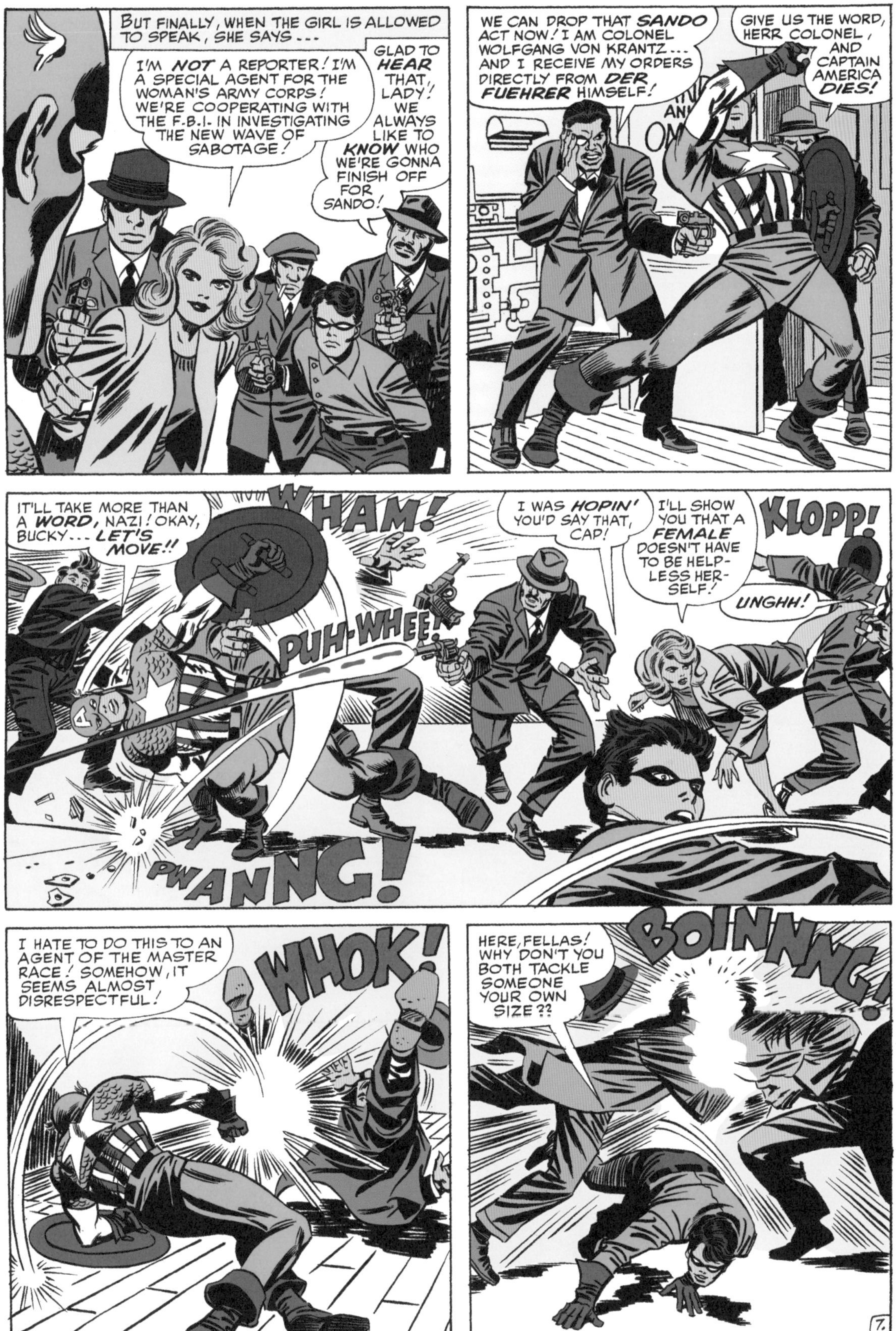
BUT FINALLY, WHEN THE GIRL IS ALLOWED TO SPEAK, SHE SAYS ...
I'M NOT A REPORTER! I'M A SPECIAL AGENT FOR THE WOMAN'S ARMY CORPS! WE'RE COOPERATING WITH THE F.B.I. IN INVESTIGATING THE NEW WAVE OF SABOTAGE!
GLAD TO HEAR THAT, LADY! WE ALWAYS LIKE TO KNOW WHO WE'RE GONNA FINISH OFF FOR SANDO!
WE CAN DROP THAT SANDO ACT NOW! I AM COLONEL WOLFGANG VON KRANTZ ... AND I RECEIVE MY ORDERS DIRECTLY FROM DER FUEHRER HIMSELF!
GIVE US THE WORD, HERR COLONEL, AND CAPTAIN AMERICA DIES!
IT'LL TAKE MORE THAN A WORD, NAZI! OKAY, BUCKY ... LET'S MOVE!!
WHAM!
PUH-WHEE!
PWANNG!
I WAS HOPIN' YOU'D SAY THAT, CAP!
I'LL SHOW YOU THAT A FEMALE DOESN'T HAVE TO BE HELP-LESS HER-SELF!
KLOPP!
UNGHH!
I HATE TO DO THIS TO AN AGENT OF THE MASTER RACE! SOMEHOW, IT SEEMS ALMOST DISRESPECTFUL!
WHOK!
HERE, FELLAS! WHY DON'T YOU BOTH TACKLE SOMEONE YOUR OWN SIZE??
BOINNNG!
7.

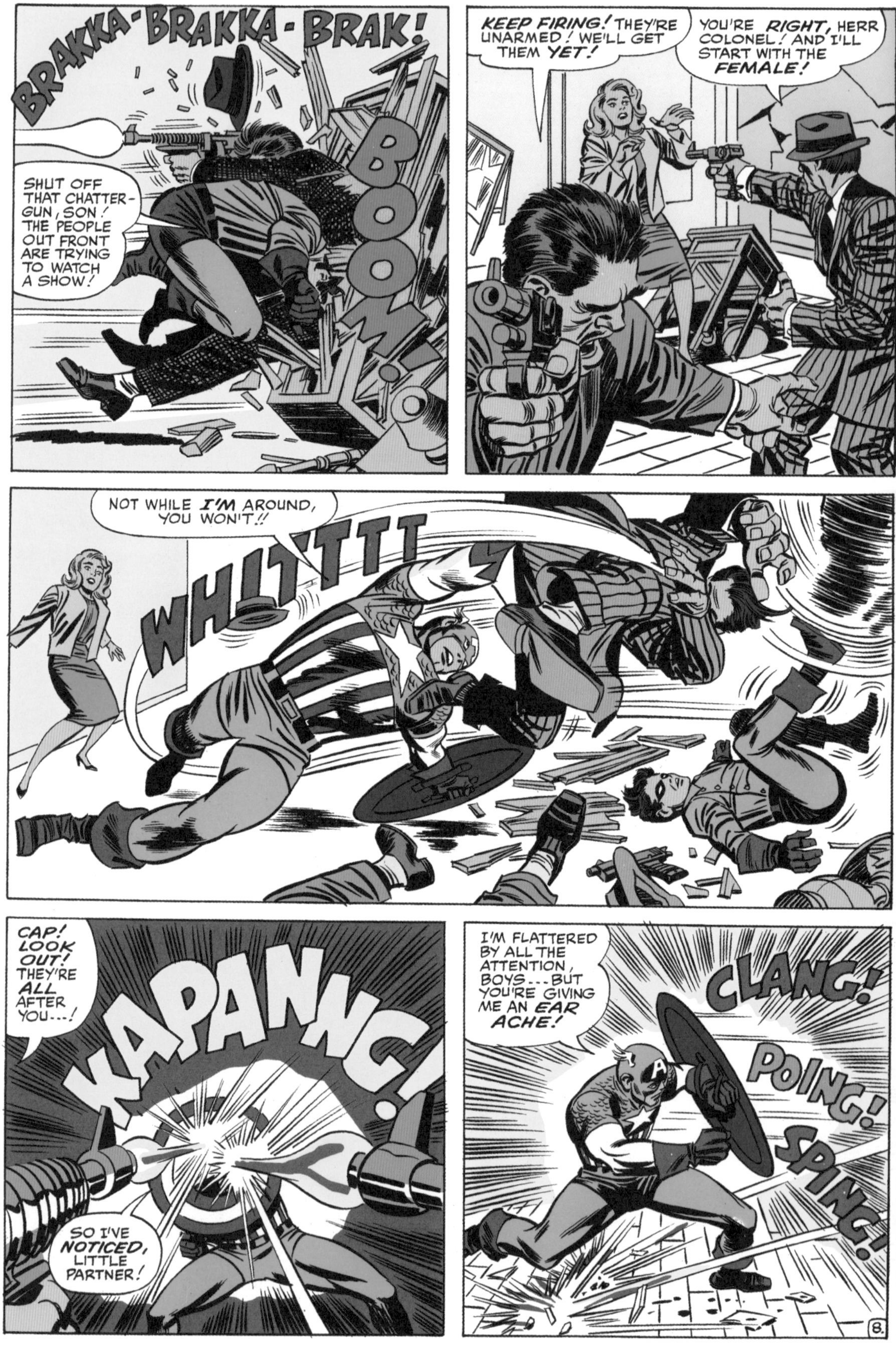
BRAKKA-BRAKKA-BRAK!
BOOM!
SHUT OFF THAT CHATTER-GUN, SON! THE PEOPLE OUT FRONT ARE TRYING TO WATCH A SHOW!
KEEP FIRING! THEY'RE UNARMED! WE'LL GET THEM YET!
YOU'RE RIGHT, HERR COLONEL! AND I'LL START WITH THE FEMALE!
NOT WHILE I'M AROUND, YOU WON'T!!
WHIITTTT
CAP! LOOK OUT! THEY'RE ALL AFTER YOU...!
KAPANNG!
SO I'VE NOTICED, LITTLE PARTNER!
I'M FLATTERED BY ALL THE ATTENTION, BOYS... BUT YOU'RE GIVING ME AN EAR ACHE!
CLANG!
POING!
SPING!
8.

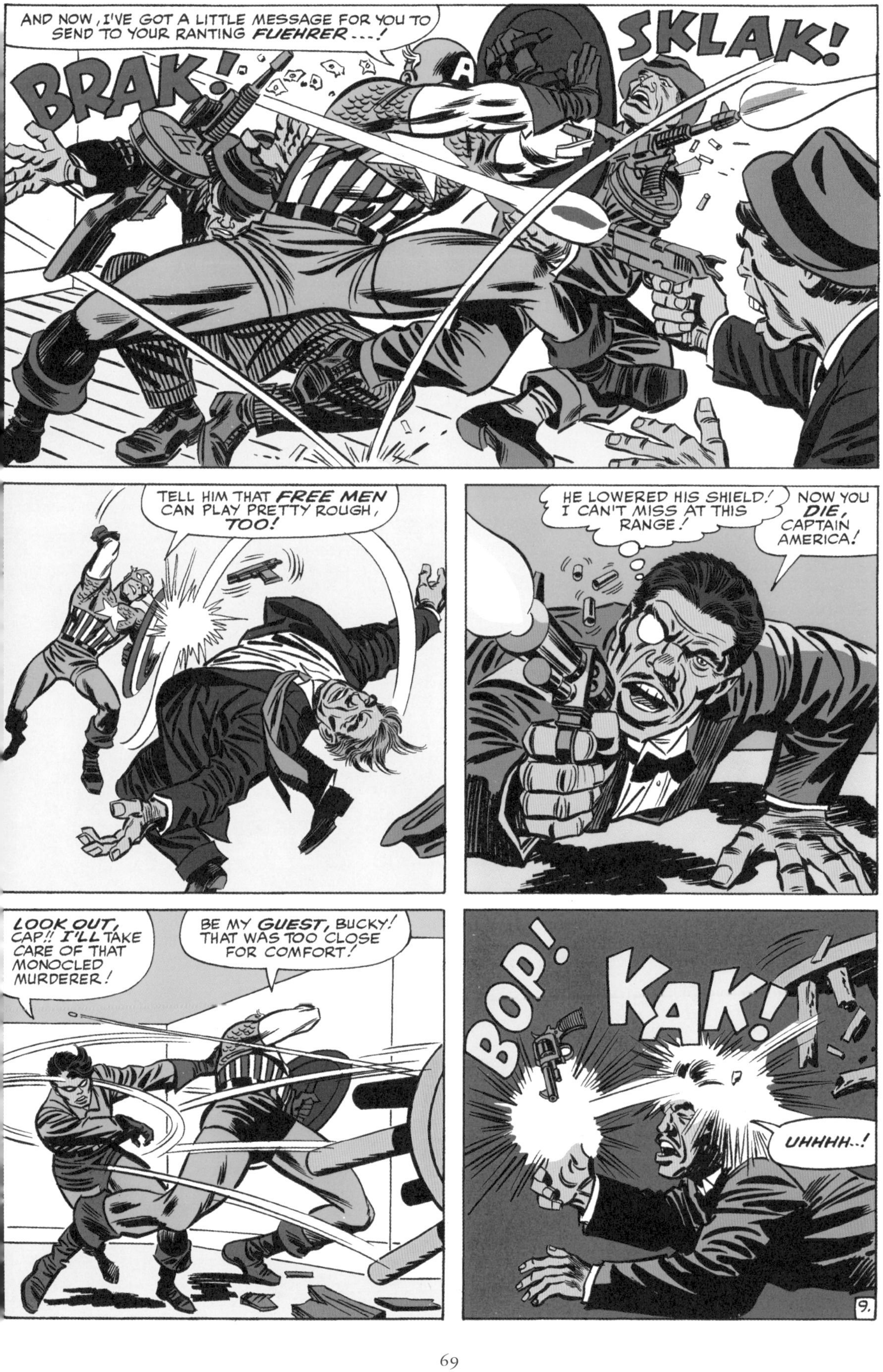
AND NOW, I'VE GOT A LITTLE MESSAGE FOR YOU TO SEND TO YOUR RANTING FUEHRER...!
BRAK!
SKLAK!
TELL HIM THAT FREE MEN CAN PLAY PRETTY ROUGH, TOO!
HE LOWERED HIS SHIELD! I CAN'T MISS AT THIS RANGE!
NOW YOU DIE, CAPTAIN AMERICA!
LOOK OUT, CAP!! I'LL TAKE CARE OF THAT MONOCLED MURDERER!
BE MY GUEST, BUCKY! THAT WAS TOO CLOSE FOR COMFORT!
BOP!
KAK!
UHHHH..!
9.

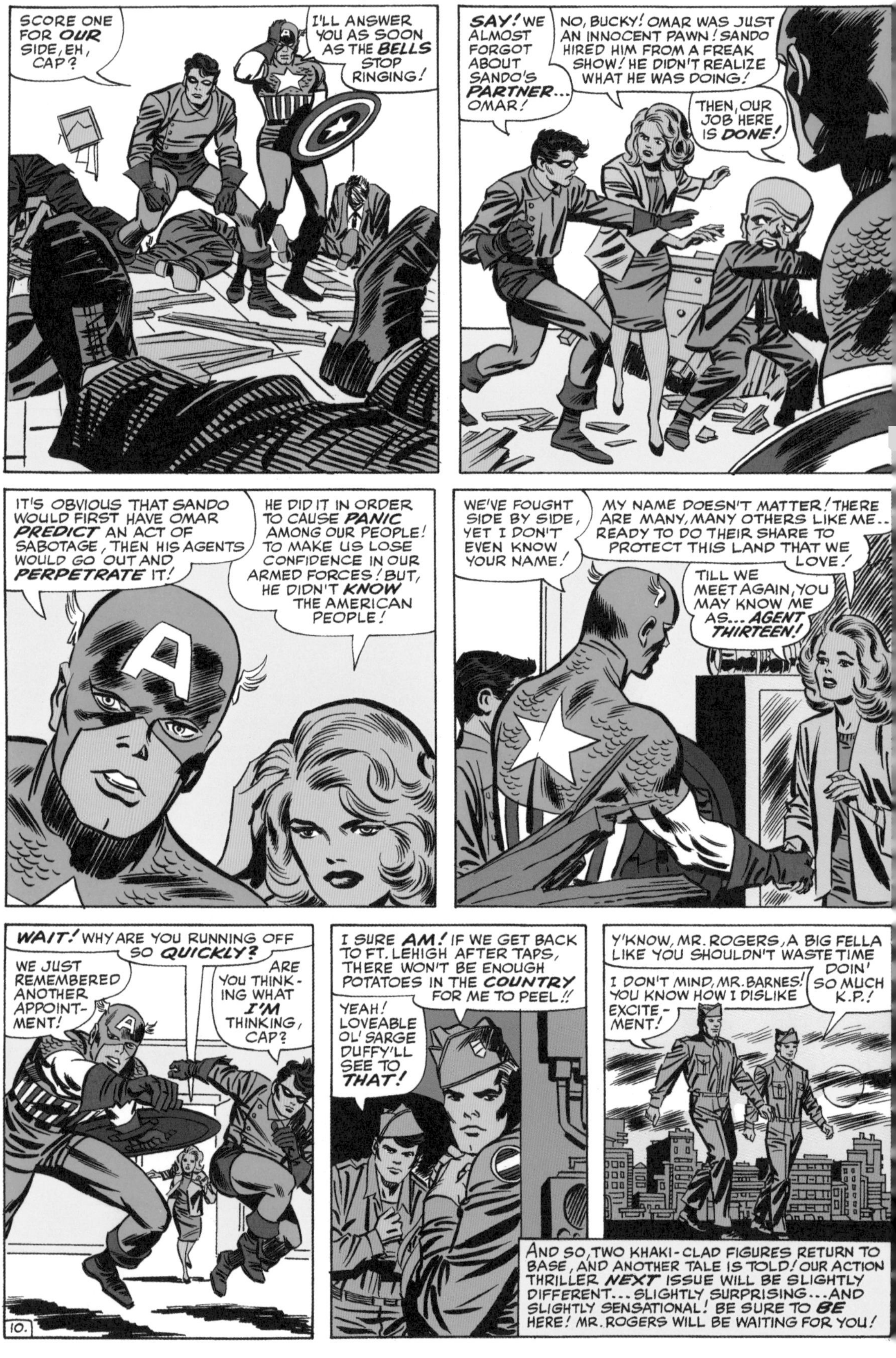
SCORE ONE FOR OUR SIDE, EH, CAP?
I'LL ANSWER YOU AS SOON AS THE BELLS STOP RINGING!
SAY! WE ALMOST FORGOT ABOUT SANDO'S PARTNER... OMAR!
NO, BUCKY! OMAR WAS JUST AN INNOCENT PAWN! SANDO HIRED HIM FROM A FREAK SHOW! HE DIDN'T REALIZE WHAT HE WAS DOING!
THEN, OUR JOB HERE IS DONE!
IT'S OBVIOUS THAT SANDO WOULD FIRST HAVE OMAR PREDICT AN ACT OF SABOTAGE, THEN HIS AGENTS WOULD GO OUT AND PERPETRATE IT!
HE DID IT IN ORDER TO CAUSE PANIC AMONG OUR PEOPLE! TO MAKE US LOSE CONFIDENCE IN OUR ARMED FORCES! BUT, HE DIDN'T KNOW THE AMERICAN PEOPLE!
WE'VE FOUGHT SIDE BY SIDE, YET I DON'T EVEN KNOW YOUR NAME!
MY NAME DOESN'T MATTER! THERE ARE MANY, MANY OTHERS LIKE ME.. READY TO DO THEIR SHARE TO PROTECT THIS LAND THAT WE LOVE!
TILL WE MEET AGAIN, YOU MAY KNOW ME AS... AGENT THIRTEEN!
WAIT! WHY ARE YOU RUNNING OFF SO QUICKLY?
WE JUST REMEMBERED ANOTHER APPOINTMENT!
ARE YOU THINKING WHAT I'M THINKING, CAP?
10.
I SURE AM! IF WE GET BACK TO FT. LEHIGH AFTER TAPS, THERE WON'T BE ENOUGH POTATOES IN THE COUNTRY FOR ME TO PEEL!!
YEAH! LOVEABLE OL' SARGE DUFFY'LL SEE TO THAT!
Y'KNOW, MR. ROGERS, A BIG FELLA LIKE YOU SHOULDN'T WASTE TIME DOIN' SO MUCH K.P.!
I DON'T MIND, MR. BARNES! YOU KNOW HOW I DISLIKE EXCITEMENT!
AND SO, TWO KHAKI-CLAD FIGURES RETURN TO BASE, AND ANOTHER TALE IS TOLD! OUR ACTION THRILLER NEXT ISSUE WILL BE SLIGHTLY DIFFERENT... SLIGHTLY SURPRISING... AND SLIGHTLY SENSATIONAL! BE SURE TO BE HERE! MR. ROGERS WILL BE WAITING FOR YOU!

Mails of SUSPENSE

SEND YOUR LETTERS TO:

THE MARVEL COMICS GROUP, SECOND FLOOR
625 MADISON AVE., NEW YORK, N.Y. 10022

Dear Stan and Jack,

In my opinion the "new" Captain America is far better than the Golden Age version. He has more depth and more reality than he used to have. This is due primarily to the death of Bucky Barnes and the effect it had on Cap. Now I never did like Bucky too much. He had his purpose—to instill patriotism in young boys. He was an obvious war effort. However, we are not at war at this time and there is no reason for Cap to be followed by a metal-scrap-and surplus-paper-collecting Teen Brigade. It is, in fact, ludicrous and does not do justice to the image that Cap projects. The pathos of Captain America is due to his grief over Bucky's demise. It gives him dignity and causes the reader to feel very emotionally involved in his attempts to avenge his sidekick's death. If Rick were to take Bucky's place, half of Cap's appeal would be lost. In SUSPENSE #60 Rick's hanging around doing nothing was really a drag. Cap was so machine-like in that story had no depth as in the AVENGERS series. If you want an example compare different panels in AVENGERS and SUSPENSE. Cap should not be a fighting robot type—a flat character like those that belong in Brand X comics. Keep Cap a loner, an unhappy hero with a heavy load on his mind yet the guts to keep on fighting for what he believes in. Please?

Cathi Manfredi, Shimer College
Mt. Carroll, Ill.

At the time you sent us your letter, Cathi, our new World War II series of Cap and Bucky's adventures hadn't appeared in print yet. Now that you've had a chance to see them, we'd be very interested in knowing if your opinion still stands! So, drop us another line, okay?

Dear Stan and Don and Jack,

I just wanted to say that I saw Stan's newest edition of MONSTERS TO LAUGH WITH. At first I wasn't going to buy it, but the magic name of Stan Lee changed my mind. It was just great, Stan—how about another one?

David Banks, 1912 W. 3rd St.
Williamsport, Pa.

Sure! Sure! M.T.L.W. #3 is on sale right now. But, how about saying something about SUSPENSE in your letter, for goodness sake!

Dear Stan and Don and Jack,

SUSPENSE #61 had one of the best Iron Man stories I have ever read. Although it was little more than a preview to the big battle that came later in #62, it nevertheless demanded the highest accolade I can give it—wow! Captain America's tale, on the other hand, lacked that certain something—Bucky. See SGT. FURY #13 and you'll get what I mean. You have got to bring this boy back. Rick Jones will not do! I tell you, this kid will be the greatest boon to Marvel since Cap himself! You'll probably say that this would give Cap no incentive to fight. I say you're wrong because with Bucky at his side, Cap would fight even harder, knowing that the boy he had loved as a brother, then lost, was once again fighting with him. Anyone who has ever read a Captain America mag or SGT. FURY #13 is bound to agree with me.

Donald Taylor, 4031 Wichita St.
Houston, Tex.

Well, Don, you've got to admit that your suggestion received some prompt action! We haven't really brought Bucky back to life, but we tried to do the next best thing! And, you might be interested in knowing that thousands of fans have made the same "Bring Bucky back!" request!

Dear Stan and Don and Jack,

I enjoy Captain America very much. Do people know Cap's secret identity? Why doesn't he change clothes and go downtown or go to work like Giant-Man, Iron Man and Thor do?

John Burchfield, 1500 So. Eudora
Denver, Colo.

As far as we know, Johnny, he's still collecting unemployment insurance! But, we'll figure out some sort of civilian identity for him sooner or later. (Knowing us, it'll probably be later!)

THE MIGHTY MARVEL CHECKLIST
A Line-Up Of Some Of The Marvel-ous Mags On Sale Right Now!

FANTASTIC FOUR #37: For sheer spectacle and imaginative fantasy, you won't want to miss "Behold! A Distant Star!" in which the world's top super-team finds undreamed-of dangers on a faraway star! It's sheer Marvel magic!

SPIDER-MAN #23: This one's a rare treat! Stan and Steve have combined the super-villainy of the exciting Green Goblin with the down-to-earth menace of a deadly gang of criminals, to give Spidey one of his toughest battles yet!

AVENGERS #14: Another off-beat sensation for the world's mightiest costumed heroes! This one takes them to the farthest reaches of earth, pitting them against a menace like none they have ever fought before! You'll love it!

X-MEN #10: Possibly the greatest X-MEN saga of all time, introducing a fabulous character who will take your breath away! This one is so terrific that it'll make you realize why we simply can't produce an issue faster than every two months!

THOR #114: The mighty Thunder God finally battles a foe who is every bit as powerful as Thor himself! In fact, in some ways, our newest villain actually has the advantage! This one's a shocker!

STRANGE TALES #131: See why all of comicdom is talking about Bob Powell's takeover of the Torch/Thing strip. This talented whiz really makes them live! And Doctor Strange is still on the run! Two action-packed thrillers!

ASTONISH #66: A real surprise is in store for you when Giant-Man is trapped by the awesome Madam Macabre! And wait till you see the Wasp fighting for their lives; Top it all off with the latest Hulk rampage behind the iron curtain! Wow-EEE!

SGT. FURY #16: This one will clearly demonstrate why the Howling Commandos are the most popular, most talked-about war mag heroes in the world today! It features our own brand of batty battling action in the mysterious tinderbox of North Africa! It's got everything!

SPECIAL ANNOUNCEMENTS SECTION:

—Well, don't just sit there! Grab those pens and let us know how you liked the new Black Widow—as well as the old Hawkeye! And, while you're at it, if you haven't yet done so, you might as well fill out the ol' M.M.M.S. coupon and get it over with!

—We've some big news for you for next ish! In SUSPENSE #64, we're going to present the most famous villain Captain America ever fought—a villain whom the older readers will remember, and who is just a legendary name to our younger fans! (No, not Zemo—someone far more notorious! Someone you haven't yet seen in the new Marvel Age of Comics!) We'll present his origin next ish—and then follow up with some of the greatest Captain America thrills of all time! We want to keep you in suspense, so we won't mention his name now, but we'll tell you this much—he was the Dr. Doom of the Golden Age of Comics!

—As for our next Iron Man yarn, it's a real doozy! It's filled with surprises, too—but this we've got to tell you—you'll see the original big, bulky, heavy Iron Man again, as well as today's modern, sleek, streamlined Shell-Head! There, that's all we'll say—you figure out the rest!

—So, till our sensational next ish, keep your transistors all charged up and don't forget to wear your M.M.M.S. button wherever you go—we want everyone to see what a great group our readers are!

TALES OF SUSPENSE #65,

MAY 1965,

"THE RED SKULL STRIKES!"

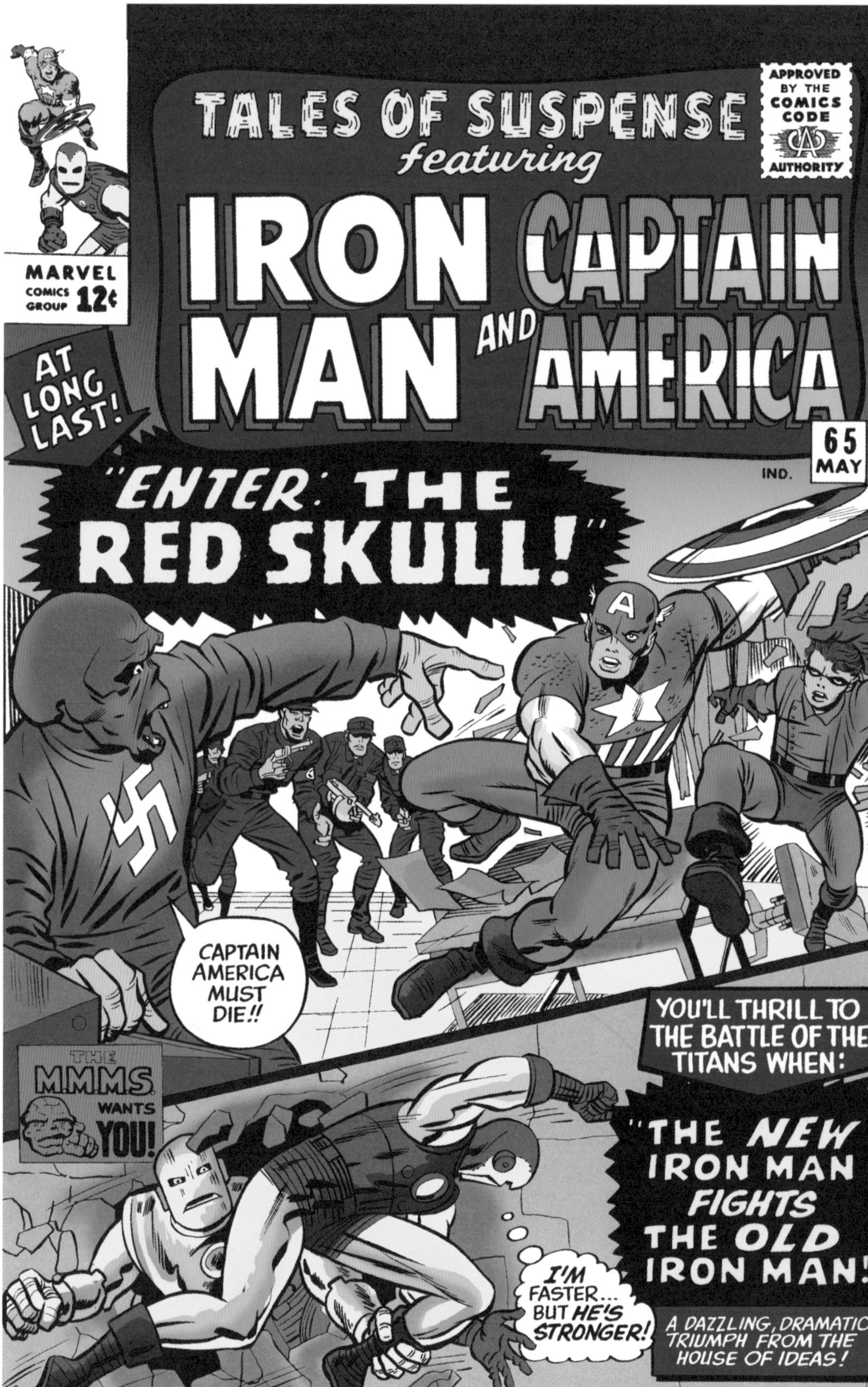

TALES OF SUSPENSE
featuring
IRON MAN AND CAPTAIN AMERICA
APPROVED BY THE COMICS CODE AUTHORITY
MARVEL COMICS GROUP 12¢
AT LONG LAST!
65 MAY
IND.
"ENTER: THE RED SKULL!"
CAPTAIN AMERICA MUST DIE!!
YOU'LL THRILL TO THE BATTLE OF THE TITANS WHEN:
THE M.M.M.S. WANTS YOU!
"THE NEW IRON MAN FIGHTS THE OLD IRON MAN!"
I'M FASTER... BUT HE'S STRONGER!
A DAZZLING, DRAMATIC TRIUMPH FROM THE HOUSE OF IDEAS!

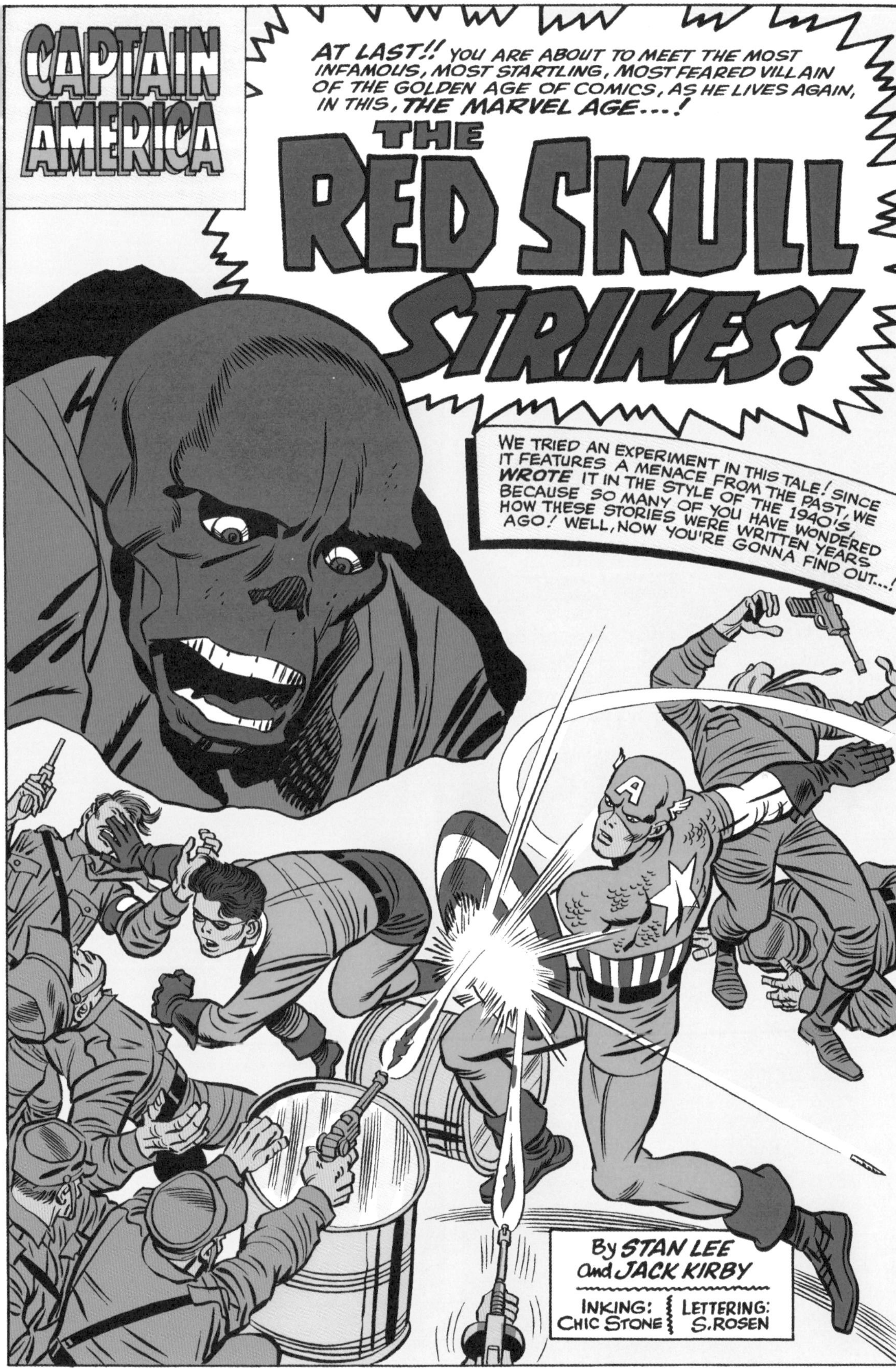
CAPTAIN AMERICA
AT LAST!! YOU ARE ABOUT TO MEET THE MOST INFAMOUS, MOST STARTLING, MOST FEARED VILLAIN OF THE GOLDEN AGE OF COMICS, AS HE LIVES AGAIN, IN THIS, THE MARVEL AGE...!
THE RED SKULL STRIKES!
WE TRIED AN EXPERIMENT IN THIS TALE! SINCE IT FEATURES A MENACE FROM THE PAST, WE WROTE IT IN THE STYLE OF THE 1940'S, BECAUSE SO MANY OF YOU HAVE WONDERED HOW THESE STORIES WERE WRITTEN YEARS AGO! WELL, NOW YOU'RE GONNA FIND OUT...!
By STAN LEE and JACK KIRBY
INKING: CHIC STONE
LETTERING: S.ROSEN

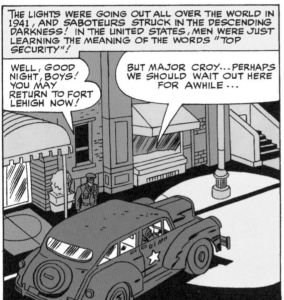

THE LIGHTS WERE GOING OUT ALL OVER THE WORLD IN 1941, AND SABOTEURS STRUCK IN THE DESCENDING DARKNESS! IN THE UNITED STATES, MEN WERE JUST LEARNING THE MEANING OF THE WORDS "TOP SECURITY"!

WELL, GOOD NIGHT, BOYS! YOU MAY RETURN TO FORT LEHIGH NOW!

BUT MAJOR CROY...PERHAPS WE SHOULD WAIT OUT HERE FOR AWHILE...

YOU'RE INVOLVED IN A VERY IMPORTANT ARMY PROJECT, AND...

NONSENSE!! PRIVATE ROGERS AND MASCOT BARNES, YOU ARE BOTH DISMISSED!

BOY! IF THE MAJOR EVER SUSPECTED WHO HE'S REALLY TALKING TO!

U.S. ARMY VEHICLE 127544

GOSH, STEVE... I KNOW WE'RE NOT YET AT WAR WITH THE NAZIS... BUT THE MAJOR OUGHT TO REALIZE THAT HITLER'S AGENTS ARE ALREADY ON THE PROWL!

WELL...YOU HEARD HIS ORDER... IT'S BACK TO BARRACKS FOR US!

AT THAT MOMENT, IN MAJOR CROY'S STUDY, THE SHADOW OF DREAD WAS NOWHERE TO BE FELT IN THE ATMOSPHERE OF RELAXATION AND COMFORT...

BUT DREAD THERE WAS--- IN SILENT AND SINISTER SHAPE...DRAWING CLOSER...CLOSER...

GOOD EVENING, MAJOR CROY! LEAVING YOUR WINDOW OPEN WAS A FATAL MISTAKE!

WHO IN BLAZES ARE YOU?

2.

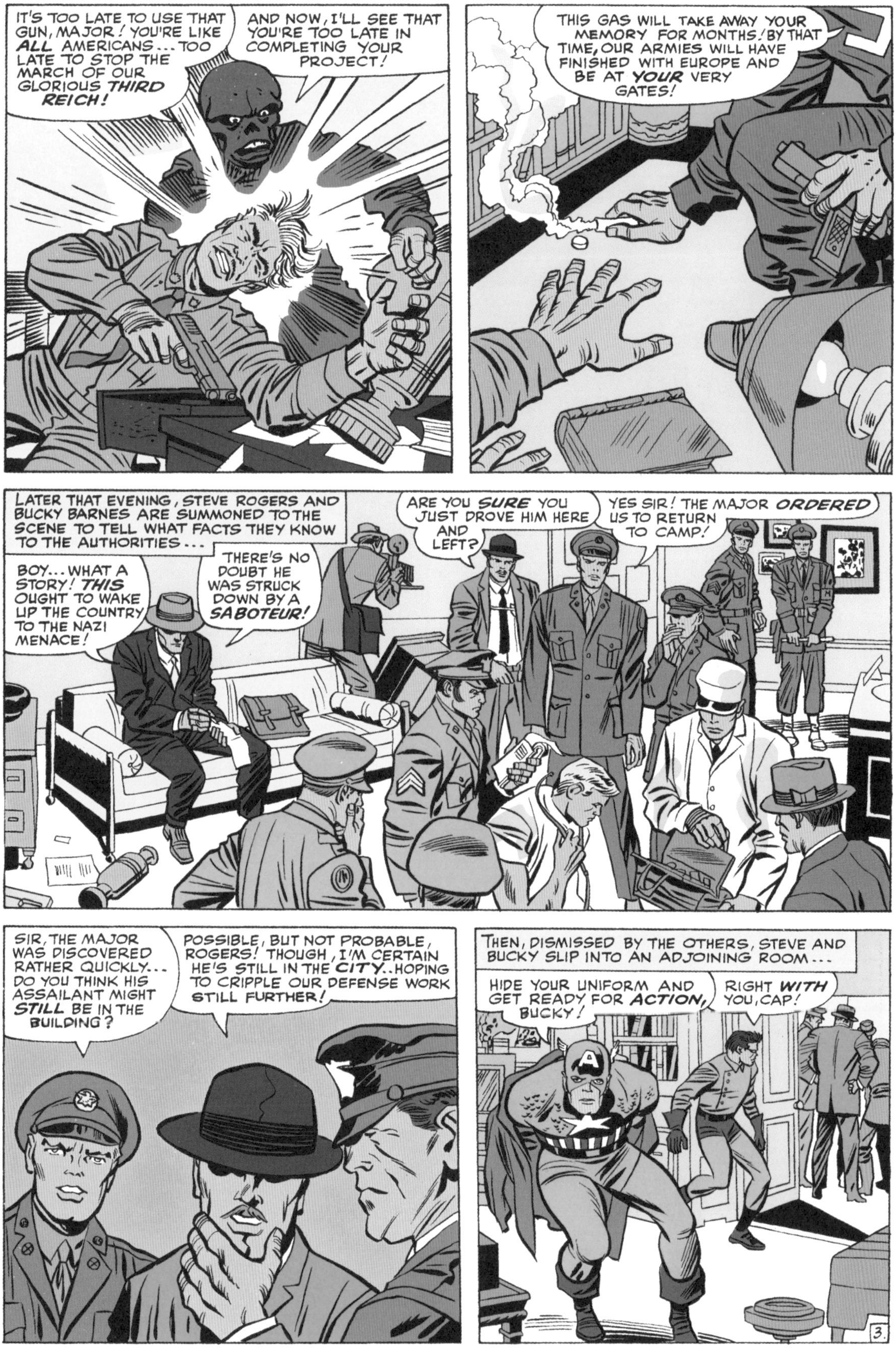
IT'S TOO LATE TO USE THAT GUN, MAJOR! YOU'RE LIKE ALL AMERICANS... TOO LATE TO STOP THE MARCH OF OUR GLORIOUS THIRD REICH!
AND NOW, I'LL SEE THAT YOU'RE TOO LATE IN COMPLETING YOUR PROJECT!
THIS GAS WILL TAKE AWAY YOUR MEMORY FOR MONTHS! BY THAT TIME, OUR ARMIES WILL HAVE FINISHED WITH EUROPE AND BE AT YOUR VERY GATES!
LATER THAT EVENING, STEVE ROGERS AND BUCKY BARNES ARE SUMMONED TO THE SCENE TO TELL WHAT FACTS THEY KNOW TO THE AUTHORITIES...
BOY... WHAT A STORY! THIS OUGHT TO WAKE UP THE COUNTRY TO THE NAZI MENACE!
THERE'S NO DOUBT HE WAS STRUCK DOWN BY A SABOTEUR!
ARE YOU SURE YOU JUST DROVE HIM HERE AND LEFT?
YES SIR! THE MAJOR ORDERED US TO RETURN TO CAMP!
SIR, THE MAJOR WAS DISCOVERED RATHER QUICKLY... DO YOU THINK HIS ASSAILANT MIGHT STILL BE IN THE BUILDING?
POSSIBLE, BUT NOT PROBABLE, ROGERS! THOUGH, I'M CERTAIN HE'S STILL IN THE CITY.. HOPING TO CRIPPLE OUR DEFENSE WORK STILL FURTHER!
THEN, DISMISSED BY THE OTHERS, STEVE AND BUCKY SLIP INTO AN ADJOINING ROOM...
HIDE YOUR UNIFORM AND GET READY FOR ACTION, BUCKY!
RIGHT WITH YOU, CAP!
3.

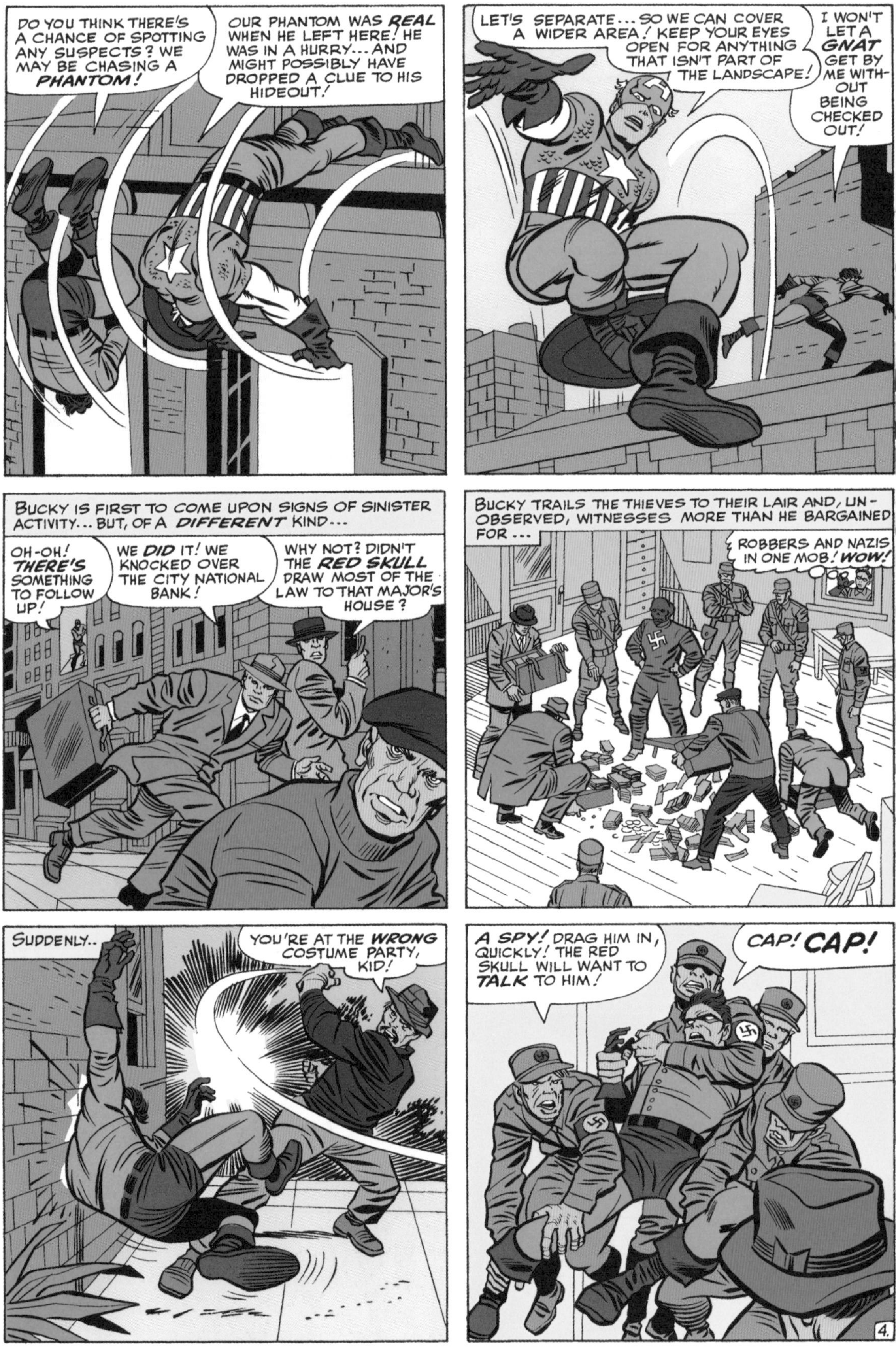
DO YOU THINK THERE'S A CHANCE OF SPOTTING ANY SUSPECTS? WE MAY BE CHASING A PHANTOM!
OUR PHANTOM WAS REAL WHEN HE LEFT HERE! HE WAS IN A HURRY... AND MIGHT POSSIBLY HAVE DROPPED A CLUE TO HIS HIDEOUT!
LET'S SEPARATE... SO WE CAN COVER A WIDER AREA! KEEP YOUR EYES OPEN FOR ANYTHING THAT ISN'T PART OF THE LANDSCAPE!
I WON'T LET A GNAT GET BY ME WITHOUT BEING CHECKED OUT!
BUCKY IS FIRST TO COME UPON SIGNS OF SINISTER ACTIVITY... BUT, OF A DIFFERENT KIND...
OH-OH! THERE'S SOMETHING TO FOLLOW UP!
WE DID IT! WE KNOCKED OVER THE CITY NATIONAL BANK!
WHY NOT? DIDN'T THE RED SKULL DRAW MOST OF THE LAW TO THAT MAJOR'S HOUSE?
BUCKY TRAILS THE THIEVES TO THEIR LAIR AND, UNOBSERVED, WITNESSES MORE THAN HE BARGAINED FOR...
ROBBERS AND NAZIS IN ONE MOB! WOW!
SUDDENLY..
YOU'RE AT THE WRONG COSTUME PARTY, KID!
A SPY! DRAG HIM IN, QUICKLY! THE RED SKULL WILL WANT TO TALK TO HIM!
CAP! CAP!
4.

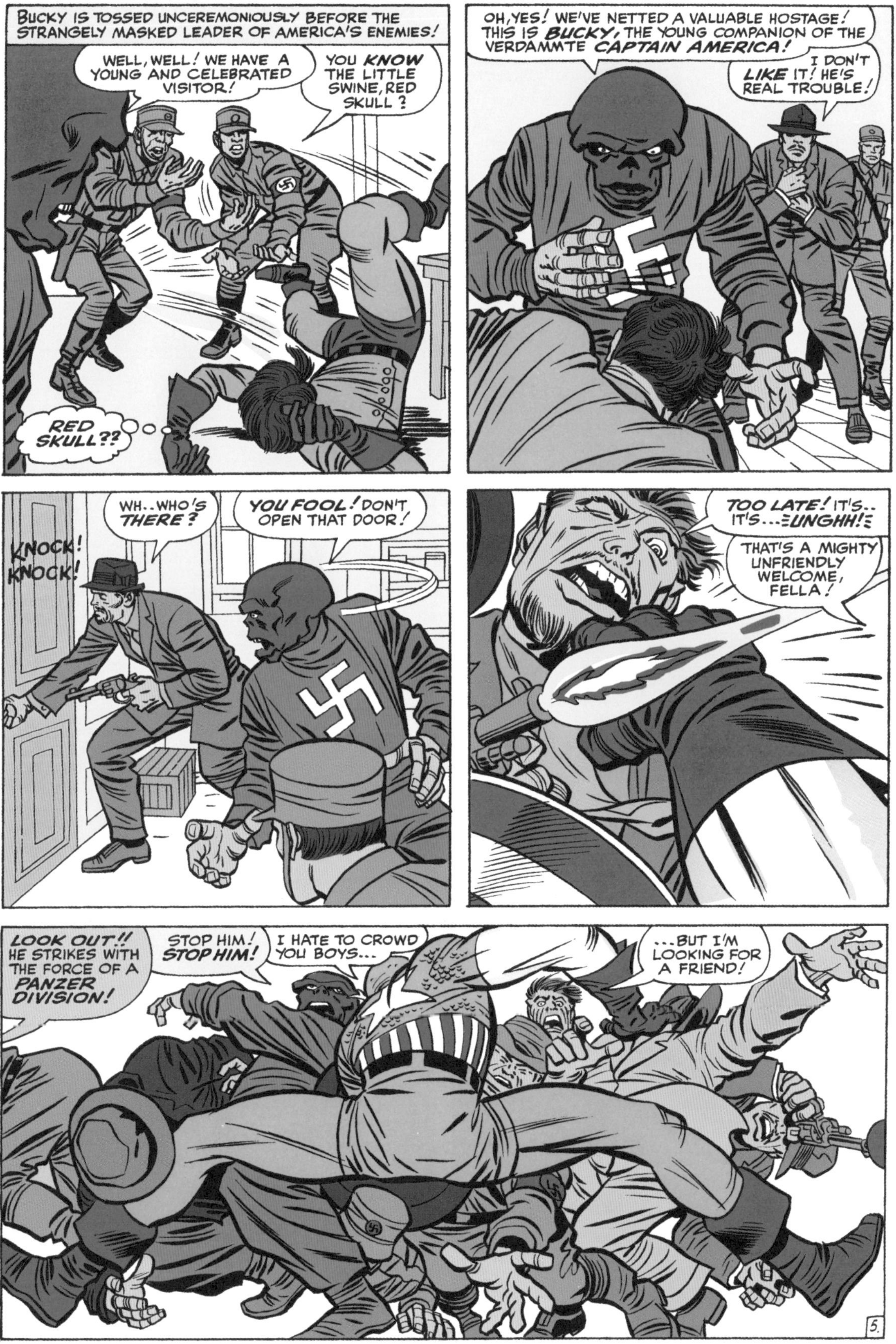
BUCKY IS TOSSED UNCEREMONIOUSLY BEFORE THE STRANGELY MASKED LEADER OF AMERICA'S ENEMIES!
WELL, WELL! WE HAVE A YOUNG AND CELEBRATED VISITOR!
YOU KNOW THE LITTLE SWINE, RED SKULL?
RED SKULL??
OH, YES! WE'VE NETTED A VALUABLE HOSTAGE! THIS IS BUCKY, THE YOUNG COMPANION OF THE VERDAMMTE CAPTAIN AMERICA!
I DON'T LIKE IT! HE'S REAL TROUBLE!
KNOCK! KNOCK!
WH..WHO'S THERE?
YOU FOOL! DON'T OPEN THAT DOOR!
TOO LATE! IT'S.. IT'S...UNGHH!
THAT'S A MIGHTY UNFRIENDLY WELCOME, FELLA!
LOOK OUT!! HE STRIKES WITH THE FORCE OF A PANZER DIVISION!
STOP HIM! STOP HIM!
I HATE TO CROWD YOU BOYS...
...BUT I'M LOOKING FOR A FRIEND!
5.

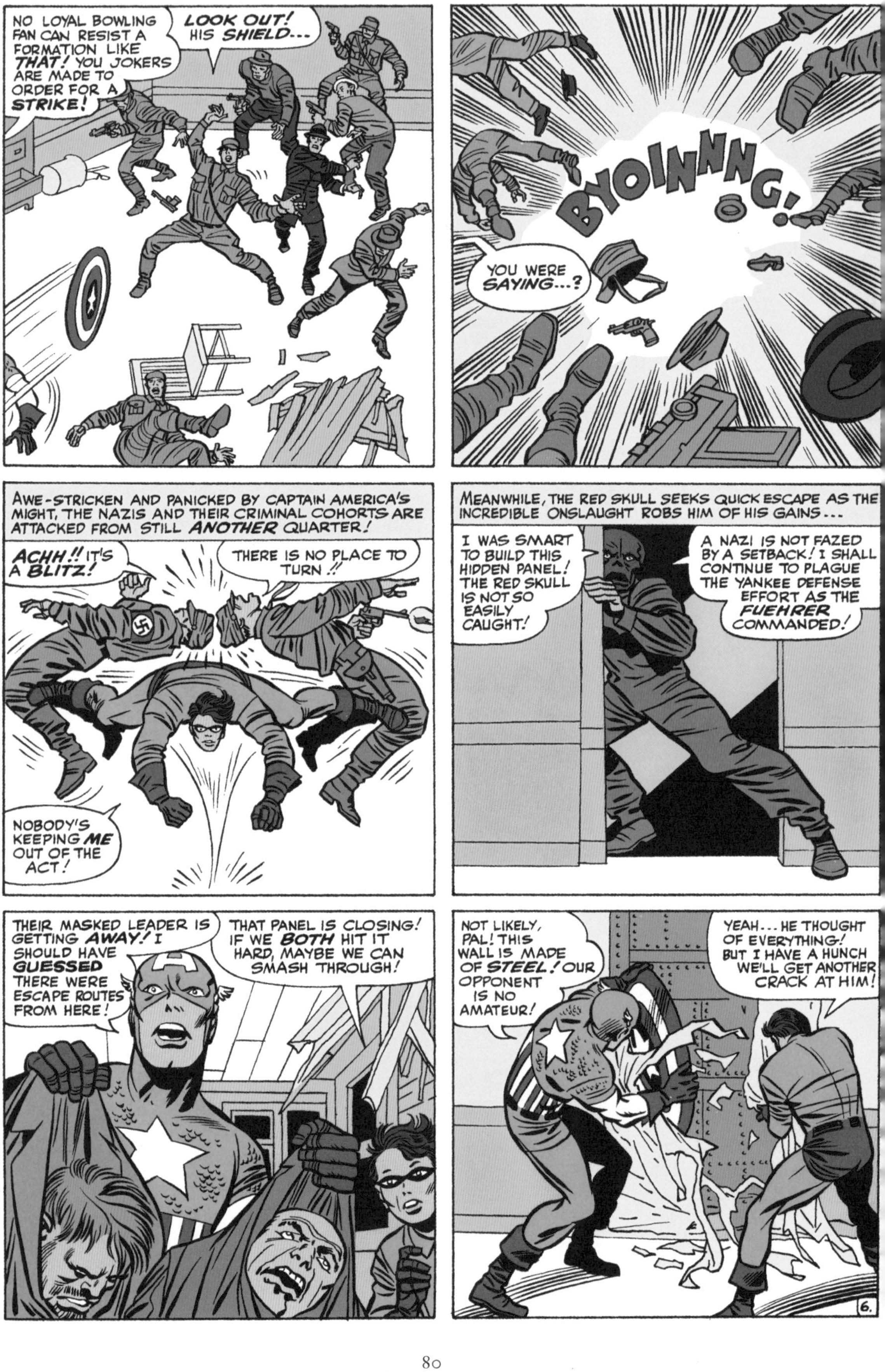
NO LOYAL BOWLING FAN CAN RESIST A FORMATION LIKE THAT! YOU JOKERS ARE MADE TO ORDER FOR A STRIKE!
LOOK OUT! HIS SHIELD...
BYOINNNG!
YOU WERE SAYING...?
AWE-STRICKEN AND PANICKED BY CAPTAIN AMERICA'S MIGHT, THE NAZIS AND THEIR CRIMINAL COHORTS ARE ATTACKED FROM STILL ANOTHER QUARTER!
ACHH!! IT'S A BLITZ!
THERE IS NO PLACE TO TURN!!
NOBODY'S KEEPING ME OUT OF THE ACT!
MEANWHILE, THE RED SKULL SEEKS QUICK ESCAPE AS THE INCREDIBLE ONSLAUGHT ROBS HIM OF HIS GAINS...
I WAS SMART TO BUILD THIS HIDDEN PANEL! THE RED SKULL IS NOT SO EASILY CAUGHT!
A NAZI IS NOT FAZED BY A SETBACK! I SHALL CONTINUE TO PLAGUE THE YANKEE DEFENSE EFFORT AS THE FUEHRER COMMANDED!
THEIR MASKED LEADER IS GETTING AWAY! I SHOULD HAVE GUESSED THERE WERE ESCAPE ROUTES FROM HERE!
THAT PANEL IS CLOSING! IF WE BOTH HIT IT HARD, MAYBE WE CAN SMASH THROUGH!
NOT LIKELY, PAL! THIS WALL IS MADE OF STEEL! OUR OPPONENT IS NO AMATEUR!
YEAH... HE THOUGHT OF EVERYTHING! BUT I HAVE A HUNCH WE'LL GET ANOTHER CRACK AT HIM!
6.

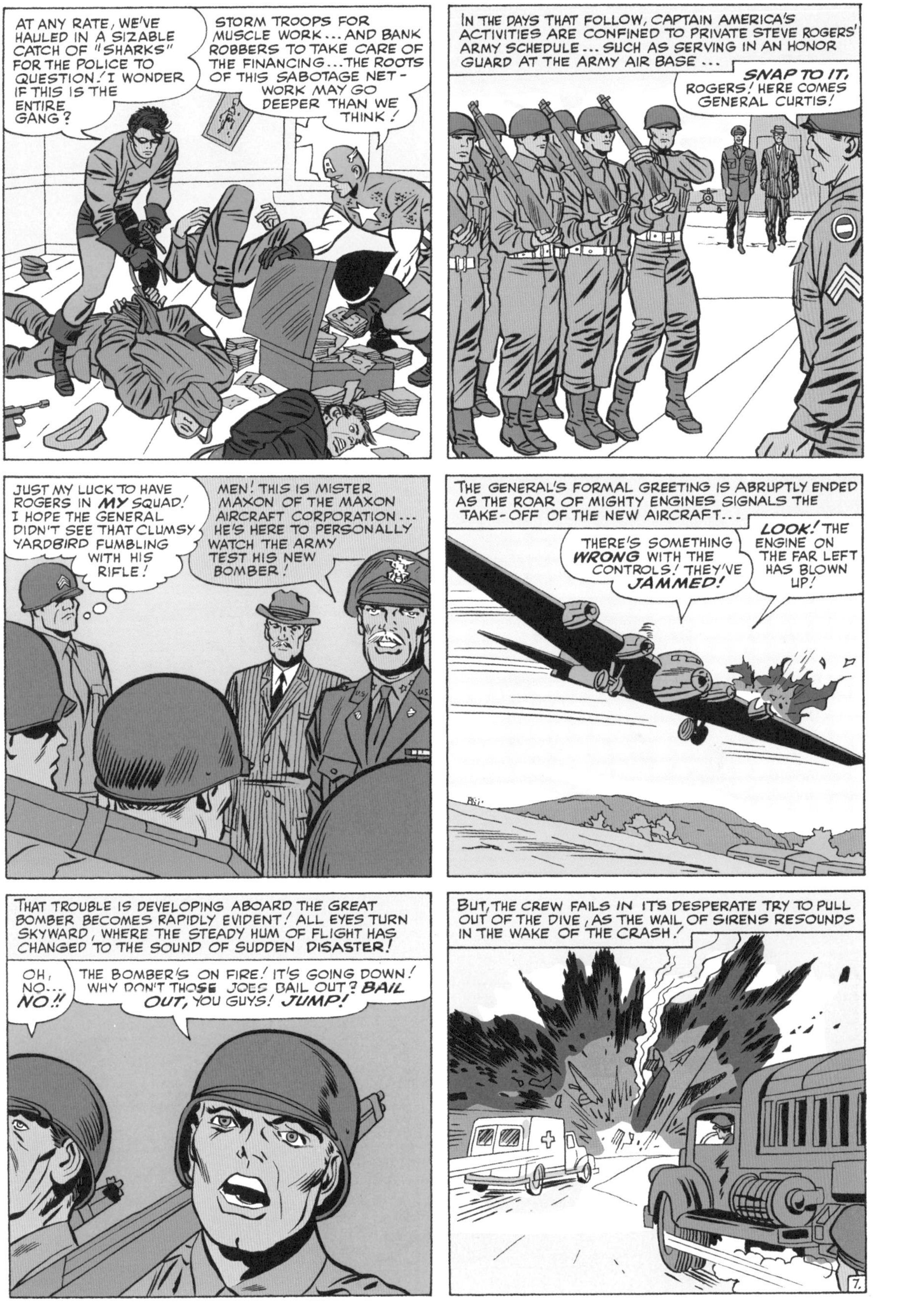

AT ANY RATE, WE'VE HAULED IN A SIZABLE CATCH OF "SHARKS" FOR THE POLICE TO QUESTION! I WONDER IF THIS IS THE ENTIRE GANG?
STORM TROOPS FOR MUSCLE WORK... AND BANK ROBBERS TO TAKE CARE OF THE FINANCING... THE ROOTS OF THIS SABOTAGE NET-WORK MAY GO DEEPER THAN WE THINK!
IN THE DAYS THAT FOLLOW, CAPTAIN AMERICA'S ACTIVITIES ARE CONFINED TO PRIVATE STEVE ROGERS' ARMY SCHEDULE... SUCH AS SERVING IN AN HONOR GUARD AT THE ARMY AIR BASE...
SNAP TO IT, ROGERS! HERE COMES GENERAL CURTIS!
JUST MY LUCK TO HAVE ROGERS IN MY SQUAD! I HOPE THE GENERAL DIDN'T SEE THAT CLUMSY YARDBIRD FUMBLING WITH HIS RIFLE!
MEN! THIS IS MISTER MAXON OF THE MAXON AIRCRAFT CORPORATION... HE'S HERE TO PERSONALLY WATCH THE ARMY TEST HIS NEW BOMBER!
THE GENERAL'S FORMAL GREETING IS ABRUPTLY ENDED AS THE ROAR OF MIGHTY ENGINES SIGNALS THE TAKE-OFF OF THE NEW AIRCRAFT...
THERE'S SOMETHING WRONG WITH THE CONTROLS! THEY'VE JAMMED!
LOOK! THE ENGINE ON THE FAR LEFT HAS BLOWN UP!
THAT TROUBLE IS DEVELOPING ABOARD THE GREAT BOMBER BECOMES RAPIDLY EVIDENT! ALL EYES TURN SKYWARD, WHERE THE STEADY HUM OF FLIGHT HAS CHANGED TO THE SOUND OF SUDDEN DISASTER!
OH, NO... NO!!
THE BOMBER'S ON FIRE! IT'S GOING DOWN! WHY DON'T THOSE JOES BAIL OUT? BAIL OUT, YOU GUYS! JUMP!
BUT, THE CREW FAILS IN ITS DESPERATE TRY TO PULL OUT OF THE DIVE, AS THE WAIL OF SIRENS RESOUNDS IN THE WAKE OF THE CRASH!
7.

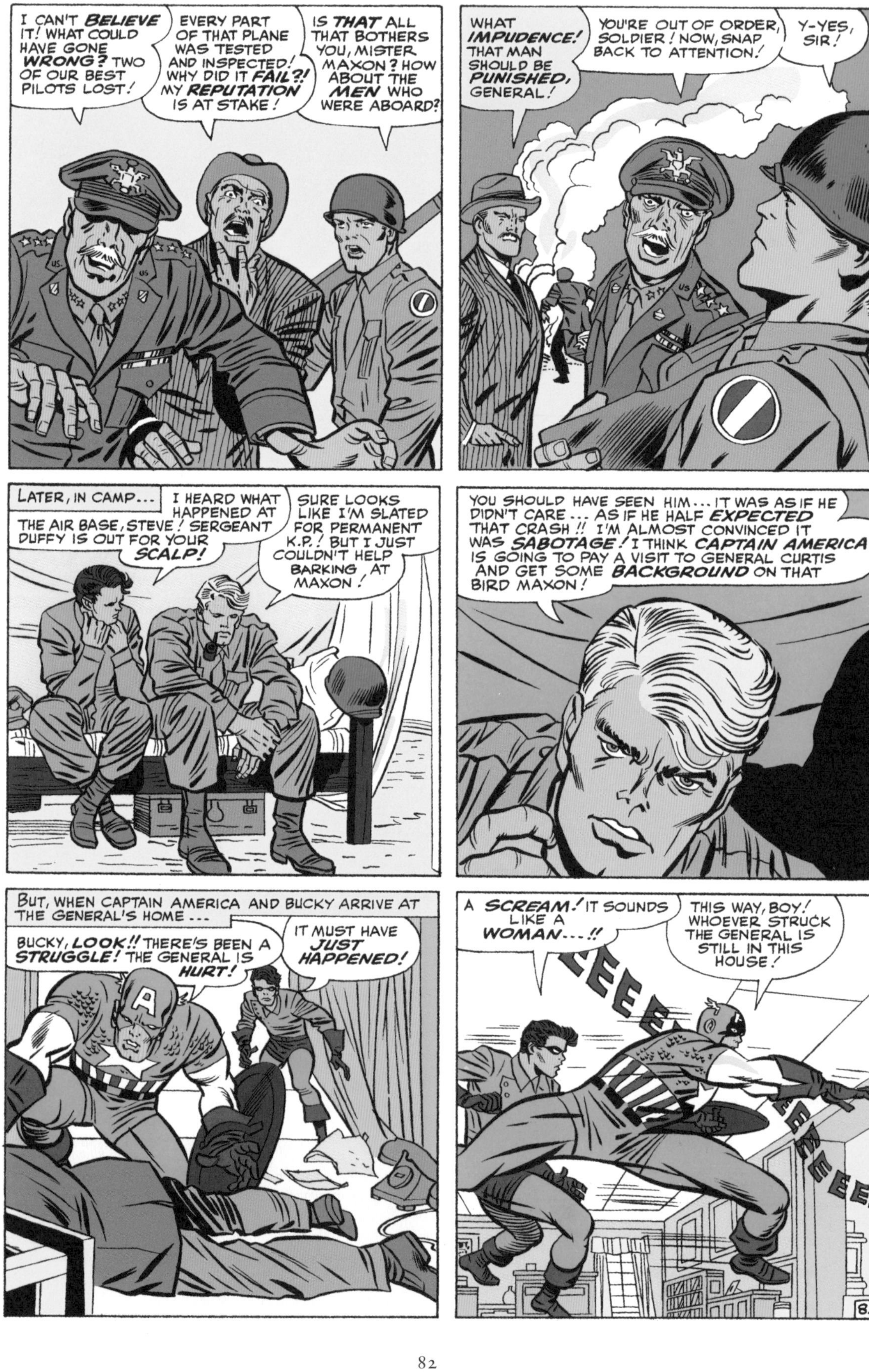
I CAN'T **BELIEVE** IT! WHAT COULD HAVE GONE **WRONG?** TWO OF OUR BEST PILOTS LOST!
EVERY PART OF THAT PLANE WAS TESTED AND INSPECTED! WHY DID IT **FAIL?!** MY **REPUTATION** IS AT STAKE!
IS **THAT** ALL THAT BOTHERS YOU, MISTER MAXON? HOW ABOUT THE **MEN** WHO WERE ABOARD?
WHAT **IMPUDENCE!** THAT MAN SHOULD BE **PUNISHED,** GENERAL!
YOU'RE OUT OF ORDER, SOLDIER! NOW, SNAP BACK TO ATTENTION!
Y-YES, SIR!
LATER, IN CAMP...
I HEARD WHAT HAPPENED AT THE AIR BASE, STEVE! SERGEANT DUFFY IS OUT FOR YOUR **SCALP!**
SURE LOOKS LIKE I'M SLATED FOR PERMANENT K.P.! BUT I JUST COULDN'T HELP BARKING AT MAXON!
YOU SHOULD HAVE SEEN HIM... IT WAS AS IF HE DIDN'T CARE... AS IF HE HALF **EXPECTED** THAT CRASH!! I'M ALMOST CONVINCED IT WAS **SABOTAGE!** I THINK **CAPTAIN AMERICA** IS GOING TO PAY A VISIT TO GENERAL CURTIS AND GET SOME **BACKGROUND** ON THAT BIRD MAXON!
BUT, WHEN CAPTAIN AMERICA AND BUCKY ARRIVE AT THE GENERAL'S HOME ...
BUCKY, **LOOK!!** THERE'S BEEN A **STRUGGLE!** THE GENERAL IS **HURT!**
IT MUST HAVE **JUST HAPPENED!**
A **SCREAM!** IT SOUNDS LIKE A **WOMAN...!!**
THIS WAY, BOY! WHOEVER STRUCK THE GENERAL IS STILL IN THIS HOUSE!
8.

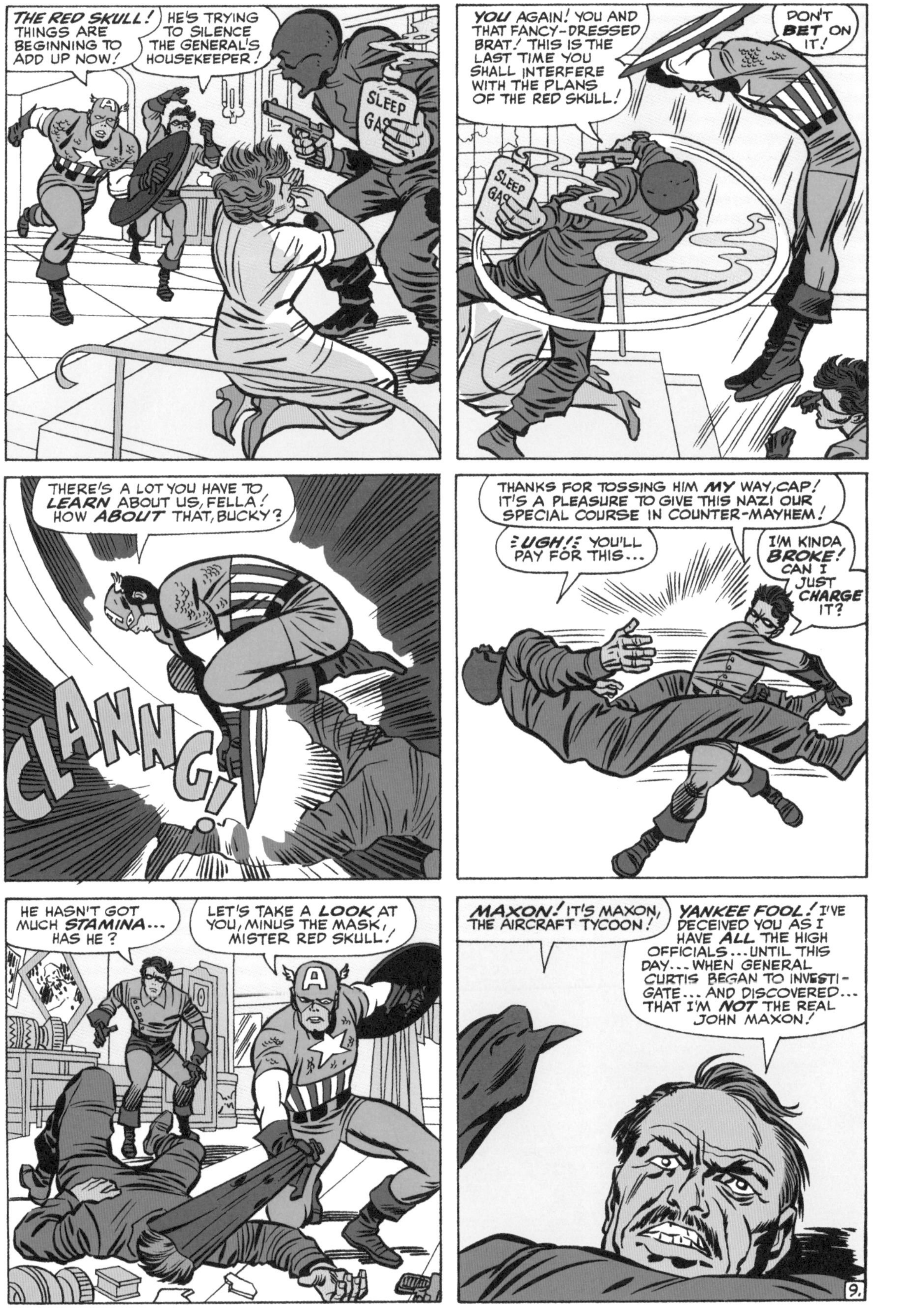
THE RED SKULL! THINGS ARE BEGINNING TO ADD UP NOW!
HE'S TRYING TO SILENCE THE GENERAL'S HOUSEKEEPER!
SLEEP GAS
YOU AGAIN! YOU AND THAT FANCY-DRESSED BRAT! THIS IS THE LAST TIME YOU SHALL INTERFERE WITH THE PLANS OF THE RED SKULL!
DON'T BET ON IT!
SLEEP GAS
THERE'S A LOT YOU HAVE TO LEARN ABOUT US, FELLA! HOW ABOUT THAT, BUCKY?
CLANNG!
THANKS FOR TOSSING HIM MY WAY, CAP! IT'S A PLEASURE TO GIVE THIS NAZI OUR SPECIAL COURSE IN COUNTER-MAYHEM!
UGH! YOU'LL PAY FOR THIS...
I'M KINDA BROKE! CAN I JUST CHARGE IT?
HE HASN'T GOT MUCH STAMINA... HAS HE?
LET'S TAKE A LOOK AT YOU, MINUS THE MASK, MISTER RED SKULL!
MAXON! IT'S MAXON, THE AIRCRAFT TYCOON!
YANKEE FOOL! I'VE DECEIVED YOU AS I HAVE ALL THE HIGH OFFICIALS... UNTIL THIS DAY... WHEN GENERAL CURTIS BEGAN TO INVESTI-GATE... AND DISCOVERED... THAT I'M NOT THE REAL JOHN MAXON!
9.

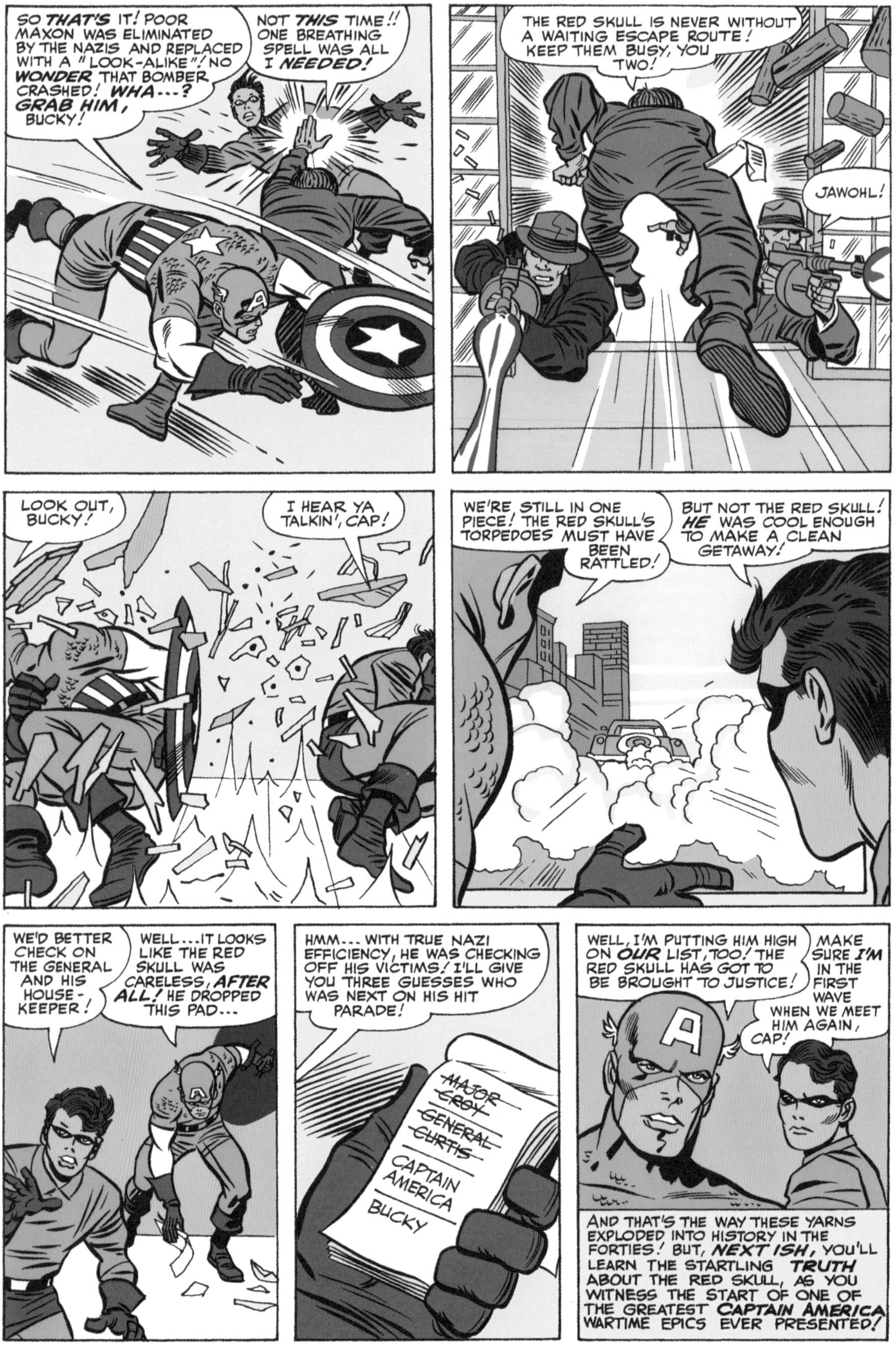
SO THAT'S IT! POOR MAXON WAS ELIMINATED BY THE NAZIS AND REPLACED WITH A "LOOK-ALIKE"! NO WONDER THAT BOMBER CRASHED! WHA...? GRAB HIM, BUCKY!
NOT THIS TIME!! ONE BREATHING SPELL WAS ALL I NEEDED!
THE RED SKULL IS NEVER WITHOUT A WAITING ESCAPE ROUTE! KEEP THEM BUSY, YOU TWO!
JAWOHL!
LOOK OUT, BUCKY!
I HEAR YA TALKIN', CAP!
WE'RE STILL IN ONE PIECE! THE RED SKULL'S TORPEDOES MUST HAVE BEEN RATTLED!
BUT NOT THE RED SKULL! HE WAS COOL ENOUGH TO MAKE A CLEAN GETAWAY!
WE'D BETTER CHECK ON THE GENERAL AND HIS HOUSE-KEEPER!
WELL...IT LOOKS LIKE THE RED SKULL WAS CARELESS, AFTER ALL! HE DROPPED THIS PAD...
HMM... WITH TRUE NAZI EFFICIENCY, HE WAS CHECKING OFF HIS VICTIMS! I'LL GIVE YOU THREE GUESSES WHO WAS NEXT ON HIS HIT PARADE!
MAJOR CROY
GENERAL CURTIS
CAPTAIN AMERICA
BUCKY
WELL, I'M PUTTING HIM HIGH ON OUR LIST, TOO! THE RED SKULL HAS GOT TO BE BROUGHT TO JUSTICE!
MAKE SURE I'M IN THE FIRST WAVE WHEN WE MEET HIM AGAIN, CAP!
AND THAT'S THE WAY THESE YARNS EXPLODED INTO HISTORY IN THE FORTIES! BUT, NEXT ISH, YOU'LL LEARN THE STARTLING TRUTH ABOUT THE RED SKULL, AS YOU WITNESS THE START OF ONE OF THE GREATEST CAPTAIN AMERICA WARTIME EPICS EVER PRESENTED!

TALES OF SUSPENSE #66,

JUNE 1965,

"THE FANTASTIC ORIGIN OF

THE RED SKULL"

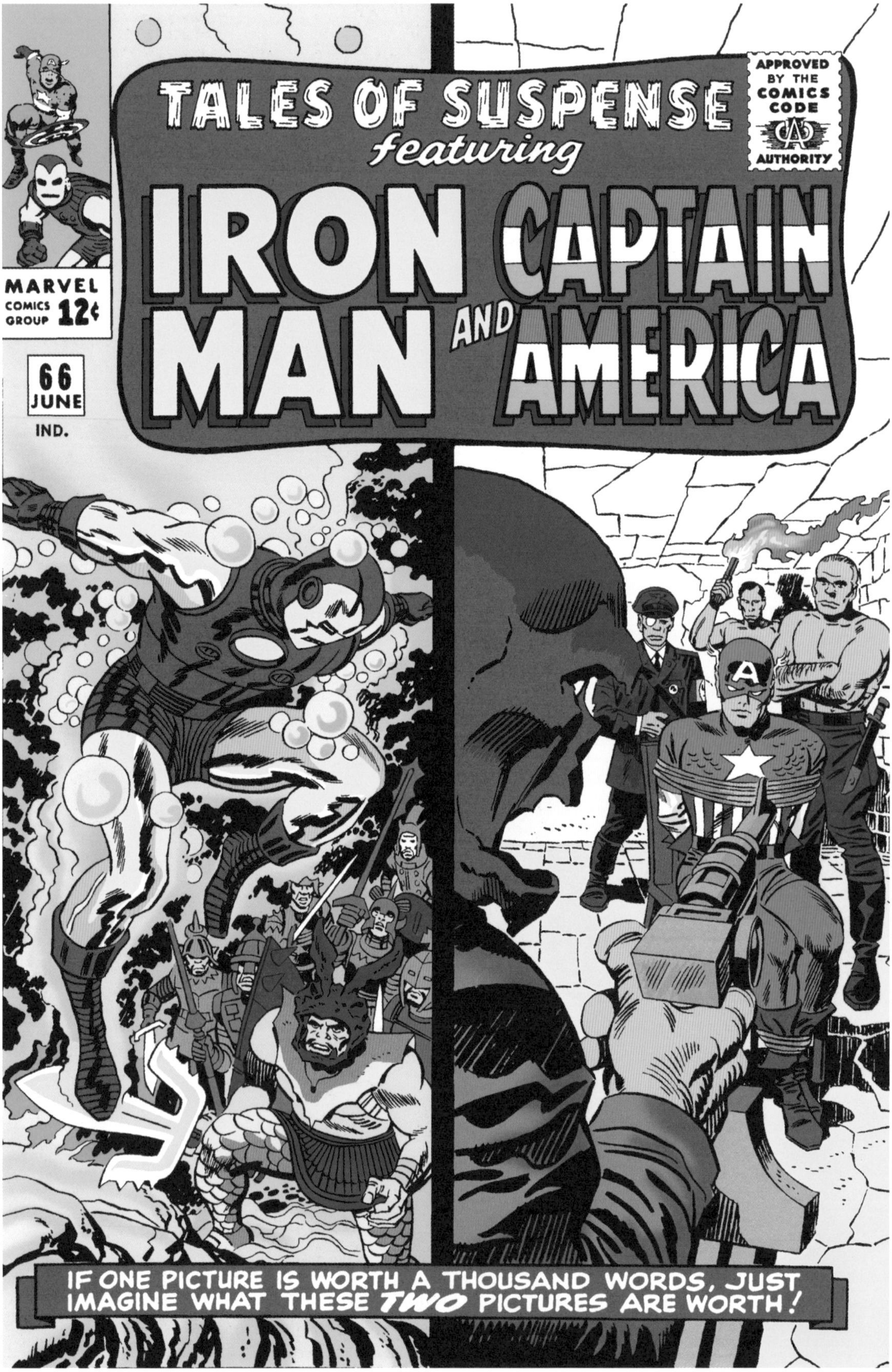
TALES OF SUSPENSE featuring
IRON MAN AND CAPTAIN AMERICA
APPROVED BY THE COMICS CODE AUTHORITY
MARVEL COMICS GROUP 12¢
66 JUNE
IND.
IF ONE PICTURE IS WORTH A THOUSAND WORDS, JUST IMAGINE WHAT THESE TWO PICTURES ARE WORTH!

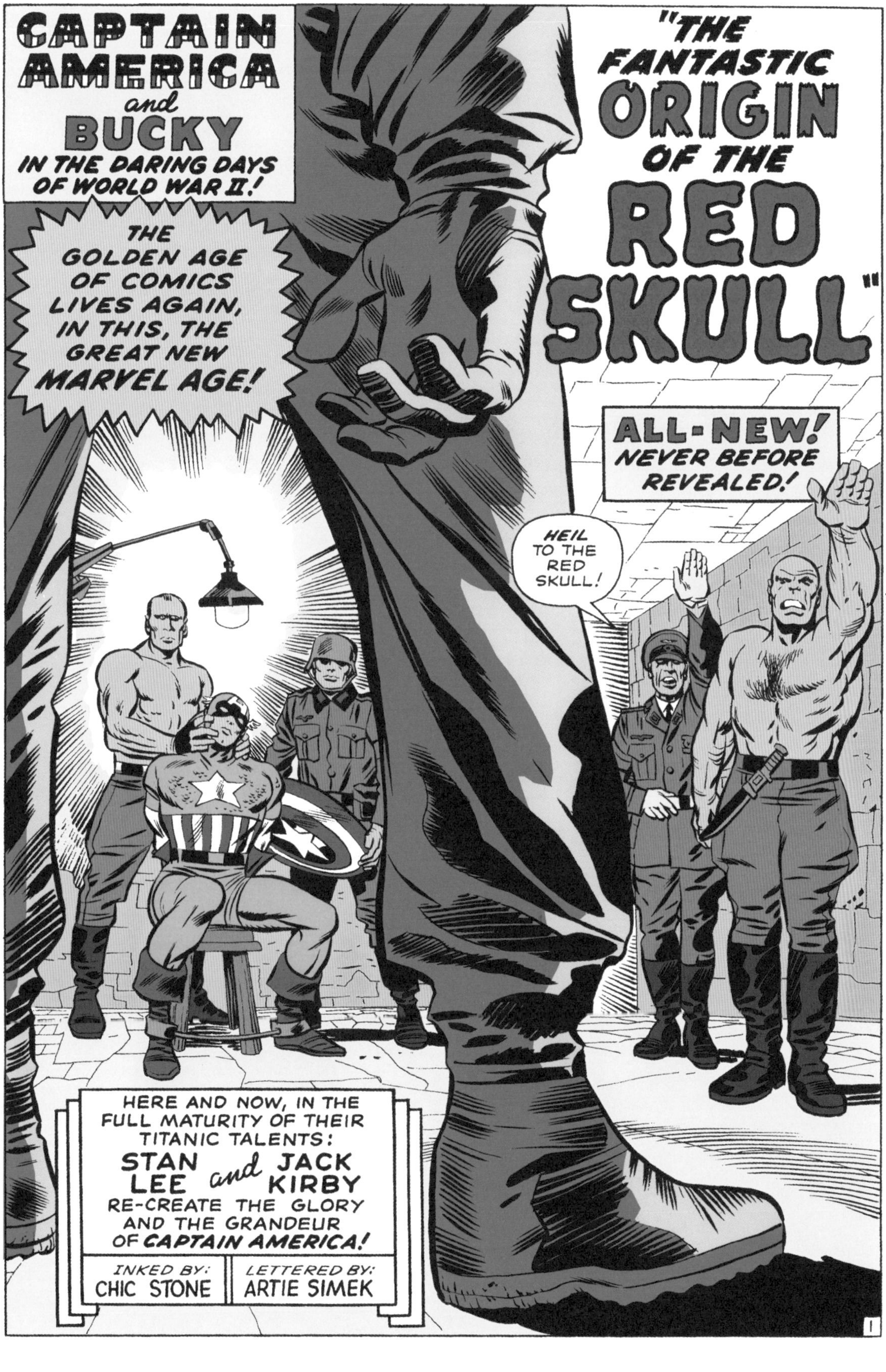

CAPTAIN AMERICA and BUCKY
IN THE DARING DAYS OF WORLD WAR II!
THE GOLDEN AGE OF COMICS LIVES AGAIN, IN THIS, THE GREAT NEW MARVEL AGE!
"THE FANTASTIC ORIGIN OF THE RED SKULL"
ALL-NEW! NEVER BEFORE REVEALED!
HEIL TO THE RED SKULL!
HERE AND NOW, IN THE FULL MATURITY OF THEIR TITANIC TALENTS: STAN LEE and JACK KIRBY RE-CREATE THE GLORY AND THE GRANDEUR OF CAPTAIN AMERICA!
INKED BY: CHIC STONE
LETTERED BY: ARTIE SIMEK
1

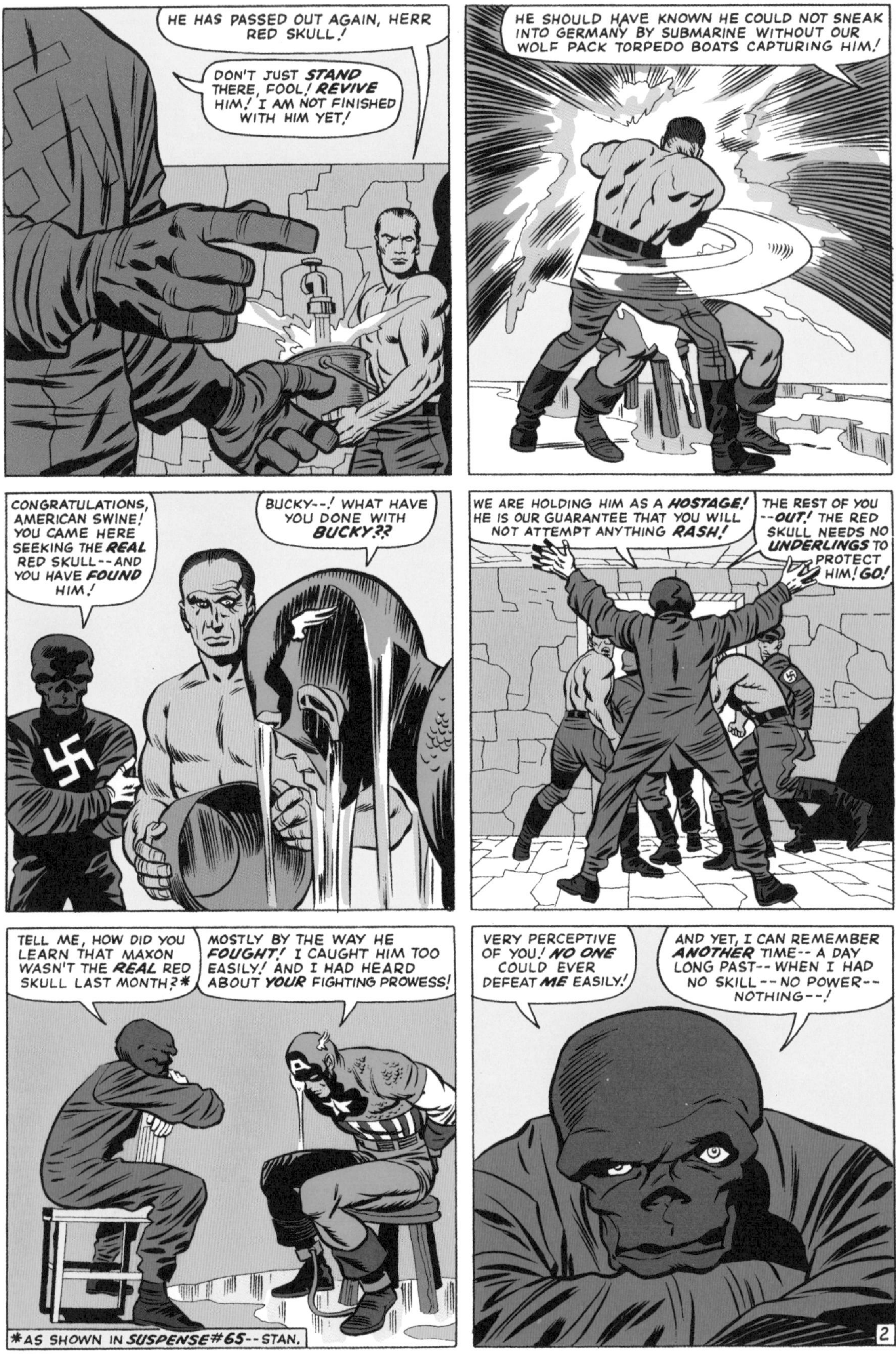
HE HAS PASSED OUT AGAIN, HERR RED SKULL!
DON'T JUST STAND THERE, FOOL! REVIVE HIM! I AM NOT FINISHED WITH HIM YET!
HE SHOULD HAVE KNOWN HE COULD NOT SNEAK INTO GERMANY BY SUBMARINE WITHOUT OUR WOLF PACK TORPEDO BOATS CAPTURING HIM!
CONGRATULATIONS, AMERICAN SWINE! YOU CAME HERE SEEKING THE REAL RED SKULL--AND YOU HAVE FOUND HIM!
BUCKY--! WHAT HAVE YOU DONE WITH BUCKY??
WE ARE HOLDING HIM AS A HOSTAGE! HE IS OUR GUARANTEE THAT YOU WILL NOT ATTEMPT ANYTHING RASH!
THE REST OF YOU --OUT! THE RED SKULL NEEDS NO UNDERLINGS TO PROTECT HIM! GO!
TELL ME, HOW DID YOU LEARN THAT MAXON WASN'T THE REAL RED SKULL LAST MONTH?*
MOSTLY BY THE WAY HE FOUGHT! I CAUGHT HIM TOO EASILY! AND I HAD HEARD ABOUT YOUR FIGHTING PROWESS!
*AS SHOWN IN SUSPENSE #65--STAN.
VERY PERCEPTIVE OF YOU! NO ONE COULD EVER DEFEAT ME EASILY!
AND YET, I CAN REMEMBER ANOTHER TIME-- A DAY LONG PAST--WHEN I HAD NO SKILL--NO POWER--NOTHING--!
2

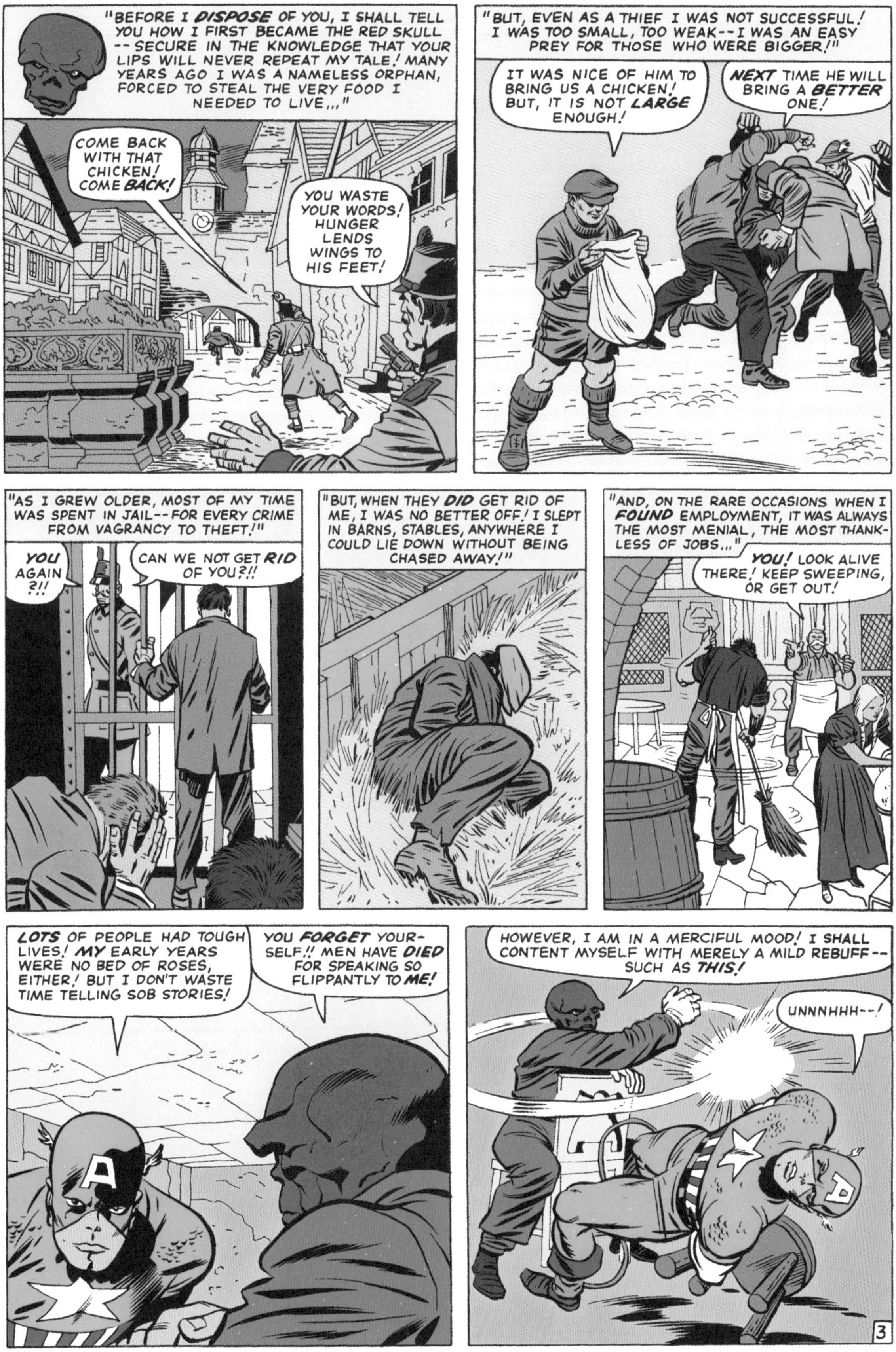
"BEFORE I DISPOSE OF YOU, I SHALL TELL YOU HOW I FIRST BECAME THE RED SKULL -- SECURE IN THE KNOWLEDGE THAT YOUR LIPS WILL NEVER REPEAT MY TALE! MANY YEARS AGO I WAS A NAMELESS ORPHAN, FORCED TO STEAL THE VERY FOOD I NEEDED TO LIVE..."
COME BACK WITH THAT CHICKEN! COME BACK!
YOU WASTE YOUR WORDS! HUNGER LENDS WINGS TO HIS FEET!
"BUT, EVEN AS A THIEF I WAS NOT SUCCESSFUL! I WAS TOO SMALL, TOO WEAK--I WAS AN EASY PREY FOR THOSE WHO WERE BIGGER!"
IT WAS NICE OF HIM TO BRING US A CHICKEN! BUT, IT IS NOT LARGE ENOUGH!
NEXT TIME HE WILL BRING A BETTER ONE!
"AS I GREW OLDER, MOST OF MY TIME WAS SPENT IN JAIL--FOR EVERY CRIME FROM VAGRANCY TO THEFT!"
YOU AGAIN ?!!
CAN WE NOT GET RID OF YOU?!!
"BUT, WHEN THEY DID GET RID OF ME, I WAS NO BETTER OFF! I SLEPT IN BARNS, STABLES, ANYWHERE I COULD LIE DOWN WITHOUT BEING CHASED AWAY!"
"AND, ON THE RARE OCCASIONS WHEN I FOUND EMPLOYMENT, IT WAS ALWAYS THE MOST MENIAL, THE MOST THANKLESS OF JOBS..."
YOU! LOOK ALIVE THERE! KEEP SWEEPING, OR GET OUT!
LOTS OF PEOPLE HAD TOUGH LIVES! MY EARLY YEARS WERE NO BED OF ROSES, EITHER! BUT I DON'T WASTE TIME TELLING SOB STORIES!
YOU FORGET YOURSELF!! MEN HAVE DIED FOR SPEAKING SO FLIPPANTLY TO ME!
HOWEVER, I AM IN A MERCIFUL MOOD! I SHALL CONTENT MYSELF WITH MERELY A MILD REBUFF -- SUCH AS THIS!
UNNNHHH--!
3

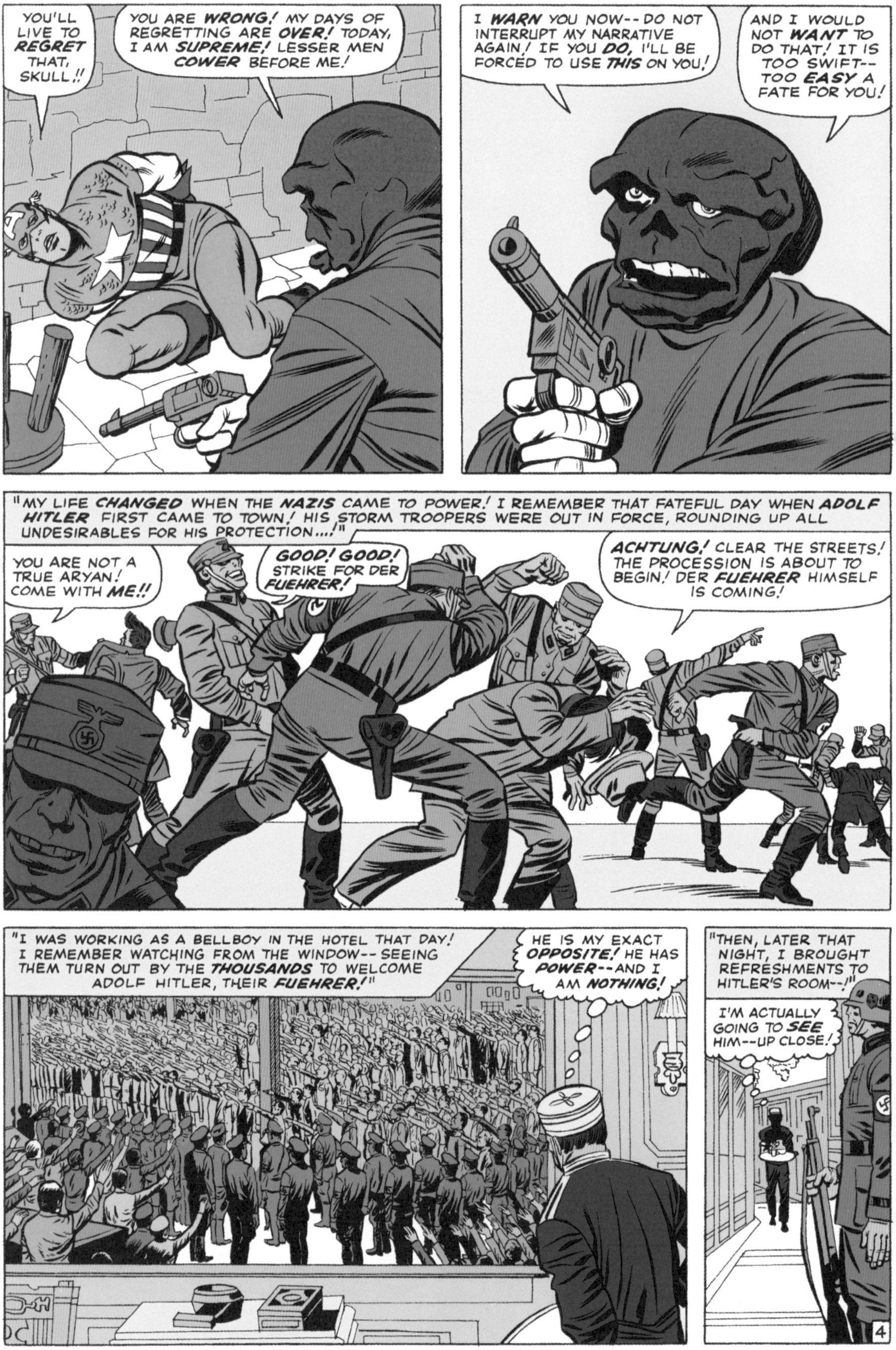
YOU'LL LIVE TO **REGRET** THAT, SKULL!!
YOU ARE **WRONG!** MY DAYS OF REGRETTING ARE **OVER!** TODAY, I AM **SUPREME!** LESSER MEN **COWER** BEFORE ME!
I **WARN** YOU NOW-- DO NOT INTERRUPT MY NARRATIVE AGAIN! IF YOU **DO**, I'LL BE FORCED TO USE **THIS** ON YOU!
AND I WOULD NOT **WANT** TO DO THAT! IT IS TOO SWIFT-- TOO **EASY** A FATE FOR YOU!
"MY LIFE **CHANGED** WHEN THE **NAZIS** CAME TO POWER! I REMEMBER THAT FATEFUL DAY WHEN **ADOLF HITLER** FIRST CAME TO TOWN! HIS STORM TROOPERS WERE OUT IN FORCE, ROUNDING UP ALL UNDESIRABLES FOR HIS PROTECTION...!"
YOU ARE NOT A TRUE ARYAN! COME WITH **ME!!**
GOOD! GOOD! STRIKE FOR DER **FUEHRER!**
ACHTUNG! CLEAR THE STREETS! THE PROCESSION IS ABOUT TO BEGIN! DER **FUEHRER** HIMSELF IS COMING!
"I WAS WORKING AS A BELLBOY IN THE HOTEL THAT DAY! I REMEMBER WATCHING FROM THE WINDOW-- SEEING THEM TURN OUT BY THE **THOUSANDS** TO WELCOME ADOLF HITLER, THEIR **FUEHRER!**"
HE IS MY EXACT **OPPOSITE!** HE HAS **POWER**--AND I AM **NOTHING!**
"THEN, LATER THAT NIGHT, I BROUGHT REFRESHMENTS TO HITLER'S ROOM--!"
I'M ACTUALLY GOING TO **SEE** HIM--UP CLOSE!
4

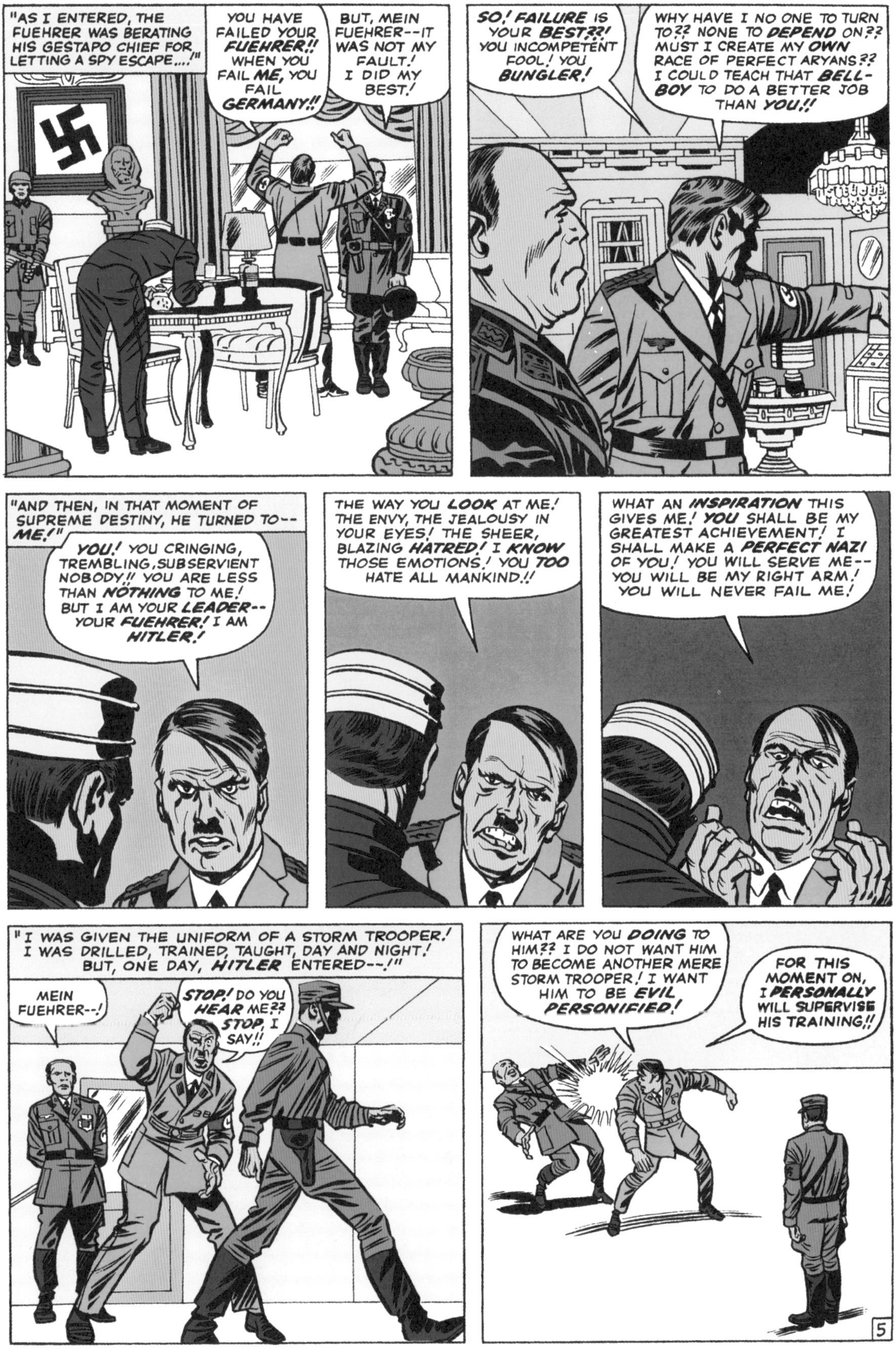
"AS I ENTERED, THE FUEHRER WAS BERATING HIS GESTAPO CHIEF FOR LETTING A SPY ESCAPE....!"
YOU HAVE FAILED YOUR FUEHRER!! WHEN YOU FAIL ME, YOU FAIL GERMANY!!
BUT, MEIN FUEHRER--IT WAS NOT MY FAULT! I DID MY BEST!
SO! FAILURE IS YOUR BEST??! YOU INCOMPETENT FOOL! YOU BUNGLER!
WHY HAVE I NO ONE TO TURN TO?? NONE TO DEPEND ON?? MUST I CREATE MY OWN RACE OF PERFECT ARYANS?? I COULD TEACH THAT BELL-BOY TO DO A BETTER JOB THAN YOU!!
"AND THEN, IN THAT MOMENT OF SUPREME DESTINY, HE TURNED TO--ME!"
YOU! YOU CRINGING, TREMBLING, SUBSERVIENT NOBODY!! YOU ARE LESS THAN NOTHING TO ME! BUT I AM YOUR LEADER--YOUR FUEHRER! I AM HITLER!
THE WAY YOU LOOK AT ME! THE ENVY, THE JEALOUSY IN YOUR EYES! THE SHEER, BLAZING HATRED! I KNOW THOSE EMOTIONS! YOU TOO HATE ALL MANKIND!!
WHAT AN INSPIRATION THIS GIVES ME! YOU SHALL BE MY GREATEST ACHIEVEMENT! I SHALL MAKE A PERFECT NAZI OF YOU! YOU WILL SERVE ME--YOU WILL BE MY RIGHT ARM! YOU WILL NEVER FAIL ME!
"I WAS GIVEN THE UNIFORM OF A STORM TROOPER! I WAS DRILLED, TRAINED, TAUGHT, DAY AND NIGHT! BUT, ONE DAY, HITLER ENTERED--!"
MEIN FUEHRER--!
STOP! DO YOU HEAR ME?? STOP, I SAY!!
WHAT ARE YOU DOING TO HIM?? I DO NOT WANT HIM TO BECOME ANOTHER MERE STORM TROOPER! I WANT HIM TO BE EVIL PERSONIFIED!
FOR THIS MOMENT ON, I PERSONALLY WILL SUPERVISE HIS TRAINING!!
5

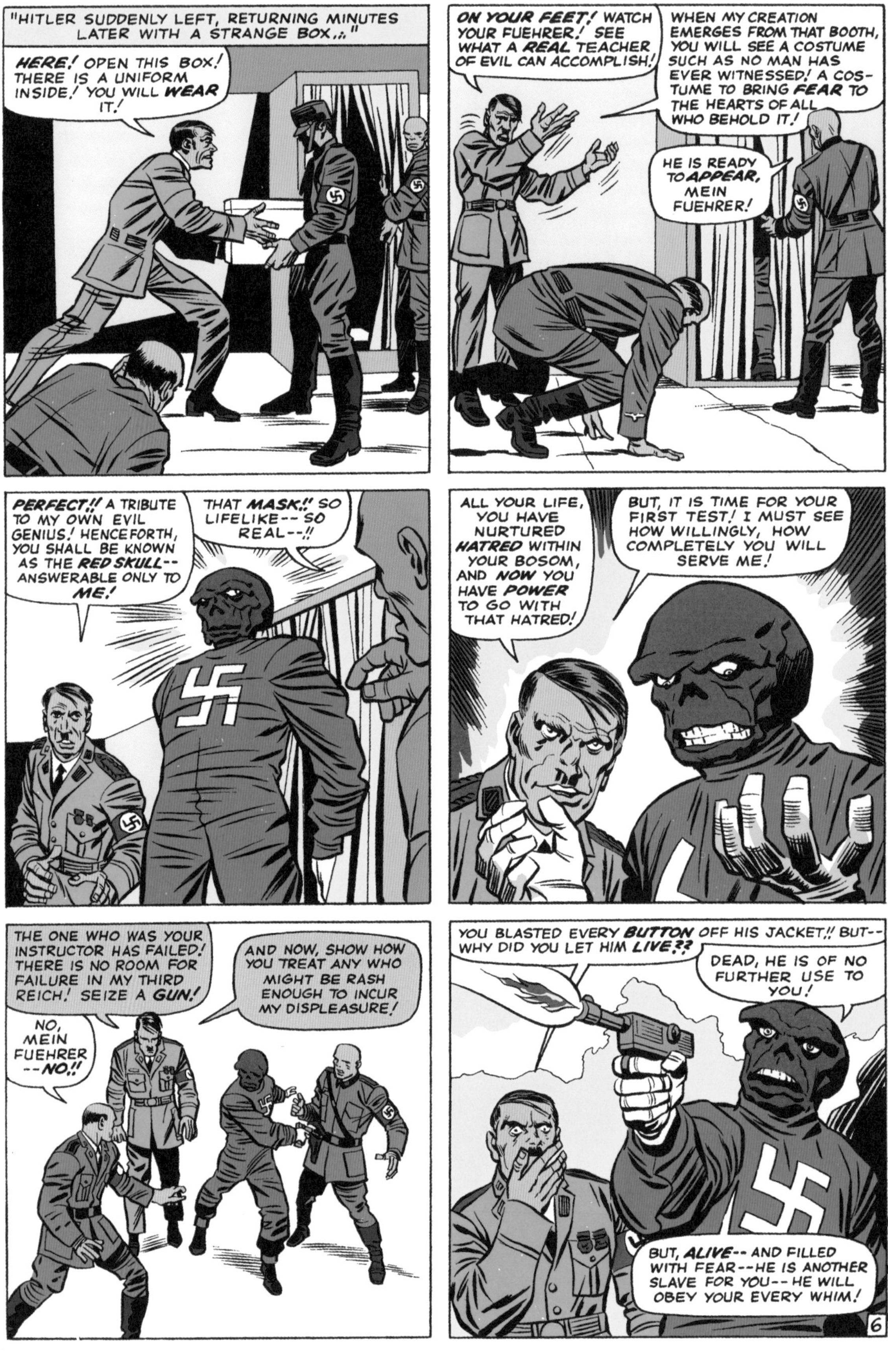
"HITLER SUDDENLY LEFT, RETURNING MINUTES LATER WITH A STRANGE BOX..."
HERE! OPEN THIS BOX! THERE IS A UNIFORM INSIDE! YOU WILL WEAR IT!
ON YOUR FEET! WATCH YOUR FUEHRER! SEE WHAT A REAL TEACHER OF EVIL CAN ACCOMPLISH!
WHEN MY CREATION EMERGES FROM THAT BOOTH, YOU WILL SEE A COSTUME SUCH AS NO MAN HAS EVER WITNESSED! A COSTUME TO BRING FEAR TO THE HEARTS OF ALL WHO BEHOLD IT!
HE IS READY TO APPEAR, MEIN FUEHRER!
PERFECT!! A TRIBUTE TO MY OWN EVIL GENIUS! HENCEFORTH, YOU SHALL BE KNOWN AS THE RED SKULL-- ANSWERABLE ONLY TO ME!
THAT MASK!! SO LIFELIKE-- SO REAL--!!
ALL YOUR LIFE, YOU HAVE NURTURED HATRED WITHIN YOUR BOSOM, AND NOW YOU HAVE POWER TO GO WITH THAT HATRED!
BUT, IT IS TIME FOR YOUR FIRST TEST! I MUST SEE HOW WILLINGLY, HOW COMPLETELY YOU WILL SERVE ME!
THE ONE WHO WAS YOUR INSTRUCTOR HAS FAILED! THERE IS NO ROOM FOR FAILURE IN MY THIRD REICH! SEIZE A GUN!
AND NOW, SHOW HOW YOU TREAT ANY WHO MIGHT BE RASH ENOUGH TO INCUR MY DISPLEASURE!
NO, MEIN FUEHRER --NO!!
YOU BLASTED EVERY BUTTON OFF HIS JACKET!! BUT-- WHY DID YOU LET HIM LIVE??
DEAD, HE IS OF NO FURTHER USE TO YOU!
BUT, ALIVE-- AND FILLED WITH FEAR--HE IS ANOTHER SLAVE FOR YOU-- HE WILL OBEY YOUR EVERY WHIM!
6

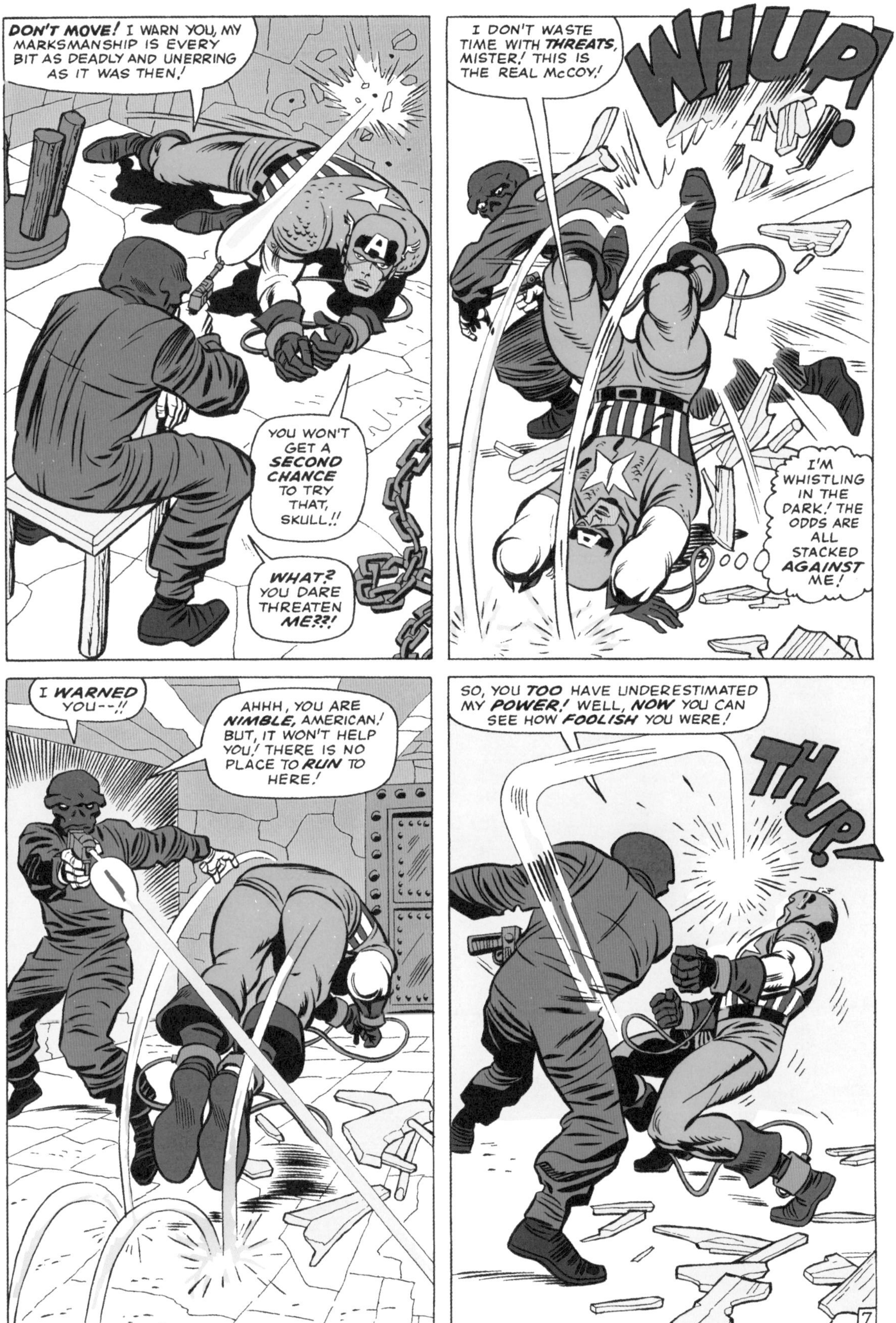
DON'T MOVE! I WARN YOU, MY MARKSMANSHIP IS EVERY BIT AS DEADLY AND UNERRING AS IT WAS THEN.!
YOU WON'T GET A SECOND CHANCE TO TRY THAT, SKULL.!!
WHAT? YOU DARE THREATEN ME??!
I DON'T WASTE TIME WITH THREATS, MISTER.! THIS IS THE REAL McCOY.!
WHUP!
I'M WHISTLING IN THE DARK.! THE ODDS ARE ALL STACKED AGAINST ME.!
I WARNED YOU--!!
AHHH, YOU ARE NIMBLE, AMERICAN.! BUT, IT WON'T HELP YOU.! THERE IS NO PLACE TO RUN TO HERE.!
SO, YOU TOO HAVE UNDERESTIMATED MY POWER.! WELL, NOW YOU CAN SEE HOW FOOLISH YOU WERE.!
THUP!
7

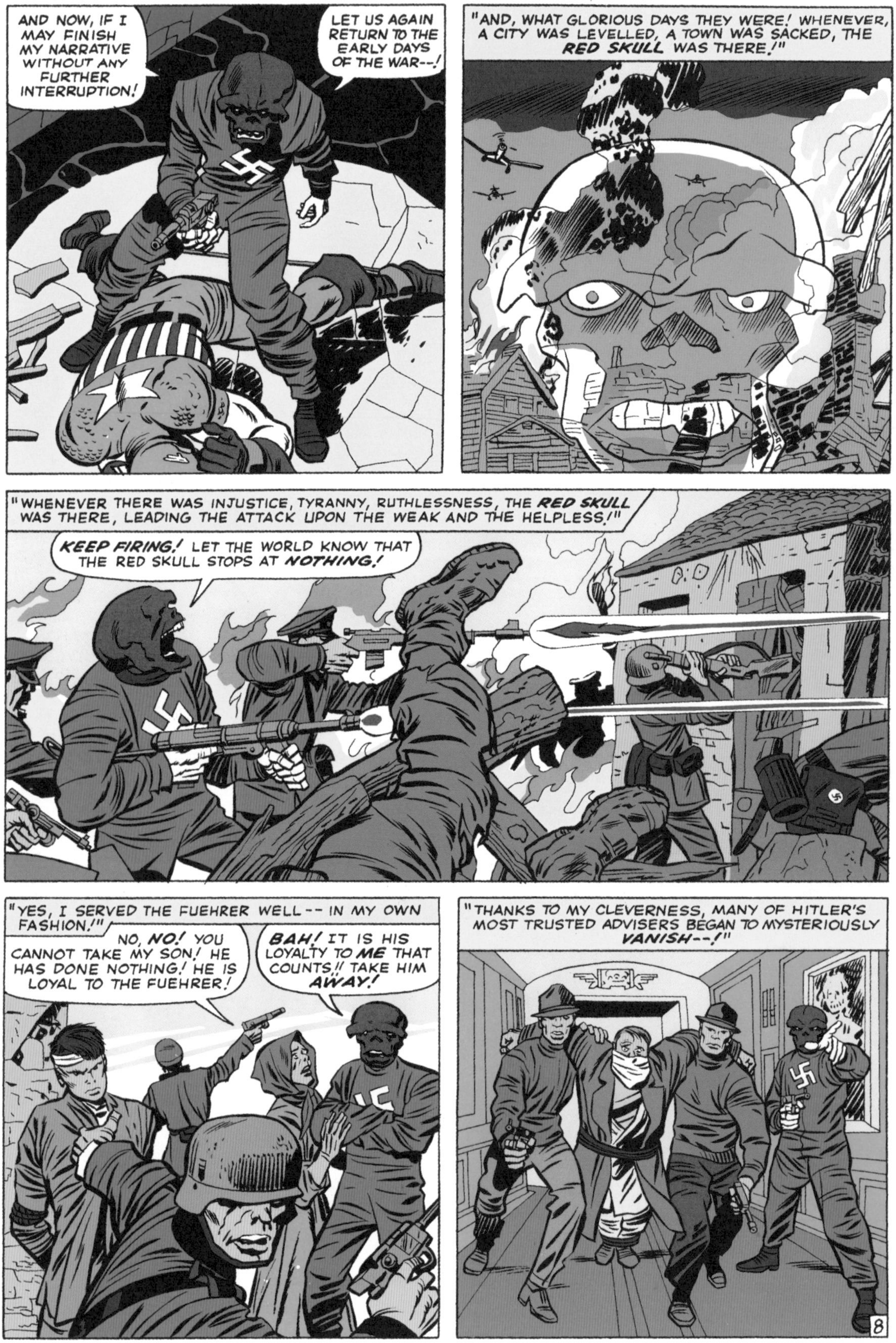
AND NOW, IF I MAY FINISH MY NARRATIVE WITHOUT ANY FURTHER INTERRUPTION!
LET US AGAIN RETURN TO THE EARLY DAYS OF THE WAR--!
"AND, WHAT GLORIOUS DAYS THEY WERE! WHENEVER, A CITY WAS LEVELLED, A TOWN WAS SACKED, THE RED SKULL WAS THERE!"
"WHENEVER THERE WAS INJUSTICE, TYRANNY, RUTHLESSNESS, THE RED SKULL WAS THERE, LEADING THE ATTACK UPON THE WEAK AND THE HELPLESS!"
KEEP FIRING! LET THE WORLD KNOW THAT THE RED SKULL STOPS AT NOTHING!
"YES, I SERVED THE FUEHRER WELL -- IN MY OWN FASHION!"
NO, NO! YOU CANNOT TAKE MY SON! HE HAS DONE NOTHING! HE IS LOYAL TO THE FUEHRER!
BAH! IT IS HIS LOYALTY TO ME THAT COUNTS!! TAKE HIM AWAY!
"THANKS TO MY CLEVERNESS, MANY OF HITLER'S MOST TRUSTED ADVISERS BEGAN TO MYSTERIOUSLY VANISH--!"
8

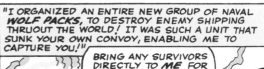

DAY BY DAY MY POWER GREW, UNTIL I WAS SECOND ONLY TO HITLER HIMSELF IN SUPREME AUTHORITY! AT MY COMMAND, CITIES WOULD FALL, ARMIES WOULD BE DESTROYED!

"I ORGANIZED AN ENTIRE NEW GROUP OF NAVAL *WOLF PACKS*, TO DESTROY ENEMY SHIPPING THRUOUT THE WORLD! IT WAS SUCH A UNIT THAT SUNK YOUR OWN CONVOY, ENABLING ME TO CAPTURE YOU!"

BRING ANY SURVIVORS DIRECTLY TO *ME* FOR QUESTIONING! IF ANY ESCAPE, YOU *DIE!*

BUT, YOU SEEM TO GROW *RESTLESS!* CAN IT BE THAT MY LITTLE TALE HAS *BORED* YOU? PERHAPS I SHOULD TRY TO REVIVE YOUR INTEREST AGAIN--!

YOU'RE A *FOOL*, NAZI! GLOATING OVER A HELPLESS PRISONER IS A SIGN OF *WEAKNESS*, NOT STRENGTH!

YOU'VE *MADE* YOUR POINT, SKULL! I'VE HEARD THAT EVEN *HITLER* FEARS YOU! EVEN *HE* CAN NO LONGER CONTROL YOU-- FOR YOU'VE GROWN TOO POWERFUL!

BUT I'M *NOT* HITLER! I'M AN *AMERICAN*--

AND *MY BREED* JUST DOESN'T SCARE EASILY!

BRAVE WORDS, CAPTAIN AMERICA! TOO BAD YOU HAVE NOT THE *STRENGTH* TO BACK THEM UP!

WHA-WHAT'S *HAPPENING* TO ME?? MY LEGS WON'T SUPPORT ME--! THE ROOM IS SPINNING--!

9

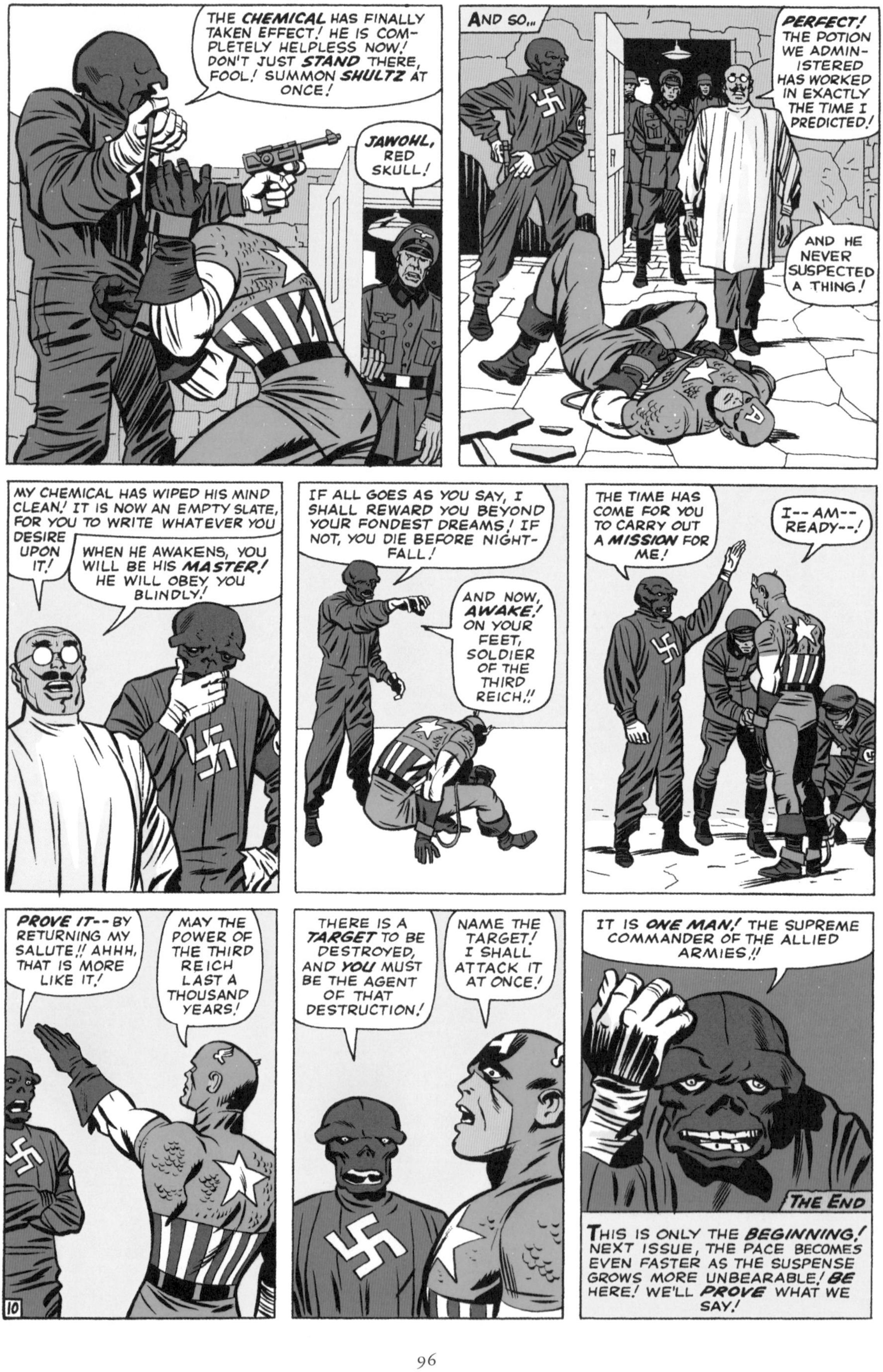
THE CHEMICAL HAS FINALLY TAKEN EFFECT! HE IS COMPLETELY HELPLESS NOW! DON'T JUST STAND THERE, FOOL! SUMMON SHULTZ AT ONCE!
JAWOHL, RED SKULL!
AND SO...
PERFECT! THE POTION WE ADMINISTERED HAS WORKED IN EXACTLY THE TIME I PREDICTED!
AND HE NEVER SUSPECTED A THING!
MY CHEMICAL HAS WIPED HIS MIND CLEAN! IT IS NOW AN EMPTY SLATE, FOR YOU TO WRITE WHATEVER YOU DESIRE UPON IT!
WHEN HE AWAKENS, YOU WILL BE HIS MASTER! HE WILL OBEY YOU BLINDLY!
IF ALL GOES AS YOU SAY, I SHALL REWARD YOU BEYOND YOUR FONDEST DREAMS! IF NOT, YOU DIE BEFORE NIGHTFALL!
AND NOW, AWAKE! ON YOUR FEET, SOLDIER OF THE THIRD REICH!!
THE TIME HAS COME FOR YOU TO CARRY OUT A MISSION FOR ME!
I-- AM-- READY--!
PROVE IT-- BY RETURNING MY SALUTE!! AHHH, THAT IS MORE LIKE IT!
MAY THE POWER OF THE THIRD REICH LAST A THOUSAND YEARS!
10
THERE IS A TARGET TO BE DESTROYED, AND YOU MUST BE THE AGENT OF THAT DESTRUCTION!
NAME THE TARGET! I SHALL ATTACK IT AT ONCE!
IT IS ONE MAN! THE SUPREME COMMANDER OF THE ALLIED ARMIES!!
THE END
THIS IS ONLY THE BEGINNING! NEXT ISSUE, THE PACE BECOMES EVEN FASTER AS THE SUSPENSE GROWS MORE UNBEARABLE! BE HERE! WE'LL PROVE WHAT WE SAY!

Mails of SUSPENSE

SEND YOUR
LETTERS TO: THE MARVEL COMICS GROUP, SECOND FLOOR 625 MADISON AVE., NEW YORK, N. Y. 10022

— If you think THIS ish was something, wait'll you see our next humdinger! But, we want to warn you — it's so good, you'll probably feel guilty taking the mag for only 12¢! However, try to curb your natural impulse to offer the dealer more money—you'll only spoil him if you do! And now, we've talked long enough! Let's hear what YOU have to say —

Dear Stan and Don and Jack,

For months I've been hounding you about the art and stories in Marvel Comics. My wish was granted in TALES OF SUSPENSE #63 with "the Origin of Captain America." This is truly the greatest work to come from the Marvel bullpen yet. The reason I liked it so well is the fact that Stan's story reminded me of the "Glory Days" for the simple reason that it did not use the usual slang and guest stars that are so prevalent in other Marvel comics. Another big reason is the beautiful detailed artwork that Jack Kirby is famous for. Frank Ray has captured his style better than any one yet. I was thrilled to hear that from now on the sentinel of liberty and his young companion will once again be engaged in their cloak-and-dagger adventures. The art in Iron Man is much better than it used to be, but the stories have me worried. Like most other Marvel stories, they are too involved with super villains and personal problems. Speaking for myself, I would prefer to have something different that stands out in the crowd. My suggestion is to let Iron Man be more concerned with the threat of Communism instead of your ordinary costumed villains.   Jerry Pritchett, 38 Carlson Ave. Danville, Va.

Jer, you know we never make a move until we hear what the rest of our frantic fans have to say! So be patient, pal—we'll clue you in on the results of the letters which we receive in answer to yours.

Dear Stan and Jack,

Regarding a fan's letter in issue #63, I say, sure, give Captain America his own mag. I say this only to keep him from cluttering up an otherwise great magazine. In the words of Flash Thompson, he's just a big zero! Does he have an interesting personal life like Spider-Man or Iron Man? Nope! Does he have a unique and exciting super ability? Nope! All he can do is fight. Even your explanation of his superhuman fighting ability as caused by some chemical doesn't help. Get rid of him, and Iron Man will be much better off in the company of someone who isn't better (?) than the F.F., greater than the Avengers and more agile (?) than Daredevil and Spider-Man.
Jim Poreliski, 4306 Deyo Brookfield, Ill.

Hmmmm! If we didn't know better, Jimmy, we'd think you don't like Captain America! But of course, that's impossible! Even our competitors read him on the sly!

— You've probably noticed that we gave a full page to our M.M.M.S. announcement this ish. It looks as though we'll have to make a habit of it from now on. Starting next month, there are so many exciting announcements about The Fan Club To End All Fan Clubs that we really should devote an entire ish to it — but you know us — we hate to be greedy!

Dear Stan and Don and Jack,

I've got a problem! Marvel Comics are about the greatest thing that's ever happened to me. And now that Cap and Shell-Head share the same mag, I've just got to buy it. The trouble is that I get a meager allowance, and, if I spend most of it on your great comics, I won't be able to join the M.M.M.S.! Please help me, guys — what can I do!!
Larry Libby, 240 Marion Lane Eugene, Ore.

Tell you what, Larry—your problem is so heart-rending and tragic that even wonderful we can't solve it! So, we'll toss it at our readers—and if we get any inspirational answers, we'll print the best ones! Fair 'nuff?

Dear Stan and Jack and Don,

TALES OF SUSPENSE #63 again illustrated the great

change in Iron Man. Both the writing and art were top notch. Though I thought the return of Stark was a little too soon, this did not detract from my enjoyment of the story. "The Origin of Captain America" was just what I would expect from Marvel: the best—what else?! By some miracle you managed to cover a span of time without crowding the story. I was delighted to see the return of Bucky, as I am a great fan of the original Captain America as he appeared in the '40's. I am looking forward to some great stories in the future.
Derrill Rothermich, Univ. of Missouri 606 W. 11th St., Rolla, Mo.

So are we, Derrie! Know where we can find some?

SPECIAL NOTE: Many of you have written to say that the Marvel mags in your town sell out so rapidly and you have trouble finding them! Only you can solve that earth-shaking problem! If enough of you tell your magazine dealers how much you want Marvel's marvel-ous mags, and if enough of you tell your dealers to display the Marvel masterpieces right up front, and to order an extra-large supply so that there'll be plenty to go around, your dealer should start getting the message after a while! So it's up to you! In the immortal words of Irving Forbush, be sure to tell your dealer: MAKE MINE MARVEL!

THE MIGHTY MARVEL CHECKLIST
A Line-Up Of Some Of The Marvel-ous Mags On Sale Right Now!

FANTASTIC FOUR #39: With their super powers gone, the F.F. must fight Dr. Doom, the most dangerous arch-villain of all! Guest-starring the fearless Daredevil, "A Blind Man Shall Lead Them!" is possibly one of the ten greatest thrillers you will ever read!

SPIDER-MAN #25: It was bound to happen sooner or later! The title is self-explanatory: "Captured By J. Jonah Jameson!" And, we promise you this—it's everything you hope it will be, and more! It's Ditko's dazzling artistry at its dramatic best!

AVENGERS #16: The biggest surprise of the season! Only mighty Marvel would dare attempt such a startling change! You are about to see a brand new line-up of stars take shape! Definitely not to be missed!

X-MEN #11: Another shocker from the House of Ideas! This one was specially produced in answer to many of your earnest requests, and it finally presents the end of the evil mutants! Also, wait till you meet The Stranger!

THOR #116: If this were a movie, it could only have been produced by Cecil B. DeMille! Spectacle follows spectacle as you marvel at "The Trial Of The Gods!" Special Note: You'll find more sensational guest stars in this issue than ever before!

STRANGE TALES #155: Don't even try to guess the ending of this month's pulse-pounding Torch and Thing epic! Just sit back and enjoy Trumbo's Terrible Toys! As for Dr. Strange, only Steve Ditko could create the mystic mood of "A Nameless Land, A Timeless Time!" It's sheer Marvel magic!

ASTONISH #68: At last! The King is back! See the Hulk, more incredible than ever under the enchanted pencil of Jack Kirby! And the New Giant-Man again faces his most sinister foe in "Peril From The Long-Dead Past!" This will show why all fandom is agog over Bob Powell's rendition of the titanic Avenger!

SGT. FURY #18: Once again tragedy strikes our little cast of characters in one of the most stirring battle sagas of all time! Be prepared for the year's most powerful climax as you learn, with shattering force, why readers everywhere have made Fury's Howlers the world's most famous battle squad!

— Now, whatever you do, don't dare miss SUSPENSE #67—unless you want to miss Shell Head's most unusual adventure of the year, or Cap's most dangerous dilemma at the hands of the Red Skull! Remember—SUSPENSE #67—the most fun you can have without laughing!

TALES OF SUSPENSE #67,

JULY 1965,

"LEST TYRANNY TRIUMPH!"

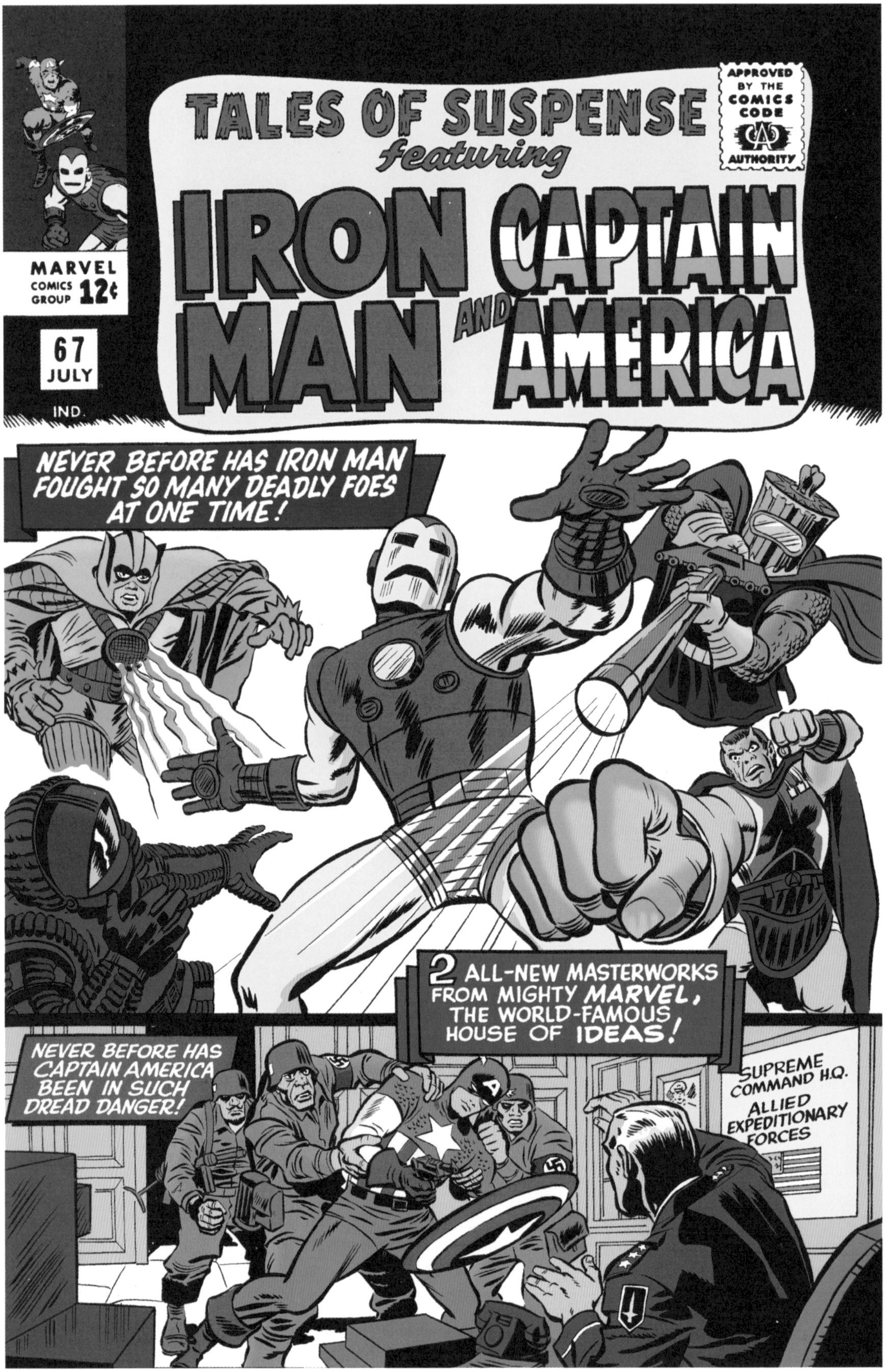

TALES OF SUSPENSE
featuring
IRON MAN AND CAPTAIN AMERICA
MARVEL COMICS GROUP 12¢
67 JULY
IND.
APPROVED BY THE COMICS CODE AUTHORITY
NEVER BEFORE HAS IRON MAN FOUGHT SO MANY DEADLY FOES AT ONE TIME!
2 ALL-NEW MASTERWORKS FROM MIGHTY MARVEL, THE WORLD-FAMOUS HOUSE OF IDEAS!
NEVER BEFORE HAS CAPTAIN AMERICA BEEN IN SUCH DREAD DANGER!
SUPREME COMMAND H.Q.
ALLIED EXPEDITIONARY FORCES

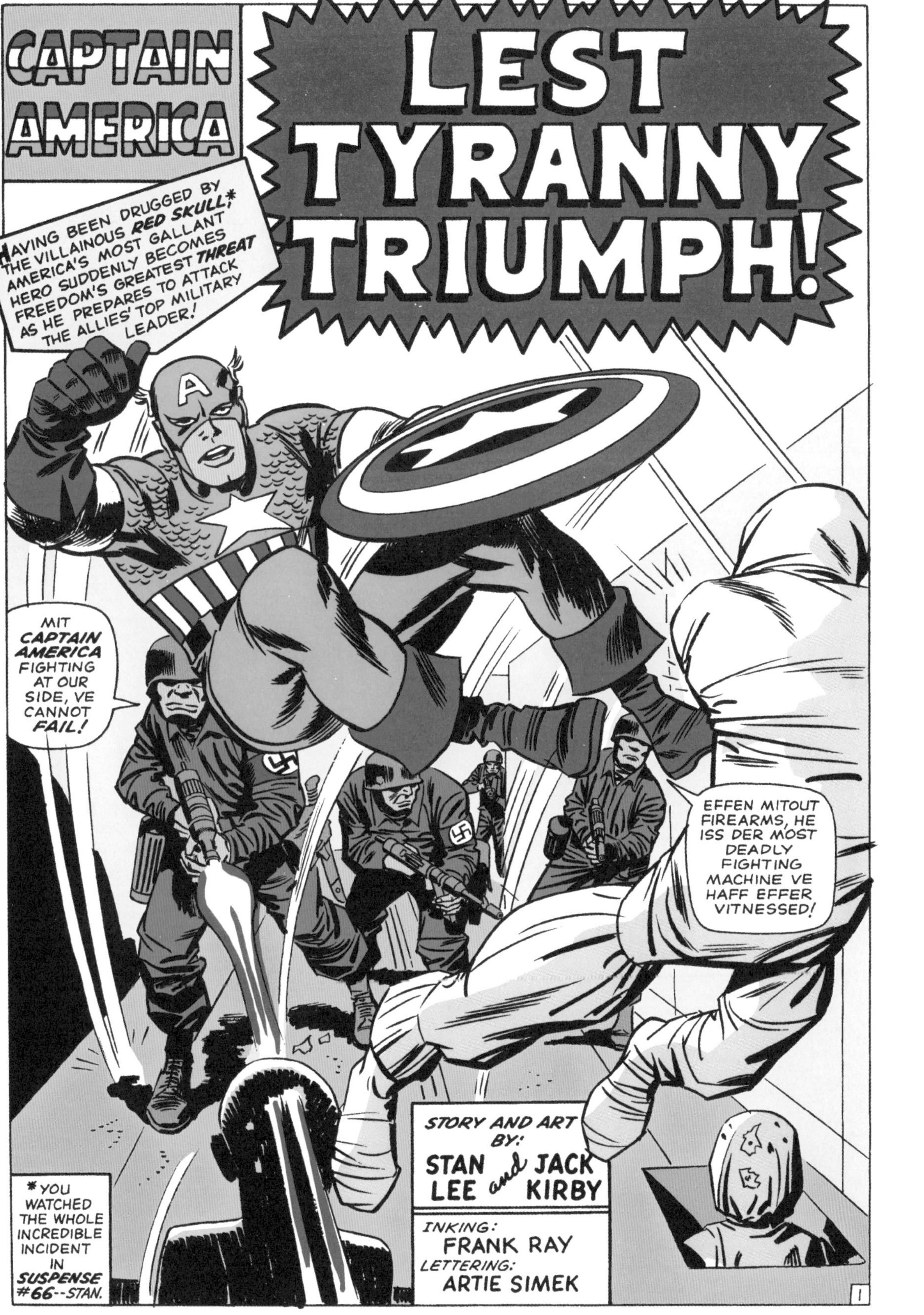

CAPTAIN AMERICA
LEST TYRANNY TRIUMPH!
HAVING BEEN DRUGGED BY THE VILLAINOUS RED SKULL,* AMERICA'S MOST GALLANT HERO SUDDENLY BECOMES FREEDOM'S GREATEST THREAT AS HE PREPARES TO ATTACK THE ALLIES' TOP MILITARY LEADER!
MIT CAPTAIN AMERICA FIGHTING AT OUR SIDE, VE CANNOT FAIL!
EFFEN MITOUT FIREARMS, HE ISS DER MOST DEADLY FIGHTING MACHINE VE HAFF EFFER VITNESSED!
*YOU WATCHED THE WHOLE INCREDIBLE INCIDENT IN SUSPENSE #66--STAN.
STORY AND ART BY: STAN LEE and JACK KIRBY
INKING: FRANK RAY
LETTERING: ARTIE SIMEK
1

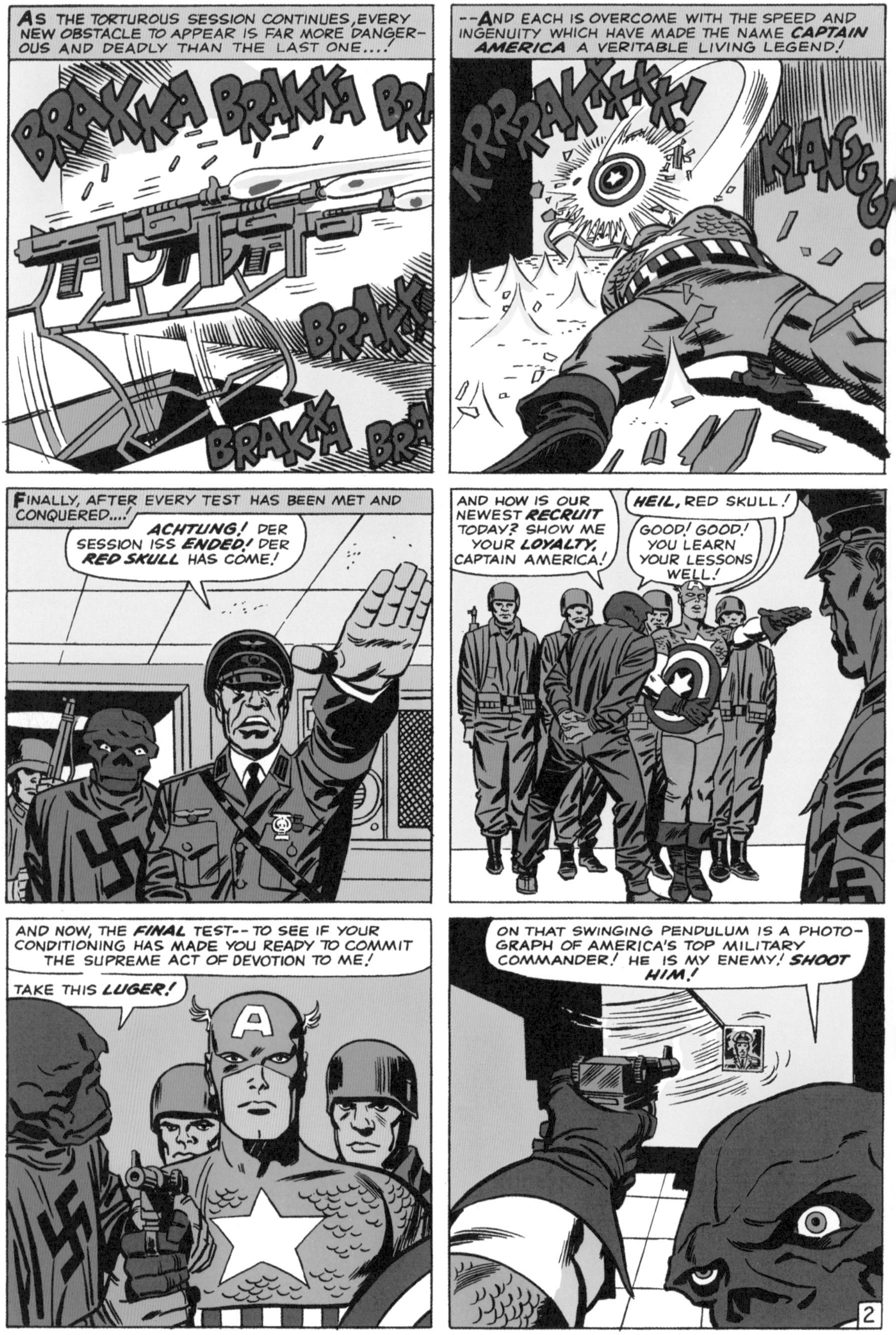
AS THE TORTUROUS SESSION CONTINUES, EVERY NEW OBSTACLE TO APPEAR IS FAR MORE DANGEROUS AND DEADLY THAN THE LAST ONE....!
BRAKKA BRAKKA BRA
BRAKKA
BRAKKA BRA
--AND EACH IS OVERCOME WITH THE SPEED AND INGENUITY WHICH HAVE MADE THE NAME CAPTAIN AMERICA A VERITABLE LIVING LEGEND!
KRRRAKKKKK!
KLANGG!
FINALLY, AFTER EVERY TEST HAS BEEN MET AND CONQUERED...!
ACHTUNG! DER SESSION ISS ENDED! DER RED SKULL HAS COME!
AND HOW IS OUR NEWEST RECRUIT TODAY? SHOW ME YOUR LOYALTY, CAPTAIN AMERICA!
HEIL, RED SKULL!
GOOD! GOOD! YOU LEARN YOUR LESSONS WELL!
AND NOW, THE FINAL TEST--TO SEE IF YOUR CONDITIONING HAS MADE YOU READY TO COMMIT THE SUPREME ACT OF DEVOTION TO ME!
TAKE THIS LUGER!
ON THAT SWINGING PENDULUM IS A PHOTOGRAPH OF AMERICA'S TOP MILITARY COMMANDER! HE IS MY ENEMY! SHOOT HIM!
2

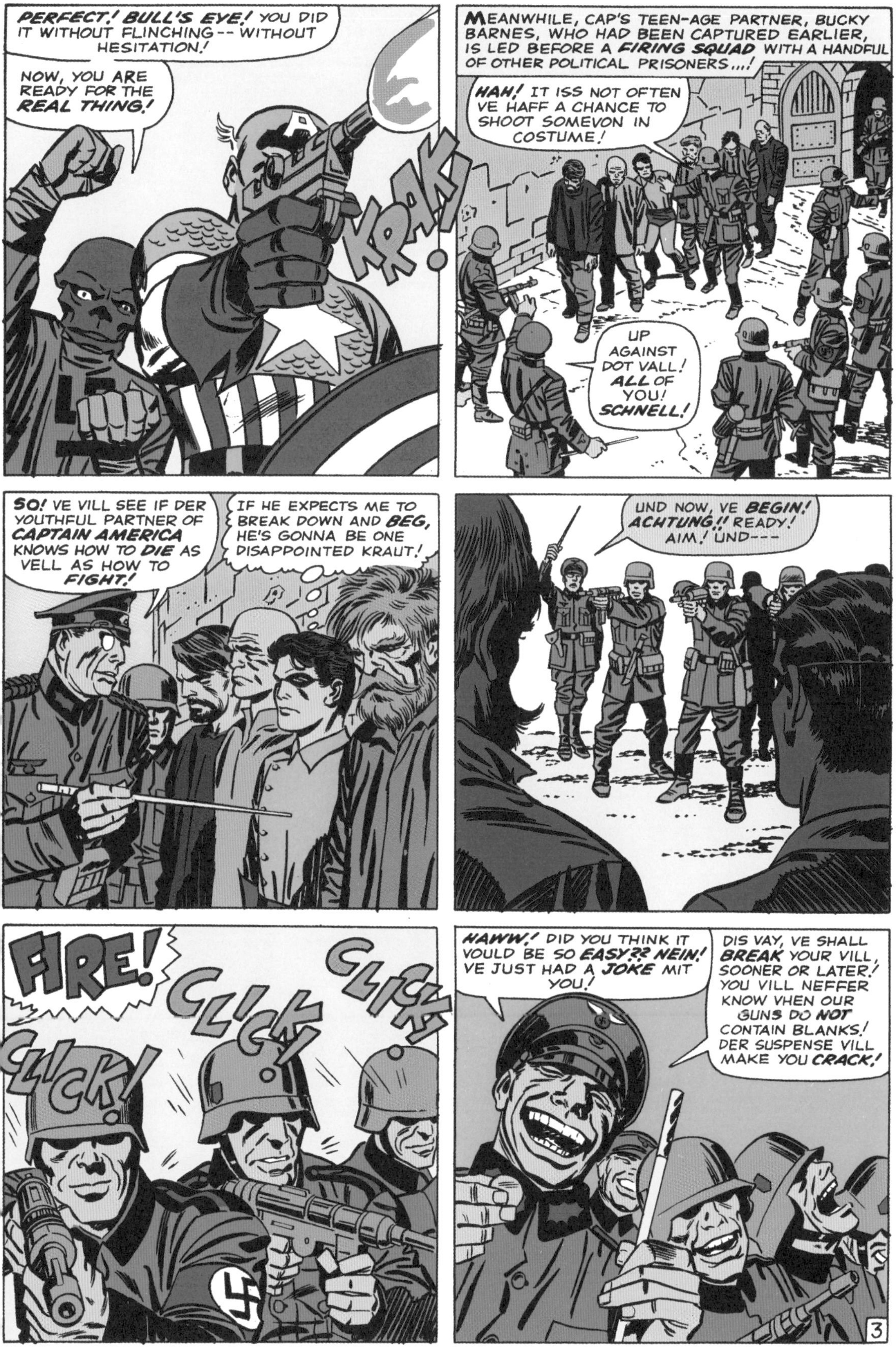
PERFECT! BULL'S EYE! YOU DID IT WITHOUT FLINCHING -- WITHOUT HESITATION!
NOW, YOU ARE READY FOR THE REAL THING!
KRAK!
MEANWHILE, CAP'S TEEN-AGE PARTNER, BUCKY BARNES, WHO HAD BEEN CAPTURED EARLIER, IS LED BEFORE A FIRING SQUAD WITH A HANDFUL OF OTHER POLITICAL PRISONERS...!
HAH! IT ISS NOT OFTEN VE HAFF A CHANCE TO SHOOT SOMEVON IN COSTUME!
UP AGAINST DOT VALL! ALL OF YOU! SCHNELL!
SO! VE VILL SEE IF DER YOUTHFUL PARTNER OF CAPTAIN AMERICA KNOWS HOW TO DIE AS VELL AS HOW TO FIGHT!
IF HE EXPECTS ME TO BREAK DOWN AND BEG, HE'S GONNA BE ONE DISAPPOINTED KRAUT!
UND NOW, VE BEGIN! ACHTUNG!! READY! AIM! UND---
FIRE!
CLICK!
CLICK!
CLICK!
HAWW! DID YOU THINK IT VOULD BE SO EASY?? NEIN! VE JUST HAD A JOKE MIT YOU!
DIS VAY, VE SHALL BREAK YOUR VILL, SOONER OR LATER! YOU VILL NEFFER KNOW VHEN OUR GUNS DO NOT CONTAIN BLANKS! DER SUSPENSE VILL MAKE YOU CRACK!
3

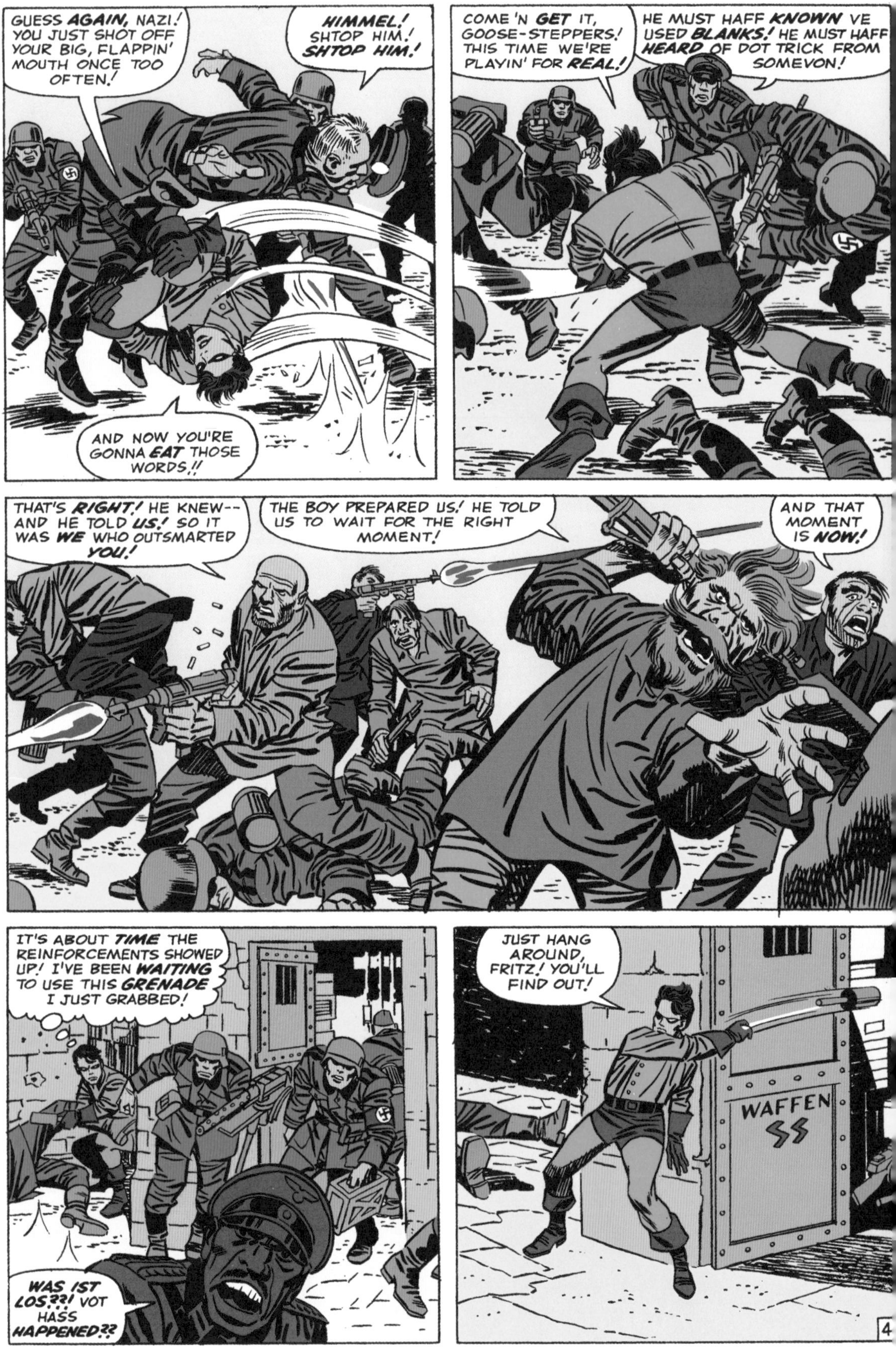
GUESS AGAIN, NAZI! YOU JUST SHOT OFF YOUR BIG, FLAPPIN' MOUTH ONCE TOO OFTEN!
HIMMEL! SHTOP HIM! SHTOP HIM!
AND NOW YOU'RE GONNA EAT THOSE WORDS!!
COME 'N GET IT, GOOSE-STEPPERS! THIS TIME WE'RE PLAYIN' FOR REAL!
HE MUST HAFF KNOWN VE USED BLANKS! HE MUST HAFF HEARD OF DOT TRICK FROM SOMEVON!
THAT'S RIGHT! HE KNEW-- AND HE TOLD US! SO IT WAS WE WHO OUTSMARTED YOU!
THE BOY PREPARED US! HE TOLD US TO WAIT FOR THE RIGHT MOMENT!
AND THAT MOMENT IS NOW!
IT'S ABOUT TIME THE REINFORCEMENTS SHOWED UP! I'VE BEEN WAITING TO USE THIS GRENADE I JUST GRABBED!
WAS IST LOS??! VOT HASS HAPPENED??
JUST HANG AROUND, FRITZ! YOU'LL FIND OUT!
WAFFEN SS
4

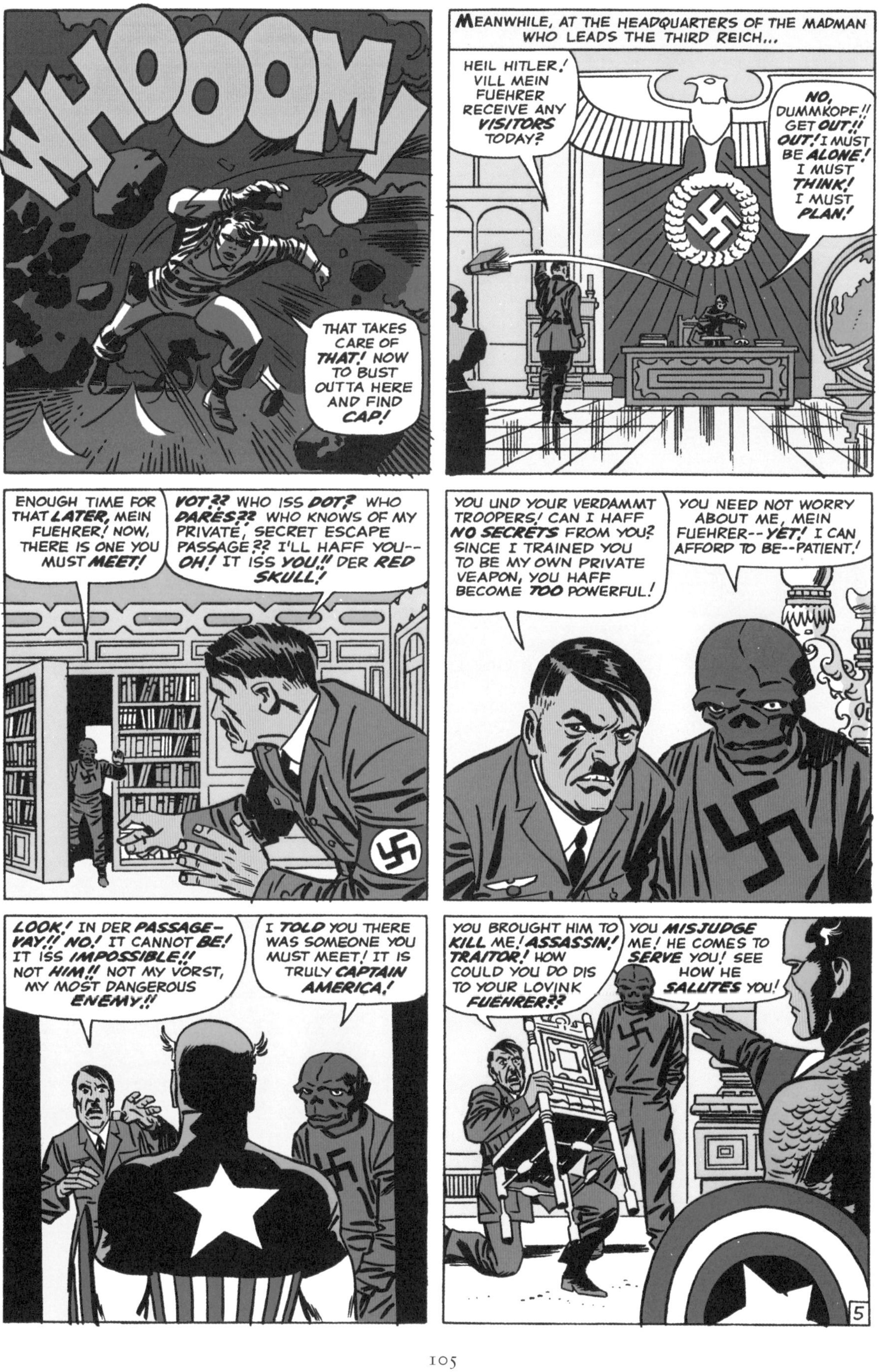
WHOOOM!
THAT TAKES CARE OF THAT! NOW TO BUST OUTTA HERE AND FIND CAP!
MEANWHILE, AT THE HEADQUARTERS OF THE MADMAN WHO LEADS THE THIRD REICH...
HEIL HITLER! VILL MEIN FUEHRER RECEIVE ANY VISITORS TODAY?
NO, DUMMKOPF!! GET OUT!! OUT! I MUST BE ALONE! I MUST THINK! I MUST PLAN!
ENOUGH TIME FOR THAT LATER, MEIN FUEHRER! NOW, THERE IS ONE YOU MUST MEET!
VOT?? WHO ISS DOT? WHO DARES?? WHO KNOWS OF MY PRIVATE, SECRET ESCAPE PASSAGE?? I'LL HAFF YOU-- OH! IT ISS YOU!! DER RED SKULL!
YOU UND YOUR VERDAMMT TROOPERS! CAN I HAFF NO SECRETS FROM YOU? SINCE I TRAINED YOU TO BE MY OWN PRIVATE VEAPON, YOU HAFF BECOME TOO POWERFUL!
YOU NEED NOT WORRY ABOUT ME, MEIN FUEHRER--YET! I CAN AFFORD TO BE--PATIENT!
LOOK! IN DER PASSAGE-VAY!! NO! IT CANNOT BE! IT ISS IMPOSSIBLE!! NOT HIM!! NOT MY VORST, MY MOST DANGEROUS ENEMY!!
I TOLD YOU THERE WAS SOMEONE YOU MUST MEET! IT IS TRULY CAPTAIN AMERICA!
YOU BROUGHT HIM TO KILL ME! ASSASSIN! TRAITOR! HOW COULD YOU DO DIS TO YOUR LOVINK FUEHRER??
YOU MISJUDGE ME! HE COMES TO SERVE YOU! SEE HOW HE SALUTES YOU!
5

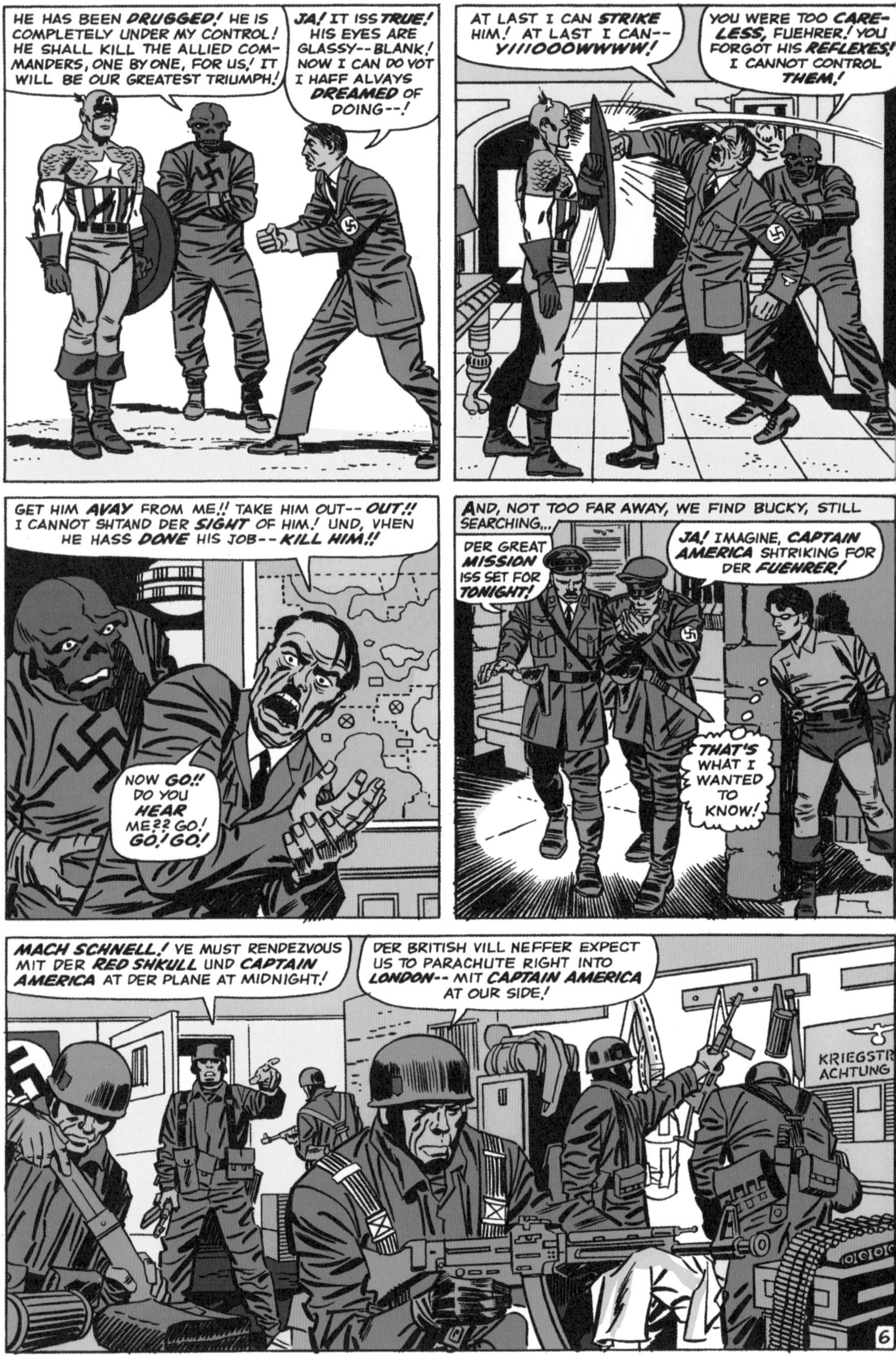
HE HAS BEEN DRUGGED! HE IS COMPLETELY UNDER MY CONTROL! HE SHALL KILL THE ALLIED COMMANDERS, ONE BY ONE, FOR US! IT WILL BE OUR GREATEST TRIUMPH!
JA! IT ISS TRUE! HIS EYES ARE GLASSY--BLANK! NOW I CAN DO VOT I HAFF ALVAYS DREAMED OF DOING--!
AT LAST I CAN STRIKE HIM! AT LAST I CAN-- YIIIOOOWWWW!
YOU WERE TOO CARELESS, FUEHRER! YOU FORGOT HIS REFLEXES! I CANNOT CONTROL THEM!
GET HIM AVAY FROM ME!! TAKE HIM OUT-- OUT!! I CANNOT SHTAND DER SIGHT OF HIM! UND, VHEN HE HASS DONE HIS JOB-- KILL HIM!!
NOW GO!! DO YOU HEAR ME?? GO! GO! GO!
AND, NOT TOO FAR AWAY, WE FIND BUCKY, STILL SEARCHING...
DER GREAT MISSION ISS SET FOR TONIGHT!
JA! IMAGINE, CAPTAIN AMERICA SHTRIKING FOR DER FUEHRER!
THAT'S WHAT I WANTED TO KNOW!
MACH SCHNELL! VE MUST RENDEZVOUS MIT DER RED SHKULL UND CAPTAIN AMERICA AT DER PLANE AT MIDNIGHT!
DER BRITISH VILL NEFFER EXPECT US TO PARACHUTE RIGHT INTO LONDON-- MIT CAPTAIN AMERICA AT OUR SIDE!
KRIEGSTR
ACHTUNG
6

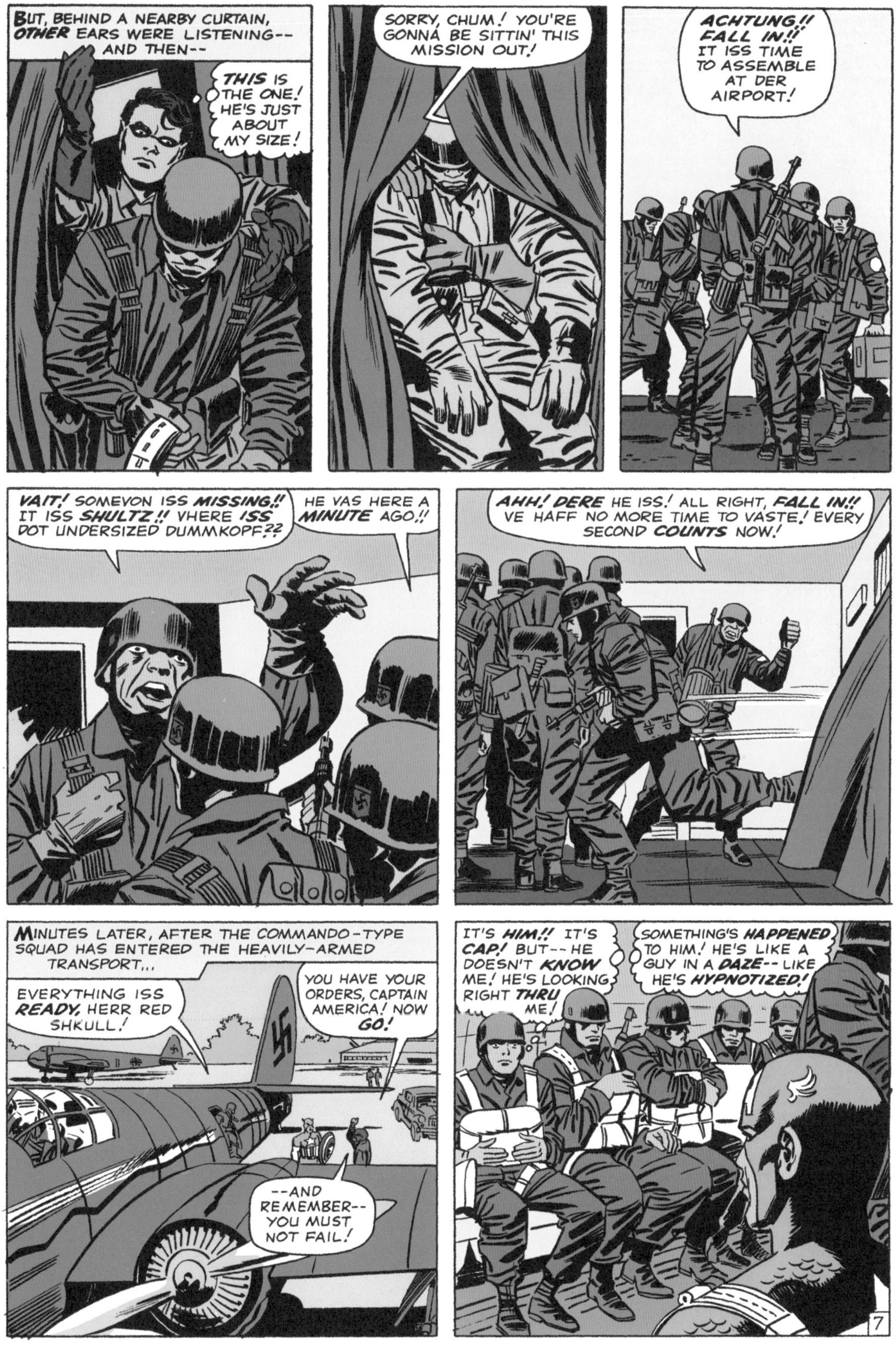
BUT, BEHIND A NEARBY CURTAIN, OTHER EARS WERE LISTENING-- AND THEN--
THIS IS THE ONE! HE'S JUST ABOUT MY SIZE!
SORRY, CHUM! YOU'RE GONNA BE SITTIN' THIS MISSION OUT!
ACHTUNG!! FALL IN!! IT ISS TIME TO ASSEMBLE AT DER AIRPORT!
VAIT! SOMEVON ISS MISSING!! IT ISS SHULTZ!! VHERE ISS DOT UNDERSIZED DUMMKOPF??
HE VAS HERE A MINUTE AGO!!
AHH! DERE HE ISS! ALL RIGHT, FALL IN!! VE HAFF NO MORE TIME TO VASTE! EVERY SECOND COUNTS NOW!
MINUTES LATER, AFTER THE COMMANDO-TYPE SQUAD HAS ENTERED THE HEAVILY-ARMED TRANSPORT...
EVERYTHING ISS READY, HERR RED SHKULL!
YOU HAVE YOUR ORDERS, CAPTAIN AMERICA! NOW GO!
--AND REMEMBER-- YOU MUST NOT FAIL!
IT'S HIM!! IT'S CAP! BUT--HE DOESN'T KNOW ME! HE'S LOOKING RIGHT THRU ME!
SOMETHING'S HAPPENED TO HIM! HE'S LIKE A GUY IN A DAZE-- LIKE HE'S HYPNOTIZED!
7

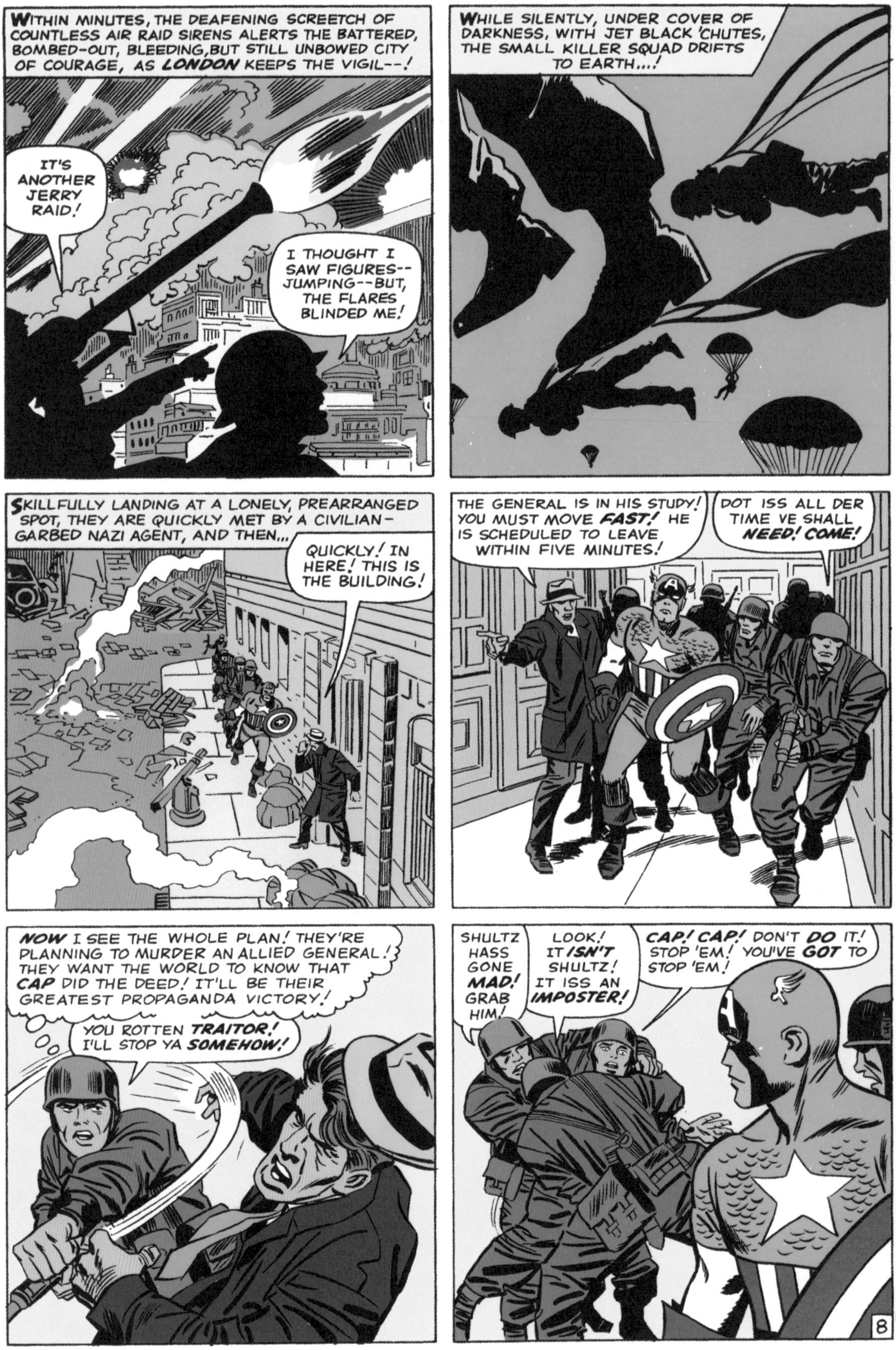
WITHIN MINUTES, THE DEAFENING SCREETCH OF COUNTLESS AIR RAID SIRENS ALERTS THE BATTERED, BOMBED-OUT, BLEEDING, BUT STILL UNBOWED CITY OF COURAGE, AS LONDON KEEPS THE VIGIL--!
IT'S ANOTHER JERRY RAID!
I THOUGHT I SAW FIGURES--JUMPING--BUT, THE FLARES BLINDED ME!
WHILE SILENTLY, UNDER COVER OF DARKNESS, WITH JET BLACK 'CHUTES, THE SMALL KILLER SQUAD DRIFTS TO EARTH...!
SKILLFULLY LANDING AT A LONELY, PREARRANGED SPOT, THEY ARE QUICKLY MET BY A CIVILIAN-GARBED NAZI AGENT, AND THEN...
QUICKLY! IN HERE! THIS IS THE BUILDING!
THE GENERAL IS IN HIS STUDY! YOU MUST MOVE FAST! HE IS SCHEDULED TO LEAVE WITHIN FIVE MINUTES!
DOT ISS ALL DER TIME VE SHALL NEED! COME!
NOW I SEE THE WHOLE PLAN! THEY'RE PLANNING TO MURDER AN ALLIED GENERAL! THEY WANT THE WORLD TO KNOW THAT CAP DID THE DEED! IT'LL BE THEIR GREATEST PROPAGANDA VICTORY!
YOU ROTTEN TRAITOR! I'LL STOP YA SOMEHOW!
SHULTZ HASS GONE MAD! GRAB HIM!
LOOK! IT ISN'T SHULTZ! IT ISS AN IMPOSTER!
CAP! CAP! DON'T DO IT! STOP 'EM! YOU'VE GOT TO STOP 'EM!
8

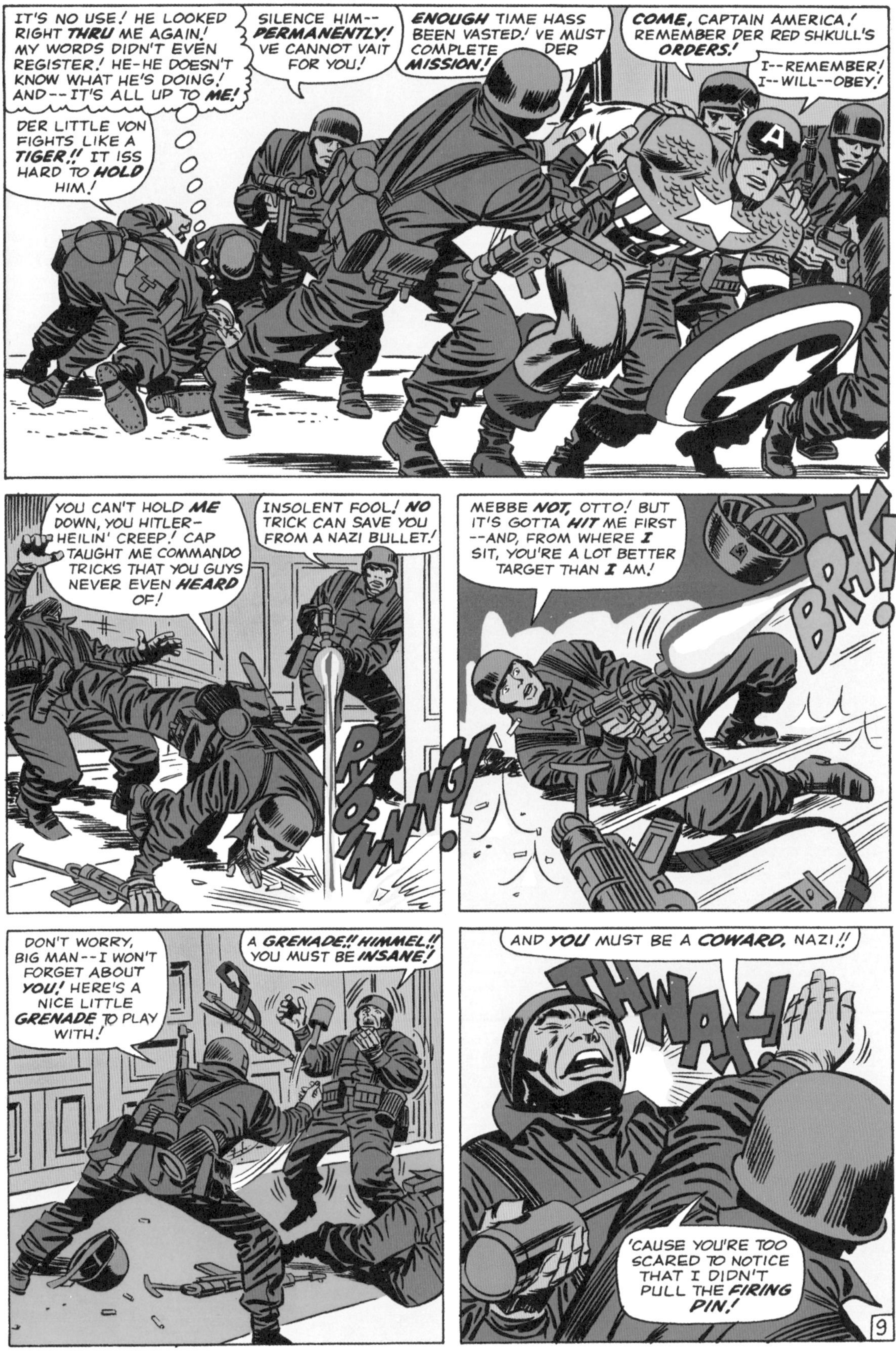
IT'S NO USE! HE LOOKED RIGHT THRU ME AGAIN! MY WORDS DIDN'T EVEN REGISTER! HE-HE DOESN'T KNOW WHAT HE'S DOING! AND--IT'S ALL UP TO ME!
SILENCE HIM--PERMANENTLY! VE CANNOT VAIT FOR YOU!
ENOUGH TIME HASS BEEN VASTED! VE MUST COMPLETE DER MISSION!
COME, CAPTAIN AMERICA! REMEMBER DER RED SHKULL'S ORDERS!
I--REMEMBER! I--WILL--OBEY!
DER LITTLE VON FIGHTS LIKE A TIGER!! IT ISS HARD TO HOLD HIM!
YOU CAN'T HOLD ME DOWN, YOU HITLER-HEILIN' CREEP! CAP TAUGHT ME COMMANDO TRICKS THAT YOU GUYS NEVER EVEN HEARD OF!
INSOLENT FOOL! NO TRICK CAN SAVE YOU FROM A NAZI BULLET!
PTYOINNNG!
MEBBE NOT, OTTO! BUT IT'S GOTTA HIT ME FIRST --AND, FROM WHERE I SIT, YOU'RE A LOT BETTER TARGET THAN I AM!
BRAK!
DON'T WORRY, BIG MAN--I WON'T FORGET ABOUT YOU! HERE'S A NICE LITTLE GRENADE TO PLAY WITH!
A GRENADE!! HIMMEL!! YOU MUST BE INSANE!
AND YOU MUST BE A COWARD, NAZI!!
THWAK!
'CAUSE YOU'RE TOO SCARED TO NOTICE THAT I DIDN'T PULL THE FIRING PIN!
9

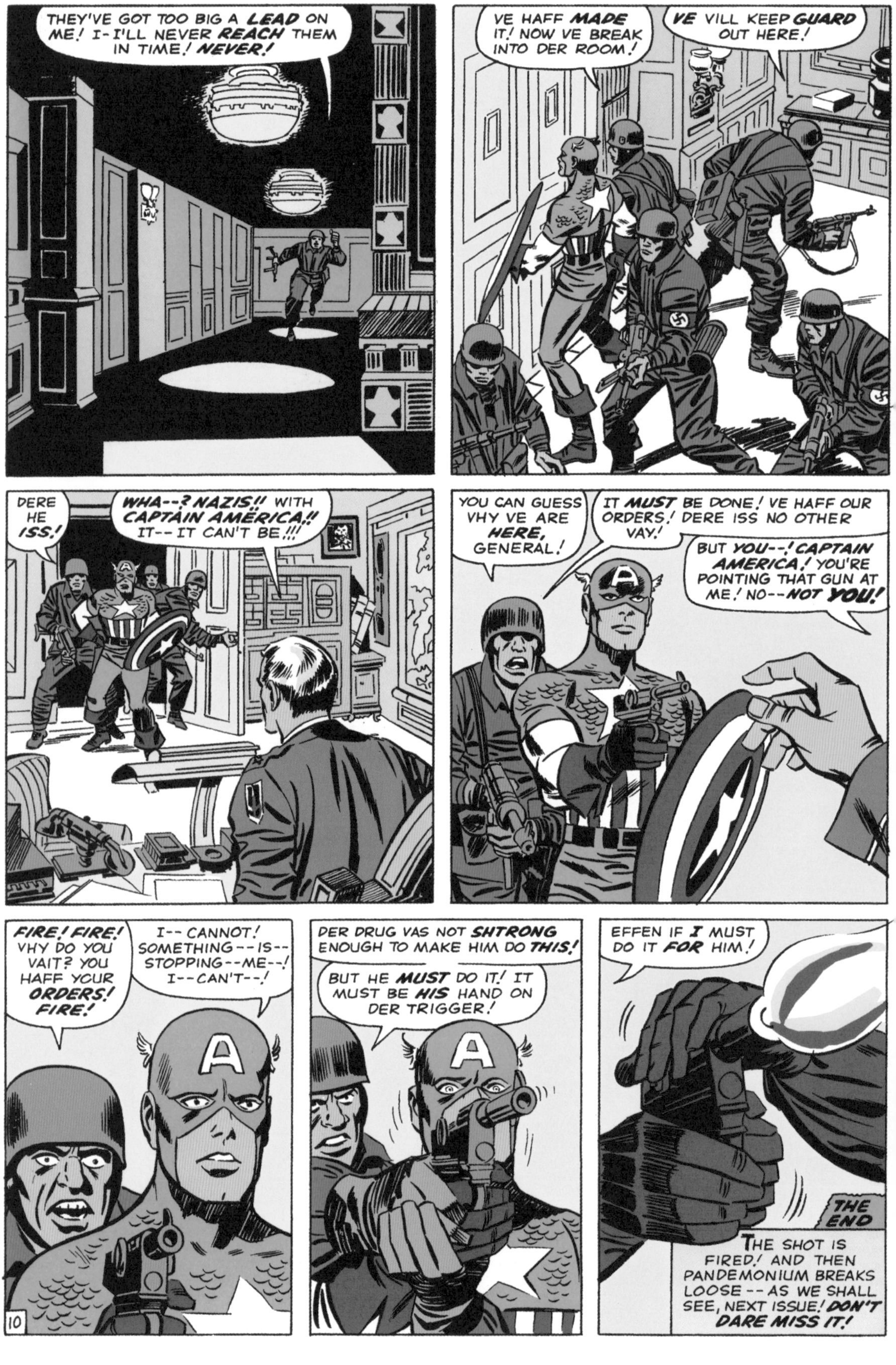
THEY'VE GOT TOO BIG A LEAD ON ME! I-I'LL NEVER REACH THEM IN TIME! NEVER!
VE HAFF MADE IT! NOW VE BREAK INTO DER ROOM!
VE VILL KEEP GUARD OUT HERE!
DERE HE ISS!
WHA--? NAZIS!! WITH CAPTAIN AMËRICA!! IT-- IT CAN'T BE!!!
YOU CAN GUESS VHY VE ARE HERE, GENERAL!
IT MUST BE DONE! VE HAFF OUR ORDERS! DERE ISS NO OTHER VAY!
BUT YOU--! CAPTAIN AMERICA! YOU'RE POINTING THAT GUN AT ME! NO--NOT YOU!
FIRE! FIRE! VHY DO YOU VAIT? YOU HAFF YOUR ORDERS! FIRE!
I-- CANNOT! SOMETHING--IS--STOPPING--ME--! I--CAN'T--!
10
DER DRUG VAS NOT SHTRONG ENOUGH TO MAKE HIM DO THIS!
BUT HE MUST DO IT! IT MUST BE HIS HAND ON DER TRIGGER!
EFFEN IF I MUST DO IT FOR HIM!
THE END
THE SHOT IS FIRED! AND THEN PANDEMONIUM BREAKS LOOSE -- AS WE SHALL SEE, NEXT ISSUE! DON'T DARE MISS IT!

Mails of SUSPENSE

SEND YOUR
LETTERS TO: THE MARVEL COMICS GROUP, SECOND FLOOR 625 MADISON AVE., NEW YORK, N. Y. 10022

—How about that? Ol' Shell-head finally had a happy ending for once! As for Cap, he's only happy when he's in trouble, so he's probably laughing like mad right now! Anyway, let's get to your letters real fast, because it gives us our one wonderful chance to talk back to you!!"

Dear Stan and Jack,

I have just read SUSPENSE #63. The origin of Captain America was very disappointing. I always thought he was a normal man trained to the peak of perfection. Here you come out and say he took some potion to make him the way he is now. I thought the idea of bringing back the old war tales was great, but the idea of the potion has ruined Captain America in my opinion. Splitting a comic up into two strips is a poor idea also. It doesn't leave room for enough action. Careful—don't ruin Iron Man too! Jerry Rogers, 1855 Carolina Ave. Butte, Montana

Jer, after reading your letter, it looks as though we must have studied a book called "How To Do Everything Wrong" before writing SUSPENSE! But, it merely underscores the occasional hazards of trying to give you fans what you want. We only presented Cap's origin because thousands of you asked for it— and naturally, in order not to deceive you, we did it just as it had been presented in the forties! So what happened? Now a lot of you are disappointed! (Although, we must admit that a lot more of you flipped over it!) Anyway, you'll be happy to know that Cap eventually *lost* the effects of the serum which was injected into him during his origin, and today he's just a fun-loving, typical, American, Marvel-type, average, everyday super-hero! (We have more details about this cataclysmic subject in future C.A. strips, so watch for 'em).

Dear Stan and Group,

I've just finished TALES OF SUSPENSE #63. I think it was a great mag. I was never happier at one of your announcements than that you planned to revive Bucky Barnes. I had never known the origin of Cap before and enjoyed it very much. I think you truly outdid yourselves in this ish. I mainly enjoy all of your Marvel mags. I think your mags would be better if you stopped dividing your covers as I go bats trying to decide which one of the stories to read first. Guess that's all the ways I can think of to improve your already all-but-perfect mags. David Welch, Box 126 Simpson, So. Car.

So you're having trouble deciding which of our minor masterpieces to read first, eh Davey? We've a suggestion to make—but, it's so staggering in its stark simplicity that it may overwhelm you! Why not just start with Page 1 and keep reading till you reach the end of the mag? We hate to sound like radicals, but it just may solve the problem! Let us know what happens, huh?

—Remember, each ish of SUSPENSE will feature an M.M.M.S. special announcements page, with every type of unexpected goodie we can dream up. And, for those of you who haven't joined our ranks yet, there's still time to fill out the coupon in this issue! We'll wait for you—because, as every Marvel madman knows, we're all heart! (And we're still pantin' for your buck!)

Dear Stan and Don and Jack

You guys are artists! I believe in all your characters, especially Captain America. Hooo boy, he's just great. Oh whee! I wish he had a whole magazine to himself! The madmen on your staff have created a convention of artistic liberty which makes use of many of the so-called "discoveries" of modern expressionism. You are not held to the narrow limits of the official art-world, and as a consequence you produce a consistent body of remarkable

work that creates its own artistic and literary forms within the framework of a pure and living myth, and it embodies the most precise simulacrum of the spirit of American Primitivism that can be found in any art today! Nelson B. Richardson, South 403 Amherst College, Amherst, Mass.

We're not sure we dig what you're saying, Nelse, but if it's a compliment we're much obliged! (And if it isn't, we won't worry about it—who'd ever know?)

THE MIGHTY MARVEL CHECKLIST
A Line-Up Of Some Of The Marvel-ous Mags On Sale Right Now!

FANTASTIC FOUR #40: If you read no other magazine all month, you must read this one! It's the thriller you've been waiting for—"The Battle of The Baxter Building!", in which the fabulous F.F. wages a no-holds-barred free-for-all against the most dangerous villain of all time— Doctor Doom! It's like WOW!

SPIDER-MAN #26: Not only is Spidey one of the greatest action characters in the Marvel line-up, but we've now added the element of MYSTERY to his tales! You're sure to go batty as you try to figure out the secret of "The Man In The Crime-Master's Mask!"

AVENGERS #17: When a mag is this good, it's almost a shame to say anything about it! This one has everything! A brand new line-up of Avengers! Captain America more heroic than ever before! And, to top it all off, the sensational theme is: "The Search For The Hulk!" How great can a comic mag get!

X-MEN #11: Another shocker from the House of Ideas! This one was specially produced in answer to many of your earnest requests, and it finally presents the end of the evil mutants! Also, wait till you meet The Stranger!

DAREDEVIL #8: For those of you who've wondered what we could possibly come up with to top our previous sensational D.D. thrillers, here's your answer—in spades! D.D. battles the most off-beat villain of the month (ANY month) when he tackles the startling, stupifying Stiltman! You'll have a ball!

THOR #117: This unforgettable epic is entitled: "Into The Blaze Of Battle!" and you'd better hang onto your seat when you read it! It features Thor's quest for an enchanted packet—a quest which brings him face-to-face with tragedy on an Asiatic battlefield! It's drenched with glory!

STRANGE TALES #134: This month's Torch and Thing thriller features a long-awaited surprise! The title will give you the idea: "Enter—the Watcher!" As for Dr. Strange, he's up to his amulet in all kinds of magical mishaps! This ish is for you!

ASTONISH #69: Giant-Man finally catches up with the Human Top, and their battle is a joy to behold! As for the incredible Hulk, it's so full of strange surprises that the only thing we'll tell now is that ol' green skin is winning every popularity poll in town hands down!

SGT. FURY #19: Those of you who were shaken up by the death of Pamela Hawley last ish, (and that includes 'most everybody) won't want to miss "An Eye For An Eye" in which Nick Fury meets up with the man responsible for Pam's death! It's stark, gripping drama as only Marvel can present it!

—Let's try something new now! We won't tell you how great next ish will be! We'll merely say that it features a new type of Iron Man drama, and the usual brand of Captain America thrills. If you want to miss it, go ahead! (But, don't write to us for back issues later on—we're betting it'll be a sellout!) See? We don't always boast! (Sometimes we merely brag!) Anyway, those of you who are lucky enough, and sagatious enough to latch onto SUSPENSE #68 will find us here to welcome you with the greatest 12¢ reading value we can create! So, till then, may your dreams be delightful, and your shield never tarnish!

TALES OF SUSPENSE #68,

AUGUST 1965,

"THE SENTINEL AND THE SPY!"

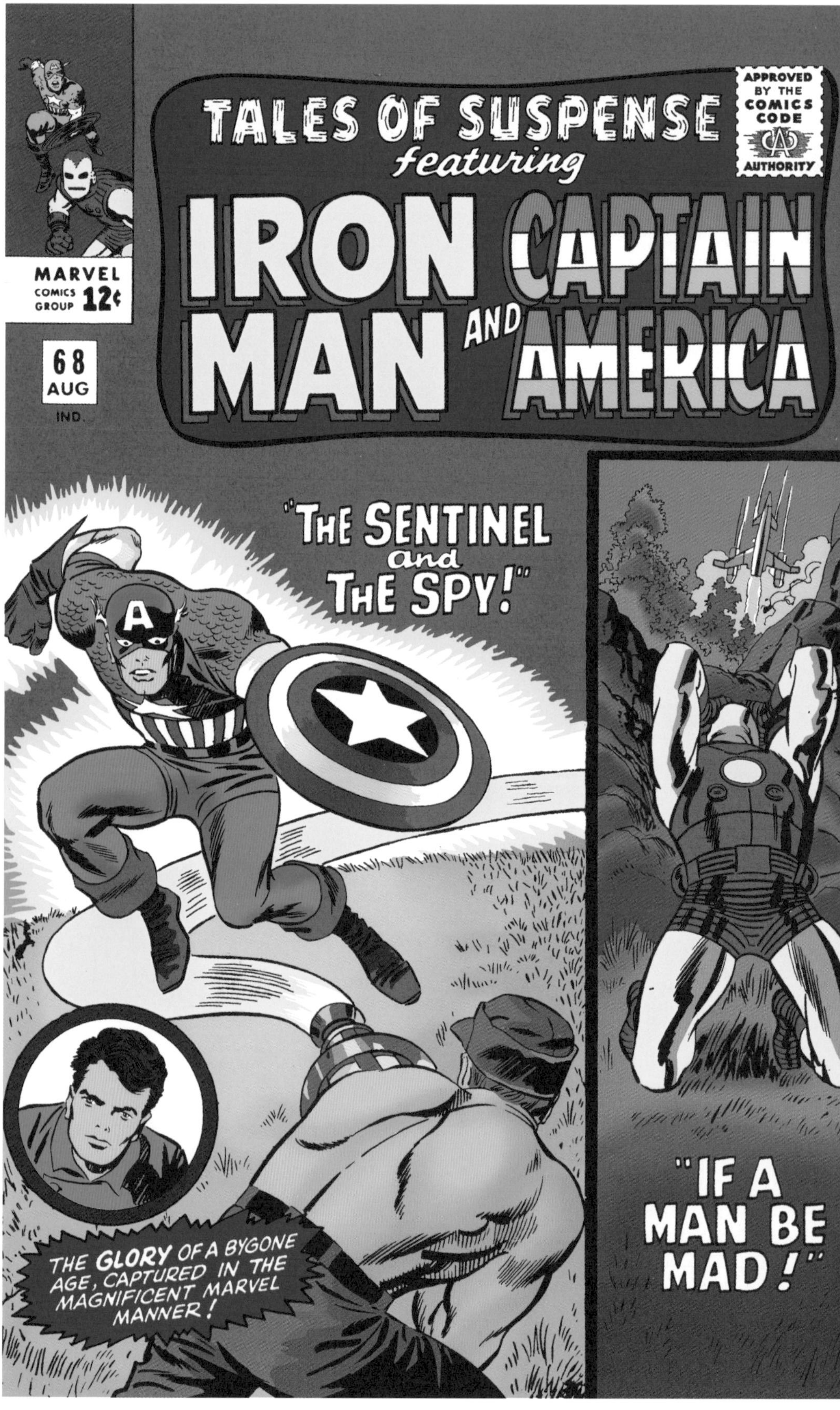
MARVEL COMICS GROUP 12¢
68 AUG
IND.
APPROVED BY THE COMICS CODE AUTHORITY
TALES OF SUSPENSE featuring
IRON MAN AND CAPTAIN AMERICA
"THE SENTINEL and THE SPY!"
THE GLORY OF A BYGONE AGE, CAPTURED IN THE MAGNIFICENT MARVEL MANNER!
"IF A MAN BE MAD!"

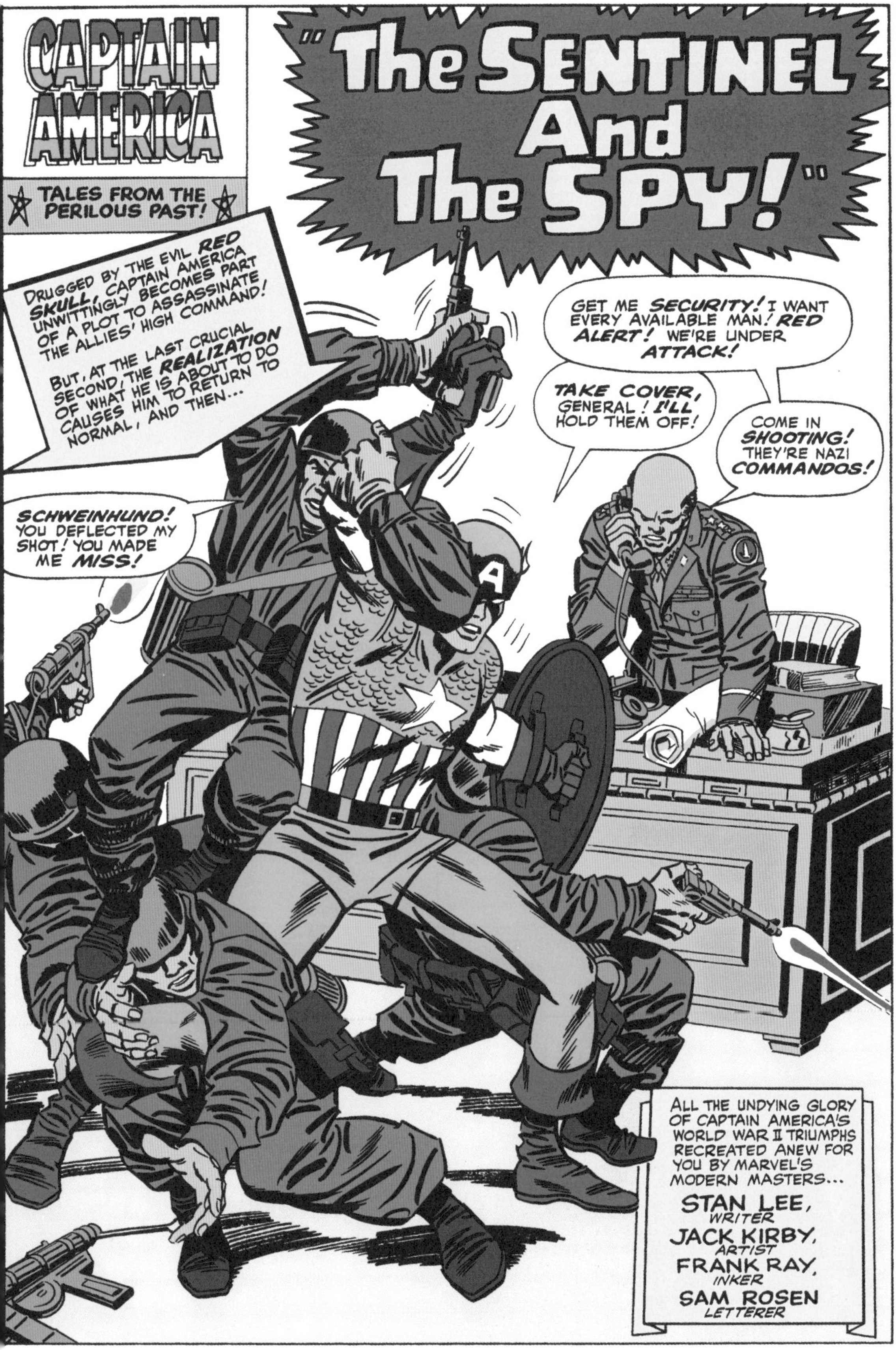
CAPTAIN AMERICA
"The SENTINEL And The SPY!"
TALES FROM THE PERILOUS PAST!
DRUGGED BY THE EVIL RED SKULL, CAPTAIN AMERICA UNWITTINGLY BECOMES PART OF A PLOT TO ASSASSINATE THE ALLIES' HIGH COMMAND!
BUT, AT THE LAST CRUCIAL SECOND, THE REALIZATION OF WHAT HE IS ABOUT TO DO CAUSES HIM TO RETURN TO NORMAL, AND THEN...
GET ME SECURITY! I WANT EVERY AVAILABLE MAN! RED ALERT! WE'RE UNDER ATTACK!
TAKE COVER, GENERAL! I'LL HOLD THEM OFF!
COME IN SHOOTING! THEY'RE NAZI COMMANDOS!
SCHWEINHUND! YOU DEFLECTED MY SHOT! YOU MADE ME MISS!
ALL THE UNDYING GLORY OF CAPTAIN AMERICA'S WORLD WAR II TRIUMPHS RECREATED ANEW FOR YOU BY MARVEL'S MODERN MASTERS...
STAN LEE, WRITER
JACK KIRBY, ARTIST
FRANK RAY, INKER
SAM ROSEN LETTERER

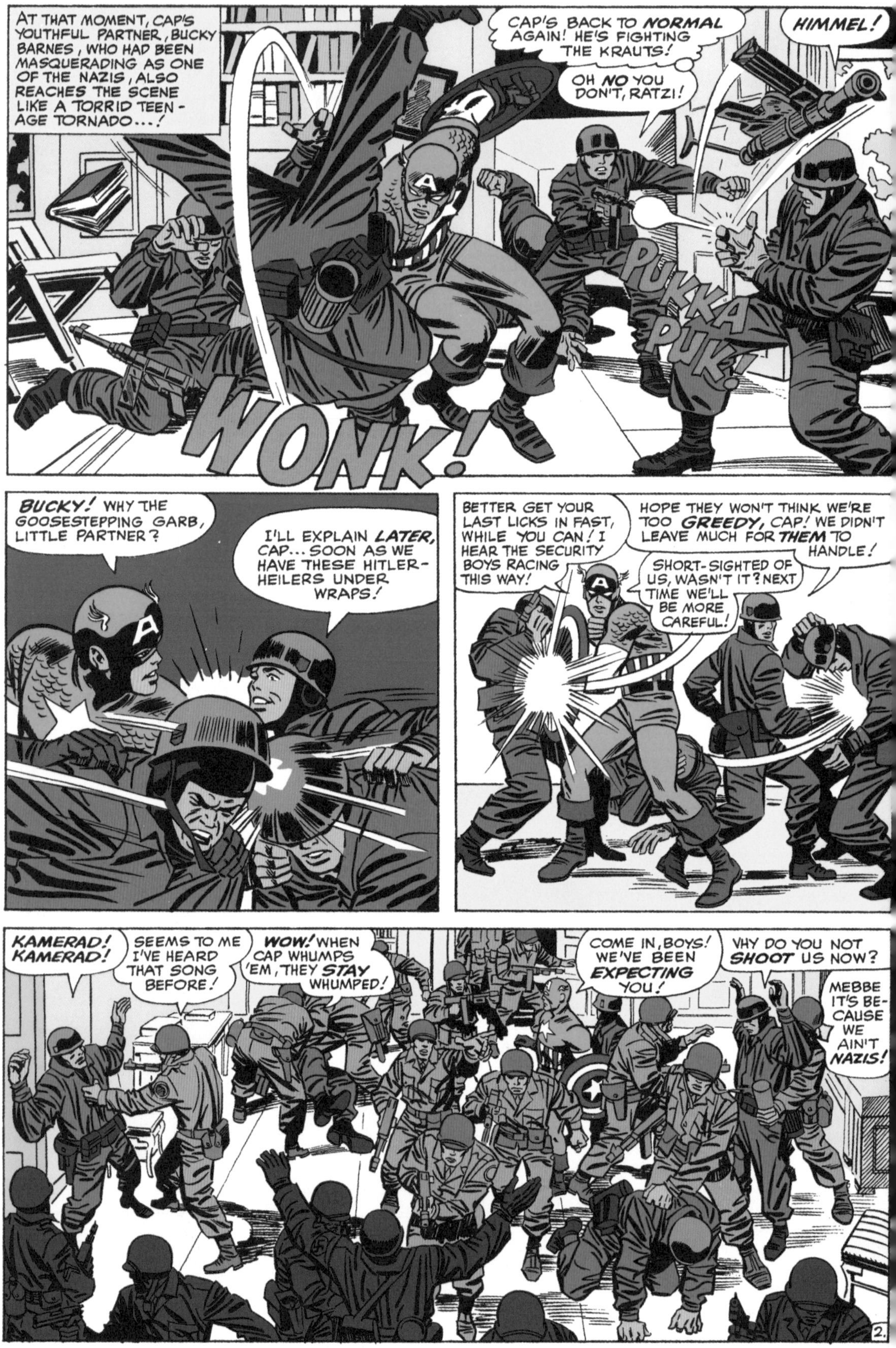
AT THAT MOMENT, CAP'S YOUTHFUL PARTNER, BUCKY BARNES, WHO HAD BEEN MASQUERADING AS ONE OF THE NAZIS, ALSO REACHES THE SCENE LIKE A TORRID TEEN-AGE TORNADO...!
CAP'S BACK TO NORMAL AGAIN! HE'S FIGHTING THE KRAUTS!
OH NO YOU DON'T, RATZI!
HIMMEL!
PUKKA PUKKA PUK!
WONK!
BUCKY! WHY THE GOOSESTEPPING GARB, LITTLE PARTNER?
I'LL EXPLAIN LATER, CAP... SOON AS WE HAVE THESE HITLER-HEILERS UNDER WRAPS!
BETTER GET YOUR LAST LICKS IN FAST, WHILE YOU CAN! I HEAR THE SECURITY BOYS RACING THIS WAY!
HOPE THEY WON'T THINK WE'RE TOO GREEDY, CAP! WE DIDN'T LEAVE MUCH FOR THEM TO HANDLE!
SHORT-SIGHTED OF US, WASN'T IT? NEXT TIME WE'LL BE MORE CAREFUL!
KAMERAD! KAMERAD!
SEEMS TO ME I'VE HEARD THAT SONG BEFORE!
WOW! WHEN CAP WHUMPS 'EM, THEY STAY WHUMPED!
COME IN, BOYS! WE'VE BEEN EXPECTING YOU!
VHY DO YOU NOT SHOOT US NOW?
MEBBE IT'S BE-CAUSE WE AIN'T NAZIS!
2.

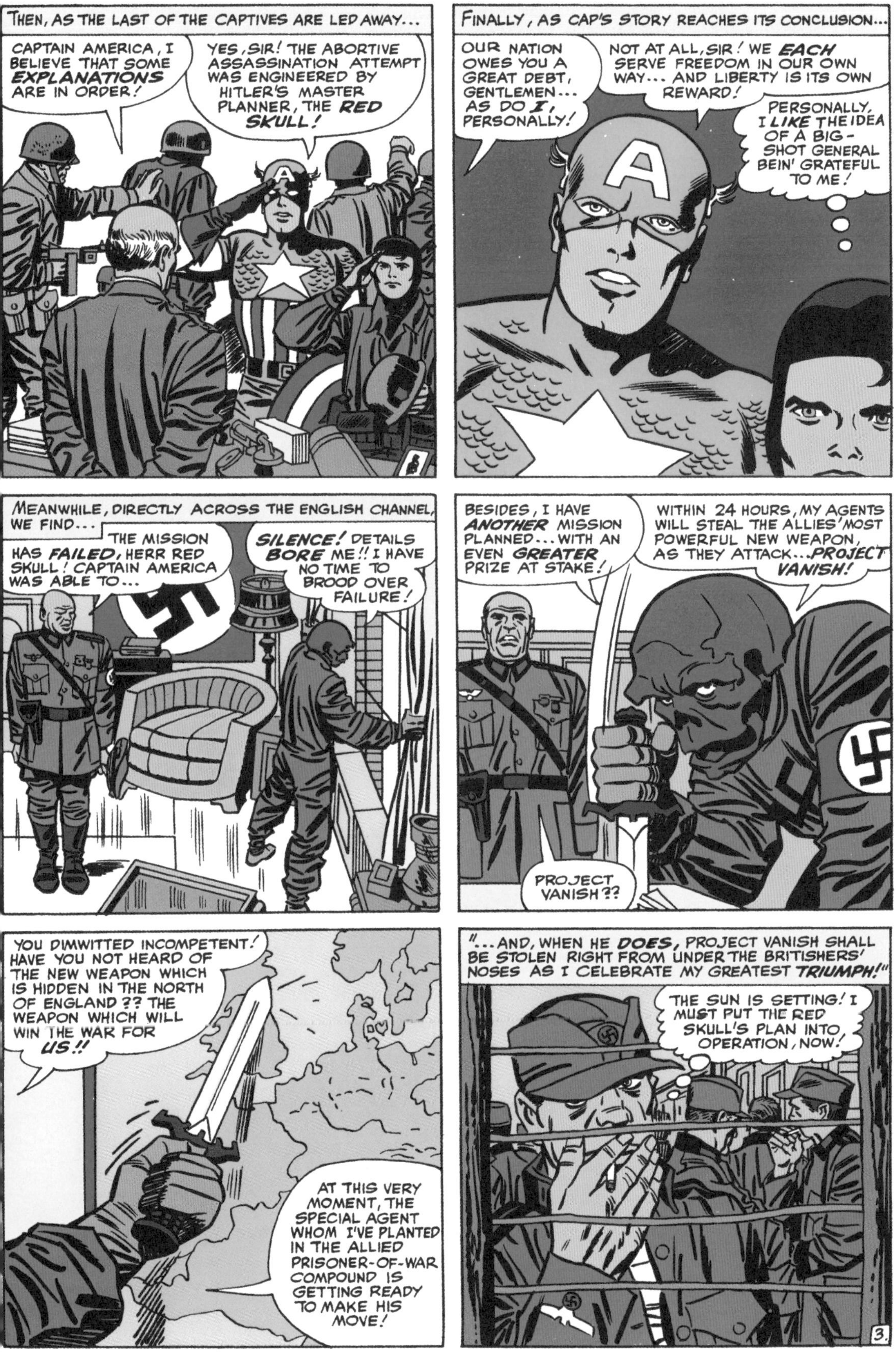
THEN, AS THE LAST OF THE CAPTIVES ARE LED AWAY...
CAPTAIN AMERICA, I BELIEVE THAT SOME EXPLANATIONS ARE IN ORDER!
YES, SIR! THE ABORTIVE ASSASSINATION ATTEMPT WAS ENGINEERED BY HITLER'S MASTER PLANNER, THE RED SKULL!
FINALLY, AS CAP'S STORY REACHES ITS CONCLUSION...
OUR NATION OWES YOU A GREAT DEBT, GENTLEMEN... AS DO I, PERSONALLY!
NOT AT ALL, SIR! WE EACH SERVE FREEDOM IN OUR OWN WAY... AND LIBERTY IS ITS OWN REWARD!
PERSONALLY, I LIKE THE IDEA OF A BIG-SHOT GENERAL BEIN' GRATEFUL TO ME!
MEANWHILE, DIRECTLY ACROSS THE ENGLISH CHANNEL, WE FIND...
THE MISSION HAS FAILED, HERR RED SKULL! CAPTAIN AMERICA WAS ABLE TO...
SILENCE! DETAILS BORE ME!! I HAVE NO TIME TO BROOD OVER FAILURE!
BESIDES, I HAVE ANOTHER MISSION PLANNED... WITH AN EVEN GREATER PRIZE AT STAKE!
WITHIN 24 HOURS, MY AGENTS WILL STEAL THE ALLIES' MOST POWERFUL NEW WEAPON, AS THEY ATTACK... PROJECT VANISH!
PROJECT VANISH??
YOU DIMWITTED INCOMPETENT! HAVE YOU NOT HEARD OF THE NEW WEAPON WHICH IS HIDDEN IN THE NORTH OF ENGLAND?? THE WEAPON WHICH WILL WIN THE WAR FOR US!!
AT THIS VERY MOMENT, THE SPECIAL AGENT WHOM I'VE PLANTED IN THE ALLIED PRISONER-OF-WAR COMPOUND IS GETTING READY TO MAKE HIS MOVE!
"...AND, WHEN HE DOES, PROJECT VANISH SHALL BE STOLEN RIGHT FROM UNDER THE BRITISHERS' NOSES AS I CELEBRATE MY GREATEST TRIUMPH!"
THE SUN IS SETTING! I MUST PUT THE RED SKULL'S PLAN INTO OPERATION, NOW!
3.

WOLFGANG! I HAVE CHOSEN *YOU!* YOU MUST TRY TO *ESCAPE* NOW!

NO! *NO!* DON'T MAKE ME DO IT! I DON'T *WANT* TO! THEY'LL *SHOOT* ME!

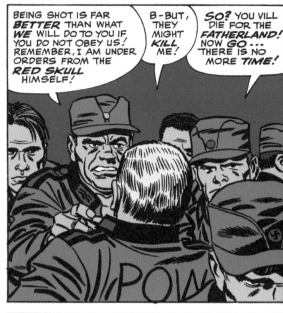

BEING SHOT IS FAR *BETTER* THAN WHAT *WE* WILL DO TO YOU IF YOU DO NOT OBEY US! REMEMBER, I AM UNDER ORDERS FROM THE *RED SKULL* HIMSELF!

B-BUT, THEY MIGHT *KILL* ME!

SO? YOU VILL DIE FOR THE *FATHERLAND!* NOW GO... THERE IS NO MORE *TIME!*

I HAVE NO OTHER *CHOICE!* IF I REFUSE, *THEY* WILL MURDER ME BEFORE THE SUN RISES! AT LEAST THE AMERICAN GUARDS MAY BE MORE MERCIFUL!

SO FAR, SO GOOD! HE IS *CERTAIN* TO BE SHOT... AND THEN *I* WILL REPLACE HIM ON THE SUPPLY TRUCK!

A PRISONER... TRYING TO ESCAPE... RIGHT PAST OUR SENTRY POST! HE MUST BE *MAD!*

HALT! HALT... OR I'LL *FIRE!*

I MUST KEEP RUNNING..OR THE *OTHERS* WILL KILL ME!

CAN'T LET HIM *ESCAPE*... BUT THERE'S NO NEED TO TAKE HIS LIFE! I'LL GET HIM IN THE *LEG!*

KRAK!

UHHH!

THUS, EARLY THE NEXT MORNING, PRIVATE STEVE ROGERS AND COMPANY MASCOT BUCKY BARNES GUARD THE NEW PRISONER WHO IS REPLACING THE WOUNDED WOLFGANG...

WHAT A JOB FOR A BATTLE-TRAINED COMBAT MAN... GUARDING A HELPLESS PRISONER!

THAT NEW KRAUT IS SOME MEAN-LOOKING EGG! HASN'T SAID A WORD ALL MORNING!

4.

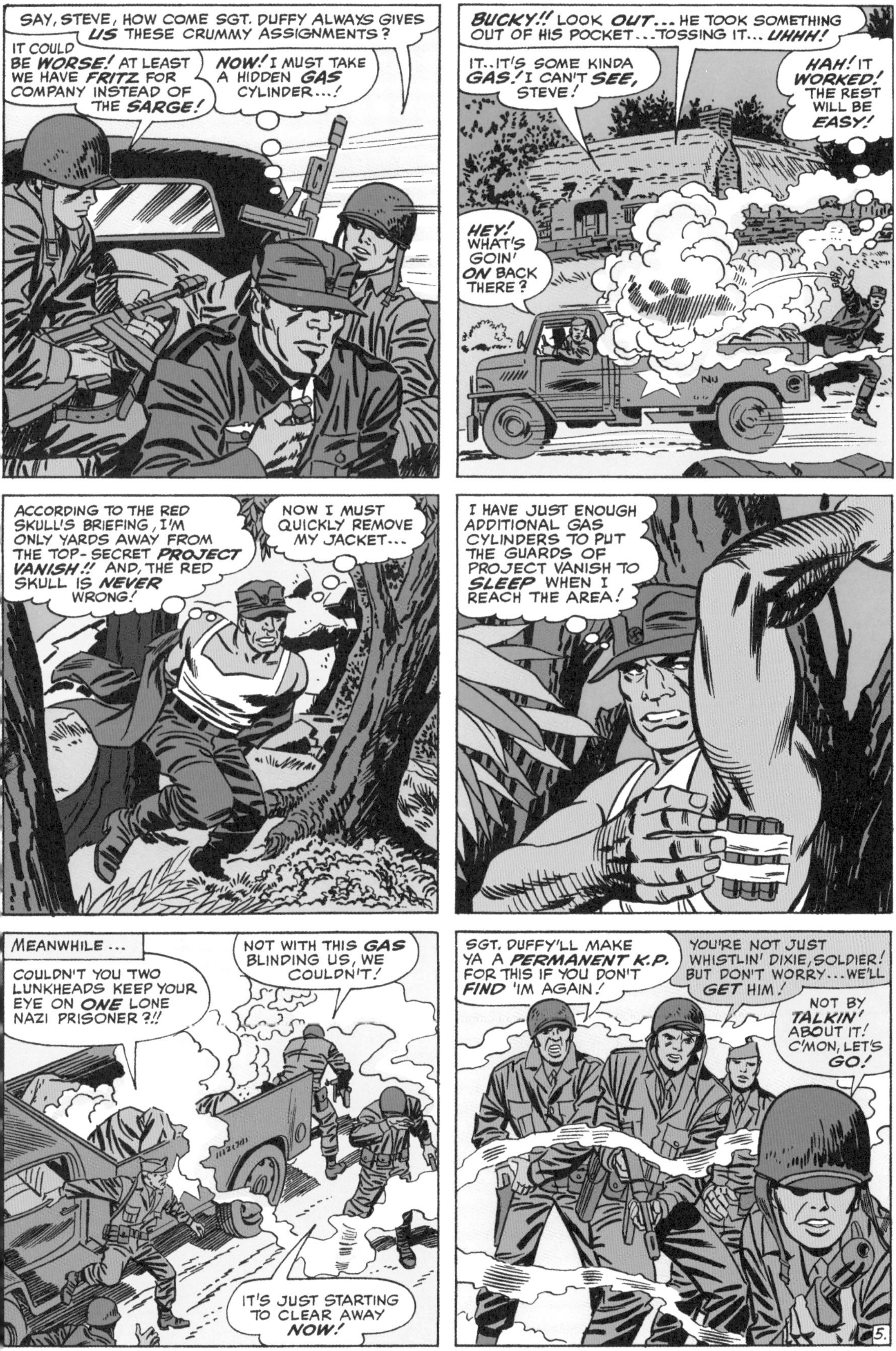
SAY, STEVE, HOW COME SGT. DUFFY ALWAYS GIVES US THESE CRUMMY ASSIGNMENTS?
IT COULD BE WORSE! AT LEAST WE HAVE FRITZ FOR COMPANY INSTEAD OF THE SARGE!
NOW! I MUST TAKE A HIDDEN GAS CYLINDER...!
BUCKY!! LOOK OUT... HE TOOK SOMETHING OUT OF HIS POCKET...TOSSING IT... UHHH!
IT..IT'S SOME KINDA GAS! I CAN'T SEE, STEVE!
HAH! IT WORKED! THE REST WILL BE EASY!
HEY! WHAT'S GOIN' ON BACK THERE?
ACCORDING TO THE RED SKULL'S BRIEFING, I'M ONLY YARDS AWAY FROM THE TOP-SECRET PROJECT VANISH!! AND, THE RED SKULL IS NEVER WRONG!
NOW I MUST QUICKLY REMOVE MY JACKET...
I HAVE JUST ENOUGH ADDITIONAL GAS CYLINDERS TO PUT THE GUARDS OF PROJECT VANISH TO SLEEP WHEN I REACH THE AREA!
MEANWHILE...
COULDN'T YOU TWO LUNKHEADS KEEP YOUR EYE ON ONE LONE NAZI PRISONER?!!
NOT WITH THIS GAS BLINDING US, WE COULDN'T!
IT'S JUST STARTING TO CLEAR AWAY NOW!
SGT. DUFFY'LL MAKE YA A PERMANENT K.P. FOR THIS IF YOU DON'T FIND 'IM AGAIN!
YOU'RE NOT JUST WHISTLIN' DIXIE, SOLDIER! BUT DON'T WORRY...WE'LL GET HIM!
NOT BY TALKIN' ABOUT IT! C'MON, LET'S GO!
5.

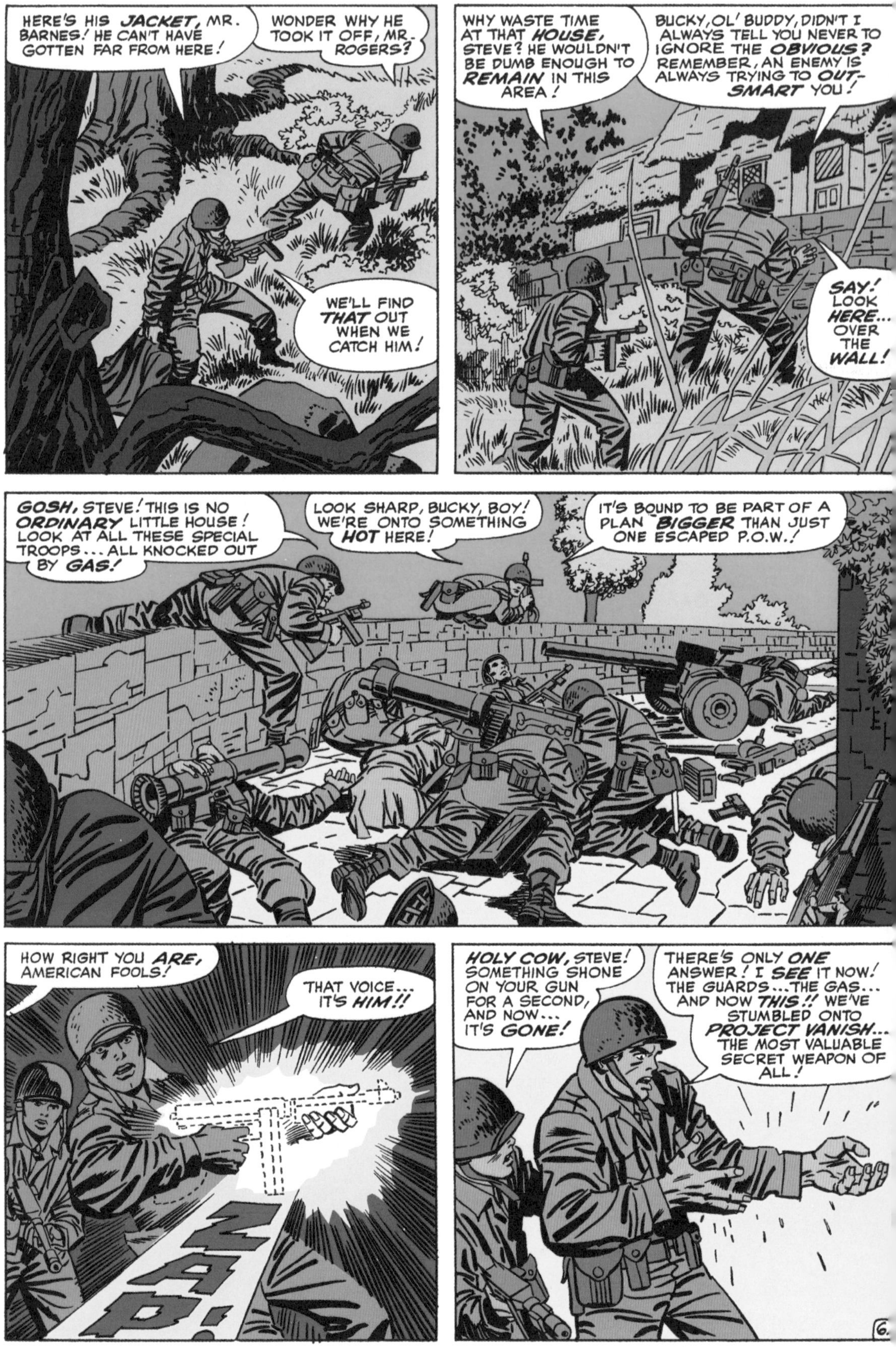
HERE'S HIS JACKET, MR. BARNES! HE CAN'T HAVE GOTTEN FAR FROM HERE!
WONDER WHY HE TOOK IT OFF, MR. ROGERS?
WE'LL FIND THAT OUT WHEN WE CATCH HIM!
WHY WASTE TIME AT THAT HOUSE, STEVE? HE WOULDN'T BE DUMB ENOUGH TO REMAIN IN THIS AREA!
BUCKY, OL' BUDDY, DIDN'T I ALWAYS TELL YOU NEVER TO IGNORE THE OBVIOUS? REMEMBER, AN ENEMY IS ALWAYS TRYING TO OUT-SMART YOU!
SAY! LOOK HERE... OVER THE WALL!
GOSH, STEVE! THIS IS NO ORDINARY LITTLE HOUSE! LOOK AT ALL THESE SPECIAL TROOPS... ALL KNOCKED OUT BY GAS!
LOOK SHARP, BUCKY, BOY! WE'RE ONTO SOMETHING HOT HERE!
IT'S BOUND TO BE PART OF A PLAN BIGGER THAN JUST ONE ESCAPED P.O.W.!
HOW RIGHT YOU ARE, AMERICAN FOOLS!
THAT VOICE... IT'S HIM!!
ZAP!
HOLY COW, STEVE! SOMETHING SHONE ON YOUR GUN FOR A SECOND, AND NOW... IT'S GONE!
THERE'S ONLY ONE ANSWER! I SEE IT NOW! THE GUARDS... THE GAS... AND NOW THIS!! WE'VE STUMBLED ONTO PROJECT VANISH... THE MOST VALUABLE SECRET WEAPON OF ALL!
6.

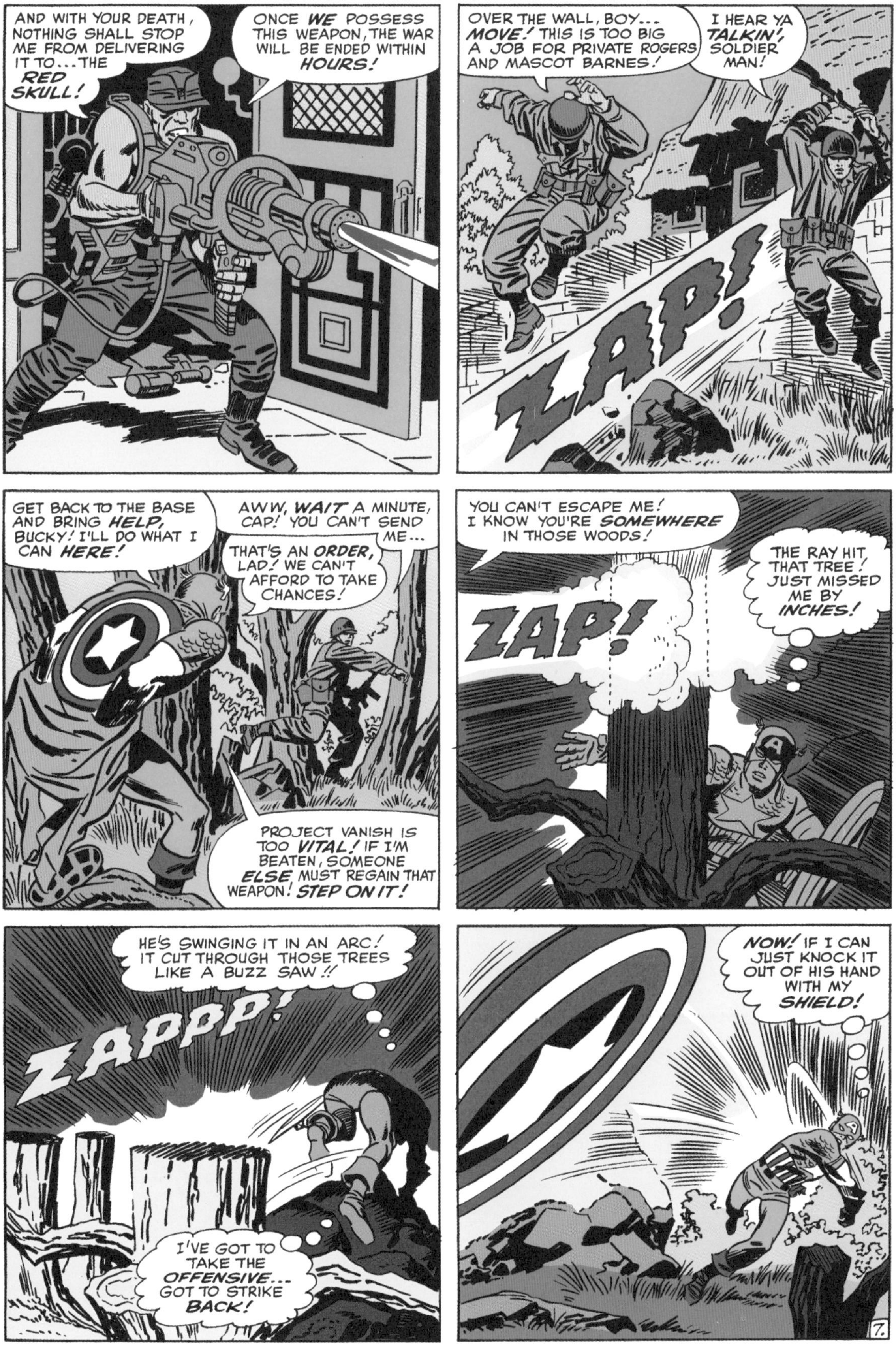
AND WITH YOUR DEATH, NOTHING SHALL STOP ME FROM DELIVERING IT TO... THE RED SKULL!
ONCE WE POSSESS THIS WEAPON, THE WAR WILL BE ENDED WITHIN HOURS!
OVER THE WALL, BOY... MOVE! THIS IS TOO BIG A JOB FOR PRIVATE ROGERS AND MASCOT BARNES!
I HEAR YA TALKIN', SOLDIER MAN!
ZAP!
GET BACK TO THE BASE AND BRING HELP, BUCKY! I'LL DO WHAT I CAN HERE!
AWW, WAIT A MINUTE, CAP! YOU CAN'T SEND ME...
THAT'S AN ORDER, LAD! WE CAN'T AFFORD TO TAKE CHANCES!
PROJECT VANISH IS TOO VITAL! IF I'M BEATEN, SOMEONE ELSE MUST REGAIN THAT WEAPON! STEP ON IT!
YOU CAN'T ESCAPE ME! I KNOW YOU'RE SOMEWHERE IN THOSE WOODS!
THE RAY HIT THAT TREE! JUST MISSED ME BY INCHES!
ZAP!
HE'S SWINGING IT IN AN ARC! IT CUT THROUGH THOSE TREES LIKE A BUZZ SAW!!
ZAPPP!
I'VE GOT TO TAKE THE OFFENSIVE... GOT TO STRIKE BACK!
NOW! IF I CAN JUST KNOCK IT OUT OF HIS HAND WITH MY SHIELD!
7.

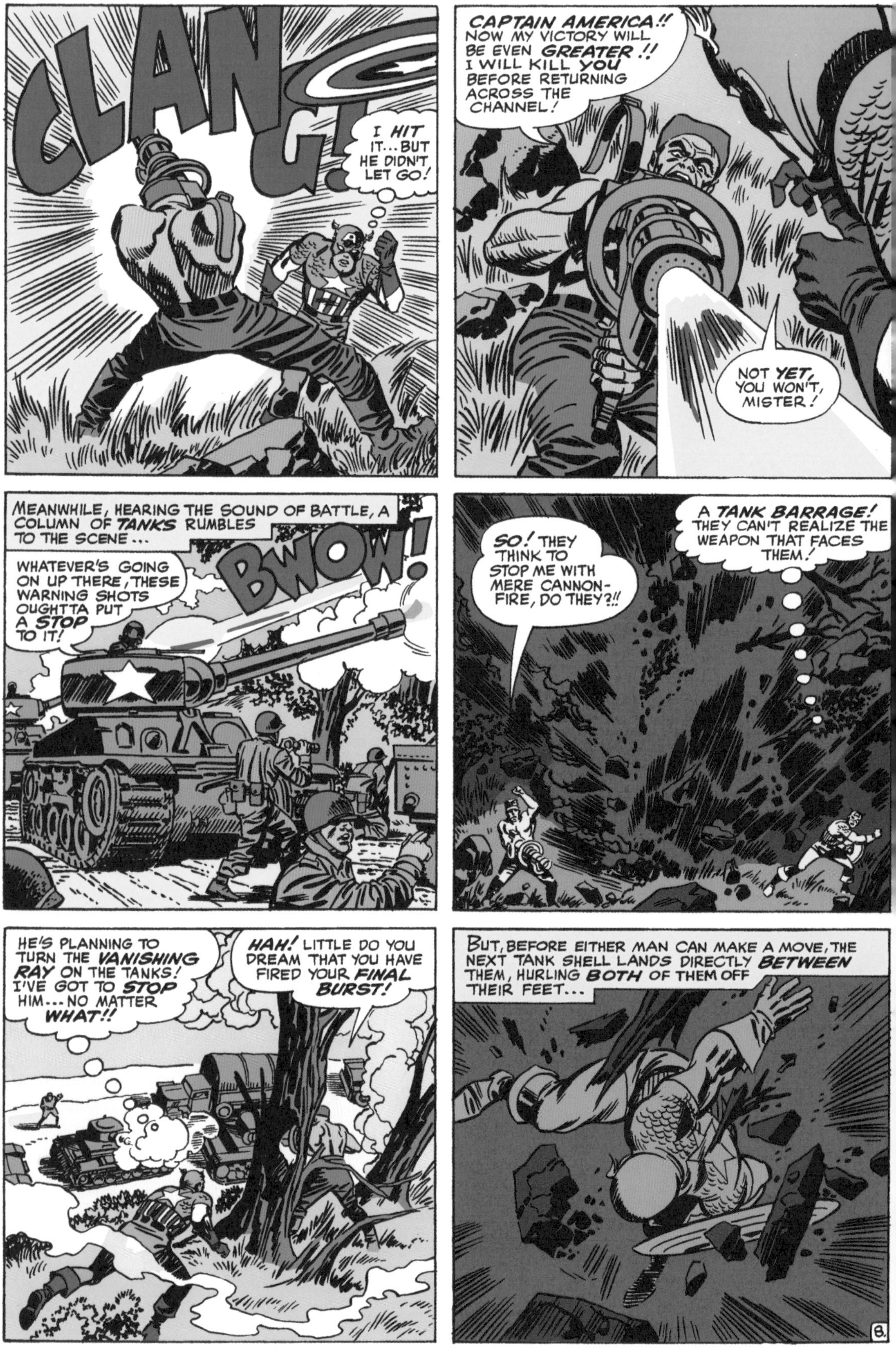
CLANG!
I HIT IT... BUT HE DIDN'T LET GO!
CAPTAIN AMERICA!! NOW MY VICTORY WILL BE EVEN GREATER!! I WILL KILL YOU BEFORE RETURNING ACROSS THE CHANNEL!
NOT YET, YOU WON'T, MISTER!
MEANWHILE, HEARING THE SOUND OF BATTLE, A COLUMN OF TANKS RUMBLES TO THE SCENE...
WHATEVER'S GOING ON UP THERE, THESE WARNING SHOTS OUGHTTA PUT A STOP TO IT!
BWOW!
SO! THEY THINK TO STOP ME WITH MERE CANNON-FIRE, DO THEY?!!
A TANK BARRAGE! THEY CAN'T REALIZE THE WEAPON THAT FACES THEM!
HE'S PLANNING TO TURN THE VANISHING RAY ON THE TANKS! I'VE GOT TO STOP HIM... NO MATTER WHAT!!
HAH! LITTLE DO YOU DREAM THAT YOU HAVE FIRED YOUR FINAL BURST!
BUT, BEFORE EITHER MAN CAN MAKE A MOVE, THE NEXT TANK SHELL LANDS DIRECTLY BETWEEN THEM, HURLING BOTH OF THEM OFF THEIR FEET...
8.

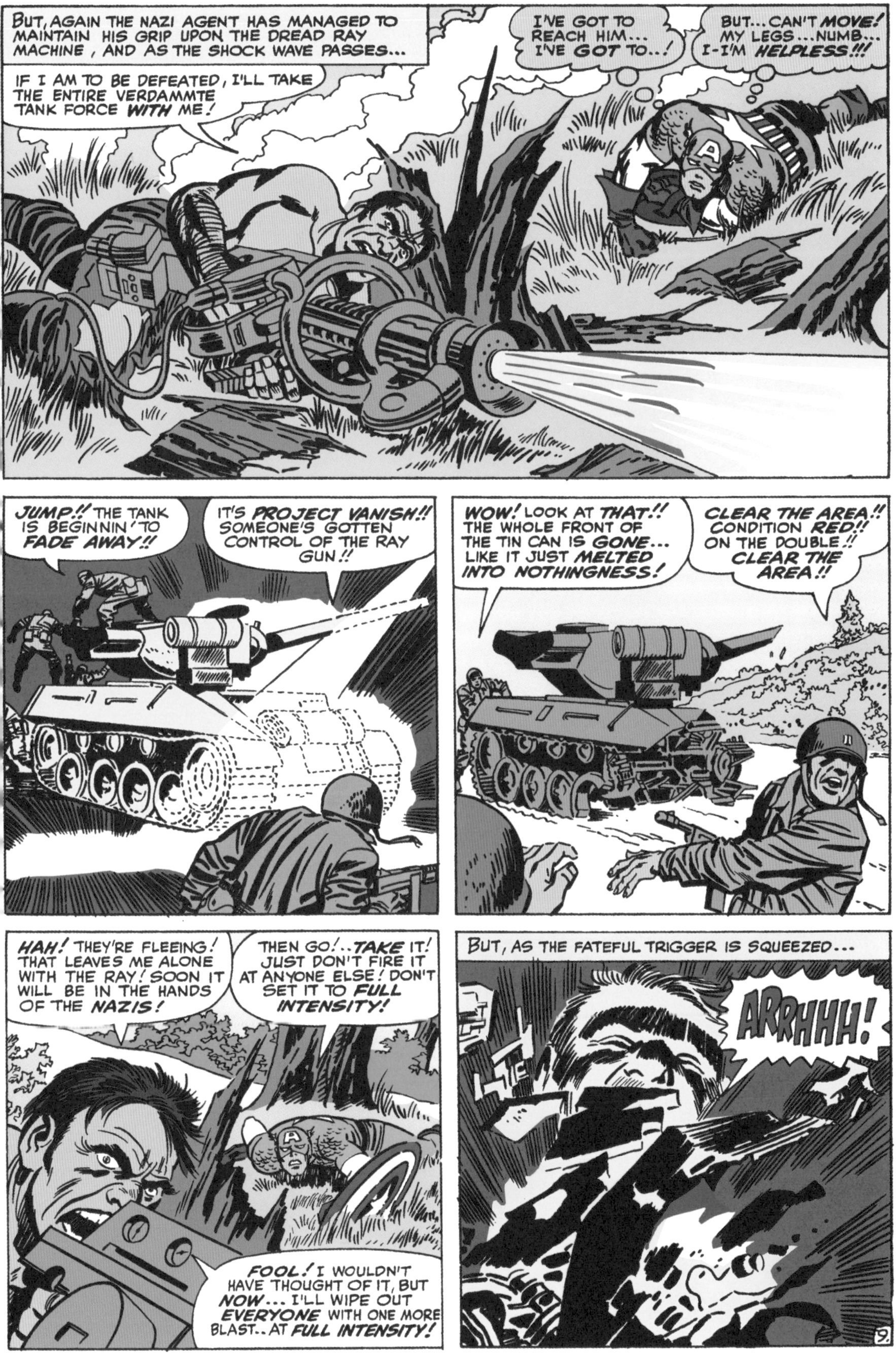
BUT, AGAIN THE NAZI AGENT HAS MANAGED TO MAINTAIN HIS GRIP UPON THE DREAD RAY MACHINE, AND AS THE SHOCK WAVE PASSES...
IF I AM TO BE DEFEATED, I'LL TAKE THE ENTIRE VERDAMMTE TANK FORCE WITH ME!
I'VE GOT TO REACH HIM... I'VE GOT TO...!
BUT...CAN'T MOVE! MY LEGS...NUMB... I-I'M HELPLESS!!!
JUMP!! THE TANK IS BEGINNIN' TO FADE AWAY!!
IT'S PROJECT VANISH!! SOMEONE'S GOTTEN CONTROL OF THE RAY GUN!!
WOW! LOOK AT THAT!! THE WHOLE FRONT OF THE TIN CAN IS GONE... LIKE IT JUST MELTED INTO NOTHINGNESS!
CLEAR THE AREA!! CONDITION RED!! ON THE DOUBLE!! CLEAR THE AREA!!
HAH! THEY'RE FLEEING! THAT LEAVES ME ALONE WITH THE RAY! SOON IT WILL BE IN THE HANDS OF THE NAZIS!
THEN GO!..TAKE IT! JUST DON'T FIRE IT AT ANYONE ELSE! DON'T SET IT TO FULL INTENSITY!
FOOL! I WOULDN'T HAVE THOUGHT OF IT, BUT NOW... I'LL WIPE OUT EVERYONE WITH ONE MORE BLAST.. AT FULL INTENSITY!
BUT, AS THE FATEFUL TRIGGER IS SQUEEZED...
ARRHHH!
9.

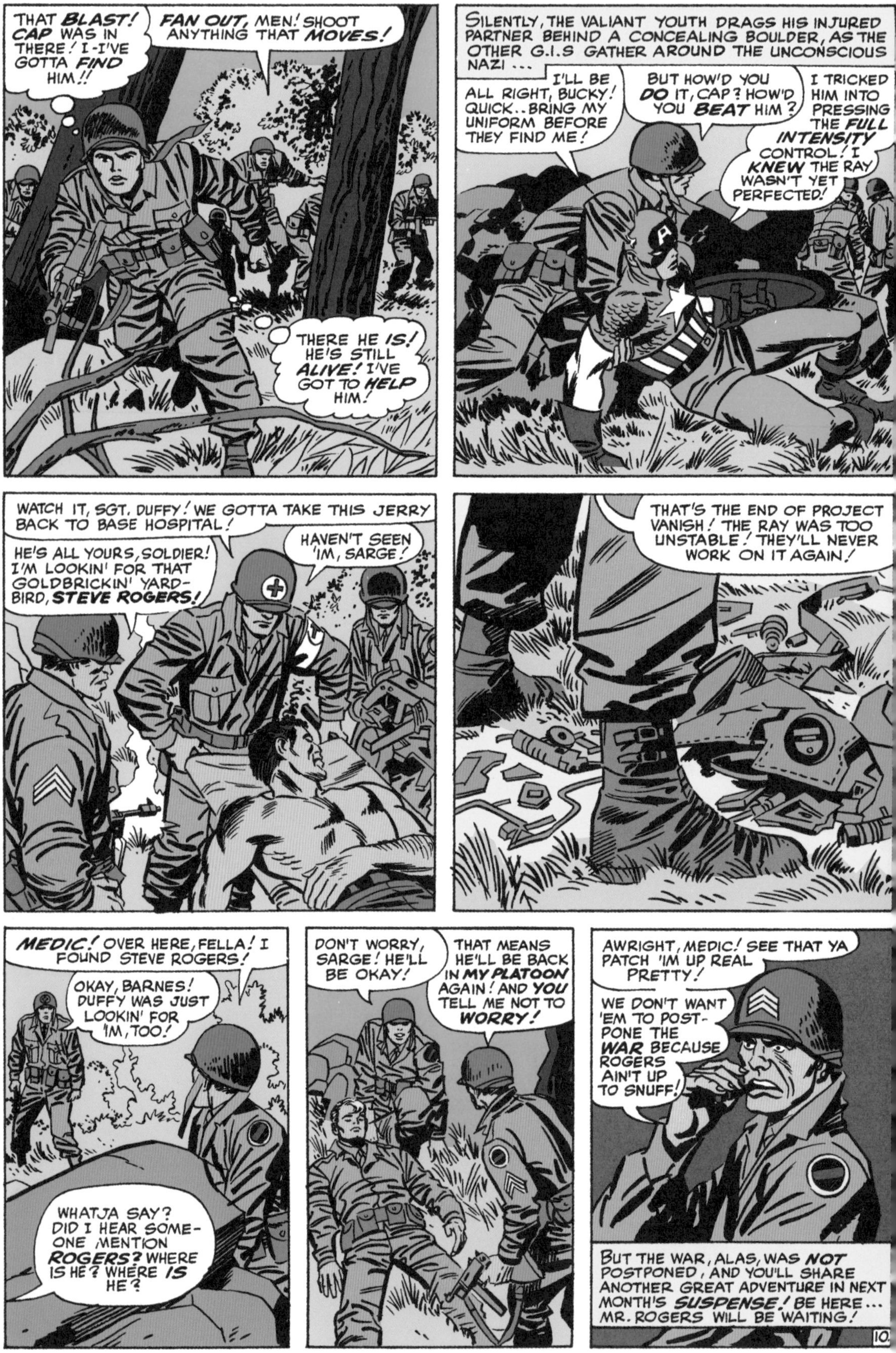
THAT BLAST! CAP WAS IN THERE! I-I'VE GOTTA FIND HIM!!
FAN OUT, MEN! SHOOT ANYTHING THAT MOVES!
THERE HE IS! HE'S STILL ALIVE! I'VE GOT TO HELP HIM!
SILENTLY, THE VALIANT YOUTH DRAGS HIS INJURED PARTNER BEHIND A CONCEALING BOULDER, AS THE OTHER G.I.S GATHER AROUND THE UNCONSCIOUS NAZI ...
I'LL BE ALL RIGHT, BUCKY! QUICK.. BRING MY UNIFORM BEFORE THEY FIND ME!
BUT HOW'D YOU DO IT, CAP? HOW'D YOU BEAT HIM?
I TRICKED HIM INTO PRESSING THE FULL INTENSITY CONTROL! I KNEW THE RAY WASN'T YET PERFECTED!
WATCH IT, SGT. DUFFY! WE GOTTA TAKE THIS JERRY BACK TO BASE HOSPITAL!
HE'S ALL YOURS, SOLDIER! I'M LOOKIN' FOR THAT GOLDBRICKIN' YARD-BIRD, STEVE ROGERS!
HAVEN'T SEEN 'IM, SARGE!
THAT'S THE END OF PROJECT VANISH! THE RAY WAS TOO UNSTABLE! THEY'LL NEVER WORK ON IT AGAIN!
MEDIC! OVER HERE, FELLA! I FOUND STEVE ROGERS!
OKAY, BARNES! DUFFY WAS JUST LOOKIN' FOR 'IM, TOO!
WHATJA SAY? DID I HEAR SOME-ONE MENTION ROGERS? WHERE IS HE? WHERE IS HE?
DON'T WORRY, SARGE! HE'LL BE OKAY!
THAT MEANS HE'LL BE BACK IN MY PLATOON AGAIN! AND YOU TELL ME NOT TO WORRY!
AWRIGHT, MEDIC! SEE THAT YA PATCH 'IM UP REAL PRETTY!
WE DON'T WANT 'EM TO POST-PONE THE WAR BECAUSE ROGERS AIN'T UP TO SNUFF!
BUT THE WAR, ALAS, WAS NOT POSTPONED, AND YOU'LL SHARE ANOTHER GREAT ADVENTURE IN NEXT MONTH'S SUSPENSE! BE HERE... MR. ROGERS WILL BE WAITING!
10.

Mails of SUSPENSE

SEND YOUR LETTERS TO: THE MARVEL COMICS GROUP, SECOND FLOOR 625 MADISON AVE., NEW YORK, N. Y. 10022

Dear Stan and Don and Jack,

SUSPENSE #65 was great! Knock off those balloons on the covers, o.k.? Iron Man was superb, and it was really a thrill seeing Tony's old armor again. Kudos to Stan for a great story—I had thought that someone had found his old armor when it was the other way around! Sorry, Stan, but I'd never heard of the Red Skull. Say, this story seems that you took a Cap story of the 1940's and just drew it. Let's keep your own style of the 1960's!! By the way, I gave a speech on Marvel in Public Speaking class and I got an "A"! I love my M.M.M.S. stuff! Stan, how does a comic script look? Does it tell the artist what to draw in each panel or does it just tell the dialogue? You do me a large enough favor simply by putting out your superb comic magazines. Thanks for existing!!

Rick Wrigley, 5505 Virginia
Kansas City, Mo. 64110

And you, sir, are welcome! It's kinda difficult to describe what a mixed-up Marvel script looks like, Rick. Actually, it's mostly a series of hastily scribbed notes, because the stories are usually created by batting them around in the bullpen, and then, after the artist has gone wild with the drawings, Stan swoops down and polishes up the dialogue. If it sounds rather disorganized to you, that's *it!*

Dear Stan and Don,

I have all your Marvels that say "May" on them. All the rest were up to your extremely high standards of good writing and art, and some above, but, by far, the best is SUSPENSE #65. Words cannot suffice. It showed the raw power of Iron Man's old suit and the strength of his new suit when used without a conscience. I hope, although I don't want to see that cheap punk Weasel Wills again, that you can have the old and new suits clashing again. Have a parallel dimension where there is an old, bad Iron Man and have him defeated. After all, the new suit wants to win, too. On rereading this, I realize I haven't shown my emotion regarding it too clearly so I hope this will suffice—should anything happen to my copy, I'm taking the precaution of buying another two copies. Another ish like this and I'll get a life subscription!

Arthur Metz, 35 Ogston Terr.
Malverne, N. Y. 11565

Another few fans like you, Art, who buy three copies of an ish, and we may be able to start *paying* the gang in the bullpen! Thanks a heap, pal!

Dear Stan and Don and Jack,

TALES OF SUSPENSE #65 was your best mag since issue #59. Don's art and Mickey Demeo's inking are great! I have a question that has been bothering me for some time—I have seen Cap and Bucky in their army uniforms walking down the street—then something happens and they are in their costumes and Cap has his shield. Where does it pop up from?

Tim Reiser, 7 Cross St.
Pittsburgh, Pa. 15205

He wears it strapped to his back, Tim. If you keep watching SUSPENSE and the AVENGERS, we'll try to do an illustration depicting how it works. Okay?

THE BIGGEST NEWS YET! When mighty Marvel changes the line-ups in a couple of already successful titles, that's news! But when the changes are as great as these, that's a sensation! We'll give it to you fast, straight, and unvarnished—because nothing we can say could possibly add to the genuine luster of these two fabulous strips! Starting with the issues now on sale, STRANGE TALES will feature "Nick Fury, Agent of S.H.I.E.L.D.", while TALES TO ASTONISH stars "Prince Namor, the Sub-Mariner"! See what we mean? What more can we say, except—don't dare miss 'em!

Dear Stan and Don and Jack,

No, no, no, no!! You can't give us a bunch of Captain America stuff from the forties! We want to see Cap as he is today! Now if you gave Cap his own mag it might be different because then we'd still have tales from today. But as long as SUSPENSE is the only place Cap appears, it's best to keep the forties in the forties and the sixties in the sixties.

Mark Leader, 1501 Ladd St.
Silver Spring, Md. 20902

Golly, Mark, where've you been? Haven't you heard of the adorable AVENGERS? Cap stars in each ish, every single month—and they're as modern and up-to-date as Iron Man's transistors! So, if you want present day stories of our red-white-and-blue Galahad, don't miss a single ish of the AVENGERS—and leave SUSPENSE for those of us who are more the sentimental type!

—You've got to do us one favor! Promise that you won't wear your inimitable Iron Man T-shirt when you're reading a Brand-X mag! But, aside from that, you're on your own! It's your T-shirt—enjoy it! And you'll never have to worry about its transistors running down!

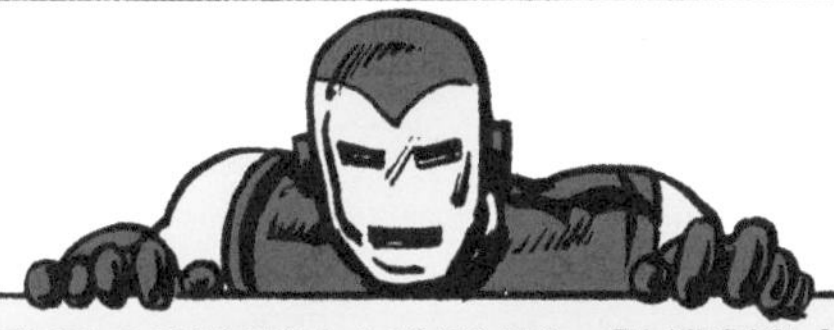

THE MIGHTY MARVEL CHECKLIST

A Line-Up Of Some Of The Marvel-ous Mags On Sale Right Now!

FANTASTIC FOUR #41: Is this the end of the fabulous F. F. at last? The mighty Thing has gone! The remaining three are on the verge of splitting up! And then, the most unexpected danger of all appears! This is truly Marvel's supreme achievement!

SPIDER-MAN #27: Featuring the long-awaited secret of Frederick Foswell—and it won't be what you are expecting! If that doesn't grab you, nothing will!

AVENGERS #18: Marvel's most surprising, mightiest super-team finds an incredible danger behind the iron curtain! See why Captain America's new fighting band is the talk of comicdom today!

X-MEN #12: At last! The long-awaited origin of Professor X—plus the most dramatic introduction of a mysterious new villain that you've ever seen! Stan and Jack pulled out all the stops on this one!

THOR #18: For the first time in recorded history, Goldilocks faces a super-foe who is not only as strong as he—but actually STRONGER! Possibly the greatest new menace ever presented will meet your startled eyes in this epic-making issue!

STRANGE TALES #135: The secret's out at last! Mighty Marvel has bowed to your demands! This ish will be a collector's item before the year's end, for it features the start of the most off-beat series of all: Nick Fury, Agent of S.H.I.E.L.D.! Written by our leader, and drawn by King Kirby! 'Nuff said!

ASTONISH #70: Bursting on the scene with the shock of a thunderclap comes the most famous hero-villain of all time—Sub-Mariner, beginning the most dramatic, spectacular series yet! We predict that the powerful combo of Prince Namor, followed by the incredible Hulk, will make ASTONISH the fastest Marvel sell-out of the month!

SGT. FURY #20: We promised they'd be back, and here they are! The fantastic Blitz Squad of Baron Strucker returns for the most exciting hand-to-hand battle with the Howlers that we've ever presented! It's a real combat shocker!

—Next ish ol' Shell-Head finally faces a foe who is actually more powerful than he! It's the start of a whole new drama-packed problem, so be sure you get in at the beginning! As for Cap, we have a somewhat off-beat type of yarn for him! You'll find it all in SUSPENSE #69, so **join us—you'll recognize** us by our Marvel T-shirts!

BACK AND FORWARD:
TALES OF SUSPENSE #69–74

Lee and Kirby clearly felt more creative confidence placing the solo Captain America in a World War II setting, but the reaction of fans was mixed. Bob Drew's letter (published in *Tales of Suspense* #70) was typical of many. "My only complaint is that all of Cap's episodes are now in the past," he writes, in an otherwise appreciative letter regarding the Red Skull story arc. "I like the Golden Age relived and I'm crazy about Red Skull, but I'd just like to see Cap without Bucky, battling enemies of modern day America."

By the time this letter saw print, Lee and Kirby's own enthusiasm for the war-era stories may also have been flagging, because they were now looking to other genres for inspiration. Thus, while the story arc in *Tales of Suspense* #69–71—based on Kirby's layouts and finished by other artists—is set during the 1940s, it partakes heavily of visual tropes derived from the cinematic traditions of gothic horror; the treasonous British villain is a clichéd "mad scientist" who lives in a remote castle with a laboratory that would make a Hollywood Doctor Frankenstein proud. Then, with issues #71–74, "in answer to your requests" (as Stan noted in a caption), the storyline shifts to the present, at least ostensibly. But the nature of the menace undermines the stated goal. Cap battles a series of "Sleeper" robots constructed by the Red Skull in the 1940s, hidden in Bavaria, and reactivated by Nazi loyalists (who continue to wear their old uniforms)—so the story still feels very much like a World War II adventure.

Both story arcs are also marred by errors of continuity that suggest a degree of distraction on the part of the two primary creators. For example, early in the first tale the mad scientist is shown to have a mechanical hand, the result of a prior laboratory accident—but Kirby and his finishers often seem to forget this detail, occasionally drawing the character with two normal hands. Meanwhile, the second arc ends with one of the more notorious gaffes of Marvel comics history. Having destroyed the Sleeper robots in midair, Cap opens a parachute and floats safely away.

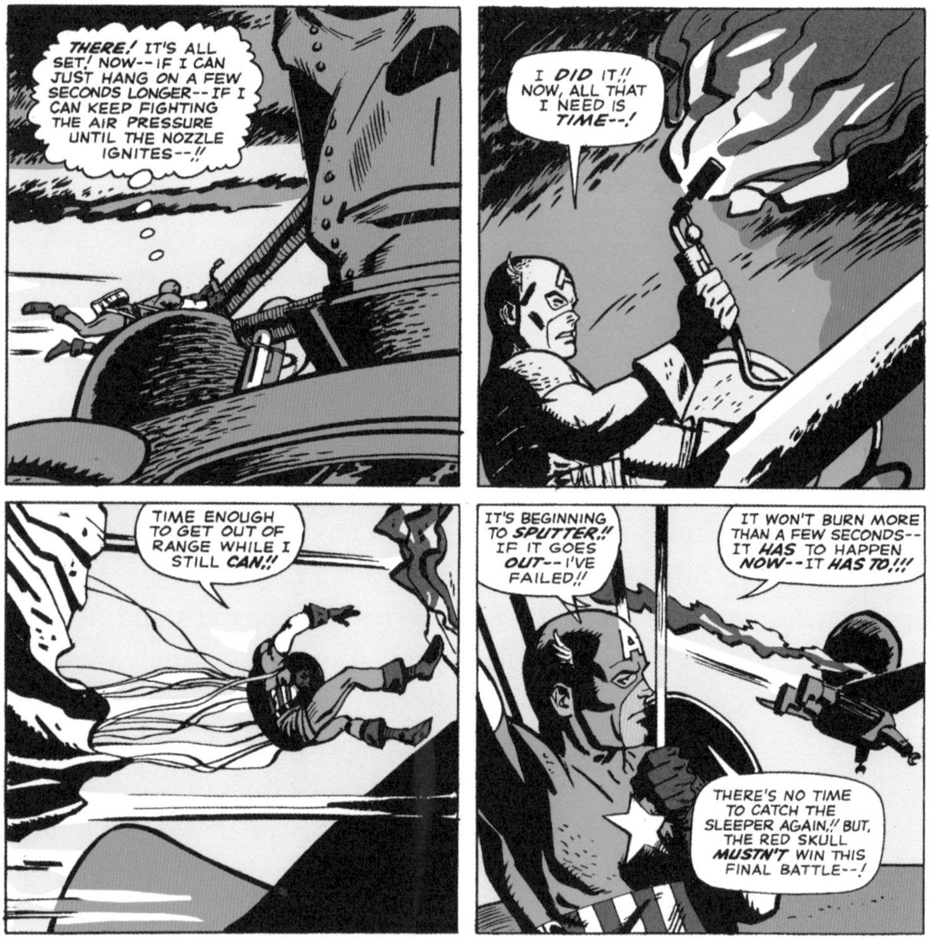
THERE! IT'S ALL SET! NOW--IF I CAN JUST HANG ON A FEW SECONDS LONGER--IF I CAN KEEP FIGHTING THE AIR PRESSURE UNTIL THE NOZZLE IGNITES--!!
I DID IT!! NOW, ALL THAT I NEED IS TIME--!
TIME ENOUGH TO GET OUT OF RANGE WHILE I STILL CAN!!
IT'S BEGINNING TO SPUTTER!! IF IT GOES OUT--I'VE FAILED!!
IT WON'T BURN MORE THAN A FEW SECONDS--IT HAS TO HAPPEN NOW--IT HAS TO!!!
THERE'S NO TIME TO CATCH THE SLEEPER AGAIN!! BUT, THE RED SKULL MUSTN'T WIN THIS FINAL BATTLE--!

But the following month (as you will see in the opening pages of "30 Minutes to Live!" from *Tales of Suspense* #75), the parachute has inconveniently disappeared.

Although these mistakes originated in the increasingly breakneck speed of production as the Marvel brand enjoyed more success, they also suggest something of Lee and Kirby's struggle to produce exciting contemporary tales about a character whose center of gravity always seemed to tilt him in the direction of the past. Over the next few issues they would begin to explore this tension more self-consciously—once again turning their biggest creative problem into an active theme of the work.

TALES OF SUSPENSE #75,

MARCH 1966,

"30 MINUTES TO LIVE!"

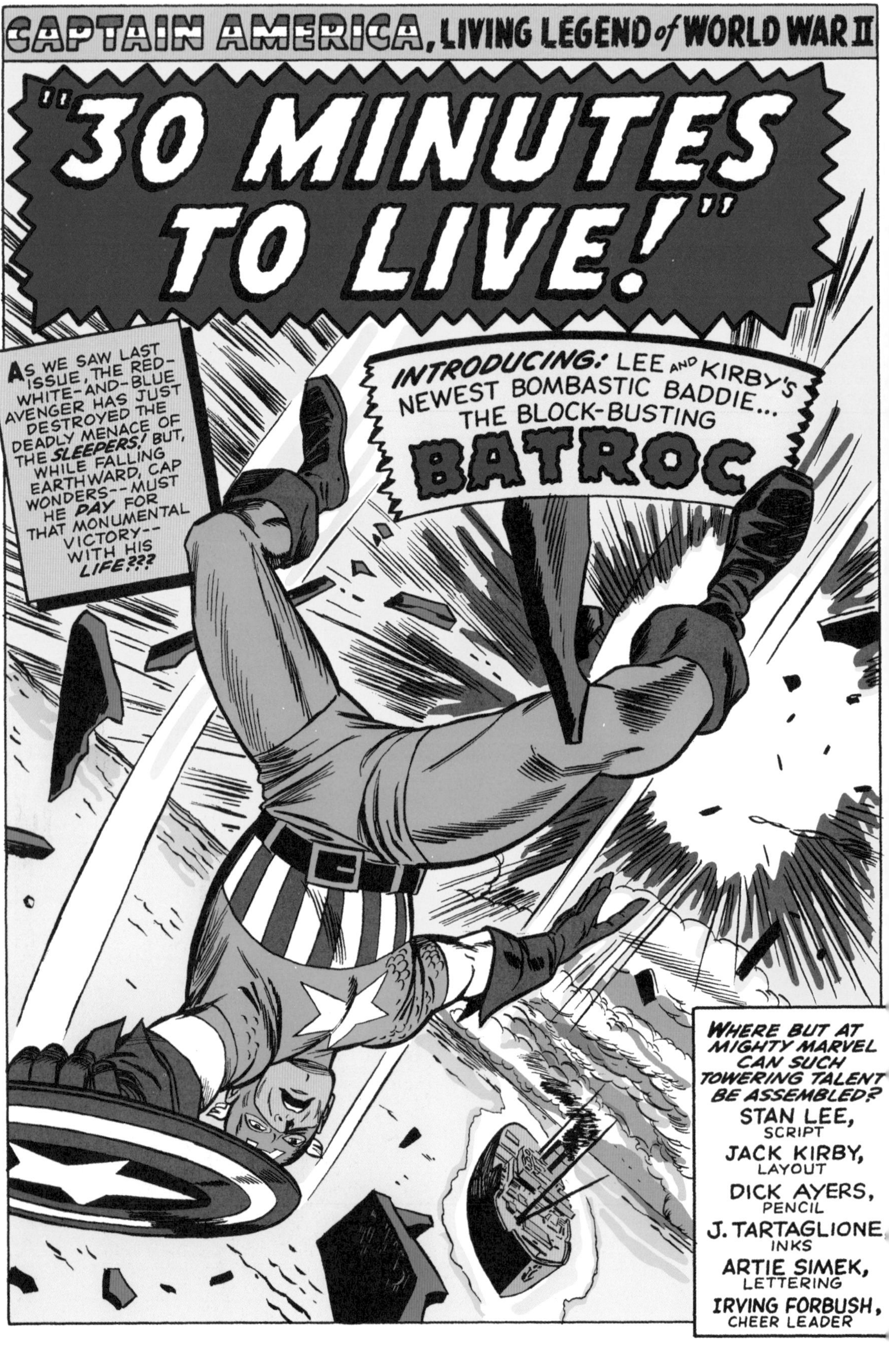
CAPTAIN AMERICA, LIVING LEGEND of WORLD WAR II
"30 MINUTES TO LIVE!"
AS WE SAW LAST ISSUE, THE RED-WHITE-AND-BLUE AVENGER HAS JUST DESTROYED THE DEADLY MENACE OF THE SLEEPERS! BUT, WHILE FALLING EARTHWARD, CAP WONDERS--MUST HE PAY FOR THAT MONUMENTAL VICTORY--WITH HIS LIFE???
INTRODUCING: LEE AND KIRBY'S NEWEST BOMBASTIC BADDIE... THE BLOCK-BUSTING BATROC
WHERE BUT AT MIGHTY MARVEL CAN SUCH TOWERING TALENT BE ASSEMBLED? STAN LEE, SCRIPT JACK KIRBY, LAYOUT DICK AYERS, PENCIL J. TARTAGLIONE, INKS ARTIE SIMEK, LETTERING IRVING FORBUSH, CHEER LEADER

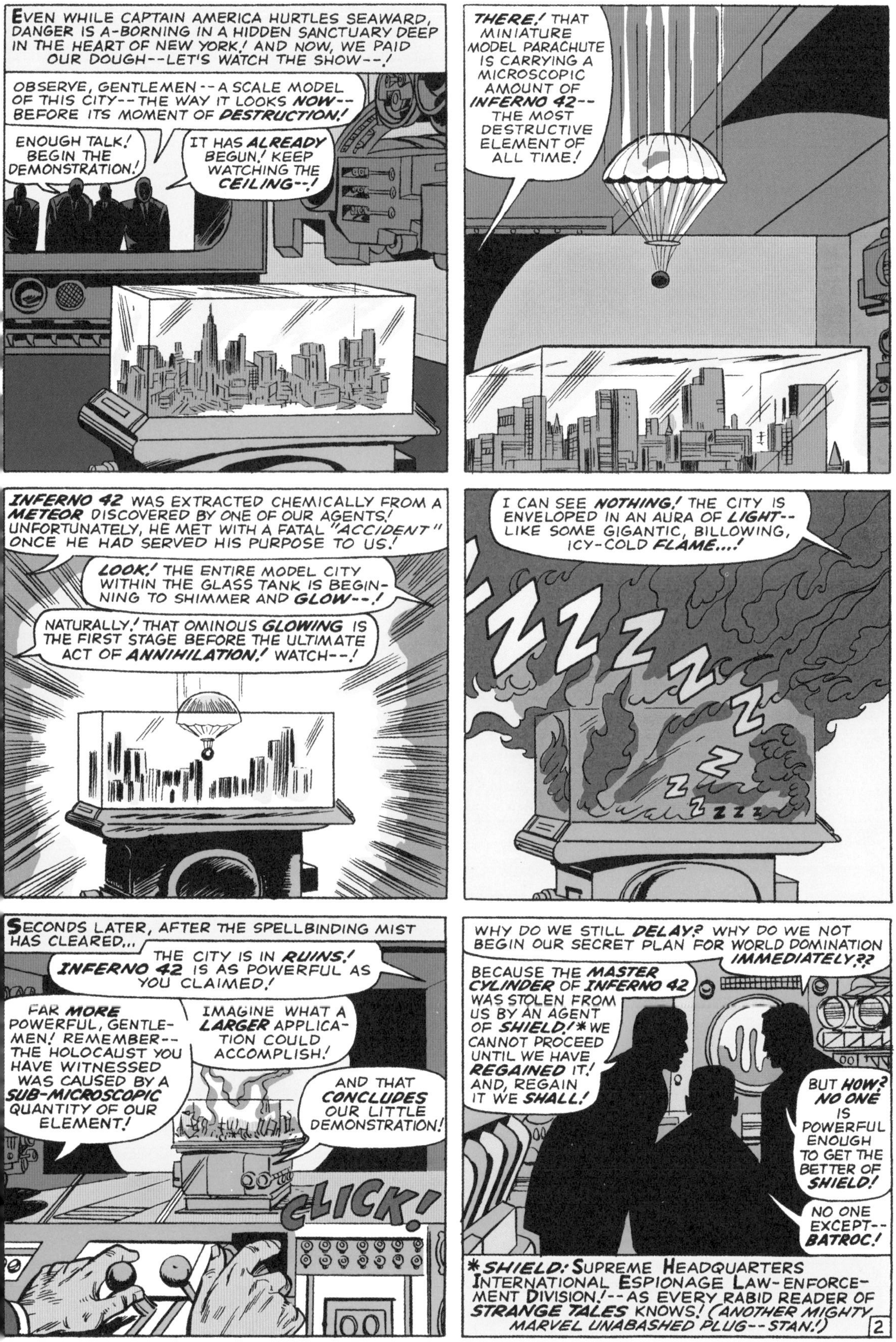
EVEN WHILE CAPTAIN AMERICA HURTLES SEAWARD, DANGER IS A-BORNING IN A HIDDEN SANCTUARY DEEP IN THE HEART OF NEW YORK! AND NOW, WE PAID OUR DOUGH--LET'S WATCH THE SHOW--!
OBSERVE, GENTLEMEN--A SCALE MODEL OF THIS CITY--THE WAY IT LOOKS NOW--BEFORE ITS MOMENT OF DESTRUCTION!
ENOUGH TALK! BEGIN THE DEMONSTRATION!
IT HAS ALREADY BEGUN! KEEP WATCHING THE CEILING--!
THERE! THAT MINIATURE MODEL PARACHUTE IS CARRYING A MICROSCOPIC AMOUNT OF INFERNO 42--THE MOST DESTRUCTIVE ELEMENT OF ALL TIME!
INFERNO 42 WAS EXTRACTED CHEMICALLY FROM A METEOR DISCOVERED BY ONE OF OUR AGENTS! UNFORTUNATELY, HE MET WITH A FATAL "ACCIDENT" ONCE HE HAD SERVED HIS PURPOSE TO US!
LOOK! THE ENTIRE MODEL CITY WITHIN THE GLASS TANK IS BEGINNING TO SHIMMER AND GLOW--!
NATURALLY! THAT OMINOUS GLOWING IS THE FIRST STAGE BEFORE THE ULTIMATE ACT OF ANNIHILATION! WATCH--!
I CAN SEE NOTHING! THE CITY IS ENVELOPED IN AN AURA OF LIGHT--LIKE SOME GIGANTIC, BILLOWING, ICY-COLD FLAME...!
ZZZZZZZZZZZZ
SECONDS LATER, AFTER THE SPELLBINDING MIST HAS CLEARED...
THE CITY IS IN RUINS! INFERNO 42 IS AS POWERFUL AS YOU CLAIMED!
FAR MORE POWERFUL, GENTLEMEN! REMEMBER--THE HOLOCAUST YOU HAVE WITNESSED WAS CAUSED BY A SUB-MICROSCOPIC QUANTITY OF OUR ELEMENT!
IMAGINE WHAT A LARGER APPLICATION COULD ACCOMPLISH!
AND THAT CONCLUDES OUR LITTLE DEMONSTRATION!
CLICK!
WHY DO WE STILL DELAY? WHY DO WE NOT BEGIN OUR SECRET PLAN FOR WORLD DOMINATION IMMEDIATELY??
BECAUSE THE MASTER CYLINDER OF INFERNO 42 WAS STOLEN FROM US BY AN AGENT OF SHIELD!* WE CANNOT PROCEED UNTIL WE HAVE REGAINED IT! AND, REGAIN IT WE SHALL!
BUT HOW? NO ONE IS POWERFUL ENOUGH TO GET THE BETTER OF SHIELD!
NO ONE EXCEPT--BATROC!
*SHIELD: SUPREME HEADQUARTERS INTERNATIONAL ESPIONAGE LAW-ENFORCEMENT DIVISION!--AS EVERY RABID READER OF STRANGE TALES KNOWS! (ANOTHER MIGHTY MARVEL UNABASHED PLUG--STAN!)
2

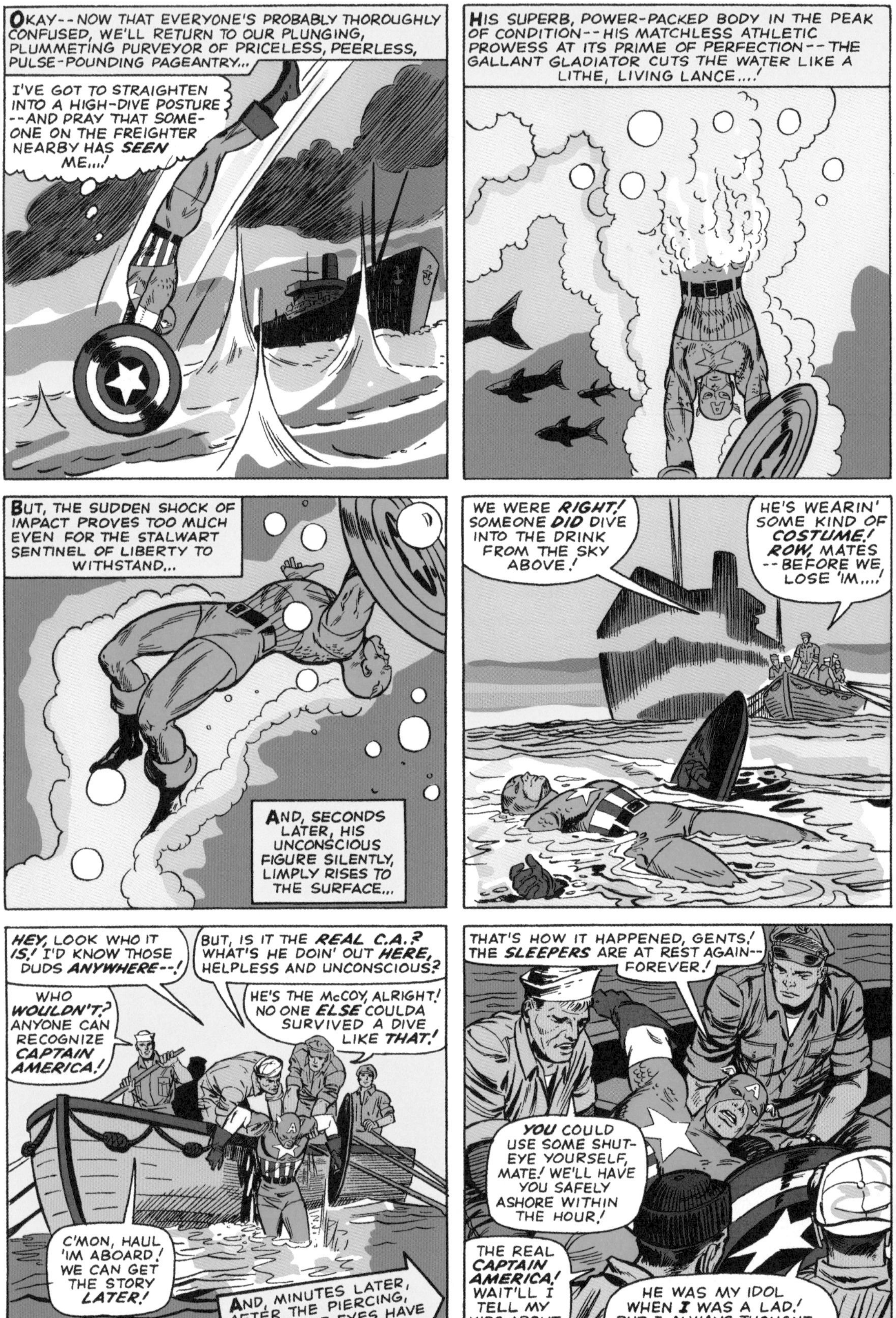
OKAY--NOW THAT EVERYONE'S PROBABLY THOROUGHLY CONFUSED, WE'LL RETURN TO OUR PLUNGING, PLUMMETING PURVEYOR OF PRICELESS, PEERLESS, PULSE-POUNDING PAGEANTRY...
I'VE GOT TO STRAIGHTEN INTO A HIGH-DIVE POSTURE --AND PRAY THAT SOME-ONE ON THE FREIGHTER NEARBY HAS SEEN ME...!
HIS SUPERB, POWER-PACKED BODY IN THE PEAK OF CONDITION--HIS MATCHLESS ATHLETIC PROWESS AT ITS PRIME OF PERFECTION--THE GALLANT GLADIATOR CUTS THE WATER LIKE A LITHE, LIVING LANCE...!
BUT, THE SUDDEN SHOCK OF IMPACT PROVES TOO MUCH EVEN FOR THE STALWART SENTINEL OF LIBERTY TO WITHSTAND...
AND, SECONDS LATER, HIS UNCONSCIOUS FIGURE SILENTLY, LIMPLY RISES TO THE SURFACE...
WE WERE RIGHT! SOMEONE DID DIVE INTO THE DRINK FROM THE SKY ABOVE!
HE'S WEARIN' SOME KIND OF COSTUME! ROW, MATES --BEFORE WE LOSE 'IM...!
HEY, LOOK WHO IT IS! I'D KNOW THOSE DUDS ANYWHERE--!
BUT, IS IT THE REAL C.A.? WHAT'S HE DOIN' OUT HERE, HELPLESS AND UNCONSCIOUS?
WHO WOULDN'T? ANYONE CAN RECOGNIZE CAPTAIN AMERICA!
HE'S THE McCOY, ALRIGHT! NO ONE ELSE COULDA SURVIVED A DIVE LIKE THAT!
C'MON, HAUL 'IM ABOARD! WE CAN GET THE STORY LATER!
AND, MINUTES LATER, AFTER THE PIERCING, STEEL-BLUE EYES HAVE OPENED ONCE MORE...
THAT'S HOW IT HAPPENED, GENTS! THE SLEEPERS ARE AT REST AGAIN--FOREVER!
YOU COULD USE SOME SHUT-EYE YOURSELF, MATE! WE'LL HAVE YOU SAFELY ASHORE WITHIN THE HOUR!
THE REAL CAPTAIN AMERICA! WAIT'LL I TELL MY KIDS ABOUT THIS!
HE WAS MY IDOL WHEN I WAS A LAD! BUT I ALWAYS THOUGHT HE WAS JUST A LEGEND!
3

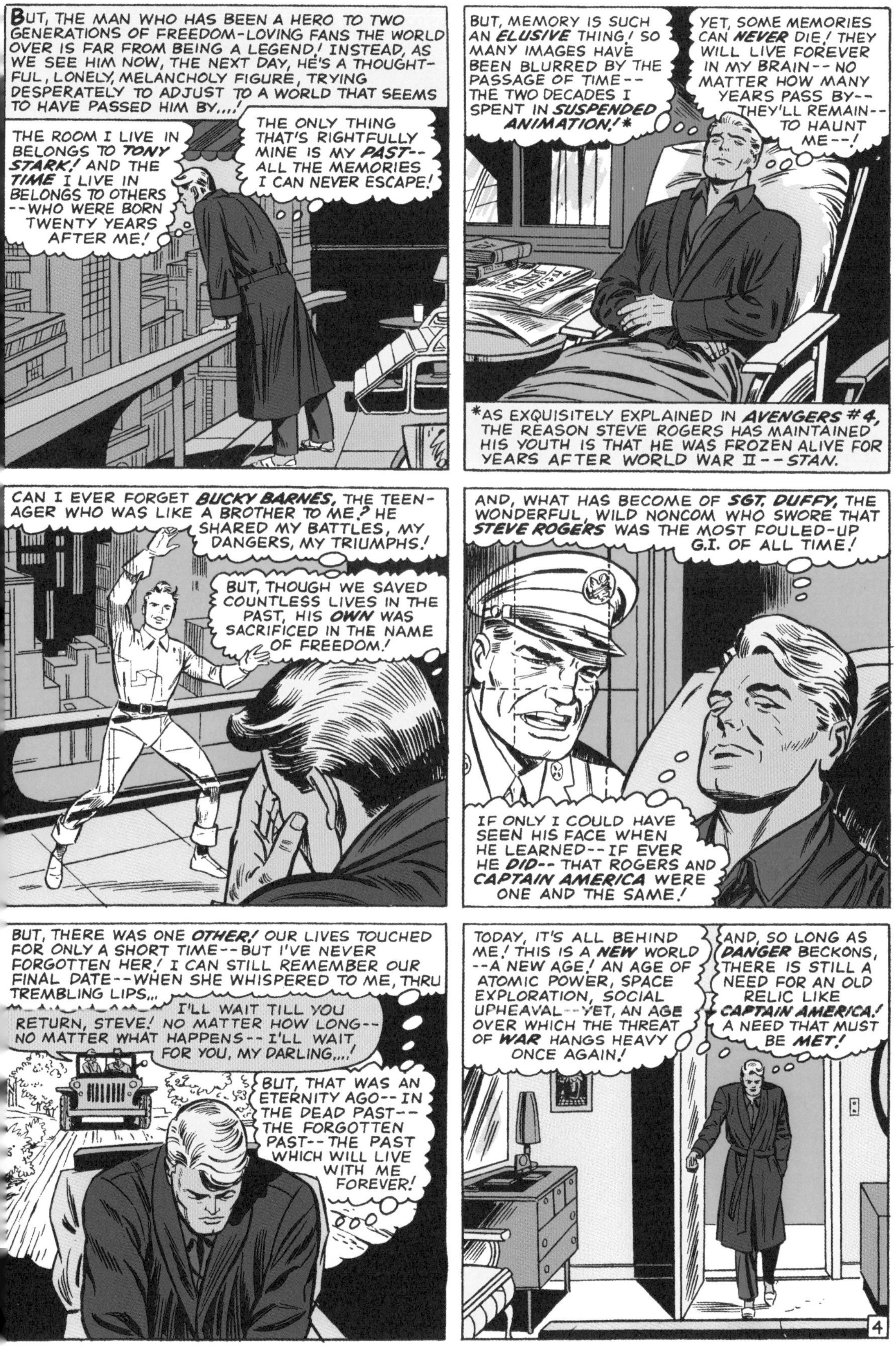
BUT, THE MAN WHO HAS BEEN A HERO TO TWO GENERATIONS OF FREEDOM-LOVING FANS THE WORLD OVER IS FAR FROM BEING A LEGEND! INSTEAD, AS WE SEE HIM NOW, THE NEXT DAY, HE'S A THOUGHTFUL, LONELY, MELANCHOLY FIGURE, TRYING DESPERATELY TO ADJUST TO A WORLD THAT SEEMS TO HAVE PASSED HIM BY...!
THE ROOM I LIVE IN BELONGS TO TONY STARK! AND THE TIME I LIVE IN BELONGS TO OTHERS --WHO WERE BORN TWENTY YEARS AFTER ME!
THE ONLY THING THAT'S RIGHTFULLY MINE IS MY PAST-- ALL THE MEMORIES I CAN NEVER ESCAPE!
BUT, MEMORY IS SUCH AN ELUSIVE THING! SO MANY IMAGES HAVE BEEN BLURRED BY THE PASSAGE OF TIME-- THE TWO DECADES I SPENT IN SUSPENDED ANIMATION!*
YET, SOME MEMORIES CAN NEVER DIE! THEY WILL LIVE FOREVER IN MY BRAIN-- NO MATTER HOW MANY YEARS PASS BY-- THEY'LL REMAIN-- TO HAUNT ME--!
*AS EXQUISITELY EXPLAINED IN AVENGERS #4, THE REASON STEVE ROGERS HAS MAINTAINED HIS YOUTH IS THAT HE WAS FROZEN ALIVE FOR YEARS AFTER WORLD WAR II --STAN.
CAN I EVER FORGET BUCKY BARNES, THE TEEN-AGER WHO WAS LIKE A BROTHER TO ME? HE SHARED MY BATTLES, MY DANGERS, MY TRIUMPHS!
BUT, THOUGH WE SAVED COUNTLESS LIVES IN THE PAST, HIS OWN WAS SACRIFICED IN THE NAME OF FREEDOM!
AND, WHAT HAS BECOME OF SGT. DUFFY, THE WONDERFUL, WILD NONCOM WHO SWORE THAT STEVE ROGERS WAS THE MOST FOULED-UP G.I. OF ALL TIME!
IF ONLY I COULD HAVE SEEN HIS FACE WHEN HE LEARNED-- IF EVER HE DID-- THAT ROGERS AND CAPTAIN AMERICA WERE ONE AND THE SAME!
BUT, THERE WAS ONE OTHER! OUR LIVES TOUCHED FOR ONLY A SHORT TIME--BUT I'VE NEVER FORGOTTEN HER! I CAN STILL REMEMBER OUR FINAL DATE--WHEN SHE WHISPERED TO ME, THRU TREMBLING LIPS...
I'LL WAIT TILL YOU RETURN, STEVE! NO MATTER HOW LONG-- NO MATTER WHAT HAPPENS-- I'LL WAIT FOR YOU, MY DARLING...!
BUT, THAT WAS AN ETERNITY AGO-- IN THE DEAD PAST-- THE FORGOTTEN PAST-- THE PAST WHICH WILL LIVE WITH ME FOREVER!
TODAY, IT'S ALL BEHIND ME! THIS IS A NEW WORLD --A NEW AGE! AN AGE OF ATOMIC POWER, SPACE EXPLORATION, SOCIAL UPHEAVAL--YET, AN AGE OVER WHICH THE THREAT OF WAR HANGS HEAVY ONCE AGAIN!
AND, SO LONG AS DANGER BECKONS, THERE IS STILL A NEED FOR AN OLD RELIC LIKE CAPTAIN AMERICA! A NEED THAT MUST BE MET!
4

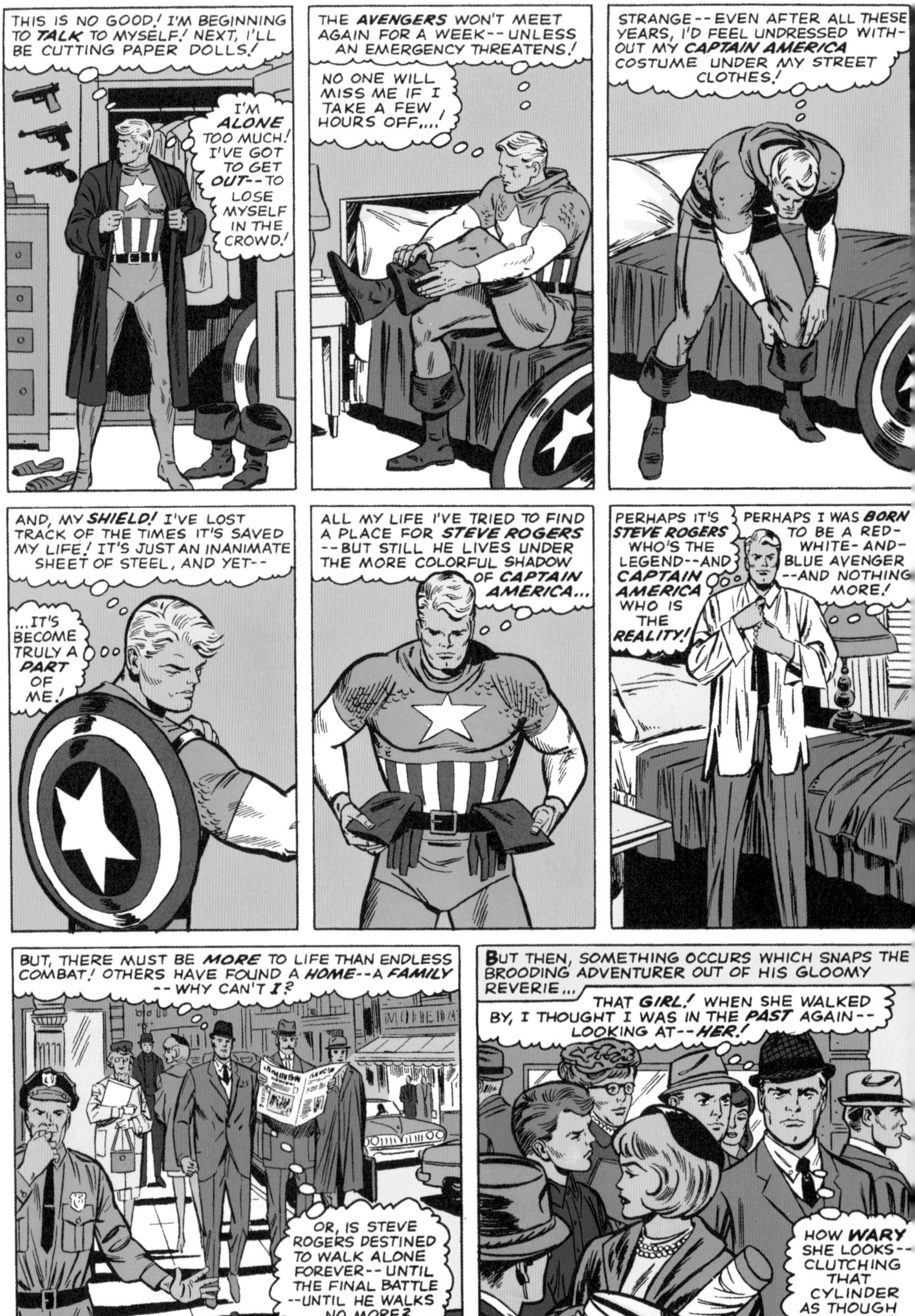
THIS IS NO GOOD! I'M BEGINNING TO TALK TO MYSELF! NEXT, I'LL BE CUTTING PAPER DOLLS!
I'M ALONE TOO MUCH! I'VE GOT TO GET OUT--TO LOSE MYSELF IN THE CROWD!
THE AVENGERS WON'T MEET AGAIN FOR A WEEK--UNLESS AN EMERGENCY THREATENS!
NO ONE WILL MISS ME IF I TAKE A FEW HOURS OFF...!
STRANGE--EVEN AFTER ALL THESE YEARS, I'D FEEL UNDRESSED WITHOUT MY CAPTAIN AMERICA COSTUME UNDER MY STREET CLOTHES!
AND, MY SHIELD! I'VE LOST TRACK OF THE TIMES IT'S SAVED MY LIFE! IT'S JUST AN INANIMATE SHEET OF STEEL, AND YET--
...IT'S BECOME TRULY A PART OF ME!
ALL MY LIFE I'VE TRIED TO FIND A PLACE FOR STEVE ROGERS--BUT STILL HE LIVES UNDER THE MORE COLORFUL SHADOW OF CAPTAIN AMERICA...
PERHAPS IT'S STEVE ROGERS WHO'S THE LEGEND--AND CAPTAIN AMERICA WHO IS THE REALITY!
PERHAPS I WAS BORN TO BE A RED-WHITE-AND-BLUE AVENGER--AND NOTHING MORE!
BUT, THERE MUST BE MORE TO LIFE THAN ENDLESS COMBAT! OTHERS HAVE FOUND A HOME--A FAMILY--WHY CAN'T I?
OR, IS STEVE ROGERS DESTINED TO WALK ALONE FOREVER--UNTIL THE FINAL BATTLE--UNTIL HE WALKS NO MORE?
BUT THEN, SOMETHING OCCURS WHICH SNAPS THE BROODING ADVENTURER OUT OF HIS GLOOMY REVERIE...
THAT GIRL! WHEN SHE WALKED BY, I THOUGHT I WAS IN THE PAST AGAIN--LOOKING AT--HER!
HOW WARY SHE LOOKS--CLUTCHING THAT CYLINDER AS THOUGH HER LIFE DEPENDS UPON IT!
5

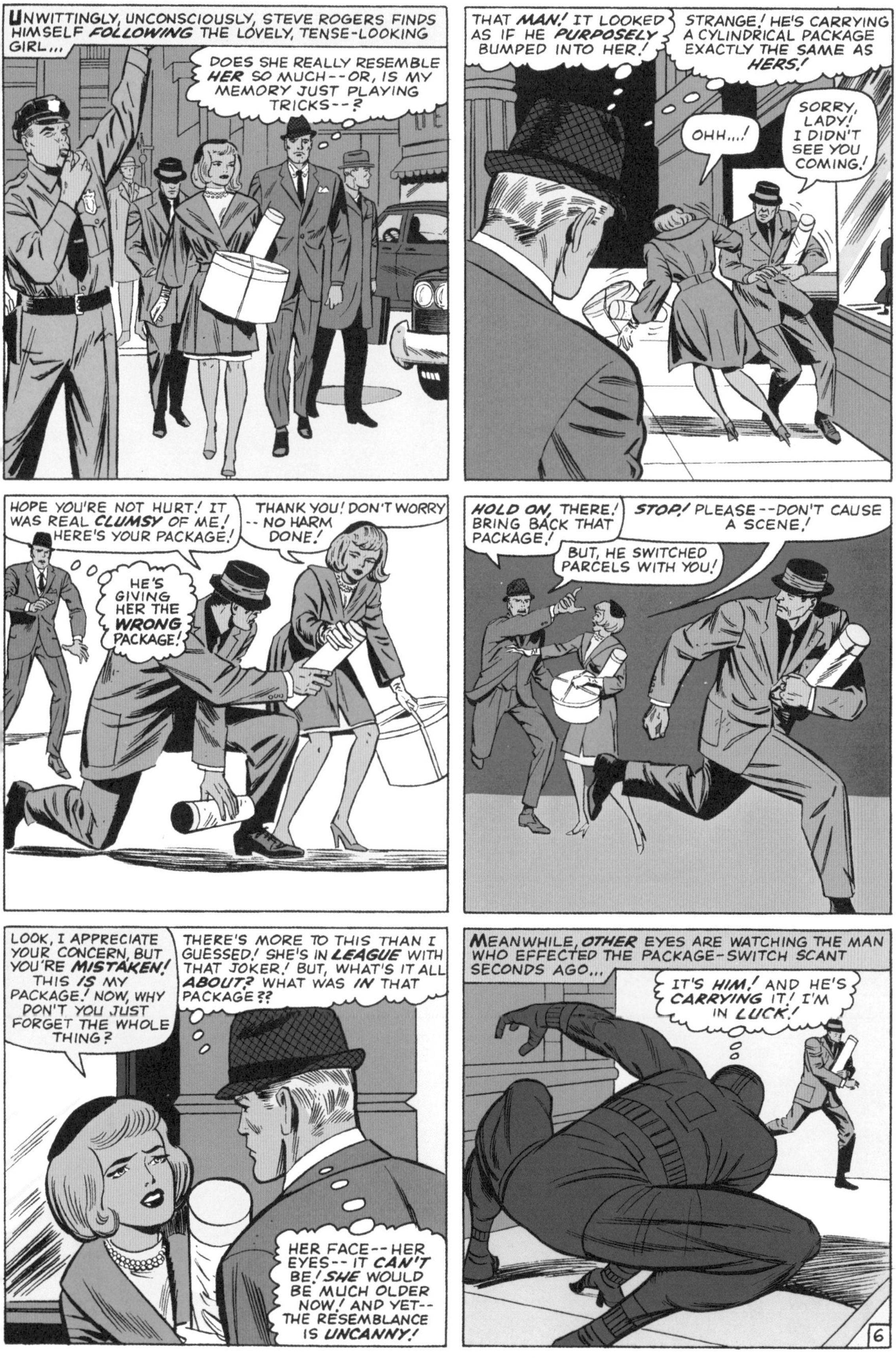
UNWITTINGLY, UNCONSCIOUSLY, STEVE ROGERS FINDS HIMSELF FOLLOWING THE LOVELY, TENSE-LOOKING GIRL...
DOES SHE REALLY RESEMBLE HER SO MUCH--OR, IS MY MEMORY JUST PLAYING TRICKS--?
THAT MAN! IT LOOKED AS IF HE PURPOSELY BUMPED INTO HER!
STRANGE! HE'S CARRYING A CYLINDRICAL PACKAGE EXACTLY THE SAME AS HERS!
OHH...!
SORRY, LADY! I DIDN'T SEE YOU COMING!
HOPE YOU'RE NOT HURT! IT WAS REAL CLUMSY OF ME! HERE'S YOUR PACKAGE!
THANK YOU! DON'T WORRY --NO HARM DONE!
HE'S GIVING HER THE WRONG PACKAGE!
HOLD ON, THERE! BRING BACK THAT PACKAGE!
STOP! PLEASE--DON'T CAUSE A SCENE!
BUT, HE SWITCHED PARCELS WITH YOU!
LOOK, I APPRECIATE YOUR CONCERN, BUT YOU'RE MISTAKEN! THIS IS MY PACKAGE! NOW, WHY DON'T YOU JUST FORGET THE WHOLE THING?
THERE'S MORE TO THIS THAN I GUESSED! SHE'S IN LEAGUE WITH THAT JOKER! BUT, WHAT'S IT ALL ABOUT? WHAT WAS IN THAT PACKAGE??
HER FACE--HER EYES--IT CAN'T BE! SHE WOULD BE MUCH OLDER NOW! AND YET--THE RESEMBLANCE IS UNCANNY!
MEANWHILE, OTHER EYES ARE WATCHING THE MAN WHO EFFECTED THE PACKAGE-SWITCH SCANT SECONDS AGO...
IT'S HIM! AND HE'S CARRYING IT! I'M IN LUCK!
6

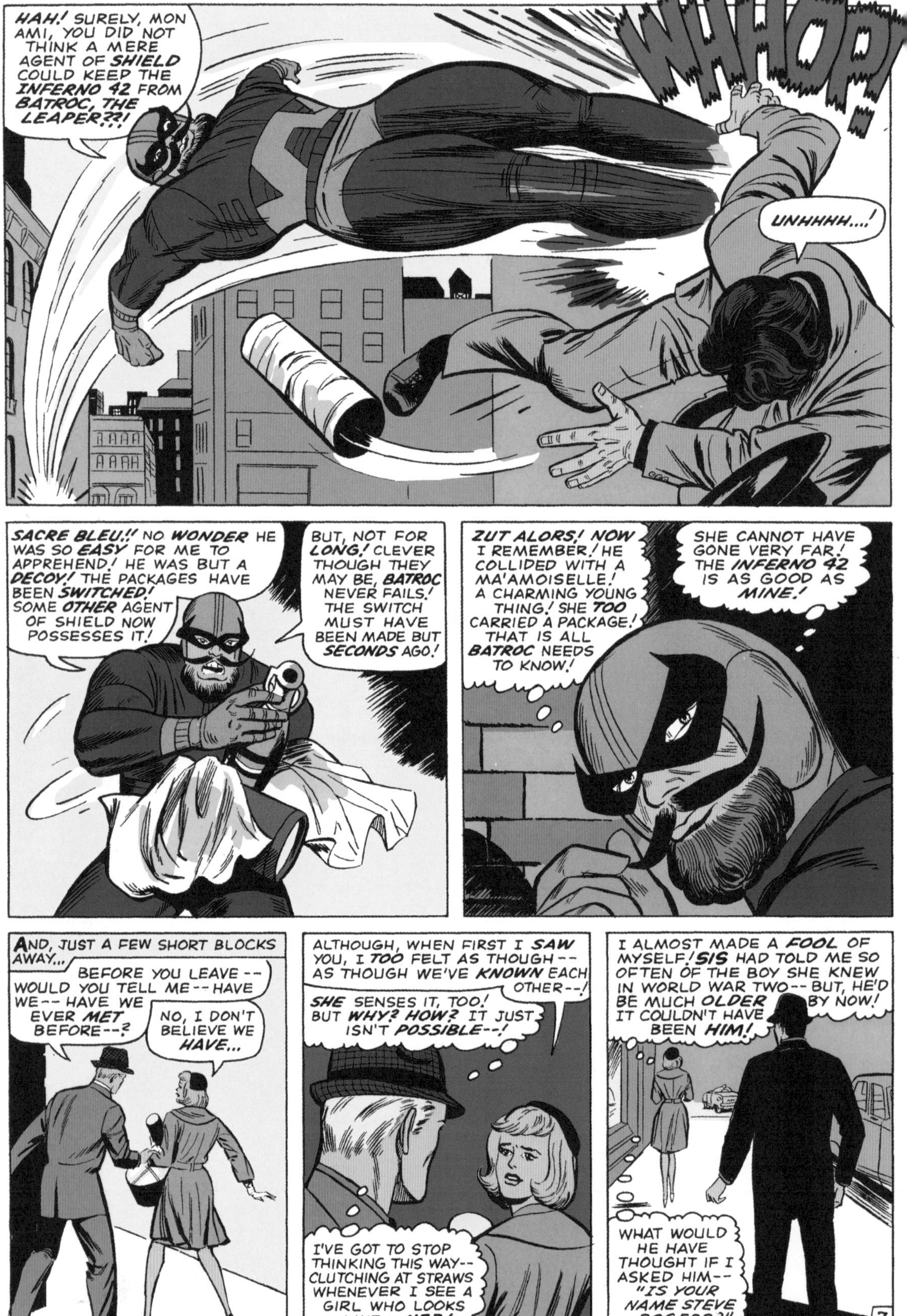

HAH! SURELY, MON AMI, YOU DID NOT THINK A MERE AGENT OF SHIELD COULD KEEP THE INFERNO 42 FROM BATROC, THE LEAPER??!
WHHOP!
UNHHHH...!
SACRE BLEU!! NO WONDER HE WAS SO EASY FOR ME TO APPREHEND! HE WAS BUT A DECOY! THE PACKAGES HAVE BEEN SWITCHED! SOME OTHER AGENT OF SHIELD NOW POSSESSES IT!
BUT, NOT FOR LONG! CLEVER THOUGH THEY MAY BE, BATROC NEVER FAILS! THE SWITCH MUST HAVE BEEN MADE BUT SECONDS AGO!
ZUT ALORS! NOW I REMEMBER! HE COLLIDED WITH A MA'AMOISELLE! A CHARMING YOUNG THING! SHE TOO CARRIED A PACKAGE! THAT IS ALL BATROC NEEDS TO KNOW!
SHE CANNOT HAVE GONE VERY FAR! THE INFERNO 42 IS AS GOOD AS MINE!
AND, JUST A FEW SHORT BLOCKS AWAY...
BEFORE YOU LEAVE -- WOULD YOU TELL ME -- HAVE WE -- HAVE WE EVER MET BEFORE --?
NO, I DON'T BELIEVE WE HAVE...
ALTHOUGH, WHEN FIRST I SAW YOU, I TOO FELT AS THOUGH -- AS THOUGH WE'VE KNOWN EACH OTHER --!
SHE SENSES IT, TOO! BUT WHY? HOW? IT JUST ISN'T POSSIBLE--!
I'VE GOT TO STOP THINKING THIS WAY-- CLUTCHING AT STRAWS WHENEVER I SEE A GIRL WHO LOOKS LIKE-- HER!
I ALMOST MADE A FOOL OF MYSELF! SIS HAD TOLD ME SO OFTEN OF THE BOY SHE KNEW IN WORLD WAR TWO-- BUT, HE'D BE MUCH OLDER BY NOW! IT COULDN'T HAVE BEEN HIM!
WHAT WOULD HE HAVE THOUGHT IF I ASKED HIM-- "IS YOUR NAME STEVE ROGERS?"
7

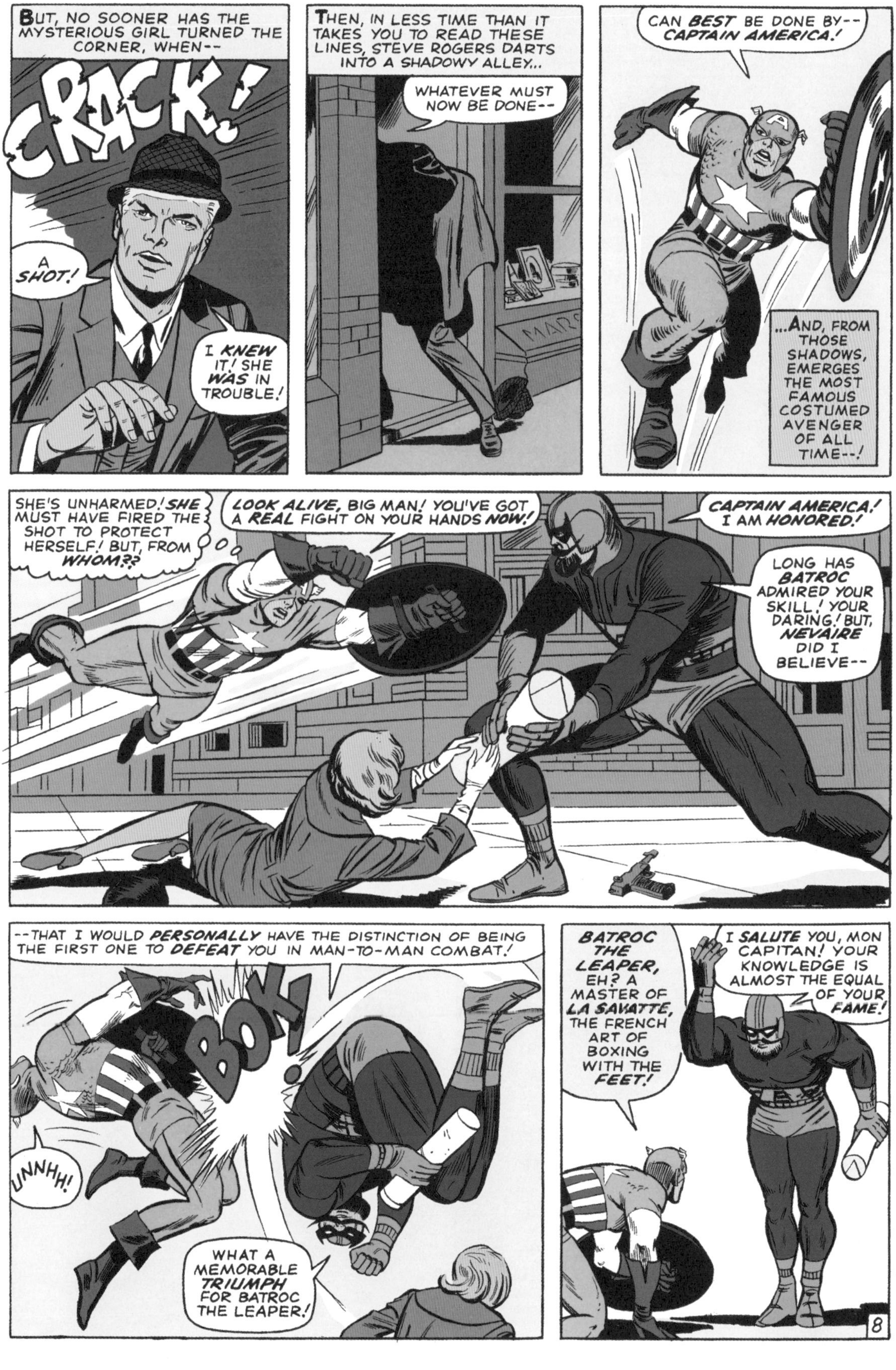
BUT, NO SOONER HAS THE MYSTERIOUS GIRL TURNED THE CORNER, WHEN--
CRACK!
A SHOT!
I KNEW IT! SHE WAS IN TROUBLE!
THEN, IN LESS TIME THAN IT TAKES YOU TO READ THESE LINES, STEVE ROGERS DARTS INTO A SHADOWY ALLEY...
WHATEVER MUST NOW BE DONE--
CAN BEST BE DONE BY--CAPTAIN AMERICA!
...AND, FROM THOSE SHADOWS, EMERGES THE MOST FAMOUS COSTUMED AVENGER OF ALL TIME--!
SHE'S UNHARMED! SHE MUST HAVE FIRED THE SHOT TO PROTECT HERSELF! BUT, FROM WHOM??
LOOK ALIVE, BIG MAN! YOU'VE GOT A REAL FIGHT ON YOUR HANDS NOW!
CAPTAIN AMERICA! I AM HONORED!
LONG HAS BATROC ADMIRED YOUR SKILL! YOUR DARING! BUT, NEVAIRE DID I BELIEVE--
--THAT I WOULD PERSONALLY HAVE THE DISTINCTION OF BEING THE FIRST ONE TO DEFEAT YOU IN MAN-TO-MAN COMBAT!
BOK!
UNNHH!
WHAT A MEMORABLE TRIUMPH FOR BATROC THE LEAPER!
BATROC THE LEAPER, EH? A MASTER OF LA SAVATTE, THE FRENCH ART OF BOXING WITH THE FEET!
I SALUTE YOU, MON CAPITAN! YOUR KNOWLEDGE IS ALMOST THE EQUAL OF YOUR FAME!
8

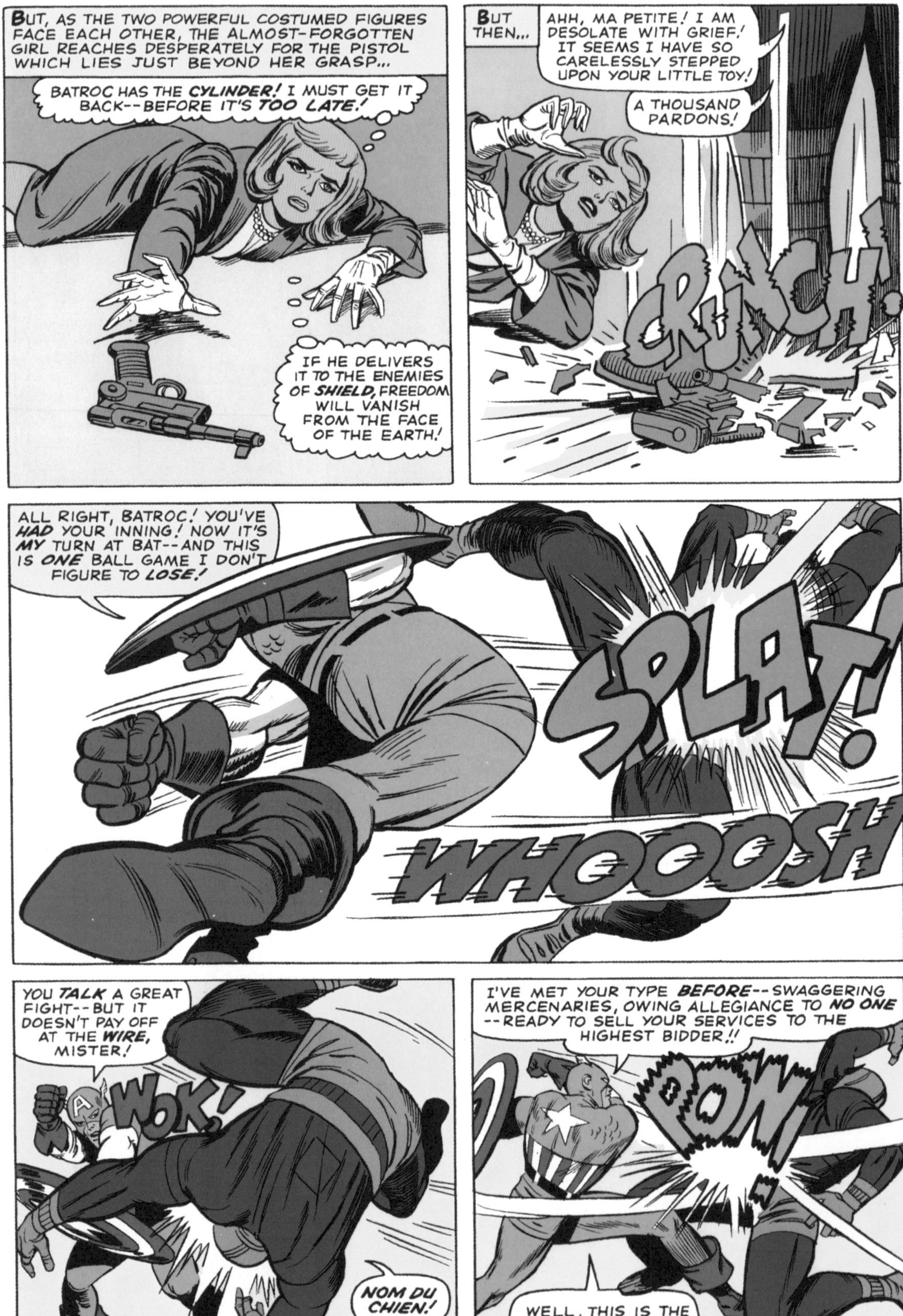
BUT, AS THE TWO POWERFUL COSTUMED FIGURES FACE EACH OTHER, THE ALMOST-FORGOTTEN GIRL REACHES DESPERATELY FOR THE PISTOL WHICH LIES JUST BEYOND HER GRASP...
BATROC HAS THE CYLINDER! I MUST GET IT BACK--BEFORE IT'S TOO LATE!
IF HE DELIVERS IT TO THE ENEMIES OF SHIELD, FREEDOM WILL VANISH FROM THE FACE OF THE EARTH!
BUT THEN...
AHH, MA PETITE! I AM DESOLATE WITH GRIEF! IT SEEMS I HAVE SO CARELESSLY STEPPED UPON YOUR LITTLE TOY!
A THOUSAND PARDONS!
CRUNCH!
ALL RIGHT, BATROC! YOU'VE HAD YOUR INNING! NOW IT'S MY TURN AT BAT--AND THIS IS ONE BALL GAME I DON'T FIGURE TO LOSE!
SPLAT!
WHOOOSH
YOU TALK A GREAT FIGHT--BUT IT DOESN'T PAY OFF AT THE WIRE, MISTER!
WOK!
NOM DU CHIEN!
I'VE MET YOUR TYPE BEFORE--SWAGGERING MERCENARIES, OWING ALLEGIANCE TO NO ONE--READY TO SELL YOUR SERVICES TO THE HIGHEST BIDDER!!
POW!
WELL, THIS IS THE ONLY PAY-OFF YOU DESERVE!
9

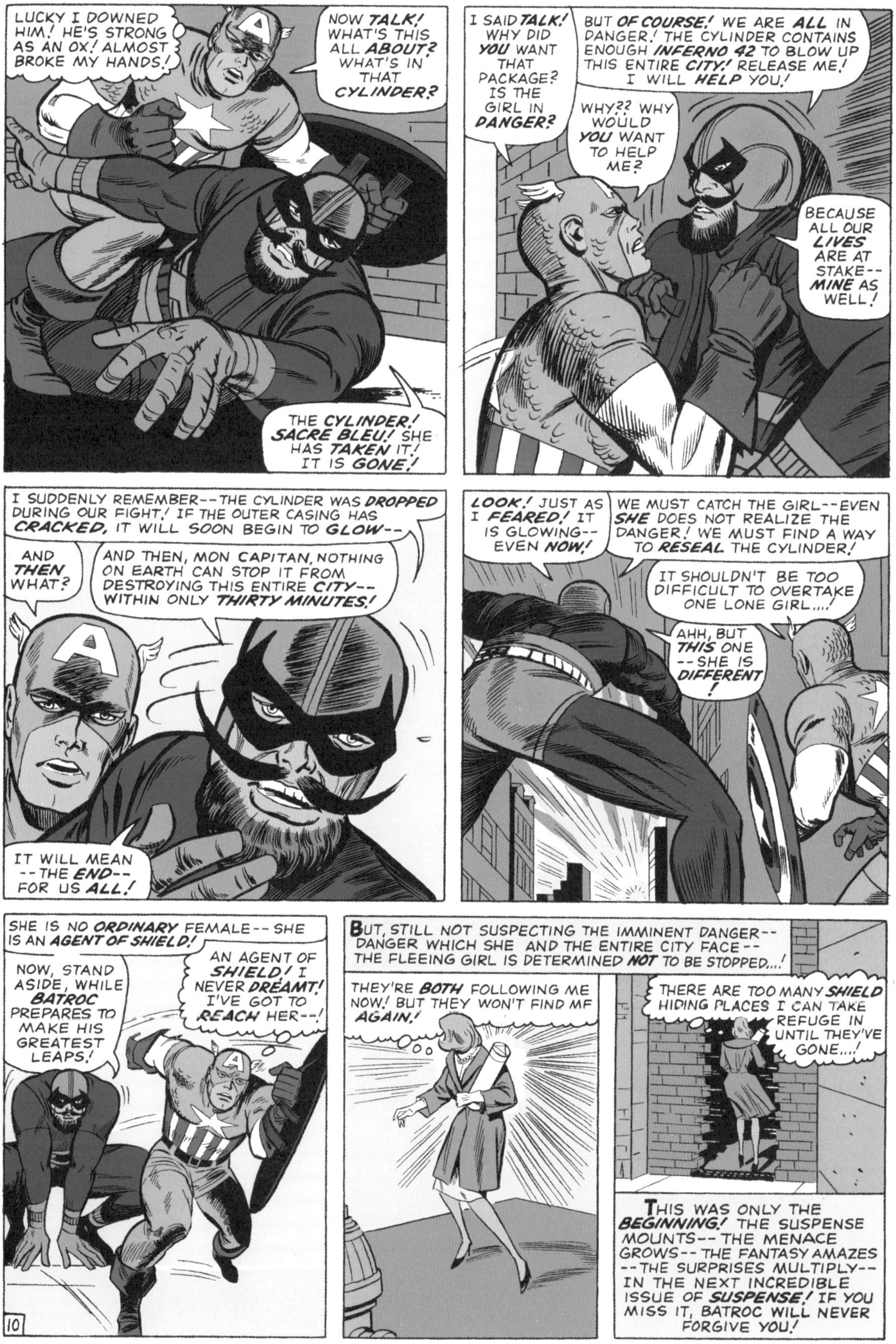
LUCKY I DOWNED HIM! HE'S STRONG AS AN OX! ALMOST BROKE MY HANDS!
NOW TALK! WHAT'S THIS ALL ABOUT? WHAT'S IN THAT CYLINDER?
THE CYLINDER! SACRE BLEU! SHE HAS TAKEN IT! IT IS GONE!
I SAID TALK! WHY DID YOU WANT THAT PACKAGE? IS THE GIRL IN DANGER?
BUT OF COURSE! WE ARE ALL IN DANGER! THE CYLINDER CONTAINS ENOUGH INFERNO 42 TO BLOW UP THIS ENTIRE CITY! RELEASE ME! I WILL HELP YOU!
WHY?? WHY WOULD YOU WANT TO HELP ME?
BECAUSE ALL OUR LIVES ARE AT STAKE-- MINE AS WELL!
I SUDDENLY REMEMBER--THE CYLINDER WAS DROPPED DURING OUR FIGHT! IF THE OUTER CASING HAS CRACKED, IT WILL SOON BEGIN TO GLOW--
AND THEN WHAT?
AND THEN, MON CAPITAN, NOTHING ON EARTH CAN STOP IT FROM DESTROYING THIS ENTIRE CITY-- WITHIN ONLY THIRTY MINUTES!
IT WILL MEAN --THE END-- FOR US ALL!
LOOK! JUST AS I FEARED! IT IS GLOWING-- EVEN NOW!
WE MUST CATCH THE GIRL--EVEN SHE DOES NOT REALIZE THE DANGER! WE MUST FIND A WAY TO RESEAL THE CYLINDER!
IT SHOULDN'T BE TOO DIFFICULT TO OVERTAKE ONE LONE GIRL....!
AHH, BUT THIS ONE --SHE IS DIFFERENT!
SHE IS NO ORDINARY FEMALE-- SHE IS AN AGENT OF SHIELD!
NOW, STAND ASIDE, WHILE BATROC PREPARES TO MAKE HIS GREATEST LEAPS!
AN AGENT OF SHIELD! I NEVER DREAMT! I'VE GOT TO REACH HER--!
10
BUT, STILL NOT SUSPECTING THE IMMINENT DANGER-- DANGER WHICH SHE AND THE ENTIRE CITY FACE-- THE FLEEING GIRL IS DETERMINED NOT TO BE STOPPED...!
THEY'RE BOTH FOLLOWING ME NOW! BUT THEY WON'T FIND ME AGAIN!
THERE ARE TOO MANY SHIELD HIDING PLACES I CAN TAKE REFUGE IN UNTIL THEY'VE GONE...!
THIS WAS ONLY THE BEGINNING! THE SUSPENSE MOUNTS-- THE MENACE GROWS-- THE FANTASY AMAZES --THE SURPRISES MULTIPLY-- IN THE NEXT INCREDIBLE ISSUE OF SUSPENSE! IF YOU MISS IT, BATROC WILL NEVER FORGIVE YOU!

TALES OF SUSPENSE #76,
APRIL 1966,
"THE GLADIATOR, THE GIRL,
AND THE GLORY!"

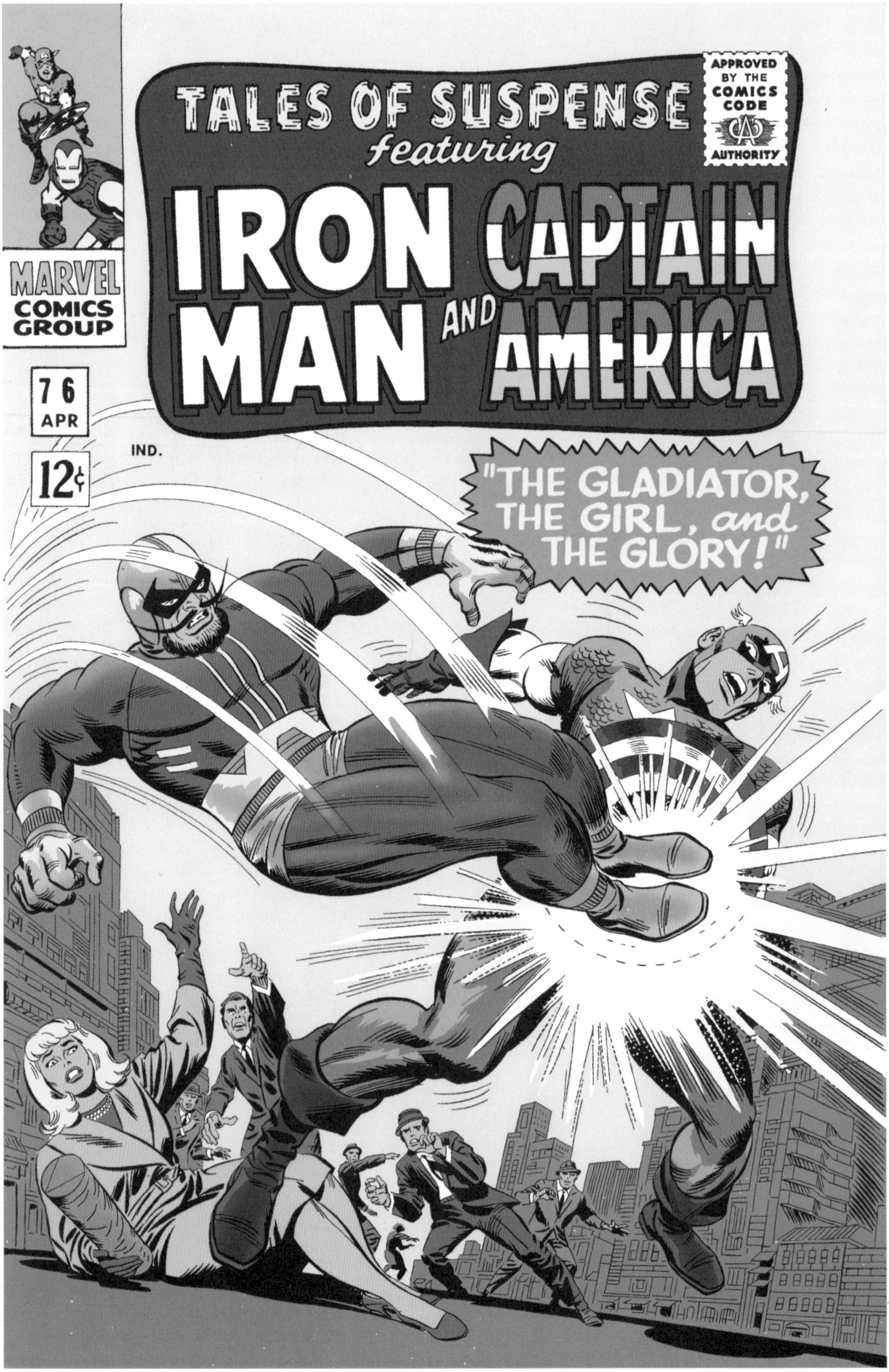
APPROVED BY THE COMICS CODE AUTHORITY
TALES OF SUSPENSE
featuring
IRON MAN AND CAPTAIN AMERICA
MARVEL COMICS GROUP
76 APR
IND.
12¢
"THE GLADIATOR, THE GIRL, and THE GLORY!"

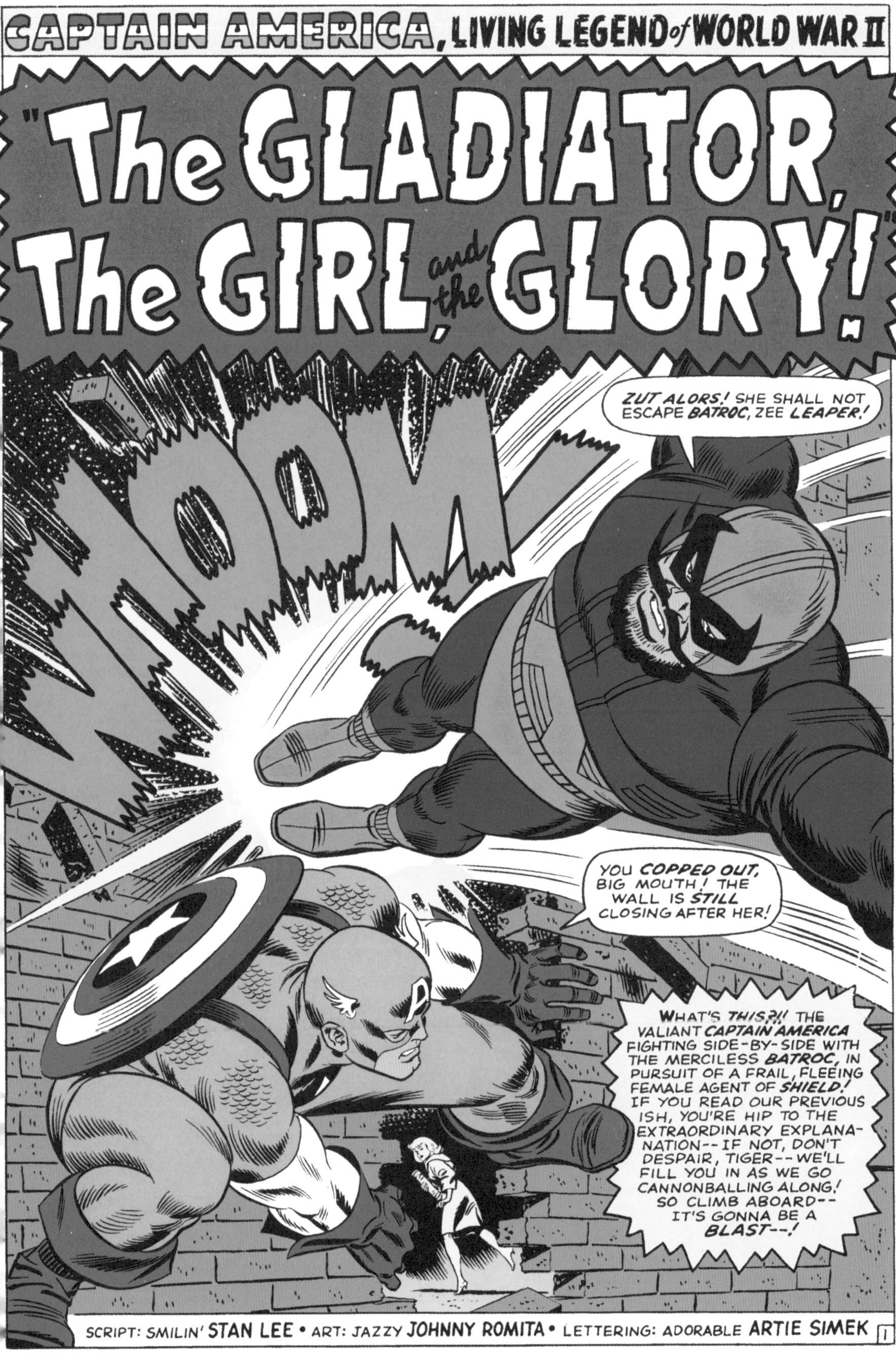
CAPTAIN AMERICA, LIVING LEGEND of WORLD WAR II
"The GLADIATOR, The GIRL, and the GLORY!"
WHOOM
ZUT ALORS! SHE SHALL NOT ESCAPE BATROC, ZEE LEAPER!
YOU COPPED OUT, BIG MOUTH! THE WALL IS STILL CLOSING AFTER HER!
WHAT'S THIS?!! THE VALIANT CAPTAIN AMERICA FIGHTING SIDE-BY-SIDE WITH THE MERCILESS BATROC, IN PURSUIT OF A FRAIL, FLEEING FEMALE AGENT OF SHIELD! IF YOU READ OUR PREVIOUS ISH, YOU'RE HIP TO THE EXTRAORDINARY EXPLANA-NATION--IF NOT, DON'T DESPAIR, TIGER--WE'LL FILL YOU IN AS WE GO CANNONBALLING ALONG! SO CLIMB ABOARD--IT'S GONNA BE A BLAST--!
SCRIPT: SMILIN' STAN LEE • ART: JAZZY JOHNNY ROMITA • LETTERING: ADORABLE ARTIE SIMEK
1

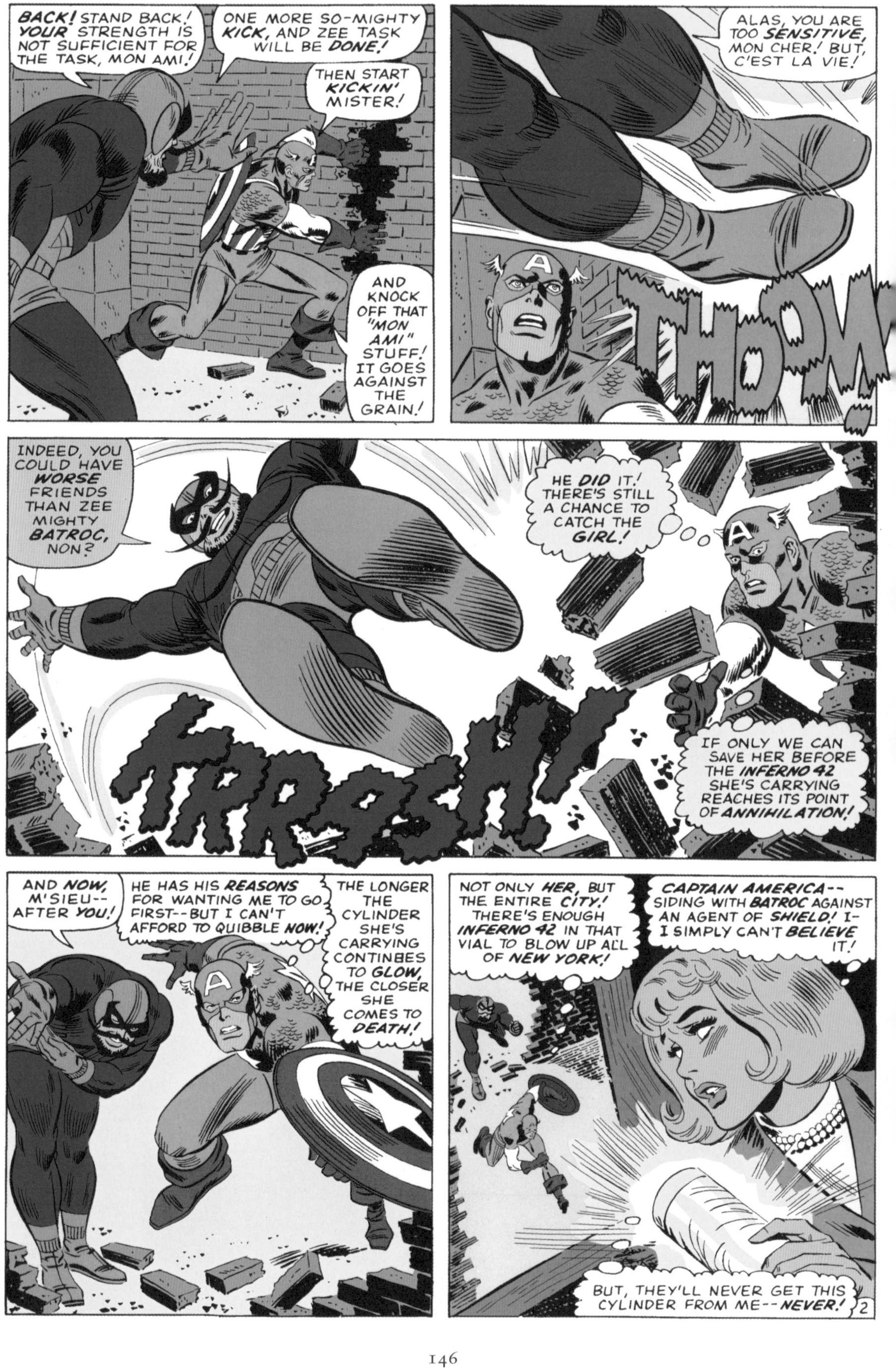
BACK! STAND BACK! YOUR STRENGTH IS NOT SUFFICIENT FOR THE TASK, MON AMI!
ONE MORE SO-MIGHTY KICK, AND ZEE TASK WILL BE DONE!
THEN START KICKIN' MISTER!
AND KNOCK OFF THAT "MON AMI" STUFF! IT GOES AGAINST THE GRAIN!
ALAS, YOU ARE TOO SENSITIVE, MON CHER! BUT, C'EST LA VIE!
THOOM!
INDEED, YOU COULD HAVE WORSE FRIENDS THAN ZEE MIGHTY BATROC, NON?
HE DID IT! THERE'S STILL A CHANCE TO CATCH THE GIRL!
TRRASH!
IF ONLY WE CAN SAVE HER BEFORE THE INFERNO 42 SHE'S CARRYING REACHES ITS POINT OF ANNIHILATION!
AND NOW, M'SIEU-- AFTER YOU!
HE HAS HIS REASONS FOR WANTING ME TO GO FIRST--BUT I CAN'T AFFORD TO QUIBBLE NOW!
THE LONGER THE CYLINDER SHE'S CARRYING CONTINBES TO GLOW, THE CLOSER SHE COMES TO DEATH!
NOT ONLY HER, BUT THE ENTIRE CITY! THERE'S ENOUGH INFERNO 42 IN THAT VIAL TO BLOW UP ALL OF NEW YORK!
CAPTAIN AMERICA-- SIDING WITH BATROC AGAINST AN AGENT OF SHIELD! I-I SIMPLY CAN'T BELIEVE IT!
BUT, THEY'LL NEVER GET THIS CYLINDER FROM ME--NEVER!
2

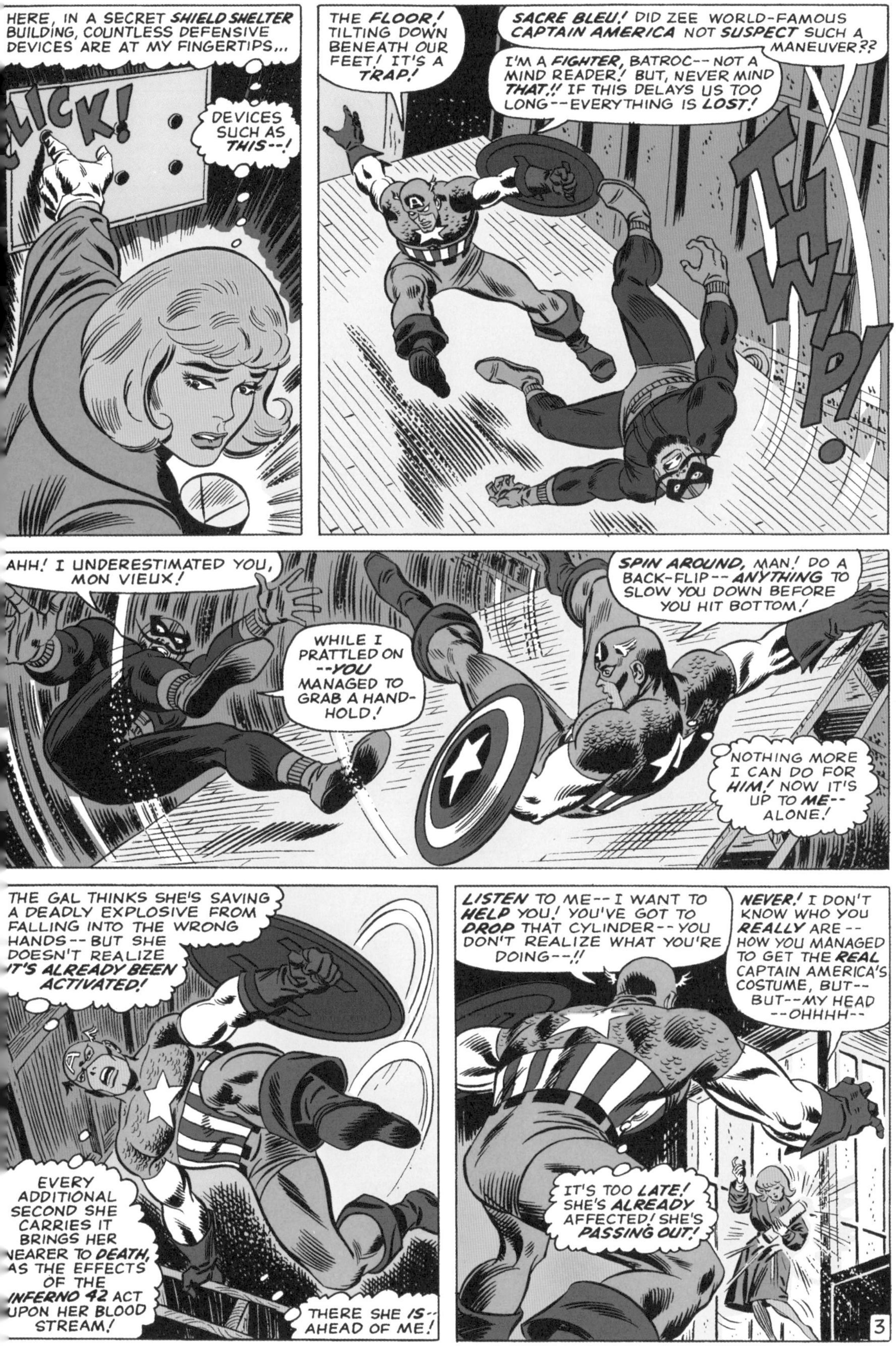

HERE, IN A SECRET SHIELD SHELTER BUILDING, COUNTLESS DEFENSIVE DEVICES ARE AT MY FINGERTIPS...
CLICK!
DEVICES SUCH AS THIS--!
THE FLOOR! TILTING DOWN BENEATH OUR FEET! IT'S A TRAP!
SACRE BLEU! DID ZEE WORLD-FAMOUS CAPTAIN AMERICA NOT SUSPECT SUCH A MANEUVER??
I'M A FIGHTER, BATROC-- NOT A MIND READER! BUT, NEVER MIND THAT!! IF THIS DELAYS US TOO LONG--EVERYTHING IS LOST!
THWIP!
AHH! I UNDERESTIMATED YOU, MON VIEUX!
WHILE I PRATTLED ON --YOU MANAGED TO GRAB A HAND-HOLD!
SPIN AROUND, MAN! DO A BACK-FLIP--ANYTHING TO SLOW YOU DOWN BEFORE YOU HIT BOTTOM!
NOTHING MORE I CAN DO FOR HIM! NOW IT'S UP TO ME-- ALONE!
THE GAL THINKS SHE'S SAVING A DEADLY EXPLOSIVE FROM FALLING INTO THE WRONG HANDS-- BUT SHE DOESN'T REALIZE IT'S ALREADY BEEN ACTIVATED!
EVERY ADDITIONAL SECOND SHE CARRIES IT BRINGS HER NEARER TO DEATH, AS THE EFFECTS OF THE INFERNO 42 ACT UPON HER BLOOD STREAM!
THERE SHE IS-- AHEAD OF ME!
LISTEN TO ME-- I WANT TO HELP YOU! YOU'VE GOT TO DROP THAT CYLINDER-- YOU DON'T REALIZE WHAT YOU'RE DOING--!!
NEVER! I DON'T KNOW WHO YOU REALLY ARE-- HOW YOU MANAGED TO GET THE REAL CAPTAIN AMERICA'S COSTUME, BUT-- BUT--MY HEAD --OHHHH--
IT'S TOO LATE! SHE'S ALREADY AFFECTED! SHE'S PASSING OUT!
3

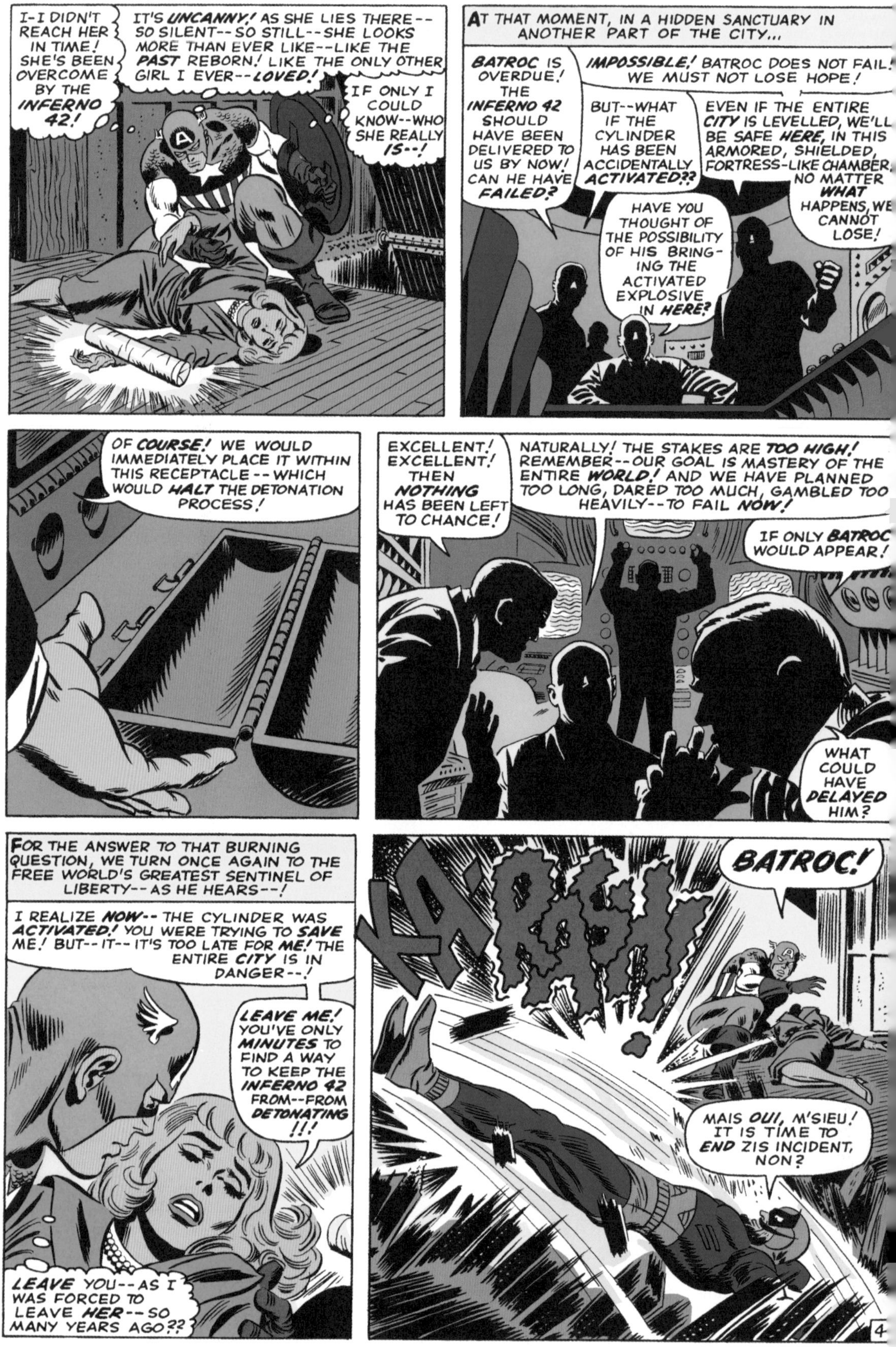
I-I DIDN'T REACH HER IN TIME! SHE'S BEEN OVERCOME BY THE INFERNO 42!
IT'S UNCANNY! AS SHE LIES THERE-- SO SILENT-- SO STILL--SHE LOOKS MORE THAN EVER LIKE--LIKE THE PAST REBORN! LIKE THE ONLY OTHER GIRL I EVER--LOVED!
IF ONLY I COULD KNOW--WHO SHE REALLY IS--!
AT THAT MOMENT, IN A HIDDEN SANCTUARY IN ANOTHER PART OF THE CITY...
BATROC IS OVERDUE! THE INFERNO 42 SHOULD HAVE BEEN DELIVERED TO US BY NOW! CAN HE HAVE FAILED?
IMPOSSIBLE! BATROC DOES NOT FAIL! WE MUST NOT LOSE HOPE!
BUT--WHAT IF THE CYLINDER HAS BEEN ACCIDENTALLY ACTIVATED??
EVEN IF THE ENTIRE CITY IS LEVELLED, WE'LL BE SAFE HERE, IN THIS ARMORED, SHIELDED, FORTRESS-LIKE CHAMBER, NO MATTER WHAT HAPPENS, WE CANNOT LOSE!
HAVE YOU THOUGHT OF THE POSSIBILITY OF HIS BRINGING THE ACTIVATED EXPLOSIVE IN HERE?
OF COURSE! WE WOULD IMMEDIATELY PLACE IT WITHIN THIS RECEPTACLE--WHICH WOULD HALT THE DETONATION PROCESS!
EXCELLENT! EXCELLENT! THEN NOTHING HAS BEEN LEFT TO CHANCE!
NATURALLY! THE STAKES ARE TOO HIGH! REMEMBER--OUR GOAL IS MASTERY OF THE ENTIRE WORLD! AND WE HAVE PLANNED TOO LONG, DARED TOO MUCH, GAMBLED TOO HEAVILY--TO FAIL NOW!
IF ONLY BATROC WOULD APPEAR!
WHAT COULD HAVE DELAYED HIM?
FOR THE ANSWER TO THAT BURNING QUESTION, WE TURN ONCE AGAIN TO THE FREE WORLD'S GREATEST SENTINEL OF LIBERTY--AS HE HEARS--!
I REALIZE NOW-- THE CYLINDER WAS ACTIVATED! YOU WERE TRYING TO SAVE ME! BUT--IT--IT'S TOO LATE FOR ME! THE ENTIRE CITY IS IN DANGER--!
LEAVE ME! YOU'VE ONLY MINUTES TO FIND A WAY TO KEEP THE INFERNO 42 FROM--FROM DETONATING!!!
LEAVE YOU--AS I WAS FORCED TO LEAVE HER--SO MANY YEARS AGO??
KA-RASH
BATROC!
MAIS OUI, M'SIEU! IT IS TIME TO END ZIS INCIDENT, NON?
4

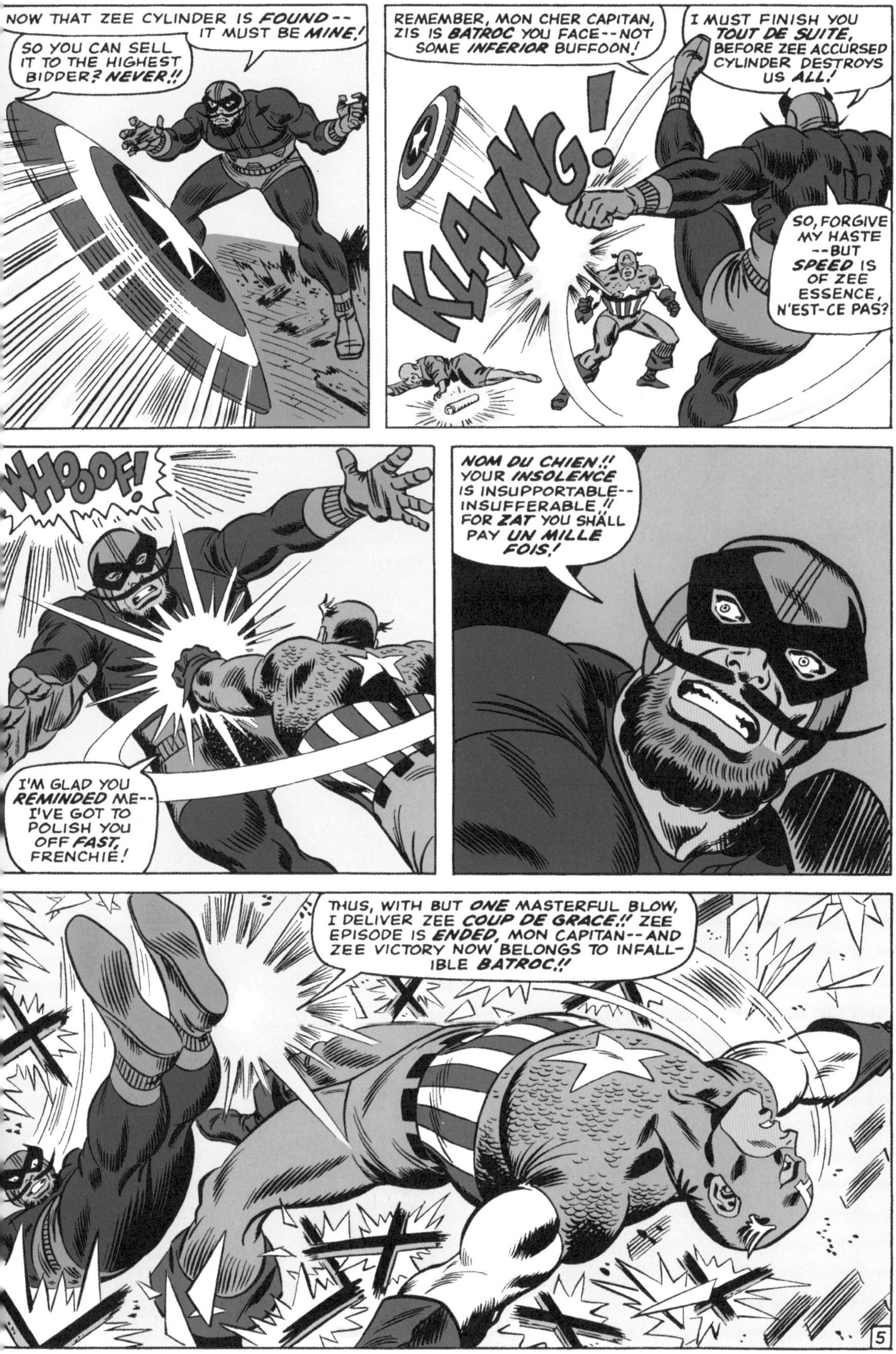
NOW THAT ZEE CYLINDER IS FOUND-- IT MUST BE MINE!
SO YOU CAN SELL IT TO THE HIGHEST BIDDER? NEVER!!
REMEMBER, MON CHER CAPITAN, ZIS IS BATROC YOU FACE--NOT SOME INFERIOR BUFFOON!
I MUST FINISH YOU TOUT DE SUITE, BEFORE ZEE ACCURSED CYLINDER DESTROYS US ALL!
KLANG!
SO, FORGIVE MY HASTE --BUT SPEED IS OF ZEE ESSENCE, N'EST-CE PAS?
WHOOOF!
I'M GLAD YOU REMINDED ME-- I'VE GOT TO POLISH YOU OFF FAST, FRENCHIE!
NOM DU CHIEN!! YOUR INSOLENCE IS INSUPPORTABLE-- INSUFFERABLE!! FOR ZAT YOU SHALL PAY UN MILLE FOIS!
THUS, WITH BUT ONE MASTERFUL BLOW, I DELIVER ZEE COUP DE GRACE!! ZEE EPISODE IS ENDED, MON CAPITAN--AND ZEE VICTORY NOW BELONGS TO INFALLIBLE BATROC!!
5

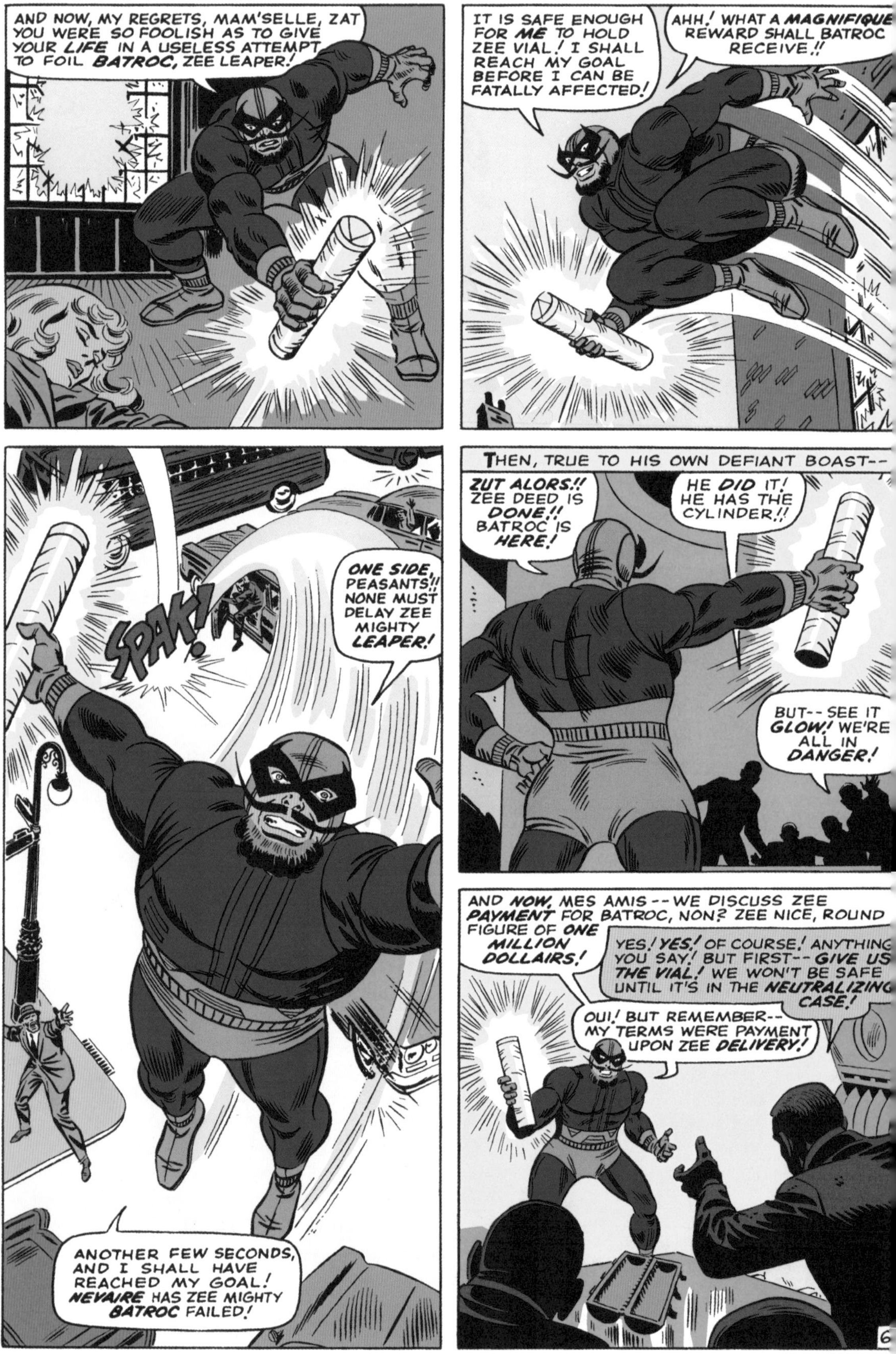
AND NOW, MY REGRETS, MAM'SELLE, ZAT YOU WERE SO FOOLISH AS TO GIVE YOUR LIFE IN A USELESS ATTEMPT TO FOIL BATROC, ZEE LEAPER!
IT IS SAFE ENOUGH FOR ME TO HOLD ZEE VIAL! I SHALL REACH MY GOAL BEFORE I CAN BE FATALLY AFFECTED!
AHH! WHAT A MAGNIFIQUE REWARD SHALL BATROC RECEIVE!!
SPAK!
ONE SIDE, PEASANTS!! NONE MUST DELAY ZEE MIGHTY LEAPER!
ANOTHER FEW SECONDS, AND I SHALL HAVE REACHED MY GOAL! NEVAIRE HAS ZEE MIGHTY BATROC FAILED!
THEN, TRUE TO HIS OWN DEFIANT BOAST--
ZUT ALORS!! ZEE DEED IS DONE!! BATROC IS HERE!
HE DID IT! HE HAS THE CYLINDER!!
BUT-- SEE IT GLOW! WE'RE ALL IN DANGER!
AND NOW, MES AMIS -- WE DISCUSS ZEE PAYMENT FOR BATROC, NON? ZEE NICE, ROUND FIGURE OF ONE MILLION DOLLAIRS!
YES! YES! OF COURSE! ANYTHING YOU SAY! BUT FIRST-- GIVE US THE VIAL! WE WON'T BE SAFE UNTIL IT'S IN THE NEUTRALIZING CASE!
OUI! BUT REMEMBER-- MY TERMS WERE PAYMENT UPON ZEE DELIVERY!
6

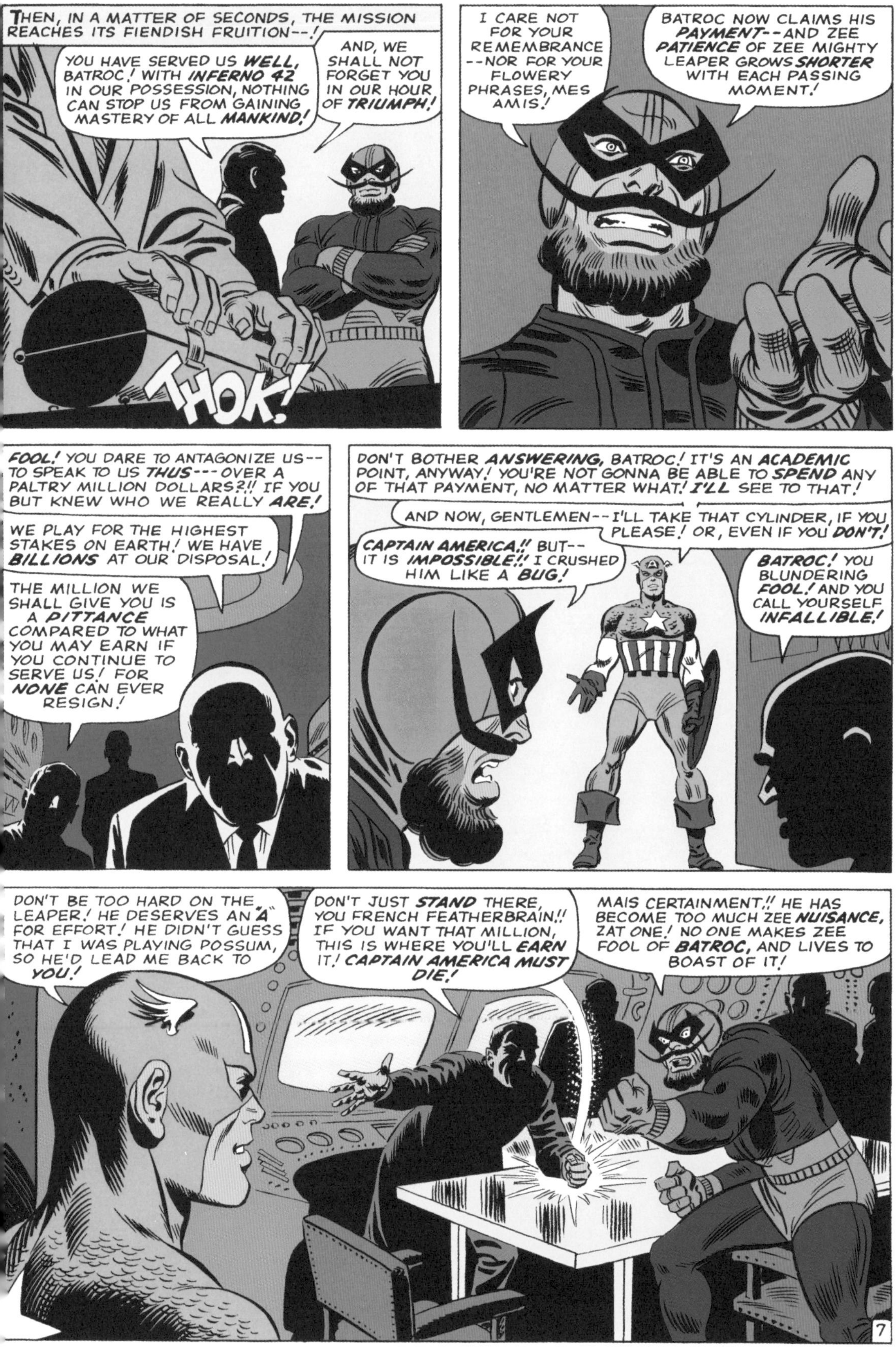
THEN, IN A MATTER OF SECONDS, THE MISSION REACHES ITS FIENDISH FRUITION--!
YOU HAVE SERVED US WELL, BATROC! WITH INFERNO 42 IN OUR POSSESSION, NOTHING CAN STOP US FROM GAINING MASTERY OF ALL MANKIND!
AND, WE SHALL NOT FORGET YOU IN OUR HOUR OF TRIUMPH!
THOK!
I CARE NOT FOR YOUR REMEMBRANCE --NOR FOR YOUR FLOWERY PHRASES, MES AMIS!
BATROC NOW CLAIMS HIS PAYMENT--AND ZEE PATIENCE OF ZEE MIGHTY LEAPER GROWS SHORTER WITH EACH PASSING MOMENT!
FOOL! YOU DARE TO ANTAGONIZE US--TO SPEAK TO US THUS---OVER A PALTRY MILLION DOLLARS?!! IF YOU BUT KNEW WHO WE REALLY ARE!
WE PLAY FOR THE HIGHEST STAKES ON EARTH! WE HAVE BILLIONS AT OUR DISPOSAL!
THE MILLION WE SHALL GIVE YOU IS A PITTANCE COMPARED TO WHAT YOU MAY EARN IF YOU CONTINUE TO SERVE US! FOR NONE CAN EVER RESIGN!
DON'T BOTHER ANSWERING, BATROC! IT'S AN ACADEMIC POINT, ANYWAY! YOU'RE NOT GONNA BE ABLE TO SPEND ANY OF THAT PAYMENT, NO MATTER WHAT! I'LL SEE TO THAT!
AND NOW, GENTLEMEN--I'LL TAKE THAT CYLINDER, IF YOU PLEASE! OR, EVEN IF YOU DON'T!
CAPTAIN AMERICA!! BUT--IT IS IMPOSSIBLE!! I CRUSHED HIM LIKE A BUG!
BATROC! YOU BLUNDERING FOOL! AND YOU CALL YOURSELF INFALLIBLE!
DON'T BE TOO HARD ON THE LEAPER! HE DESERVES AN "A" FOR EFFORT! HE DIDN'T GUESS THAT I WAS PLAYING POSSUM, SO HE'D LEAD ME BACK TO YOU!
DON'T JUST STAND THERE, YOU FRENCH FEATHERBRAIN!! IF YOU WANT THAT MILLION, THIS IS WHERE YOU'LL EARN IT! CAPTAIN AMERICA MUST DIE!
MAIS CERTAINMENT!! HE HAS BECOME TOO MUCH ZEE NUISANCE, ZAT ONE! NO ONE MAKES ZEE FOOL OF BATROC, AND LIVES TO BOAST OF IT!
7

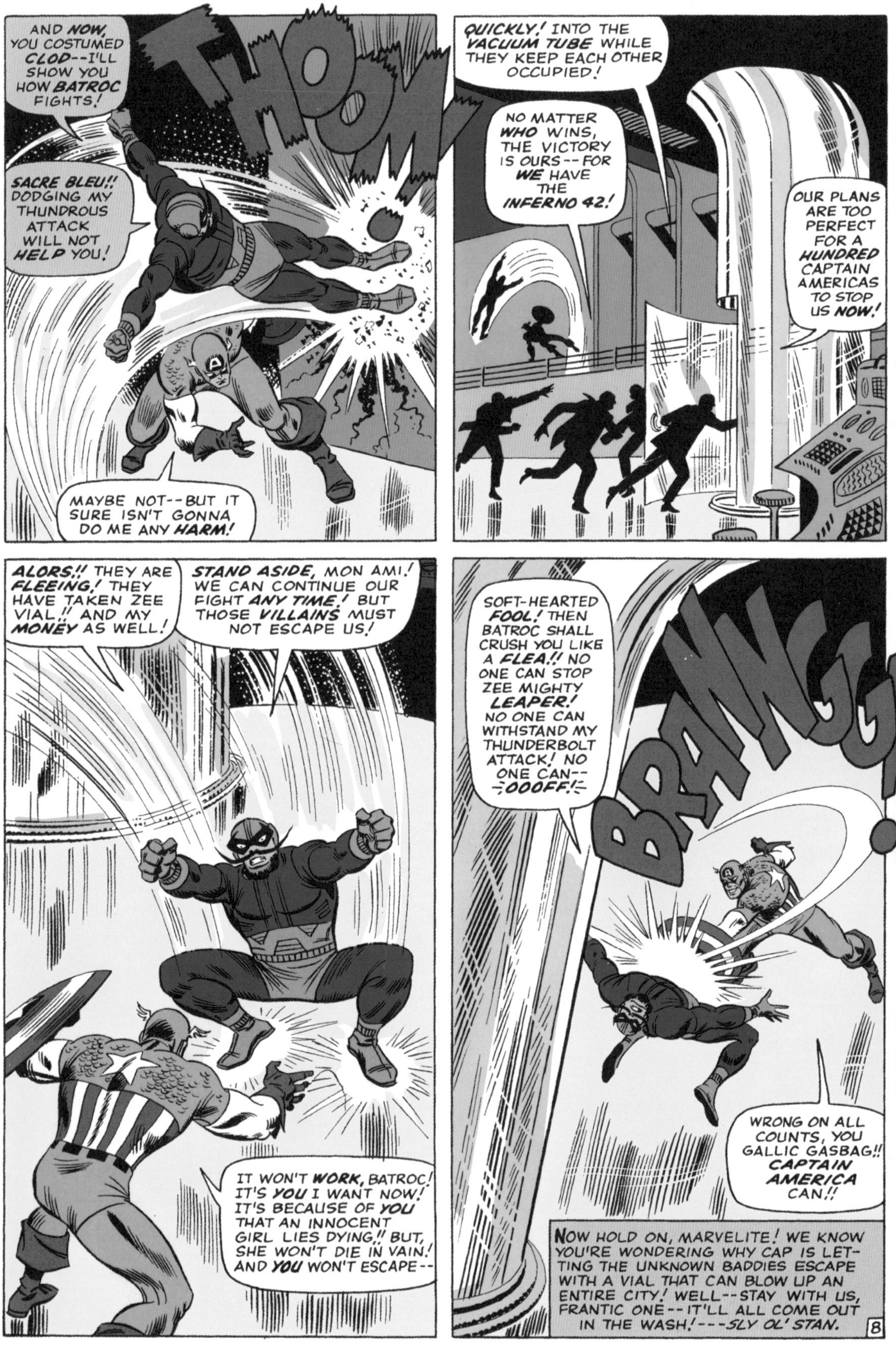
AND NOW, YOU COSTUMED CLOD--I'LL SHOW YOU HOW BATROC FIGHTS!
THOOM
SACRE BLEU!! DODGING MY THUNDROUS ATTACK WILL NOT HELP YOU!
MAYBE NOT--BUT IT SURE ISN'T GONNA DO ME ANY HARM!
QUICKLY! INTO THE VACUUM TUBE WHILE THEY KEEP EACH OTHER OCCUPIED!
NO MATTER WHO WINS, THE VICTORY IS OURS--FOR WE HAVE THE INFERNO 42!
OUR PLANS ARE TOO PERFECT FOR A HUNDRED CAPTAIN AMERICAS TO STOP US NOW!
ALORS!! THEY ARE FLEEING! THEY HAVE TAKEN ZEE VIAL!! AND MY MONEY AS WELL!
STAND ASIDE, MON AMI! WE CAN CONTINUE OUR FIGHT ANY TIME! BUT THOSE VILLAINS MUST NOT ESCAPE US!
IT WON'T WORK, BATROC! IT'S YOU I WANT NOW! IT'S BECAUSE OF YOU THAT AN INNOCENT GIRL LIES DYING!! BUT, SHE WON'T DIE IN VAIN! AND YOU WON'T ESCAPE--
SOFT-HEARTED FOOL! THEN BATROC SHALL CRUSH YOU LIKE A FLEA!! NO ONE CAN STOP ZEE MIGHTY LEAPER! NO ONE CAN WITHSTAND MY THUNDERBOLT ATTACK! NO ONE CAN-- -OOOFF!-
BRANGG
WRONG ON ALL COUNTS, YOU GALLIC GASBAG!! CAPTAIN AMERICA CAN!!
NOW HOLD ON, MARVELITE! WE KNOW YOU'RE WONDERING WHY CAP IS LETTING THE UNKNOWN BADDIES ESCAPE WITH A VIAL THAT CAN BLOW UP AN ENTIRE CITY! WELL--STAY WITH US, FRANTIC ONE--IT'LL ALL COME OUT IN THE WASH!---SLY OL' STAN.
8

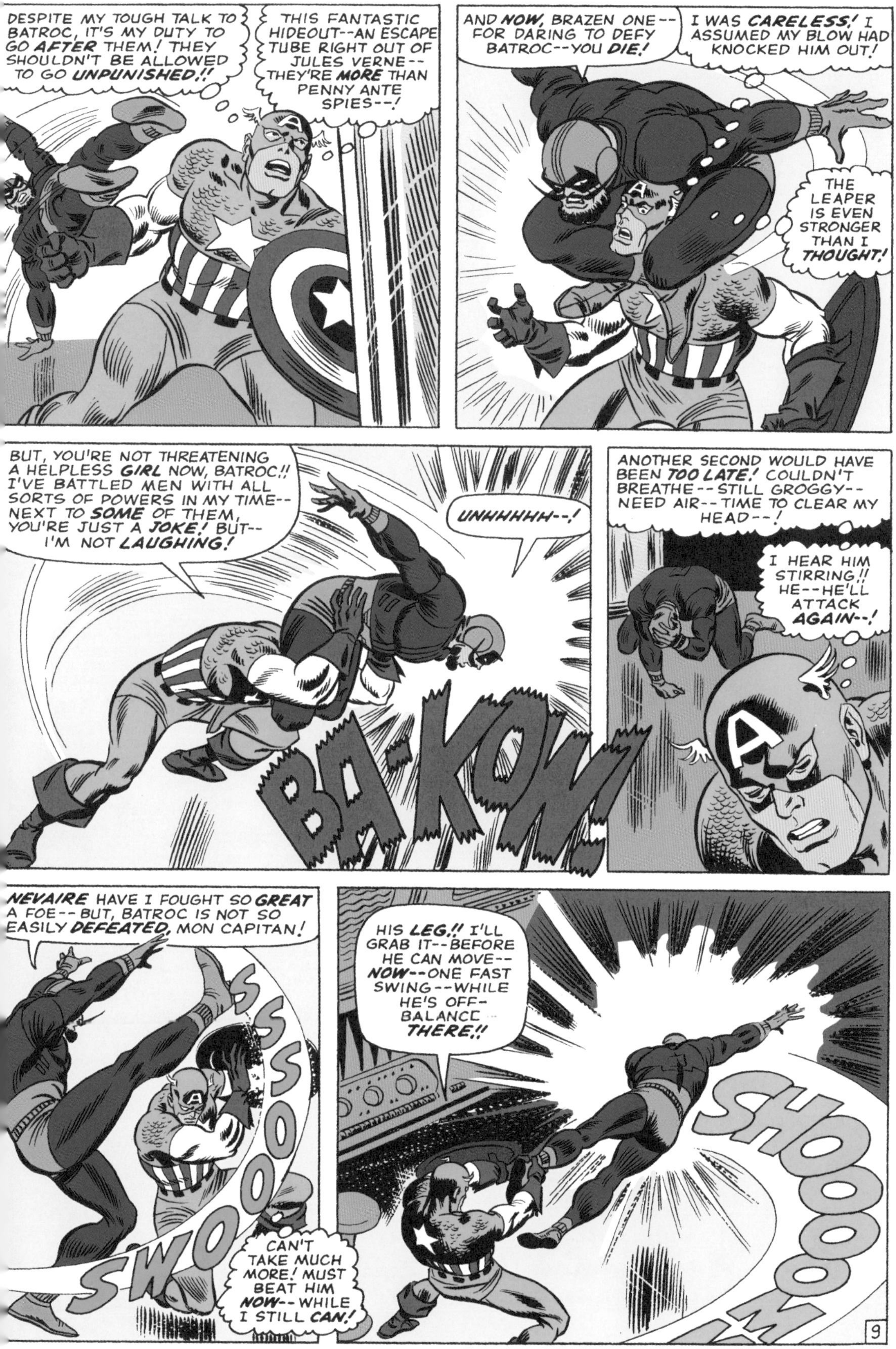
DESPITE MY TOUGH TALK TO BATROC, IT'S MY DUTY TO GO AFTER THEM! THEY SHOULDN'T BE ALLOWED TO GO UNPUNISHED!!
THIS FANTASTIC HIDEOUT--AN ESCAPE TUBE RIGHT OUT OF JULES VERNE--THEY'RE MORE THAN PENNY ANTE SPIES--!
AND NOW, BRAZEN ONE--FOR DARING TO DEFY BATROC--YOU DIE!
I WAS CARELESS! I ASSUMED MY BLOW HAD KNOCKED HIM OUT!
THE LEAPER IS EVEN STRONGER THAN I THOUGHT!
BUT, YOU'RE NOT THREATENING A HELPLESS GIRL NOW, BATROC!! I'VE BATTLED MEN WITH ALL SORTS OF POWERS IN MY TIME--NEXT TO SOME OF THEM, YOU'RE JUST A JOKE! BUT--I'M NOT LAUGHING!
UNHHHHH--!
BA-KOW!
ANOTHER SECOND WOULD HAVE BEEN TOO LATE! COULDN'T BREATHE--STILL GROGGY--NEED AIR--TIME TO CLEAR MY HEAD--!
I HEAR HIM STIRRING!! HE--HE'LL ATTACK AGAIN--!
NEVAIRE HAVE I FOUGHT SO GREAT A FOE--BUT, BATROC IS NOT SO EASILY DEFEATED, MON CAPITAN!
SSSOOOOSWOO
CAN'T TAKE MUCH MORE! MUST BEAT HIM NOW--WHILE I STILL CAN!
HIS LEG!! I'LL GRAB IT--BEFORE HE CAN MOVE--NOW--ONE FAST SWING--WHILE HE'S OFF-BALANCE--THERE!!
SHOOOOOM
9

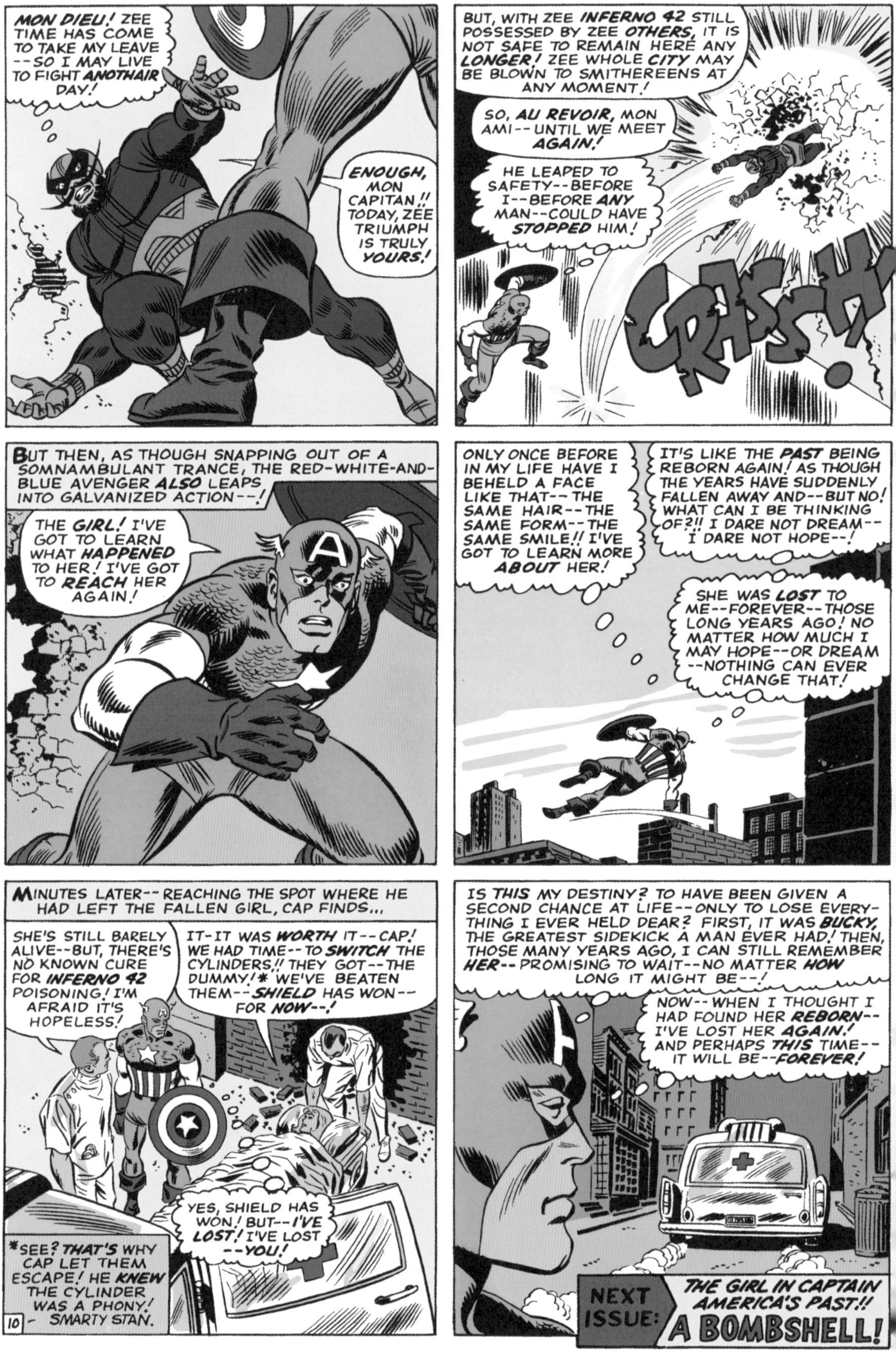

MON DIEU! ZEE TIME HAS COME TO TAKE MY LEAVE --SO I MAY LIVE TO FIGHT ANOTHAIR DAY!
ENOUGH, MON CAPITAN!! TODAY, ZEE TRIUMPH IS TRULY YOURS!
BUT, WITH ZEE INFERNO 42 STILL POSSESSED BY ZEE OTHERS, IT IS NOT SAFE TO REMAIN HERE ANY LONGER! ZEE WHOLE CITY MAY BE BLOWN TO SMITHEREENS AT ANY MOMENT!
SO, AU REVOIR, MON AMI--UNTIL WE MEET AGAIN!
HE LEAPED TO SAFETY--BEFORE I--BEFORE ANY MAN--COULD HAVE STOPPED HIM!
CRASSH!
BUT THEN, AS THOUGH SNAPPING OUT OF A SOMNAMBULANT TRANCE, THE RED-WHITE-AND-BLUE AVENGER ALSO LEAPS INTO GALVANIZED ACTION--!
THE GIRL! I'VE GOT TO LEARN WHAT HAPPENED TO HER! I'VE GOT TO REACH HER AGAIN!
ONLY ONCE BEFORE IN MY LIFE HAVE I BEHELD A FACE LIKE THAT--THE SAME HAIR--THE SAME FORM--THE SAME SMILE!! I'VE GOT TO LEARN MORE ABOUT HER!
IT'S LIKE THE PAST BEING REBORN AGAIN! AS THOUGH THE YEARS HAVE SUDDENLY FALLEN AWAY AND--BUT NO! WHAT CAN I BE THINKING OF?!! I DARE NOT DREAM--I DARE NOT HOPE--!
SHE WAS LOST TO ME--FOREVER--THOSE LONG YEARS AGO! NO MATTER HOW MUCH I MAY HOPE--OR DREAM--NOTHING CAN EVER CHANGE THAT!
MINUTES LATER--REACHING THE SPOT WHERE HE HAD LEFT THE FALLEN GIRL, CAP FINDS...
SHE'S STILL BARELY ALIVE--BUT, THERE'S NO KNOWN CURE FOR INFERNO 42 POISONING! I'M AFRAID IT'S HOPELESS!
IT-IT WAS WORTH IT--CAP! WE HAD TIME--TO SWITCH THE CYLINDERS!! THEY GOT--THE DUMMY!* WE'VE BEATEN THEM--SHIELD HAS WON--FOR NOW--!
YES, SHIELD HAS WON! BUT--I'VE LOST! I'VE LOST--YOU!
*SEE? THAT'S WHY CAP LET THEM ESCAPE! HE KNEW THE CYLINDER WAS A PHONY! - SMARTY STAN.
10
IS THIS MY DESTINY? TO HAVE BEEN GIVEN A SECOND CHANCE AT LIFE--ONLY TO LOSE EVERYTHING I EVER HELD DEAR? FIRST, IT WAS BUCKY, THE GREATEST SIDEKICK A MAN EVER HAD! THEN, THOSE MANY YEARS AGO, I CAN STILL REMEMBER HER--PROMISING TO WAIT--NO MATTER HOW LONG IT MIGHT BE--!
NOW--WHEN I THOUGHT I HAD FOUND HER REBORN--I'VE LOST HER AGAIN! AND PERHAPS THIS TIME--IT WILL BE--FOREVER!
NEXT ISSUE: THE GIRL IN CAPTAIN AMERICA'S PAST!! A BOMBSHELL!

TALES OF SUSPENSE #77,

MAY 1966,

"IF A HOSTAGE SHOULD DIE!"

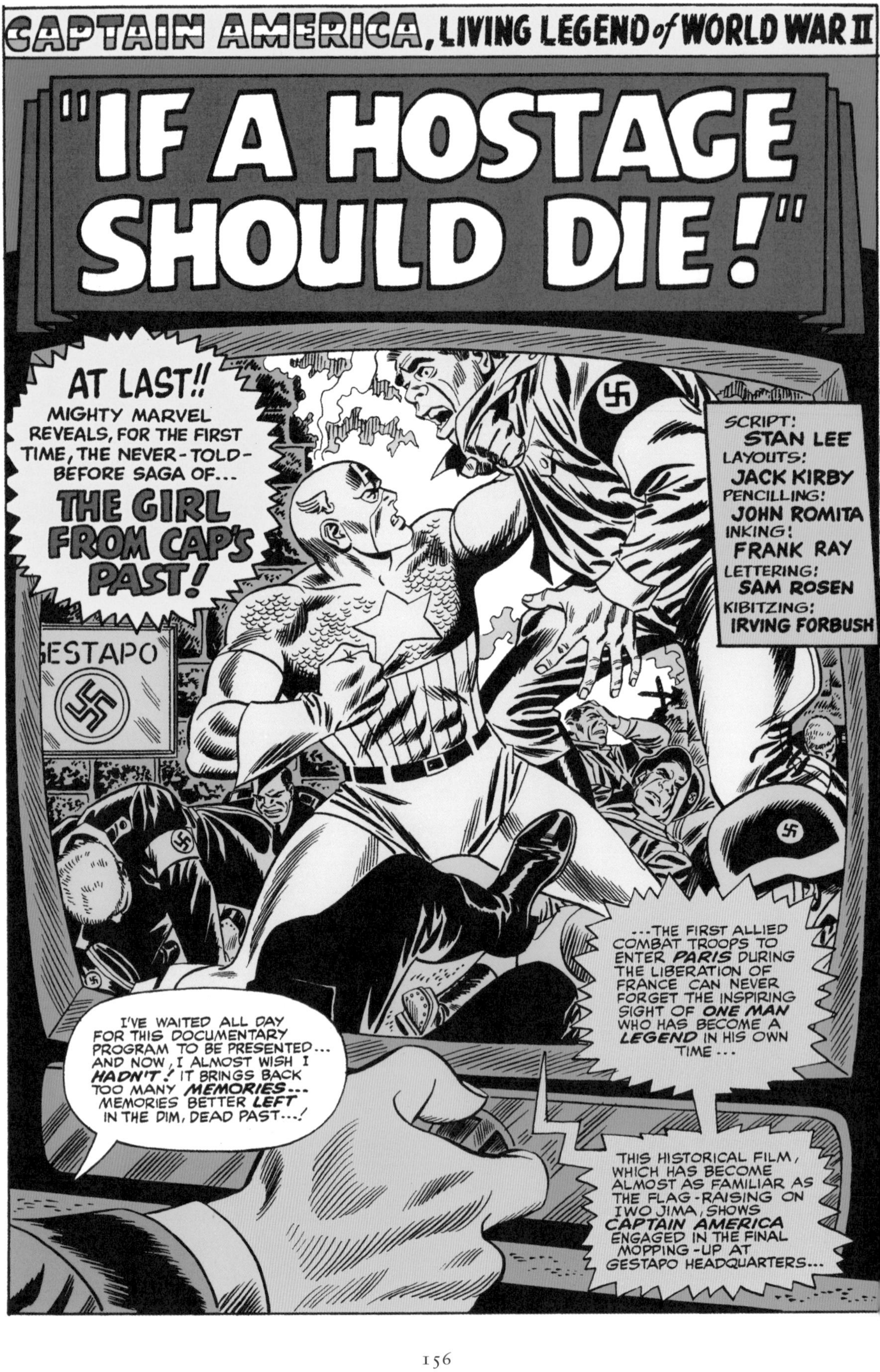
CAPTAIN AMERICA, LIVING LEGEND of WORLD WAR II
"IF A HOSTAGE SHOULD DIE!"
AT LAST!! MIGHTY MARVEL REVEALS, FOR THE FIRST TIME, THE NEVER-TOLD-BEFORE SAGA OF... THE GIRL FROM CAP'S PAST!
SCRIPT: STAN LEE LAYOUTS: JACK KIRBY PENCILLING: JOHN ROMITA INKING: FRANK RAY LETTERING: SAM ROSEN KIBITZING: IRVING FORBUSH
GESTAPO
...THE FIRST ALLIED COMBAT TROOPS TO ENTER PARIS DURING THE LIBERATION OF FRANCE CAN NEVER FORGET THE INSPIRING SIGHT OF ONE MAN WHO HAS BECOME A LEGEND IN HIS OWN TIME...
I'VE WAITED ALL DAY FOR THIS DOCUMENTARY PROGRAM TO BE PRESENTED... AND NOW, I ALMOST WISH I HADN'T! IT BRINGS BACK TOO MANY MEMORIES--- MEMORIES BETTER LEFT IN THE DIM, DEAD PAST...!
THIS HISTORICAL FILM, WHICH HAS BECOME ALMOST AS FAMILIAR AS THE FLAG-RAISING ON IWO JIMA, SHOWS CAPTAIN AMERICA ENGAGED IN THE FINAL MOPPING-UP AT GESTAPO HEADQUARTERS...

ONE OF THE MANY UNEXPLAINED *MYSTERIES* OF THAT FATEFUL EVENT WAS THE *REACTION* OF CAPTAIN AMERICA WHEN HE SAW THE ALLIED TROOPS!

INSTEAD OF WEARING THE TRIUMPHANT SMILE ONE WOULD *EXPECT* TO SEE... HE APPEARED SHOCKED... DISTRAUGHT... ALMOST ON THE VERGE OF *PANIC!*

SO IT WAS *OBVIOUS* TO ALL OF THEM...!

FINALLY, AMERICA'S MOST GALLANT SENTINEL OF LIBERTY FREED HIMSELF FROM THE CHEERING G.I.'S WHO HAD HAPPILY LIFTED HIM UPON THEIR SHOULDERS ... AND WITHIN BRIEF MOMENTS, HE HAD LOST HIMSELF IN THE CROWD!

BUT, IT WASN'T SOON *ENOUGH!* I WAS STILL *TOO LATE!*

...TOO LATE EVER TO SEE *HER* AGAIN!

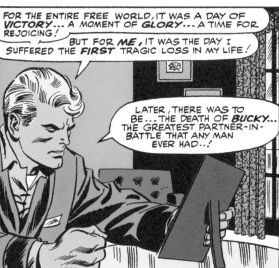

FOR THE ENTIRE FREE WORLD, IT WAS A DAY OF *VICTORY*... A MOMENT OF *GLORY*... A TIME FOR REJOICING!

BUT FOR *ME*, IT WAS THE DAY I SUFFERED THE *FIRST* TRAGIC LOSS IN MY LIFE!

LATER, THERE WAS TO BE... THE DEATH OF *BUCKY*... THE GREATEST PARTNER-IN-BATTLE THAT ANY MAN EVER HAD...!

BUT THAT DAY, AT THE LAST FEW MOMENTS OF FIGHTING ... WHEN THE VICTORY HAD FINALLY BEEN WON... I LOST *HER*... FOREVER!

I NEVER KNEW FOR CERTAIN WHETHER SHE HAD BEEN *KILLED*-- OR IF-- BUT, IT'S BEEN MORE THAN *TWENTY YEARS* SINCE THEN...

...IF SHE WERE STILL ALIVE, SURELY SHE'D HAVE *FOUND* ME BY NOW!

I NEVER *TOLD* THEM ... THAT IT WAS BECAUSE OF *YOU* I WAS SO DESPERATE ON THAT FATAL DAY!

I WANTED TO *FIND* YOU... TO TEAR ALL OF *PARIS* APART UNTIL WE WERE TOGETHER AGAIN... BUT, IT WAS *TOO LATE*, MY DARLING... I HAD *LOST* YOU... FOREVER!

THAT LIGHTNING AND THUNDER ... IT'S LIKE THE ANGRY ROAR OF THE *PAST*... TRYING TO CAPTURE ME AGAIN!

IF ONLY I *COULD* RETURN TO THAT DAY... IF ONLY I *COULD* GO BACK... AND HAVE A SECOND CHANCE..!

2.

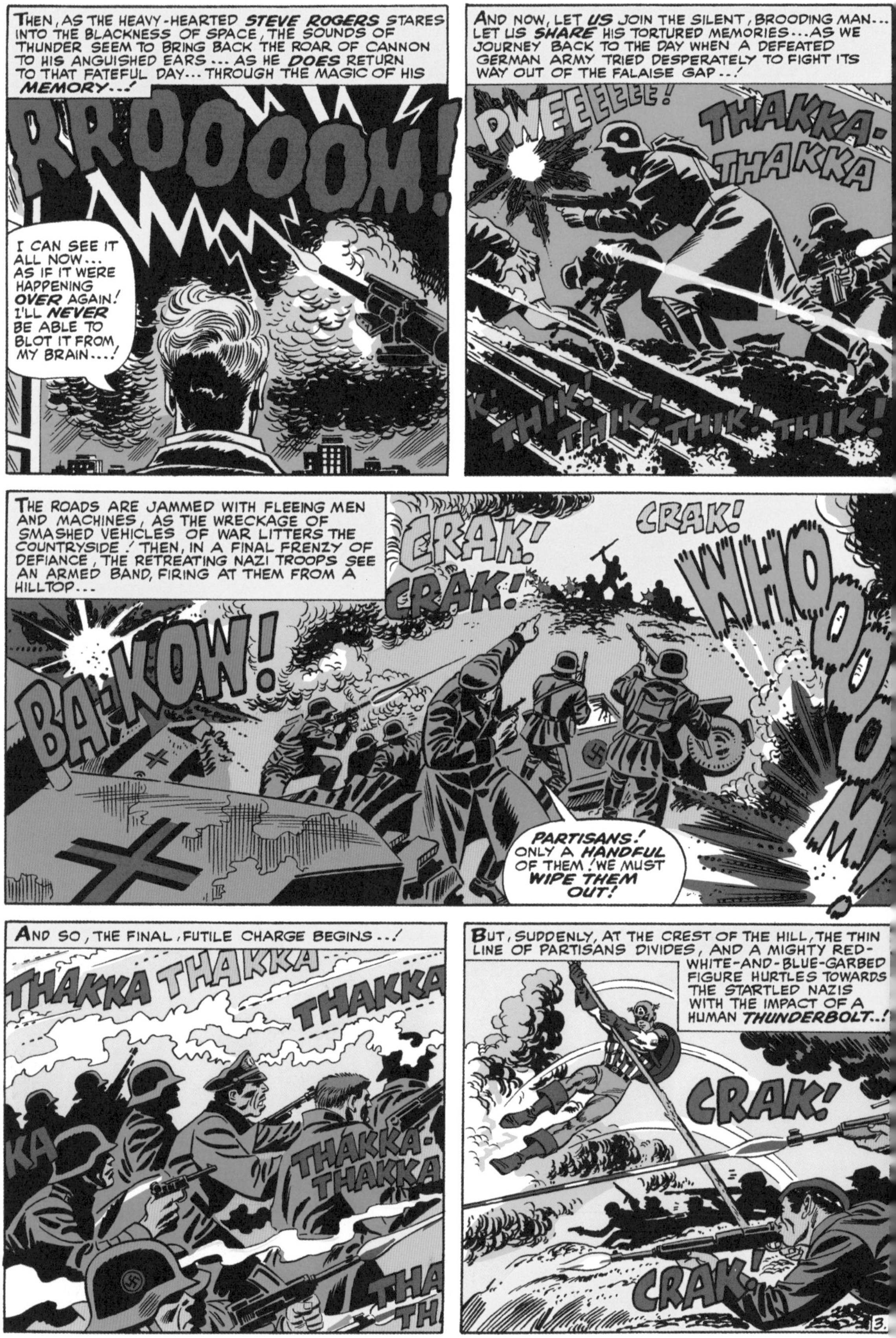

THEN, AS THE HEAVY-HEARTED STEVE ROGERS STARES INTO THE BLACKNESS OF SPACE, THE SOUNDS OF THUNDER SEEM TO BRING BACK THE ROAR OF CANNON TO HIS ANGUISHED EARS... AS HE DOES RETURN TO THAT FATEFUL DAY... THROUGH THE MAGIC OF HIS MEMORY...!
RROOOOOM!
I CAN SEE IT ALL NOW... AS IF IT WERE HAPPENING OVER AGAIN! I'LL NEVER BE ABLE TO BLOT IT FROM MY BRAIN...!
AND NOW, LET US JOIN THE SILENT, BROODING MAN... LET US SHARE HIS TORTURED MEMORIES... AS WE JOURNEY BACK TO THE DAY WHEN A DEFEATED GERMAN ARMY TRIED DESPERATELY TO FIGHT ITS WAY OUT OF THE FALAISE GAP...!
PWEEEEEEE!
THAKKA-THAKKA
THIK! THIK! THIK! THIK!
THE ROADS ARE JAMMED WITH FLEEING MEN AND MACHINES, AS THE WRECKAGE OF SMASHED VEHICLES OF WAR LITTERS THE COUNTRYSIDE! THEN, IN A FINAL FRENZY OF DEFIANCE, THE RETREATING NAZI TROOPS SEE AN ARMED BAND, FIRING AT THEM FROM A HILLTOP...
CRAK!
CRAK!
CRAK!
BA-KOW!
WHOOOOOM!
PARTISANS! ONLY A HANDFUL OF THEM! WE MUST WIPE THEM OUT!
AND SO, THE FINAL, FUTILE CHARGE BEGINS...!
THAKKA THAKKA
THAKKA
THAKKA-THAKKA
BUT, SUDDENLY, AT THE CREST OF THE HILL, THE THIN LINE OF PARTISANS DIVIDES, AND A MIGHTY RED-WHITE-AND-BLUE-GARBED FIGURE HURTLES TOWARDS THE STARTLED NAZIS WITH THE IMPACT OF A HUMAN THUNDERBOLT..!
CRAK!
CRAK!
3.

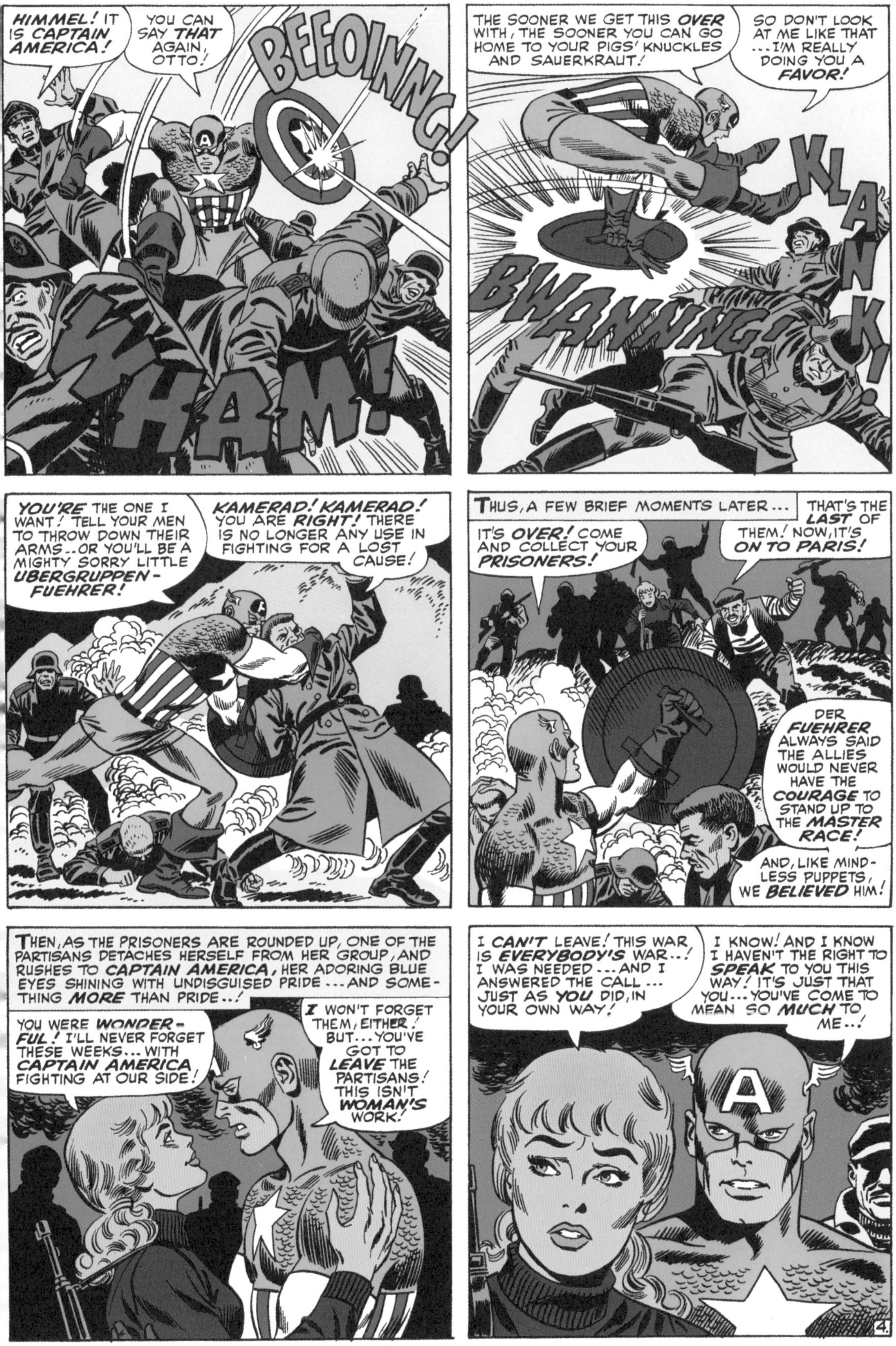
HIMMEL! IT IS CAPTAIN AMERICA!
YOU CAN SAY THAT AGAIN, OTTO!
BEEOINNG!
WHAM!
THE SOONER WE GET THIS OVER WITH, THE SOONER YOU CAN GO HOME TO YOUR PIGS' KNUCKLES AND SAUERKRAUT!
SO DON'T LOOK AT ME LIKE THAT ...I'M REALLY DOING YOU A FAVOR!
KLANK!
BWANNNG!
YOU'RE THE ONE I WANT! TELL YOUR MEN TO THROW DOWN THEIR ARMS..OR YOU'LL BE A MIGHTY SORRY LITTLE UBERGRUPPEN-FUEHRER!
KAMERAD! KAMERAD! YOU ARE RIGHT! THERE IS NO LONGER ANY USE IN FIGHTING FOR A LOST CAUSE!
THUS, A FEW BRIEF MOMENTS LATER...
IT'S OVER! COME AND COLLECT YOUR PRISONERS!
THAT'S THE LAST OF THEM! NOW, IT'S ON TO PARIS!
DER FUEHRER ALWAYS SAID THE ALLIES WOULD NEVER HAVE THE COURAGE TO STAND UP TO THE MASTER RACE!
AND, LIKE MINDLESS PUPPETS, WE BELIEVED HIM!
THEN, AS THE PRISONERS ARE ROUNDED UP, ONE OF THE PARTISANS DETACHES HERSELF FROM HER GROUP, AND RUSHES TO CAPTAIN AMERICA, HER ADORING BLUE EYES SHINING WITH UNDISGUISED PRIDE ...AND SOMETHING MORE THAN PRIDE..!
YOU WERE WONDERFUL! I'LL NEVER FORGET THESE WEEKS... WITH CAPTAIN AMERICA FIGHTING AT OUR SIDE!
I WON'T FORGET THEM, EITHER! BUT...YOU'VE GOT TO LEAVE THE PARTISANS! THIS ISN'T WOMAN'S WORK!
I CAN'T LEAVE! THIS WAR IS EVERYBODY'S WAR..! I WAS NEEDED ...AND I ANSWERED THE CALL ... JUST AS YOU DID, IN YOUR OWN WAY!
I KNOW! AND I KNOW I HAVEN'T THE RIGHT TO SPEAK TO YOU THIS WAY! IT'S JUST THAT YOU...YOU'VE COME TO MEAN SO MUCH TO ME..!
4.

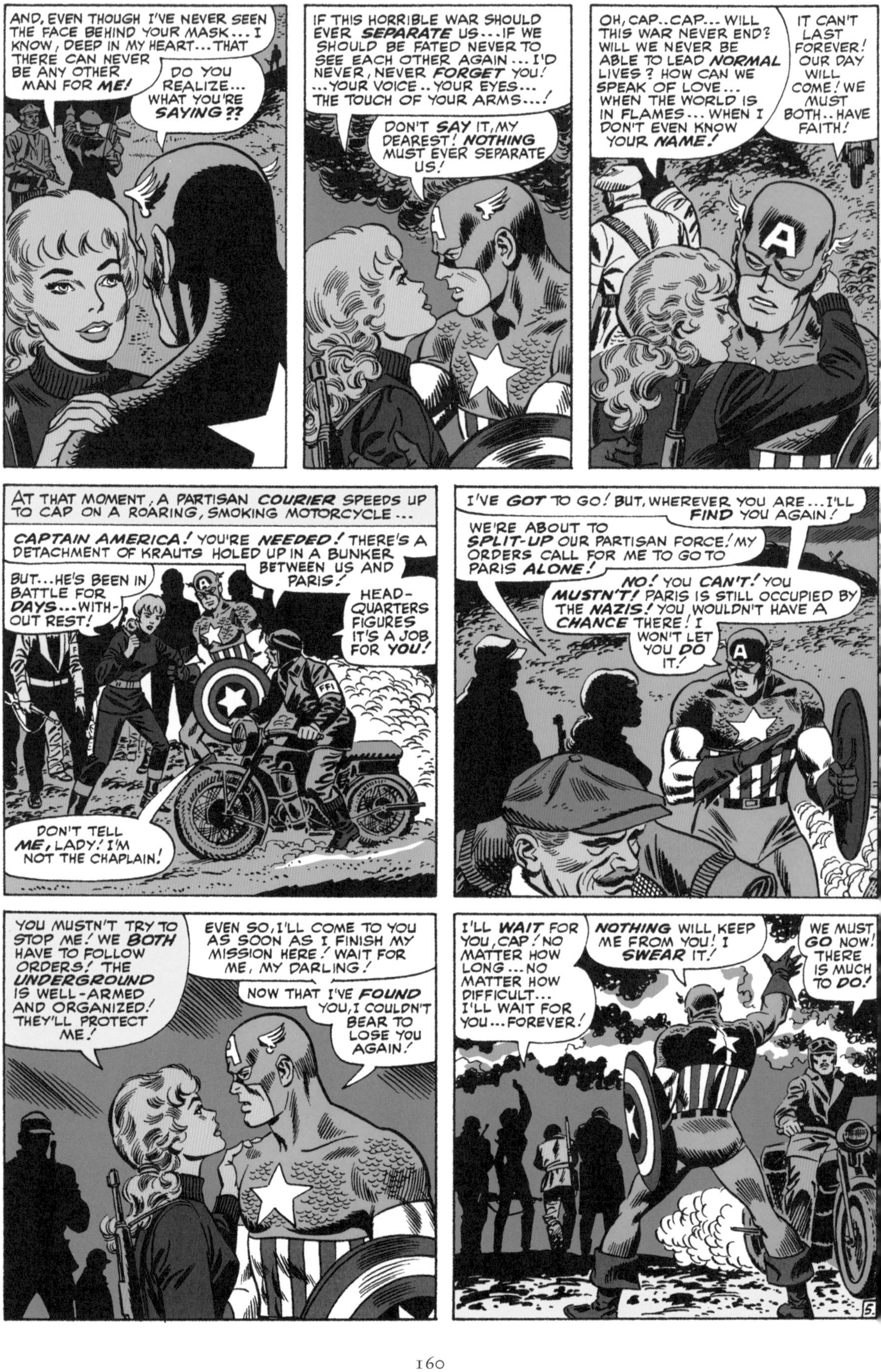
AND, EVEN THOUGH I'VE NEVER SEEN THE FACE BEHIND YOUR MASK... I KNOW, DEEP IN MY HEART... THAT THERE CAN NEVER BE ANY OTHER MAN FOR ME!
DO YOU REALIZE... WHAT YOU'RE SAYING??
IF THIS HORRIBLE WAR SHOULD EVER SEPARATE US... IF WE SHOULD BE FATED NEVER TO SEE EACH OTHER AGAIN... I'D NEVER, NEVER FORGET YOU! ...YOUR VOICE.. YOUR EYES... THE TOUCH OF YOUR ARMS...!
DON'T SAY IT, MY DEAREST! NOTHING MUST EVER SEPARATE US!
OH, CAP.. CAP... WILL THIS WAR NEVER END? WILL WE NEVER BE ABLE TO LEAD NORMAL LIVES? HOW CAN WE SPEAK OF LOVE... WHEN THE WORLD IS IN FLAMES... WHEN I DON'T EVEN KNOW YOUR NAME!
IT CAN'T LAST FOREVER! OUR DAY WILL COME! WE MUST BOTH.. HAVE FAITH!
AT THAT MOMENT, A PARTISAN COURIER SPEEDS UP TO CAP ON A ROARING, SMOKING MOTORCYCLE...
CAPTAIN AMERICA! YOU'RE NEEDED! THERE'S A DETACHMENT OF KRAUTS HOLED UP IN A BUNKER BETWEEN US AND PARIS!
BUT... HE'S BEEN IN BATTLE FOR DAYS... WITHOUT REST!
HEAD-QUARTERS FIGURES IT'S A JOB FOR YOU!
DON'T TELL ME, LADY! I'M NOT THE CHAPLAIN!
I'VE GOT TO GO! BUT, WHEREVER YOU ARE... I'LL FIND YOU AGAIN!
WE'RE ABOUT TO SPLIT-UP OUR PARTISAN FORCE! MY ORDERS CALL FOR ME TO GO TO PARIS ALONE!
NO! YOU CAN'T! YOU MUSTN'T! PARIS IS STILL OCCUPIED BY THE NAZIS! YOU WOULDN'T HAVE A CHANCE THERE! I WON'T LET YOU DO IT!
YOU MUSTN'T TRY TO STOP ME! WE BOTH HAVE TO FOLLOW ORDERS! THE UNDERGROUND IS WELL-ARMED AND ORGANIZED! THEY'LL PROTECT ME!
EVEN SO, I'LL COME TO YOU AS SOON AS I FINISH MY MISSION HERE! WAIT FOR ME, MY DARLING!
NOW THAT I'VE FOUND YOU, I COULDN'T BEAR TO LOSE YOU AGAIN!
I'LL WAIT FOR YOU, CAP! NO MATTER HOW LONG... NO MATTER HOW DIFFICULT... I'LL WAIT FOR YOU... FOREVER!
NOTHING WILL KEEP ME FROM YOU! I SWEAR IT!
WE MUST GO NOW! THERE IS MUCH TO DO!
5.

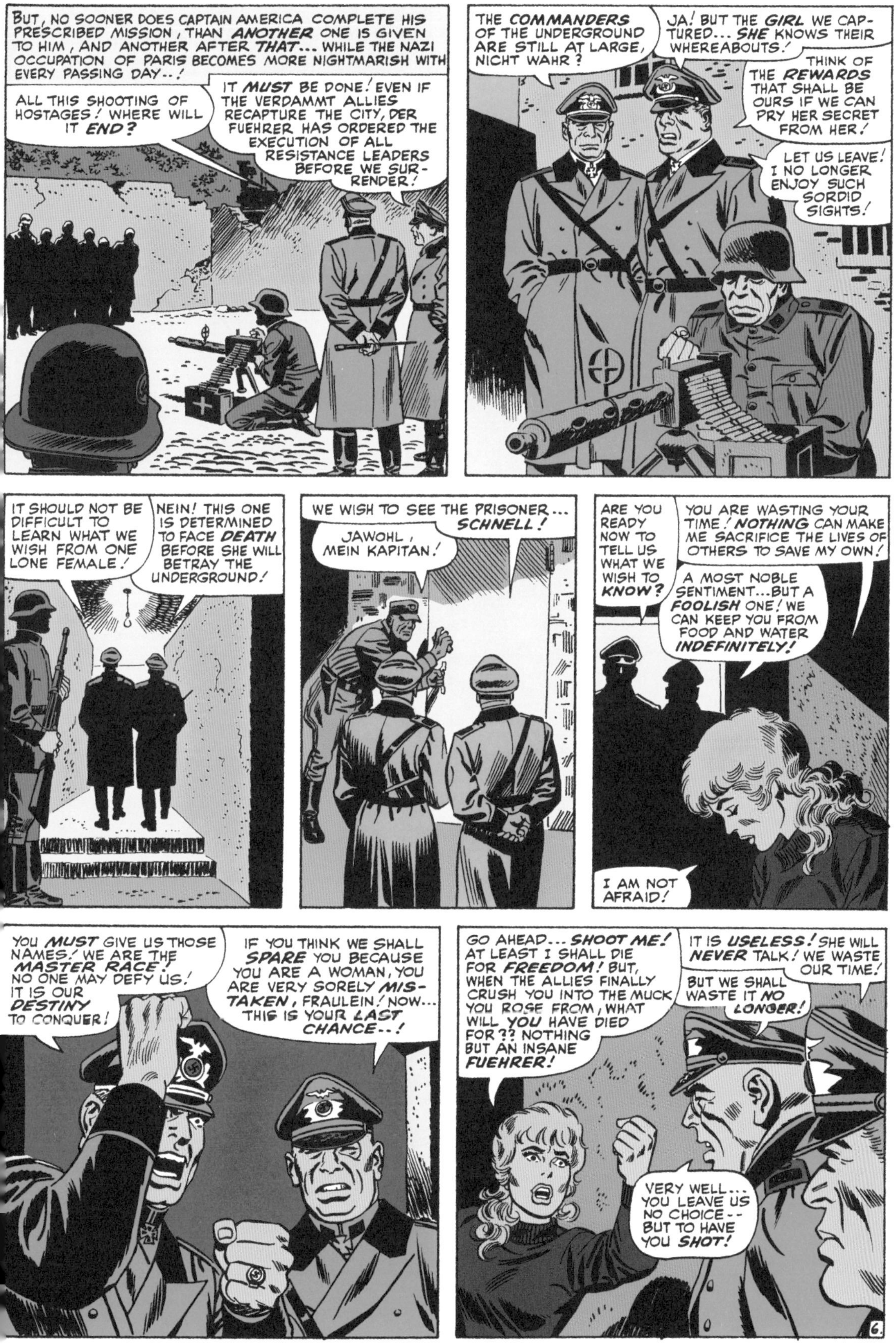
BUT, NO SOONER DOES CAPTAIN AMERICA COMPLETE HIS PRESCRIBED MISSION, THAN ANOTHER ONE IS GIVEN TO HIM, AND ANOTHER AFTER THAT... WHILE THE NAZI OCCUPATION OF PARIS BECOMES MORE NIGHTMARISH WITH EVERY PASSING DAY--!
ALL THIS SHOOTING OF HOSTAGES! WHERE WILL IT END?
IT MUST BE DONE! EVEN IF THE VERDAMMT ALLIES RECAPTURE THE CITY, DER FUEHRER HAS ORDERED THE EXECUTION OF ALL RESISTANCE LEADERS BEFORE WE SURRENDER!
THE COMMANDERS OF THE UNDERGROUND ARE STILL AT LARGE, NICHT WAHR?
JA! BUT THE GIRL WE CAPTURED... SHE KNOWS THEIR WHEREABOUTS!
THINK OF THE REWARDS THAT SHALL BE OURS IF WE CAN PRY HER SECRET FROM HER!
LET US LEAVE! I NO LONGER ENJOY SUCH SORDID SIGHTS!
IT SHOULD NOT BE DIFFICULT TO LEARN WHAT WE WISH FROM ONE LONE FEMALE!
NEIN! THIS ONE IS DETERMINED TO FACE DEATH BEFORE SHE WILL BETRAY THE UNDERGROUND!
WE WISH TO SEE THE PRISONER... SCHNELL!
JAWOHL, MEIN KAPITAN!
ARE YOU READY NOW TO TELL US WHAT WE WISH TO KNOW?
YOU ARE WASTING YOUR TIME! NOTHING CAN MAKE ME SACRIFICE THE LIVES OF OTHERS TO SAVE MY OWN!
A MOST NOBLE SENTIMENT...BUT A FOOLISH ONE! WE CAN KEEP YOU FROM FOOD AND WATER INDEFINITELY!
I AM NOT AFRAID!
YOU MUST GIVE US THOSE NAMES! WE ARE THE MASTER RACE! NO ONE MAY DEFY US! IT IS OUR DESTINY TO CONQUER!
IF YOU THINK WE SHALL SPARE YOU BECAUSE YOU ARE A WOMAN, YOU ARE VERY SORELY MISTAKEN, FRAULEIN! NOW... THIS IS YOUR LAST CHANCE--!
GO AHEAD... SHOOT ME! AT LEAST I SHALL DIE FOR FREEDOM! BUT, WHEN THE ALLIES FINALLY CRUSH YOU INTO THE MUCK YOU ROSE FROM, WHAT WILL YOU HAVE DIED FOR?? NOTHING BUT AN INSANE FUEHRER!
IT IS USELESS! SHE WILL NEVER TALK! WE WASTE OUR TIME!
BUT WE SHALL WASTE IT NO LONGER!
VERY WELL... YOU LEAVE US NO CHOICE-- BUT TO HAVE YOU SHOT!
6.

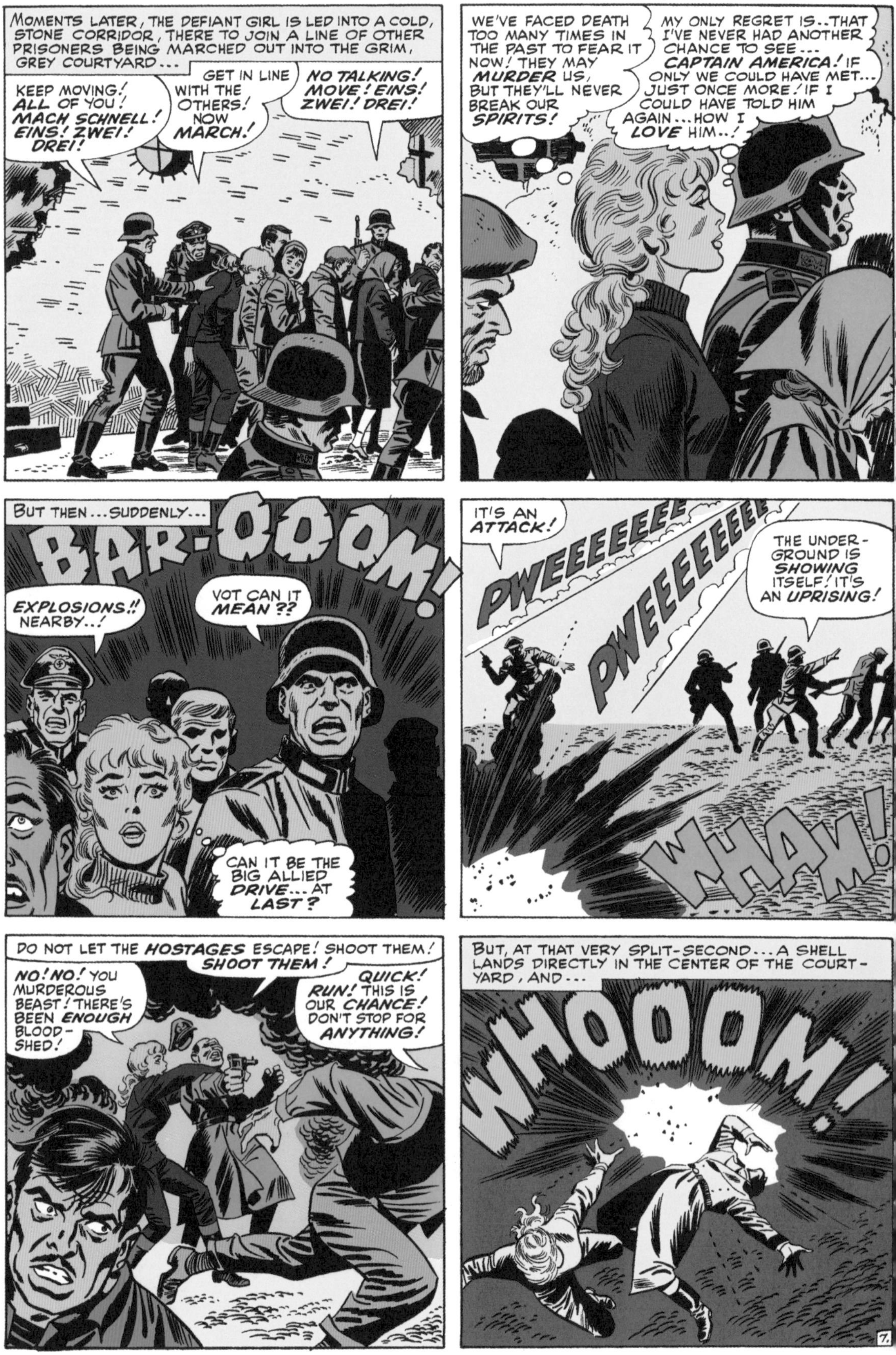
MOMENTS LATER, THE DEFIANT GIRL IS LED INTO A COLD, STONE CORRIDOR, THERE TO JOIN A LINE OF OTHER PRISONERS BEING MARCHED OUT INTO THE GRIM, GREY COURTYARD...
KEEP MOVING! ALL OF YOU! MACH SCHNELL! EINS! ZWEI! DREI!
GET IN LINE WITH THE OTHERS! NOW MARCH!
NO TALKING! MOVE! EINS! ZWEI! DREI!
WE'VE FACED DEATH TOO MANY TIMES IN THE PAST TO FEAR IT NOW! THEY MAY MURDER US, BUT THEY'LL NEVER BREAK OUR SPIRITS!
MY ONLY REGRET IS..THAT I'VE NEVER HAD ANOTHER CHANCE TO SEE... CAPTAIN AMERICA! IF ONLY WE COULD HAVE MET... JUST ONCE MORE! IF I COULD HAVE TOLD HIM AGAIN...HOW I LOVE HIM..!
BUT THEN...SUDDENLY...
BAR-OOOM!
EXPLOSIONS!! NEARBY..!
VOT CAN IT MEAN??
CAN IT BE THE BIG ALLIED DRIVE... AT LAST?
IT'S AN ATTACK!
PWEEEEEEE
PWEEEEEEEE
THE UNDER-GROUND IS SHOWING ITSELF! IT'S AN UPRISING!
WHAM!
DO NOT LET THE HOSTAGES ESCAPE! SHOOT THEM! SHOOT THEM!
NO! NO! YOU MURDEROUS BEAST! THERE'S BEEN ENOUGH BLOOD-SHED!
QUICK! RUN! THIS IS OUR CHANCE! DON'T STOP FOR ANYTHING!
BUT, AT THAT VERY SPLIT-SECOND... A SHELL LANDS DIRECTLY IN THE CENTER OF THE COURT-YARD, AND...
WHOOOM!
7.

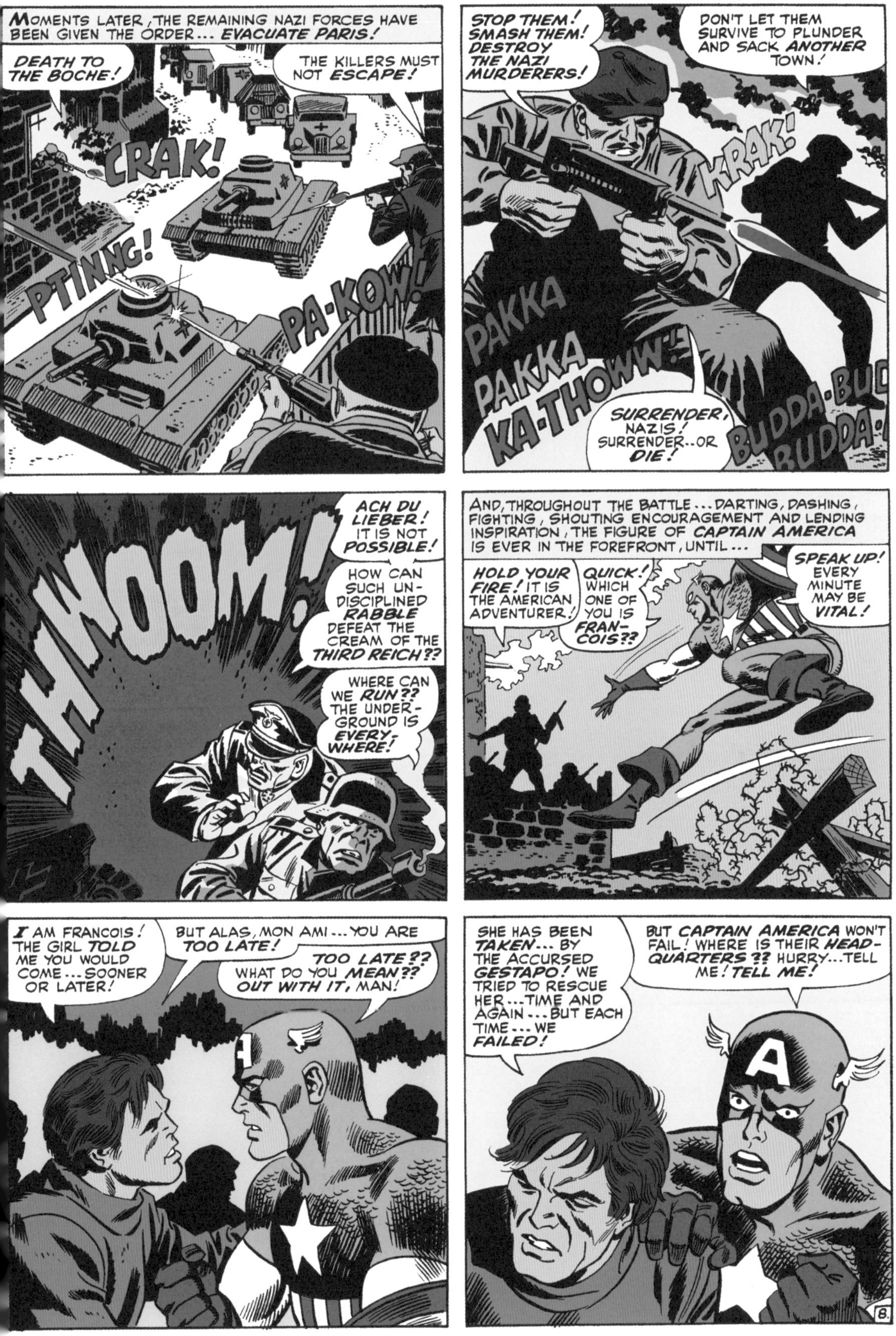
MOMENTS LATER, THE REMAINING NAZI FORCES HAVE BEEN GIVEN THE ORDER... EVACUATE PARIS!
DEATH TO THE BOCHE!
THE KILLERS MUST NOT ESCAPE!
CRAK!
PTINNG!
PA-KOW!
STOP THEM! SMASH THEM! DESTROY THE NAZI MURDERERS!
DON'T LET THEM SURVIVE TO PLUNDER AND SACK ANOTHER TOWN!
KRAK!
PAKKA
PAKKA
KA-THOWW!
SURRENDER, NAZIS! SURRENDER...OR DIE!
BUDDA-BUD
BUDDA-
THOOM!
ACH DU LIEBER! IT IS NOT POSSIBLE!
HOW CAN SUCH UN-DISCIPLINED RABBLE DEFEAT THE CREAM OF THE THIRD REICH??
WHERE CAN WE RUN?? THE UNDER-GROUND IS EVERY-WHERE!
AND, THROUGHOUT THE BATTLE... DARTING, DASHING, FIGHTING, SHOUTING ENCOURAGEMENT AND LENDING INSPIRATION, THE FIGURE OF CAPTAIN AMERICA IS EVER IN THE FOREFRONT, UNTIL...
HOLD YOUR FIRE! IT IS THE AMERICAN ADVENTURER!
QUICK! WHICH ONE OF YOU IS FRAN-COIS??
SPEAK UP! EVERY MINUTE MAY BE VITAL!
I AM FRANCOIS! THE GIRL TOLD ME YOU WOULD COME... SOONER OR LATER!
BUT ALAS, MON AMI... YOU ARE TOO LATE!
TOO LATE?? WHAT DO YOU MEAN?? OUT WITH IT, MAN!
SHE HAS BEEN TAKEN... BY THE ACCURSED GESTAPO! WE TRIED TO RESCUE HER... TIME AND AGAIN... BUT EACH TIME... WE FAILED!
BUT CAPTAIN AMERICA WON'T FAIL! WHERE IS THEIR HEAD-QUARTERS?? HURRY... TELL ME! TELL ME!
8.

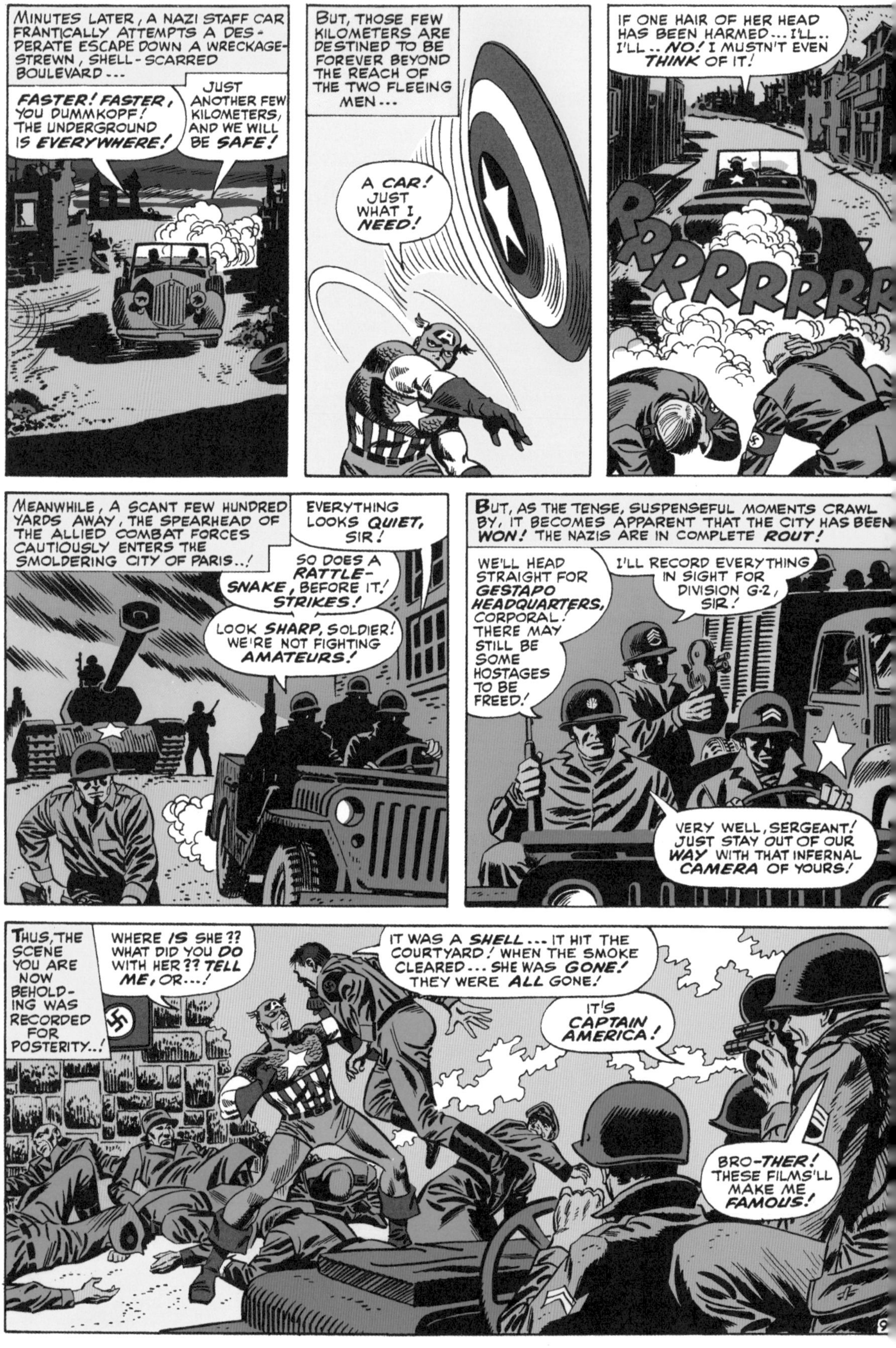

MINUTES LATER, A NAZI STAFF CAR FRANTICALLY ATTEMPTS A DESPERATE ESCAPE DOWN A WRECKAGE-STREWN, SHELL-SCARRED BOULEVARD...
FASTER! FASTER, YOU DUMMKOPF! THE UNDERGROUND IS EVERYWHERE!
JUST ANOTHER FEW KILOMETERS, AND WE WILL BE SAFE!
BUT, THOSE FEW KILOMETERS ARE DESTINED TO BE FOREVER BEYOND THE REACH OF THE TWO FLEEING MEN...
A CAR! JUST WHAT I NEED!
IF ONE HAIR OF HER HEAD HAS BEEN HARMED... I'LL.. I'LL.. NO! I MUSTN'T EVEN THINK OF IT!
RRRRRRRRR
MEANWHILE, A SCANT FEW HUNDRED YARDS AWAY, THE SPEARHEAD OF THE ALLIED COMBAT FORCES CAUTIOUSLY ENTERS THE SMOLDERING CITY OF PARIS..!
EVERYTHING LOOKS QUIET, SIR!
SO DOES A RATTLE-SNAKE, BEFORE IT STRIKES!
LOOK SHARP, SOLDIER! WE'RE NOT FIGHTING AMATEURS!
BUT, AS THE TENSE, SUSPENSEFUL MOMENTS CRAWL BY, IT BECOMES APPARENT THAT THE CITY HAS BEEN WON! THE NAZIS ARE IN COMPLETE ROUT!
WE'LL HEAD STRAIGHT FOR GESTAPO HEADQUARTERS, CORPORAL! THERE MAY STILL BE SOME HOSTAGES TO BE FREED!
I'LL RECORD EVERYTHING IN SIGHT FOR DIVISION G-2, SIR!
VERY WELL, SERGEANT! JUST STAY OUT OF OUR WAY WITH THAT INFERNAL CAMERA OF YOURS!
THUS, THE SCENE YOU ARE NOW BEHOLDING WAS RECORDED FOR POSTERITY..!
WHERE IS SHE?? WHAT DID YOU DO WITH HER?? TELL ME, OR...!
IT WAS A SHELL... IT HIT THE COURTYARD! WHEN THE SMOKE CLEARED... SHE WAS GONE! THEY WERE ALL GONE!
IT'S CAPTAIN AMERICA!
BRO-THER! THESE FILMS'LL MAKE ME FAMOUS!
9

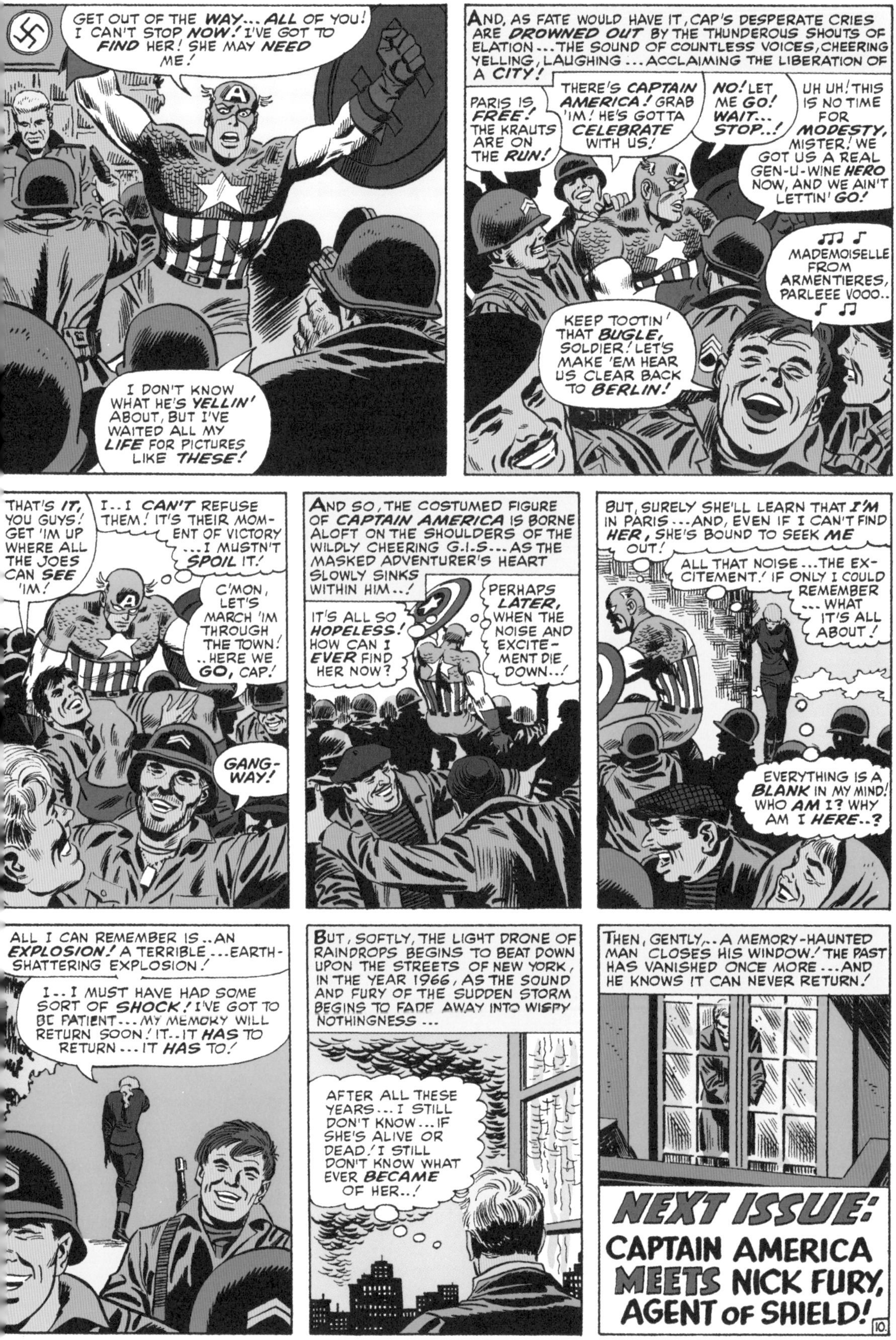
GET OUT OF THE WAY... ALL OF YOU! I CAN'T STOP NOW! I'VE GOT TO FIND HER! SHE MAY NEED ME!
I DON'T KNOW WHAT HE'S YELLIN' ABOUT, BUT I'VE WAITED ALL MY LIFE FOR PICTURES LIKE THESE!
AND, AS FATE WOULD HAVE IT, CAP'S DESPERATE CRIES ARE DROWNED OUT BY THE THUNDEROUS SHOUTS OF ELATION ...THE SOUND OF COUNTLESS VOICES, CHEERING YELLING, LAUGHING ... ACCLAIMING THE LIBERATION OF A CITY!
PARIS IS FREE! THE KRAUTS ARE ON THE RUN!
THERE'S CAPTAIN AMERICA! GRAB 'IM! HE'S GOTTA CELEBRATE WITH US!
NO! LET ME GO! WAIT... STOP...!
UH UH! THIS IS NO TIME FOR MODESTY, MISTER! WE GOT US A REAL GEN-U-WINE HERO NOW, AND WE AIN'T LETTIN' GO!
MADEMOISELLE FROM ARMENTIERES, PARLEEE VOOO..
KEEP TOOTIN' THAT BUGLE, SOLDIER! LET'S MAKE 'EM HEAR US CLEAR BACK TO BERLIN!
THAT'S IT, YOU GUYS! GET 'IM UP WHERE ALL THE JOES CAN SEE 'IM!
I..I CAN'T REFUSE THEM! IT'S THEIR MOMENT OF VICTORY ...I MUSTN'T SPOIL IT!
C'MON, LET'S MARCH 'IM THROUGH THE TOWN! ..HERE WE GO, CAP!
GANG-WAY!
AND SO, THE COSTUMED FIGURE OF CAPTAIN AMERICA IS BORNE ALOFT ON THE SHOULDERS OF THE WILDLY CHEERING G.I.S...AS THE MASKED ADVENTURER'S HEART SLOWLY SINKS WITHIN HIM..!
IT'S ALL SO HOPELESS! HOW CAN I EVER FIND HER NOW?
PERHAPS LATER, WHEN THE NOISE AND EXCITEMENT DIE DOWN..!
BUT, SURELY SHE'LL LEARN THAT I'M IN PARIS...AND, EVEN IF I CAN'T FIND HER, SHE'S BOUND TO SEEK ME OUT!
ALL THAT NOISE ...THE EXCITEMENT! IF ONLY I COULD REMEMBER ...WHAT IT'S ALL ABOUT!
EVERYTHING IS A BLANK IN MY MIND! WHO AM I? WHY AM I HERE..?
ALL I CAN REMEMBER IS..AN EXPLOSION! A TERRIBLE ...EARTH-SHATTERING EXPLOSION!
I..I MUST HAVE HAD SOME SORT OF SHOCK! I'VE GOT TO BE PATIENT... MY MEMORY WILL RETURN SOON! IT..IT HAS TO RETURN ... IT HAS TO!
BUT, SOFTLY, THE LIGHT DRONE OF RAINDROPS BEGINS TO BEAT DOWN UPON THE STREETS OF NEW YORK, IN THE YEAR 1966, AS THE SOUND AND FURY OF THE SUDDEN STORM BEGINS TO FADE AWAY INTO WISPY NOTHINGNESS ...
AFTER ALL THESE YEARS... I STILL DON'T KNOW... IF SHE'S ALIVE OR DEAD! I STILL DON'T KNOW WHAT EVER BECAME OF HER..!
THEN, GENTLY,.. A MEMORY-HAUNTED MAN CLOSES HIS WINDOW! THE PAST HAS VANISHED ONCE MORE ...AND HE KNOWS IT CAN NEVER RETURN!
NEXT ISSUE:
CAPTAIN AMERICA MEETS NICK FURY, AGENT OF SHIELD!
10.

TALES OF SUSPENSE #78,

JUNE 1966,

"THEM!"

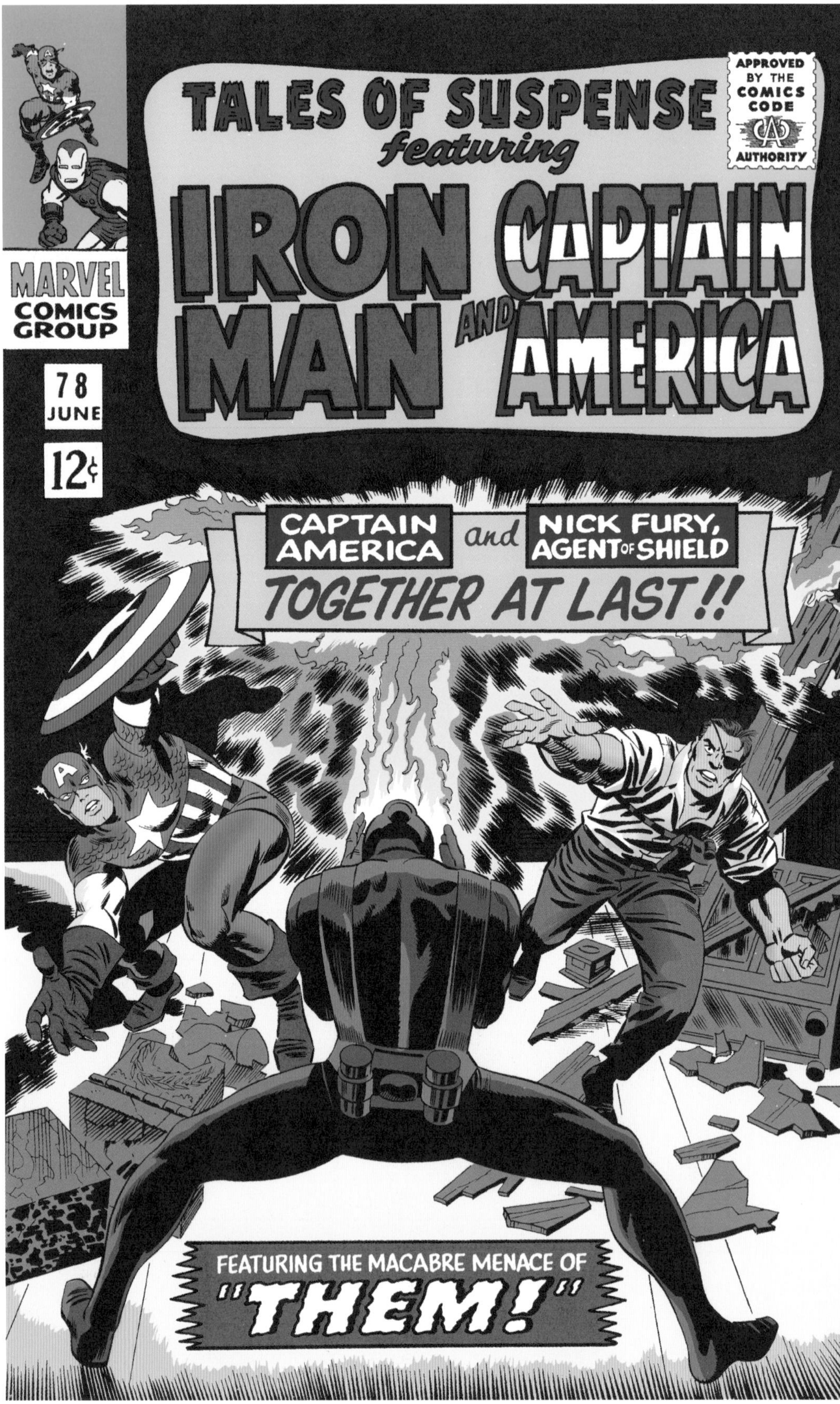
TALES OF SUSPENSE
featuring
IRON MAN AND CAPTAIN AMERICA
APPROVED BY THE COMICS CODE AUTHORITY
MARVEL COMICS GROUP
78 JUNE
12¢
CAPTAIN AMERICA and NICK FURY, AGENT OF SHIELD
TOGETHER AT LAST!!
FEATURING THE MACABRE MENACE OF
"THEM!"

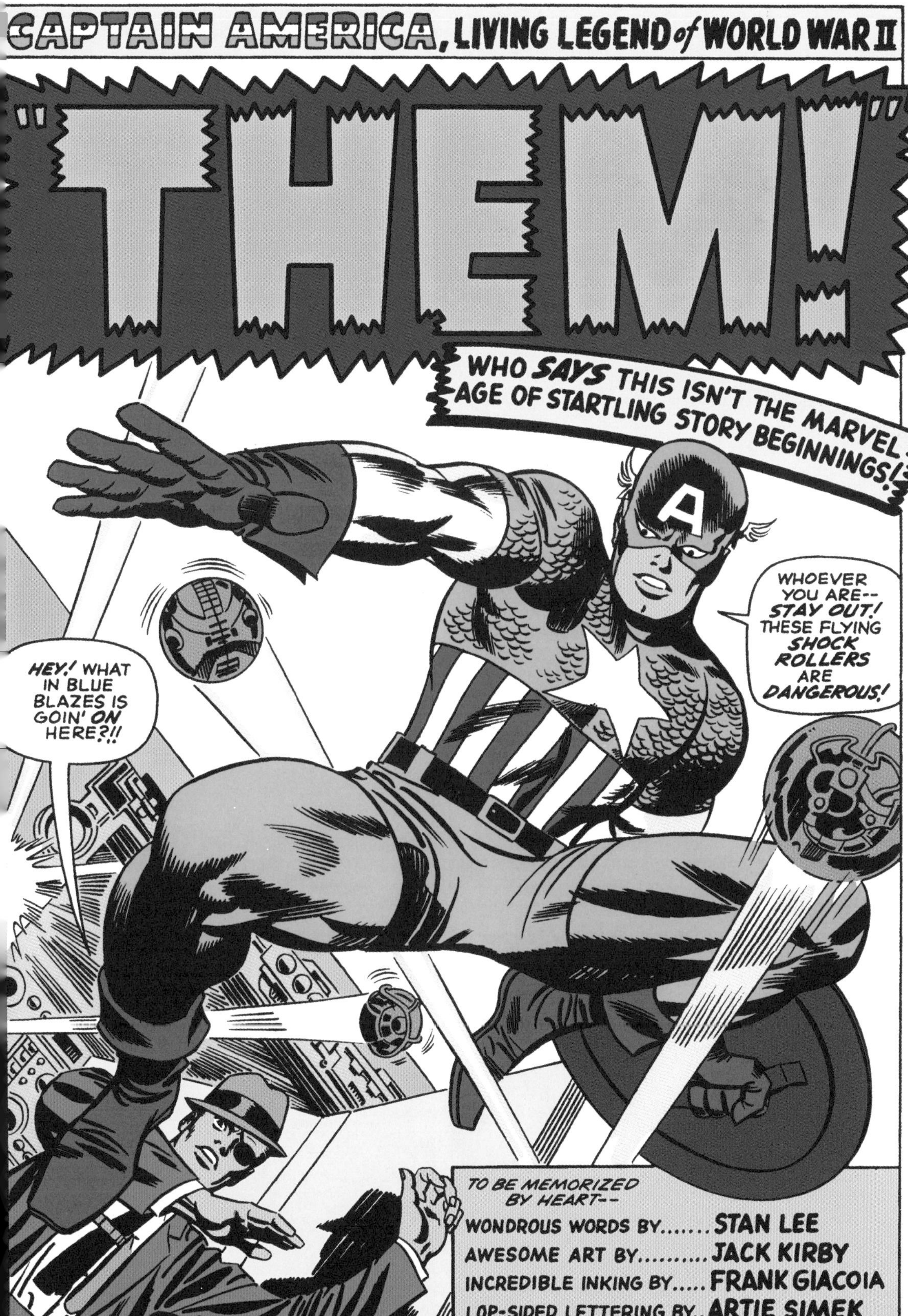

CAPTAIN AMERICA, LIVING LEGEND of WORLD WAR II
"THEM!"
WHO SAYS THIS ISN'T THE MARVEL AGE OF STARTLING STORY BEGINNINGS!
HEY! WHAT IN BLUE BLAZES IS GOIN' ON HERE?!!
WHOEVER YOU ARE-- STAY OUT! THESE FLYING SHOCK ROLLERS ARE DANGEROUS!
TO BE MEMORIZED BY HEART--
WONDROUS WORDS BY...... STAN LEE
AWESOME ART BY.......... JACK KIRBY
INCREDIBLE INKING BY..... FRANK GIACOIA
LOP-SIDED LETTERING BY.. ARTIE SIMEK
1

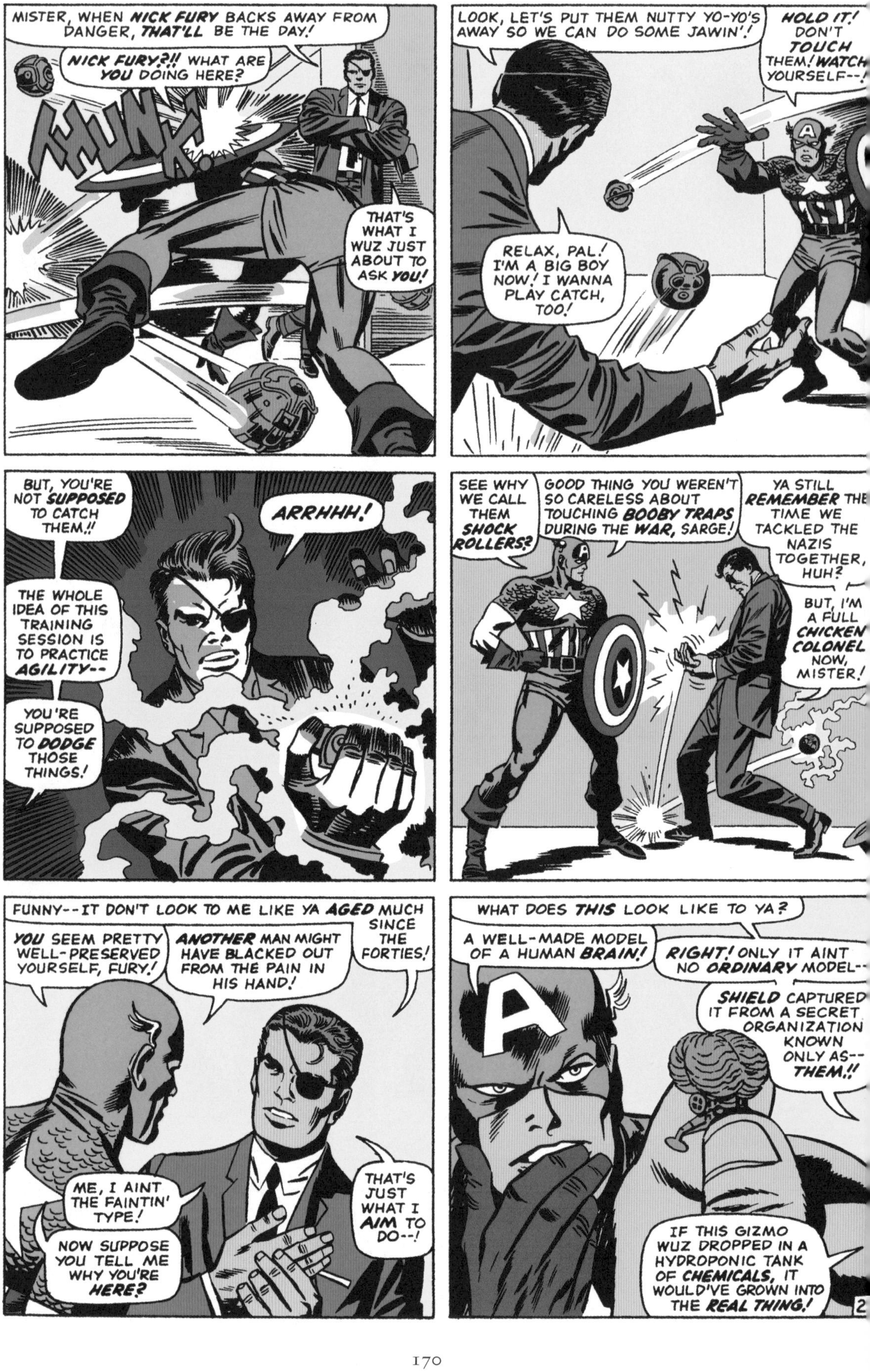

MISTER, WHEN NICK FURY BACKS AWAY FROM DANGER, THAT'LL BE THE DAY!
NICK FURY?!! WHAT ARE YOU DOING HERE?
THUNK!
THAT'S WHAT I WUZ JUST ABOUT TO ASK YOU!
LOOK, LET'S PUT THEM NUTTY YO-YO'S AWAY SO WE CAN DO SOME JAWIN'!
HOLD IT! DON'T TOUCH THEM! WATCH YOURSELF--!
RELAX, PAL! I'M A BIG BOY NOW! I WANNA PLAY CATCH, TOO!
BUT, YOU'RE NOT SUPPOSED TO CATCH THEM!!
ARRHHH!
THE WHOLE IDEA OF THIS TRAINING SESSION IS TO PRACTICE AGILITY--
YOU'RE SUPPOSED TO DODGE THOSE THINGS!
SEE WHY WE CALL THEM SHOCK ROLLERS?
GOOD THING YOU WEREN'T SO CARELESS ABOUT TOUCHING BOOBY TRAPS DURING THE WAR, SARGE!
YA STILL REMEMBER THE TIME WE TACKLED THE NAZIS TOGETHER, HUH?
BUT, I'M A FULL CHICKEN COLONEL NOW, MISTER!
FUNNY--IT DON'T LOOK TO ME LIKE YA AGED MUCH SINCE THE FORTIES!
YOU SEEM PRETTY WELL-PRESERVED YOURSELF, FURY!
ANOTHER MAN MIGHT HAVE BLACKED OUT FROM THE PAIN IN HIS HAND!
ME, I AINT THE FAINTIN' TYPE!
NOW SUPPOSE YOU TELL ME WHY YOU'RE HERE?
THAT'S JUST WHAT I AIM TO DO--!
WHAT DOES THIS LOOK LIKE TO YA?
A WELL-MADE MODEL OF A HUMAN BRAIN!
RIGHT! ONLY IT AINT NO ORDINARY MODEL--
SHIELD CAPTURED IT FROM A SECRET ORGANIZATION KNOWN ONLY AS--THEM!!
IF THIS GIZMO WUZ DROPPED IN A HYDROPONIC TANK OF CHEMICALS, IT WOULD'VE GROWN INTO THE REAL THING!
2

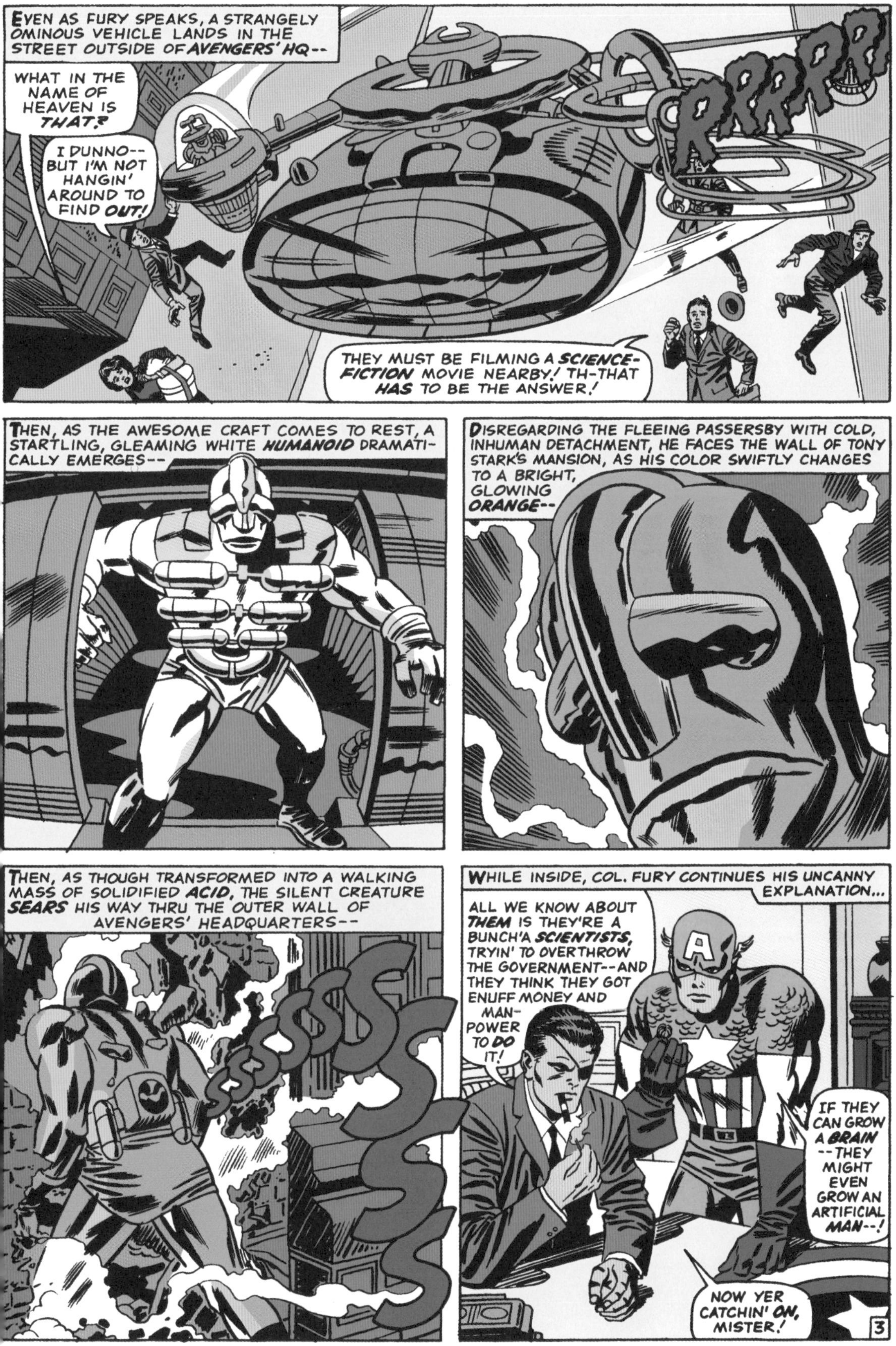
EVEN AS FURY SPEAKS, A STRANGELY OMINOUS VEHICLE LANDS IN THE STREET OUTSIDE OF AVENGERS' HQ--
WHAT IN THE NAME OF HEAVEN IS THAT?
I DUNNO-- BUT I'M NOT HANGIN' AROUND TO FIND OUT!
RRRRRR
THEY MUST BE FILMING A SCIENCE-FICTION MOVIE NEARBY! TH-THAT HAS TO BE THE ANSWER!
THEN, AS THE AWESOME CRAFT COMES TO REST, A STARTLING, GLEAMING WHITE HUMANOID DRAMATICALLY EMERGES--
DISREGARDING THE FLEEING PASSERSBY WITH COLD, INHUMAN DETACHMENT, HE FACES THE WALL OF TONY STARK'S MANSION, AS HIS COLOR SWIFTLY CHANGES TO A BRIGHT, GLOWING ORANGE--
THEN, AS THOUGH TRANSFORMED INTO A WALKING MASS OF SOLIDIFIED ACID, THE SILENT CREATURE SEARS HIS WAY THRU THE OUTER WALL OF AVENGERS' HEADQUARTERS--
SSSSSSSSS
WHILE INSIDE, COL. FURY CONTINUES HIS UNCANNY EXPLANATION...
ALL WE KNOW ABOUT THEM IS THEY'RE A BUNCH'A SCIENTISTS, TRYIN' TO OVERTHROW THE GOVERNMENT--AND THEY THINK THEY GOT ENUFF MONEY AND MAN-POWER TO DO IT!
IF THEY CAN GROW A BRAIN --THEY MIGHT EVEN GROW AN ARTIFICIAL MAN--!
NOW YER CATCHIN' ON, MISTER!
3

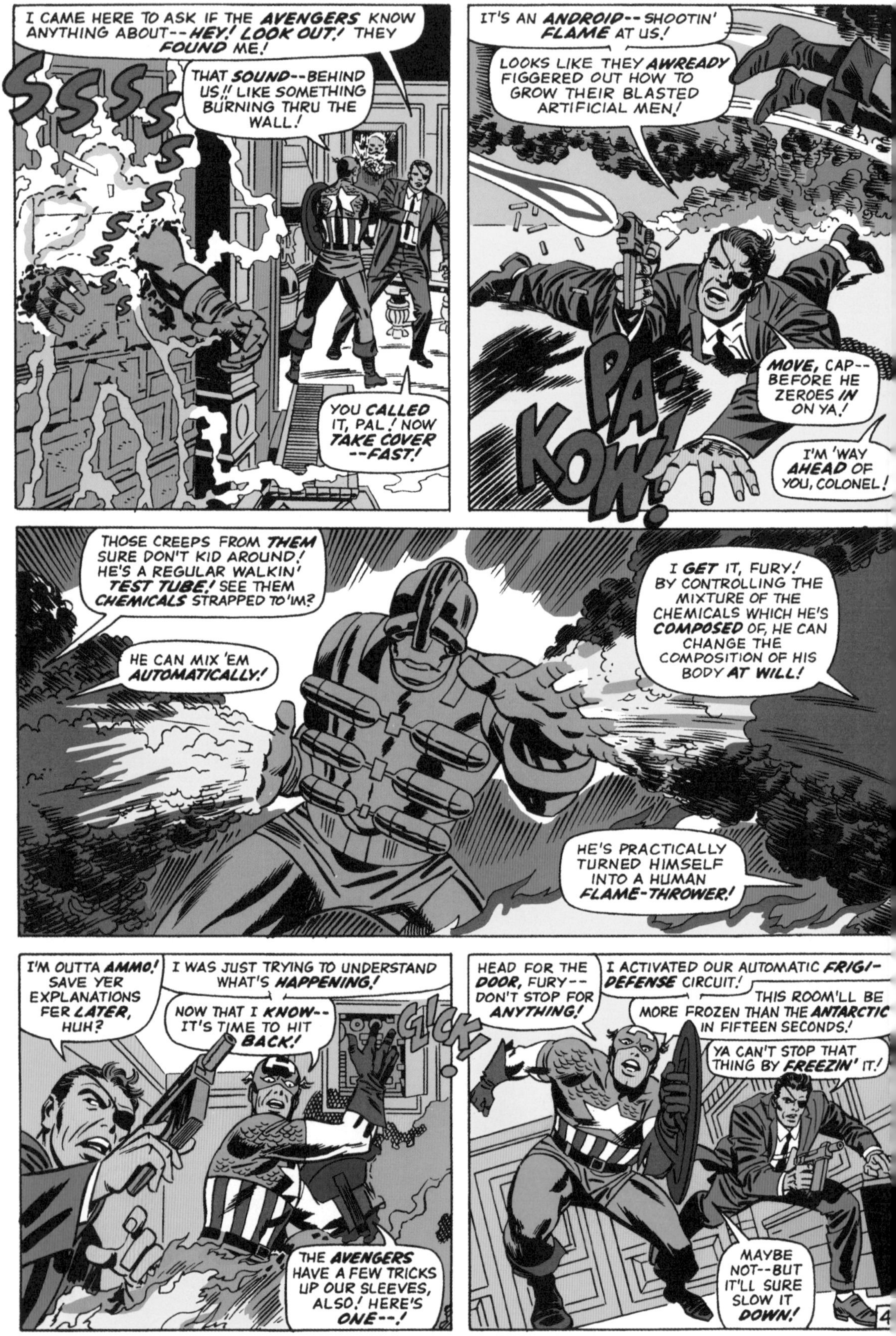
I CAME HERE TO ASK IF THE AVENGERS KNOW ANYTHING ABOUT--HEY! LOOK OUT! THEY FOUND ME!
SSSSSSSSS
THAT SOUND--BEHIND US!! LIKE SOMETHING BURNING THRU THE WALL!
YOU CALLED IT, PAL! NOW TAKE COVER --FAST!
IT'S AN ANDROID--SHOOTIN' FLAME AT US!
LOOKS LIKE THEY AWREADY FIGGERED OUT HOW TO GROW THEIR BLASTED ARTIFICIAL MEN!
PA-KOW!
MOVE, CAP-- BEFORE HE ZEROES IN ON YA!
I'M 'WAY AHEAD OF YOU, COLONEL!
THOSE CREEPS FROM THEM SURE DON'T KID AROUND! HE'S A REGULAR WALKIN' TEST TUBE! SEE THEM CHEMICALS STRAPPED TO 'IM?
HE CAN MIX 'EM AUTOMATICALLY!
I GET IT, FURY! BY CONTROLLING THE MIXTURE OF THE CHEMICALS WHICH HE'S COMPOSED OF, HE CAN CHANGE THE COMPOSITION OF HIS BODY AT WILL!
HE'S PRACTICALLY TURNED HIMSELF INTO A HUMAN FLAME-THROWER!
I'M OUTTA AMMO! SAVE YER EXPLANATIONS FER LATER, HUH?
I WAS JUST TRYING TO UNDERSTAND WHAT'S HAPPENING!
NOW THAT I KNOW-- IT'S TIME TO HIT BACK!
CLICK!
THE AVENGERS HAVE A FEW TRICKS UP OUR SLEEVES, ALSO! HERE'S ONE--!
HEAD FOR THE DOOR, FURY-- DON'T STOP FOR ANYTHING!
I ACTIVATED OUR AUTOMATIC FRIGI-DEFENSE CIRCUIT!
THIS ROOM'LL BE MORE FROZEN THAN THE ANTARCTIC IN FIFTEEN SECONDS!
YA CAN'T STOP THAT THING BY FREEZIN' IT!
MAYBE NOT--BUT IT'LL SURE SLOW IT DOWN!
4

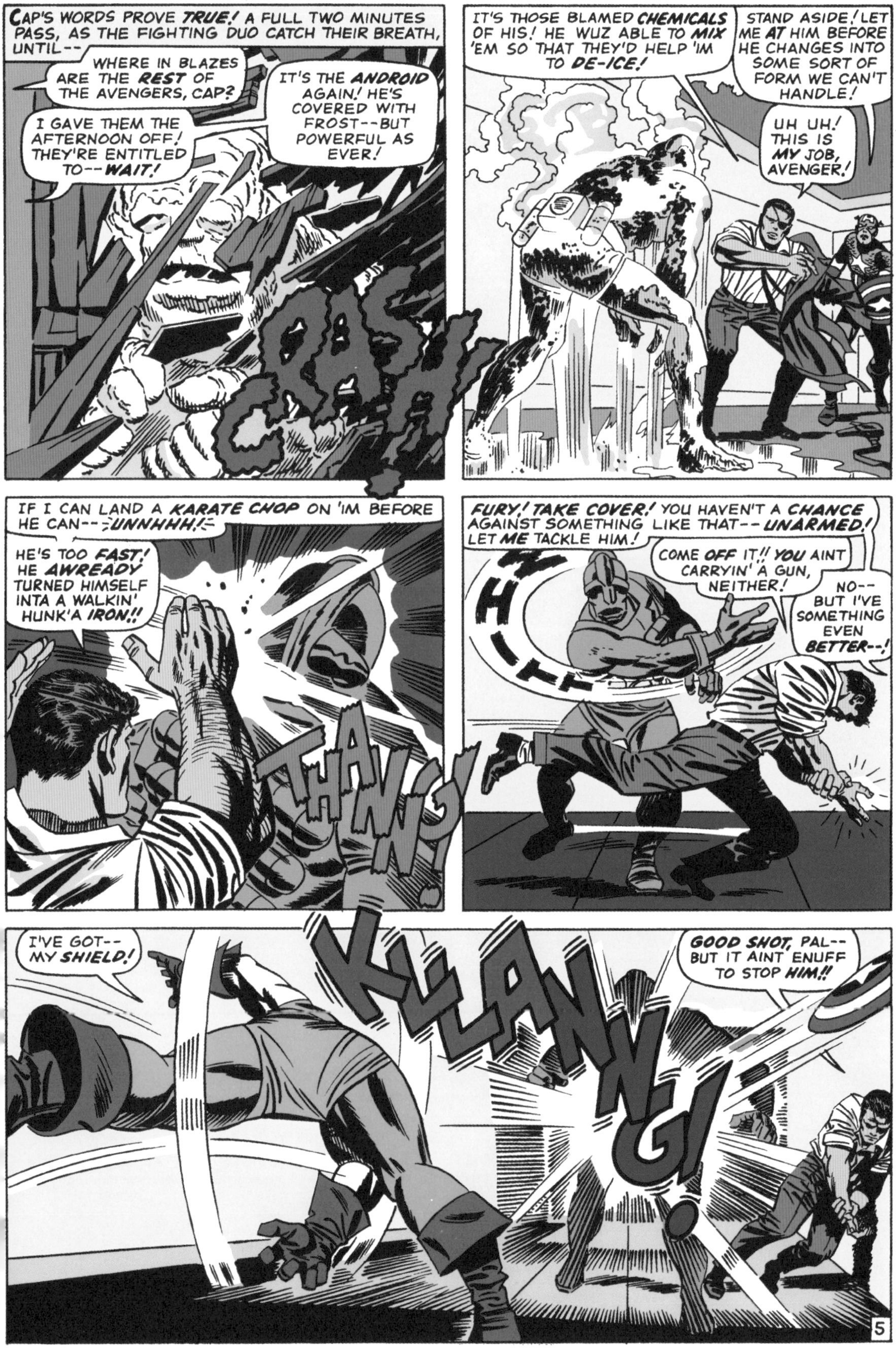
CAP'S WORDS PROVE TRUE! A FULL TWO MINUTES PASS, AS THE FIGHTING DUO CATCH THEIR BREATH, UNTIL--
WHERE IN BLAZES ARE THE REST OF THE AVENGERS, CAP?
I GAVE THEM THE AFTERNOON OFF! THEY'RE ENTITLED TO--WAIT!
IT'S THE ANDROID AGAIN! HE'S COVERED WITH FROST--BUT POWERFUL AS EVER!
CRASH
IT'S THOSE BLAMED CHEMICALS OF HIS! HE WUZ ABLE TO MIX 'EM SO THAT THEY'D HELP 'IM TO DE-ICE!
STAND ASIDE! LET ME AT HIM BEFORE HE CHANGES INTO SOME SORT OF FORM WE CAN'T HANDLE!
UH UH! THIS IS MY JOB, AVENGER!
IF I CAN LAND A KARATE CHOP ON 'IM BEFORE HE CAN--UNNHHH!
HE'S TOO FAST! HE AWREADY TURNED HIMSELF INTA A WALKIN' HUNK'A IRON!!
THANNG!
FURY! TAKE COVER! YOU HAVEN'T A CHANCE AGAINST SOMETHING LIKE THAT--UNARMED! LET ME TACKLE HIM!
COME OFF IT!! YOU AINT CARRYIN' A GUN, NEITHER!
NO--BUT I'VE SOMETHING EVEN BETTER--!
I'VE GOT--MY SHIELD!
KLLANNG!
GOOD SHOT, PAL--BUT IT AINT ENUFF TO STOP HIM!!
5

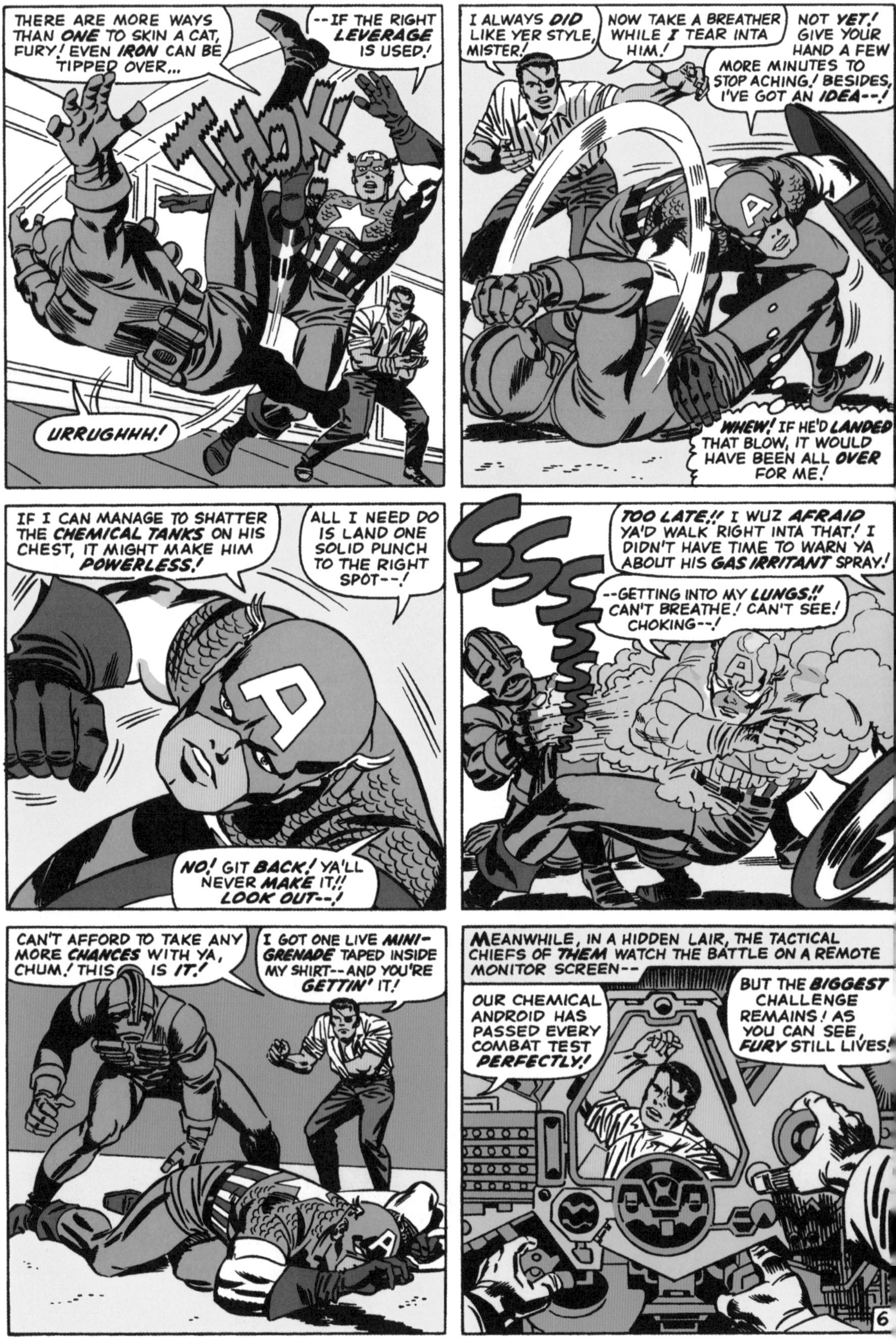
THERE ARE MORE WAYS THAN ONE TO SKIN A CAT, FURY! EVEN IRON CAN BE TIPPED OVER...
--IF THE RIGHT LEVERAGE IS USED!
THOK!
URRUGHHH!
I ALWAYS DID LIKE YER STYLE, MISTER!
NOW TAKE A BREATHER WHILE I TEAR INTA HIM!
NOT YET! GIVE YOUR HAND A FEW MORE MINUTES TO STOP ACHING! BESIDES, I'VE GOT AN IDEA--!
WHEW! IF HE'D LANDED THAT BLOW, IT WOULD HAVE BEEN ALL OVER FOR ME!
IF I CAN MANAGE TO SHATTER THE CHEMICAL TANKS ON HIS CHEST, IT MIGHT MAKE HIM POWERLESS!
ALL I NEED DO IS LAND ONE SOLID PUNCH TO THE RIGHT SPOT--!
NO! GIT BACK! YA'LL NEVER MAKE IT!! LOOK OUT--!
SSSSSSS
TOO LATE!! I WUZ AFRAID YA'D WALK RIGHT INTA THAT! I DIDN'T HAVE TIME TO WARN YA ABOUT HIS GAS IRRITANT SPRAY!
--GETTING INTO MY LUNGS!! CAN'T BREATHE! CAN'T SEE! CHOKING--!
CAN'T AFFORD TO TAKE ANY MORE CHANCES WITH YA, CHUM! THIS IS IT!
I GOT ONE LIVE MINI-GRENADE TAPED INSIDE MY SHIRT--AND YOU'RE GETTIN' IT!
MEANWHILE, IN A HIDDEN LAIR, THE TACTICAL CHIEFS OF THEM WATCH THE BATTLE ON A REMOTE MONITOR SCREEN--
OUR CHEMICAL ANDROID HAS PASSED EVERY COMBAT TEST PERFECTLY!
BUT THE BIGGEST CHALLENGE REMAINS! AS YOU CAN SEE, FURY STILL LIVES!
6

HE WON'T LIVE MUCH *LONGER!* IF OUR CHEMICAL ANDROID FAILS, WE SHALL SEND *ANOTHER* AFTER HIM!

TRUE! SOONER OR LATER, THE HEAD OF *SHIELD* MUST DIE! THEN, WITH THAT ORGANIZATION LEADERLESS, WE WILL BE ABLE TO COME OUT INTO THE OPEN!

BUT, UNTIL THAT TIME, WE MUST CONTINUE TO WEAR THESE ORNATE TRAPPINGS, TO STRIKE FEAR AND DREAD INTO THE HEARTS OF THOSE WHO SERVE US--AND THOSE WHO OPPOSE US, ALIKE!

WITH THE UNLIMITED *WEALTH* AT OUR DISPOSAL --WITH THE SCIENTIFIC GENIUSES WHO SERVE US--WE *CANNOT* FAIL!

OUR ONLY SETBACK WAS THE TIME WE ALLOWED *MENTALLO* AND THE *FIXER* TO ATTACK SHIELD IN OUR BEHALF!* WE UNDER-ESTIMATED OUR FOE DURING THAT BATTLE!

STAGE 2 ANIMATED CHEMICAL SEED

*AS VIVIDLY DEPICTED IN *STRANGE TALES* #141-143 --NOSTALGIC STAN.

BUT, NEVER AGAIN SHALL WE BE GUILTY OF SUCH A MISTAKE!

SO LONG AS WE POSSESS THE THE KNOWLEDGE TO GROW ARTIFICIAL LIFE--LIFE WHICH WILL SOON REACH *BATTALION* STRENGTH--EVEN *SHIELD* WILL BE POWERLESS TO STOP US!

STAGE 4

OUR STUDIES WITH *D.N.A.*--THE BASIC BUILDING BLOCKS OF LIFE--HAVE NOT BEEN IN VAIN!

STAGE 2

BUT, ENOUGH TALK! THE *IMPERATOR* WANTS SHIELD UTTERLY *DESTROYED,* SO THAT THE WORLD WILL SOON TREMBLE BEFORE THE POWER OF--*THEM!*

7

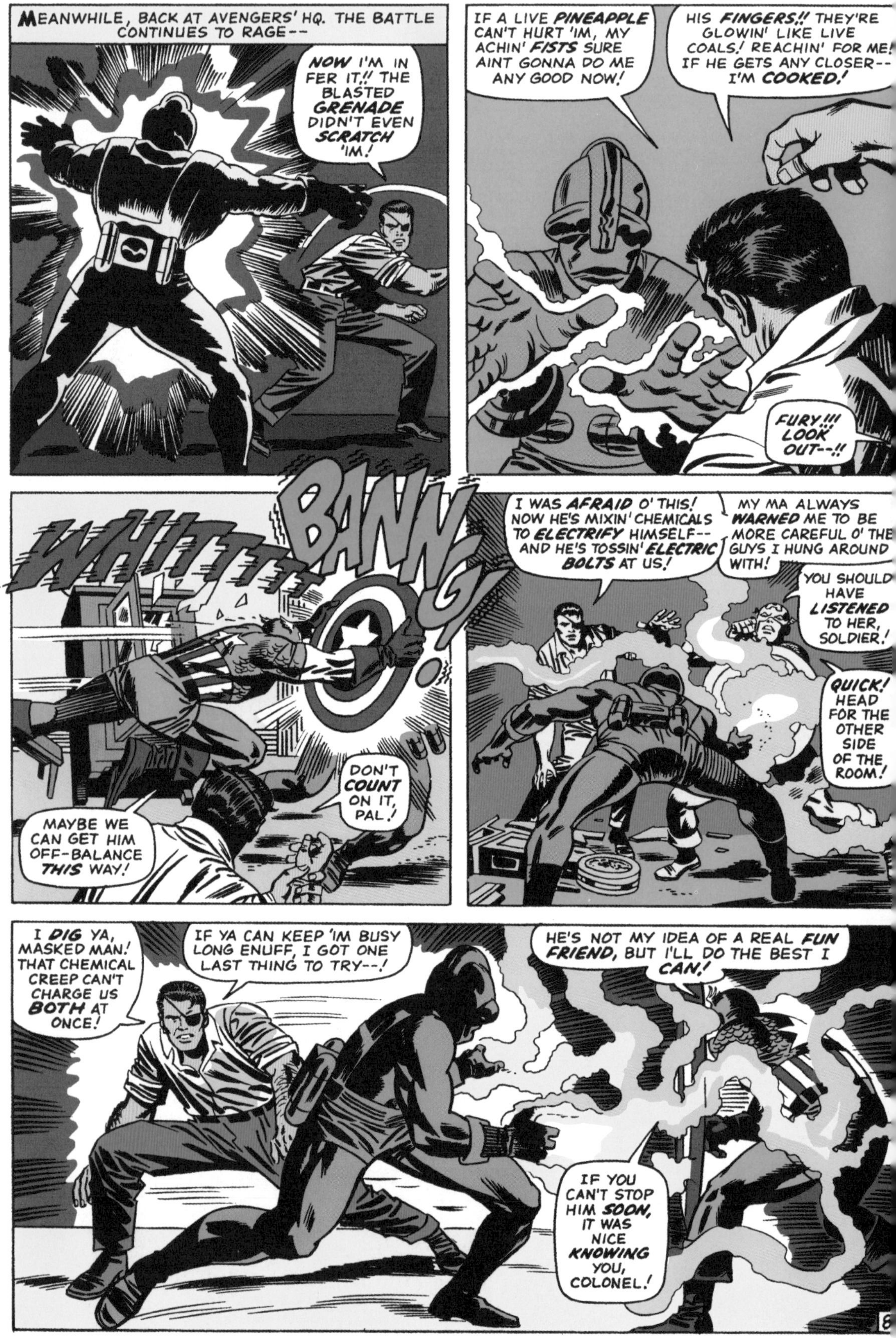
MEANWHILE, BACK AT AVENGERS' HQ. THE BATTLE CONTINUES TO RAGE--
NOW I'M IN FER IT!! THE BLASTED GRENADE DIDN'T EVEN SCRATCH 'IM!
IF A LIVE PINEAPPLE CAN'T HURT 'IM, MY ACHIN' FISTS SURE AINT GONNA DO ME ANY GOOD NOW!
HIS FINGERS!! THEY'RE GLOWIN' LIKE LIVE COALS! REACHIN' FOR ME! IF HE GETS ANY CLOSER-- I'M COOKED!
FURY!!! LOOK OUT--!!
WHITTTTT
BANNG!
DON'T COUNT ON IT, PAL.!
MAYBE WE CAN GET HIM OFF-BALANCE THIS WAY!
I WAS AFRAID O' THIS! NOW HE'S MIXIN' CHEMICALS TO ELECTRIFY HIMSELF-- AND HE'S TOSSIN' ELECTRIC BOLTS AT US!
MY MA ALWAYS WARNED ME TO BE MORE CAREFUL O' THE GUYS I HUNG AROUND WITH!
YOU SHOULD HAVE LISTENED TO HER, SOLDIER!
QUICK! HEAD FOR THE OTHER SIDE OF THE ROOM!
I DIG YA, MASKED MAN! THAT CHEMICAL CREEP CAN'T CHARGE US BOTH AT ONCE!
IF YA CAN KEEP 'IM BUSY LONG ENUFF, I GOT ONE LAST THING TO TRY--!
HE'S NOT MY IDEA OF A REAL FUN FRIEND, BUT I'LL DO THE BEST I CAN!
IF YOU CAN'T STOP HIM SOON, IT WAS NICE KNOWING YOU, COLONEL!
8

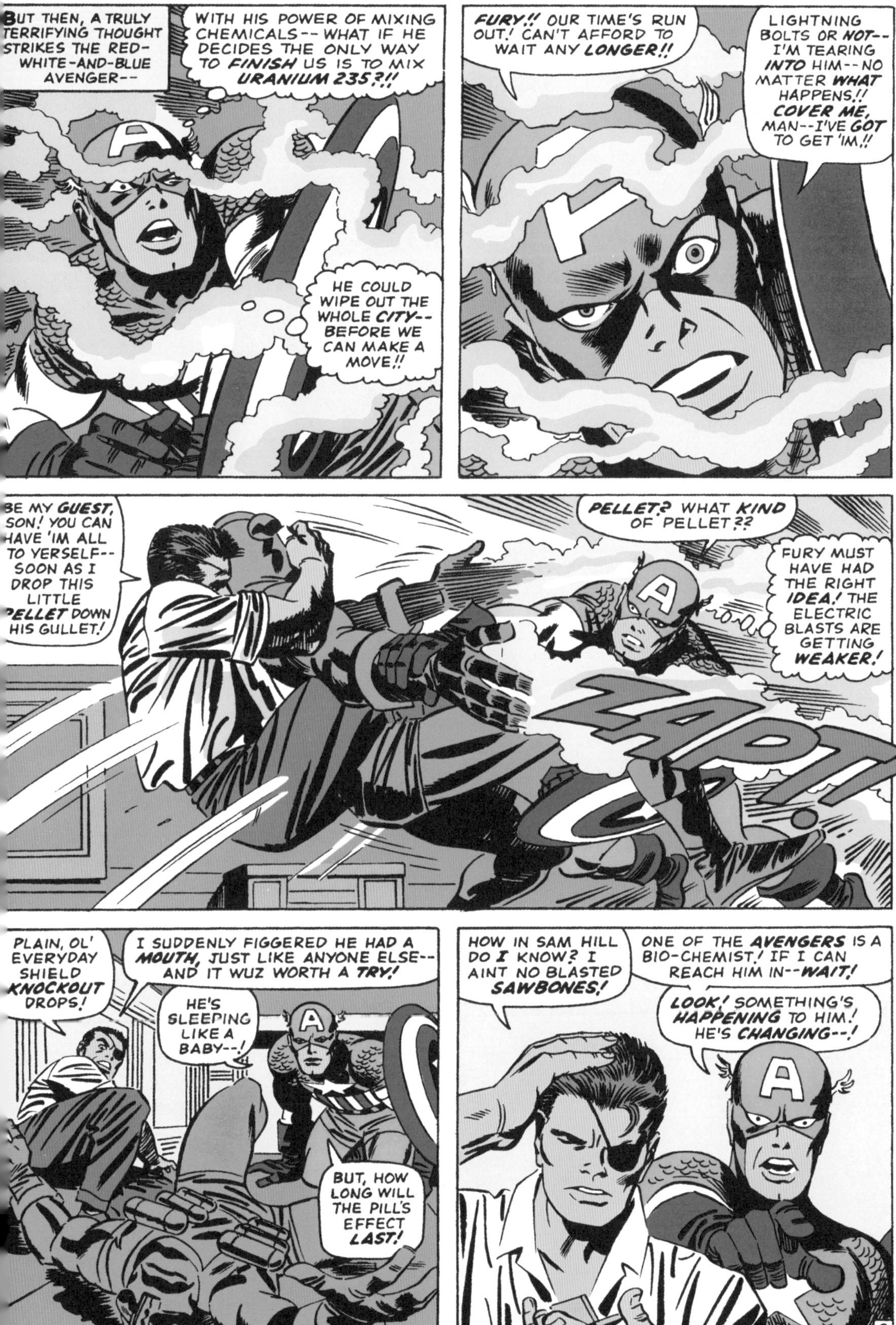

BUT THEN, A TRULY TERRIFYING THOUGHT STRIKES THE RED-WHITE-AND-BLUE AVENGER--
WITH HIS POWER OF MIXING CHEMICALS--WHAT IF HE DECIDES THE ONLY WAY TO FINISH US IS TO MIX URANIUM 235?!!
HE COULD WIPE OUT THE WHOLE CITY--BEFORE WE CAN MAKE A MOVE!!
FURY!! OUR TIME'S RUN OUT! CAN'T AFFORD TO WAIT ANY LONGER!!
LIGHTNING BOLTS OR NOT--I'M TEARING INTO HIM--NO MATTER WHAT HAPPENS!! COVER ME, MAN--I'VE GOT TO GET 'IM!!
BE MY GUEST, SON! YOU CAN HAVE 'IM ALL TO YERSELF--SOON AS I DROP THIS LITTLE PELLET DOWN HIS GULLET!
PELLET? WHAT KIND OF PELLET??
FURY MUST HAVE HAD THE RIGHT IDEA! THE ELECTRIC BLASTS ARE GETTING WEAKER!
ZAP!!
PLAIN, OL' EVERYDAY SHIELD KNOCKOUT DROPS!
I SUDDENLY FIGGERED HE HAD A MOUTH, JUST LIKE ANYONE ELSE--AND IT WUZ WORTH A TRY!
HE'S SLEEPING LIKE A BABY--!
BUT, HOW LONG WILL THE PILL'S EFFECT LAST!
HOW IN SAM HILL DO I KNOW? I AINT NO BLASTED SAWBONES!
ONE OF THE AVENGERS IS A BIO-CHEMIST! IF I CAN REACH HIM IN--WAIT!
LOOK! SOMETHING'S HAPPENING TO HIM! HE'S CHANGING--!
9

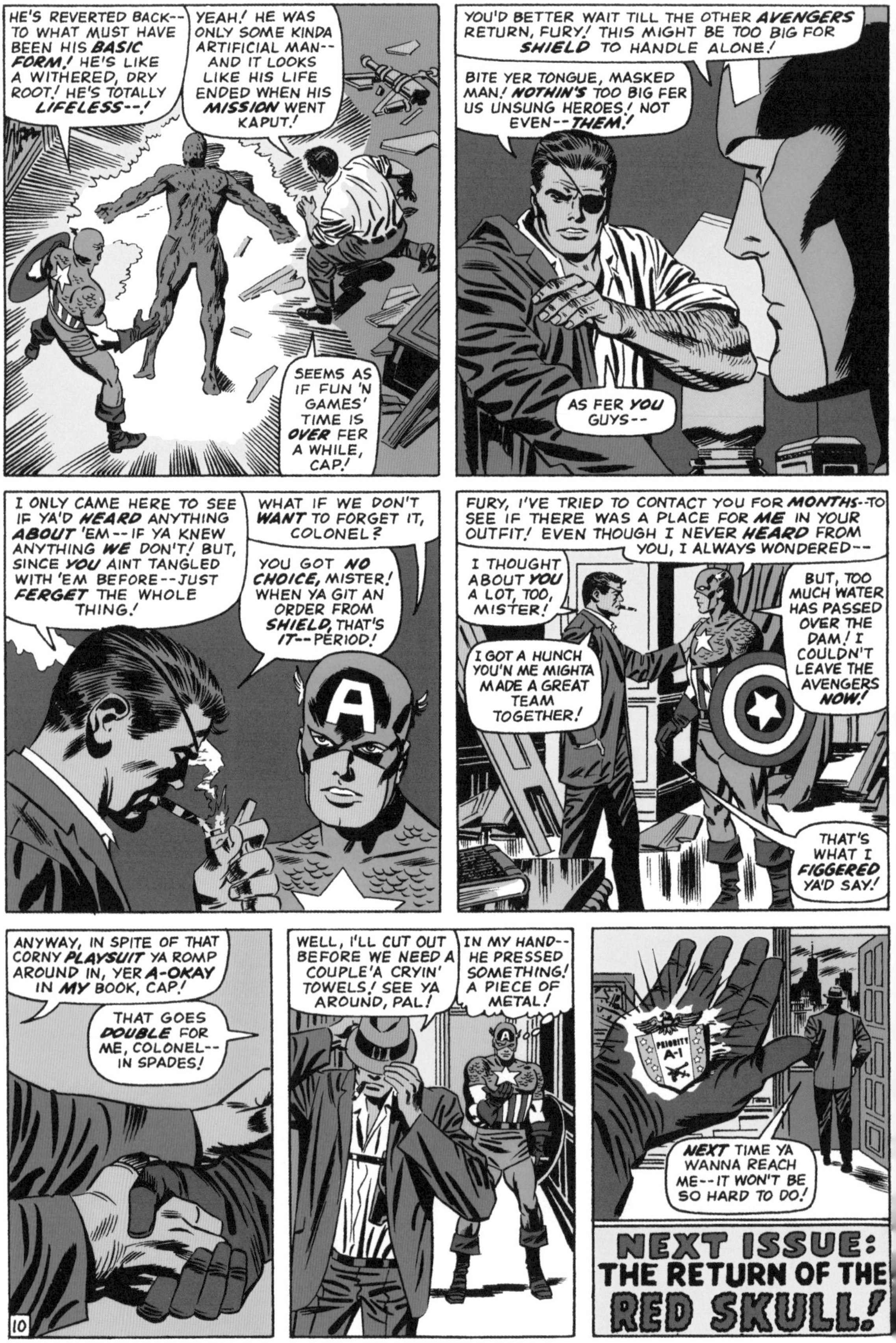
HE'S REVERTED BACK--TO WHAT MUST HAVE BEEN HIS BASIC FORM! HE'S LIKE A WITHERED, DRY ROOT! HE'S TOTALLY LIFELESS--!
YEAH! HE WAS ONLY SOME KINDA ARTIFICIAL MAN--AND IT LOOKS LIKE HIS LIFE ENDED WHEN HIS MISSION WENT KAPUT!
SEEMS AS IF FUN 'N GAMES' TIME IS OVER FER A WHILE, CAP!
YOU'D BETTER WAIT TILL THE OTHER AVENGERS RETURN, FURY! THIS MIGHT BE TOO BIG FOR SHIELD TO HANDLE ALONE!
BITE YER TONGUE, MASKED MAN! NOTHIN'S TOO BIG FER US UNSUNG HEROES! NOT EVEN--THEM!
AS FER YOU GUYS--
I ONLY CAME HERE TO SEE IF YA'D HEARD ANYTHING ABOUT 'EM--IF YA KNEW ANYTHING WE DON'T! BUT, SINCE YOU AINT TANGLED WITH 'EM BEFORE--JUST FERGET THE WHOLE THING!
WHAT IF WE DON'T WANT TO FORGET IT, COLONEL?
YOU GOT NO CHOICE, MISTER! WHEN YA GIT AN ORDER FROM SHIELD, THAT'S IT--PERIOD!
FURY, I'VE TRIED TO CONTACT YOU FOR MONTHS--TO SEE IF THERE WAS A PLACE FOR ME IN YOUR OUTFIT! EVEN THOUGH I NEVER HEARD FROM YOU, I ALWAYS WONDERED--
I THOUGHT ABOUT YOU A LOT, TOO, MISTER!
I GOT A HUNCH YOU'N ME MIGHTA MADE A GREAT TEAM TOGETHER!
BUT, TOO MUCH WATER HAS PASSED OVER THE DAM! I COULDN'T LEAVE THE AVENGERS NOW!
THAT'S WHAT I FIGGERED YA'D SAY!
ANYWAY, IN SPITE OF THAT CORNY PLAYSUIT YA ROMP AROUND IN, YER A-OKAY IN MY BOOK, CAP!
THAT GOES DOUBLE FOR ME, COLONEL--IN SPADES!
10
WELL, I'LL CUT OUT BEFORE WE NEED A COUPLE'A CRYIN' TOWELS! SEE YA AROUND, PAL!
IN MY HAND--HE PRESSED SOMETHING! A PIECE OF METAL!
PRIORITY A-1
NEXT TIME YA WANNA REACH ME--IT WON'T BE SO HARD TO DO!
NEXT ISSUE: THE RETURN OF THE RED SKULL!

TALES OF SUSPENSE #79,

JULY 1966,

"THE RED SKULL LIVES!"

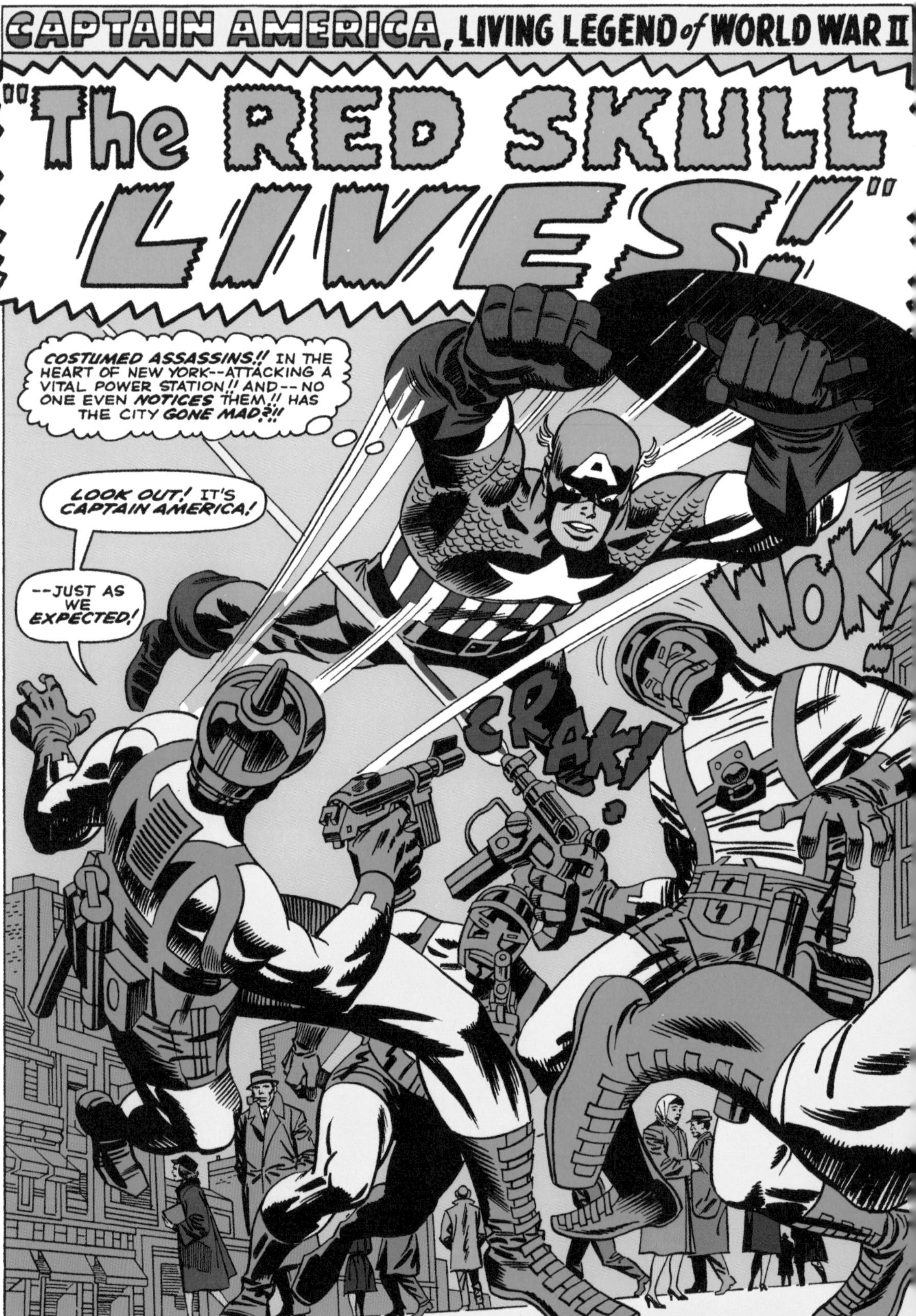

CAPTAIN AMERICA, LIVING LEGEND of WORLD WAR II
"The RED SKULL LIVES!"
COSTUMED ASSASSINS!! IN THE HEART OF NEW YORK--ATTACKING A VITAL POWER STATION!! AND--NO ONE EVEN NOTICES THEM!! HAS THE CITY GONE MAD?!!
LOOK OUT! IT'S CAPTAIN AMERICA!
--JUST AS WE EXPECTED!
WOK!
CRAK!
SCRIPT: SMILIN' STAN! ART: JOLLY JACK INKS: FRANTIC FRANKIE LETTERING: AGONIZED ARTIE

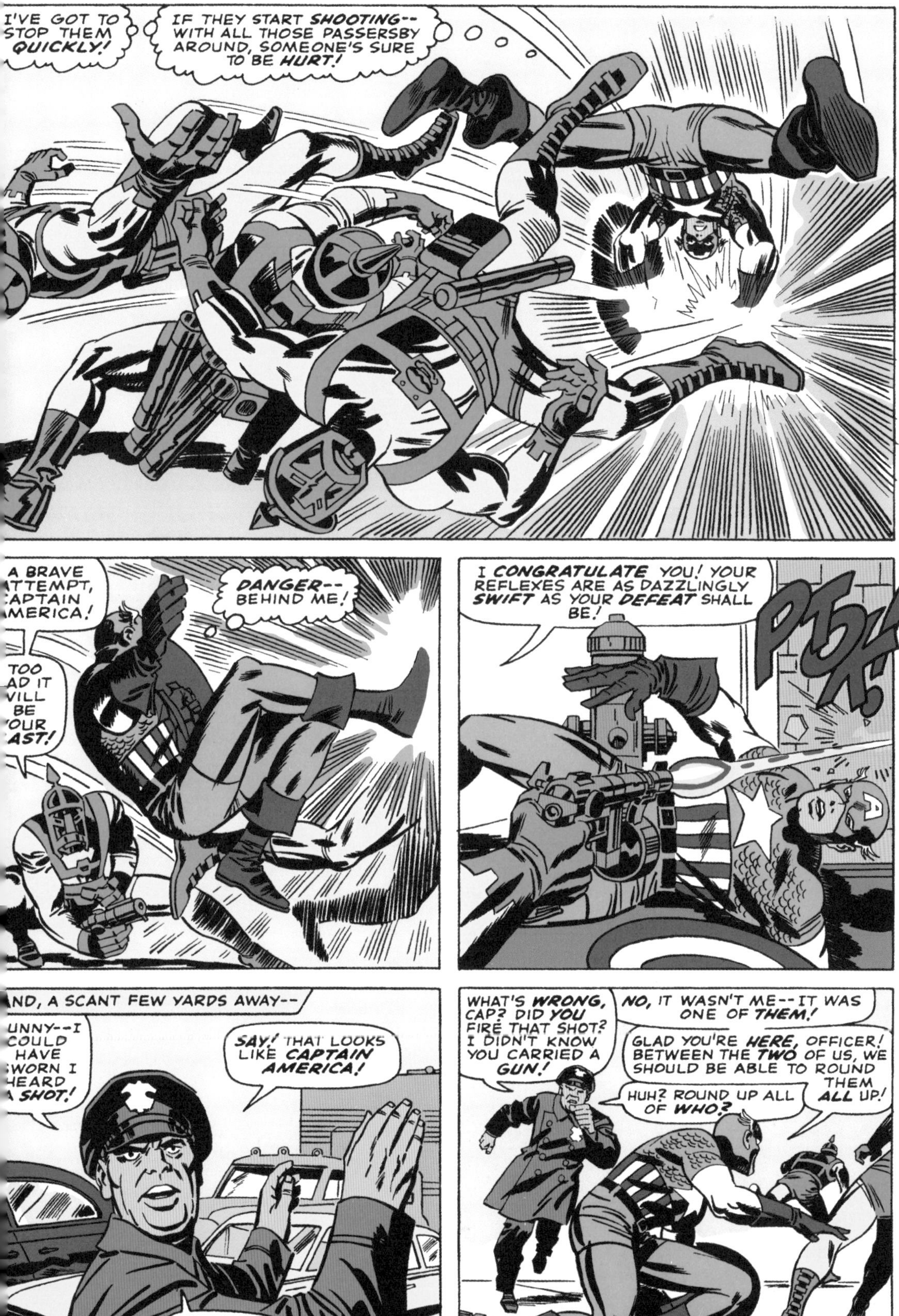
I'VE GOT TO STOP THEM QUICKLY!
IF THEY START SHOOTING-- WITH ALL THOSE PASSERSBY AROUND, SOMEONE'S SURE TO BE HURT!
A BRAVE TTEMPT, APTAIN MERICA!
TOO AD IT VILL BE OUR AST!
DANGER-- BEHIND ME!
I CONGRATULATE YOU! YOUR REFLEXES ARE AS DAZZLINGLY SWIFT AS YOUR DEFEAT SHALL BE!
PTOK!
ND, A SCANT FEW YARDS AWAY--
UNNY--I COULD HAVE WORN I HEARD A SHOT!
SAY! THAT LOOKS LIKE CAPTAIN AMERICA!
I'D BETTER SEE WHAT'S GOING ON!
WHAT'S WRONG, CAP? DID YOU FIRE THAT SHOT? I DIDN'T KNOW YOU CARRIED A GUN!
NO, IT WASN'T ME--IT WAS ONE OF THEM!
GLAD YOU'RE HERE, OFFICER! BETWEEN THE TWO OF US, WE SHOULD BE ABLE TO ROUND THEM ALL UP!
HUH? ROUND UP ALL OF WHO?
2

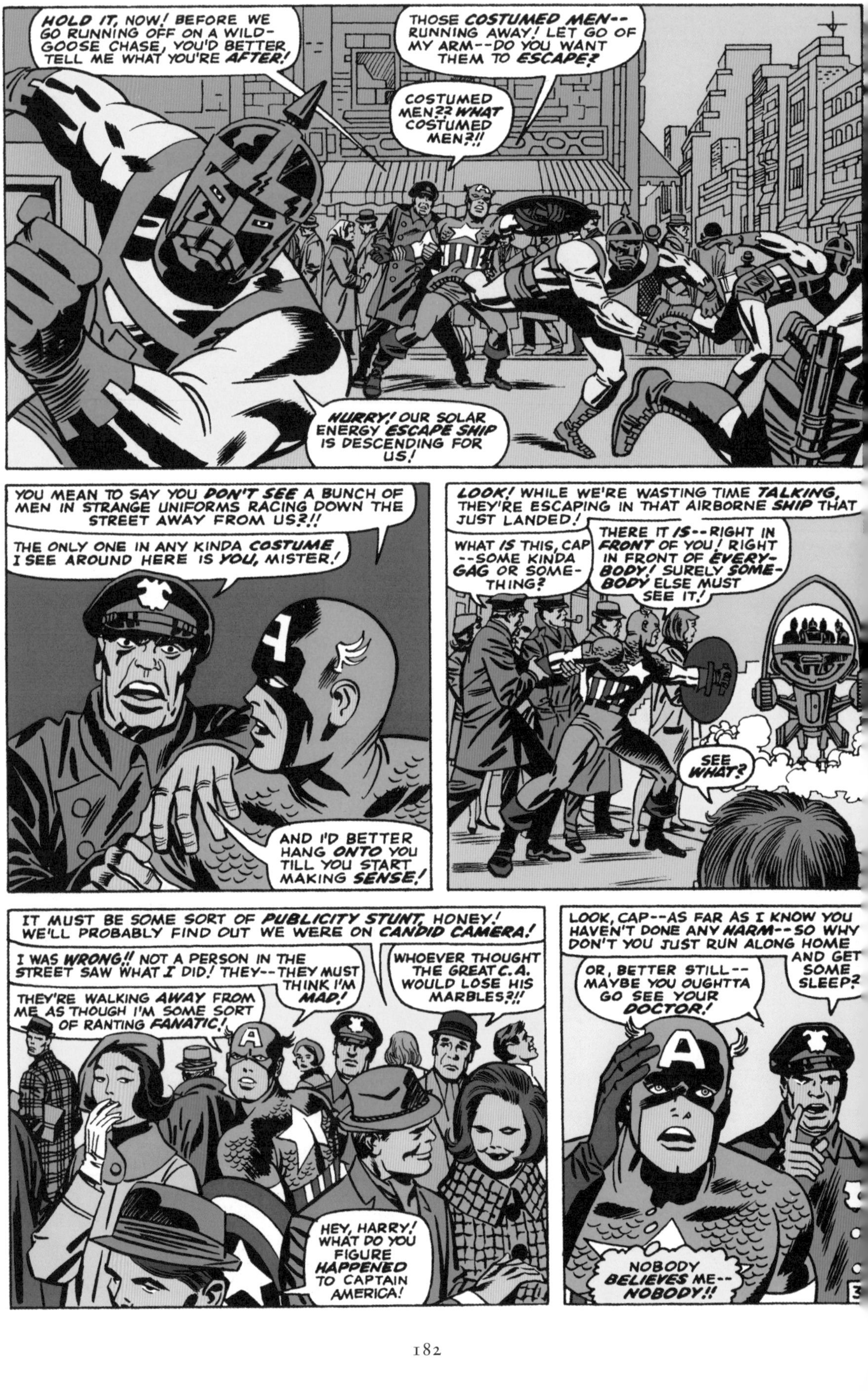

HOLD IT, NOW! BEFORE WE GO RUNNING OFF ON A WILD-GOOSE CHASE, YOU'D BETTER TELL ME WHAT YOU'RE AFTER!
THOSE COSTUMED MEN--RUNNING AWAY! LET GO OF MY ARM--DO YOU WANT THEM TO ESCAPE?
COSTUMED MEN?? WHAT COSTUMED MEN?!!
HURRY! OUR SOLAR ENERGY ESCAPE SHIP IS DESCENDING FOR US!
YOU MEAN TO SAY YOU DON'T SEE A BUNCH OF MEN IN STRANGE UNIFORMS RACING DOWN THE STREET AWAY FROM US?!!
THE ONLY ONE IN ANY KINDA COSTUME I SEE AROUND HERE IS YOU, MISTER!
AND I'D BETTER HANG ONTO YOU TILL YOU START MAKING SENSE!
LOOK! WHILE WE'RE WASTING TIME TALKING, THEY'RE ESCAPING IN THAT AIRBORNE SHIP THAT JUST LANDED!
WHAT IS THIS, CAP --SOME KINDA GAG OR SOMETHING?
THERE IT IS--RIGHT IN FRONT OF YOU! RIGHT IN FRONT OF EVERYBODY! SURELY SOMEBODY ELSE MUST SEE IT!
SEE WHAT?
IT MUST BE SOME SORT OF PUBLICITY STUNT, HONEY! WE'LL PROBABLY FIND OUT WE WERE ON CANDID CAMERA!
I WAS WRONG!! NOT A PERSON IN THE STREET SAW WHAT I DID! THEY--THEY MUST THINK I'M MAD!
THEY'RE WALKING AWAY FROM ME AS THOUGH I'M SOME SORT OF RANTING FANATIC!
WHOEVER THOUGHT THE GREAT C.A. WOULD LOSE HIS MARBLES?!!
HEY, HARRY! WHAT DO YOU FIGURE HAPPENED TO CAPTAIN AMERICA!
LOOK, CAP--AS FAR AS I KNOW YOU HAVEN'T DONE ANY HARM--SO WHY DON'T YOU JUST RUN ALONG HOME AND GET SOME SLEEP?
OR, BETTER STILL--MAYBE YOU OUGHTTA GO SEE YOUR DOCTOR!
NOBODY BELIEVES ME--NOBODY!!
3

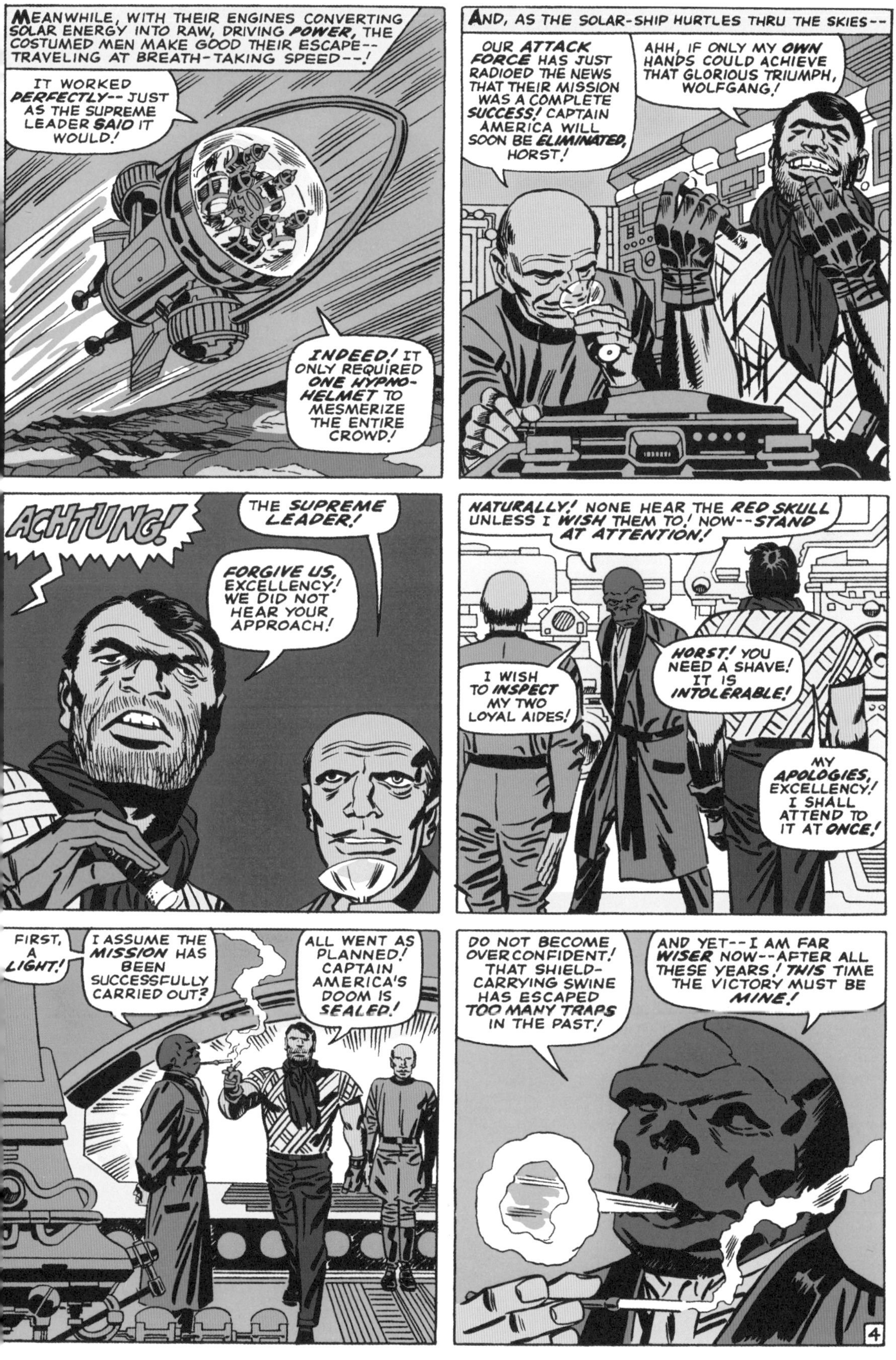
MEANWHILE, WITH THEIR ENGINES CONVERTING SOLAR ENERGY INTO RAW, DRIVING POWER, THE COSTUMED MEN MAKE GOOD THEIR ESCAPE--TRAVELING AT BREATH-TAKING SPEED--!
IT WORKED PERFECTLY-- JUST AS THE SUPREME LEADER SAID IT WOULD!
INDEED! IT ONLY REQUIRED ONE HYPNO-HELMET TO MESMERIZE THE ENTIRE CROWD!
AND, AS THE SOLAR-SHIP HURTLES THRU THE SKIES--
OUR ATTACK FORCE HAS JUST RADIOED THE NEWS THAT THEIR MISSION WAS A COMPLETE SUCCESS! CAPTAIN AMERICA WILL SOON BE ELIMINATED, HORST!
AHH, IF ONLY MY OWN HANDS COULD ACHIEVE THAT GLORIOUS TRIUMPH, WOLFGANG!
ACHTUNG!
THE SUPREME LEADER!
FORGIVE US, EXCELLENCY! WE DID NOT HEAR YOUR APPROACH!
NATURALLY! NONE HEAR THE RED SKULL UNLESS I WISH THEM TO! NOW--STAND AT ATTENTION!
I WISH TO INSPECT MY TWO LOYAL AIDES!
HORST! YOU NEED A SHAVE! IT IS INTOLERABLE!
MY APOLOGIES, EXCELLENCY! I SHALL ATTEND TO IT AT ONCE!
FIRST, A LIGHT!
I ASSUME THE MISSION HAS BEEN SUCCESSFULLY CARRIED OUT?
ALL WENT AS PLANNED! CAPTAIN AMERICA'S DOOM IS SEALED!
DO NOT BECOME OVERCONFIDENT! THAT SHIELD-CARRYING SWINE HAS ESCAPED TOO MANY TRAPS IN THE PAST!
AND YET--I AM FAR WISER NOW--AFTER ALL THESE YEARS! THIS TIME THE VICTORY MUST BE MINE!
4

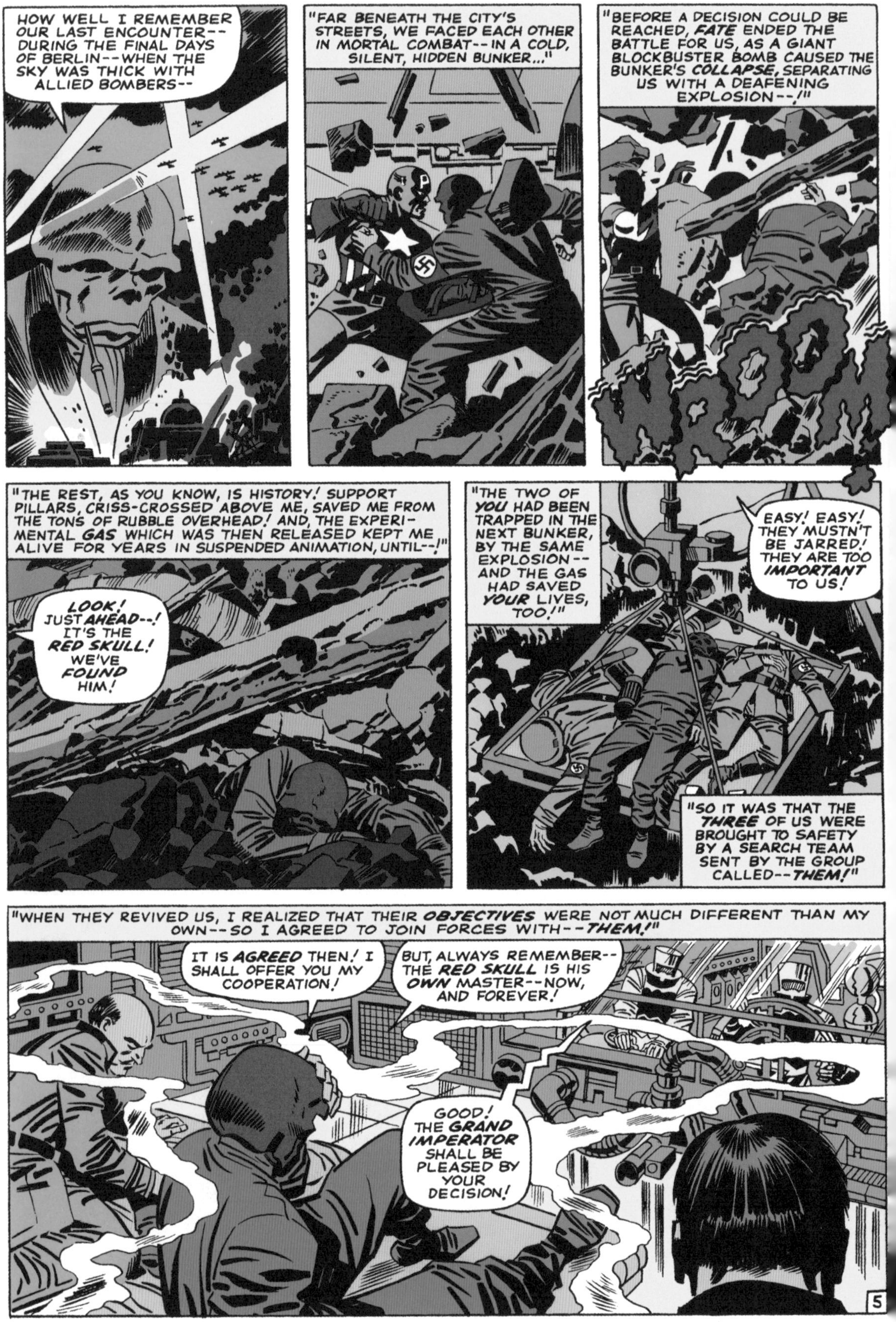
HOW WELL I REMEMBER OUR LAST ENCOUNTER-- DURING THE FINAL DAYS OF BERLIN--WHEN THE SKY WAS THICK WITH ALLIED BOMBERS--
"FAR BENEATH THE CITY'S STREETS, WE FACED EACH OTHER IN MORTAL COMBAT--IN A COLD, SILENT, HIDDEN BUNKER..."
"BEFORE A DECISION COULD BE REACHED, FATE ENDED THE BATTLE FOR US, AS A GIANT BLOCKBUSTER BOMB CAUSED THE BUNKER'S COLLAPSE, SEPARATING US WITH A DEAFENING EXPLOSION--!"
VROOM
"THE REST, AS YOU KNOW, IS HISTORY! SUPPORT PILLARS, CRISS-CROSSED ABOVE ME, SAVED ME FROM THE TONS OF RUBBLE OVERHEAD! AND, THE EXPERIMENTAL GAS WHICH WAS THEN RELEASED KEPT ME ALIVE FOR YEARS IN SUSPENDED ANIMATION, UNTIL--!"
LOOK! JUST AHEAD--! IT'S THE RED SKULL! WE'VE FOUND HIM!
"THE TWO OF YOU HAD BEEN TRAPPED IN THE NEXT BUNKER, BY THE SAME EXPLOSION--AND THE GAS HAD SAVED YOUR LIVES, TOO!"
EASY! EASY! THEY MUSTN'T BE JARRED! THEY ARE TOO IMPORTANT TO US!
"SO IT WAS THAT THE THREE OF US WERE BROUGHT TO SAFETY BY A SEARCH TEAM SENT BY THE GROUP CALLED--THEM!"
"WHEN THEY REVIVED US, I REALIZED THAT THEIR OBJECTIVES WERE NOT MUCH DIFFERENT THAN MY OWN--SO I AGREED TO JOIN FORCES WITH--THEM!"
IT IS AGREED THEN! I SHALL OFFER YOU MY COOPERATION!
BUT, ALWAYS REMEMBER--THE RED SKULL IS HIS OWN MASTER--NOW, AND FOREVER!
GOOD! THE GRAND IMPERATOR SHALL BE PLEASED BY YOUR DECISION!
5

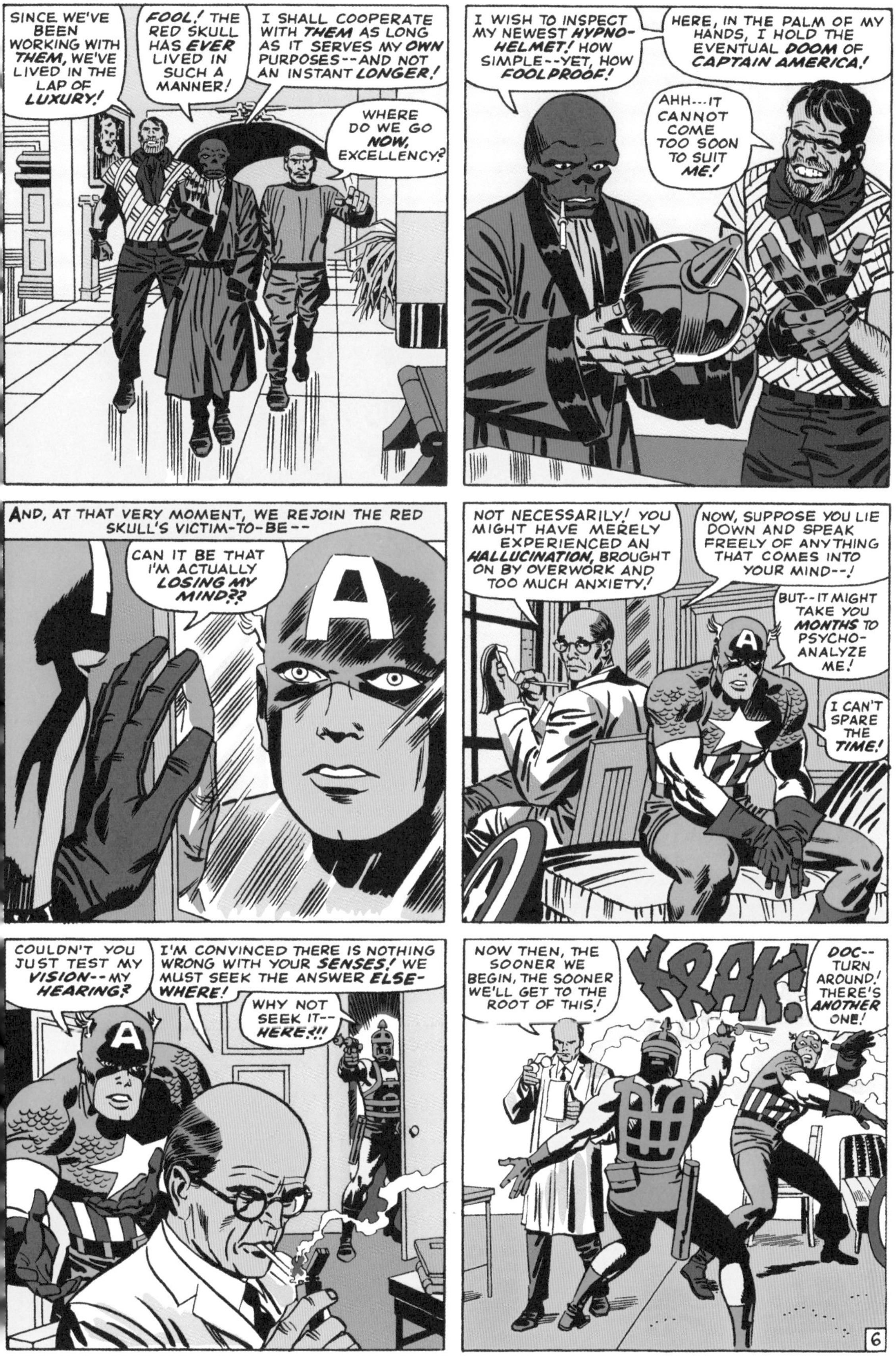
SINCE WE'VE BEEN WORKING WITH THEM, WE'VE LIVED IN THE LAP OF LUXURY!
FOOL! THE RED SKULL HAS EVER LIVED IN SUCH A MANNER!
I SHALL COOPERATE WITH THEM AS LONG AS IT SERVES MY OWN PURPOSES--AND NOT AN INSTANT LONGER!
WHERE DO WE GO NOW, EXCELLENCY?
I WISH TO INSPECT MY NEWEST HYPNO-HELMET! HOW SIMPLE--YET, HOW FOOLPROOF!
HERE, IN THE PALM OF MY HANDS, I HOLD THE EVENTUAL DOOM OF CAPTAIN AMERICA!
AHH---IT CANNOT COME TOO SOON TO SUIT ME!
AND, AT THAT VERY MOMENT, WE REJOIN THE RED SKULL'S VICTIM-TO-BE--
CAN IT BE THAT I'M ACTUALLY LOSING MY MIND??
NOT NECESSARILY! YOU MIGHT HAVE MERELY EXPERIENCED AN HALLUCINATION, BROUGHT ON BY OVERWORK AND TOO MUCH ANXIETY!
NOW, SUPPOSE YOU LIE DOWN AND SPEAK FREELY OF ANYTHING THAT COMES INTO YOUR MIND--!
BUT--IT MIGHT TAKE YOU MONTHS TO PSYCHO-ANALYZE ME!
I CAN'T SPARE THE TIME!
COULDN'T YOU JUST TEST MY VISION--MY HEARING?
I'M CONVINCED THERE IS NOTHING WRONG WITH YOUR SENSES! WE MUST SEEK THE ANSWER ELSE-WHERE!
WHY NOT SEEK IT--HERE?!!
NOW THEN, THE SOONER WE BEGIN, THE SOONER WE'LL GET TO THE ROOT OF THIS!
KRAK!
DOC--TURN AROUND! THERE'S ANOTHER ONE!
6

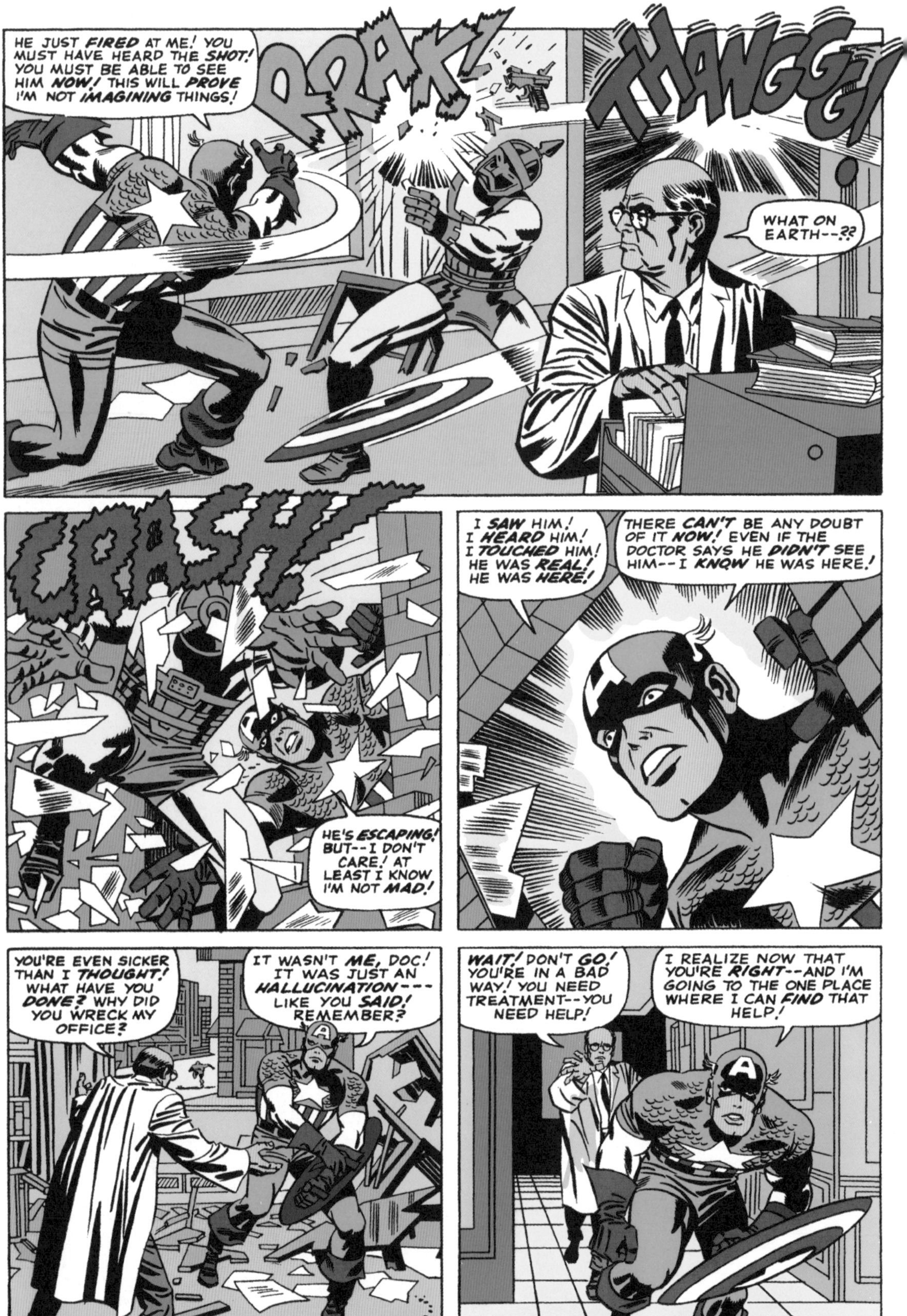
HE JUST FIRED AT ME! YOU MUST HAVE HEARD THE SHOT! YOU MUST BE ABLE TO SEE HIM NOW! THIS WILL PROVE I'M NOT IMAGINING THINGS!
RRAK!
THANGGG!
WHAT ON EARTH--??
CRASH!
HE'S ESCAPING! BUT--I DON'T CARE! AT LEAST I KNOW I'M NOT MAD!
I SAW HIM! I HEARD HIM! I TOUCHED HIM! HE WAS REAL! HE WAS HERE!
THERE CAN'T BE ANY DOUBT OF IT NOW! EVEN IF THE DOCTOR SAYS HE DIDN'T SEE HIM--I KNOW HE WAS HERE!
YOU'RE EVEN SICKER THAN I THOUGHT! WHAT HAVE YOU DONE? WHY DID YOU WRECK MY OFFICE?
IT WASN'T ME, DOC! IT WAS JUST AN HALLUCINATION---LIKE YOU SAID! REMEMBER?
WAIT! DON'T GO! YOU'RE IN A BAD WAY! YOU NEED TREATMENT--YOU NEED HELP!
I REALIZE NOW THAT YOU'RE RIGHT--AND I'M GOING TO THE ONE PLACE WHERE I CAN FIND THAT HELP!
7

AND, EVEN AS CAP RACES OFF INTO THE NIGHT...

PHASES ONE AND TWO HAVE BEEN *COMPLETED!* NOW WE ARE READY FOR *PHASE THREE* -- THE FINAL DESTRUCTION OF CAPTAIN AMERICA!

YOU MUST EXECUTE YOUR ORDERS *PERFECTLY,* HORST! THERE CAN BE NOT THE SLIGHTEST MARGIN FOR ERROR!

I SHALL NOT FAIL YOU, EXCELLENCY!

SO LONG AS YOU WEAR YOUR *HYPNO-HELMET,* YOU CAN ACCOMPLISH *ANYTHING!*

BUT *THIS* TIME YOU ARE TO HYPNOTIZE *CAPTAIN AMERICA,* AS WELL AS THE OTHERS!

I UNDERSTAND! AND, WHEN HE WAKES UP -- HE WILL BE ACCUSED OF -- *MURDER!*

CORRECT! AND IT SHALL BE THE MURDER *YOU* HAVE COMMITTED!

OF ALL MY MANY PLANS, *THIS* IS TRULY THE MOST DIABOLICALLY *PERFECT!*

FAREWELL, CAPTAIN AMERICA! THE FINAL TRIUMPH BELONGS TO *ME* AFTER ALL!

SHOOSH!

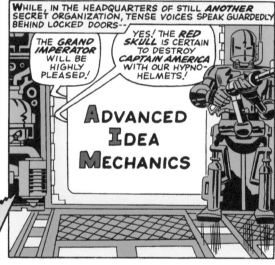

WHILE, IN THE HEADQUARTERS OF STILL *ANOTHER* SECRET ORGANIZATION, TENSE VOICES SPEAK GUARDEDLY BEHIND LOCKED DOORS --

THE *GRAND IMPERATOR* WILL BE HIGHLY PLEASED!

YES! THE *RED SKULL* IS CERTAIN TO DESTROY *CAPTAIN AMERICA* WITH OUR HYPNO-HELMETS!

ADVANCED IDEA MECHANICS

AS FOR *YOU,* COUNT ROYALE, IT WILL BE *YOUR* DUTY TO INSURE THAT *COLONEL FURY,* THE DIRECTOR OF *SHIELD,* WILL NEVER INTERFERE WITH US AGAIN!

I HAVE NEVER FAILED *YET* -- IS THAT NOT SO?*

TELL ME, BEFORE I GO -- WHAT IS *WITHIN* THAT IONIC SHELL?

*TO SEE HOW COUNT ROYALE MAKES OUT, DON'T MISS *STRANGE TALES* #146 ON SALE NOW! --SMILEY!

IT IS ENOUGH TO STAGGER THE IMAGINATION OF A *WIZARD!* WE CALL IT A *COSMIC CUBE* -- AND IT WELL MAY BE THE MOST POTENT DEVICE IN ALL THE WORLD!

YOU MUST GUARD IT WELL! IF IT SHOULD EVER FALL INTO THE HANDS OF A MADMAN LIKE THE *RED SKULL* --!

HOLD YOUR TONGUE, ROYALE! SUCH MATTERS ARE FOR *US* TO CONSIDER! THE RED SKULL SERVES THE *GRAND IMPERATOR* -- AS DO WE *ALL!*

YOU HAVE YOUR MISSION -- *PERFORM IT!*

8

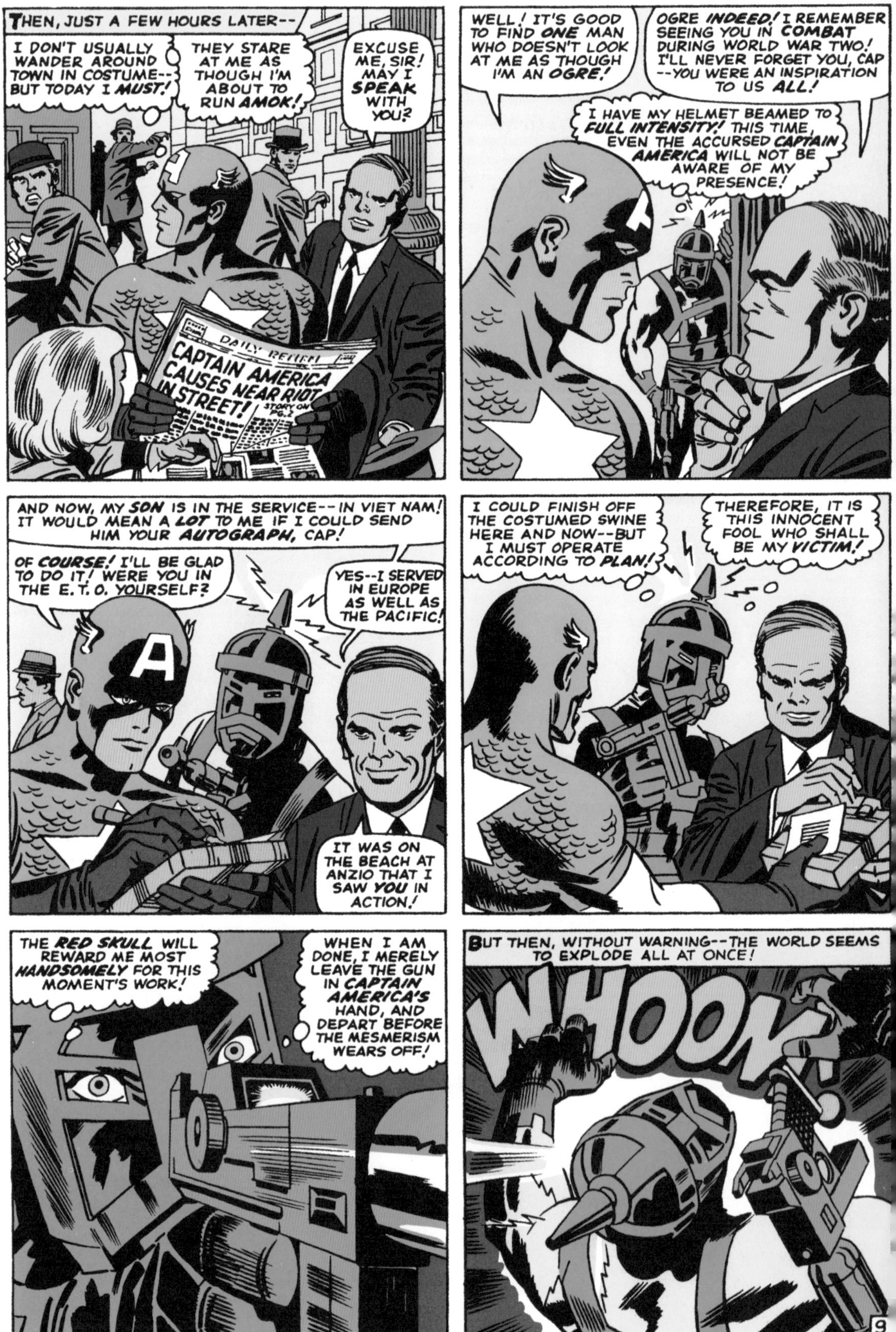
THEN, JUST A FEW HOURS LATER--
I DON'T USUALLY WANDER AROUND TOWN IN COSTUME--BUT TODAY I MUST!
THEY STARE AT ME AS THOUGH I'M ABOUT TO RUN AMOK!
EXCUSE ME, SIR! MAY I SPEAK WITH YOU?
CAPTAIN AMERICA CAUSES NEAR RIOT IN STREET!
STORY ON PG. 2
WELL! IT'S GOOD TO FIND ONE MAN WHO DOESN'T LOOK AT ME AS THOUGH I'M AN OGRE!
OGRE INDEED! I REMEMBER SEEING YOU IN COMBAT DURING WORLD WAR TWO! I'LL NEVER FORGET YOU, CAP --YOU WERE AN INSPIRATION TO US ALL!
I HAVE MY HELMET BEAMED TO FULL INTENSITY! THIS TIME, EVEN THE ACCURSED CAPTAIN AMERICA WILL NOT BE AWARE OF MY PRESENCE!
AND NOW, MY SON IS IN THE SERVICE--IN VIET NAM! IT WOULD MEAN A LOT TO ME IF I COULD SEND HIM YOUR AUTOGRAPH, CAP!
OF COURSE! I'LL BE GLAD TO DO IT! WERE YOU IN THE E.T.O. YOURSELF?
YES--I SERVED IN EUROPE AS WELL AS THE PACIFIC!
IT WAS ON THE BEACH AT ANZIO THAT I SAW YOU IN ACTION!
I COULD FINISH OFF THE COSTUMED SWINE HERE AND NOW--BUT I MUST OPERATE ACCORDING TO PLAN!
THEREFORE, IT IS THIS INNOCENT FOOL WHO SHALL BE MY VICTIM!
THE RED SKULL WILL REWARD ME MOST HANDSOMELY FOR THIS MOMENT'S WORK!
WHEN I AM DONE, I MERELY LEAVE THE GUN IN CAPTAIN AMERICA'S HAND, AND DEPART BEFORE THE MESMERISM WEARS OFF!
BUT THEN, WITHOUT WARNING--THE WORLD SEEMS TO EXPLODE ALL AT ONCE!
WHOOM
9

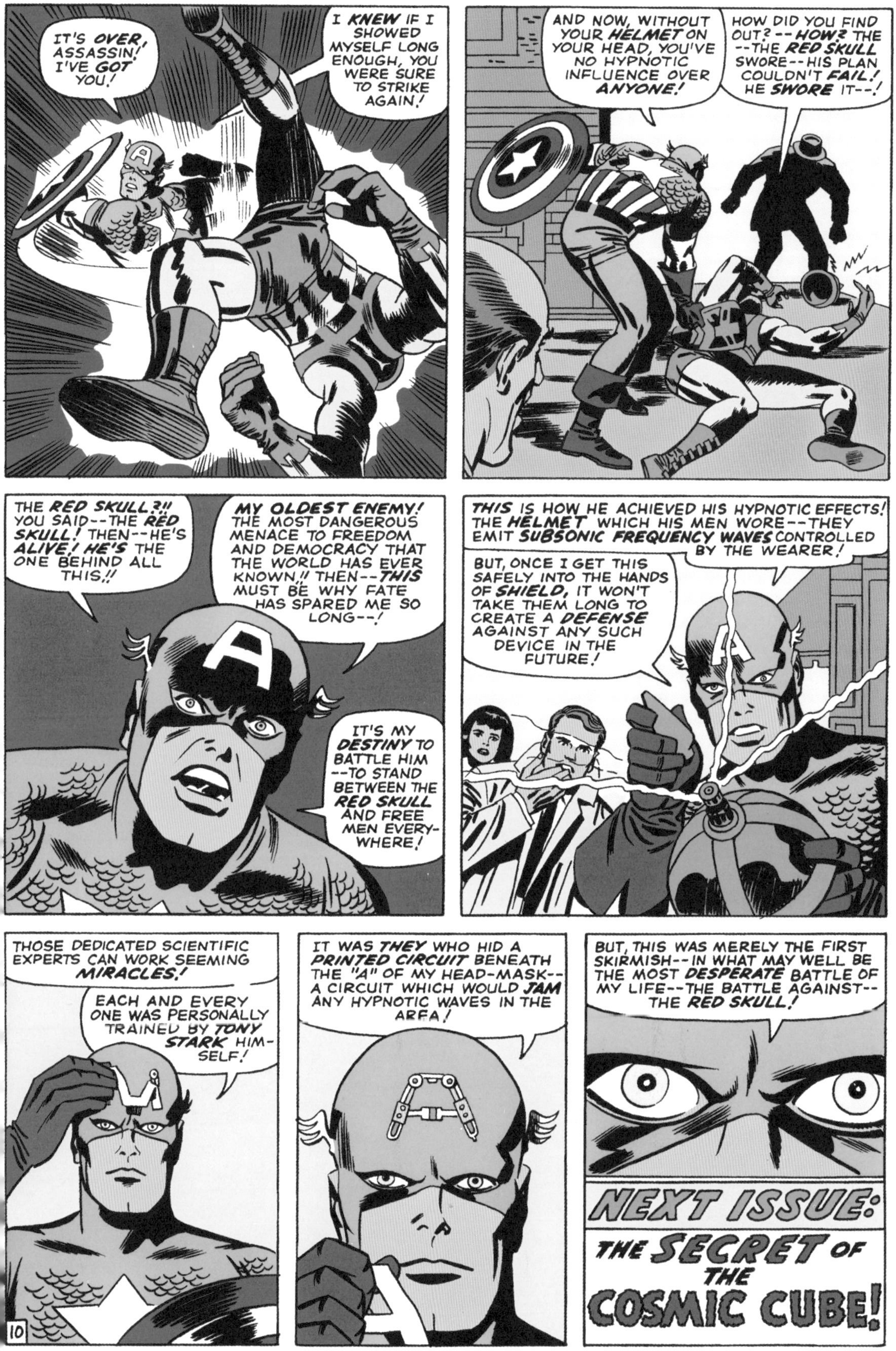

IT'S OVER, ASSASSIN! I'VE GOT YOU!
I KNEW IF I SHOWED MYSELF LONG ENOUGH, YOU WERE SURE TO STRIKE AGAIN!
AND NOW, WITHOUT YOUR HELMET ON YOUR HEAD, YOU'VE NO HYPNOTIC INFLUENCE OVER ANYONE!
HOW DID YOU FIND OUT? --HOW? THE --THE RED SKULL SWORE--HIS PLAN COULDN'T FAIL! HE SWORE IT--!
THE RED SKULL?!! YOU SAID--THE RED SKULL! THEN--HE'S ALIVE! HE'S THE ONE BEHIND ALL THIS!!
MY OLDEST ENEMY! THE MOST DANGEROUS MENACE TO FREEDOM AND DEMOCRACY THAT THE WORLD HAS EVER KNOWN!! THEN--THIS MUST BE WHY FATE HAS SPARED ME SO LONG--!
IT'S MY DESTINY TO BATTLE HIM --TO STAND BETWEEN THE RED SKULL AND FREE MEN EVERY-WHERE!
THIS IS HOW HE ACHIEVED HIS HYPNOTIC EFFECTS! THE HELMET WHICH HIS MEN WORE--THEY EMIT SUBSONIC FREQUENCY WAVES CONTROLLED BY THE WEARER!
BUT, ONCE I GET THIS SAFELY INTO THE HANDS OF SHIELD, IT WON'T TAKE THEM LONG TO CREATE A DEFENSE AGAINST ANY SUCH DEVICE IN THE FUTURE!
THOSE DEDICATED SCIENTIFIC EXPERTS CAN WORK SEEMING MIRACLES!
EACH AND EVERY ONE WAS PERSONALLY TRAINED BY TONY STARK HIM-SELF!
10
IT WAS THEY WHO HID A PRINTED CIRCUIT BENEATH THE "A" OF MY HEAD-MASK--A CIRCUIT WHICH WOULD JAM ANY HYPNOTIC WAVES IN THE AREA!
BUT, THIS WAS MERELY THE FIRST SKIRMISH--IN WHAT MAY WELL BE THE MOST DESPERATE BATTLE OF MY LIFE--THE BATTLE AGAINST--THE RED SKULL!
NEXT ISSUE:
THE SECRET OF THE COSMIC CUBE!

TALES OF SUSPENSE #80,

AUGUST 1966,

"HE WHO HOLDS

THE COSMIC CUBE!"

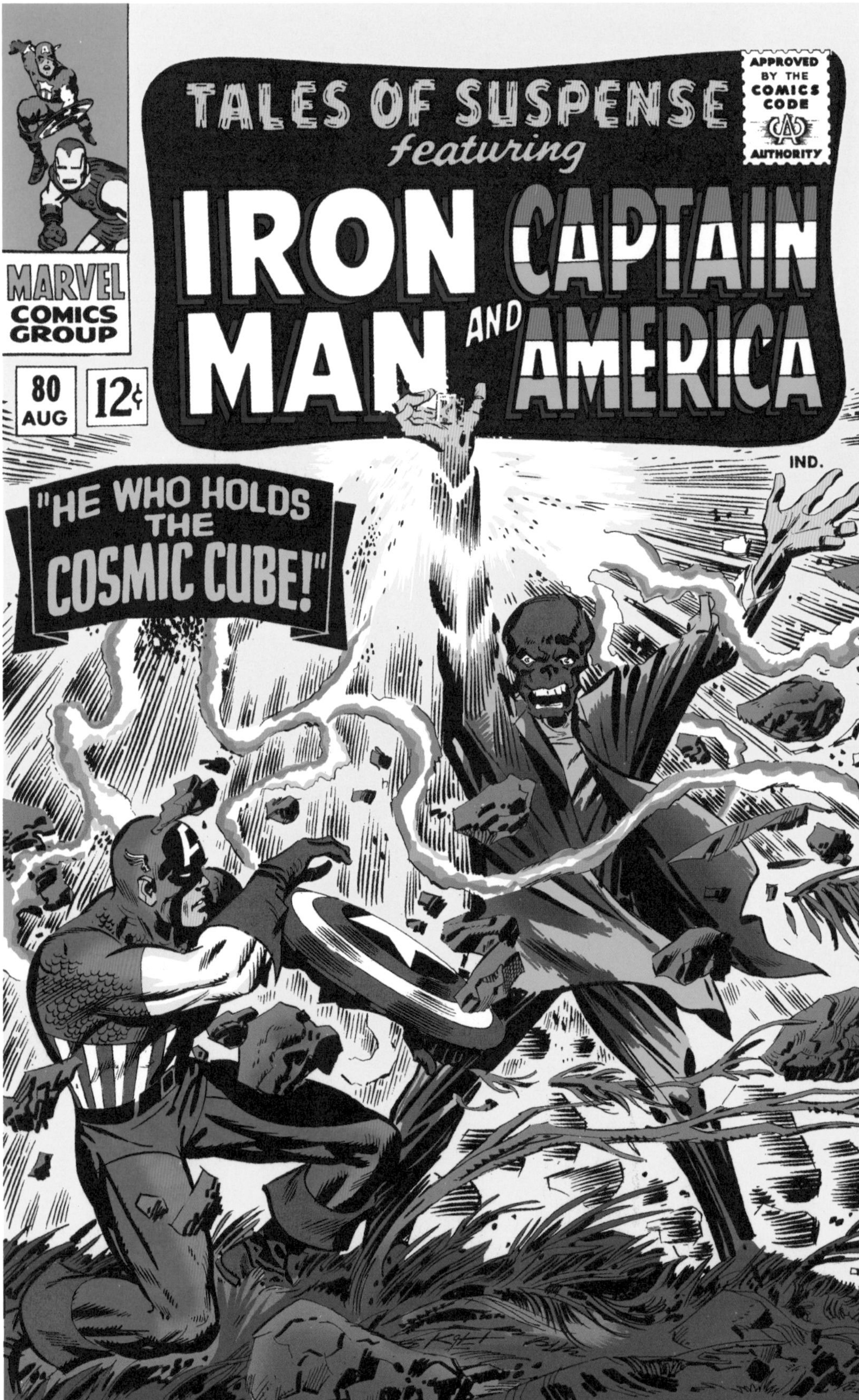
TALES OF SUSPENSE
featuring
IRON MAN AND CAPTAIN AMERICA
APPROVED BY THE COMICS CODE AUTHORITY
MARVEL COMICS GROUP
80 AUG
12¢
IND.
"HE WHO HOLDS THE COSMIC CUBE!"

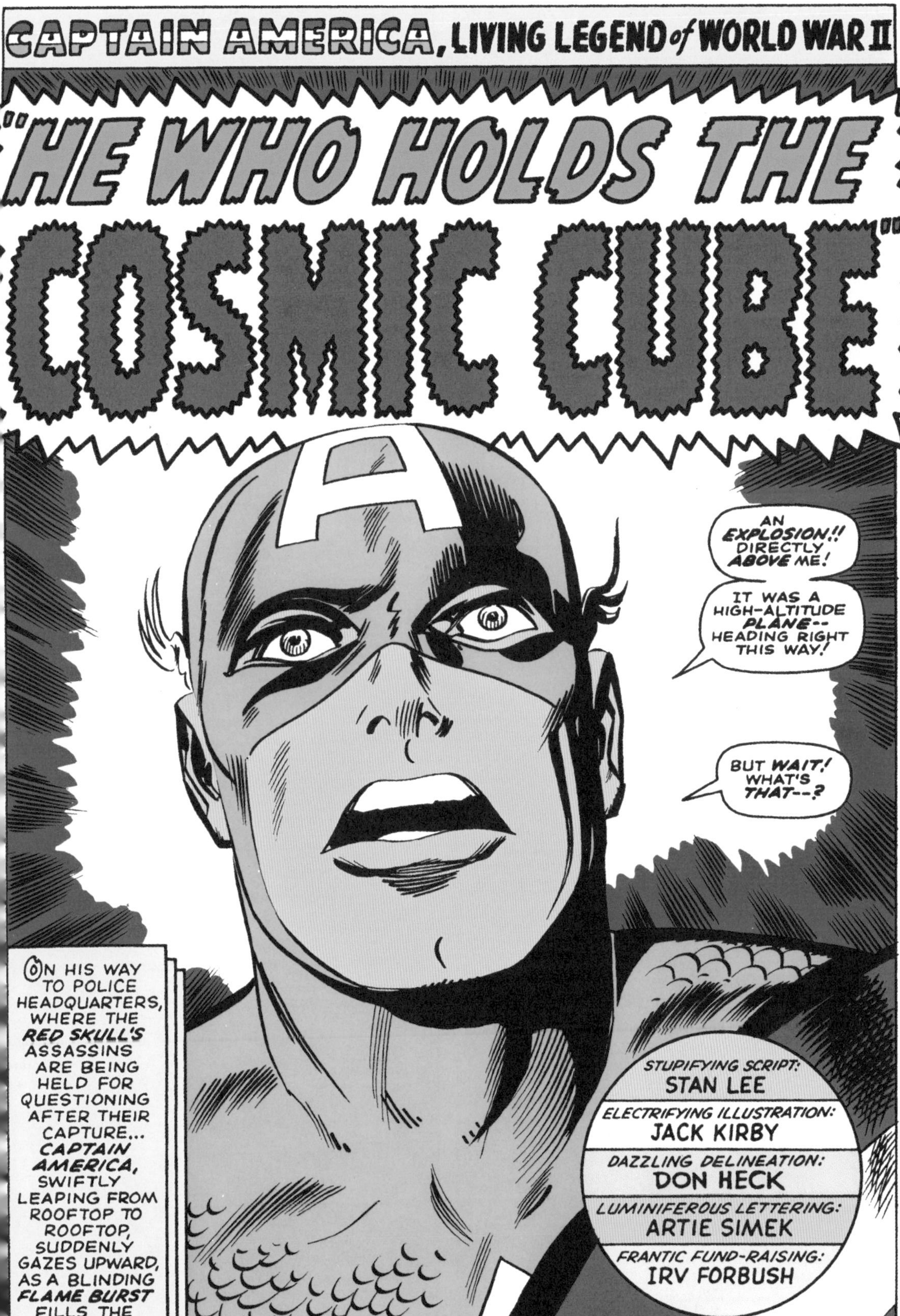

CAPTAIN AMERICA, LIVING LEGEND of WORLD WAR II
"HE WHO HOLDS THE COSMIC CUBE"
AN EXPLOSION!! DIRECTLY ABOVE ME!
IT WAS A HIGH-ALTITUDE PLANE-- HEADING RIGHT THIS WAY!
BUT WAIT! WHAT'S THAT--?
ON HIS WAY TO POLICE HEADQUARTERS, WHERE THE RED SKULL'S ASSASSINS ARE BEING HELD FOR QUESTIONING AFTER THEIR CAPTURE... CAPTAIN AMERICA, SWIFTLY LEAPING FROM ROOFTOP TO ROOFTOP, SUDDENLY GAZES UPWARD, AS A BLINDING FLAME BURST FILLS THE SKY--
STUPIFYING SCRIPT: STAN LEE
ELECTRIFYING ILLUSTRATION: JACK KIRBY
DAZZLING DELINEATION: DON HECK
LUMINIFEROUS LETTERING: ARTIE SIMEK
FRANTIC FUND-RAISING: IRV FORBUSH
1

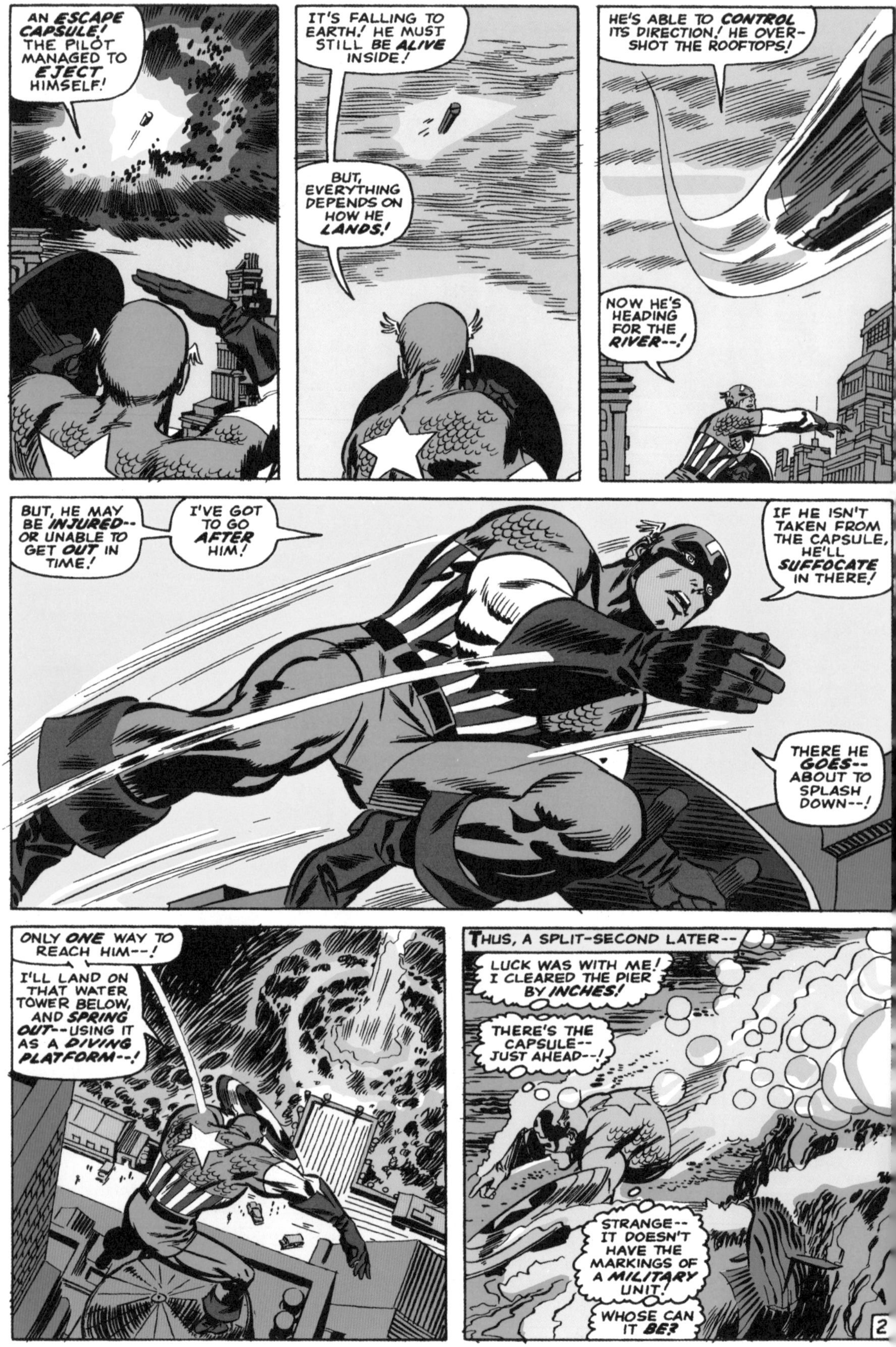

AN ESCAPE CAPSULE! THE PILOT MANAGED TO EJECT HIMSELF!
IT'S FALLING TO EARTH! HE MUST STILL BE ALIVE INSIDE!
BUT, EVERYTHING DEPENDS ON HOW HE LANDS!
HE'S ABLE TO CONTROL ITS DIRECTION! HE OVER-SHOT THE ROOFTOPS!
NOW HE'S HEADING FOR THE RIVER--!
BUT, HE MAY BE INJURED--OR UNABLE TO GET OUT IN TIME!
I'VE GOT TO GO AFTER HIM!
IF HE ISN'T TAKEN FROM THE CAPSULE, HE'LL SUFFOCATE IN THERE!
THERE HE GOES--ABOUT TO SPLASH DOWN--!
ONLY ONE WAY TO REACH HIM--!
I'LL LAND ON THAT WATER TOWER BELOW, AND SPRING OUT--USING IT AS A DIVING PLATFORM--!
THUS, A SPLIT-SECOND LATER--
LUCK WAS WITH ME! I CLEARED THE PIER BY INCHES!
THERE'S THE CAPSULE--JUST AHEAD--!
STRANGE--IT DOESN'T HAVE THE MARKINGS OF A MILITARY UNIT!
WHOSE CAN IT BE?
2

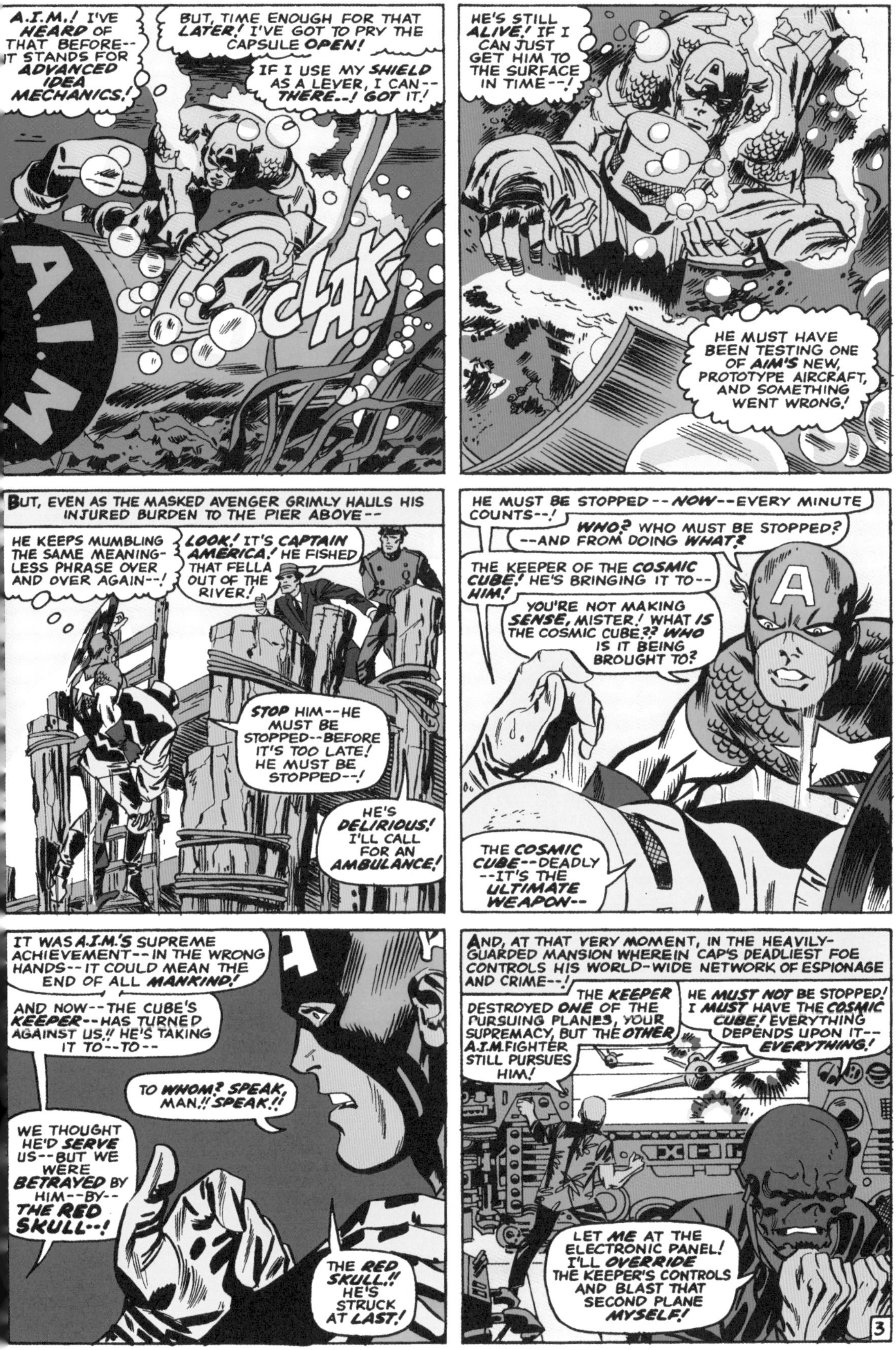
A.I.M.! I'VE HEARD OF THAT BEFORE-- IT STANDS FOR ADVANCED IDEA MECHANICS!
BUT, TIME ENOUGH FOR THAT LATER! I'VE GOT TO PRY THE CAPSULE OPEN!
IF I USE MY SHIELD AS A LEVER, I CAN-- THERE--! GOT IT!
A.I.M.
CLAK
HE'S STILL ALIVE! IF I CAN JUST GET HIM TO THE SURFACE IN TIME--!
HE MUST HAVE BEEN TESTING ONE OF AIM'S NEW, PROTOTYPE AIRCRAFT, AND SOMETHING WENT WRONG!
BUT, EVEN AS THE MASKED AVENGER GRIMLY HAULS HIS INJURED BURDEN TO THE PIER ABOVE--
HE KEEPS MUMBLING THE SAME MEANINGLESS PHRASE OVER AND OVER AGAIN--!
LOOK! IT'S CAPTAIN AMERICA! HE FISHED THAT FELLA OUT OF THE RIVER!
STOP HIM--HE MUST BE STOPPED--BEFORE IT'S TOO LATE! HE MUST BE STOPPED--!
HE'S DELIRIOUS! I'LL CALL FOR AN AMBULANCE!
HE MUST BE STOPPED--NOW--EVERY MINUTE COUNTS--!
WHO? WHO MUST BE STOPPED? --AND FROM DOING WHAT?
THE KEEPER OF THE COSMIC CUBE! HE'S BRINGING IT TO--HIM!
YOU'RE NOT MAKING SENSE, MISTER! WHAT IS THE COSMIC CUBE?? WHO IS IT BEING BROUGHT TO?
THE COSMIC CUBE--DEADLY --IT'S THE ULTIMATE WEAPON--
IT WAS A.I.M.'S SUPREME ACHIEVEMENT--IN THE WRONG HANDS--IT COULD MEAN THE END OF ALL MANKIND!
AND NOW--THE CUBE'S KEEPER--HAS TURNED AGAINST US!! HE'S TAKING IT TO--TO--
TO WHOM? SPEAK, MAN!! SPEAK!!
WE THOUGHT HE'D SERVE US--BUT WE WERE BETRAYED BY HIM--BY--THE RED SKULL--!
THE RED SKULL!! HE'S STRUCK AT LAST!
AND, AT THAT VERY MOMENT, IN THE HEAVILY-GUARDED MANSION WHEREIN CAP'S DEADLIEST FOE CONTROLS HIS WORLD-WIDE NETWORK OF ESPIONAGE AND CRIME--!
THE KEEPER DESTROYED ONE OF THE PURSUING PLANES, YOUR SUPREMACY, BUT THE OTHER A.I.M. FIGHTER STILL PURSUES HIM!
HE MUST NOT BE STOPPED! I MUST HAVE THE COSMIC CUBE! EVERYTHING DEPENDS UPON IT--EVERYTHING!
LET ME AT THE ELECTRONIC PANEL! I'LL OVERRIDE THE KEEPER'S CONTROLS AND BLAST THAT SECOND PLANE MYSELF!
3

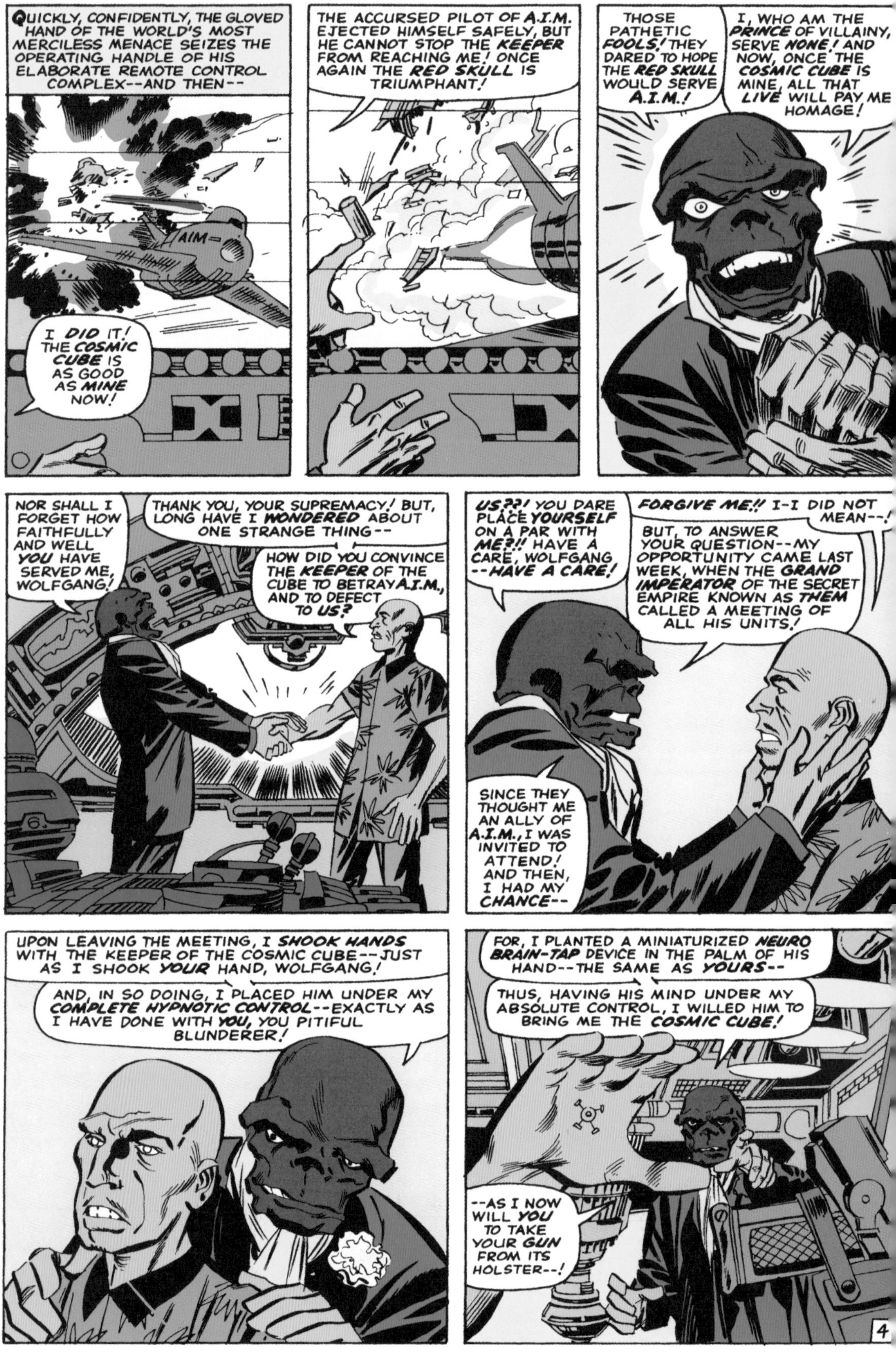
QUICKLY, CONFIDENTLY, THE GLOVED HAND OF THE WORLD'S MOST MERCILESS MENACE SEIZES THE OPERATING HANDLE OF HIS ELABORATE REMOTE CONTROL COMPLEX--AND THEN--
AIM
I DID IT! THE COSMIC CUBE IS AS GOOD AS MINE NOW!
THE ACCURSED PILOT OF A.I.M. EJECTED HIMSELF SAFELY, BUT HE CANNOT STOP THE KEEPER FROM REACHING ME! ONCE AGAIN THE RED SKULL IS TRIUMPHANT!
THOSE PATHETIC FOOLS! THEY DARED TO HOPE THE RED SKULL WOULD SERVE A.I.M.!
I, WHO AM THE PRINCE OF VILLAINY, SERVE NONE! AND NOW, ONCE THE COSMIC CUBE IS MINE, ALL THAT LIVE WILL PAY ME HOMAGE!
NOR SHALL I FORGET HOW FAITHFULLY AND WELL YOU HAVE SERVED ME, WOLFGANG!
THANK YOU, YOUR SUPREMACY! BUT, LONG HAVE I WONDERED ABOUT ONE STRANGE THING--
HOW DID YOU CONVINCE THE KEEPER OF THE CUBE TO BETRAY A.I.M., AND TO DEFECT TO US?
US??! YOU DARE PLACE YOURSELF ON A PAR WITH ME?!! HAVE A CARE, WOLFGANG --HAVE A CARE!
FORGIVE ME!! I-I DID NOT MEAN--!
BUT, TO ANSWER YOUR QUESTION--MY OPPORTUNITY CAME LAST WEEK, WHEN THE GRAND IMPERATOR OF THE SECRET EMPIRE KNOWN AS THEM CALLED A MEETING OF ALL HIS UNITS!
SINCE THEY THOUGHT ME AN ALLY OF A.I.M., I WAS INVITED TO ATTEND! AND THEN, I HAD MY CHANCE--
UPON LEAVING THE MEETING, I SHOOK HANDS WITH THE KEEPER OF THE COSMIC CUBE--JUST AS I SHOOK YOUR HAND, WOLFGANG!
AND, IN SO DOING, I PLACED HIM UNDER MY COMPLETE HYPNOTIC CONTROL--EXACTLY AS I HAVE DONE WITH YOU, YOU PITIFUL BLUNDERER!
FOR, I PLANTED A MINIATURIZED NEURO BRAIN-TAP DEVICE IN THE PALM OF HIS HAND--THE SAME AS YOURS--
THUS, HAVING HIS MIND UNDER MY ABSOLUTE CONTROL, I WILLED HIM TO BRING ME THE COSMIC CUBE!
--AS I NOW WILL YOU TO TAKE YOUR GUN FROM ITS HOLSTER--!
4

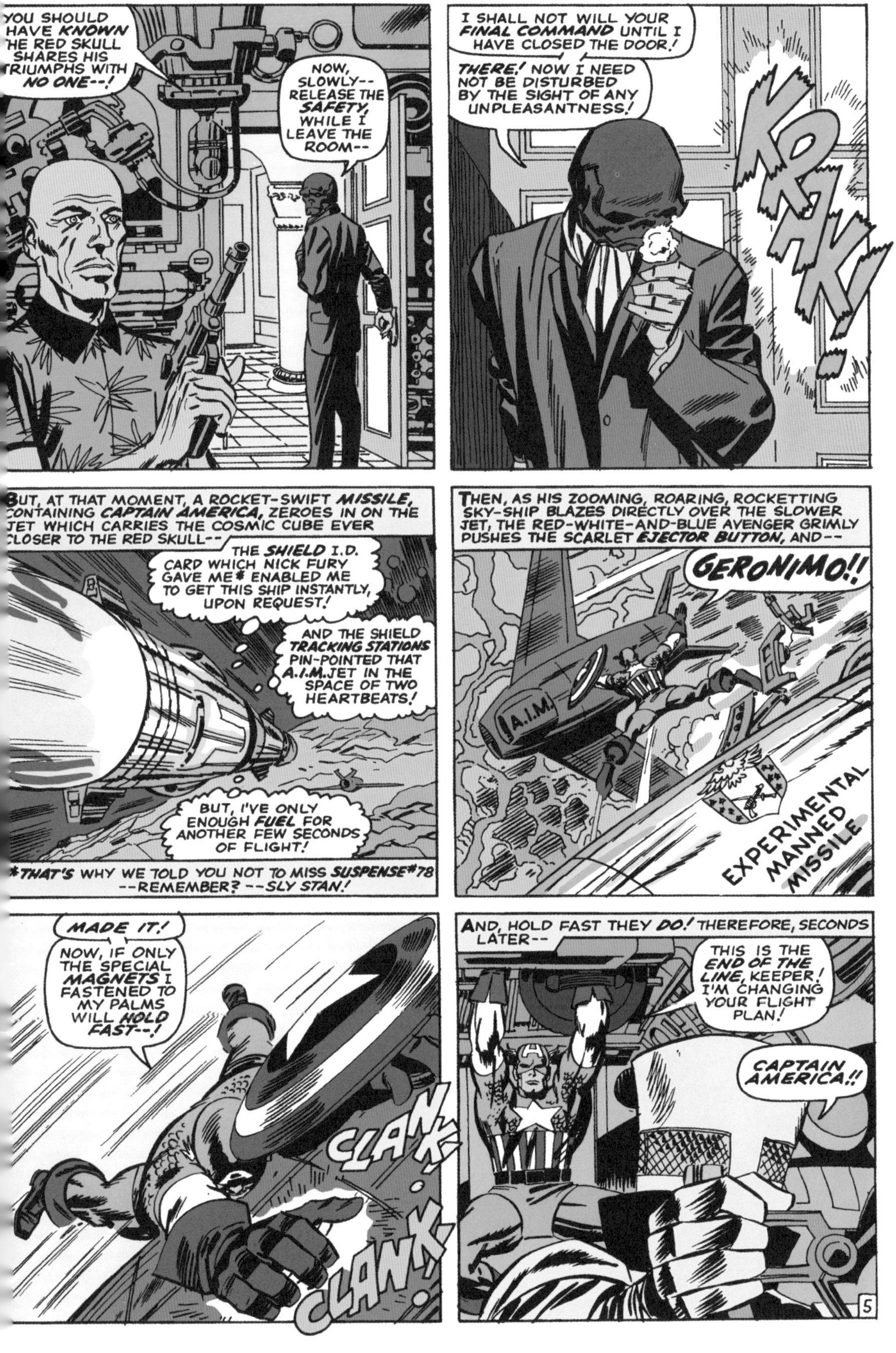
YOU SHOULD HAVE KNOWN THE RED SKULL SHARES HIS TRIUMPHS WITH NO ONE--!
NOW, SLOWLY-- RELEASE THE SAFETY, WHILE I LEAVE THE ROOM--
I SHALL NOT WILL YOUR FINAL COMMAND UNTIL I HAVE CLOSED THE DOOR!
THERE! NOW I NEED NOT BE DISTURBED BY THE SIGHT OF ANY UNPLEASANTNESS!
KRAK!
BUT, AT THAT MOMENT, A ROCKET-SWIFT MISSILE, CONTAINING CAPTAIN AMERICA, ZEROES IN ON THE JET WHICH CARRIES THE COSMIC CUBE EVER CLOSER TO THE RED SKULL--
THE SHIELD I.D. CARD WHICH NICK FURY GAVE ME* ENABLED ME TO GET THIS SHIP INSTANTLY, UPON REQUEST!
AND THE SHIELD TRACKING STATIONS PIN-POINTED THAT A.I.M. JET IN THE SPACE OF TWO HEARTBEATS!
BUT, I'VE ONLY ENOUGH FUEL FOR ANOTHER FEW SECONDS OF FLIGHT!
*THAT'S WHY WE TOLD YOU NOT TO MISS SUSPENSE #78 --REMEMBER? --SLY STAN!
THEN, AS HIS ZOOMING, ROARING, ROCKETTING SKY-SHIP BLAZES DIRECTLY OVER THE SLOWER JET, THE RED-WHITE-AND-BLUE AVENGER GRIMLY PUSHES THE SCARLET EJECTOR BUTTON, AND--
GERONIMO!!
A.I.M.
EXPERIMENTAL MANNED MISSILE
MADE IT!
NOW, IF ONLY THE SPECIAL MAGNETS I FASTENED TO MY PALMS WILL HOLD FAST--!
CLANK!
CLANK!
AND, HOLD FAST THEY DO! THEREFORE, SECONDS LATER--
THIS IS THE END OF THE LINE, KEEPER! I'M CHANGING YOUR FLIGHT PLAN!
CAPTAIN AMERICA!!
5

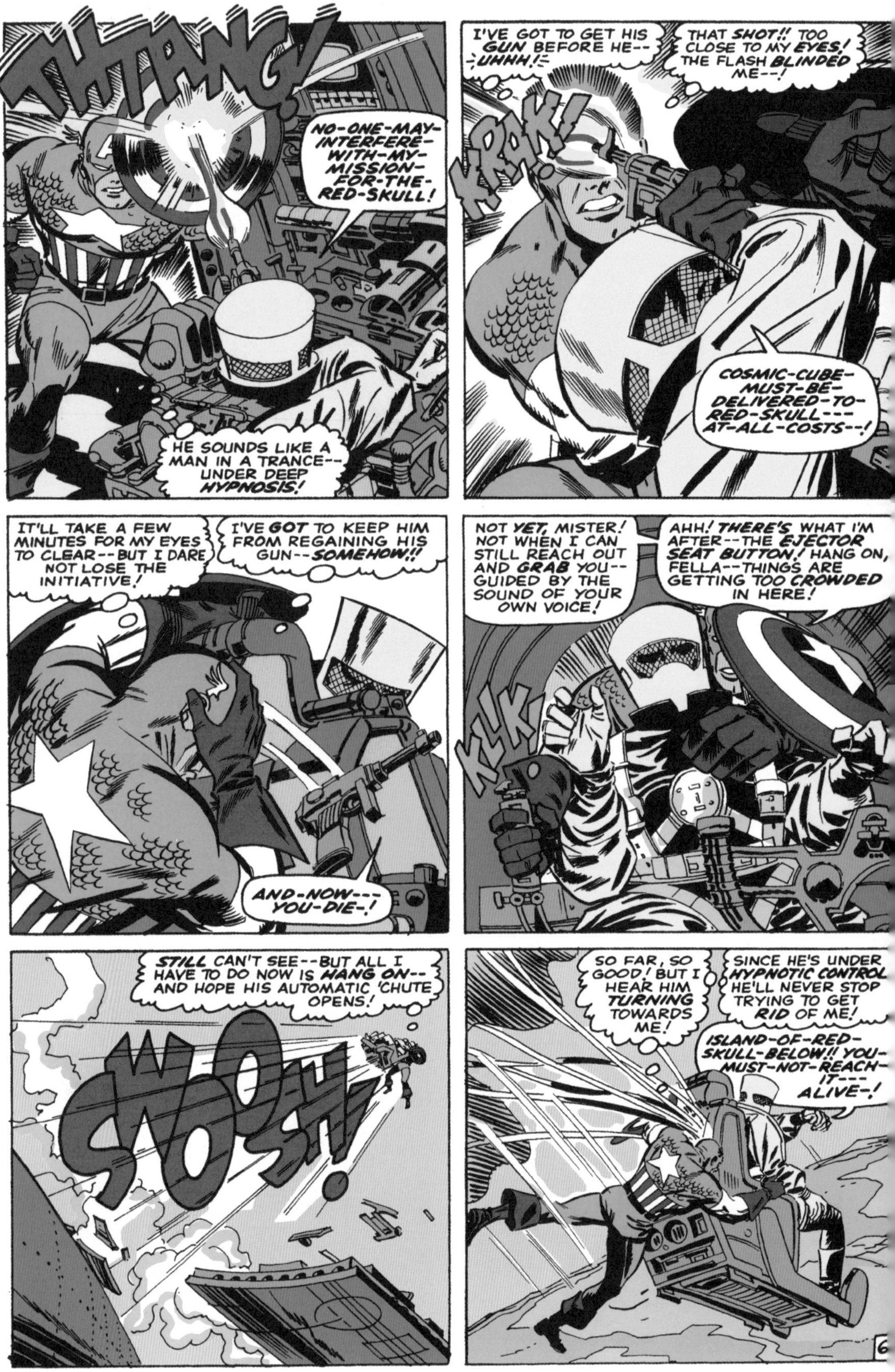
THTANG!
NO-ONE-MAY-INTERFERE-WITH-MY-MISSION-FOR-THE-RED-SKULL!
HE SOUNDS LIKE A MAN IN A TRANCE-- UNDER DEEP HYPNOSIS!
I'VE GOT TO GET HIS GUN BEFORE HE-- UHHH!
THAT SHOT!! TOO CLOSE TO MY EYES! THE FLASH BLINDED ME--!
KRAK!
COSMIC-CUBE-MUST-BE-DELIVERED-TO-RED-SKULL---AT-ALL-COSTS--!
IT'LL TAKE A FEW MINUTES FOR MY EYES TO CLEAR--BUT I DARE NOT LOSE THE INITIATIVE!
I'VE GOT TO KEEP HIM FROM REGAINING HIS GUN--SOMEHOW!!
AND-NOW---YOU-DIE-!
NOT YET, MISTER! NOT WHEN I CAN STILL REACH OUT AND GRAB YOU-- GUIDED BY THE SOUND OF YOUR OWN VOICE!
AHH! THERE'S WHAT I'M AFTER--THE EJECTOR SEAT BUTTON! HANG ON, FELLA--THINGS ARE GETTING TOO CROWDED IN HERE!
KLIK
STILL CAN'T SEE--BUT ALL I HAVE TO DO NOW IS HANG ON-- AND HOPE HIS AUTOMATIC 'CHUTE OPENS!
SWOOOSH!
SO FAR, SO GOOD! BUT I HEAR HIM TURNING TOWARDS ME!
SINCE HE'S UNDER HYPNOTIC CONTROL HE'LL NEVER STOP TRYING TO GET RID OF ME!
ISLAND-OF-RED-SKULL-BELOW!! YOU-MUST-NOT-REACH-IT---ALIVE-!
6

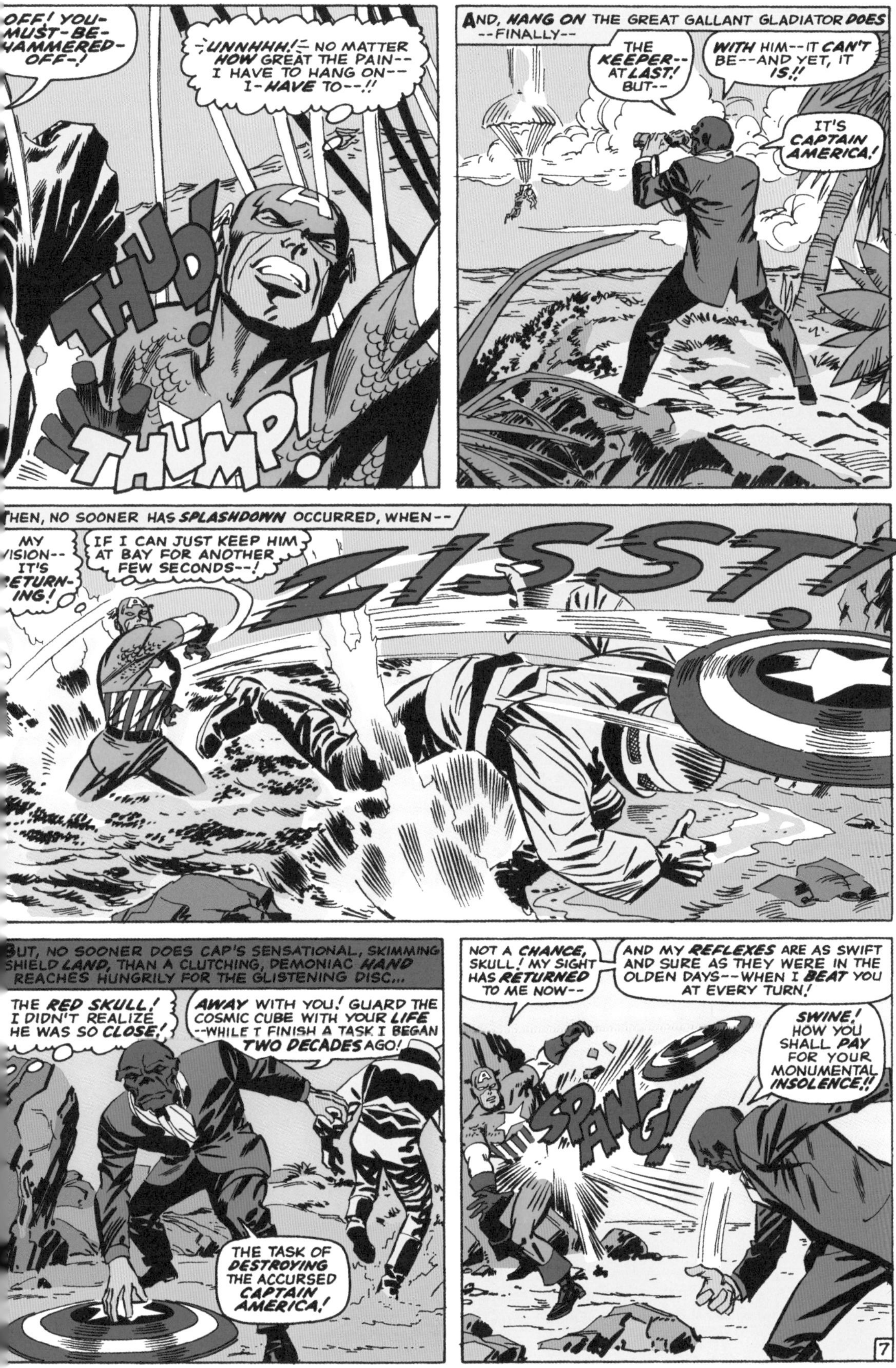
OFF! YOU-MUST-BE-HAMMERED-OFF-!
-UNNHHH!- NO MATTER HOW GREAT THE PAIN--I HAVE TO HANG ON--I-HAVE TO--!!
THUD!
THUMP!
AND, HANG ON THE GREAT GALLANT GLADIATOR DOES --FINALLY--
THE KEEPER--AT LAST! BUT--
WITH HIM--IT CAN'T BE--AND YET, IT IS!!
IT'S CAPTAIN AMERICA!
THEN, NO SOONER HAS SPLASHDOWN OCCURRED, WHEN--
MY VISION--IT'S RETURNING!
IF I CAN JUST KEEP HIM AT BAY FOR ANOTHER FEW SECONDS--!
ZISST!
BUT, NO SOONER DOES CAP'S SENSATIONAL, SKIMMING SHIELD LAND, THAN A CLUTCHING, DEMONIAC HAND REACHES HUNGRILY FOR THE GLISTENING DISC...
THE RED SKULL! I DIDN'T REALIZE HE WAS SO CLOSE!
AWAY WITH YOU! GUARD THE COSMIC CUBE WITH YOUR LIFE --WHILE I FINISH A TASK I BEGAN TWO DECADES AGO!
THE TASK OF DESTROYING THE ACCURSED CAPTAIN AMERICA!
NOT A CHANCE, SKULL! MY SIGHT HAS RETURNED TO ME NOW--
AND MY REFLEXES ARE AS SWIFT AND SURE AS THEY WERE IN THE OLDEN DAYS--WHEN I BEAT YOU AT EVERY TURN!
SWINE! HOW YOU SHALL PAY FOR YOUR MONUMENTAL INSOLENCE!!
SPANG!
7

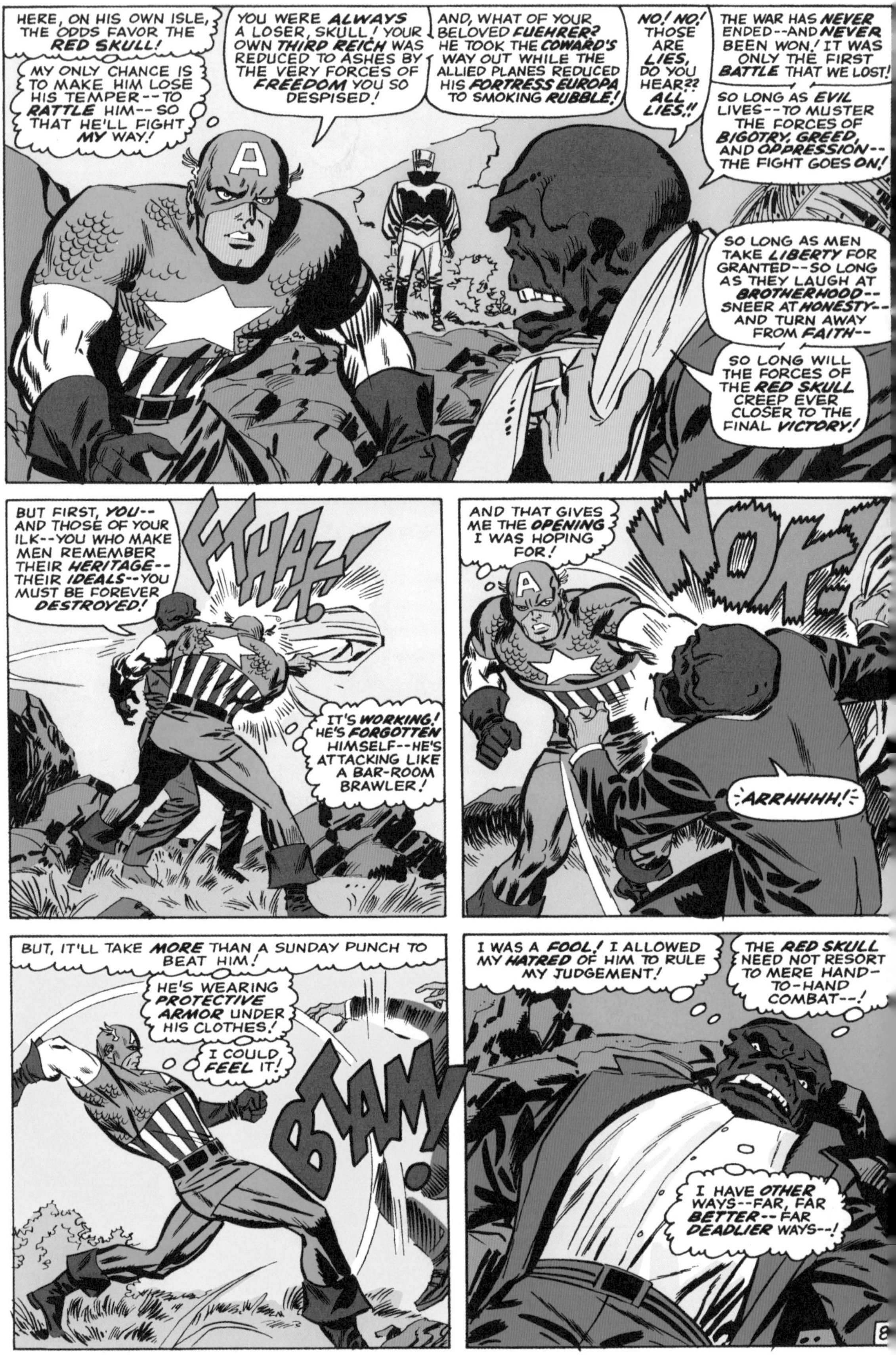
HERE, ON HIS OWN ISLE, THE ODDS FAVOR THE RED SKULL!
MY ONLY CHANCE IS TO MAKE HIM LOSE HIS TEMPER--TO RATTLE HIM--SO THAT HE'LL FIGHT MY WAY!
YOU WERE ALWAYS A LOSER, SKULL! YOUR OWN THIRD REICH WAS REDUCED TO ASHES BY THE VERY FORCES OF FREEDOM YOU SO DESPISED!
AND, WHAT OF YOUR BELOVED FUEHRER? HE TOOK THE COWARD'S WAY OUT WHILE THE ALLIED PLANES REDUCED HIS FORTRESS EUROPA TO SMOKING RUBBLE!
NO! NO! THOSE ARE LIES, DO YOU HEAR?? ALL LIES!!
THE WAR HAS NEVER ENDED--AND NEVER BEEN WON! IT WAS ONLY THE FIRST BATTLE THAT WE LOST!
SO LONG AS EVIL LIVES--TO MUSTER THE FORCES OF BIGOTRY, GREED, AND OPPRESSION--THE FIGHT GOES ON!
SO LONG AS MEN TAKE LIBERTY FOR GRANTED--SO LONG AS THEY LAUGH AT BROTHERHOOD--SNEER AT HONESTY--AND TURN AWAY FROM FAITH--
SO LONG WILL THE FORCES OF THE RED SKULL CREEP EVER CLOSER TO THE FINAL VICTORY!
BUT FIRST, YOU--AND THOSE OF YOUR ILK--YOU WHO MAKE MEN REMEMBER THEIR HERITAGE--THEIR IDEALS--YOU MUST BE FOREVER DESTROYED!
THWAK!
IT'S WORKING! HE'S FORGOTTEN HIMSELF--HE'S ATTACKING LIKE A BAR-ROOM BRAWLER!
AND THAT GIVES ME THE OPENING I WAS HOPING FOR!
WOK!
ARRHHHH!
BUT, IT'LL TAKE MORE THAN A SUNDAY PUNCH TO BEAT HIM!
HE'S WEARING PROTECTIVE ARMOR UNDER HIS CLOTHES!
I COULD FEEL IT!
BTAM!
I WAS A FOOL! I ALLOWED MY HATRED OF HIM TO RULE MY JUDGEMENT!
THE RED SKULL NEED NOT RESORT TO MERE HAND-TO-HAND COMBAT--!
I HAVE OTHER WAYS--FAR, FAR BETTER--FAR DEADLIER WAYS--!
8

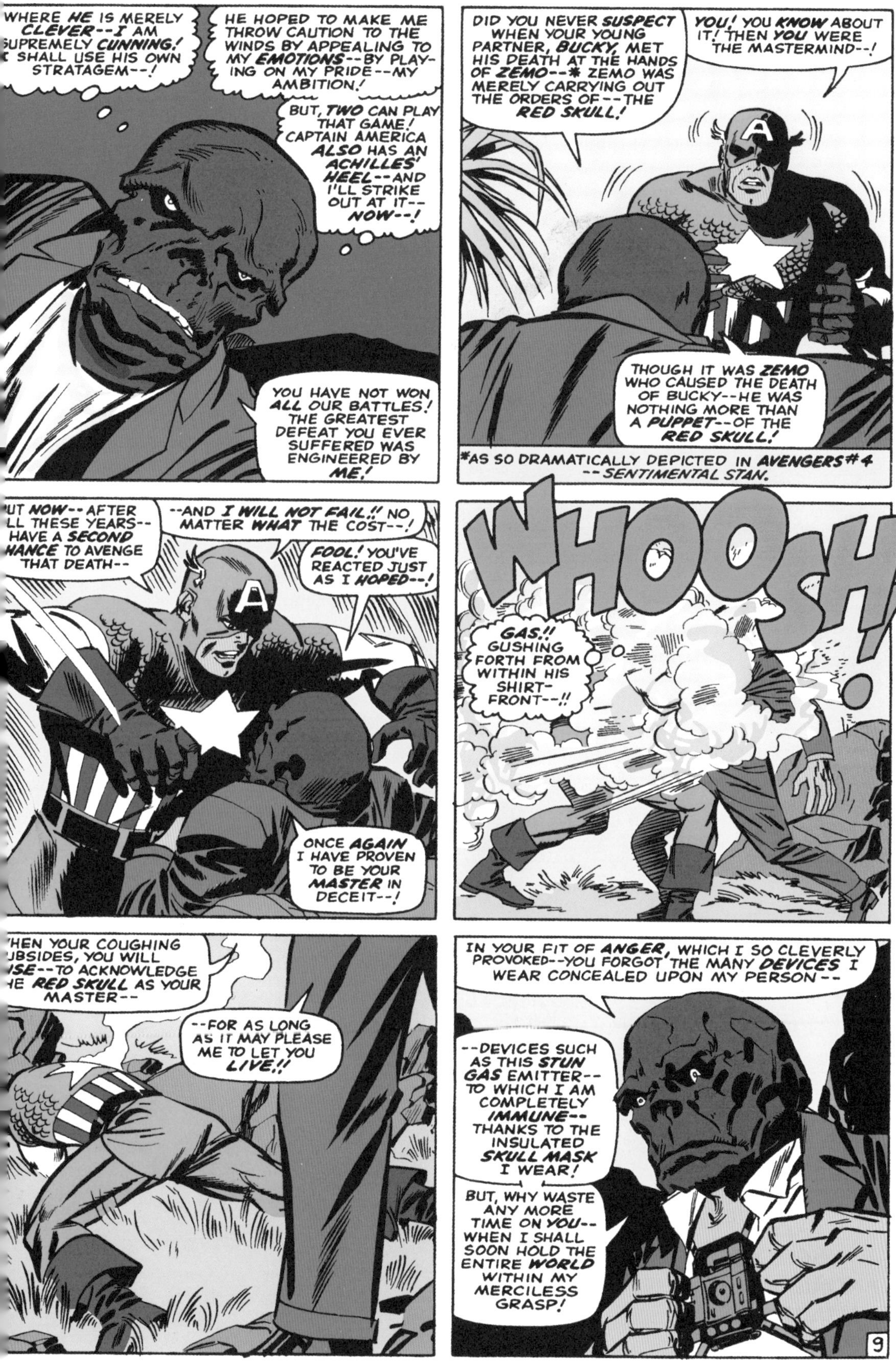
WHERE HE IS MERELY CLEVER--I AM SUPREMELY CUNNING! I SHALL USE HIS OWN STRATAGEM--!
HE HOPED TO MAKE ME THROW CAUTION TO THE WINDS BY APPEALING TO MY EMOTIONS--BY PLAYING ON MY PRIDE--MY AMBITION!
BUT, TWO CAN PLAY THAT GAME! CAPTAIN AMERICA ALSO HAS AN ACHILLES' HEEL--AND I'LL STRIKE OUT AT IT--NOW--!
YOU HAVE NOT WON ALL OUR BATTLES! THE GREATEST DEFEAT YOU EVER SUFFERED WAS ENGINEERED BY ME!
DID YOU NEVER SUSPECT WHEN YOUR YOUNG PARTNER, BUCKY, MET HIS DEATH AT THE HANDS OF ZEMO--* ZEMO WAS MERELY CARRYING OUT THE ORDERS OF--THE RED SKULL!
YOU! YOU KNOW ABOUT IT! THEN YOU WERE THE MASTERMIND--!
THOUGH IT WAS ZEMO WHO CAUSED THE DEATH OF BUCKY--HE WAS NOTHING MORE THAN A PUPPET--OF THE RED SKULL!
*AS SO DRAMATICALLY DEPICTED IN AVENGERS #4 --SENTIMENTAL STAN.
UT NOW--AFTER LL THESE YEARS--HAVE A SECOND HANCE TO AVENGE THAT DEATH--
--AND I WILL NOT FAIL!! NO MATTER WHAT THE COST--!
FOOL! YOU'VE REACTED JUST AS I HOPED--!
ONCE AGAIN I HAVE PROVEN TO BE YOUR MASTER IN DECEIT--!
WHOOSH!
GAS!! GUSHING FORTH FROM WITHIN HIS SHIRT-FRONT--!!
HEN YOUR COUGHING UBSIDES, YOU WILL ISE--TO ACKNOWLEDGE HE RED SKULL AS YOUR MASTER--
--FOR AS LONG AS IT MAY PLEASE ME TO LET YOU LIVE!!
IN YOUR FIT OF ANGER, WHICH I SO CLEVERLY PROVOKED--YOU FORGOT THE MANY DEVICES I WEAR CONCEALED UPON MY PERSON--
--DEVICES SUCH AS THIS STUN GAS EMITTER--TO WHICH I AM COMPLETELY IMMUNE--THANKS TO THE INSULATED SKULL MASK I WEAR!
BUT, WHY WASTE ANY MORE TIME ON YOU--WHEN I SHALL SOON HOLD THE ENTIRE WORLD WITHIN MY MERCILESS GRASP!
9

THE *CUBE!* BRING ME THE *COSMIC CUBE!*

I SO COMMAND!

I—HEAR—AND—OBEY—SUPREME—ONE—!

AT *LAST*—IT IS *MINE!!* THE ULTIMATE WEAPON! THE ULTIMATE SOURCE OF *POWER!*

THE ONLY SUCH ARTIFACT KNOWN TO MAN—WHICH CAN CONVERT *THOUGHT WAVES*—INTO *MATERIAL ACTION!*

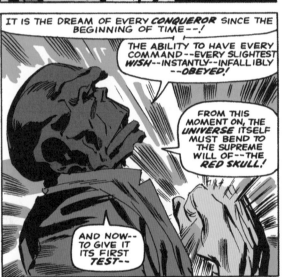

IT IS THE DREAM OF EVERY *CONQUEROR* SINCE THE BEGINNING OF TIME—!

THE ABILITY TO HAVE EVERY COMMAND—EVERY SLIGHTEST *WISH*—INSTANTLY—INFALLIBLY—*OBEYED!*

FROM THIS MOMENT ON, THE *UNIVERSE* ITSELF MUST BEND TO THE SUPREME WILL OF—THE *RED SKULL!*

AND NOW—TO GIVE IT ITS FIRST *TEST*—

YOU HAVE *SERVED* YOUR PURPOSE—I HAVE NEED OF YOU *NO LONGER!*

THEREFORE, *BEGONE!* I CONSIGN YOU TO *ANOTHER DIMENSION!*

THERE IS *NOTHING* I CANNOT DO! *NOTHING! NOTHING!*

THAT BOULDER *DISPLEASES* ME! LET IT *DEFY GRAVITY!!* LET IT *RISE*—UNTIL IT IS OUT OF SIGHT!

THE WAY HE *IGNORES* ME—AS THOUGH HE IS BEYOND ANY HARM!!

AND, NO *WONDER!* WITH THAT CUBE IN HIS HAND, HE HAS ONLY TO *THINK* OF SOMETHING—AND IT *HAPPENS!*

HE'S *NO LONGER* MERELY A DANGEROUS FOE—

—TO ALL INTENTS AND PURPOSES, THE MAN WHO IS SLOWLY *TURNING* TOWARDS ME NOW HAS BECOME—

—*INVINCIBLE!!*

CONTINUED NEXT ISSUE!

TALES OF SUSPENSE #81,

SEPTEMBER 1966,

"THE RED SKULL SUPREME!"

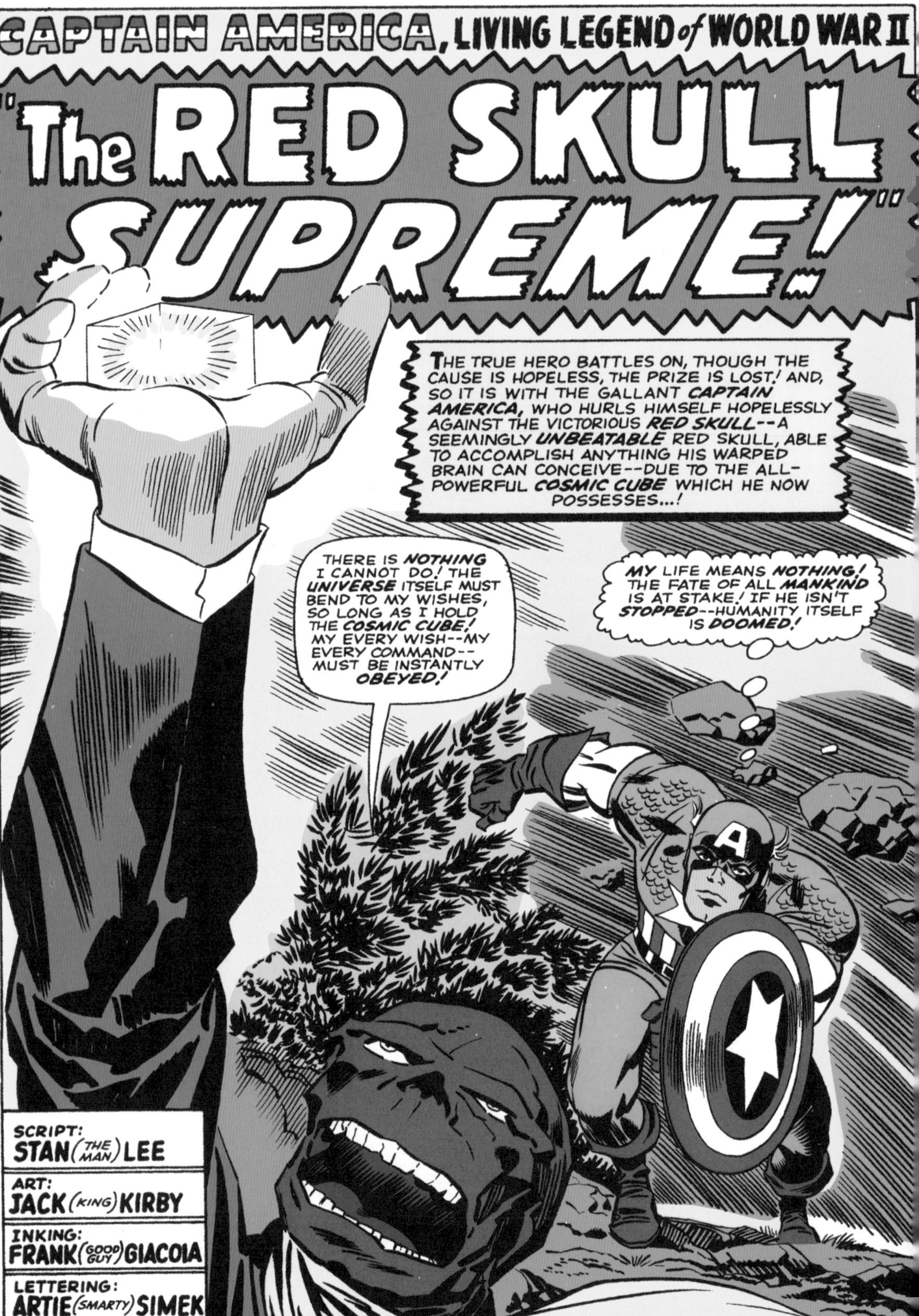
CAPTAIN AMERICA, LIVING LEGEND of WORLD WAR II
"The RED SKULL SUPREME!"
THE TRUE HERO BATTLES ON, THOUGH THE CAUSE IS HOPELESS, THE PRIZE IS LOST! AND, SO IT IS WITH THE GALLANT CAPTAIN AMERICA, WHO HURLS HIMSELF HOPELESSLY AGAINST THE VICTORIOUS RED SKULL--A SEEMINGLY UNBEATABLE RED SKULL, ABLE TO ACCOMPLISH ANYTHING HIS WARPED BRAIN CAN CONCEIVE--DUE TO THE ALL-POWERFUL COSMIC CUBE WHICH HE NOW POSSESSES...!
THERE IS NOTHING I CANNOT DO! THE UNIVERSE ITSELF MUST BEND TO MY WISHES, SO LONG AS I HOLD THE COSMIC CUBE! MY EVERY WISH--MY EVERY COMMAND--MUST BE INSTANTLY OBEYED!
MY LIFE MEANS NOTHING! THE FATE OF ALL MANKIND IS AT STAKE! IF HE ISN'T STOPPED--HUMANITY ITSELF IS DOOMED!
SCRIPT: STAN (THE MAN) LEE
ART: JACK (KING) KIRBY
INKING: FRANK (GOOD GUY) GIACOIA
LETTERING: ARTIE (SMARTY) SIMEK
RECRUITING: IRV (FALL GUY) FORBUSH
1

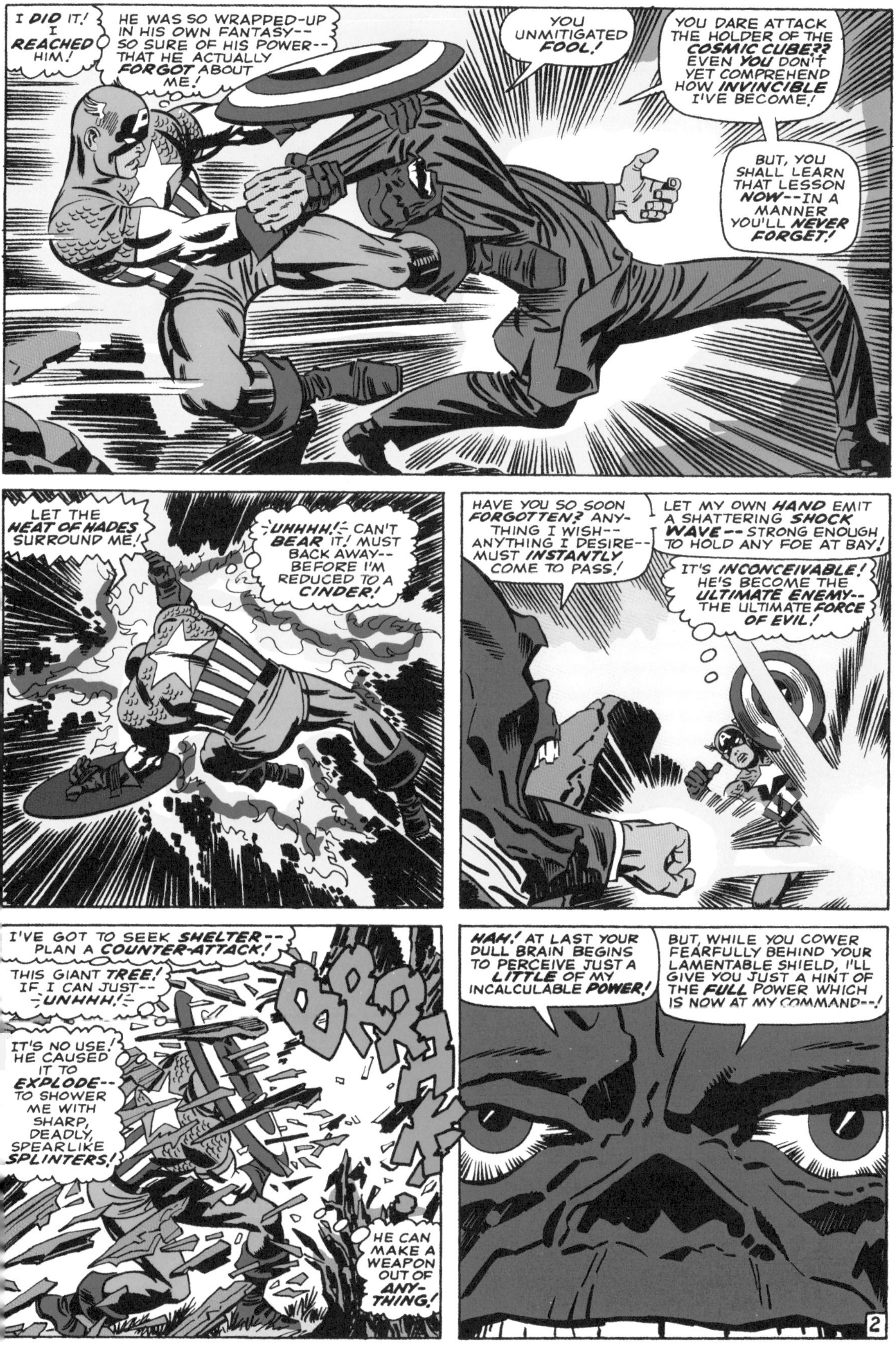
I DID IT! I REACHED HIM!
HE WAS SO WRAPPED-UP IN HIS OWN FANTASY-- SO SURE OF HIS POWER-- THAT HE ACTUALLY FORGOT ABOUT ME!
YOU UNMITIGATED FOOL!
YOU DARE ATTACK THE HOLDER OF THE COSMIC CUBE?? EVEN YOU DON'T YET COMPREHEND HOW INVINCIBLE I'VE BECOME!
BUT, YOU SHALL LEARN THAT LESSON NOW--IN A MANNER YOU'LL NEVER FORGET!
LET THE HEAT OF HADES SURROUND ME!
UNHHH! CAN'T BEAR IT! MUST BACK AWAY-- BEFORE I'M REDUCED TO A CINDER!
HAVE YOU SO SOON FORGOTTEN? ANYTHING I WISH-- ANYTHING I DESIRE-- MUST INSTANTLY COME TO PASS!
LET MY OWN HAND EMIT A SHATTERING SHOCK WAVE -- STRONG ENOUGH TO HOLD ANY FOE AT BAY!
IT'S INCONCEIVABLE! HE'S BECOME THE ULTIMATE ENEMY-- THE ULTIMATE FORCE OF EVIL!
I'VE GOT TO SEEK SHELTER-- PLAN A COUNTER-ATTACK!
THIS GIANT TREE! IF I CAN JUST-- UNHHH!
BRRAK
IT'S NO USE! HE CAUSED IT TO EXPLODE-- TO SHOWER ME WITH SHARP, DEADLY, SPEARLIKE SPLINTERS!
HE CAN MAKE A WEAPON OUT OF ANYTHING!
HAH! AT LAST YOUR DULL BRAIN BEGINS TO PERCEIVE JUST A LITTLE OF MY INCALCULABLE POWER!
BUT, WHILE YOU COWER FEARFULLY BEHIND YOUR LAMENTABLE SHIELD, I'LL GIVE YOU JUST A HINT OF THE FULL POWER WHICH IS NOW AT MY COMMAND--!
2

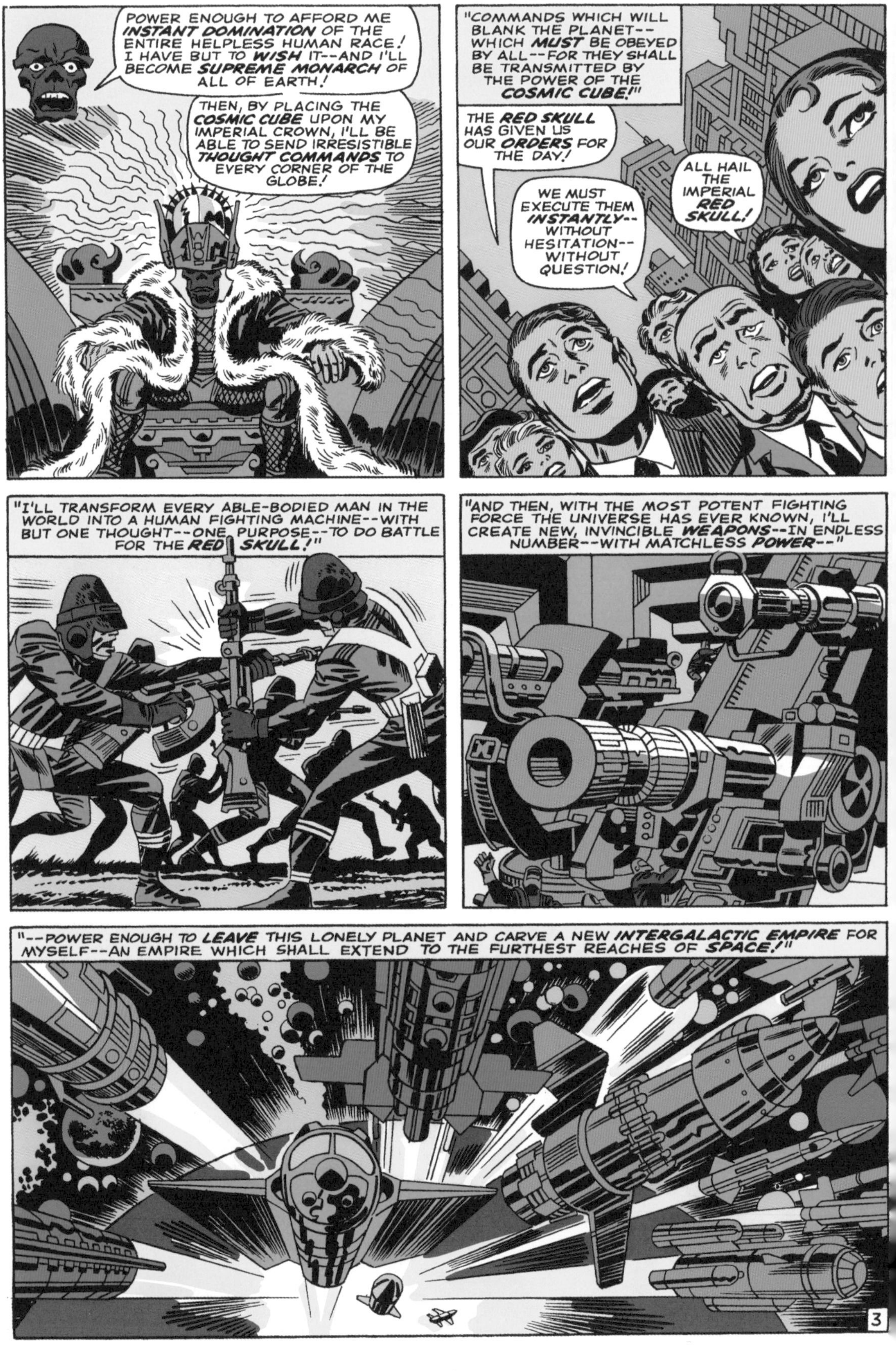
POWER ENOUGH TO AFFORD ME INSTANT DOMINATION OF THE ENTIRE HELPLESS HUMAN RACE! I HAVE BUT TO WISH IT--AND I'LL BECOME SUPREME MONARCH OF ALL OF EARTH!
THEN, BY PLACING THE COSMIC CUBE UPON MY IMPERIAL CROWN, I'LL BE ABLE TO SEND IRRESISTIBLE THOUGHT COMMANDS TO EVERY CORNER OF THE GLOBE!
"COMMANDS WHICH WILL BLANK THE PLANET--WHICH MUST BE OBEYED BY ALL--FOR THEY SHALL BE TRANSMITTED BY THE POWER OF THE COSMIC CUBE!"
THE RED SKULL HAS GIVEN US OUR ORDERS FOR THE DAY!
WE MUST EXECUTE THEM INSTANTLY--WITHOUT HESITATION--WITHOUT QUESTION!
ALL HAIL THE IMPERIAL RED SKULL!
"I'LL TRANSFORM EVERY ABLE-BODIED MAN IN THE WORLD INTO A HUMAN FIGHTING MACHINE--WITH BUT ONE THOUGHT--ONE PURPOSE--TO DO BATTLE FOR THE RED SKULL!"
"AND THEN, WITH THE MOST POTENT FIGHTING FORCE THE UNIVERSE HAS EVER KNOWN, I'LL CREATE NEW, INVINCIBLE WEAPONS--IN ENDLESS NUMBER--WITH MATCHLESS POWER--"
"--POWER ENOUGH TO LEAVE THIS LONELY PLANET AND CARVE A NEW INTERGALACTIC EMPIRE FOR MYSELF--AN EMPIRE WHICH SHALL EXTEND TO THE FURTHEST REACHES OF SPACE!"
3

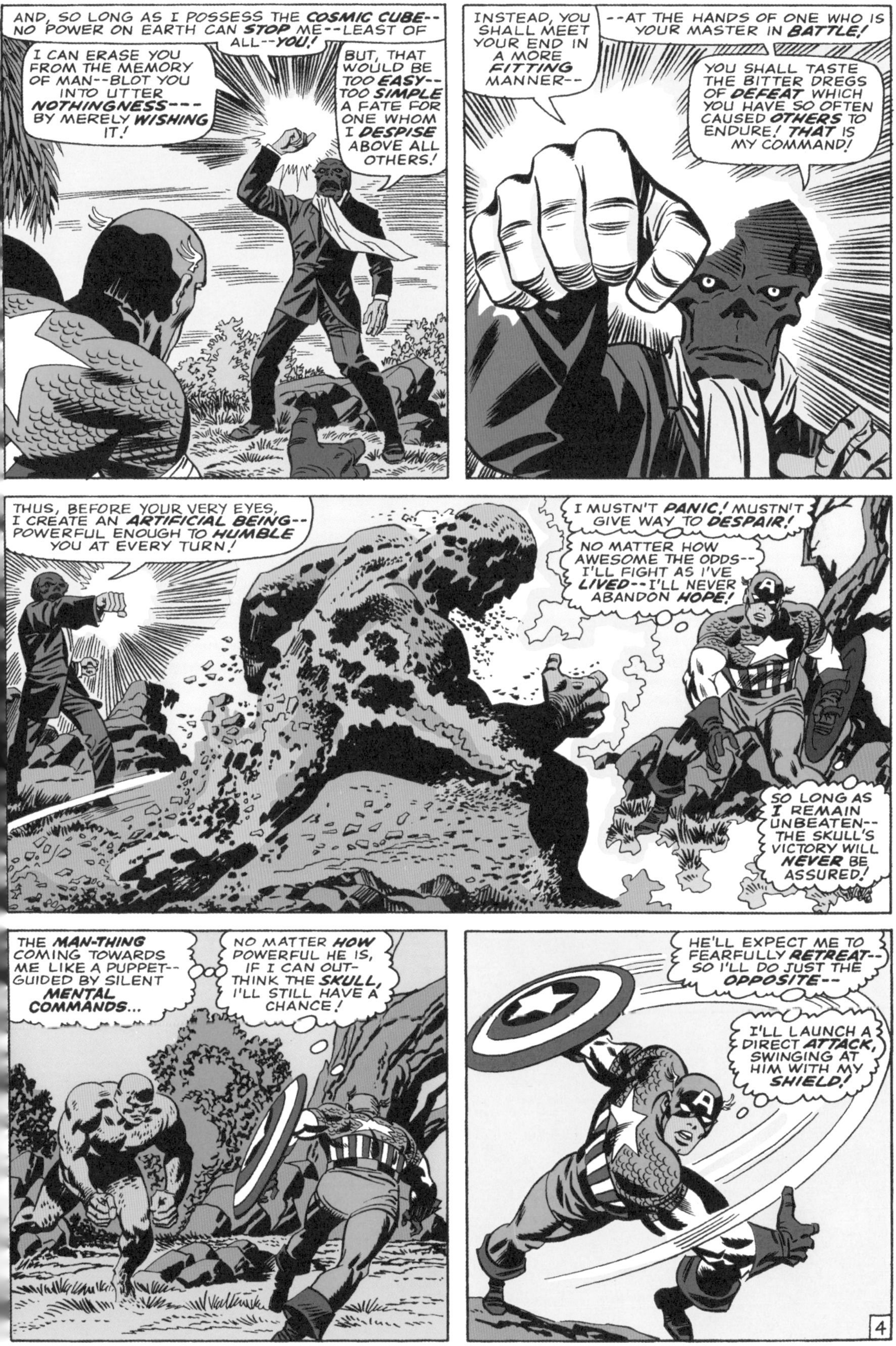
AND, SO LONG AS I POSSESS THE COSMIC CUBE-- NO POWER ON EARTH CAN STOP ME--LEAST OF ALL--YOU!
I CAN ERASE YOU FROM THE MEMORY OF MAN--BLOT YOU INTO UTTER NOTHINGNESS--- BY MERELY WISHING IT!
BUT, THAT WOULD BE TOO EASY-- TOO SIMPLE A FATE FOR ONE WHOM I DESPISE ABOVE ALL OTHERS!
INSTEAD, YOU SHALL MEET YOUR END IN A MORE FITTING MANNER--
--AT THE HANDS OF ONE WHO IS YOUR MASTER IN BATTLE!
YOU SHALL TASTE THE BITTER DREGS OF DEFEAT WHICH YOU HAVE SO OFTEN CAUSED OTHERS TO ENDURE! THAT IS MY COMMAND!
THUS, BEFORE YOUR VERY EYES, I CREATE AN ARTIFICIAL BEING-- POWERFUL ENOUGH TO HUMBLE YOU AT EVERY TURN!
I MUSTN'T PANIC! MUSTN'T GIVE WAY TO DESPAIR!
NO MATTER HOW AWESOME THE ODDS-- I'LL FIGHT AS I'VE LIVED--I'LL NEVER ABANDON HOPE!
SO LONG AS I REMAIN UNBEATEN-- THE SKULL'S VICTORY WILL NEVER BE ASSURED!
THE MAN-THING COMING TOWARDS ME LIKE A PUPPET-- GUIDED BY SILENT MENTAL COMMANDS...
NO MATTER HOW POWERFUL HE IS, IF I CAN OUT-THINK THE SKULL, I'LL STILL HAVE A CHANCE!
HE'LL EXPECT ME TO FEARFULLY RETREAT-- SO I'LL DO JUST THE OPPOSITE--
I'LL LAUNCH A DIRECT ATTACK, SWINGING AT HIM WITH MY SHIELD!
4

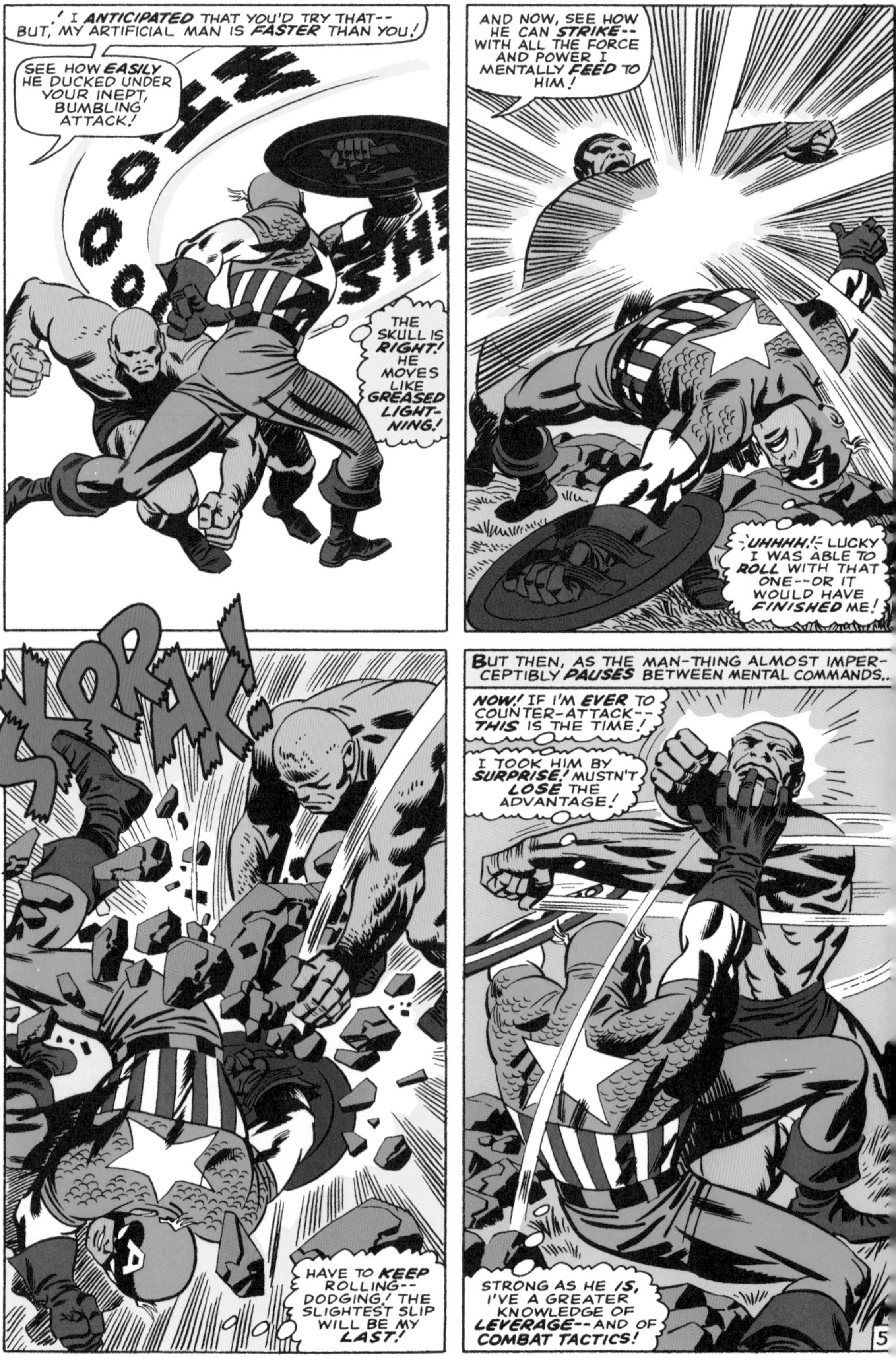

-! I ANTICIPATED THAT YOU'D TRY THAT-- BUT, MY ARTIFICIAL MAN IS FASTER THAN YOU!
SEE HOW EASILY HE DUCKED UNDER YOUR INEPT, BUMBLING ATTACK!
WHOOSH!
THE SKULL IS RIGHT! HE MOVES LIKE GREASED LIGHTNING!
AND NOW, SEE HOW HE CAN STRIKE-- WITH ALL THE FORCE AND POWER I MENTALLY FEED TO HIM!
UHHHH!-- LUCKY I WAS ABLE TO ROLL WITH THAT ONE--OR IT WOULD HAVE FINISHED ME!
SKRAK!
HAVE TO KEEP ROLLING-- DODGING! THE SLIGHTEST SLIP WILL BE MY LAST!
BUT THEN, AS THE MAN-THING ALMOST IMPERCEPTIBLY PAUSES BETWEEN MENTAL COMMANDS..
NOW! IF I'M EVER TO COUNTER-ATTACK-- THIS IS THE TIME!
I TOOK HIM BY SURPRISE! MUSTN'T LOSE THE ADVANTAGE!
STRONG AS HE IS, I'VE A GREATER KNOWLEDGE OF LEVERAGE--AND OF COMBAT TACTICS!
5

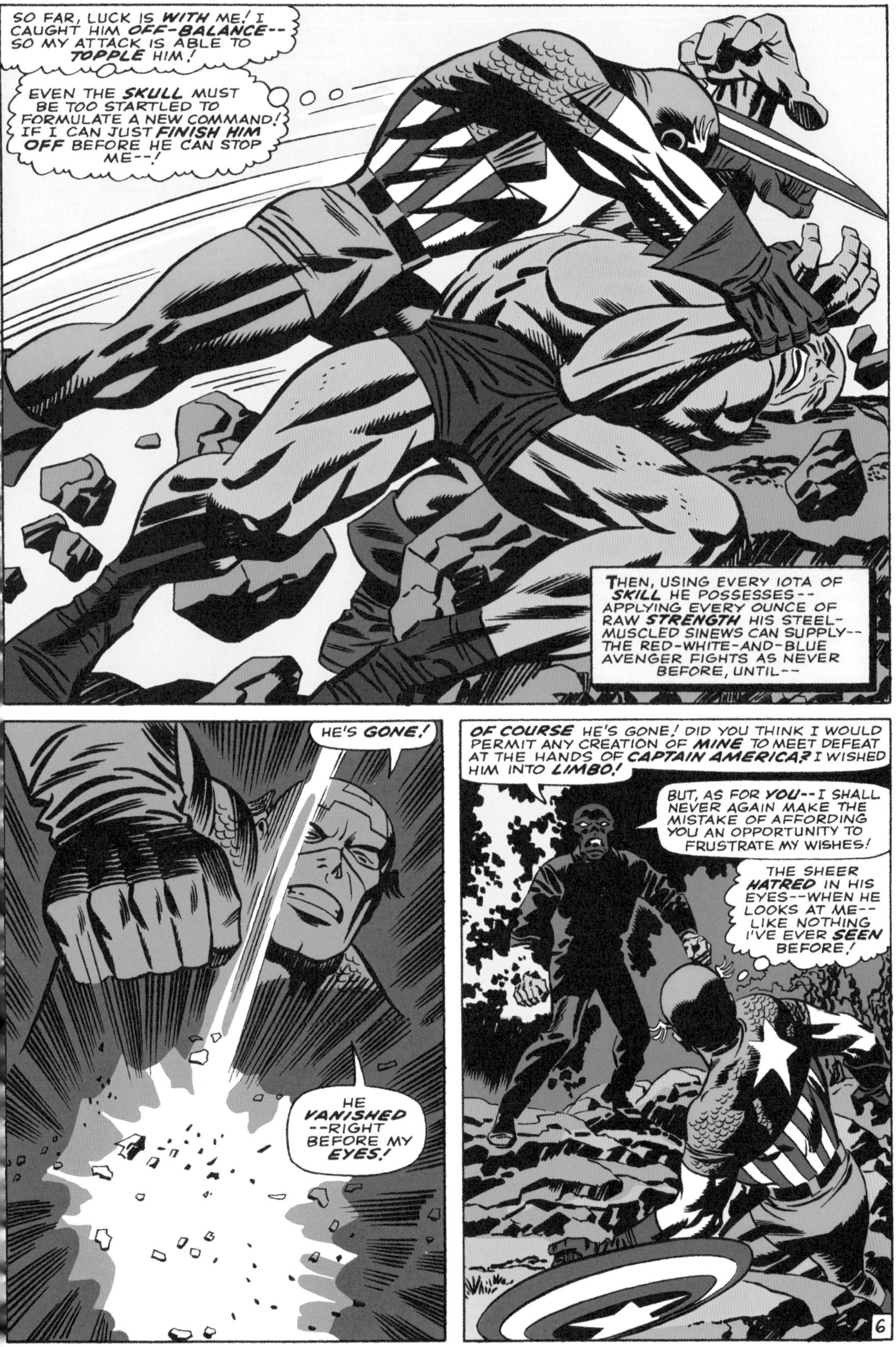

SO FAR, LUCK IS WITH ME! I CAUGHT HIM OFF-BALANCE-- SO MY ATTACK IS ABLE TO TOPPLE HIM!
EVEN THE SKULL MUST BE TOO STARTLED TO FORMULATE A NEW COMMAND! IF I CAN JUST FINISH HIM OFF BEFORE HE CAN STOP ME--!
THEN, USING EVERY IOTA OF SKILL HE POSSESSES-- APPLYING EVERY OUNCE OF RAW STRENGTH HIS STEEL-MUSCLED SINEWS CAN SUPPLY-- THE RED-WHITE-AND-BLUE AVENGER FIGHTS AS NEVER BEFORE, UNTIL--
HE'S GONE!
HE VANISHED --RIGHT BEFORE MY EYES!
OF COURSE HE'S GONE! DID YOU THINK I WOULD PERMIT ANY CREATION OF MINE TO MEET DEFEAT AT THE HANDS OF CAPTAIN AMERICA? I WISHED HIM INTO LIMBO!
BUT, AS FOR YOU-- I SHALL NEVER AGAIN MAKE THE MISTAKE OF AFFORDING YOU AN OPPORTUNITY TO FRUSTRATE MY WISHES!
THE SHEER HATRED IN HIS EYES--WHEN HE LOOKS AT ME-- LIKE NOTHING I'VE EVER SEEN BEFORE!
6

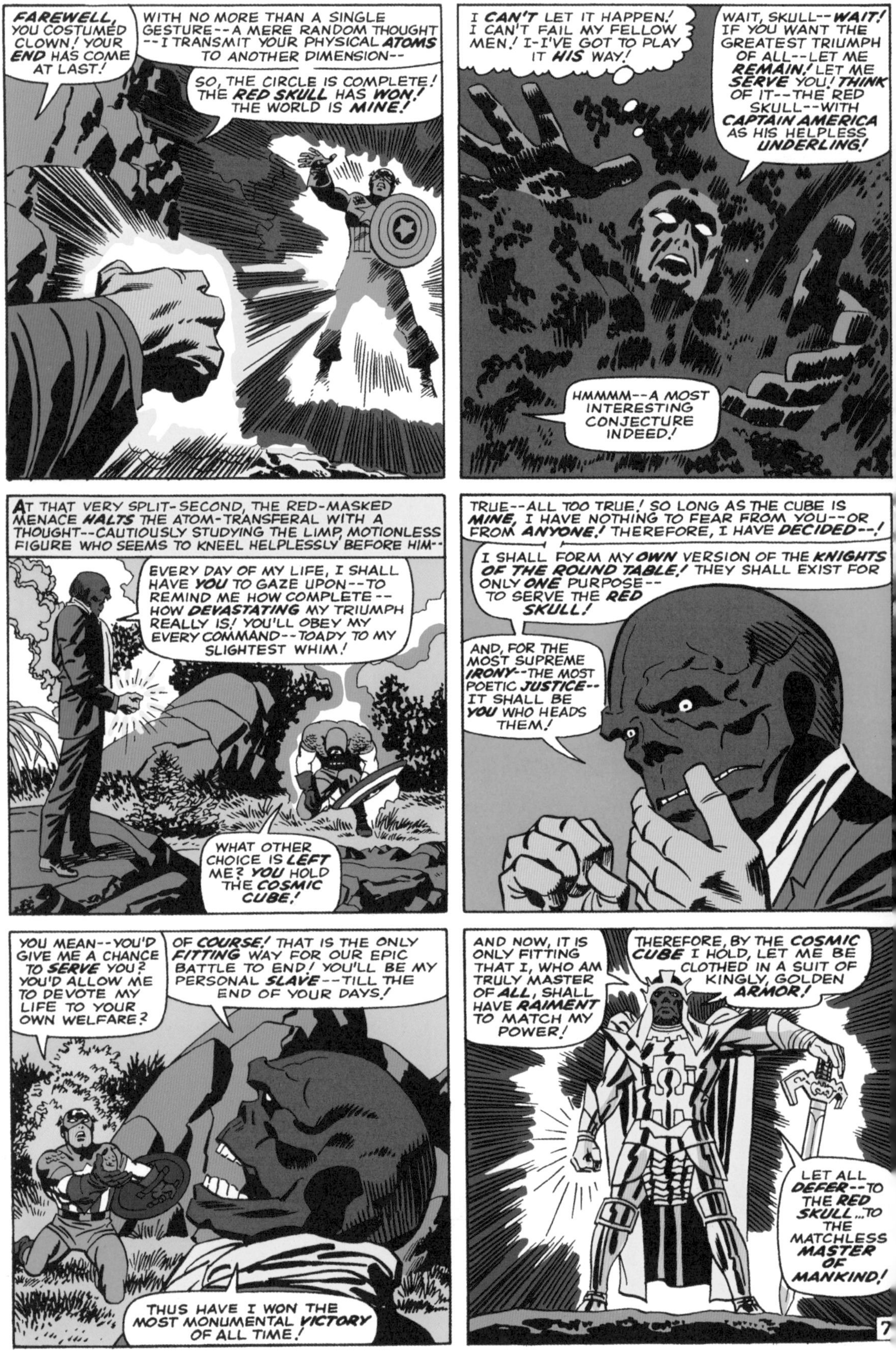
FAREWELL, YOU COSTUMED CLOWN! YOUR END HAS COME AT LAST!
WITH NO MORE THAN A SINGLE GESTURE--A MERE RANDOM THOUGHT--I TRANSMIT YOUR PHYSICAL ATOMS TO ANOTHER DIMENSION--
SO, THE CIRCLE IS COMPLETE! THE RED SKULL HAS WON! THE WORLD IS MINE!
I CAN'T LET IT HAPPEN! I CAN'T FAIL MY FELLOW MEN! I-I'VE GOT TO PLAY IT HIS WAY!
WAIT, SKULL--WAIT! IF YOU WANT THE GREATEST TRIUMPH OF ALL--LET ME REMAIN! LET ME SERVE YOU! THINK OF IT--THE RED SKULL--WITH CAPTAIN AMERICA AS HIS HELPLESS UNDERLING!
HMMMM--A MOST INTERESTING CONJECTURE INDEED!
AT THAT VERY SPLIT-SECOND, THE RED-MASKED MENACE HALTS THE ATOM-TRANSFERAL WITH A THOUGHT--CAUTIOUSLY STUDYING THE LIMP, MOTIONLESS FIGURE WHO SEEMS TO KNEEL HELPLESSLY BEFORE HIM--
EVERY DAY OF MY LIFE, I SHALL HAVE YOU TO GAZE UPON--TO REMIND ME HOW COMPLETE--HOW DEVASTATING MY TRIUMPH REALLY IS! YOU'LL OBEY MY EVERY COMMAND--TOADY TO MY SLIGHTEST WHIM!
WHAT OTHER CHOICE IS LEFT ME? YOU HOLD THE COSMIC CUBE!
TRUE--ALL TOO TRUE! SO LONG AS THE CUBE IS MINE, I HAVE NOTHING TO FEAR FROM YOU--OR FROM ANYONE! THEREFORE, I HAVE DECIDED--!
I SHALL FORM MY OWN VERSION OF THE KNIGHTS OF THE ROUND TABLE! THEY SHALL EXIST FOR ONLY ONE PURPOSE--TO SERVE THE RED SKULL!
AND, FOR THE MOST SUPREME IRONY--THE MOST POETIC JUSTICE--IT SHALL BE YOU WHO HEADS THEM!
YOU MEAN--YOU'D GIVE ME A CHANCE TO SERVE YOU? YOU'D ALLOW ME TO DEVOTE MY LIFE TO YOUR OWN WELFARE?
OF COURSE! THAT IS THE ONLY FITTING WAY FOR OUR EPIC BATTLE TO END! YOU'LL BE MY PERSONAL SLAVE--TILL THE END OF YOUR DAYS!
THUS HAVE I WON THE MOST MONUMENTAL VICTORY OF ALL TIME!
AND NOW, IT IS ONLY FITTING THAT I, WHO AM TRULY MASTER OF ALL, SHALL HAVE RAIMENT TO MATCH MY POWER!
THEREFORE, BY THE COSMIC CUBE I HOLD, LET ME BE CLOTHED IN A SUIT OF KINGLY, GOLDEN ARMOR!
LET ALL DEFER--TO THE RED SKULL...TO THE MATCHLESS MASTER OF MANKIND!
7

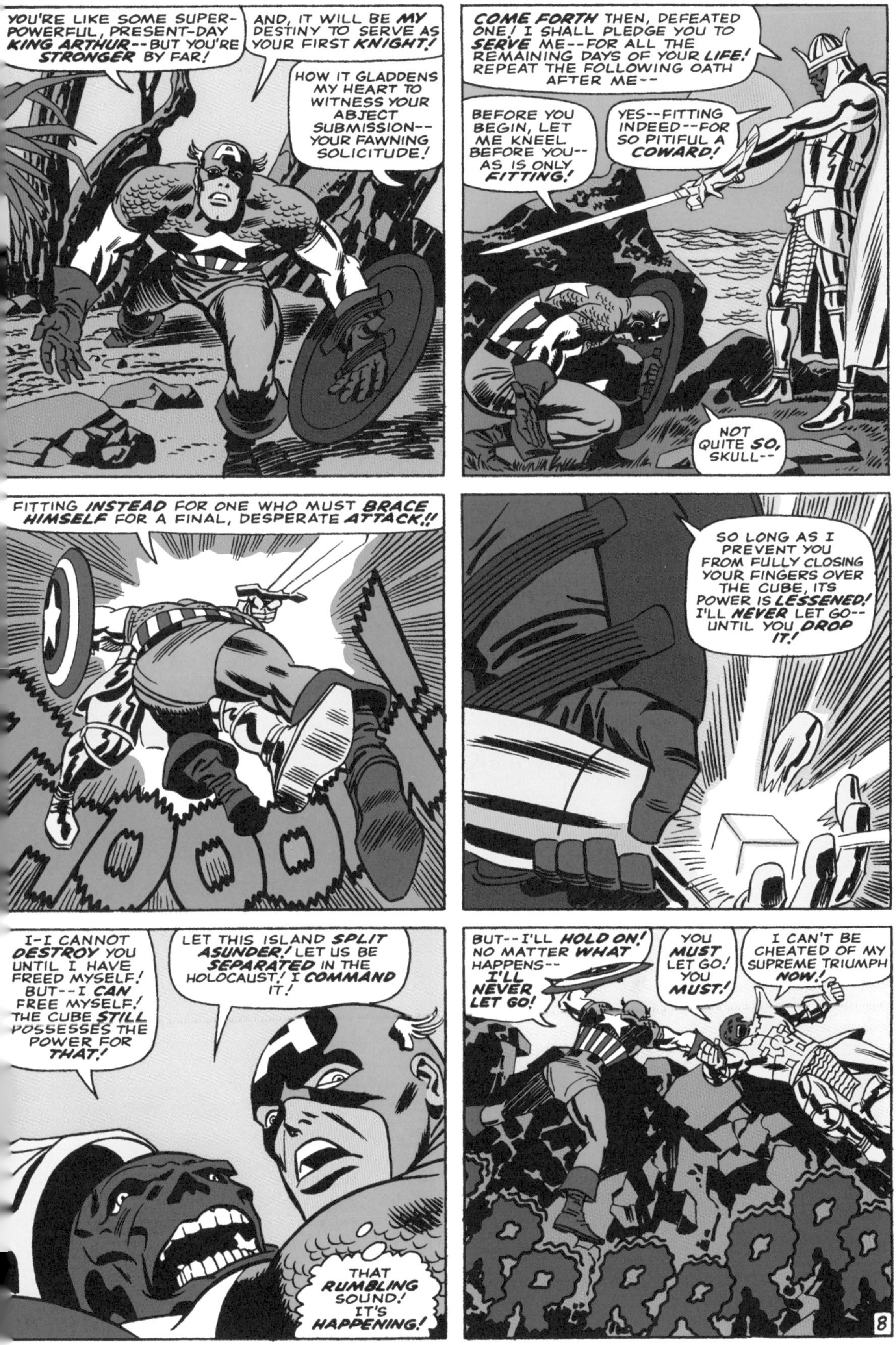
YOU'RE LIKE SOME SUPER-POWERFUL, PRESENT-DAY KING ARTHUR--BUT YOU'RE STRONGER BY FAR!
AND, IT WILL BE MY DESTINY TO SERVE AS YOUR FIRST KNIGHT!
HOW IT GLADDENS MY HEART TO WITNESS YOUR ABJECT SUBMISSION--YOUR FAWNING SOLICITUDE!
COME FORTH THEN, DEFEATED ONE! I SHALL PLEDGE YOU TO SERVE ME--FOR ALL THE REMAINING DAYS OF YOUR LIFE! REPEAT THE FOLLOWING OATH AFTER ME--
BEFORE YOU BEGIN, LET ME KNEEL BEFORE YOU--AS IS ONLY FITTING!
YES--FITTING INDEED--FOR SO PITIFUL A COWARD!
NOT QUITE SO, SKULL--
FITTING INSTEAD FOR ONE WHO MUST BRACE HIMSELF FOR A FINAL, DESPERATE ATTACK!!
SO LONG AS I PREVENT YOU FROM FULLY CLOSING YOUR FINGERS OVER THE CUBE, ITS POWER IS LESSENED! I'LL NEVER LET GO--UNTIL YOU DROP IT!
I-I CANNOT DESTROY YOU UNTIL I HAVE FREED MYSELF! BUT--I CAN FREE MYSELF! THE CUBE STILL POSSESSES THE POWER FOR THAT!
LET THIS ISLAND SPLIT ASUNDER! LET US BE SEPARATED IN THE HOLOCAUST! I COMMAND IT!
THAT RUMBLING SOUND! IT'S HAPPENING!
BUT--I'LL HOLD ON! NO MATTER WHAT HAPPENS--I'LL NEVER LET GO!
YOU MUST LET GO! YOU MUST!
I CAN'T BE CHEATED OF MY SUPREME TRIUMPH NOW!
8

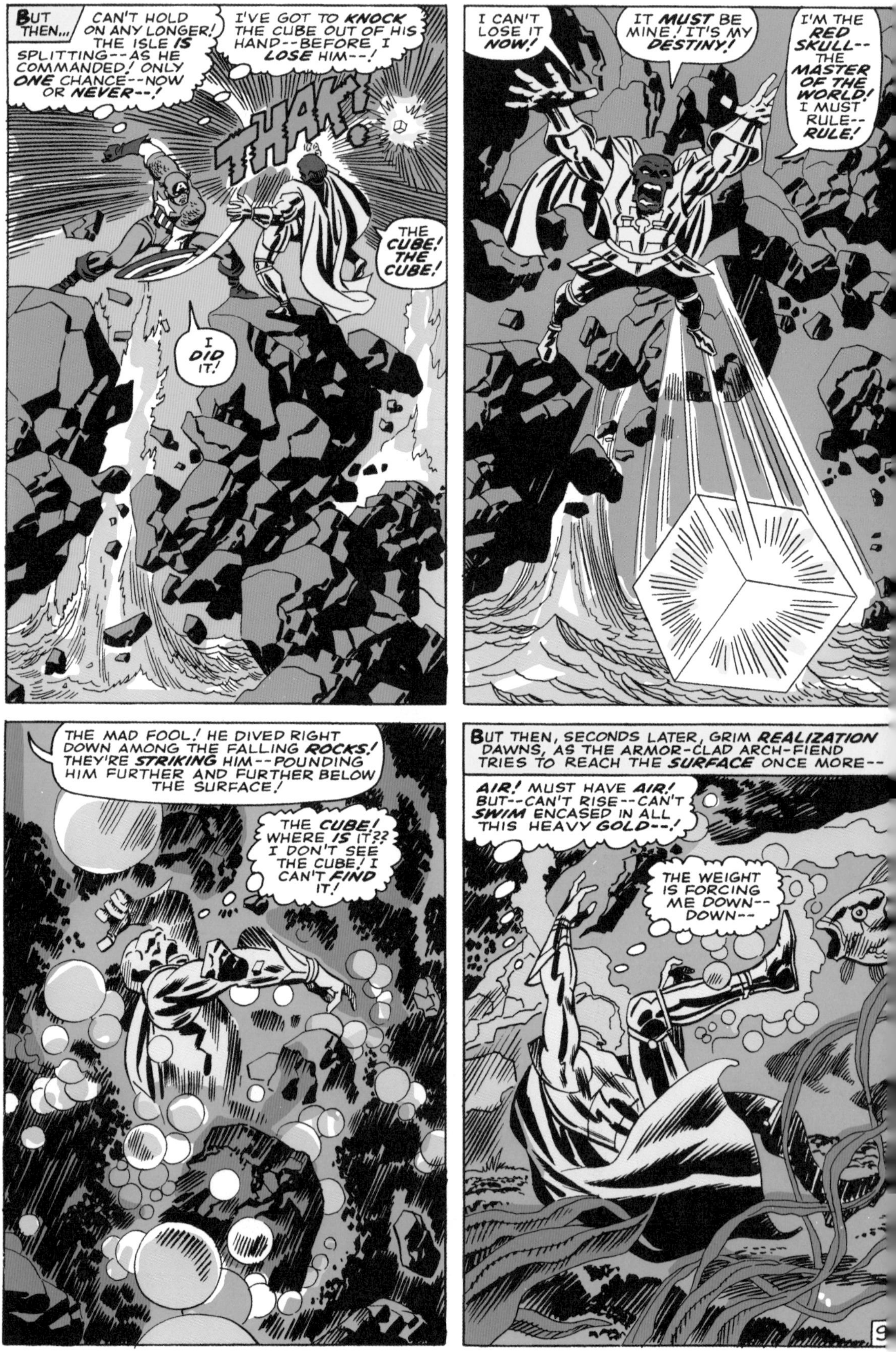
BUT THEN...
CAN'T HOLD ON ANY LONGER! THE ISLE IS SPLITTING--AS HE COMMANDED! ONLY ONE CHANCE--NOW OR NEVER--!
I'VE GOT TO KNOCK THE CUBE OUT OF HIS HAND--BEFORE I LOSE HIM--!
THAK!
THE CUBE! THE CUBE!
I DID IT!
I CAN'T LOSE IT NOW!
IT MUST BE MINE! IT'S MY DESTINY!
I'M THE RED SKULL--THE MASTER OF THE WORLD! I MUST RULE--RULE!
THE MAD FOOL! HE DIVED RIGHT DOWN AMONG THE FALLING ROCKS! THEY'RE STRIKING HIM--POUNDING HIM FURTHER AND FURTHER BELOW THE SURFACE!
THE CUBE! WHERE IS IT?? I DON'T SEE THE CUBE! I CAN'T FIND IT!
BUT THEN, SECONDS LATER, GRIM REALIZATION DAWNS, AS THE ARMOR-CLAD ARCH-FIEND TRIES TO REACH THE SURFACE ONCE MORE--
AIR! MUST HAVE AIR! BUT--CAN'T RISE--CAN'T SWIM ENCASED IN ALL THIS HEAVY GOLD--!
THE WEIGHT IS FORCING ME DOWN--DOWN--
9

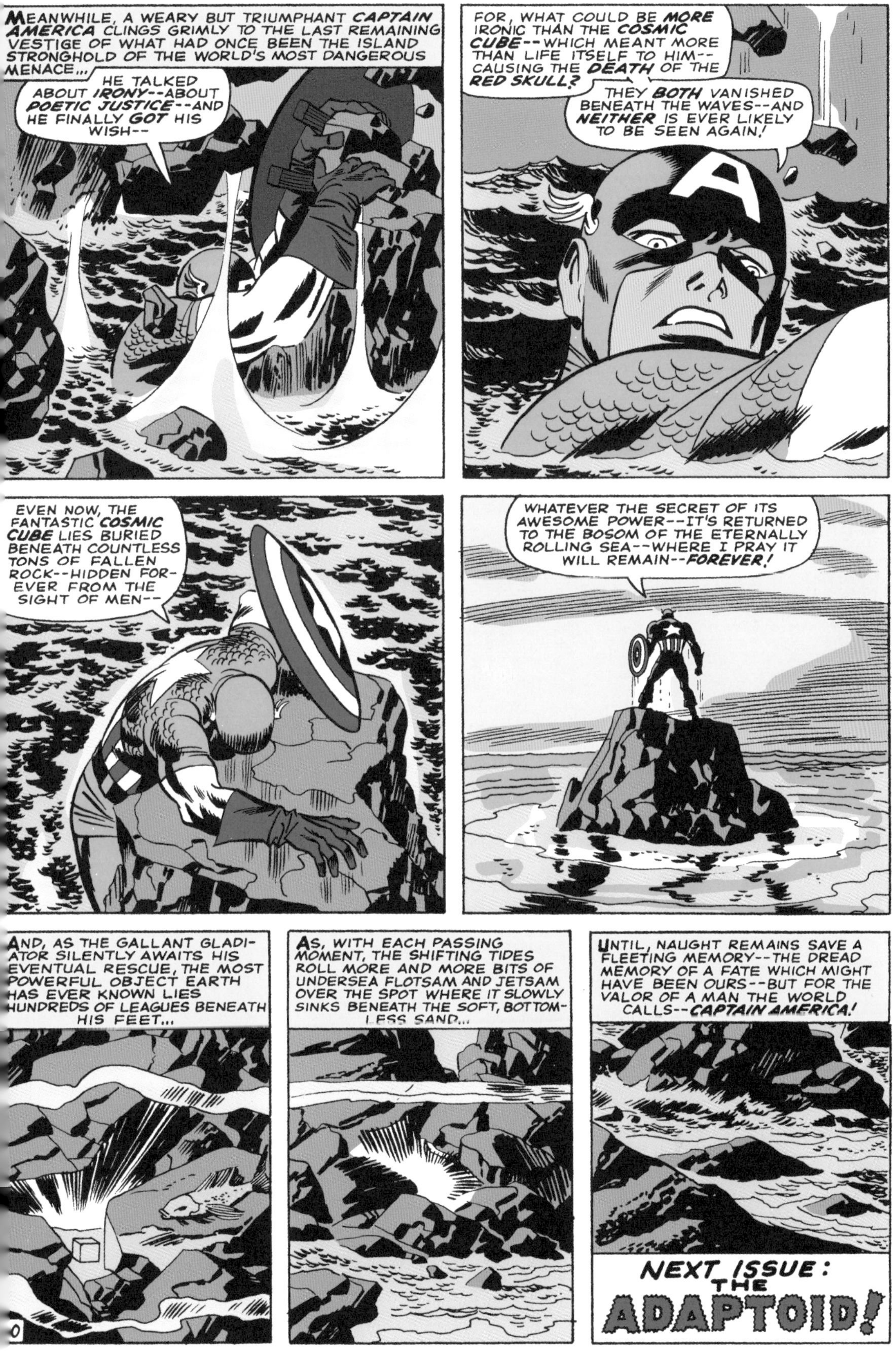
MEANWHILE, A WEARY BUT TRIUMPHANT CAPTAIN AMERICA CLINGS GRIMLY TO THE LAST REMAINING VESTIGE OF WHAT HAD ONCE BEEN THE ISLAND STRONGHOLD OF THE WORLD'S MOST DANGEROUS MENACE...
HE TALKED ABOUT IRONY--ABOUT POETIC JUSTICE--AND HE FINALLY GOT HIS WISH--
FOR, WHAT COULD BE MORE IRONIC THAN THE COSMIC CUBE--WHICH MEANT MORE THAN LIFE ITSELF TO HIM--CAUSING THE DEATH OF THE RED SKULL?
THEY BOTH VANISHED BENEATH THE WAVES--AND NEITHER IS EVER LIKELY TO BE SEEN AGAIN!
EVEN NOW, THE FANTASTIC COSMIC CUBE LIES BURIED BENEATH COUNTLESS TONS OF FALLEN ROCK--HIDDEN FOREVER FROM THE SIGHT OF MEN--
WHATEVER THE SECRET OF ITS AWESOME POWER--IT'S RETURNED TO THE BOSOM OF THE ETERNALLY ROLLING SEA--WHERE I PRAY IT WILL REMAIN--FOREVER!
AND, AS THE GALLANT GLADIATOR SILENTLY AWAITS HIS EVENTUAL RESCUE, THE MOST POWERFUL OBJECT EARTH HAS EVER KNOWN LIES HUNDREDS OF LEAGUES BENEATH HIS FEET...
AS, WITH EACH PASSING MOMENT, THE SHIFTING TIDES ROLL MORE AND MORE BITS OF UNDERSEA FLOTSAM AND JETSAM OVER THE SPOT WHERE IT SLOWLY SINKS BENEATH THE SOFT, BOTTOMLESS SAND...
UNTIL, NAUGHT REMAINS SAVE A FLEETING MEMORY--THE DREAD MEMORY OF A FATE WHICH MIGHT HAVE BEEN OURS--BUT FOR THE VALOR OF A MAN THE WORLD CALLS--CAPTAIN AMERICA!
NEXT ISSUE: THE ADAPTOID!

THE FIGHTING ACROBAT: *TALES OF SUSPENSE* #82–91

Having returned to full pencils for the Red Skull's first modern-era appearance, Kirby drew five more episodes before taking another break. The villains were the Adaptoid, an artificial life-form with the ability to mimic Cap's abilities; the Tumbler, another specialist in close combat; and (making his second appearance) Batroc the Leaper—surely one of Lee and Kirby's oddest creations—a kickboxer with a magnificently absurd mustache and a French accent to make Peter Sellers blush. All super-acrobats, these antagonists provided Kirby with a ready excuse to fill up the pages of the series with carefully choreographed fight scenes, some of which seem to have stunned even Stan Lee into silence.

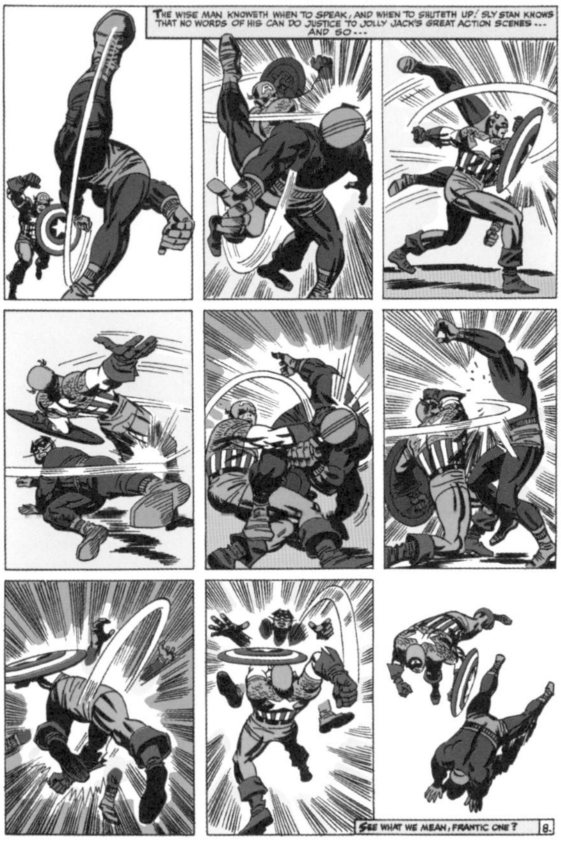
THE WISE MAN KNOWETH WHEN TO SPEAK, AND WHEN TO SHUTETH UP! SLY STAN KNOWS THAT NO WORDS OF HIS CAN DO JUSTICE TO JOLLY JACK'S GREAT ACTION SCENES... AND SO...
SEE WHAT WE MEAN, FRANTIC ONE?
8.

With *Tales of Suspense* #87, Lee and Kirby both stepped back for a fill-in issue by Roy Thomas and Jack Sparling. Lee returned with

#88 for a four-part tale illustrated by Gil Kane in which it appears that Bucky has returned; it turns out to be a robot created by the Red Skull—back again only eight months after his apparent demise in *Tales of Suspense* #81.

Lee seems to have felt that no one could really substitute for Kirby as artist and co-plotter on the strip, however, and reassigned him to produce full pencils with #92. These issues also benefited from the lush inks of Joe Sinnott—one of the few embellishers of the period capable of rendering Kirby's increasingly baroque style without compromising on detail. The result, as can be seen in the following pages, was a solo Captain America tale that (perhaps for the first time) felt entirely contemporary—filled with science-fictional elements and free from traumatic flashbacks, with a modern menace in the form of Modok.

TALES OF SUSPENSE #92,

AUGUST 1967,

"BEFORE MY EYES,

NICK FURY DIED!"

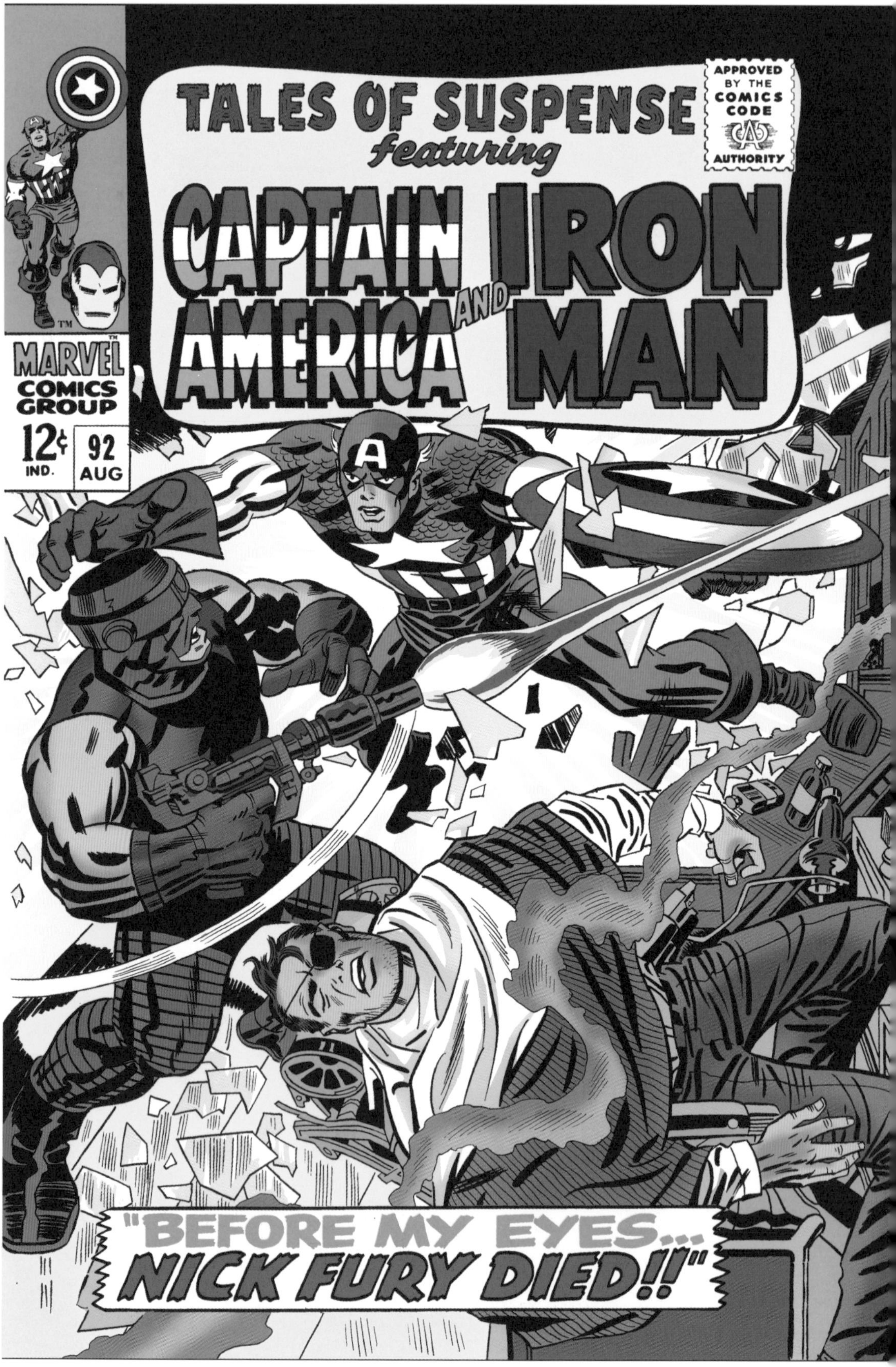
TALES OF SUSPENSE
featuring
CAPTAIN AMERICA AND IRON MAN
APPROVED BY THE COMICS CODE AUTHORITY
MARVEL COMICS GROUP
12¢ IND.
92 AUG
"BEFORE MY EYES... NICK FURY DIED!!"

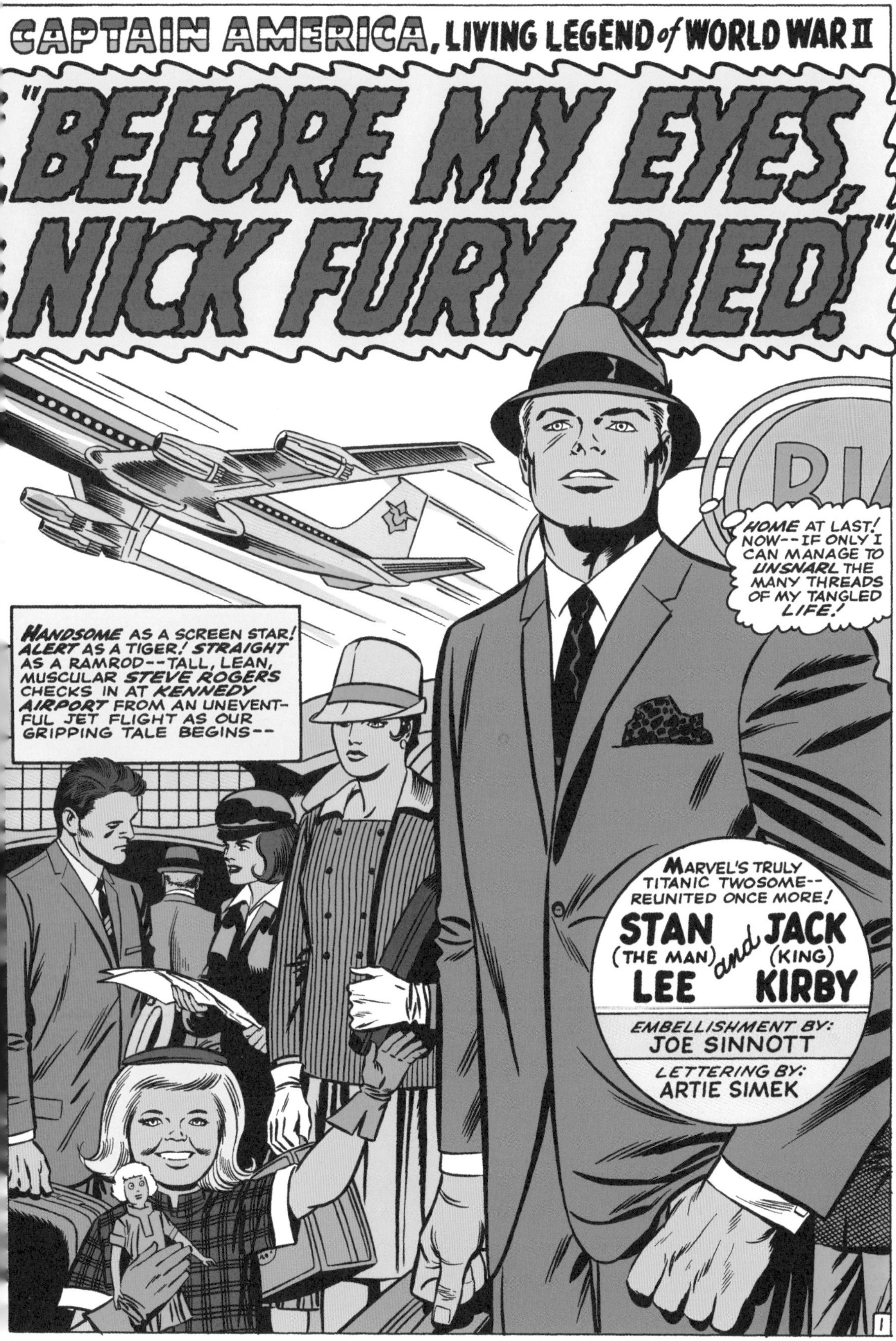

CAPTAIN AMERICA, LIVING LEGEND of WORLD WAR II
"BEFORE MY EYES, NICK FURY DIED!"
HANDSOME AS A SCREEN STAR! ALERT AS A TIGER! STRAIGHT AS A RAMROD--TALL, LEAN, MUSCULAR STEVE ROGERS CHECKS IN AT KENNEDY AIRPORT FROM AN UNEVENTFUL JET FLIGHT AS OUR GRIPPING TALE BEGINS--
HOME AT LAST! NOW--IF ONLY I CAN MANAGE TO UNSNARL THE MANY THREADS OF MY TANGLED LIFE!
MARVEL'S TRULY TITANIC TWOSOME--REUNITED ONCE MORE!
STAN (THE MAN) LEE and JACK (KING) KIRBY
EMBELLISHMENT BY: JOE SINNOTT
LETTERING BY: ARTIE SIMEK
1

BEFORE LEAVING THE AIRPORT, I'LL JUST CATCH UP ON MY *READING*, HERE IN THE LOUNGE!

OF COURSE, IT MIGHT NOT BE EXACTLY THE TYPE OF *"READING"* MATTER THAT A PASSERBY WOULD *EXPECT--*

BUT THEN, I'M HOPING THAT NO CASUAL PASSERBY WILL *NOTICE* IT!

CAPTAIN AMERICA REPORTING TO *AVENGERS!* I WAS ON TEMPORARY DUTY WITH *SHIELD* FOR A FEW DAYS AFTER LAST SEEING YOU! HAVE JUST *RETURNED!*

AM NOW AT *JFK FLIGHT LOUNGE*, CHECKING TO SEE IF ALL GOES WELL WITH MY FELLOW *ASSEMBLERS!*

GOOD TO *HEAR* FROM YOU, WING-HEAD! WELCOME BACK TO *FUN CITY!*

TRAVEL TOPICS

EVERYTHING'S FINE *NOW*, AVENGER! ESPECIALLY SINCE YOU LAST GAVE US A HAND WITH *DIABLO!**

WELL, *FACE FRONT*, LI'L FRIENDS! LEAVE A *CANDLE* BURNING IN THE WINDOW--I'M ON MY *WAY!*

SO, TILL LATER ON, THIS IS YOUR STARRY-EYED SHIELD-SLINGER SAYIN' *SO LONG!*

*IF YOU DIDN'T READ ALL ABOUT IT IN *AVENGERS #42*, NOW ON SALE, DON'T *TELL* US! YOU KNOW HOW EASILY WE *CRY!* --SENSITIVE STAN

WELL! I'VE JUST NEVER *HEARD* CAP SOUNDING SO *CHEERFUL!*

IT ALMOST *WORRIES* ME! IT'S AS THOUGH HE'S TRYING TO *CONVINCE* US THAT HE'S FEEL-ING HAPPY!

I KNOW WHAT YOU *MEAN!*

HE'S TRYING *TOO HARD!* IT MEANS THE POOR GUY IS FIGHTING ANOTHER MOOD OF *DEPRESSION!*

MORTALS! BAH! CAN YE NOT ACCEPT WHAT IS *SAID* WITHOUT SEEKING *HIDDEN* MEANINGS?

ALAS, WE'LL NEVER KNOW WHAT *ANSWER* HERCULES RECEIVED, FOR WE'VE GOT TO SWITCH SCENES AGAIN--*THIS* TIME DIVING BENEATH THE *SEA*--

WE ARE SAFELY *HIDDEN* NOW!

GIVE US YOUR *REPORT* CONCERNING COLONEL FURY!

IT WILL BE SAFE TO *ATTACK* AT 0800 HOURS!

AIM

A.I.M.

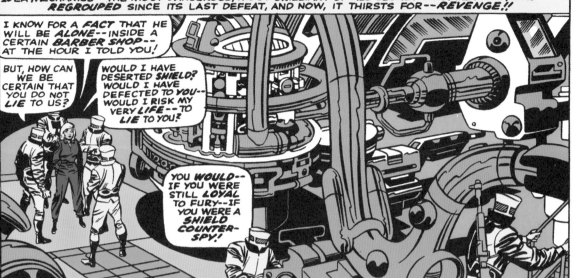

NO! YOUR EYES ARE *NOT* DECEIVING YOU! THE DEADLY MENACE OF *A.I.M.* STILL EXISTS! *A.I.M.*--ADVANCED IDEA MECHANICS--THE MOST DANGEROUS, MOST BRILLIANT OF ALL SECRET ORGANIZATIONS, HAS *REGROUPED* SINCE ITS LAST DEFEAT, AND NOW, IT THIRSTS FOR--*REVENGE!!*

I KNOW FOR A *FACT* THAT HE WILL BE *ALONE*--INSIDE A CERTAIN *BARBER SHOP*-- AT THE HOUR I TOLD YOU!

BUT, HOW CAN WE BE CERTAIN THAT YOU DO NOT *LIE* TO US?

WOULD I HAVE DESERTED *SHIELD?* WOULD I HAVE *DEFECTED* TO *YOU*-- WOULD I RISK MY VERY *LIFE*--TO *LIE* TO YOU?

YOU *WOULD*-- IF YOU WERE STILL *LOYAL* TO FURY--IF YOU WERE A *SHIELD* COUNTER-SPY!

BUT, I BROUGHT *PROOF!*

HERE IS A *TAPE RECORDING* WHICH I SECRETLY MADE!

YOU CAN HEAR IT *YOURSELF!* YOU'LL HEAR FURY'S OWN *VOICE* TELLING HIS AGENTS HE'LL BE AT THE *BARBER SHOP* IN CASE THEY *NEED* HIM!

HAND IT TO ME, WOMAN!

WHA-WHAT ARE YOU DOING?

ZZZST!

SILENCE!

THERE IS NO *NEED* TO LISTEN TO THE ROLL OF TAPE!

IF YOU HAVE *LIED* TO US, YOU CAN BE *ATOMIZED* EVEN AS YOUR TIN OF *EVIDENCE* HAS BEEN!

AND *NOW*, THRU THE SIMPLE EXPEDIENT OF OUR *ULTRA-WAVE TRANSVIEWER*, WE SHALL *LEARN* IF YOU CAN BE *TRUSTED!*

I WILL NOW RADIO THE COMMAND TO *RELEASE THE MECHNO-ASSASSIN!!*

3

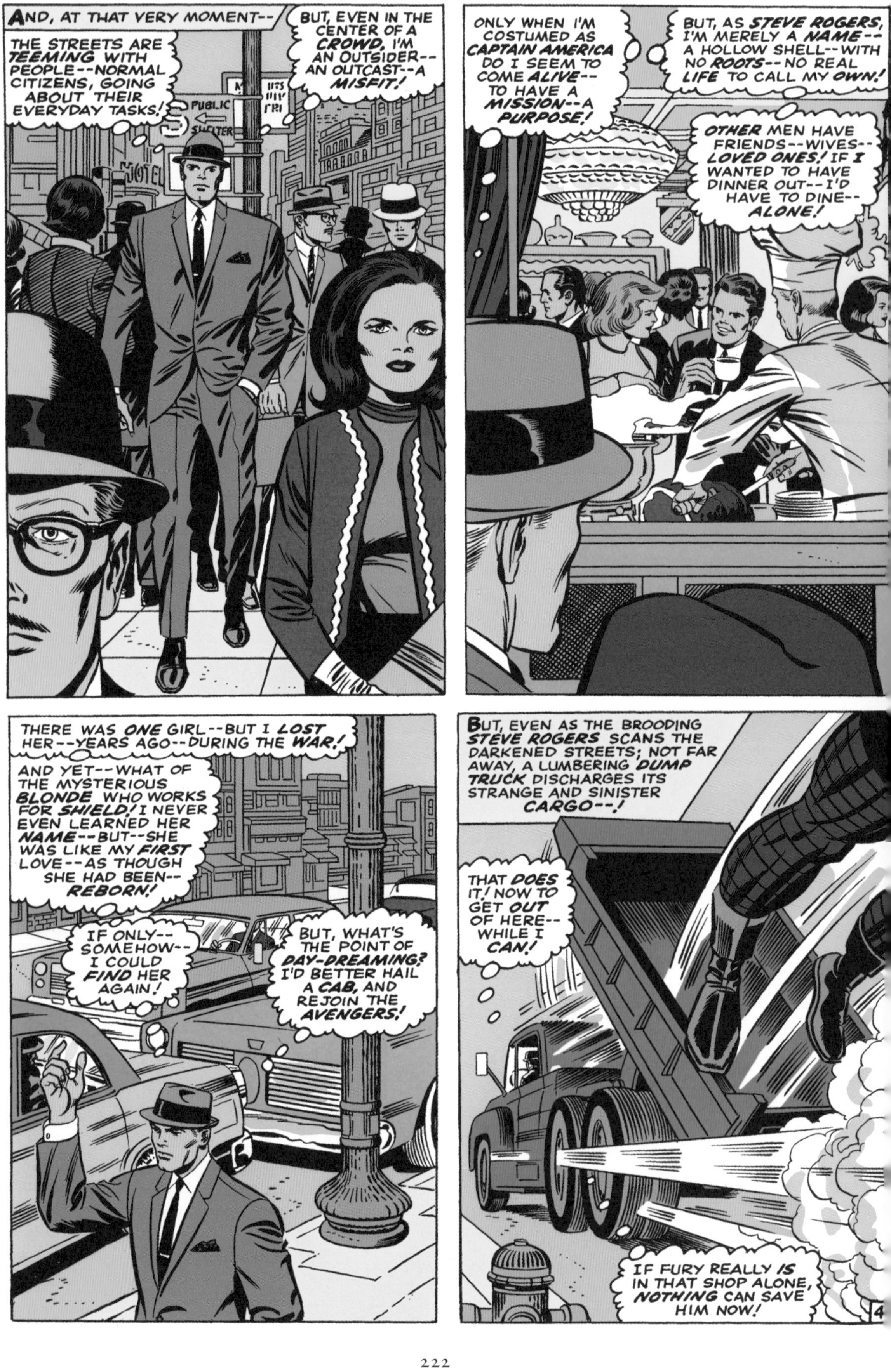
AND, AT THAT VERY MOMENT--
THE STREETS ARE TEEMING WITH PEOPLE--NORMAL CITIZENS, GOING ABOUT THEIR EVERYDAY TASKS!
BUT, EVEN IN THE CENTER OF A CROWD, I'M AN OUTSIDER--AN OUTCAST--A MISFIT!
PUBLIC SHELTER
ONLY WHEN I'M COSTUMED AS CAPTAIN AMERICA DO I SEEM TO COME ALIVE--TO HAVE A MISSION--A PURPOSE!
BUT, AS STEVE ROGERS, I'M MERELY A NAME--A HOLLOW SHELL--WITH NO ROOTS--NO REAL LIFE TO CALL MY OWN!
OTHER MEN HAVE FRIENDS--WIVES--LOVED ONES! IF I WANTED TO HAVE DINNER OUT--I'D HAVE TO DINE--ALONE!
THERE WAS ONE GIRL--BUT I LOST HER--YEARS AGO--DURING THE WAR!
AND YET--WHAT OF THE MYSTERIOUS BLONDE WHO WORKS FOR SHIELD! I NEVER EVEN LEARNED HER NAME--BUT--SHE WAS LIKE MY FIRST LOVE--AS THOUGH SHE HAD BEEN--REBORN!
IF ONLY--SOMEHOW--I COULD FIND HER AGAIN!
BUT, WHAT'S THE POINT OF DAY-DREAMING? I'D BETTER HAIL A CAB, AND REJOIN THE AVENGERS!
BUT, EVEN AS THE BROODING STEVE ROGERS SCANS THE DARKENED STREETS; NOT FAR AWAY, A LUMBERING DUMP TRUCK DISCHARGES ITS STRANGE AND SINISTER CARGO--!
THAT DOES IT! NOW TO GET OUT OF HERE--WHILE I CAN!
IF FURY REALLY IS IN THAT SHOP ALONE, NOTHING CAN SAVE HIM NOW!
4

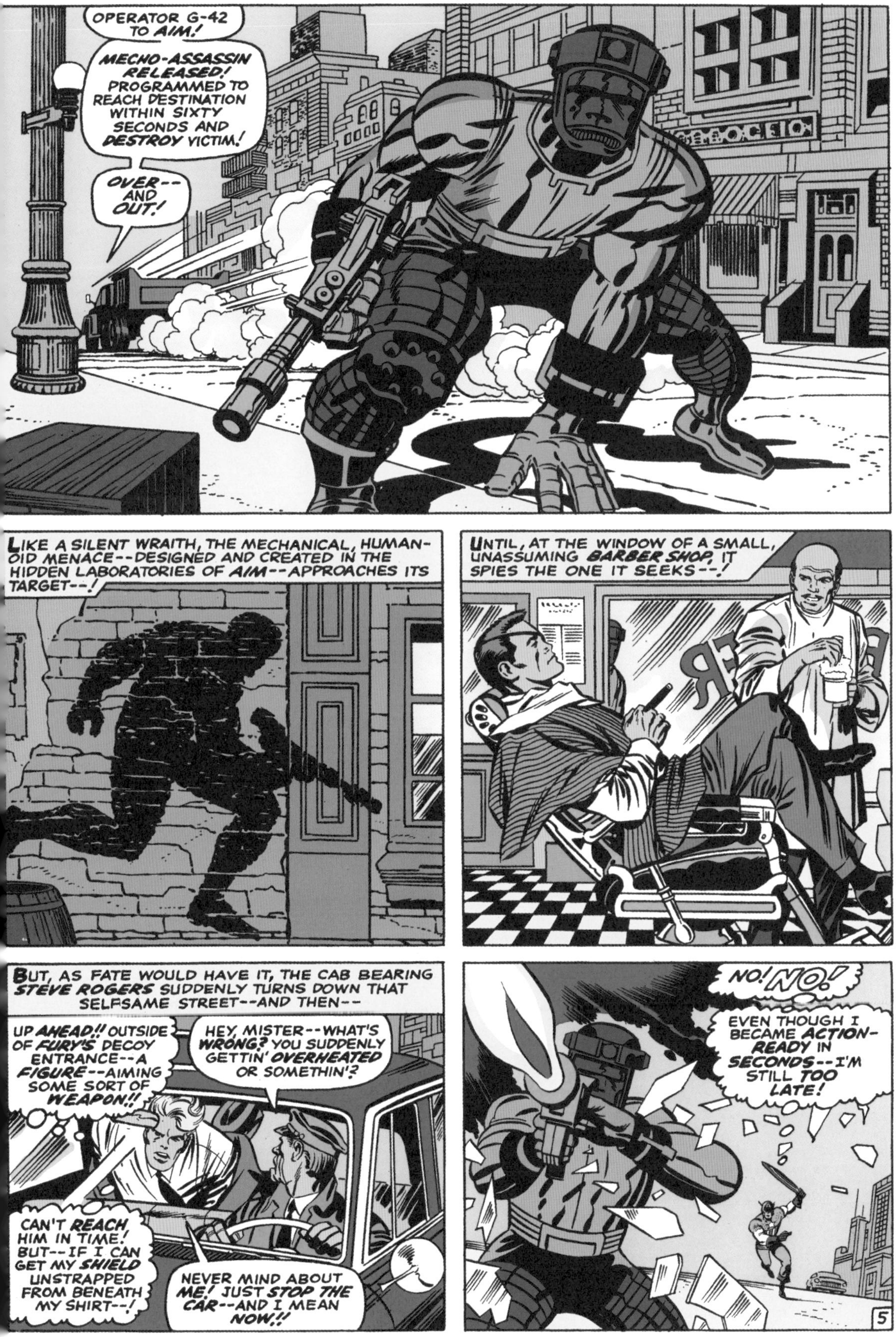
OPERATOR G-42 TO AIM!
MECHO-ASSASSIN RELEASED! PROGRAMMED TO REACH DESTINATION WITHIN SIXTY SECONDS AND DESTROY VICTIM!
OVER-- AND OUT!
LIKE A SILENT WRAITH, THE MECHANICAL, HUMAN-OID MENACE--DESIGNED AND CREATED IN THE HIDDEN LABORATORIES OF AIM--APPROACHES ITS TARGET--!
UNTIL, AT THE WINDOW OF A SMALL, UNASSUMING BARBER SHOP, IT SPIES THE ONE IT SEEKS--!
BUT, AS FATE WOULD HAVE IT, THE CAB BEARING STEVE ROGERS SUDDENLY TURNS DOWN THAT SELFSAME STREET--AND THEN--
UP AHEAD!! OUTSIDE OF FURY'S DECOY ENTRANCE--A FIGURE--AIMING SOME SORT OF WEAPON!!
HEY, MISTER--WHAT'S WRONG? YOU SUDDENLY GETTIN' OVERHEATED OR SOMETHIN'?
CAN'T REACH HIM IN TIME! BUT--IF I CAN GET MY SHIELD UNSTRAPPED FROM BENEATH MY SHIRT--!
NEVER MIND ABOUT ME! JUST STOP THE CAR--AND I MEAN NOW!!
NO! NO!
EVEN THOUGH I BECAME ACTION-READY IN SECONDS--I'M STILL TOO LATE!
5

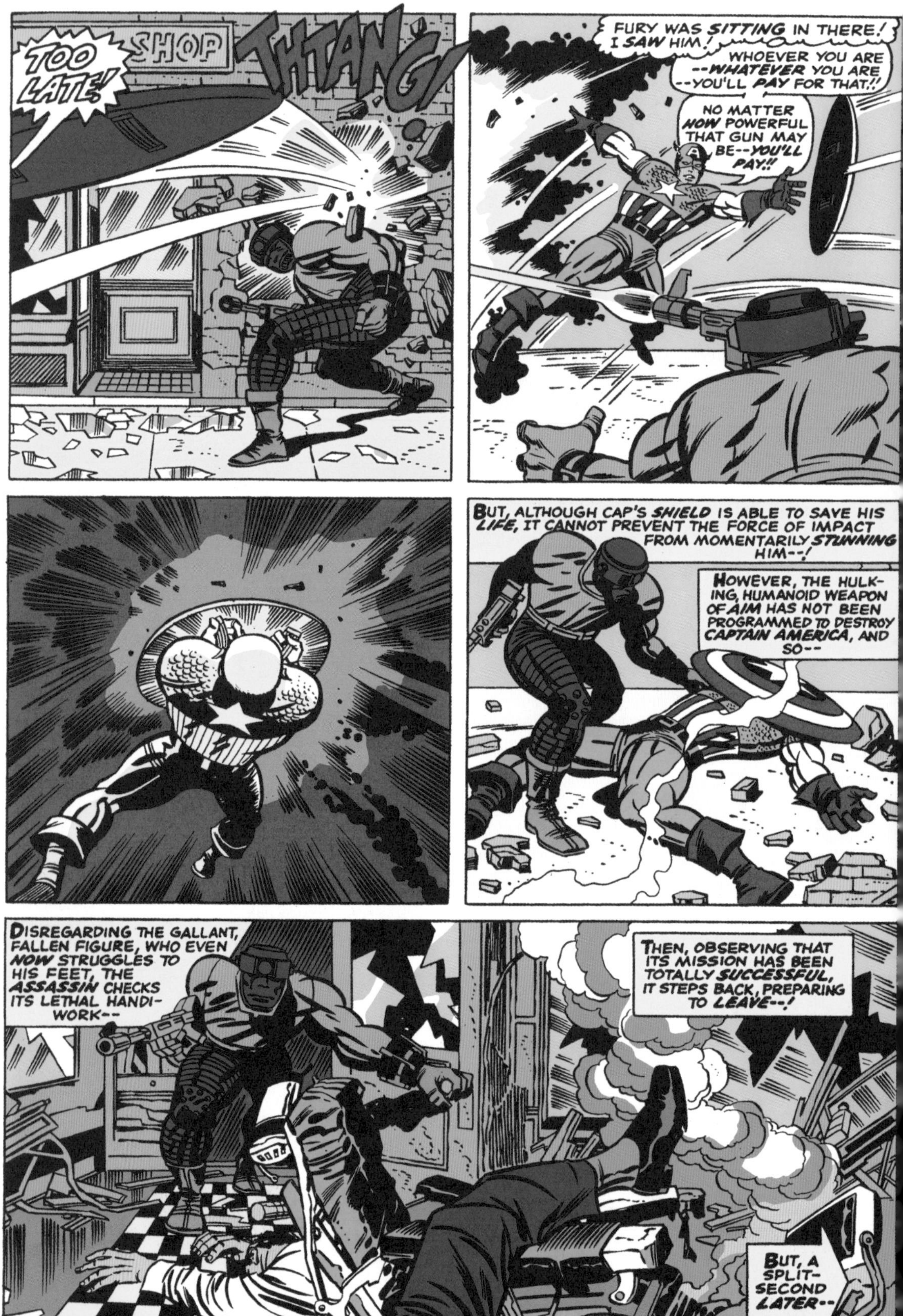
TOO LATE!
SHOP
THTANG!
FURY WAS SITTING IN THERE! I SAW HIM!
WHOEVER YOU ARE --WHATEVER YOU ARE --YOU'LL PAY FOR THAT!!
NO MATTER NOW POWERFUL THAT GUN MAY BE--YOU'LL PAY!!
BUT, ALTHOUGH CAP'S SHIELD IS ABLE TO SAVE HIS LIFE, IT CANNOT PREVENT THE FORCE OF IMPACT FROM MOMENTARILY STUNNING HIM--!
HOWEVER, THE HULKING, HUMANOID WEAPON OF AIM HAS NOT BEEN PROGRAMMED TO DESTROY CAPTAIN AMERICA, AND SO--
DISREGARDING THE GALLANT, FALLEN FIGURE, WHO EVEN NOW STRUGGLES TO HIS FEET, THE ASSASSIN CHECKS ITS LETHAL HANDIWORK--
THEN, OBSERVING THAT ITS MISSION HAS BEEN TOTALLY SUCCESSFUL, IT STEPS BACK, PREPARING TO LEAVE--!
BUT, A SPLIT-SECOND LATER--
6

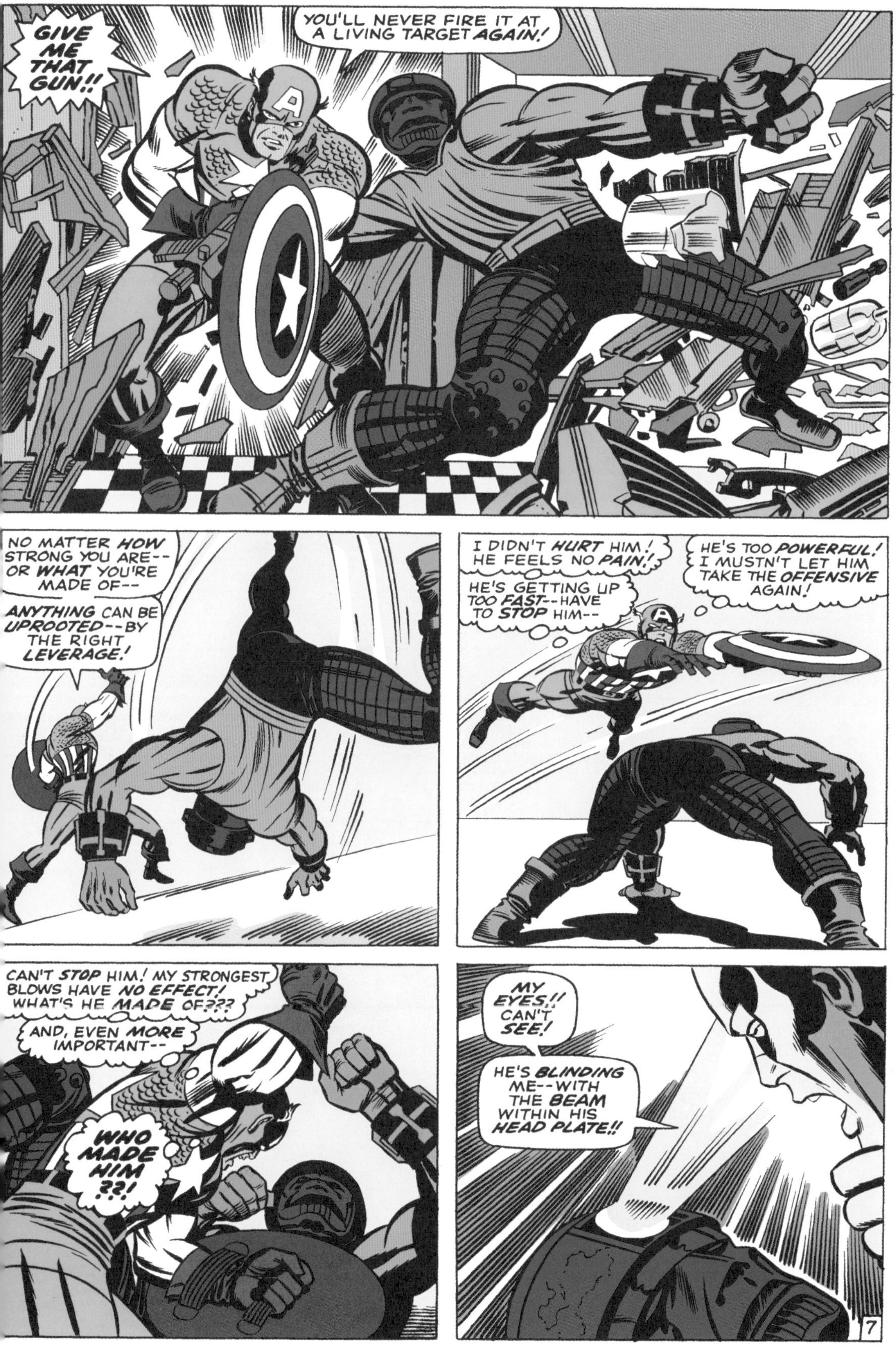

GIVE ME THAT GUN!!
YOU'LL NEVER FIRE IT AT A LIVING TARGET AGAIN!
NO MATTER HOW STRONG YOU ARE-- OR WHAT YOU'RE MADE OF--
ANYTHING CAN BE UPROOTED--BY THE RIGHT LEVERAGE!
I DIDN'T HURT HIM! HE FEELS NO PAIN!
HE'S GETTING UP TOO FAST--HAVE TO STOP HIM--
HE'S TOO POWERFUL! I MUSTN'T LET HIM TAKE THE OFFENSIVE AGAIN!
CAN'T STOP HIM! MY STRONGEST BLOWS HAVE NO EFFECT! WHAT'S HE MADE OF???
AND, EVEN MORE IMPORTANT--
WHO MADE HIM ??!
MY EYES!! CAN'T SEE!
HE'S BLINDING ME--WITH THE BEAM WITHIN HIS HEAD PLATE!!
7

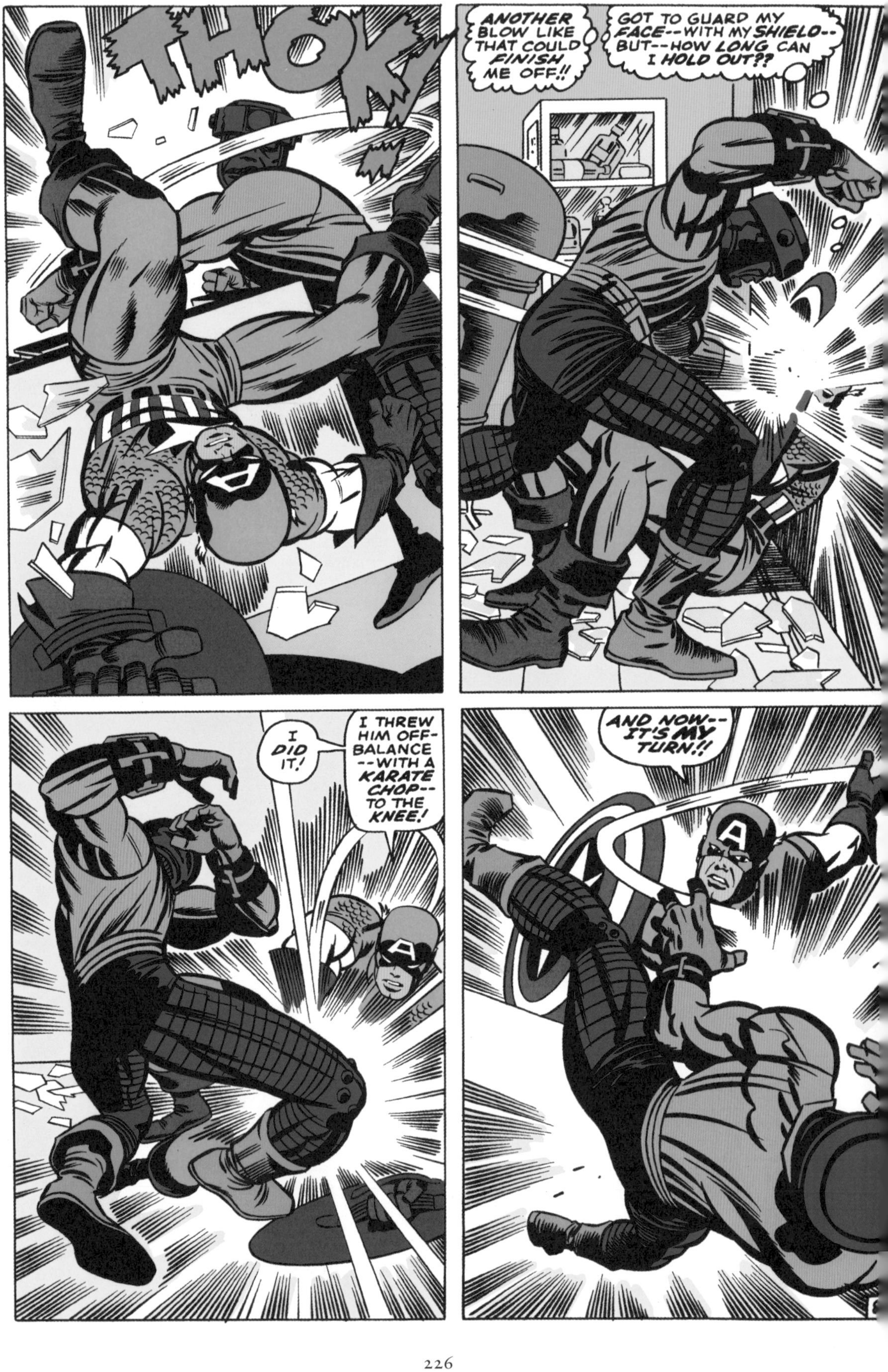
THOK
ANOTHER BLOW LIKE THAT COULD FINISH ME OFF!!
GOT TO GUARD MY FACE--WITH MY SHIELD--BUT--HOW LONG CAN I HOLD OUT??
I DID IT!
I THREW HIM OFF-BALANCE--WITH A KARATE CHOP--TO THE KNEE!
AND NOW--IT'S MY TURN!!

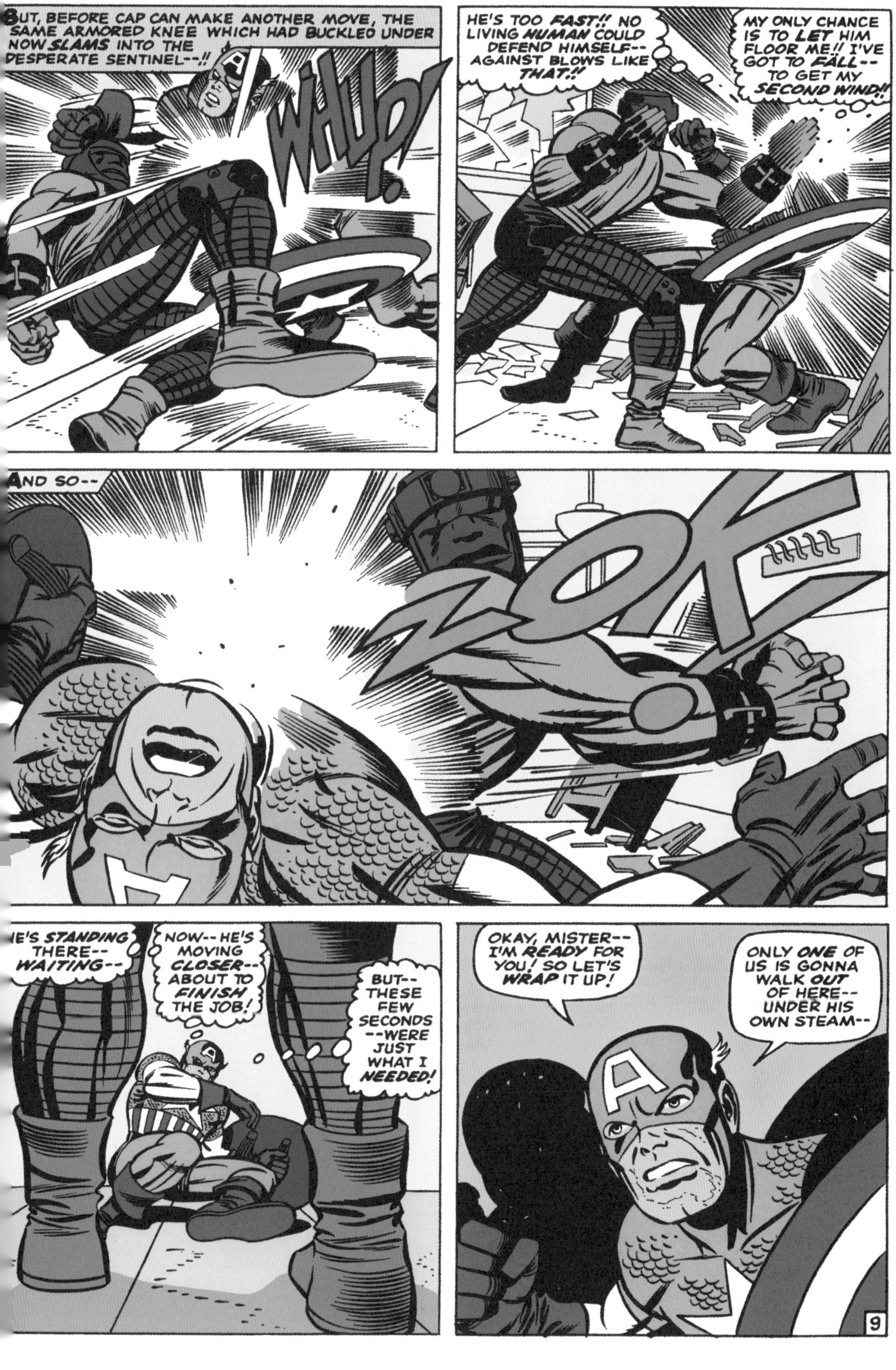
BUT, BEFORE CAP CAN MAKE ANOTHER MOVE, THE SAME ARMORED KNEE WHICH HAD BUCKLED UNDER NOW SLAMS INTO THE DESPERATE SENTINEL--!!
WHUP!
HE'S TOO FAST!! NO LIVING HUMAN COULD DEFEND HIMSELF--AGAINST BLOWS LIKE THAT!!
MY ONLY CHANCE IS TO LET HIM FLOOR ME!! I'VE GOT TO FALL--TO GET MY SECOND WIND!!
AND SO--
ZOK
HE'S STANDING THERE--WAITING--
NOW--HE'S MOVING CLOSER--ABOUT TO FINISH THE JOB!
BUT--THESE FEW SECONDS--WERE JUST WHAT I NEEDED!
OKAY, MISTER--I'M READY FOR YOU! SO LET'S WRAP IT UP!
ONLY ONE OF US IS GONNA WALK OUT OF HERE--UNDER HIS OWN STEAM--
9

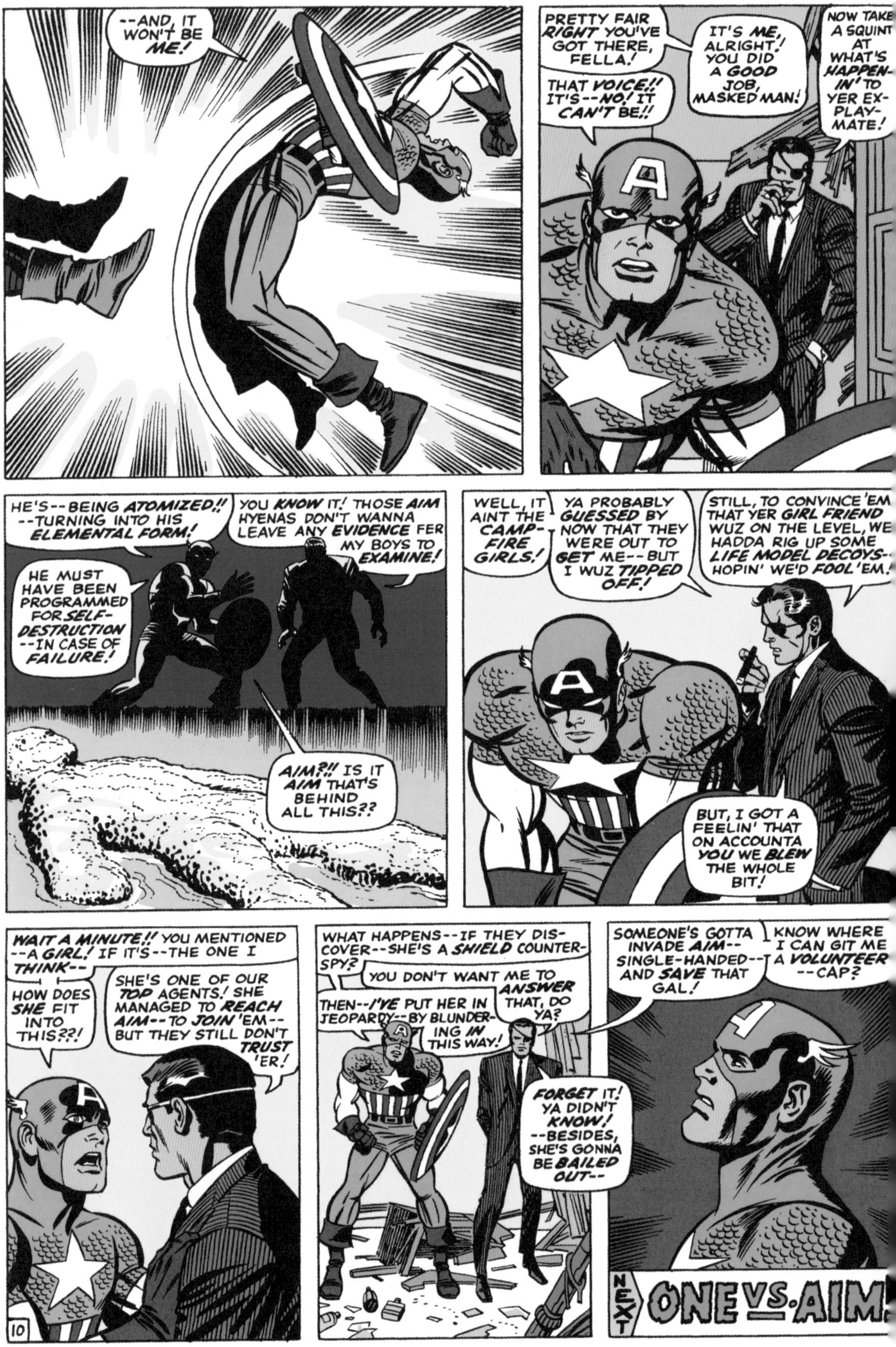
--AND, IT WON'T BE ME!
PRETTY FAIR RIGHT YOU'VE GOT THERE, FELLA!
THAT VOICE!! IT'S--NO! IT CAN'T BE!!
IT'S ME, ALRIGHT! YOU DID A GOOD JOB, MASKED MAN!
NOW TAKE A SQUINT AT WHAT'S HAPPENIN' TO YER EX-PLAYMATE!
HE'S--BEING ATOMIZED!! --TURNING INTO HIS ELEMENTAL FORM!
YOU KNOW IT! THOSE AIM HYENAS DON'T WANNA LEAVE ANY EVIDENCE FER MY BOYS TO EXAMINE!
HE MUST HAVE BEEN PROGRAMMED FOR SELF-DESTRUCTION --IN CASE OF FAILURE!
AIM?!! IS IT AIM THAT'S BEHIND ALL THIS??
WELL, IT AINT THE CAMP-FIRE GIRLS!
YA PROBABLY GUESSED BY NOW THAT THEY WERE OUT TO GET ME--BUT I WUZ TIPPED OFF!
STILL, TO CONVINCE 'EM THAT YER GIRL FRIEND WUZ ON THE LEVEL, WE HADDA RIG UP SOME LIFE MODEL DECOYS--HOPIN' WE'D FOOL 'EM!
BUT, I GOT A FEELIN' THAT ON ACCOUNTA YOU WE BLEW THE WHOLE BIT!
WAIT A MINUTE!! YOU MENTIONED --A GIRL! IF IT'S--THE ONE I THINK--
HOW DOES SHE FIT INTO THIS??!
SHE'S ONE OF OUR TOP AGENTS! SHE MANAGED TO REACH AIM--TO JOIN 'EM--BUT THEY STILL DON'T TRUST 'ER!
10
WHAT HAPPENS--IF THEY DIS-COVER--SHE'S A SHIELD COUNTER-SPY?
YOU DON'T WANT ME TO ANSWER THAT, DO YA?
THEN--I'VE PUT HER IN JEOPARDY--BY BLUNDER-ING IN THIS WAY!
FORGET IT! YA DIDN'T KNOW! --BESIDES, SHE'S GONNA BE BAILED OUT--
SOMEONE'S GOTTA INVADE AIM--SINGLE-HANDED--AND SAVE THAT GAL!
KNOW WHERE I CAN GIT ME A VOLUNTEER --CAP?
NEXT
ONE VS. AIM!

TALES OF SUSPENSE #93,
SEPTEMBER 1967,
"INTO THE JAWS . . .
OF A.I.M.!"

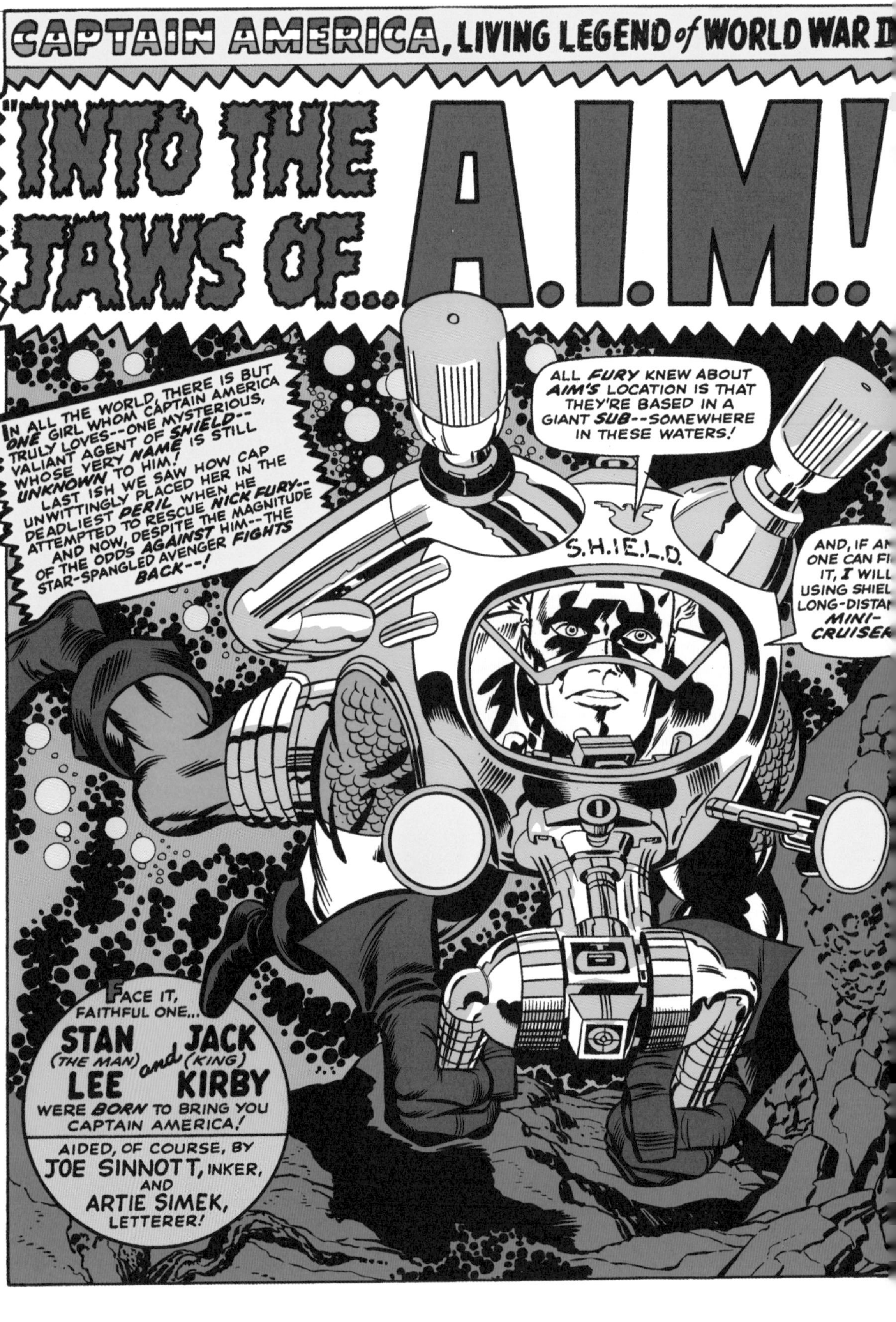
CAPTAIN AMERICA, LIVING LEGEND of WORLD WAR
"INTO THE JAWS OF... A.I.M!..
IN ALL THE WORLD, THERE IS BUT ONE GIRL WHOM CAPTAIN AMERICA TRULY LOVES--ONE MYSTERIOUS, VALIANT AGENT OF SHIELD--WHOSE VERY NAME IS STILL UNKNOWN TO HIM! LAST ISH WE SAW HOW CAP UNWITTINGLY PLACED HER IN THE DEADLIEST PERIL WHEN HE ATTEMPTED TO RESCUE NICK FURY-- AND NOW, DESPITE THE MAGNITUDE OF THE ODDS AGAINST HIM--THE STAR-SPANGLED AVENGER FIGHTS BACK--!
ALL FURY KNEW ABOUT AIM'S LOCATION IS THAT THEY'RE BASED IN A GIANT SUB--SOMEWHERE IN THESE WATERS!
S.H.I.E.L.D.
AND, IF AN ONE CAN FI IT, I WILL USING SHIEL LONG-DISTA MINI- CRUISER
FACE IT, FAITHFUL ONE... STAN (THE MAN) LEE and JACK (KING) KIRBY WERE BORN TO BRING YOU CAPTAIN AMERICA!
AIDED, OF COURSE, BY JOE SINNOTT, INKER, AND ARTIE SIMEK, LETTERER!

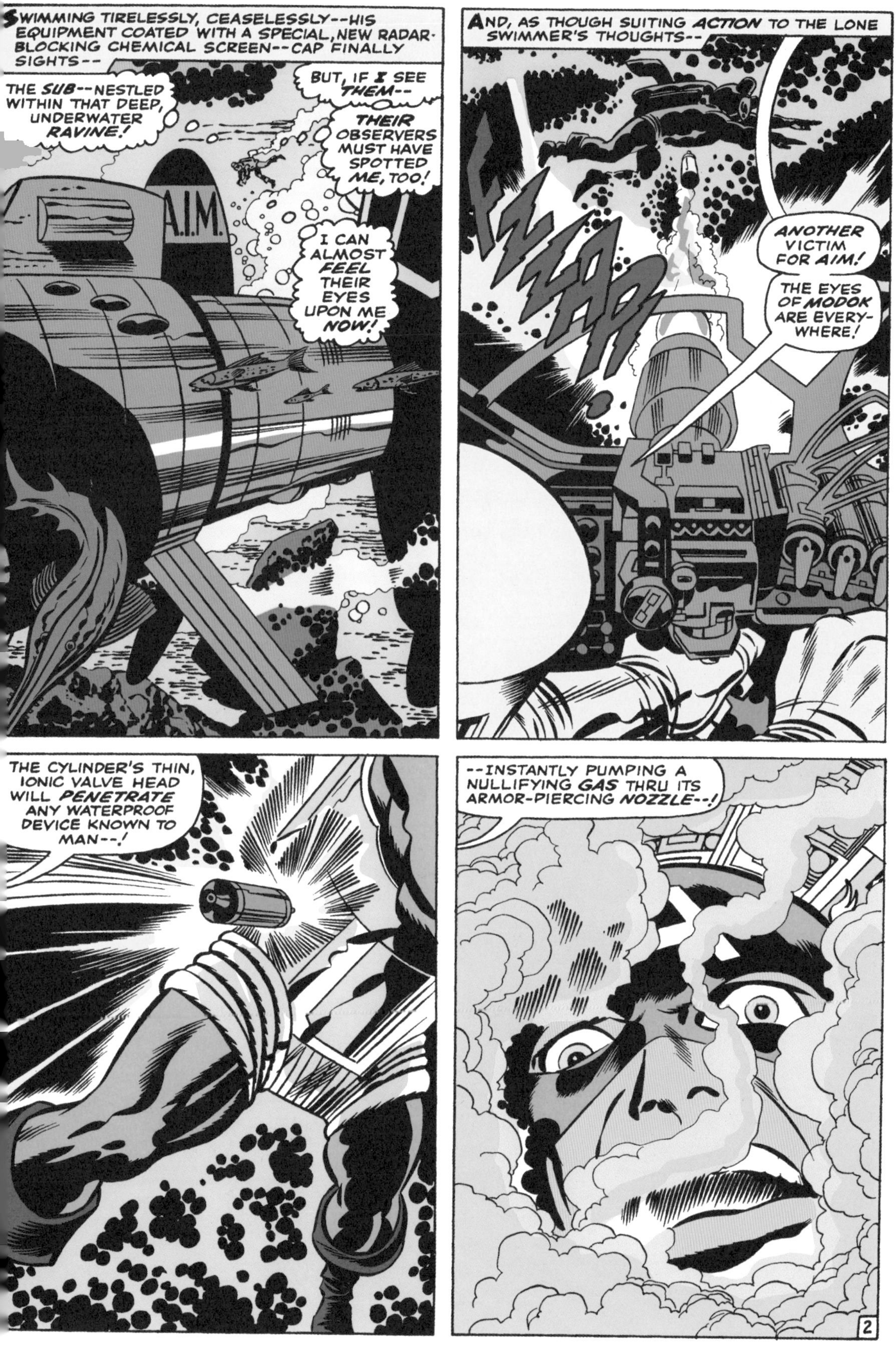

SWIMMING TIRELESSLY, CEASELESSLY--HIS EQUIPMENT COATED WITH A SPECIAL, NEW RADAR-BLOCKING CHEMICAL SCREEN--CAP FINALLY SIGHTS--
THE SUB--NESTLED WITHIN THAT DEEP, UNDERWATER RAVINE!
BUT, IF I SEE THEM--
THEIR OBSERVERS MUST HAVE SPOTTED ME, TOO!
A.I.M.
I CAN ALMOST FEEL THEIR EYES UPON ME NOW!
AND, AS THOUGH SUITING ACTION TO THE LONE SWIMMER'S THOUGHTS--
ZZZAP!
ANOTHER VICTIM FOR AIM!
THE EYES OF MODOK ARE EVERY-WHERE!
THE CYLINDER'S THIN, IONIC VALVE HEAD WILL PENETRATE ANY WATERPROOF DEVICE KNOWN TO MAN--!
--INSTANTLY PUMPING A NULLIFYING GAS THRU ITS ARMOR-PIERCING NOZZLE--!
2

WITHIN *SECONDS*, THE SUBJECT LAPSES INTO TOTAL *HELPLESSNESS*--

PLUNGING INTO AN ALL-ENGULFING SEA OF ENDLESS *NIGHT*--!

DRIFTING DEEPER--DEEPER INTO A NAMELESS, SILENT *LIMBO*--

UNTIL--!

HE'S HURLED INTO *REALITY* LIKE AN EXPLODING METEOR!!

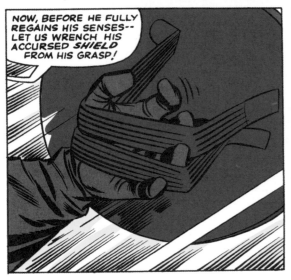

NOW, BEFORE HE FULLY REGAINS HIS SENSES-- LET US WRENCH HIS ACCURSED *SHIELD* FROM HIS GRASP!

WELCOME, CAPTAIN AMERICA!

MODOK WELCOMES YOU TO THE SUPREME WORLD OF-- *AIM, REBORN!*

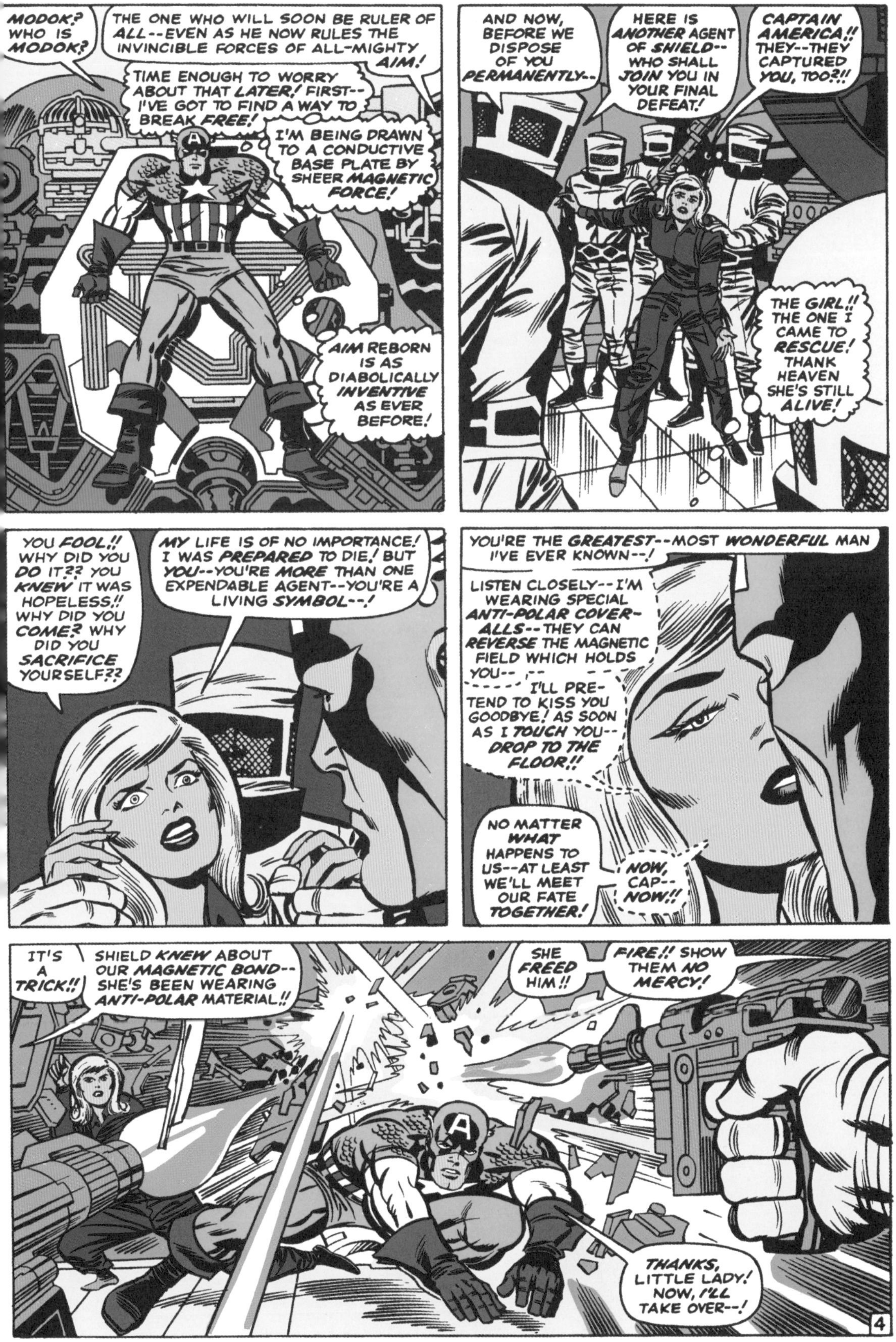
MODOK? WHO IS MODOK?
THE ONE WHO WILL SOON BE RULER OF ALL--EVEN AS HE NOW RULES THE INVINCIBLE FORCES OF ALL-MIGHTY AIM!
TIME ENOUGH TO WORRY ABOUT THAT LATER! FIRST-- I'VE GOT TO FIND A WAY TO BREAK FREE!
I'M BEING DRAWN TO A CONDUCTIVE BASE PLATE BY SHEER MAGNETIC FORCE!
AIM REBORN IS AS DIABOLICALLY INVENTIVE AS EVER BEFORE!
AND NOW, BEFORE WE DISPOSE OF YOU PERMANENTLY--
HERE IS ANOTHER AGENT OF SHIELD-- WHO SHALL JOIN YOU IN YOUR FINAL DEFEAT!
CAPTAIN AMERICA!! THEY--THEY CAPTURED YOU, TOO?!!
THE GIRL!! THE ONE I CAME TO RESCUE! THANK HEAVEN SHE'S STILL ALIVE!
YOU FOOL!! WHY DID YOU DO IT?? YOU KNEW IT WAS HOPELESS!! WHY DID YOU COME? WHY DID YOU SACRIFICE YOURSELF??
MY LIFE IS OF NO IMPORTANCE! I WAS PREPARED TO DIE! BUT YOU--YOU'RE MORE THAN ONE EXPENDABLE AGENT--YOU'RE A LIVING SYMBOL--!
YOU'RE THE GREATEST--MOST WONDERFUL MAN I'VE EVER KNOWN--!
LISTEN CLOSELY--I'M WEARING SPECIAL ANTI-POLAR COVER-ALLS--THEY CAN REVERSE THE MAGNETIC FIELD WHICH HOLDS YOU--
I'LL PRE-TEND TO KISS YOU GOODBYE! AS SOON AS I TOUCH YOU-- DROP TO THE FLOOR!!
NO MATTER WHAT HAPPENS TO US--AT LEAST WE'LL MEET OUR FATE TOGETHER!
NOW, CAP-- NOW!!
IT'S A TRICK!!
SHIELD KNEW ABOUT OUR MAGNETIC BOND-- SHE'S BEEN WEARING ANTI-POLAR MATERIAL!!
SHE FREED HIM!!
FIRE!! SHOW THEM NO MERCY!
THANKS, LITTLE LADY! NOW, I'LL TAKE OVER--!
4

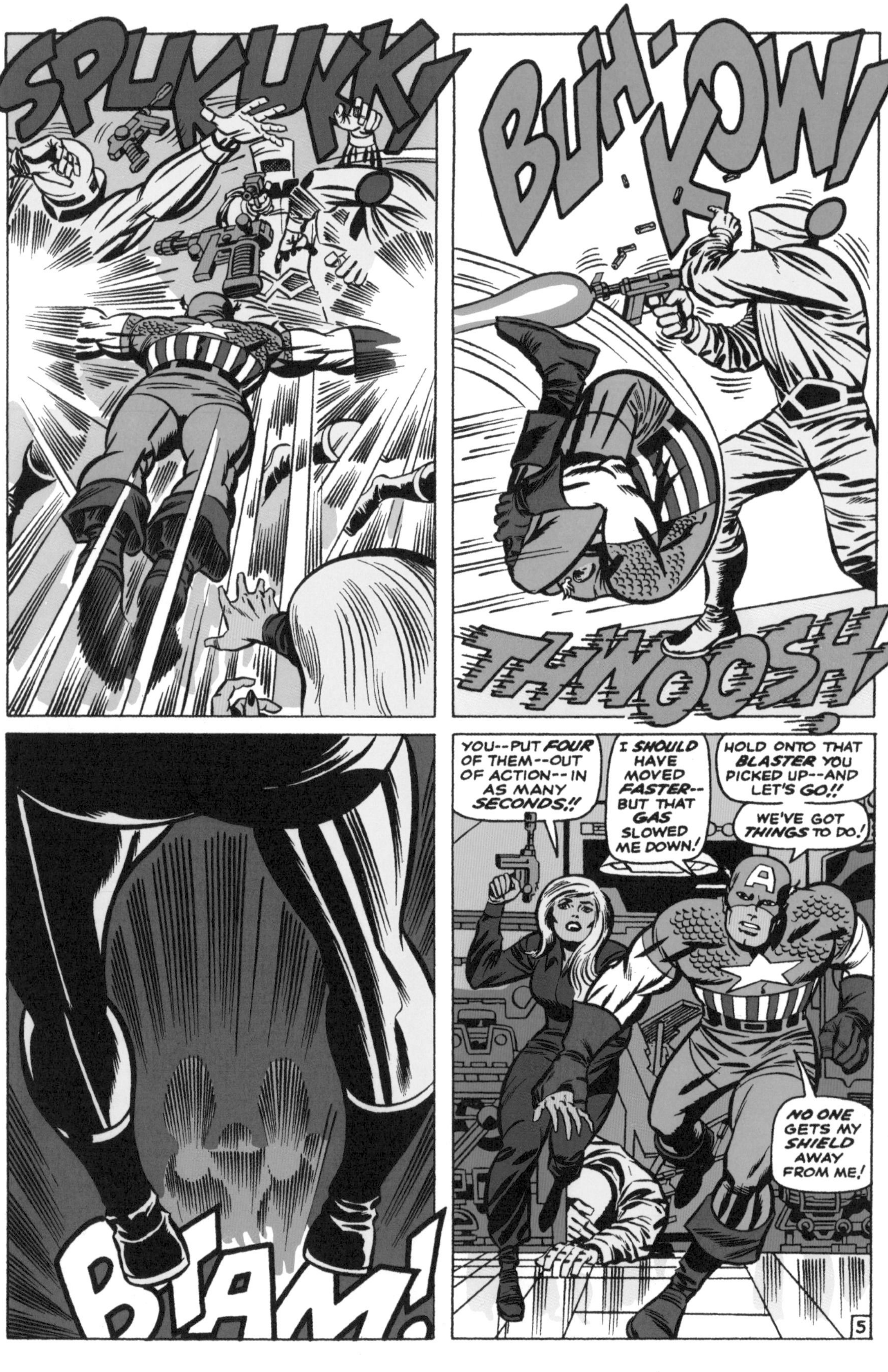
SPUKUKK!
BUH-KOW!
THWOOSH!
BLAM!
YOU--PUT FOUR OF THEM--OUT OF ACTION--IN AS MANY SECONDS!!
I SHOULD HAVE MOVED FASTER--BUT THAT GAS SLOWED ME DOWN!
HOLD ONTO THAT BLASTER YOU PICKED UP--AND LET'S GO!!
WE'VE GOT THINGS TO DO!
NO ONE GETS MY SHIELD AWAY FROM ME!
5

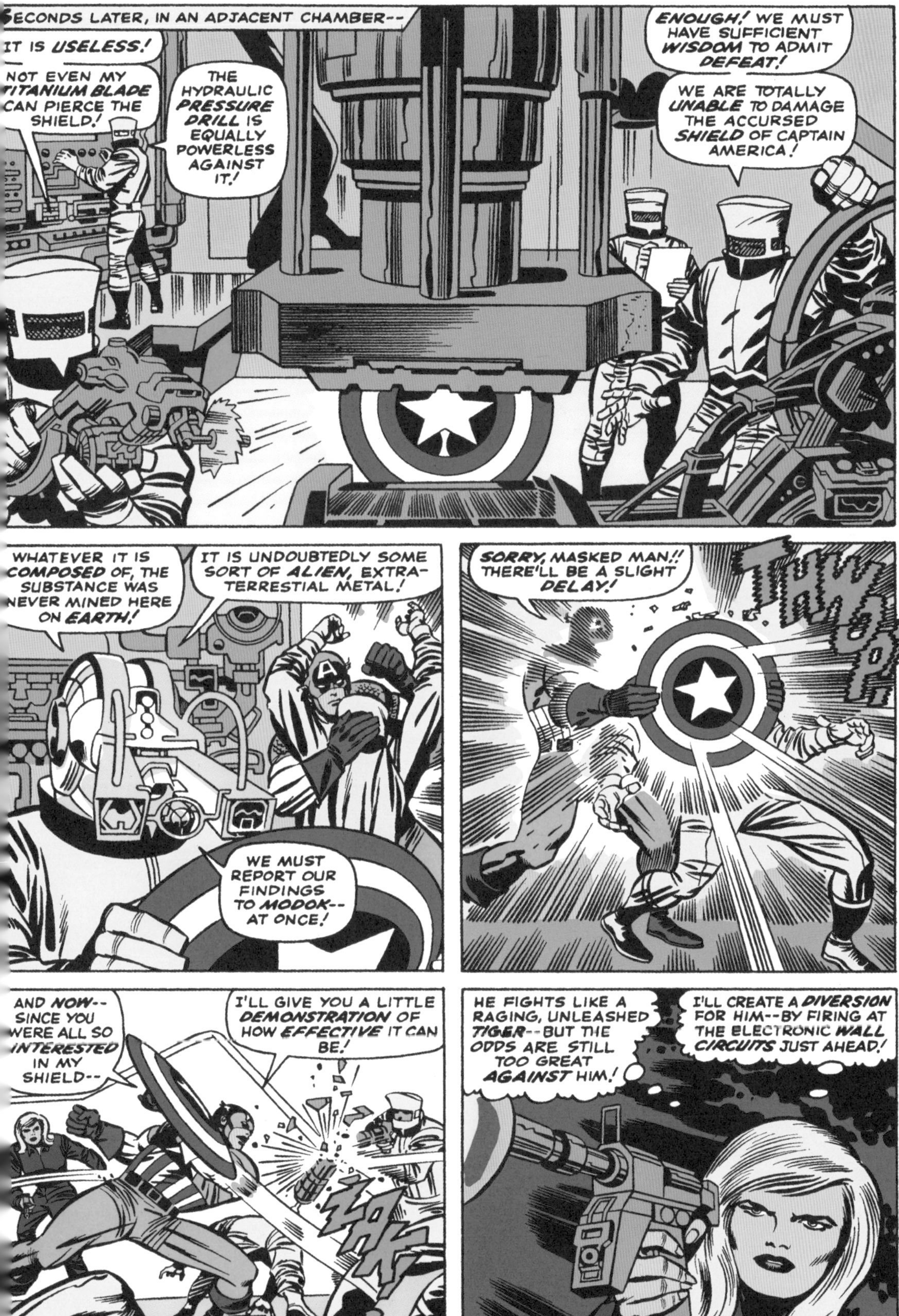

SECONDS LATER, IN AN ADJACENT CHAMBER--
IT IS USELESS!
NOT EVEN MY TITANIUM BLADE CAN PIERCE THE SHIELD!
THE HYDRAULIC PRESSURE DRILL IS EQUALLY POWERLESS AGAINST IT!
ENOUGH! WE MUST HAVE SUFFICIENT WISDOM TO ADMIT DEFEAT!
WE ARE TOTALLY UNABLE TO DAMAGE THE ACCURSED SHIELD OF CAPTAIN AMERICA!
WHATEVER IT IS COMPOSED OF, THE SUBSTANCE WAS NEVER MINED HERE ON EARTH!
IT IS UNDOUBTEDLY SOME SORT OF ALIEN, EXTRA-TERRESTIAL METAL!
WE MUST REPORT OUR FINDINGS TO MODOK--AT ONCE!
SORRY, MASKED MAN!! THERE'LL BE A SLIGHT DELAY!
THWOP!
AND NOW--SINCE YOU WERE ALL SO INTERESTED IN MY SHIELD--
I'LL GIVE YOU A LITTLE DEMONSTRATION OF HOW EFFECTIVE IT CAN BE!
ZAK
HE FIGHTS LIKE A RAGING, UNLEASHED TIGER--BUT THE ODDS ARE STILL TOO GREAT AGAINST HIM!
I'LL CREATE A DIVERSION FOR HIM--BY FIRING AT THE ELECTRONIC WALL CIRCUITS JUST AHEAD!
6

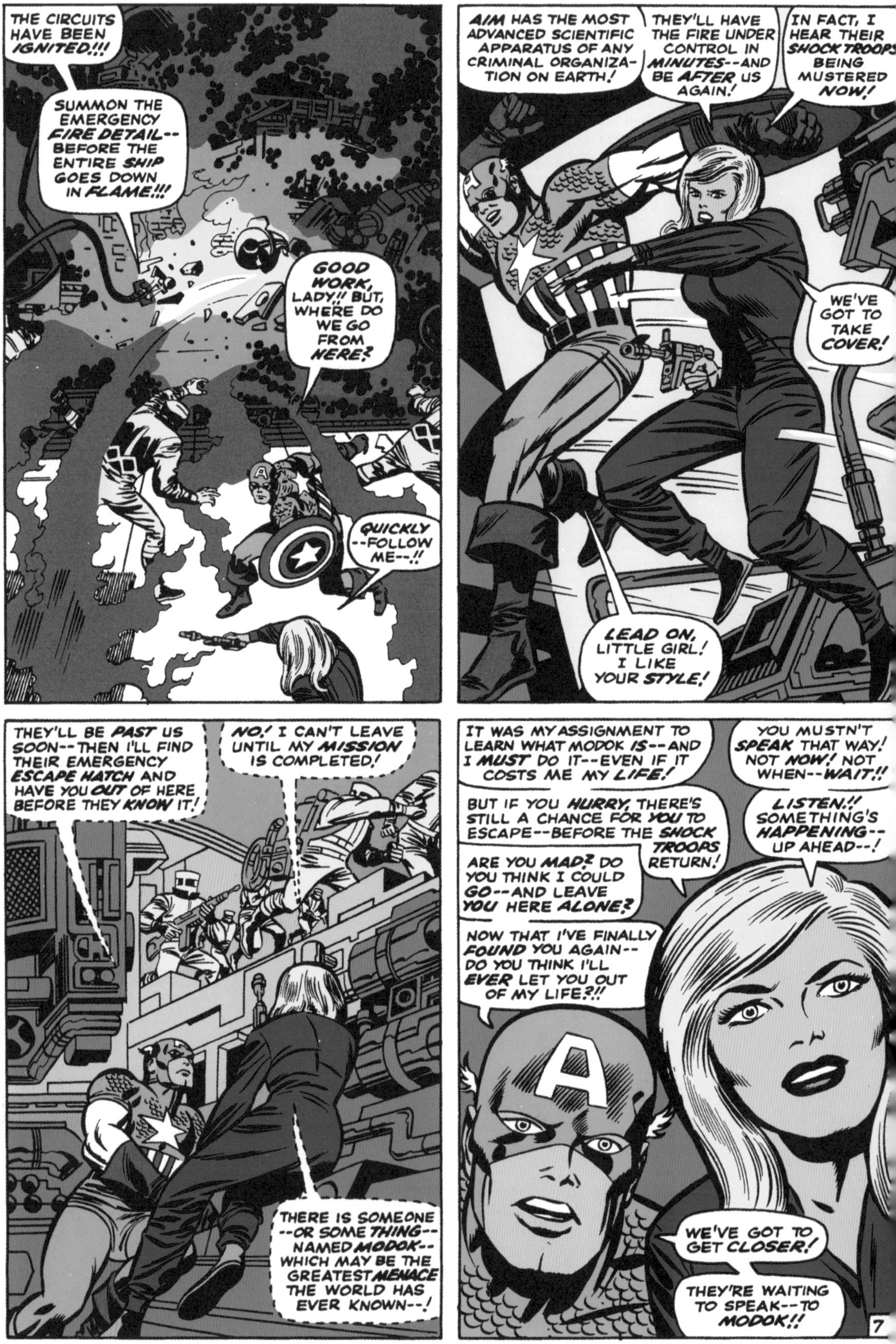
THE CIRCUITS HAVE BEEN IGNITED!!!
SUMMON THE EMERGENCY FIRE DETAIL-- BEFORE THE ENTIRE SHIP GOES DOWN IN FLAME!!!
GOOD WORK, LADY!! BUT, WHERE DO WE GO FROM HERE?
QUICKLY --FOLLOW ME--!!
AIM HAS THE MOST ADVANCED SCIENTIFIC APPARATUS OF ANY CRIMINAL ORGANIZA-TION ON EARTH!
THEY'LL HAVE THE FIRE UNDER CONTROL IN MINUTES--AND BE AFTER US AGAIN!
IN FACT, I HEAR THEIR SHOCK TROOPS BEING MUSTERED NOW!
WE'VE GOT TO TAKE COVER!
LEAD ON, LITTLE GIRL! I LIKE YOUR STYLE!
THEY'LL BE PAST US SOON--THEN I'LL FIND THEIR EMERGENCY ESCAPE HATCH AND HAVE YOU OUT OF HERE BEFORE THEY KNOW IT!
NO! I CAN'T LEAVE UNTIL MY MISSION IS COMPLETED!
THERE IS SOMEONE --OR SOME THING-- NAMED MODOK-- WHICH MAY BE THE GREATEST MENACE THE WORLD HAS EVER KNOWN--!
IT WAS MY ASSIGNMENT TO LEARN WHAT MODOK IS--AND I MUST DO IT--EVEN IF IT COSTS ME MY LIFE!
BUT IF YOU HURRY, THERE'S STILL A CHANCE FOR YOU TO ESCAPE--BEFORE THE SHOCK TROOPS RETURN!
ARE YOU MAD? DO YOU THINK I COULD GO--AND LEAVE YOU HERE ALONE?
NOW THAT I'VE FINALLY FOUND YOU AGAIN-- DO YOU THINK I'LL EVER LET YOU OUT OF MY LIFE?!!
YOU MUSTN'T SPEAK THAT WAY! NOT NOW! NOT WHEN--WAIT!!
LISTEN!! SOMETHING'S HAPPENING-- UP AHEAD--!
WE'VE GOT TO GET CLOSER!
THEY'RE WAITING TO SPEAK--TO MODOK!!
7

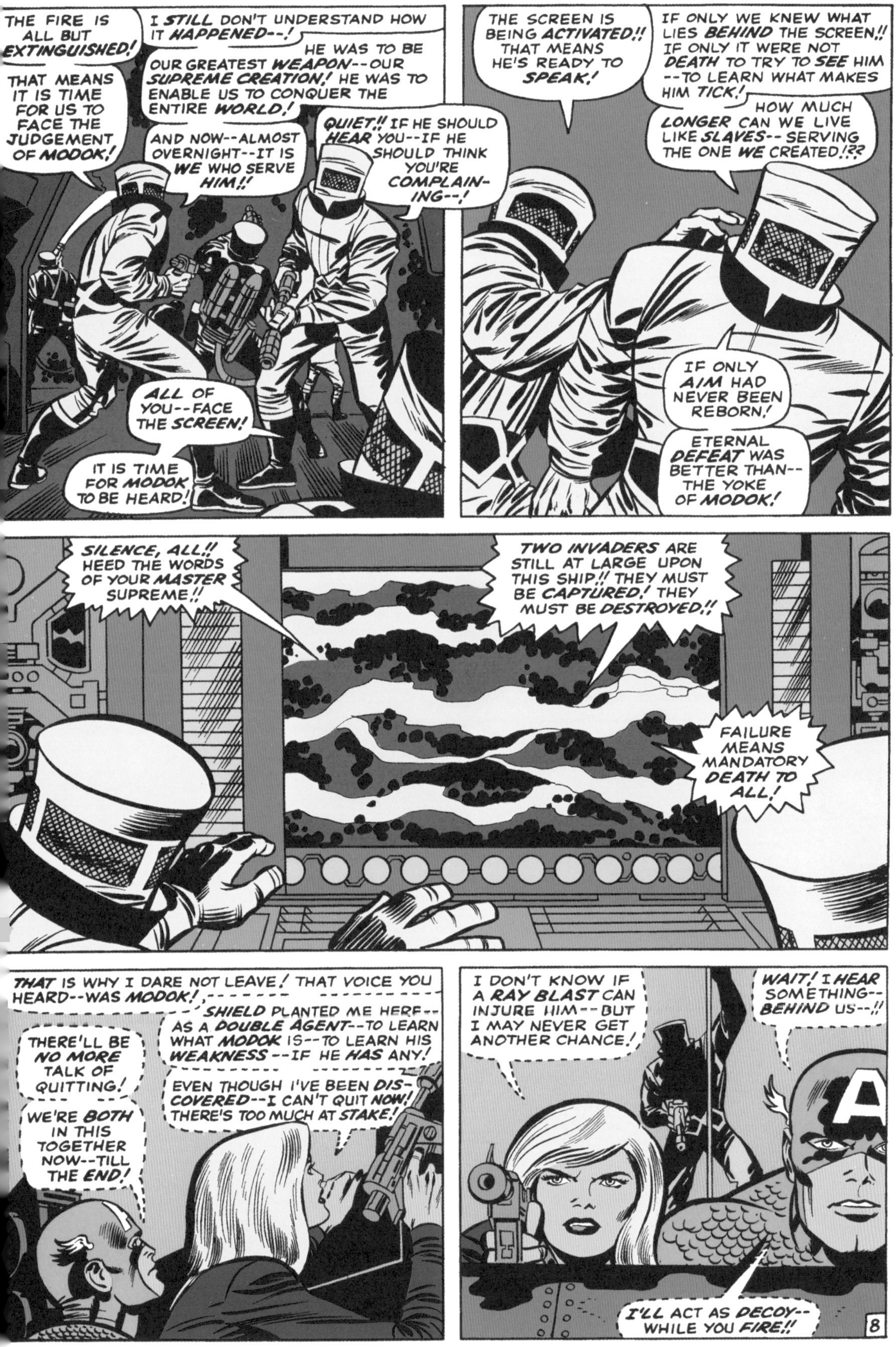
THE FIRE IS ALL BUT EXTINGUISHED!
THAT MEANS IT IS TIME FOR US TO FACE THE JUDGEMENT OF MODOK!
I STILL DON'T UNDERSTAND HOW IT HAPPENED--!
HE WAS TO BE OUR GREATEST WEAPON--OUR SUPREME CREATION! HE WAS TO ENABLE US TO CONQUER THE ENTIRE WORLD!
AND NOW--ALMOST OVERNIGHT--IT IS WE WHO SERVE HIM!!
QUIET!! IF HE SHOULD HEAR YOU--IF HE SHOULD THINK YOU'RE COMPLAINING--!
ALL OF YOU--FACE THE SCREEN!
IT IS TIME FOR MODOK TO BE HEARD!
THE SCREEN IS BEING ACTIVATED!! THAT MEANS HE'S READY TO SPEAK!
IF ONLY WE KNEW WHAT LIES BEHIND THE SCREEN!! IF ONLY IT WERE NOT DEATH TO TRY TO SEE HIM --TO LEARN WHAT MAKES HIM TICK!
HOW MUCH LONGER CAN WE LIVE LIKE SLAVES-- SERVING THE ONE WE CREATED!??
IF ONLY AIM HAD NEVER BEEN REBORN!
ETERNAL DEFEAT WAS BETTER THAN-- THE YOKE OF MODOK!
SILENCE, ALL!! HEED THE WORDS OF YOUR MASTER SUPREME!!
TWO INVADERS ARE STILL AT LARGE UPON THIS SHIP!! THEY MUST BE CAPTURED! THEY MUST BE DESTROYED!!
FAILURE MEANS MANDATORY DEATH TO ALL!
THAT IS WHY I DARE NOT LEAVE! THAT VOICE YOU HEARD--WAS MODOK!
SHIELD PLANTED ME HERE-- AS A DOUBLE AGENT--TO LEARN WHAT MODOK IS--TO LEARN HIS WEAKNESS--IF HE HAS ANY!
EVEN THOUGH I'VE BEEN DISCOVERED--I CAN'T QUIT NOW! THERE'S TOO MUCH AT STAKE!
THERE'LL BE NO MORE TALK OF QUITTING!
WE'RE BOTH IN THIS TOGETHER NOW--TILL THE END!
I DON'T KNOW IF A RAY BLAST CAN INJURE HIM--BUT I MAY NEVER GET ANOTHER CHANCE!
WAIT! I HEAR SOMETHING-- BEHIND US--!!
I'LL ACT AS DECOY-- WHILE YOU FIRE!!
8

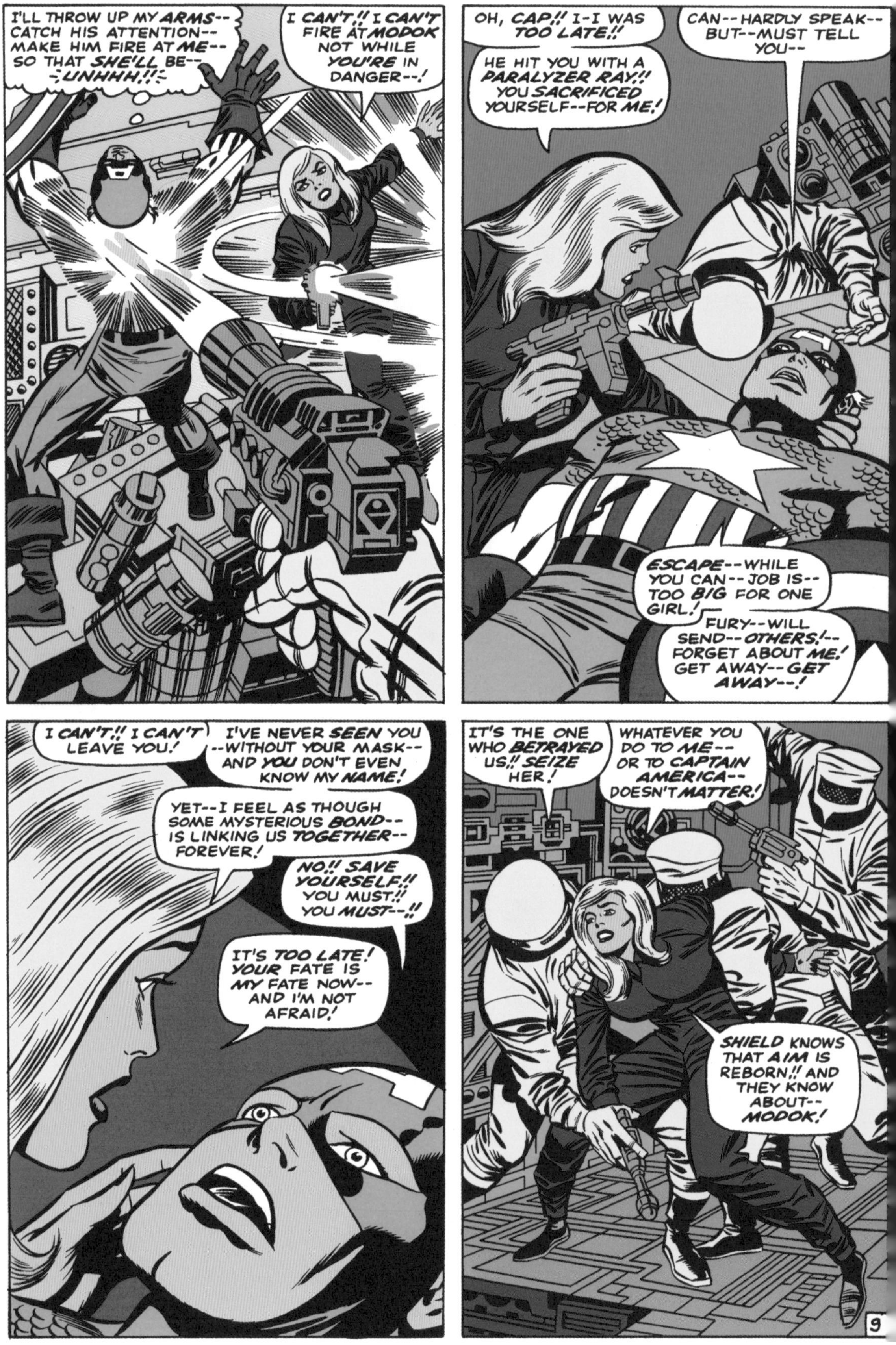
I'LL THROW UP MY ARMS--
CATCH HIS ATTENTION--
MAKE HIM FIRE AT ME--
SO THAT SHE'LL BE--
--UNHHH!!--
I CAN'T!! I CAN'T
FIRE AT MODOK
NOT WHILE
YOU'RE IN
DANGER--!
OH, CAP!! I-I WAS
TOO LATE!!
HE HIT YOU WITH A
PARALYZER RAY!!
YOU SACRIFICED
YOURSELF--FOR ME!
CAN--HARDLY SPEAK--
BUT--MUST TELL
YOU--
ESCAPE--WHILE
YOU CAN--JOB IS--
TOO BIG FOR ONE
GIRL!
FURY--WILL
SEND--OTHERS!--
FORGET ABOUT ME!
GET AWAY--GET
AWAY--!
I CAN'T!! I CAN'T
LEAVE YOU!
I'VE NEVER SEEN YOU
--WITHOUT YOUR MASK--
AND YOU DON'T EVEN
KNOW MY NAME!
YET--I FEEL AS THOUGH
SOME MYSTERIOUS BOND--
IS LINKING US TOGETHER--
FOREVER!
NO!! SAVE
YOURSELF!!
YOU MUST!!
YOU MUST--!!
IT'S TOO LATE!
YOUR FATE IS
MY FATE NOW--
AND I'M NOT
AFRAID!
IT'S THE ONE
WHO BETRAYED
US!! SEIZE
HER!
WHATEVER YOU
DO TO ME--
OR TO CAPTAIN
AMERICA--
DOESN'T MATTER!
SHIELD KNOWS
THAT AIM IS
REBORN!! AND
THEY KNOW
ABOUT--
MODOK!
9

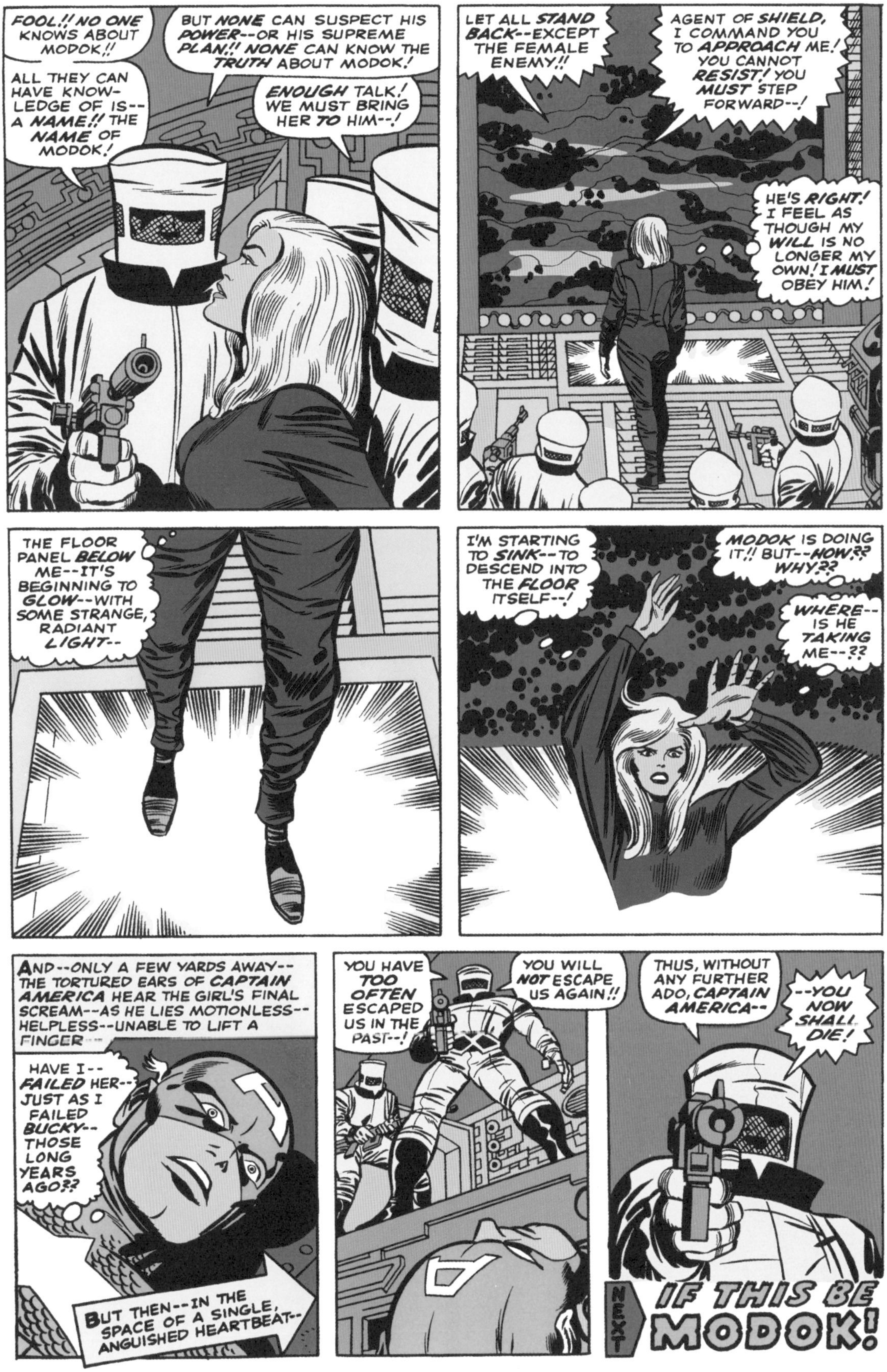
FOOL!! NO ONE KNOWS ABOUT MODOK!!
ALL THEY CAN HAVE KNOWLEDGE OF IS-- A NAME!! THE NAME OF MODOK!
BUT NONE CAN SUSPECT HIS POWER--OR HIS SUPREME PLAN!! NONE CAN KNOW THE TRUTH ABOUT MODOK!
ENOUGH TALK! WE MUST BRING HER TO HIM--!
LET ALL STAND BACK--EXCEPT THE FEMALE ENEMY!!
AGENT OF SHIELD, I COMMAND YOU TO APPROACH ME! YOU CANNOT RESIST! YOU MUST STEP FORWARD--!
HE'S RIGHT! I FEEL AS THOUGH MY WILL IS NO LONGER MY OWN! I MUST OBEY HIM!
THE FLOOR PANEL BELOW ME--IT'S BEGINNING TO GLOW--WITH SOME STRANGE, RADIANT LIGHT--
I'M STARTING TO SINK--TO DESCEND INTO THE FLOOR ITSELF--!
MODOK IS DOING IT!! BUT--HOW?? WHY??
WHERE--IS HE TAKING ME--??
AND--ONLY A FEW YARDS AWAY--THE TORTURED EARS OF CAPTAIN AMERICA HEAR THE GIRL'S FINAL SCREAM--AS HE LIES MOTIONLESS--HELPLESS--UNABLE TO LIFT A FINGER--
HAVE I--FAILED HER--JUST AS I FAILED BUCKY--THOSE LONG YEARS AGO??
BUT THEN--IN THE SPACE OF A SINGLE, ANGUISHED HEARTBEAT--
YOU HAVE TOO OFTEN ESCAPED US IN THE PAST--!
YOU WILL NOT ESCAPE US AGAIN!!
THUS, WITHOUT ANY FURTHER ADO, CAPTAIN AMERICA--
--YOU NOW SHALL DIE!
NEXT
IF THIS BE MODOK!

TALES OF SUSPENSE #94,

OCTOBER 1967,

"IF THIS BE . . .

MODOK!"

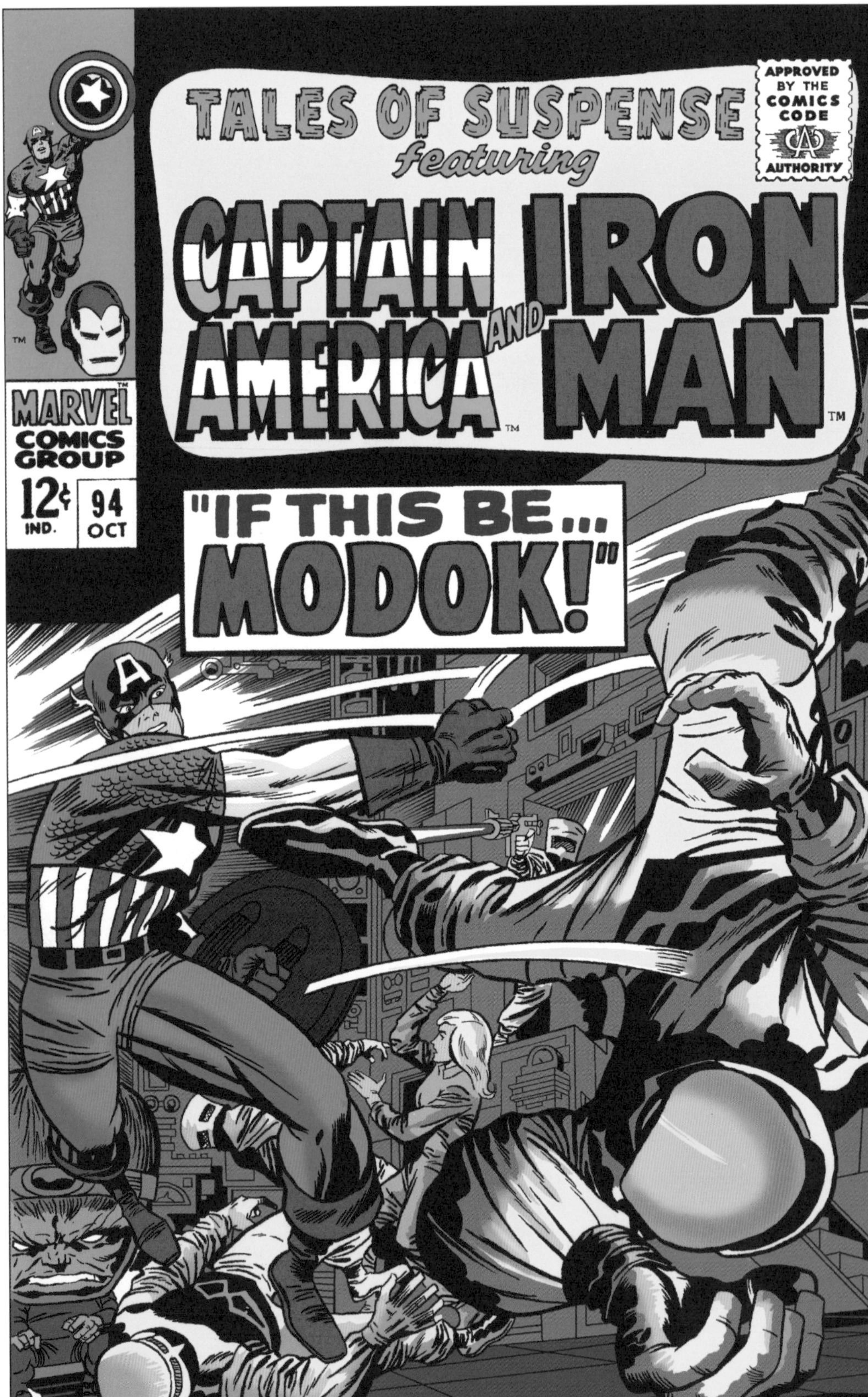
TALES OF SUSPENSE
featuring
CAPTAIN AMERICA AND IRON MAN
TM
APPROVED BY THE COMICS CODE AUTHORITY
MARVEL COMICS GROUP
12¢ IND.
94 OCT
"IF THIS BE... MODOK!"

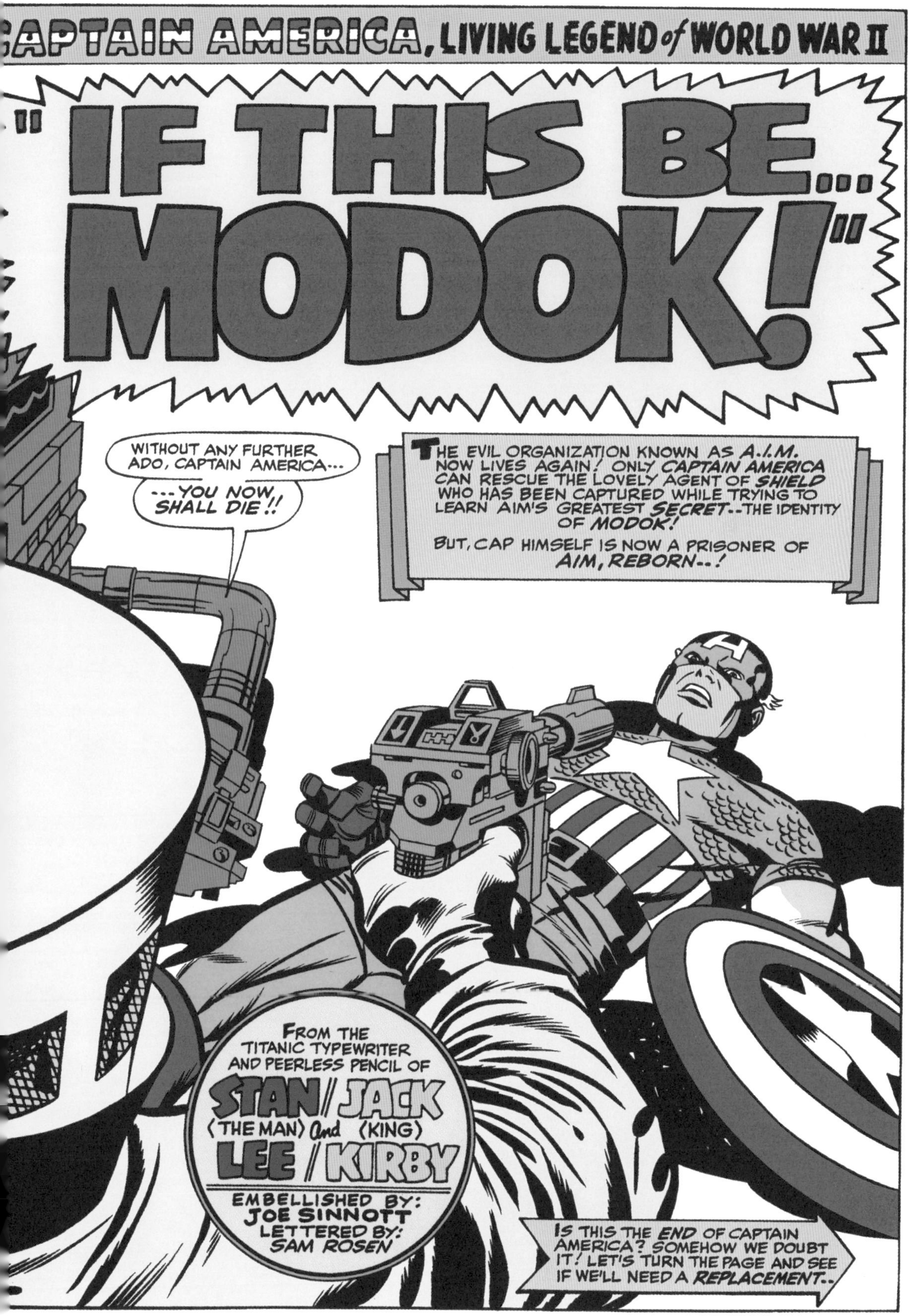
CAPTAIN AMERICA, LIVING LEGEND of WORLD WAR II
"IF THIS BE... MODOK!"
WITHOUT ANY FURTHER ADO, CAPTAIN AMERICA...
...YOU NOW, SHALL DIE!!
THE EVIL ORGANIZATION KNOWN AS A.I.M. NOW LIVES AGAIN! ONLY CAPTAIN AMERICA CAN RESCUE THE LOVELY AGENT OF SHIELD WHO HAS BEEN CAPTURED WHILE TRYING TO LEARN AIM'S GREATEST SECRET--THE IDENTITY OF MODOK!
BUT, CAP HIMSELF IS NOW A PRISONER OF AIM, REBORN--!
FROM THE TITANIC TYPEWRITER AND PEERLESS PENCIL OF STAN (THE MAN) LEE and JACK (KING) KIRBY
EMBELLISHED BY: JOE SINNOTT
LETTERED BY: SAM ROSEN
IS THIS THE END OF CAPTAIN AMERICA? SOMEHOW WE DOUBT IT! LET'S TURN THE PAGE AND SEE IF WE'LL NEED A REPLACEMENT..

STOP!! HAVE YOU FORGOTTEN **MODOK??**

HIS ORDERS ARE THAT ONLY *HE* MAY GIVE THE COMMAND TO *DISPOSE* OF A PRISONER!

MODOK! **MODOK!!** HOW MUCH *LONGER* MUST WE SERVE THE ONE WHOM *WE* OURSELVES CREATED?

WATCH YOUR *TONGUE!!* MODOK'S EARS ARE *EVERYWHERE!*

NO! IF WE ARE *EVER* TO REBEL...IT MUST BE *NOW!*

NOW..WHILE MODOK IS BUSY INTERROGATING THE FEMALE AGENT OF *SHIELD!*

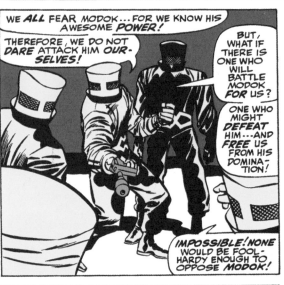

WE *ALL* FEAR MODOK...FOR WE KNOW HIS AWESOME *POWER!*

THEREFORE, WE DO NOT *DARE* ATTACK HIM *OUR-SELVES!*

BUT, WHAT IF THERE IS ONE WHO WILL BATTLE MODOK *FOR* US?

ONE WHO MIGHT *DEFEAT* HIM---AND *FREE* US FROM HIS DOMINA-TION!

IMPOSSIBLE! NONE WOULD BE FOOL-HARDY ENOUGH TO OPPOSE *MODOK!*

CAPTAIN AMERICA WOULD DO IT...IN ORDER TO SAVE THE *GIRL!*

AND, WHETHER HE *SUCCEEDS* OR NOT IS *UNIMPORTANT!*

WHAT *DOES* MATTER IS..WHILE MODOK BATTLES THE AVENGER, *WE* WILL BE FREE TO FOLLOW OUR *OWN* PLAN!

EXCELLENT!! WE'LL *DO* IT!

QUIET NOW... WHILE I *CONTACT* HIM--!

WE HAVE TAKEN CAPTAIN AMERICA *PRISONER!* DO YOU WISH TO *STUDY* HIM BEFORE HE IS.. DISPOSED OF?

I *SO* DESIRE! BRING HIM *TO* ME!

IT *WORKED!*--ONCE THEY MEET, THERE *MUST* BE A *BATTLE!*

EVEN IF IT MEANS PLAYING INTO AIM'S *HANDS*..I'VE *GOT* TO RESCUE THE GIRL FROM *MODOK!*--, I DARE NOT *FAIL!*

I'M SINKING... DOWNWARD...!

THEY'RE DISPERSING THE MOLECULES OF THE FLOOR... AS THEY DID WITH---HER!

ONLY THE INVENTIVE GENIUS OF AN OUTFIT LIKE AIM COULD HAVE CREATED SUCH A METHOD OF BRIDGING SPACE!

IF ONLY THAT SAME GENIUS WASN'T DEDICATED TO EVIL!

THE PARALYSIS RAY THAT HELD ME MOTIONLESS IS GONE!

I CAN MOVE AGAIN... I CAN FIGHT... THE SAME AS EVER!

THIS TIME... IF I DON'T COME OUT ON TOP... I'LL HAVE ONLY MYSELF TO BLAME!

WHOEVER... OR WHATEVER MODOK IS...HE MUST HAVE A WEAK SPOT...

AND, IF HE DOES... I'LL FIND IT!

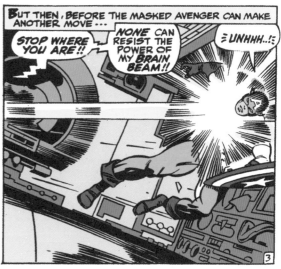

BUT THEN, BEFORE THE MASKED AVENGER CAN MAKE ANOTHER MOVE...

STOP WHERE YOU ARE!!

NONE CAN RESIST THE POWER OF MY BRAIN BEAM!!

≡UNHHH..!≡

3

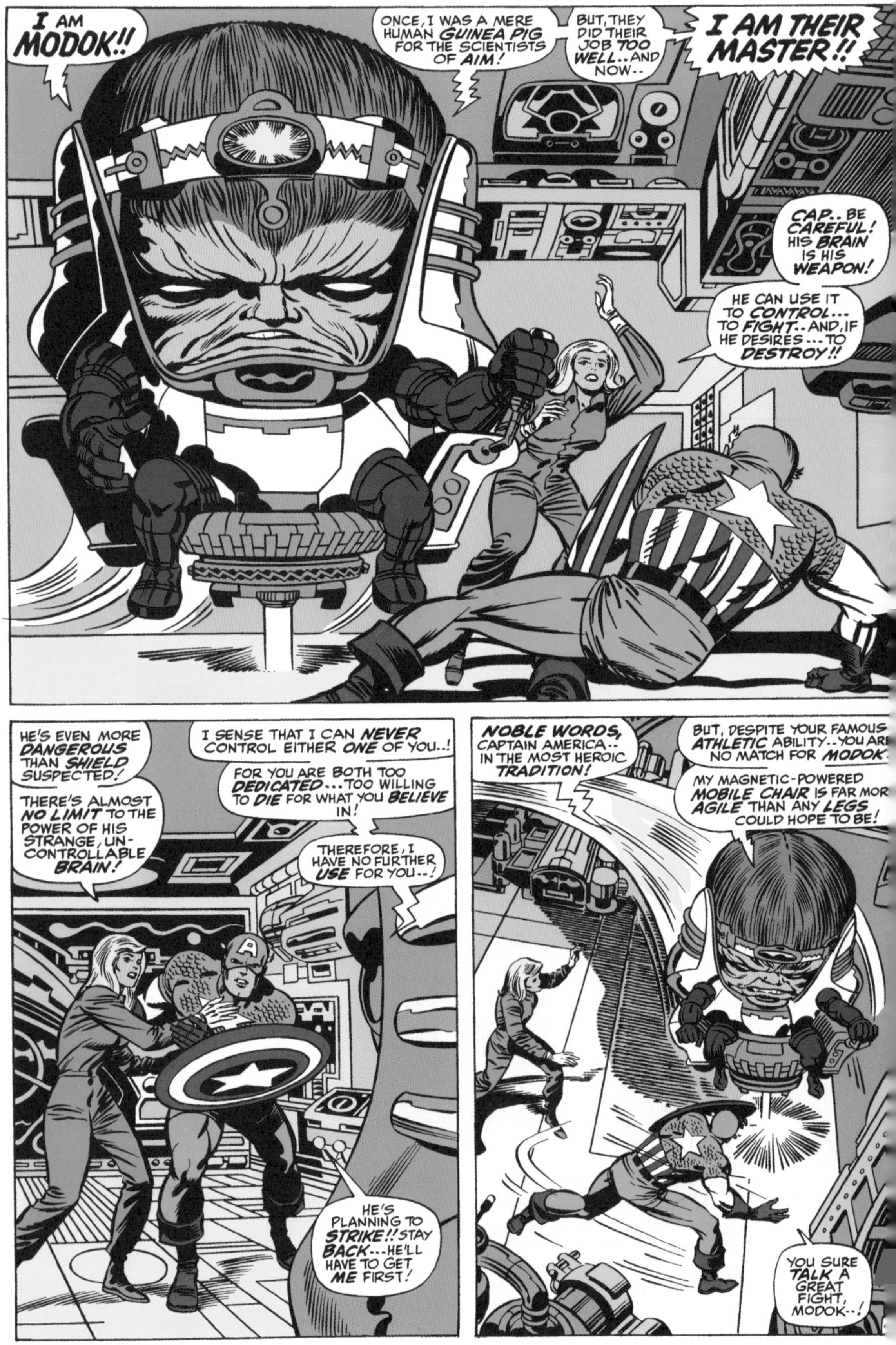

I AM MODOK!!
ONCE, I WAS A MERE HUMAN GUINEA PIG FOR THE SCIENTISTS OF AIM!
BUT, THEY DID THEIR JOB TOO WELL..AND NOW--
I AM THEIR MASTER!!
CAP.. BE CAREFUL! HIS BRAIN IS HIS WEAPON!
HE CAN USE IT TO CONTROL... TO FIGHT.. AND, IF HE DESIRES... TO DESTROY!!
HE'S EVEN MORE DANGEROUS THAN SHIELD SUSPECTED!
THERE'S ALMOST NO LIMIT TO THE POWER OF HIS STRANGE, UN-CONTROLLABLE BRAIN!
I SENSE THAT I CAN NEVER CONTROL EITHER ONE OF YOU..!
FOR YOU ARE BOTH TOO DEDICATED... TOO WILLING TO DIE FOR WHAT YOU BELIEVE IN!
THEREFORE, I HAVE NO FURTHER USE FOR YOU--!
HE'S PLANNING TO STRIKE!! STAY BACK--- HE'LL HAVE TO GET ME FIRST!
NOBLE WORDS, CAPTAIN AMERICA-- IN THE MOST HEROIC TRADITION!
BUT, DESPITE YOUR FAMOUS ATHLETIC ABILITY..YOU AR NO MATCH FOR MODOK
MY MAGNETIC-POWERED MOBILE CHAIR IS FAR MOR AGILE THAN ANY LEGS COULD HOPE TO BE!
YOU SURE TALK A GREAT FIGHT, MODOK--!

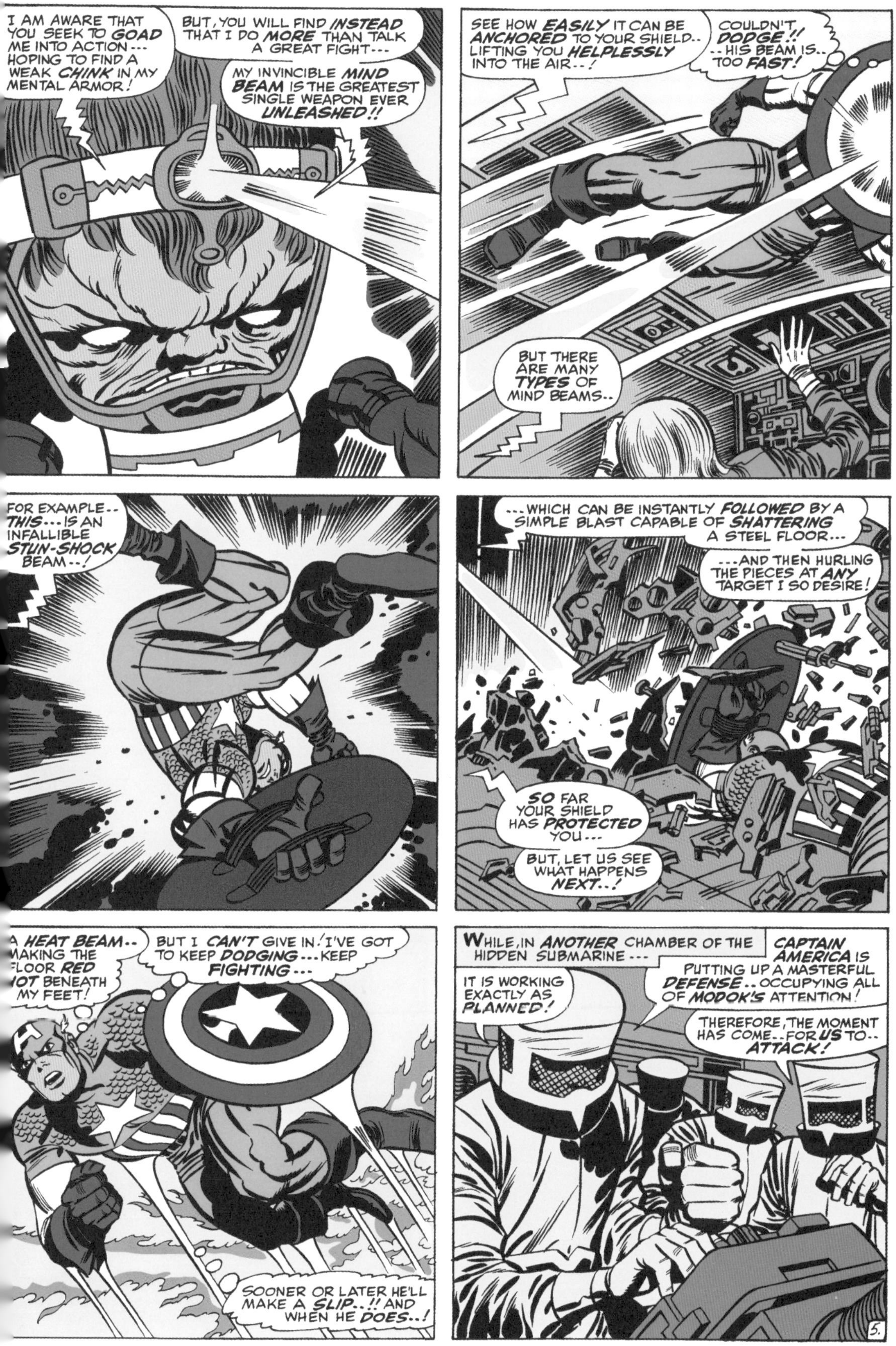
I AM AWARE THAT YOU SEEK TO GOAD ME INTO ACTION --- HOPING TO FIND A WEAK CHINK IN MY MENTAL ARMOR!
BUT, YOU WILL FIND INSTEAD THAT I DO MORE THAN TALK A GREAT FIGHT---
MY INVINCIBLE MIND BEAM IS THE GREATEST SINGLE WEAPON EVER UNLEASHED!!
SEE HOW EASILY IT CAN BE ANCHORED TO YOUR SHIELD.. LIFTING YOU HELPLESSLY INTO THE AIR--!
COULDN'T DODGE!! --HIS BEAM IS.. TOO FAST!
BUT THERE ARE MANY TYPES OF MIND BEAMS..
FOR EXAMPLE-- THIS---IS AN INFALLIBLE STUN-SHOCK BEAM--!
---WHICH CAN BE INSTANTLY FOLLOWED BY A SIMPLE BLAST CAPABLE OF SHATTERING A STEEL FLOOR---
---AND THEN HURLING THE PIECES AT ANY TARGET I SO DESIRE!
SO FAR YOUR SHIELD HAS PROTECTED YOU---
BUT, LET US SEE WHAT HAPPENS NEXT--!
A HEAT BEAM-- MAKING THE FLOOR RED HOT BENEATH MY FEET!
BUT I CAN'T GIVE IN! I'VE GOT TO KEEP DODGING---KEEP FIGHTING---
SOONER OR LATER HE'LL MAKE A SLIP..!! AND WHEN HE DOES..!
WHILE, IN ANOTHER CHAMBER OF THE HIDDEN SUBMARINE---
IT IS WORKING EXACTLY AS PLANNED!
CAPTAIN AMERICA IS PUTTING UP A MASTERFUL DEFENSE.. OCCUPYING ALL OF MODOK'S ATTENTION!
THEREFORE, THE MOMENT HAS COME..FOR US TO.. ATTACK!
5.

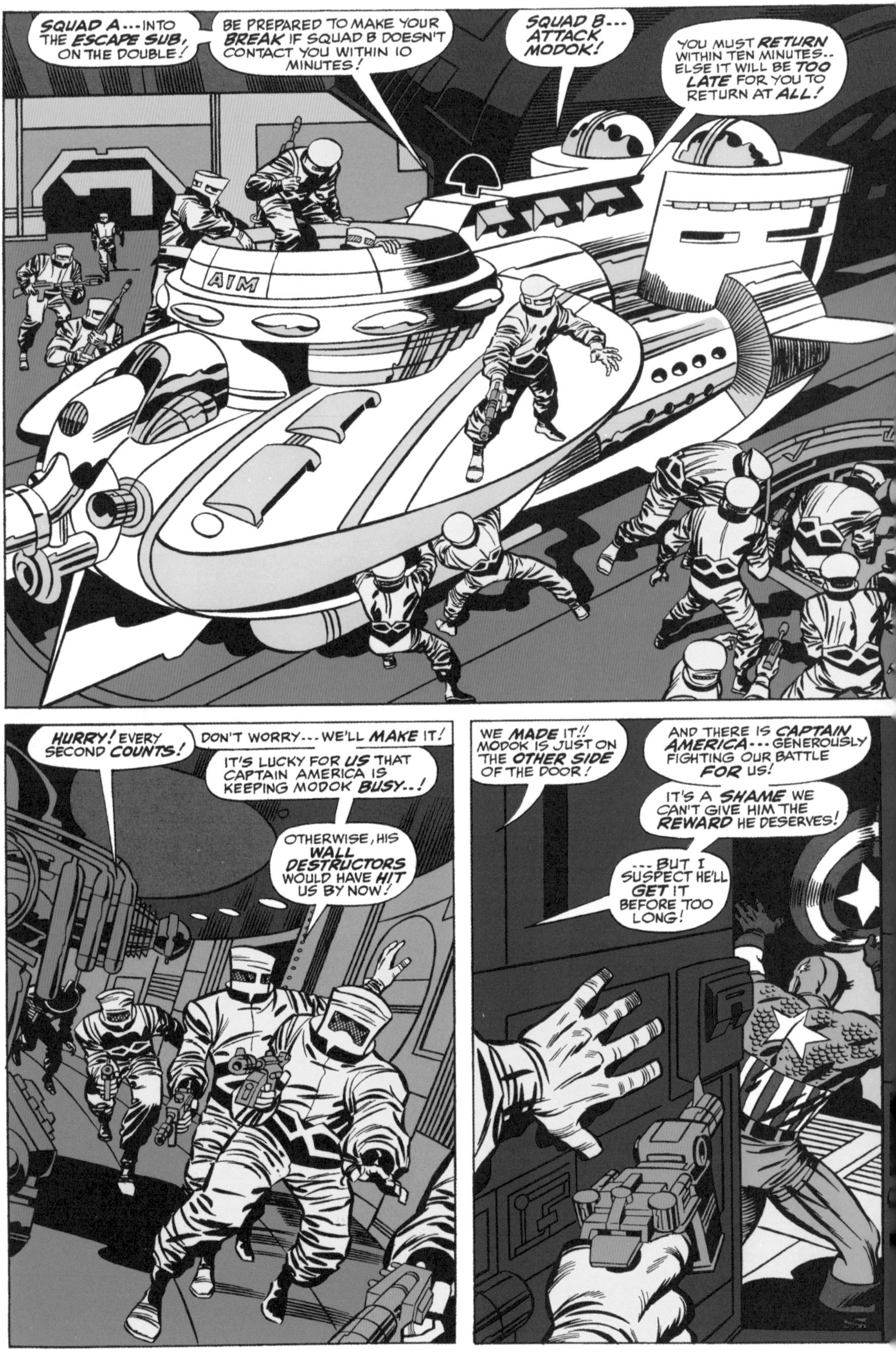
SQUAD A... INTO THE ESCAPE SUB, ON THE DOUBLE!
BE PREPARED TO MAKE YOUR BREAK IF SQUAD B DOESN'T CONTACT YOU WITHIN 10 MINUTES!
SQUAD B... ATTACK MODOK!
YOU MUST RETURN WITHIN TEN MINUTES.. ELSE IT WILL BE TOO LATE FOR YOU TO RETURN AT ALL!
AIM
HURRY! EVERY SECOND COUNTS!
DON'T WORRY... WE'LL MAKE IT!
IT'S LUCKY FOR US THAT CAPTAIN AMERICA IS KEEPING MODOK BUSY..!
OTHERWISE, HIS WALL DESTRUCTORS WOULD HAVE HIT US BY NOW!
WE MADE IT!! MODOK IS JUST ON THE OTHER SIDE OF THE DOOR!
AND THERE IS CAPTAIN AMERICA... GENEROUSLY FIGHTING OUR BATTLE FOR US!
IT'S A SHAME WE CAN'T GIVE HIM THE REWARD HE DESERVES!
...BUT I SUSPECT HE'LL GET IT BEFORE TOO LONG!

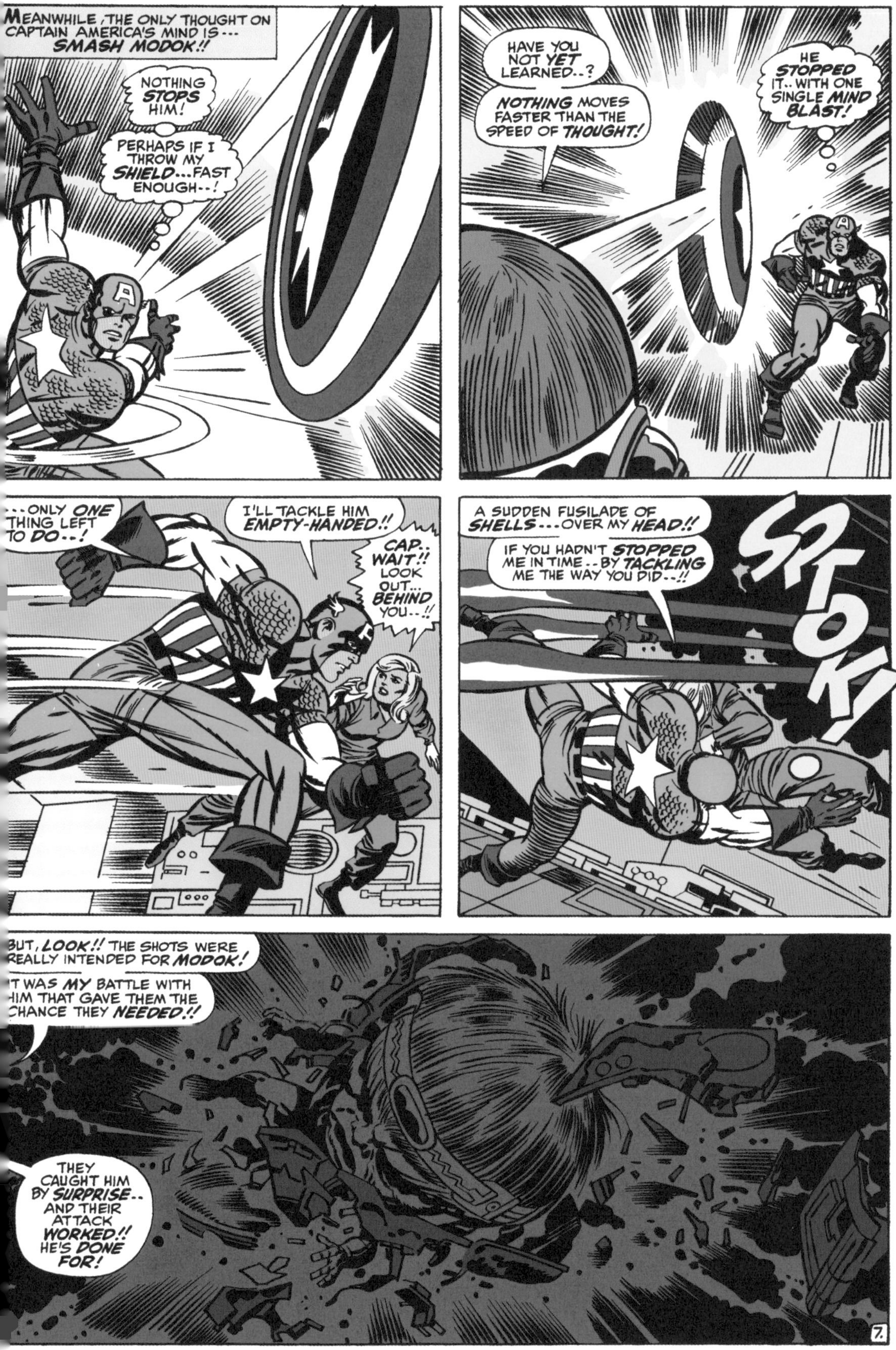
MEANWHILE, THE ONLY THOUGHT ON CAPTAIN AMERICA'S MIND IS--- SMASH MODOK!!
NOTHING STOPS HIM!
PERHAPS IF I THROW MY SHIELD...FAST ENOUGH--!
HAVE YOU NOT YET LEARNED--?
NOTHING MOVES FASTER THAN THE SPEED OF THOUGHT!
HE STOPPED IT.. WITH ONE SINGLE MIND BLAST!
...ONLY ONE THING LEFT TO DO--!
I'LL TACKLE HIM EMPTY-HANDED!!
CAP.. WAIT!! LOOK OUT... BEHIND YOU--!!
A SUDDEN FUSILADE OF SHELLS---OVER MY HEAD!!
IF YOU HADN'T STOPPED ME IN TIME..BY TACKLING ME THE WAY YOU DID--!!
SPTOK!
BUT, LOOK!! THE SHOTS WERE REALLY INTENDED FOR MODOK!
IT WAS MY BATTLE WITH HIM THAT GAVE THEM THE CHANCE THEY NEEDED!!
THEY CAUGHT HIM BY SURPRISE.. AND THEIR ATTACK WORKED!! HE'S DONE FOR!
7.

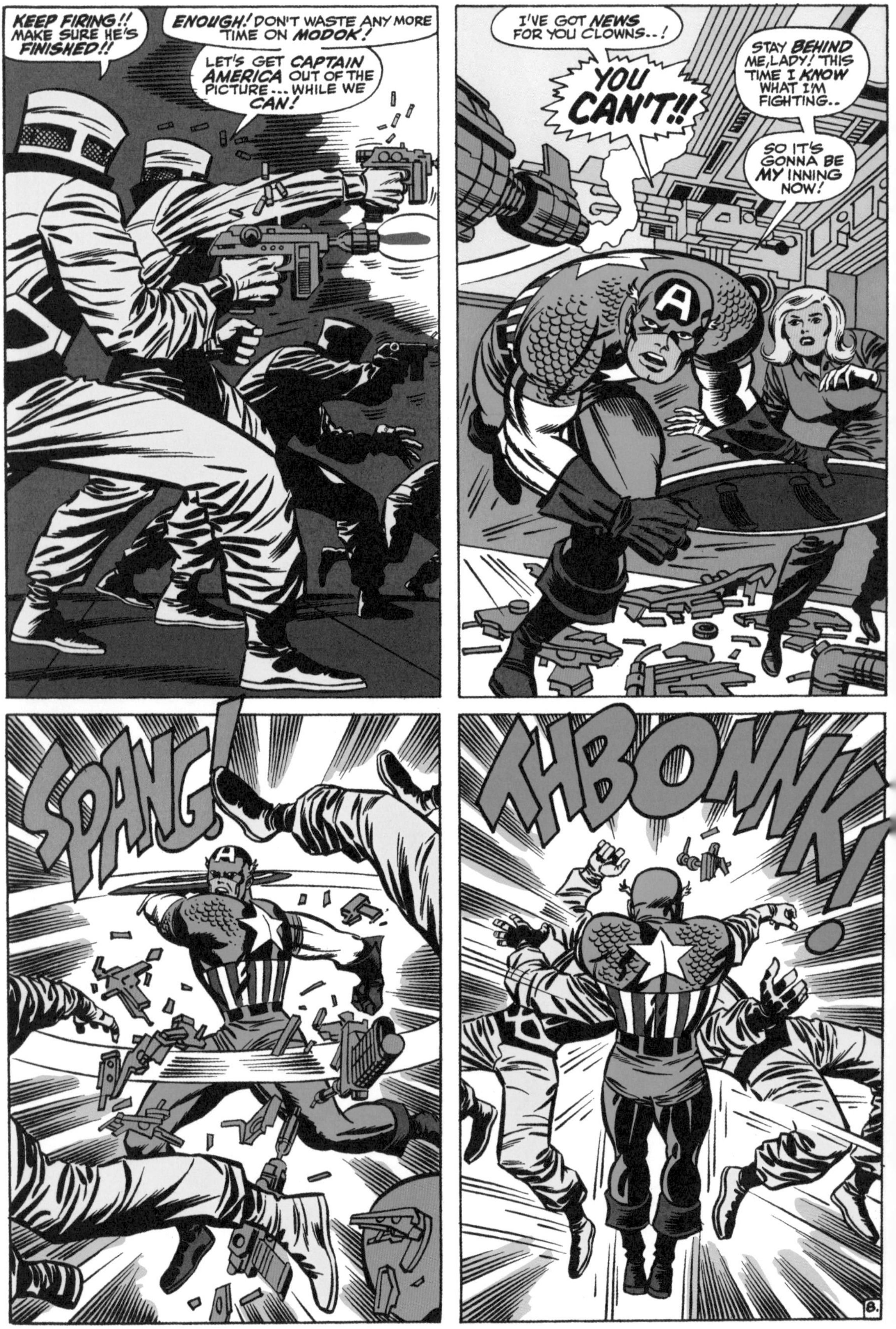
KEEP FIRING!! MAKE SURE HE'S FINISHED!!
ENOUGH! DON'T WASTE ANY MORE TIME ON MODOK!
LET'S GET CAPTAIN AMERICA OUT OF THE PICTURE ... WHILE WE CAN!
I'VE GOT NEWS FOR YOU CLOWNS..!
YOU CAN'T!!
STAY BEHIND ME, LADY! THIS TIME I KNOW WHAT I'M FIGHTING..
SO IT'S GONNA BE MY INNING NOW!
SPANG!
KHBONNK!
8.

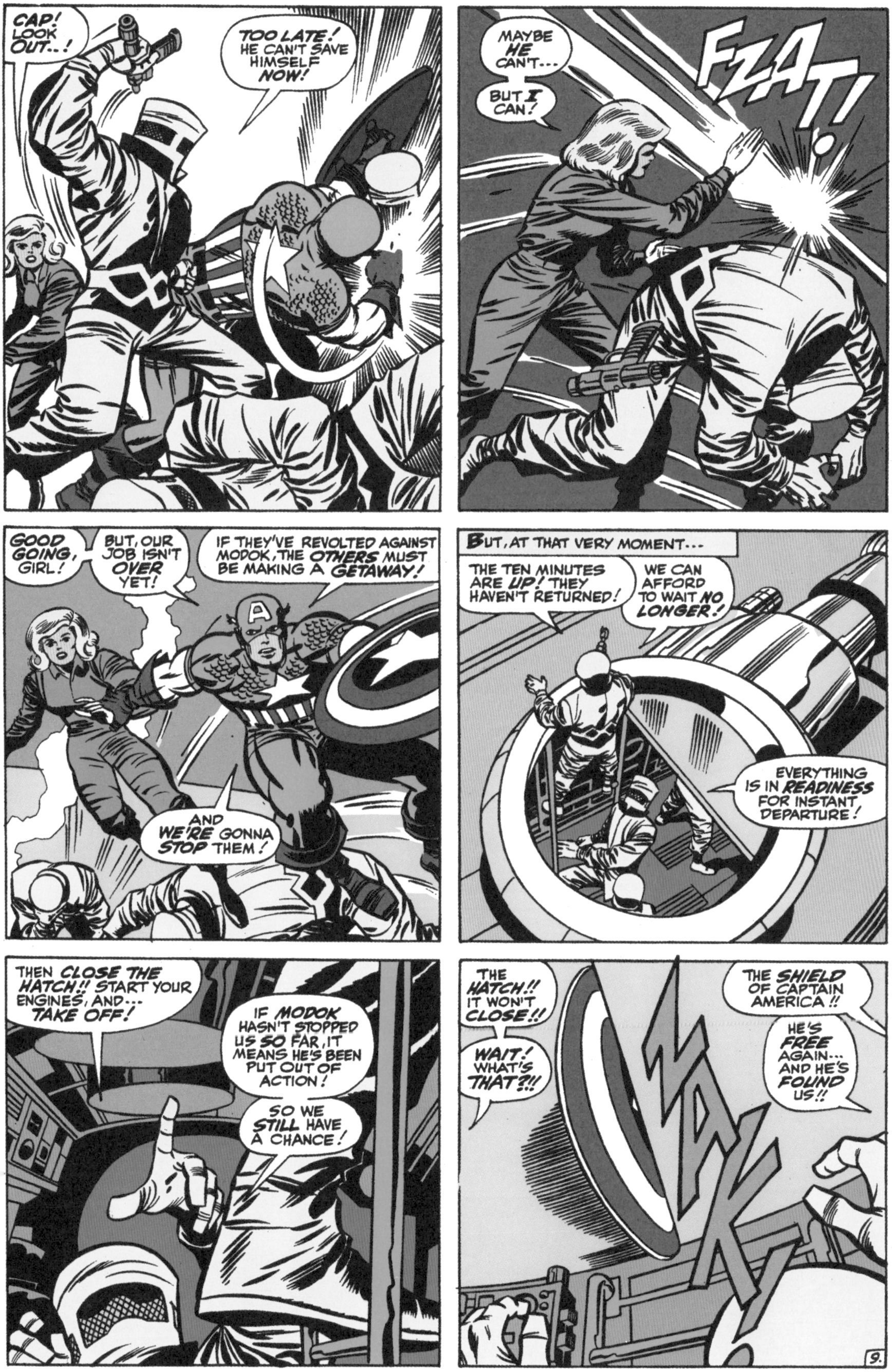
CAP! LOOK OUT..!
TOO LATE! HE CAN'T SAVE HIMSELF NOW!
MAYBE HE CAN'T...
BUT I CAN!
FZAT!
GOOD GOING, GIRL!
BUT, OUR JOB ISN'T OVER YET!
IF THEY'VE REVOLTED AGAINST MODOK, THE OTHERS MUST BE MAKING A GETAWAY!
AND WE'RE GONNA STOP THEM!
BUT, AT THAT VERY MOMENT...
THE TEN MINUTES ARE UP! THEY HAVEN'T RETURNED!
WE CAN AFFORD TO WAIT NO LONGER!
EVERYTHING IS IN READINESS FOR INSTANT DEPARTURE!
THEN CLOSE THE HATCH!! START YOUR ENGINES, AND... TAKE OFF!
IF MODOK HASN'T STOPPED US SO FAR, IT MEANS HE'S BEEN PUT OUT OF ACTION!
SO WE STILL HAVE A CHANCE!
THE HATCH!! IT WON'T CLOSE!!
WAIT! WHAT'S THAT?!!
THE SHIELD OF CAPTAIN AMERICA!!
HE'S FREE AGAIN... AND HE'S FOUND US!!
ZAK!
9.

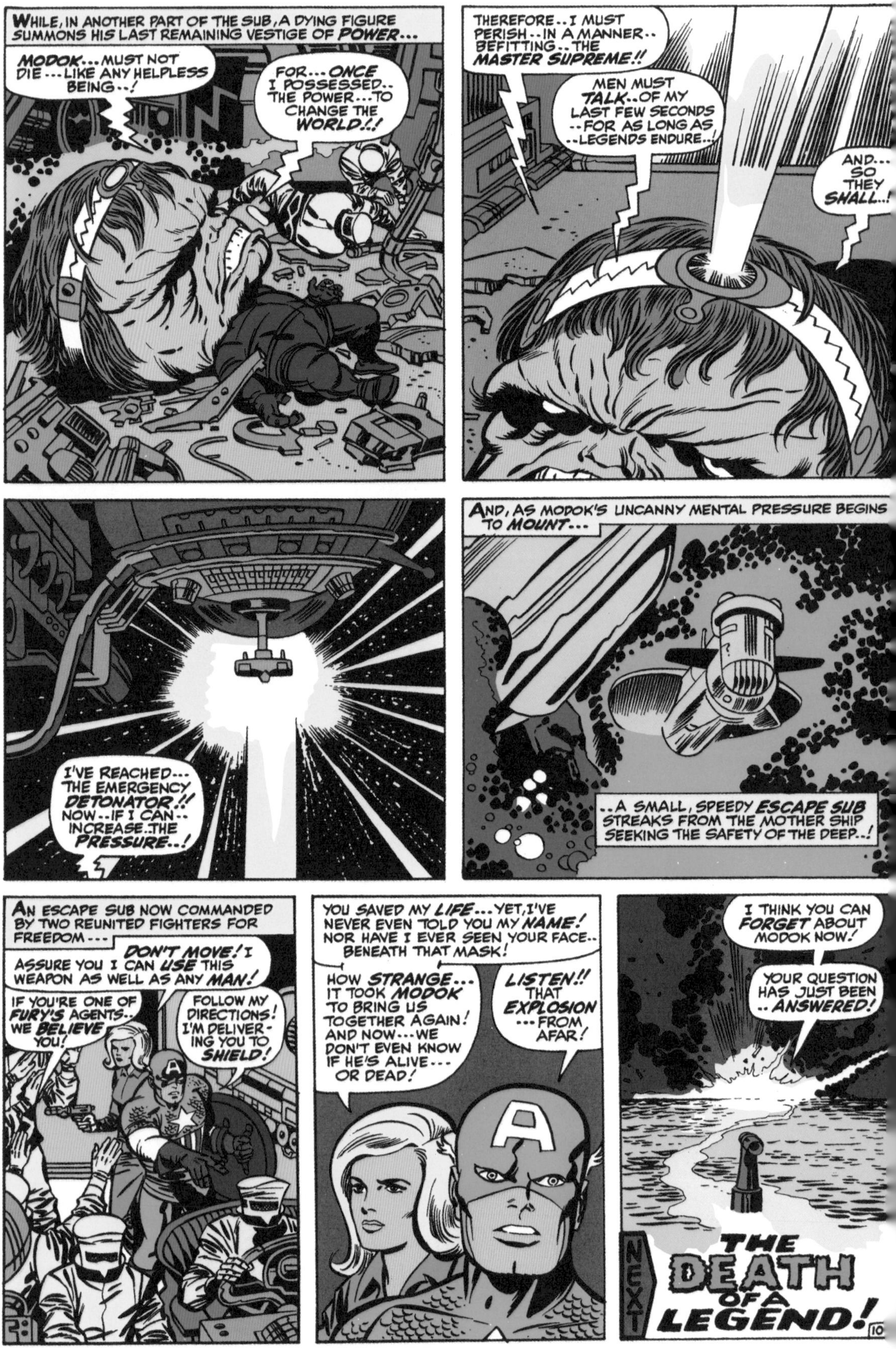
WHILE, IN ANOTHER PART OF THE SUB, A DYING FIGURE SUMMONS HIS LAST REMAINING VESTIGE OF POWER...
MODOK... MUST NOT DIE... LIKE ANY HELPLESS BEING..!
FOR... ONCE I POSSESSED.. THE POWER... TO CHANGE THE WORLD.!.!
THEREFORE.. I MUST PERISH.. IN A MANNER.. BEFITTING.. THE MASTER SUPREME!!
MEN MUST TALK..OF MY LAST FEW SECONDS ..FOR AS LONG AS ..LEGENDS ENDURE..!
AND... SO THEY SHALL..!
I'VE REACHED... THE EMERGENCY DETONATOR.!! NOW..IF I CAN.. INCREASE..THE PRESSURE..!
AND, AS MODOK'S UNCANNY MENTAL PRESSURE BEGINS TO MOUNT...
..A SMALL, SPEEDY ESCAPE SUB STREAKS FROM THE MOTHER SHIP SEEKING THE SAFETY OF THE DEEP..!
AN ESCAPE SUB NOW COMMANDED BY TWO REUNITED FIGHTERS FOR FREEDOM...
DON'T MOVE! I ASSURE YOU I CAN USE THIS WEAPON AS WELL AS ANY MAN!
IF YOU'RE ONE OF FURY'S AGENTS.. WE BELIEVE YOU!
FOLLOW MY DIRECTIONS! I'M DELIVERING YOU TO SHIELD!
YOU SAVED MY LIFE... YET, I'VE NEVER EVEN TOLD YOU MY NAME! NOR HAVE I EVER SEEN YOUR FACE.. BENEATH THAT MASK!
HOW STRANGE... IT TOOK MODOK TO BRING US TOGETHER AGAIN! AND NOW... WE DON'T EVEN KNOW IF HE'S ALIVE... OR DEAD!
LISTEN!! THAT EXPLOSION ... FROM AFAR!
I THINK YOU CAN FORGET ABOUT MODOK NOW!
YOUR QUESTION HAS JUST BEEN .. ANSWERED!
NEXT
THE DEATH OF A LEGEND!
10

TALES OF SUSPENSE #95,

NOVEMBER 1967,

"A TIME TO DIE . . .

A TIME TO LIVE!"

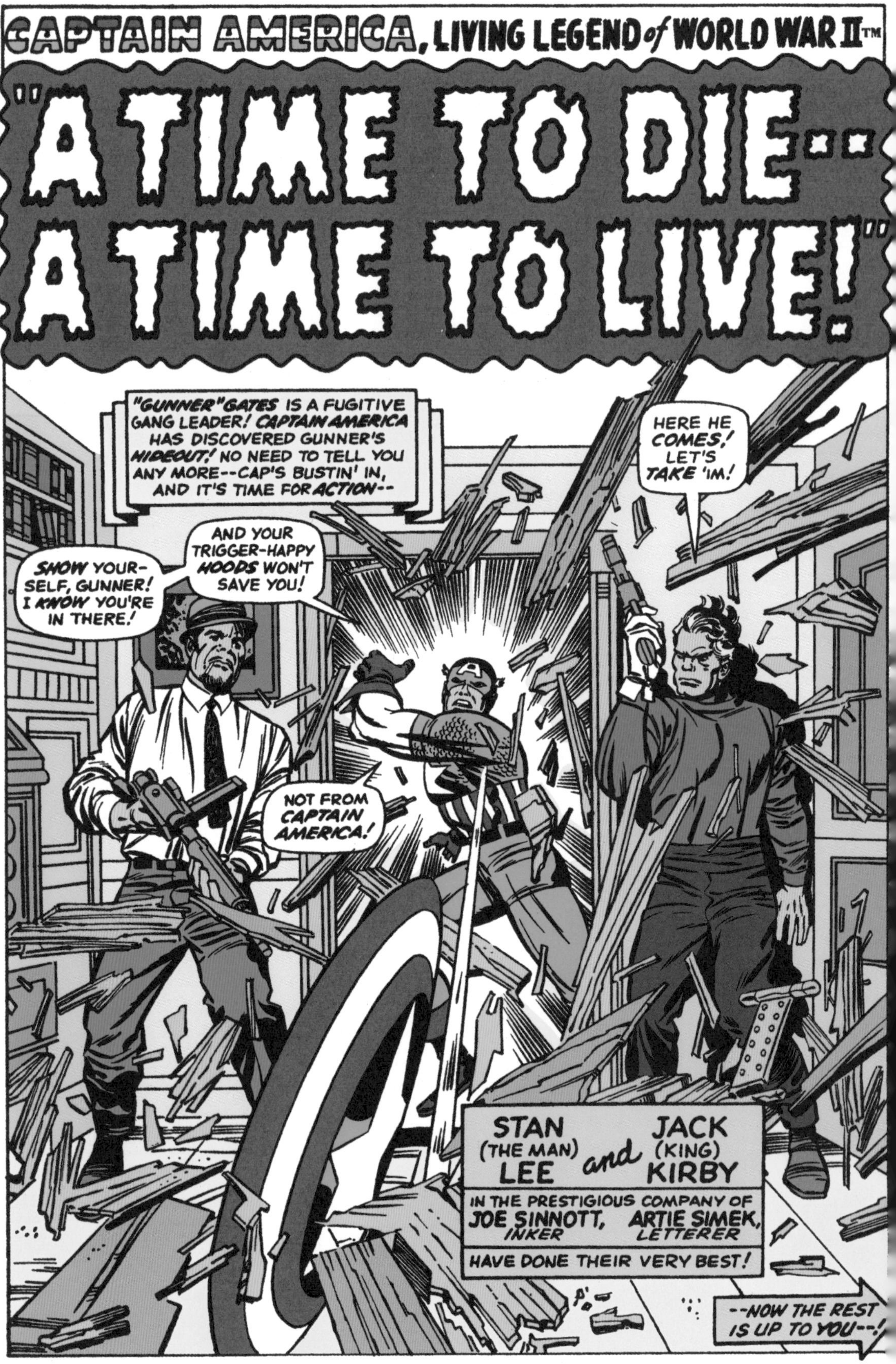

CAPTAIN AMERICA, LIVING LEGEND of WORLD WAR II™
"A TIME TO DIE-- A TIME TO LIVE!"
"GUNNER" GATES IS A FUGITIVE GANG LEADER! CAPTAIN AMERICA HAS DISCOVERED GUNNER'S HIDEOUT! NO NEED TO TELL YOU ANY MORE--CAP'S BUSTIN' IN, AND IT'S TIME FOR ACTION--
HERE HE COMES! LET'S TAKE 'IM!
SHOW YOURSELF, GUNNER! I KNOW YOU'RE IN THERE!
AND YOUR TRIGGER-HAPPY HOODS WON'T SAVE YOU!
NOT FROM CAPTAIN AMERICA!
STAN (THE MAN) LEE and JACK (KING) KIRBY
IN THE PRESTIGIOUS COMPANY OF JOE SINNOTT, INKER ARTIE SIMEK, LETTERER
HAVE DONE THEIR VERY BEST!
--NOW THE REST IS UP TO YOU--!

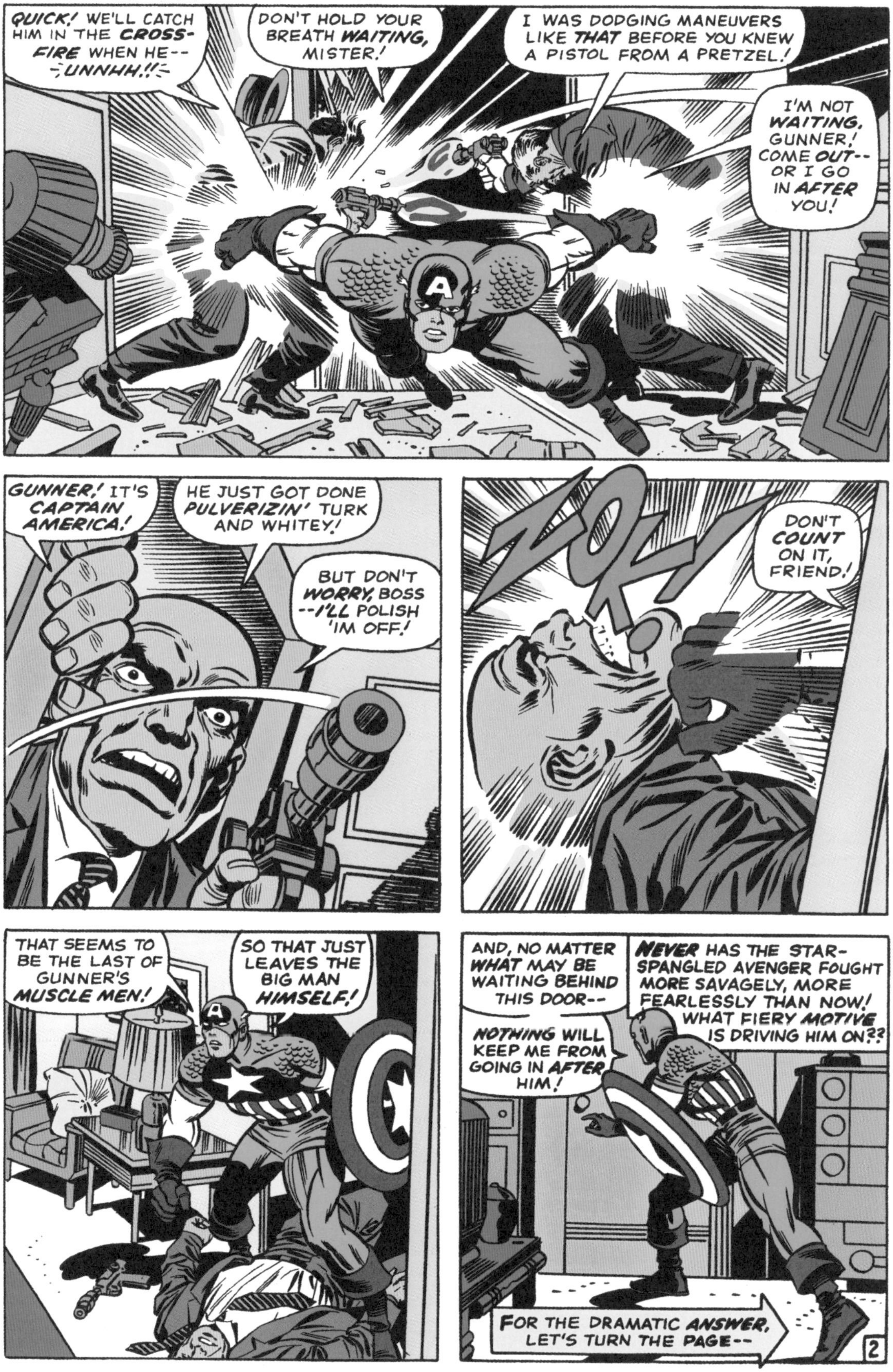
QUICK! WE'LL CATCH HIM IN THE CROSS-FIRE WHEN HE-- UNNHH!!
DON'T HOLD YOUR BREATH WAITING, MISTER!
I WAS DODGING MANEUVERS LIKE THAT BEFORE YOU KNEW A PISTOL FROM A PRETZEL!
I'M NOT WAITING, GUNNER! COME OUT-- OR I GO IN AFTER YOU!
GUNNER! IT'S CAPTAIN AMERICA!
HE JUST GOT DONE PULVERIZIN' TURK AND WHITEY!
BUT DON'T WORRY, BOSS --I'LL POLISH 'IM OFF!
ZOK!
DON'T COUNT ON IT, FRIEND!
THAT SEEMS TO BE THE LAST OF GUNNER'S MUSCLE MEN!
SO THAT JUST LEAVES THE BIG MAN HIMSELF!
AND, NO MATTER WHAT MAY BE WAITING BEHIND THIS DOOR--
NOTHING WILL KEEP ME FROM GOING IN AFTER HIM!
NEVER HAS THE STAR-SPANGLED AVENGER FOUGHT MORE SAVAGELY, MORE FEARLESSLY THAN NOW! WHAT FIERY MOTIVE IS DRIVING HIM ON??
FOR THE DRAMATIC ANSWER, LET'S TURN THE PAGE--
2

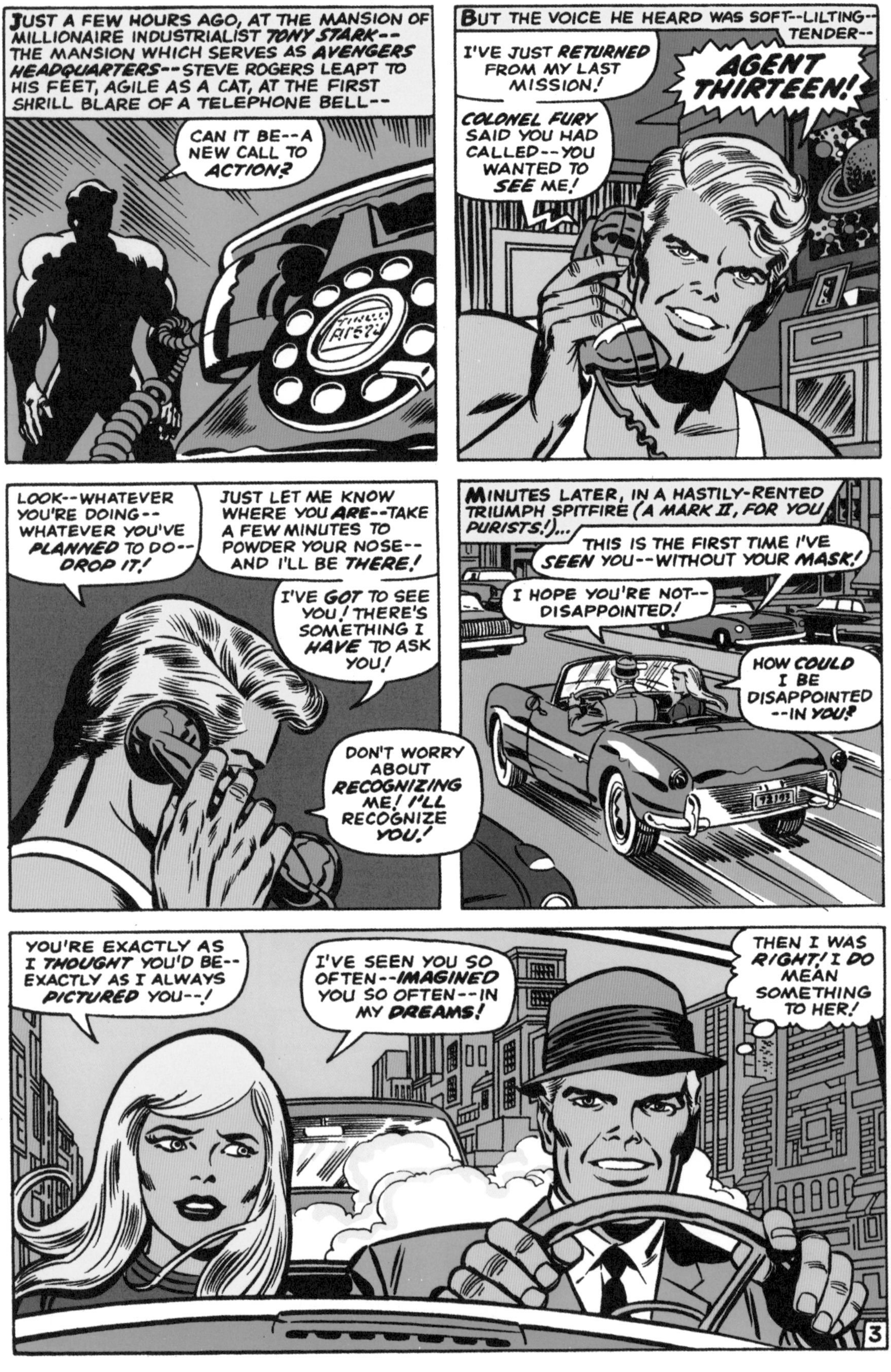
JUST A FEW HOURS AGO, AT THE MANSION OF MILLIONAIRE INDUSTRIALIST TONY STARK-- THE MANSION WHICH SERVES AS AVENGERS HEADQUARTERS--STEVE ROGERS LEAPT TO HIS FEET, AGILE AS A CAT, AT THE FIRST SHRILL BLARE OF A TELEPHONE BELL--
CAN IT BE--A NEW CALL TO ACTION?
BUT THE VOICE HE HEARD WAS SOFT--LILTING--TENDER--
I'VE JUST RETURNED FROM MY LAST MISSION!
AGENT THIRTEEN!
COLONEL FURY SAID YOU HAD CALLED--YOU WANTED TO SEE ME!
LOOK--WHATEVER YOU'RE DOING--WHATEVER YOU'VE PLANNED TO DO--DROP IT!
JUST LET ME KNOW WHERE YOU ARE--TAKE A FEW MINUTES TO POWDER YOUR NOSE--AND I'LL BE THERE!
I'VE GOT TO SEE YOU! THERE'S SOMETHING I HAVE TO ASK YOU!
DON'T WORRY ABOUT RECOGNIZING ME! I'LL RECOGNIZE YOU!
MINUTES LATER, IN A HASTILY-RENTED TRIUMPH SPITFIRE (A MARK II, FOR YOU PURISTS!)...
THIS IS THE FIRST TIME I'VE SEEN YOU--WITHOUT YOUR MASK!
I HOPE YOU'RE NOT--DISAPPOINTED!
HOW COULD I BE DISAPPOINTED--IN YOU?
YOU'RE EXACTLY AS I THOUGHT YOU'D BE--EXACTLY AS I ALWAYS PICTURED YOU--!
I'VE SEEN YOU SO OFTEN--IMAGINED YOU SO OFTEN--IN MY DREAMS!
THEN I WAS RIGHT! I DO MEAN SOMETHING TO HER!
3

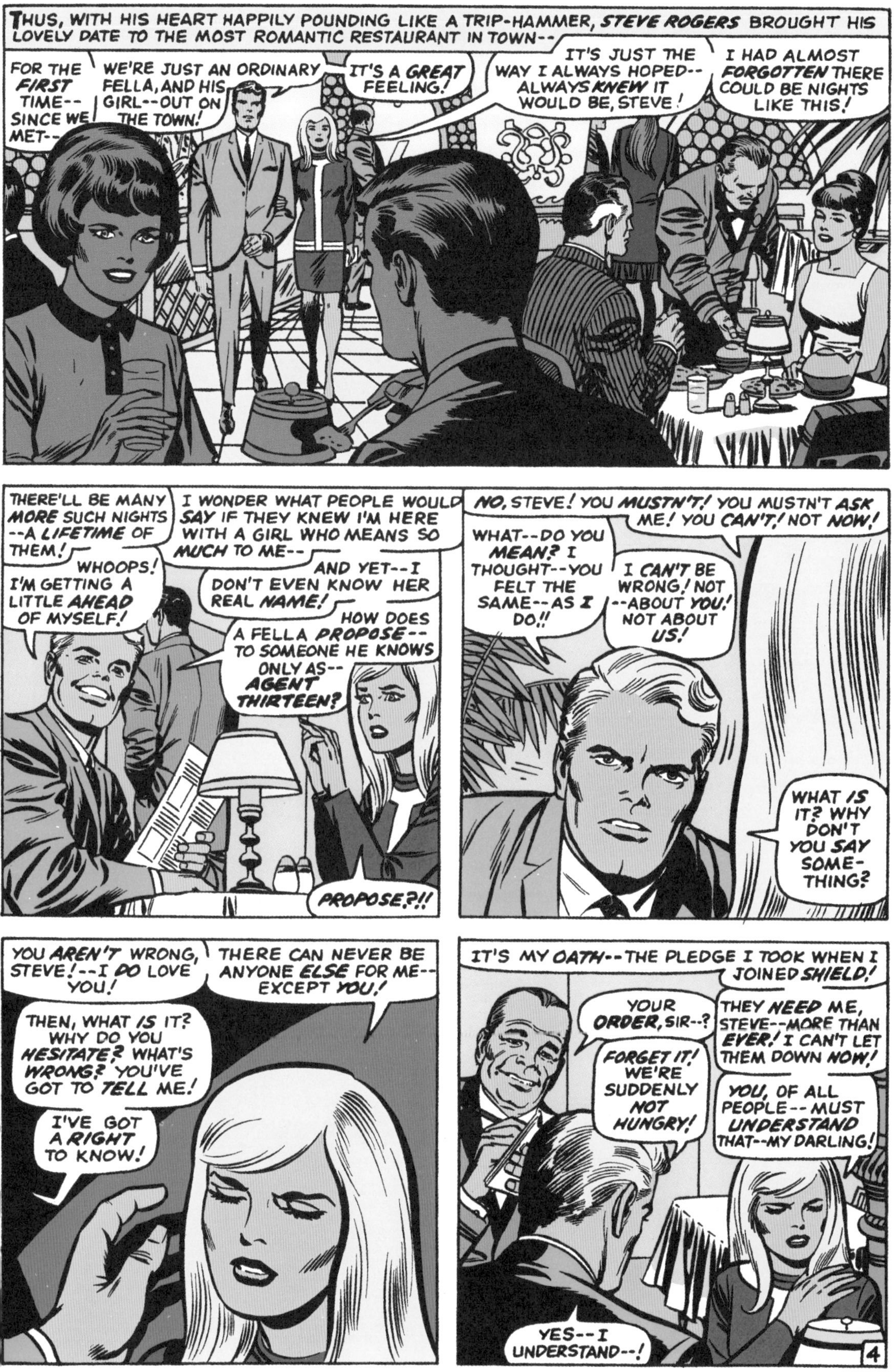
THUS, WITH HIS HEART HAPPILY POUNDING LIKE A TRIP-HAMMER, STEVE ROGERS BROUGHT HIS LOVELY DATE TO THE MOST ROMANTIC RESTAURANT IN TOWN--
FOR THE FIRST TIME-- SINCE WE MET--
WE'RE JUST AN ORDINARY FELLA, AND HIS GIRL--OUT ON THE TOWN!
IT'S A GREAT FEELING!
IT'S JUST THE WAY I ALWAYS HOPED-- ALWAYS KNEW IT WOULD BE, STEVE!
I HAD ALMOST FORGOTTEN THERE COULD BE NIGHTS LIKE THIS!
THERE'LL BE MANY MORE SUCH NIGHTS --A LIFETIME OF THEM!
WHOOPS! I'M GETTING A LITTLE AHEAD OF MYSELF!
I WONDER WHAT PEOPLE WOULD SAY IF THEY KNEW I'M HERE WITH A GIRL WHO MEANS SO MUCH TO ME--
AND YET--I DON'T EVEN KNOW HER REAL NAME!
HOW DOES A FELLA PROPOSE-- TO SOMEONE HE KNOWS ONLY AS-- AGENT THIRTEEN?
PROPOSE?!!
NO, STEVE! YOU MUSTN'T! YOU MUSTN'T ASK ME! YOU CAN'T! NOT NOW!
WHAT--DO YOU MEAN? I THOUGHT--YOU FELT THE SAME--AS I DO!!
I CAN'T BE WRONG! NOT --ABOUT YOU! NOT ABOUT US!
WHAT IS IT? WHY DON'T YOU SAY SOME-THING?
YOU AREN'T WRONG, STEVE!--I DO LOVE YOU!
THERE CAN NEVER BE ANYONE ELSE FOR ME-- EXCEPT YOU!
THEN, WHAT IS IT? WHY DO YOU HESITATE? WHAT'S WRONG? YOU'VE GOT TO TELL ME!
I'VE GOT A RIGHT TO KNOW!
IT'S MY OATH--THE PLEDGE I TOOK WHEN I JOINED SHIELD!
YOUR ORDER, SIR--?
THEY NEED ME, STEVE--MORE THAN EVER! I CAN'T LET THEM DOWN NOW!
FORGET IT! WE'RE SUDDENLY NOT HUNGRY!
YOU, OF ALL PEOPLE--MUST UNDERSTAND THAT--MY DARLING!
YES--I UNDERSTAND--!
4

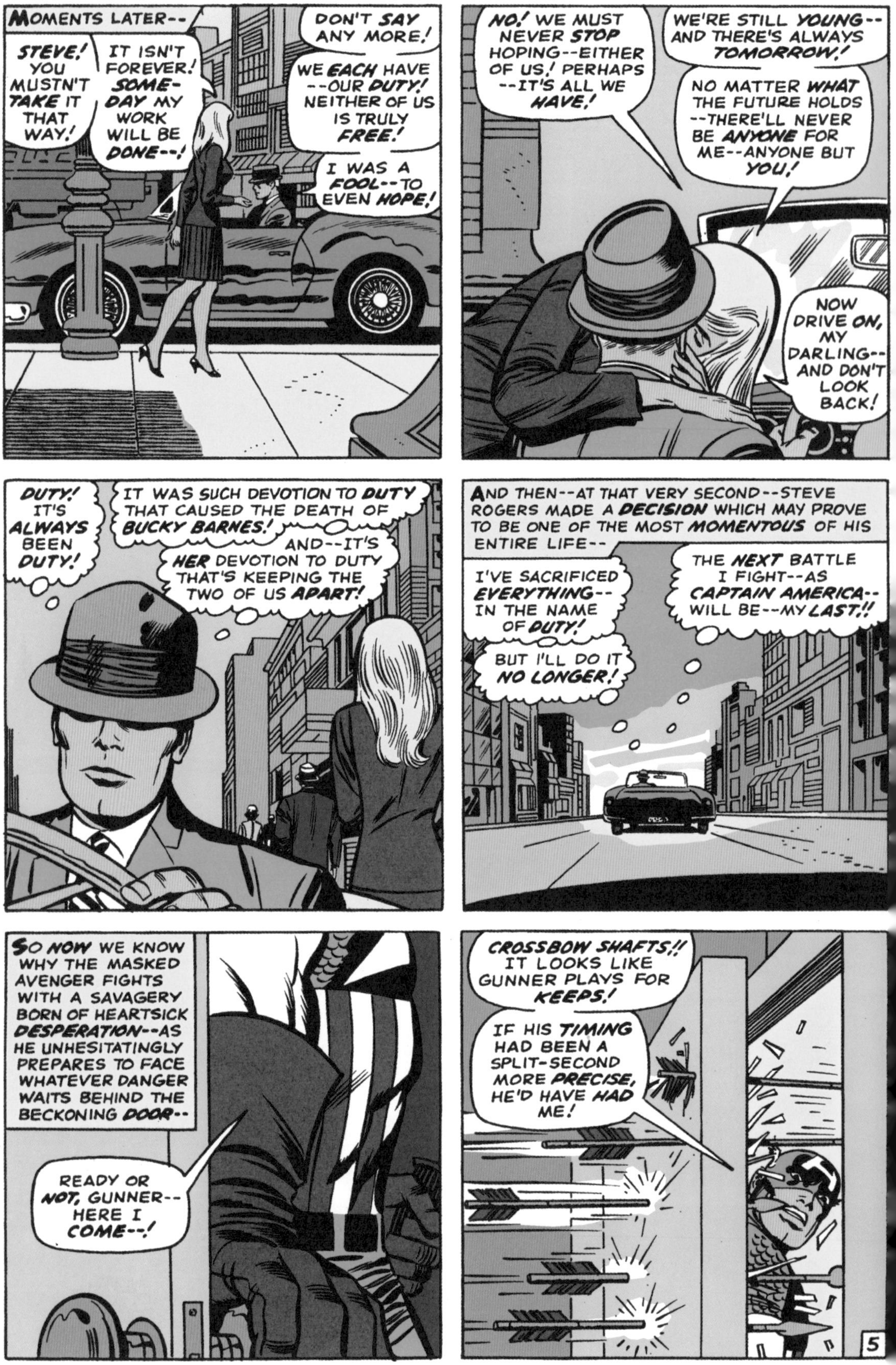
MOMENTS LATER--
STEVE! YOU MUSTN'T TAKE IT THAT WAY!
IT ISN'T FOREVER! SOME-DAY MY WORK WILL BE DONE--!
DON'T SAY ANY MORE!
WE EACH HAVE --OUR DUTY! NEITHER OF US IS TRULY FREE!
I WAS A FOOL--TO EVEN HOPE!
NO! WE MUST NEVER STOP HOPING--EITHER OF US! PERHAPS --IT'S ALL WE HAVE!
WE'RE STILL YOUNG-- AND THERE'S ALWAYS TOMORROW!
NO MATTER WHAT THE FUTURE HOLDS --THERE'LL NEVER BE ANYONE FOR ME--ANYONE BUT YOU!
NOW DRIVE ON, MY DARLING-- AND DON'T LOOK BACK!
DUTY! IT'S ALWAYS BEEN DUTY!
IT WAS SUCH DEVOTION TO DUTY THAT CAUSED THE DEATH OF BUCKY BARNES!
AND--IT'S HER DEVOTION TO DUTY THAT'S KEEPING THE TWO OF US APART!
AND THEN--AT THAT VERY SECOND--STEVE ROGERS MADE A DECISION WHICH MAY PROVE TO BE ONE OF THE MOST MOMENTOUS OF HIS ENTIRE LIFE--
I'VE SACRIFICED EVERYTHING-- IN THE NAME OF DUTY!
BUT I'LL DO IT NO LONGER!
THE NEXT BATTLE I FIGHT--AS CAPTAIN AMERICA-- WILL BE--MY LAST!!
SO NOW WE KNOW WHY THE MASKED AVENGER FIGHTS WITH A SAVAGERY BORN OF HEARTSICK DESPERATION--AS HE UNHESITATINGLY PREPARES TO FACE WHATEVER DANGER WAITS BEHIND THE BECKONING DOOR--
READY OR NOT, GUNNER-- HERE I COME--!
CROSSBOW SHAFTS!! IT LOOKS LIKE GUNNER PLAYS FOR KEEPS!
IF HIS TIMING HAD BEEN A SPLIT-SECOND MORE PRECISE, HE'D HAVE HAD ME!
5

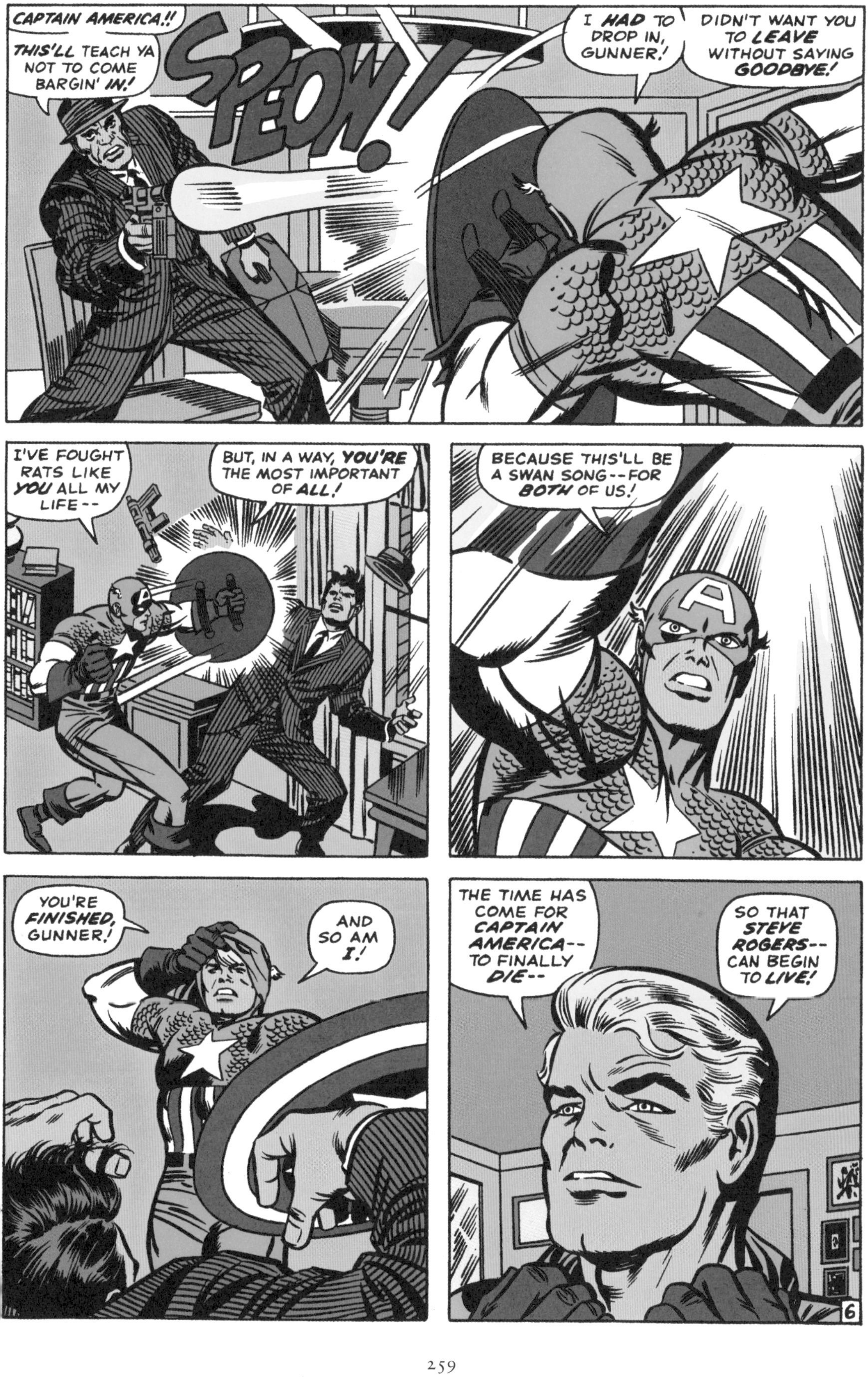
CAPTAIN AMERICA!!
THIS'LL TEACH YA NOT TO COME BARGIN' IN!
SPEOW!
I HAD TO DROP IN, GUNNER!
DIDN'T WANT YOU TO LEAVE WITHOUT SAYING GOODBYE!
I'VE FOUGHT RATS LIKE YOU ALL MY LIFE--
BUT, IN A WAY, YOU'RE THE MOST IMPORTANT OF ALL!
BECAUSE THIS'LL BE A SWAN SONG--FOR BOTH OF US!
YOU'RE FINISHED, GUNNER!
AND SO AM I!
THE TIME HAS COME FOR CAPTAIN AMERICA--TO FINALLY DIE--
SO THAT STEVE ROGERS--CAN BEGIN TO LIVE!
6

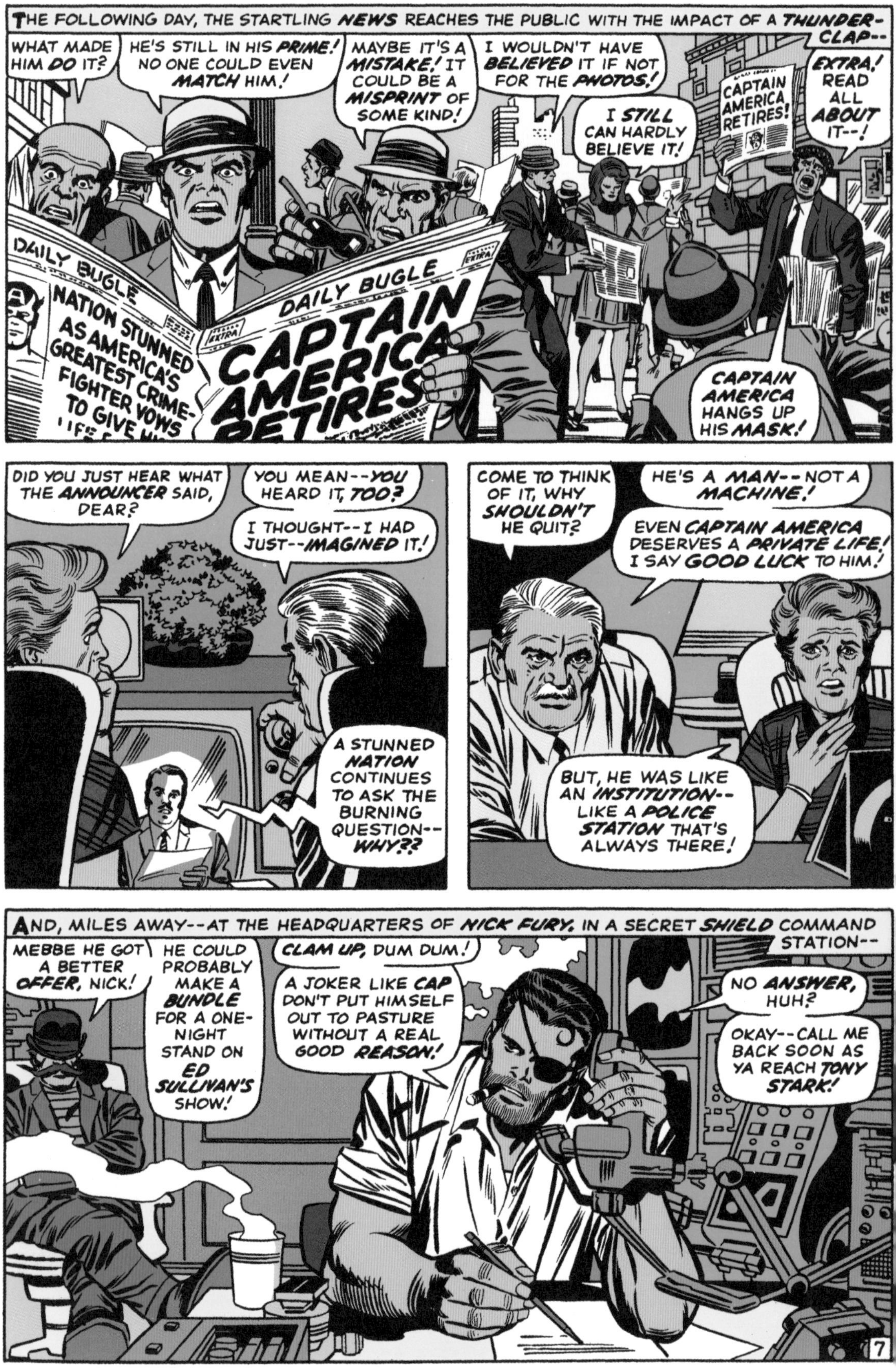

THE FOLLOWING DAY, THE STARTLING NEWS REACHES THE PUBLIC WITH THE IMPACT OF A THUNDER-CLAP--
WHAT MADE HIM DO IT?
HE'S STILL IN HIS PRIME! NO ONE COULD EVEN MATCH HIM!
MAYBE IT'S A MISTAKE! IT COULD BE A MISPRINT OF SOME KIND!
I WOULDN'T HAVE BELIEVED IT IF NOT FOR THE PHOTOS!
I STILL CAN HARDLY BELIEVE IT!
CAPTAIN AMERICA RETIRES!
EXTRA! READ ALL ABOUT IT--!
DAILY BUGLE
NATION STUNNED AS AMERICA'S GREATEST CRIME-FIGHTER VOWS TO GIVE
DAILY BUGLE
EXTRA
CAPTAIN AMERICA RETIRES
CAPTAIN AMERICA HANGS UP HIS MASK!
DID YOU JUST HEAR WHAT THE ANNOUNCER SAID, DEAR?
YOU MEAN--YOU HEARD IT, TOO?
I THOUGHT--I HAD JUST--IMAGINED IT!
A STUNNED NATION CONTINUES TO ASK THE BURNING QUESTION--WHY??
COME TO THINK OF IT, WHY SHOULDN'T HE QUIT?
HE'S A MAN--NOT A MACHINE!
EVEN CAPTAIN AMERICA DESERVES A PRIVATE LIFE! I SAY GOOD LUCK TO HIM!
BUT, HE WAS LIKE AN INSTITUTION--LIKE A POLICE STATION THAT'S ALWAYS THERE!
AND, MILES AWAY--AT THE HEADQUARTERS OF NICK FURY, IN A SECRET SHIELD COMMAND STATION--
MEBBE HE GOT A BETTER OFFER, NICK!
HE COULD PROBABLY MAKE A BUNDLE FOR A ONE-NIGHT STAND ON ED SULLIVAN'S SHOW!
CLAM UP, DUM DUM!
A JOKER LIKE CAP DON'T PUT HIMSELF OUT TO PASTURE WITHOUT A REAL GOOD REASON!
NO ANSWER, HUH?
OKAY--CALL ME BACK SOON AS YA REACH TONY STARK!
7

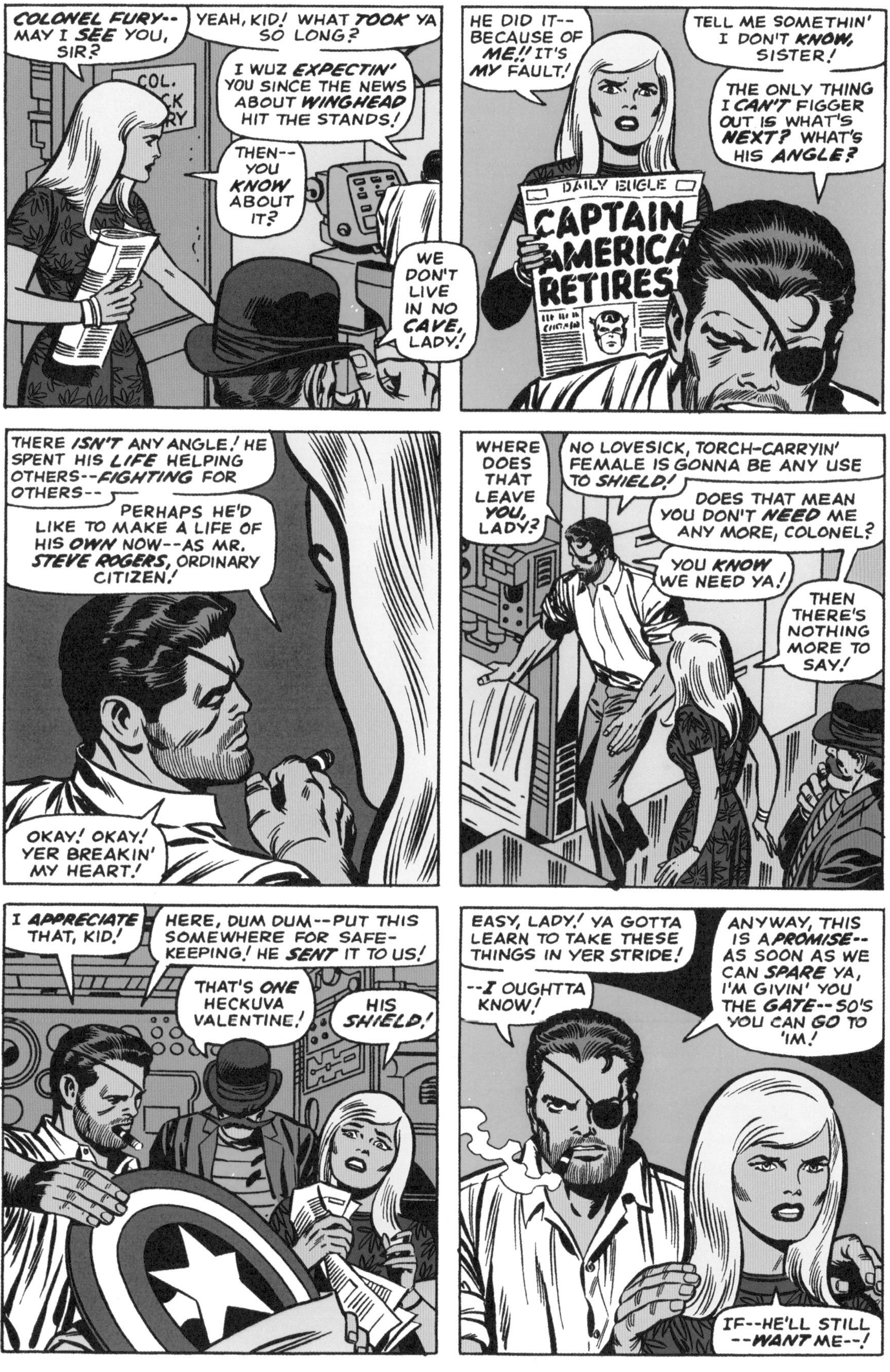

COLONEL FURY-- MAY I SEE YOU, SIR?
YEAH, KID! WHAT TOOK YA SO LONG?
I WUZ EXPECTIN' YOU SINCE THE NEWS ABOUT WINGHEAD HIT THE STANDS!
THEN-- YOU KNOW ABOUT IT?
WE DON'T LIVE IN NO CAVE, LADY!
HE DID IT-- BECAUSE OF ME!! IT'S MY FAULT!
TELL ME SOMETHIN' I DON'T KNOW, SISTER!
THE ONLY THING I CAN'T FIGGER OUT IS WHAT'S NEXT? WHAT'S HIS ANGLE?
DAILY BUGLE
CAPTAIN AMERICA RETIRES
THERE ISN'T ANY ANGLE! HE SPENT HIS LIFE HELPING OTHERS--FIGHTING FOR OTHERS--
PERHAPS HE'D LIKE TO MAKE A LIFE OF HIS OWN NOW--AS MR. STEVE ROGERS, ORDINARY CITIZEN!
OKAY! OKAY! YER BREAKIN' MY HEART!
WHERE DOES THAT LEAVE YOU, LADY?
NO LOVESICK, TORCH-CARRYIN' FEMALE IS GONNA BE ANY USE TO SHIELD!
DOES THAT MEAN YOU DON'T NEED ME ANY MORE, COLONEL?
YOU KNOW WE NEED YA!
THEN THERE'S NOTHING MORE TO SAY!
I APPRECIATE THAT, KID!
HERE, DUM DUM--PUT THIS SOMEWHERE FOR SAFE-KEEPING! HE SENT IT TO US!
THAT'S ONE HECKUVA VALENTINE!
HIS SHIELD!
EASY, LADY! YA GOTTA LEARN TO TAKE THESE THINGS IN YER STRIDE!
--I OUGHTTA KNOW!
ANYWAY, THIS IS A PROMISE-- AS SOON AS WE CAN SPARE YA, I'M GIVIN' YOU THE GATE--SO'S YOU CAN GO TO 'IM!
IF--HE'LL STILL --WANT ME--!

WHILE BACK AT THE MANSION OF PLAYBOY MILLIONAIRE, *TONY STARK*--

BY *NOW*, ANYONE WHO CAN *READ* KNOWS THAT *STEVE ROGERS* AND *CAPTAIN AMERICA* ARE ONE AND THE SAME!

ARE YOU *SURE* YOU'RE DOING THE RIGHT THING? HAVE YOU THOUGHT IT ALL *OUT*?

WHY *NOT*, STARK? WHY KEEP A SECRET IF THERE'S NO *REASON* FOR IT?

I WORRIED ABOUT THE *RIGHT THING* ALL MY LIFE!

FROM NOW ON-- I COULDN'T CARE *LESS*!

BE SURE TO GIVE ME TWO DEEP *VENTS* IN THE JACKET, FRIEND!

HOW WILL THE *AVENGERS* TAKE IT WHEN THEY CONVENE?

THEY'LL SURVIVE! THEY'VE GOT ENOUGH MEMBERS *NOW* TO START A *COLONY*!

OF COURSE, I'M NOT SAYING I WON'T *MISS* THEM--OR YOU--!

YOU'VE BEEN A GOOD *FRIEND*, STARK! I'LL ALWAYS BE GRATEFUL!

IT'S TOO BAD *YOU* COULDN'T HAVE BEEN AN *AVENGER*! BUT, YOU HELPED IN THE ONLY WAY YOU *COULD*--

--WITH YOUR *MONEY*!

YES--I HELPED --THE BEST I *COULD*!

IN A WAY, I CAN EVEN *UNDERSTAND* WHAT YOU'RE DOING, STEVE!

SOONER OR LATER, *EACH* OF US MUST REACH A *TURNING POINT* IN OUR LIVES!

GOODBYE, OLD FRIEND--IT'S TIME FOR *CAPTAIN AMERICA* TO LEARN WHO *STEVE ROGERS* REALLY IS!

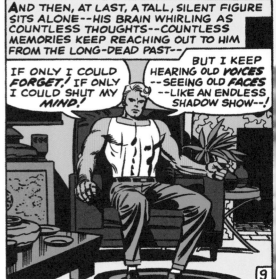

AND THEN, AT LAST, A TALL, SILENT FIGURE SITS ALONE--HIS BRAIN WHIRLING AS COUNTLESS THOUGHTS--COUNTLESS MEMORIES KEEP REACHING OUT TO HIM FROM THE LONG-DEAD PAST--

IF ONLY I COULD *FORGET*! IF ONLY I COULD SHUT MY *MIND*!

BUT I KEEP HEARING OLD *VOICES* --SEEING OLD *FACES* --LIKE AN ENDLESS SHADOW SHOW--!

9

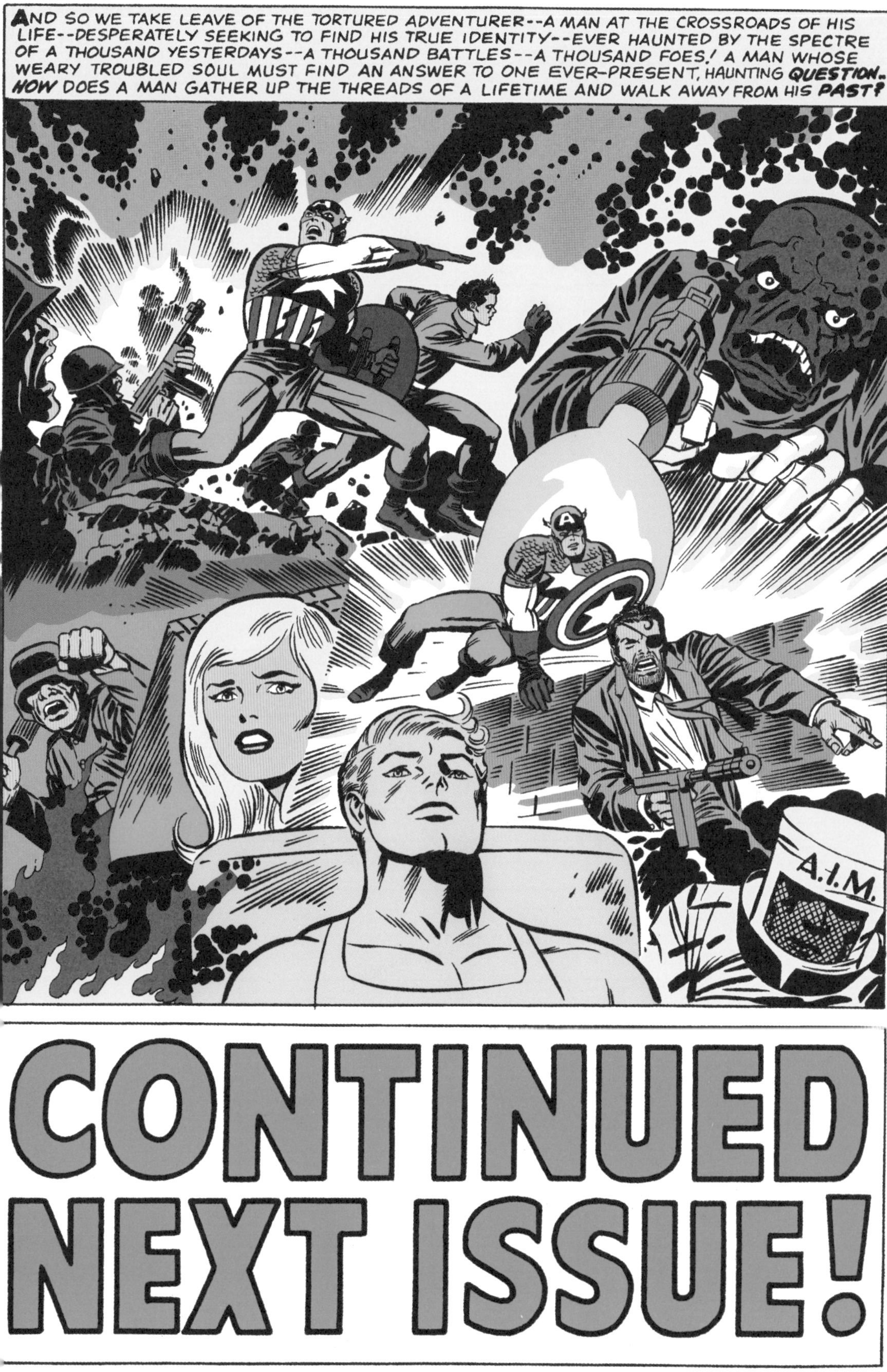
AND SO WE TAKE LEAVE OF THE TORTURED ADVENTURER--A MAN AT THE CROSSROADS OF HIS LIFE--DESPERATELY SEEKING TO FIND HIS TRUE IDENTITY--EVER HAUNTED BY THE SPECTRE OF A THOUSAND YESTERDAYS--A THOUSAND BATTLES--A THOUSAND FOES! A MAN WHOSE WEARY TROUBLED SOUL MUST FIND AN ANSWER TO ONE EVER-PRESENT, HAUNTING **QUESTION**.. **HOW** DOES A MAN GATHER UP THE THREADS OF A LIFETIME AND WALK AWAY FROM HIS **PAST?**
A.I.M.
CONTINUED NEXT ISSUE!

OLD FOES RETURN:
TALES OF SUSPENSE #96–99,
CAPTAIN AMERICA #100–109

Cap's "retirement" in #95 does not last long; in fact, he decides to pick up his shield again at the end of #96. But the psychological conflict that drove him to consider retirement in the first place—his desire to "gather up the threads of a lifetime and walk away from his past"—remained unresolved. Over the next year, Cap would continue to find himself flashing back at inconvenient moments to the traumas of war and the events of Bucky's death, while caught up in battles with old foes from the past such as Baron Zemo and the Red Skull.

Issues #97–99 are notable for the first team-up between Cap and the Black Panther (also the first appearance of the Panther since his debut in the pages of The Fantastic Four in 1966). Unfortunately, Joe Sinnott rotated off the book one episode into this storyline, to be replaced by Syd Shores—a competent professional whose years of experience with the character went back to the 1940s, but whose heavy brushwork sometimes obscured the details of Kirby's pencils.

With #100, the title of the series changed from Tales of Suspense to Captain America; readers would now enjoy a book-length Cap adventure every month (as would fans of Iron Man, who was also given a new title of his own). This move was obviously a sign of Marvel's continued success on the newsstands, but the relationships between the key creators who had propelled that success were becoming strained. According to numerous accounts, Kirby was dissatisfied; he was also increasingly embittered over Lee's growing celebrity, feeling that his own vital role in co-creating the Marvel Universe was not as widely recognized.[1]

Not yet ready to quit the company, Kirby decided to recycle older concepts rather than give away new ideas. Consequently, the next few months saw the return (again) of the Red Skull with a Sleeper robot; another battle with Batroc the Leaper; another issue exploring Cap's guilt over Bucky's death; an appearance by the Trapster (a villain Kirby had first created with Lee in the pages of The Fantastic Four); and yet another retelling of Cap's origin (the fourth since the character's resurrection in 1963).

The standard of execution remained high; despite Shores's sometimes muddy inking, the pencils from any issue during this period are consummate examples of Kirby's mature style, and Lee's talent for melodrama remained undiminished. The story exploring Cap's survivor guilt included a nightmare scene with perhaps the most terrifying spectral vision of Bucky to date.

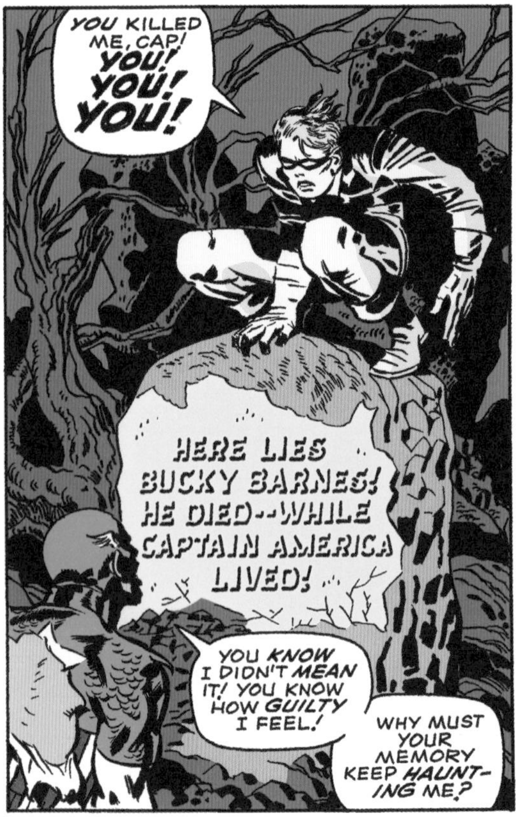
YOU KILLED ME, CAP! YOU! YOU! YOU!
HERE LIES BUCKY BARNES! HE DIED--WHILE CAPTAIN AMERICA LIVED!
YOU KNOW I DIDN'T MEAN IT! YOU KNOW HOW GUILTY I FEEL!
WHY MUST YOUR MEMORY KEEP HAUNTING ME?

The retelling of Cap's origin was also notable for providing (for the first time) some perspective on Steve Rogers's thoughts and motivations *prior* to the experiment that changes him into a super hero.

Nevertheless, the series was in danger of becoming trapped within the dramatic formula that Lee and Kirby had established, in which Cap would start to seem more at home in the world of the present, only to find himself dragged down once again by the ghosts of the past. Kirby wanted to move on, and Lee knew that he could not be replaced by just anyone. He turned for help to a man who was, at the time, one of the biggest stars of the field—Jim Steranko.

CAPTAIN AMERICA #110,

FEBRUARY 1969,

"THE HERO THAT WAS!"

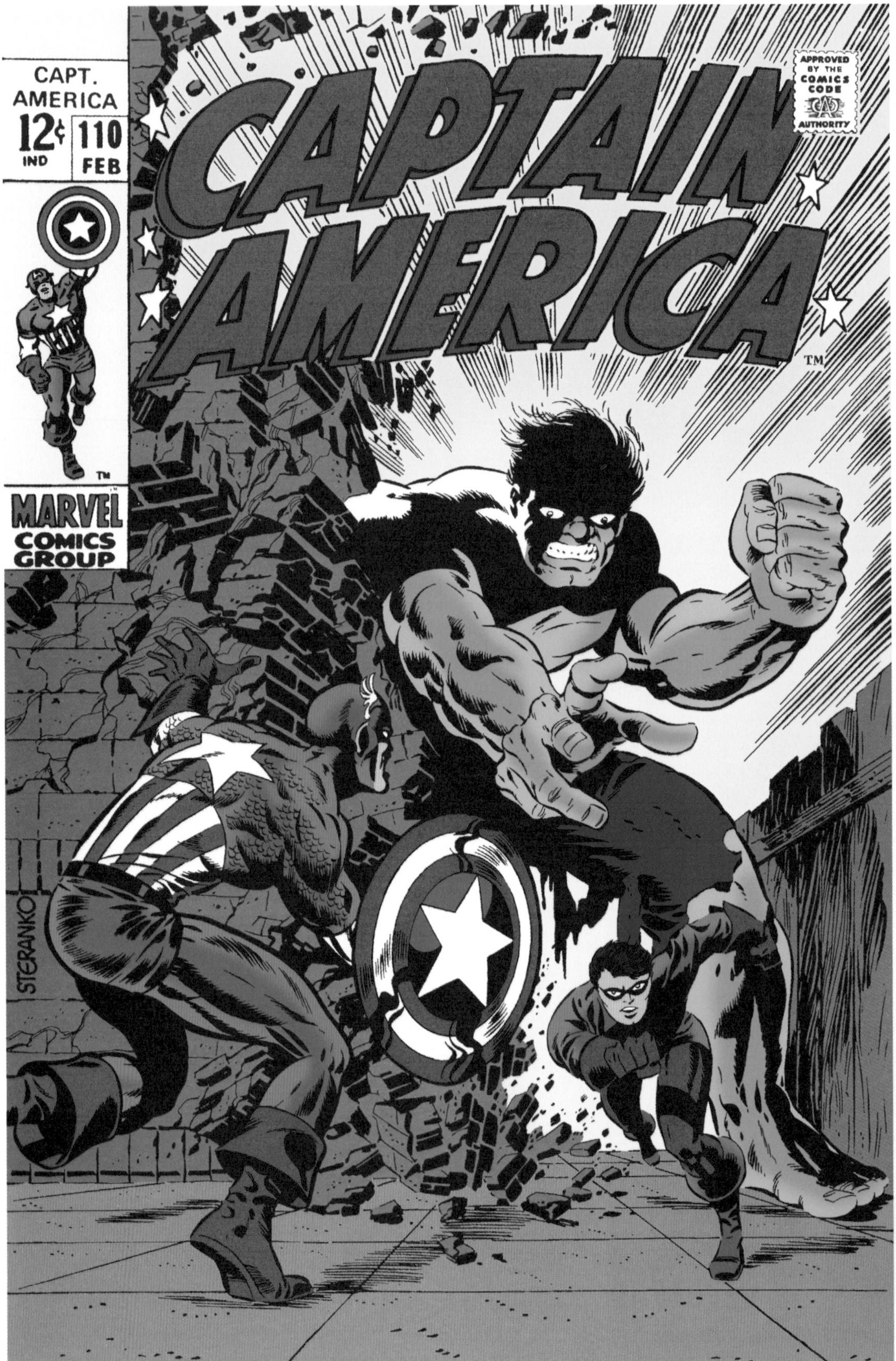
CAPT.
AMERICA
12¢ IND
110 FEB
APPROVED BY THE COMICS CODE AUTHORITY
CAPTAIN AMERICA
MARVEL COMICS GROUP
STERANKO

SLOWLY, FALTER-INGLY, HE WALKS THRU THE NIGHT...

A LONE, SILENT FIGURE...HAUNTED BY THE PAST...

PLAGUED BY MEMO-RIES SUCH AS FEW HAVE EVER KNOWN...

EVER TORTURED BY DOUBT...YET DRIVEN BY DUTY...

AND NOW HE STANDS BEFORE US...THIS MAN STEVE ROGERS!

STAN LEE-STERANKO
ASSOCIATION UNLIMITED
PRESENT...

NO LONGER ALONE!

IN PERSON!

JOE SINNOTT, INKER WAS HERE

BENEFIT PERFO

LETTERED BY:
SAM ROSEN

269

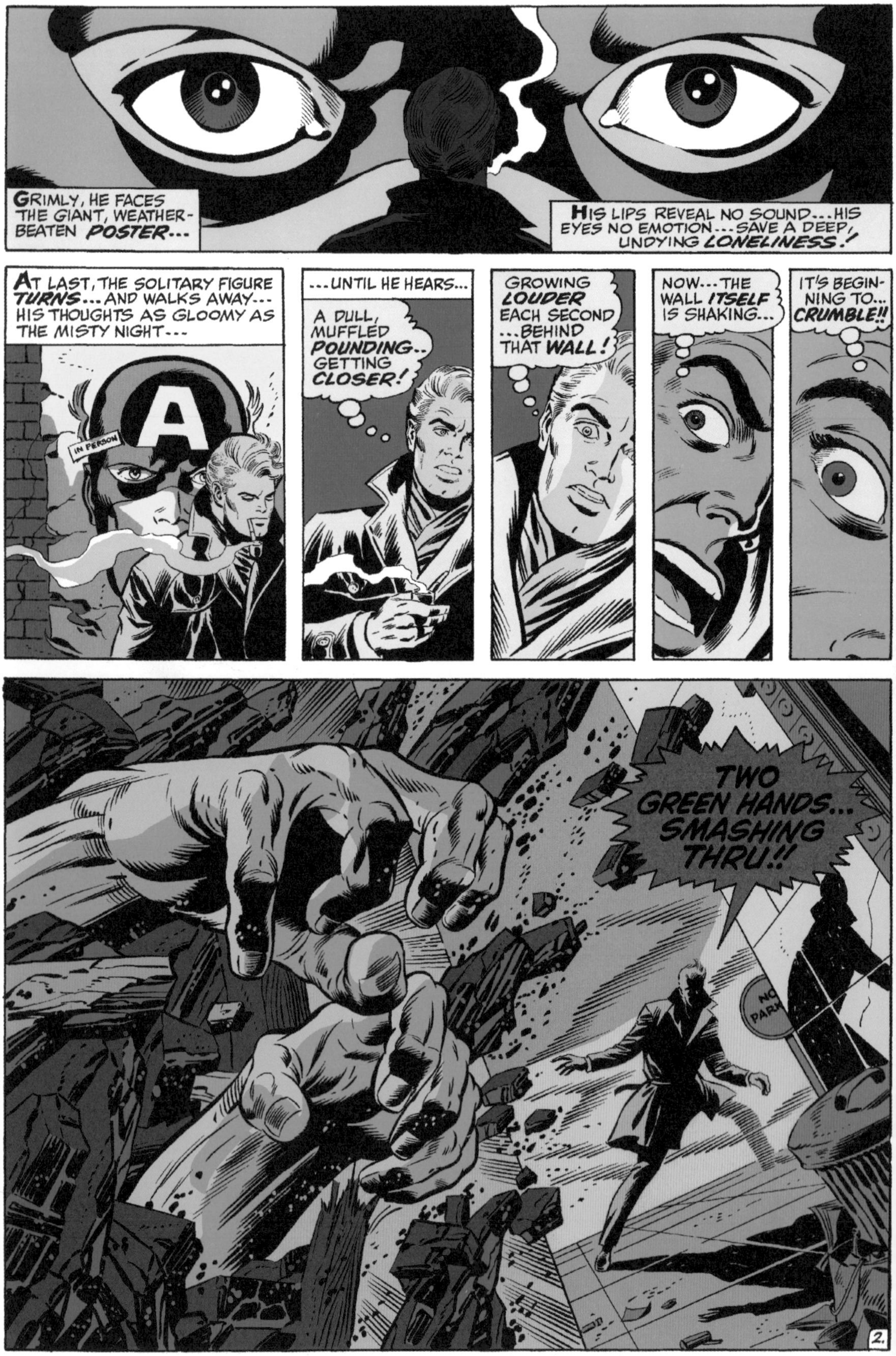
GRIMLY, HE FACES THE GIANT, WEATHER-BEATEN POSTER...
HIS LIPS REVEAL NO SOUND...HIS EYES NO EMOTION...SAVE A DEEP, UNDYING LONELINESS!
AT LAST, THE SOLITARY FIGURE TURNS...AND WALKS AWAY...HIS THOUGHTS AS GLOOMY AS THE MISTY NIGHT---
IN PERSON
...UNTIL HE HEARS...
A DULL, MUFFLED POUNDING.. GETTING CLOSER!
GROWING LOUDER EACH SECOND ...BEHIND THAT WALL!
NOW...THE WALL ITSELF IS SHAKING...
IT'S BEGINNING TO...CRUMBLE!!
TWO GREEN HANDS... SMASHING THRU!!
2.

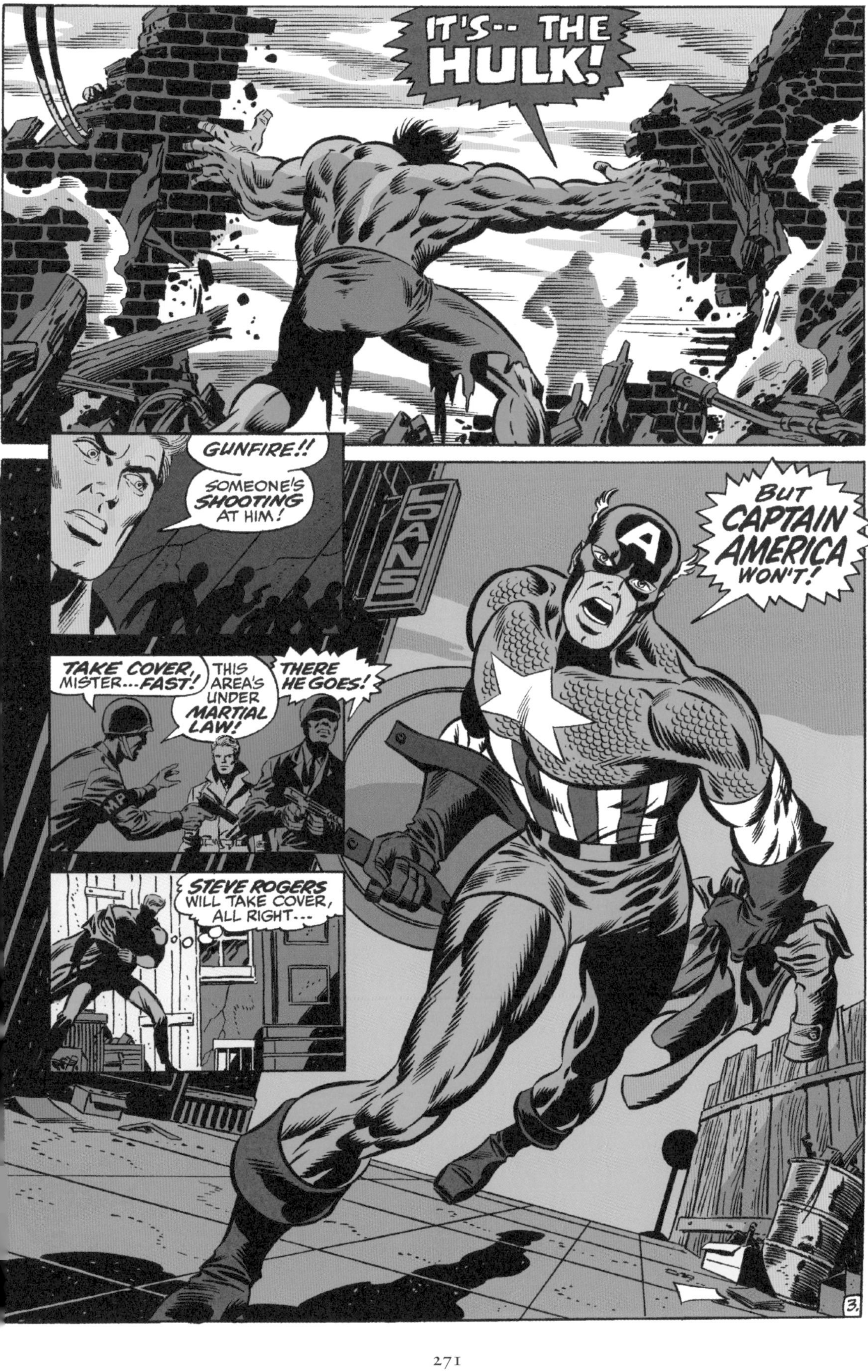
IT'S-- THE HULK!
GUNFIRE!!
SOMEONE'S SHOOTING AT HIM!
TAKE COVER, MISTER...FAST!
THIS AREA'S UNDER MARTIAL LAW!
THERE HE GOES!
STEVE ROGERS WILL TAKE COVER, ALL RIGHT--
LOANS
BUT CAPTAIN AMERICA WON'T!
3.

AND, EVEN AS THE STAR-SPANGLED *AVENGER* ATTEMPTS TO LOCATE THE SWIFTLY LUMBERING, GREEN-SKINNED TITAN...

SOLDIERS!! ALL AROUND ME!!

BRINGING UP *BIG GUN*.!.!

TRYING TO KILL HULK!

SET FOR *MINIMUM RANGE*... *MAXIMUM VELOCITY!*

AT MY COMMAND... *PREPARE TO FIRE!*

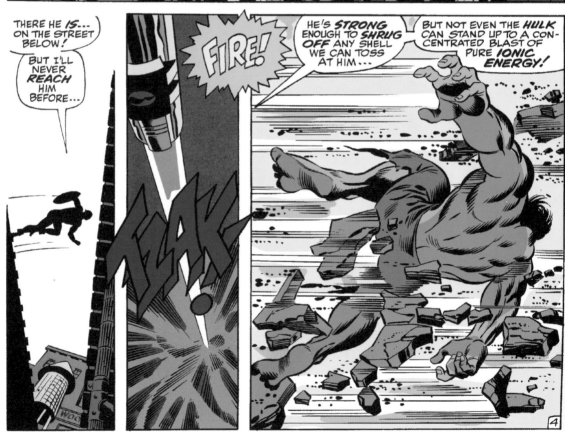

THERE HE *IS*... ON THE STREET BELOW!

BUT I'LL NEVER *REACH* HIM BEFORE...

FIRE!

HE'S *STRONG* ENOUGH TO *SHRUG OFF* ANY SHELL WE CAN TOSS AT HIM...

BUT NOT EVEN THE *HULK* CAN STAND UP TO A CONCENTRATED BLAST OF PURE *IONIC ENERGY!*

FLAK

4

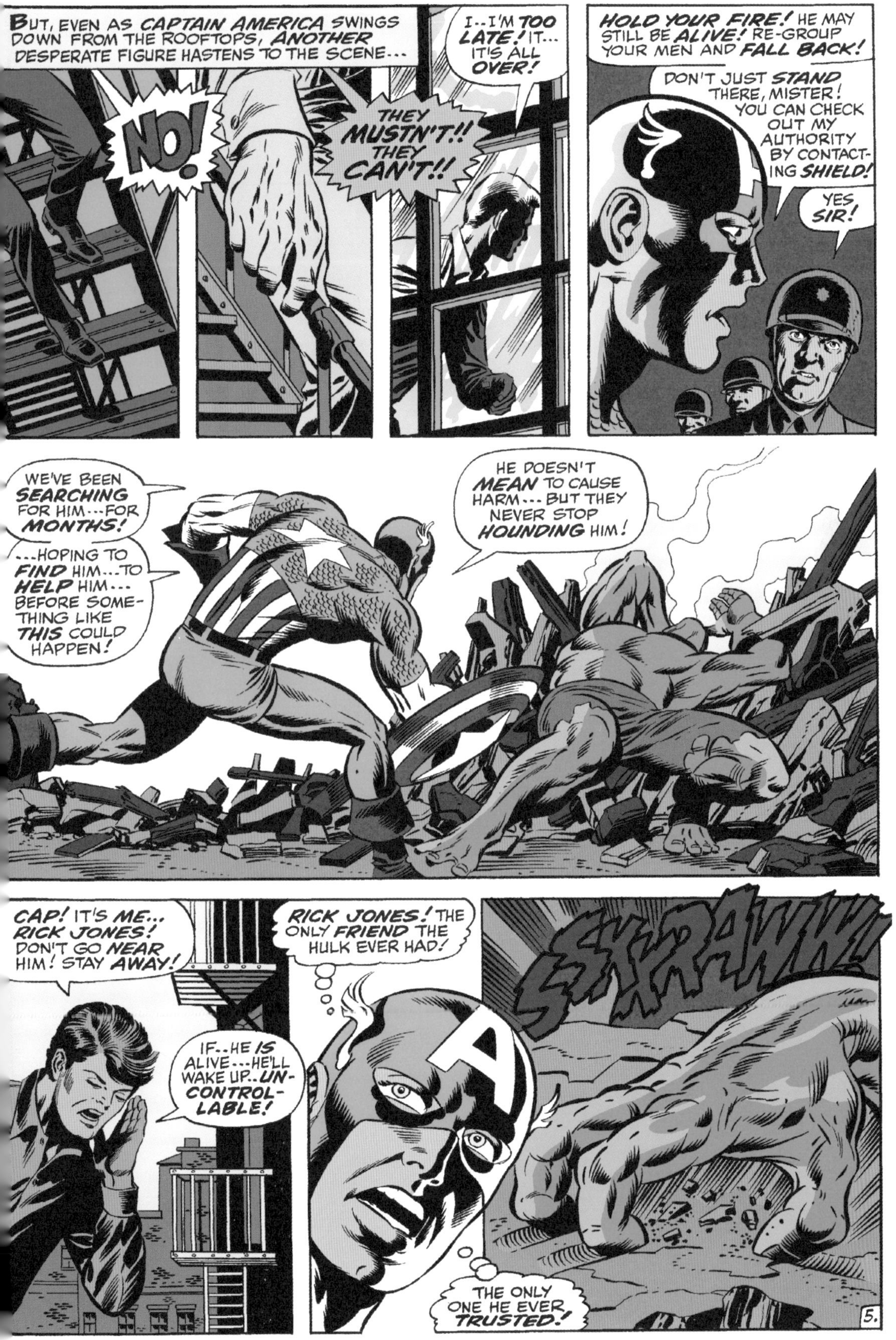
BUT, EVEN AS CAPTAIN AMERICA SWINGS DOWN FROM THE ROOFTOPS, ANOTHER DESPERATE FIGURE HASTENS TO THE SCENE...
NO!
THEY MUSTN'T!! THEY CAN'T!!
I..I'M TOO LATE! IT... IT'S ALL OVER!
HOLD YOUR FIRE! HE MAY STILL BE ALIVE! RE-GROUP YOUR MEN AND FALL BACK!
DON'T JUST STAND THERE, MISTER! YOU CAN CHECK OUT MY AUTHORITY BY CONTACTING SHIELD!
YES SIR!
WE'VE BEEN SEARCHING FOR HIM...FOR MONTHS!
...HOPING TO FIND HIM...TO HELP HIM... BEFORE SOMETHING LIKE THIS COULD HAPPEN!
HE DOESN'T MEAN TO CAUSE HARM... BUT THEY NEVER STOP HOUNDING HIM!
CAP! IT'S ME... RICK JONES! DON'T GO NEAR HIM! STAY AWAY!
IF..HE IS ALIVE...HE'LL WAKE UP..UNCONTROLLABLE!
RICK JONES! THE ONLY FRIEND THE HULK EVER HAD!
THE ONLY ONE HE EVER TRUSTED!
SKRAWK!
5.

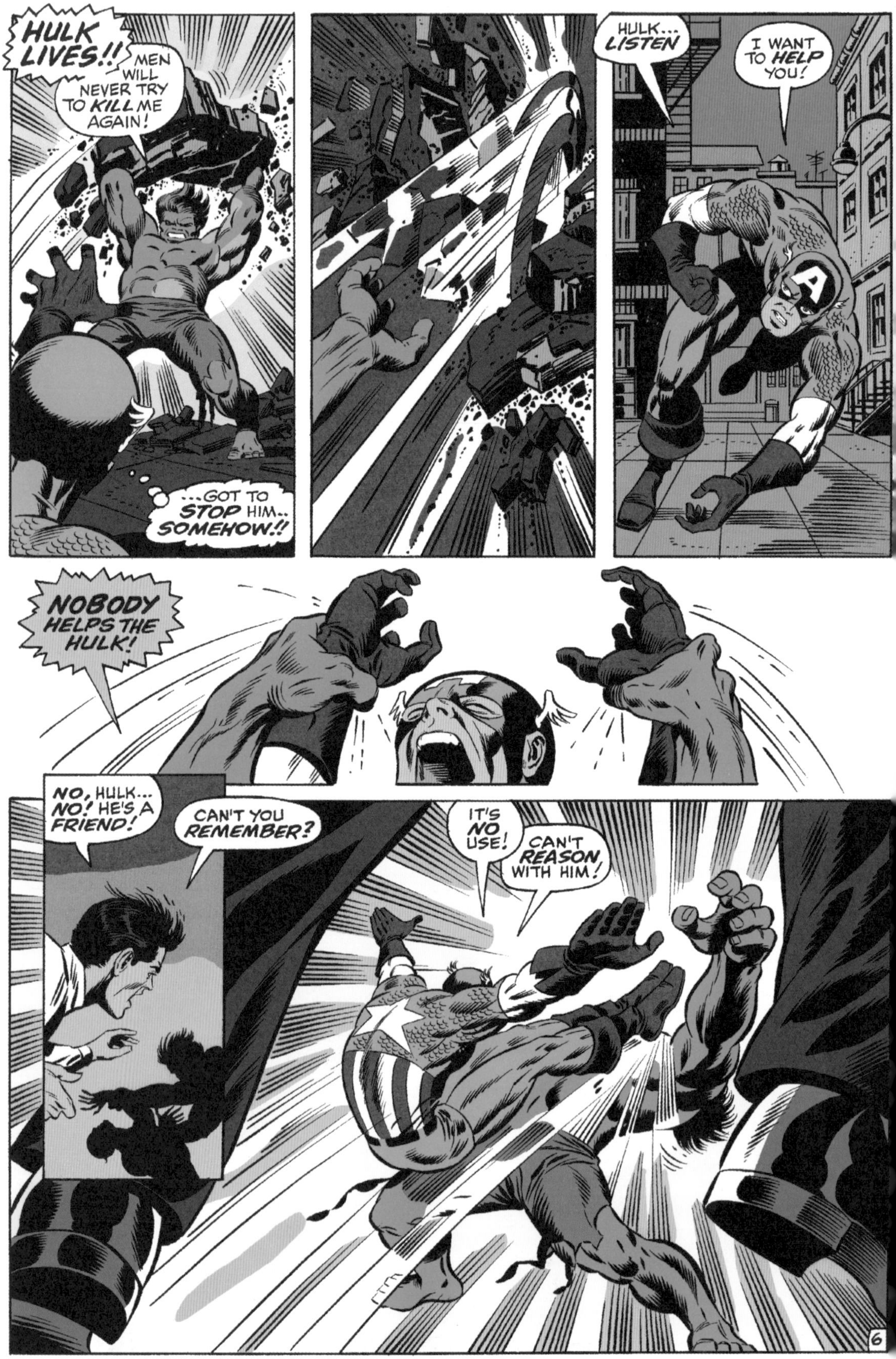
HULK LIVES!!
MEN WILL NEVER TRY TO KILL ME AGAIN!
...GOT TO STOP HIM.. SOMEHOW!!
HULK... LISTEN
I WANT TO HELP YOU!
NOBODY HELPS THE HULK!
NO, HULK... NO! HE'S A FRIEND!
CAN'T YOU REMEMBER?
IT'S NO USE!
CAN'T REASON WITH HIM!
6

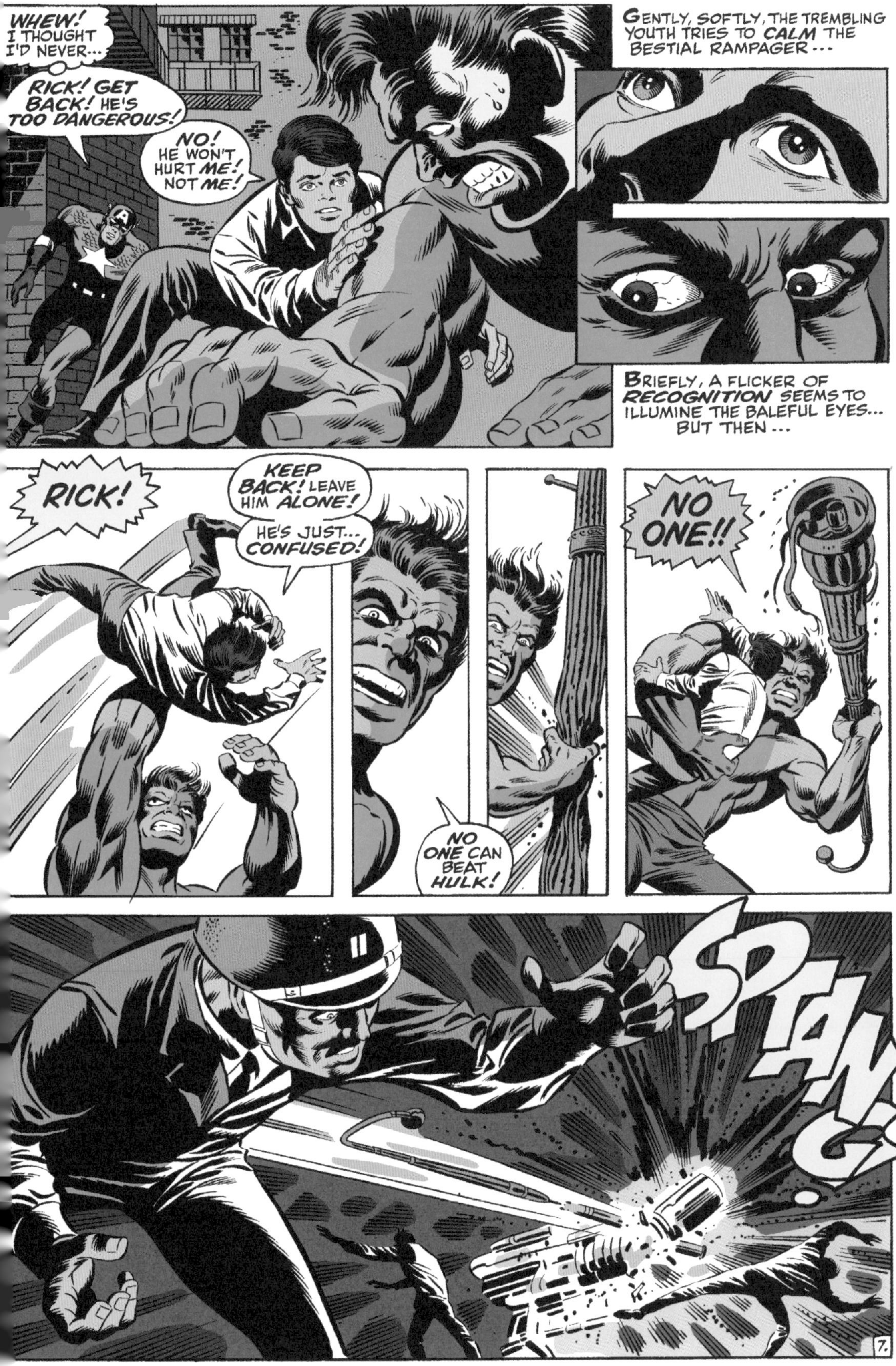
WHEW! I THOUGHT I'D NEVER...
RICK! GET BACK! HE'S TOO DANGEROUS!
NO! HE WON'T HURT ME! NOT ME!
GENTLY, SOFTLY, THE TREMBLING YOUTH TRIES TO CALM THE BESTIAL RAMPAGER...
BRIEFLY, A FLICKER OF RECOGNITION SEEMS TO ILLUMINE THE BALEFUL EYES... BUT THEN...
RICK!
KEEP BACK! LEAVE HIM ALONE!
HE'S JUST... CONFUSED!
NO ONE CAN BEAT HULK!
NO ONE!!
SPTANG
7.

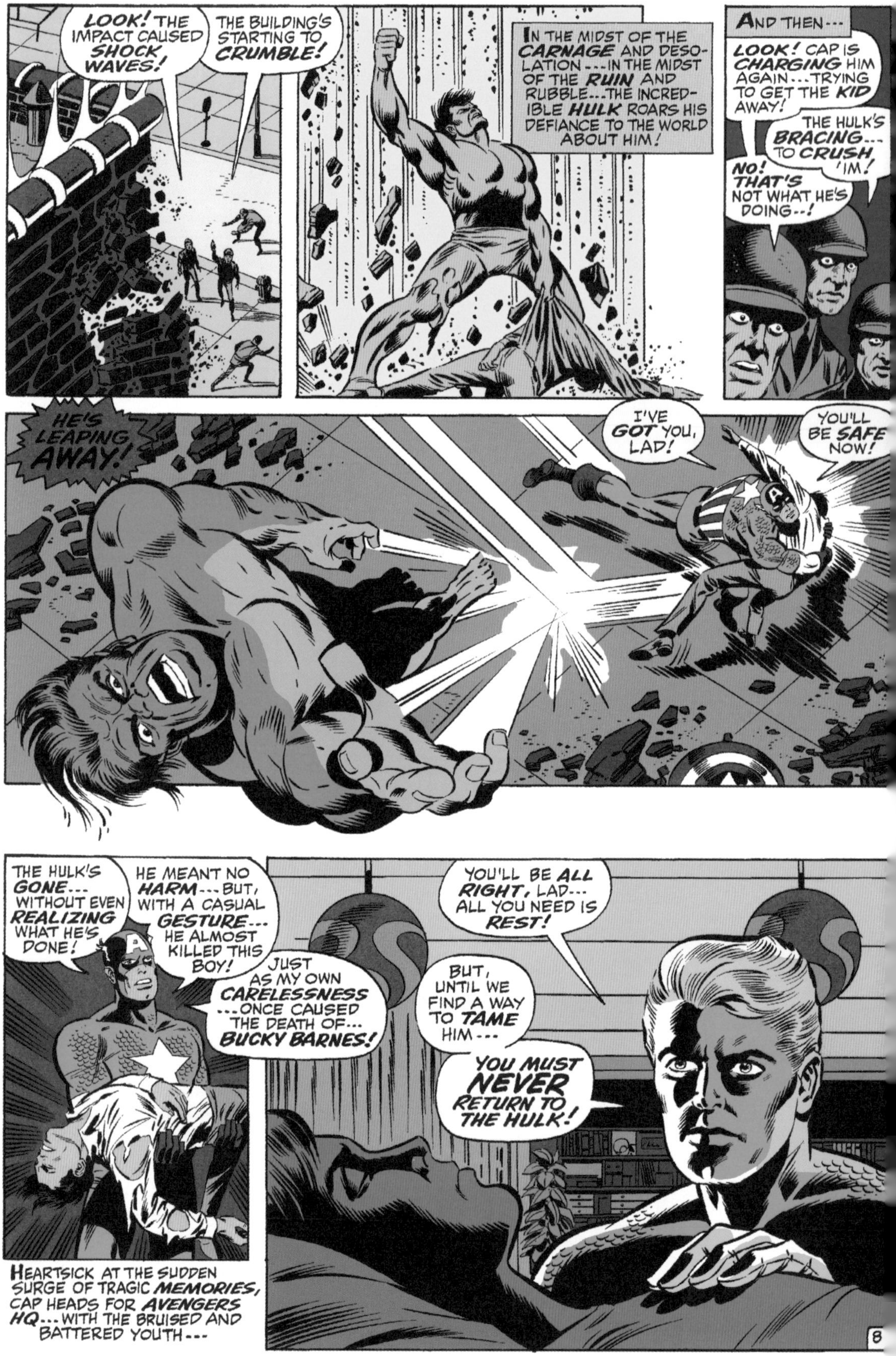
LOOK! THE IMPACT CAUSED SHOCK WAVES!
THE BUILDING'S STARTING TO CRUMBLE!
IN THE MIDST OF THE CARNAGE AND DESOLATION --- IN THE MIDST OF THE RUIN AND RUBBLE --- THE INCREDIBLE HULK ROARS HIS DEFIANCE TO THE WORLD ABOUT HIM!
AND THEN ---
LOOK! CAP IS CHARGING HIM AGAIN --- TRYING TO GET THE KID AWAY!
THE HULK'S BRACING --- TO CRUSH 'IM!
NO! THAT'S NOT WHAT HE'S DOING --!
HE'S LEAPING AWAY!
I'VE GOT YOU, LAD!
YOU'LL BE SAFE NOW!
THE HULK'S GONE --- WITHOUT EVEN REALIZING WHAT HE'S DONE!
HE MEANT NO HARM --- BUT, WITH A CASUAL GESTURE --- HE ALMOST KILLED THIS BOY!
JUST AS MY OWN CARELESSNESS --- ONCE CAUSED THE DEATH OF --- BUCKY BARNES!
HEARTSICK AT THE SUDDEN SURGE OF TRAGIC MEMORIES, CAP HEADS FOR AVENGERS HQ --- WITH THE BRUISED AND BATTERED YOUTH ---
YOU'LL BE ALL RIGHT, LAD --- ALL YOU NEED IS REST!
BUT, UNTIL WE FIND A WAY TO TAME HIM ---
YOU MUST NEVER RETURN TO THE HULK!
8

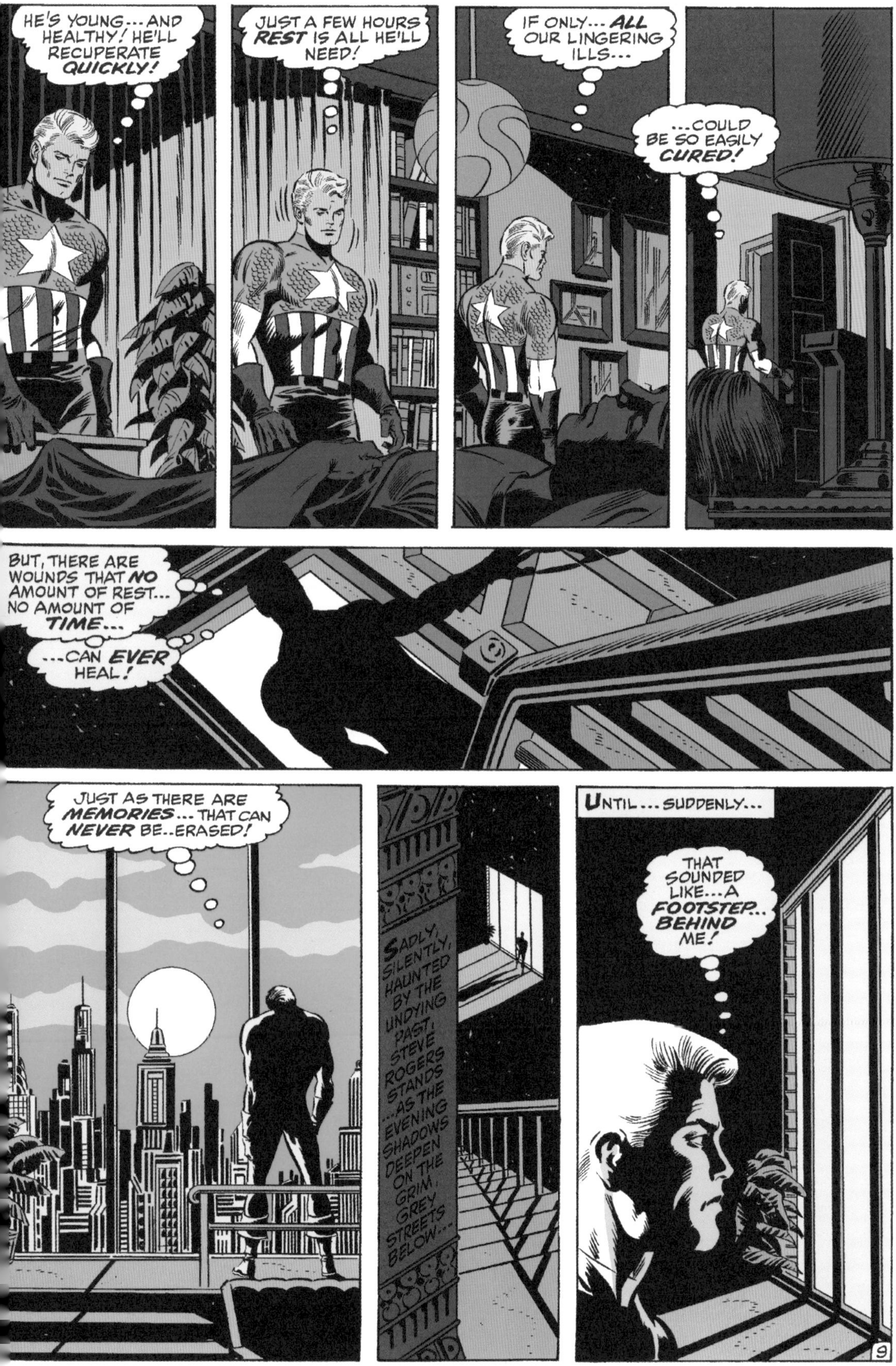
HE'S YOUNG... AND HEALTHY! HE'LL RECUPERATE QUICKLY!
JUST A FEW HOURS REST IS ALL HE'LL NEED!
IF ONLY... ALL OUR LINGERING ILLS...
...COULD BE SO EASILY CURED!
BUT, THERE ARE WOUNDS THAT NO AMOUNT OF REST... NO AMOUNT OF TIME...
...CAN EVER HEAL!
JUST AS THERE ARE MEMORIES... THAT CAN NEVER BE..ERASED!
SADLY, SILENTLY, HAUNTED BY THE UNDYING PAST, STEVE ROGERS STANDS ...AS THE EVENING SHADOWS DEEPEN ON THE GRIM, GREY STREETS BELOW...
UNTIL... SUDDENLY...
THAT SOUNDED LIKE...A FOOTSTEP... BEHIND ME!
9

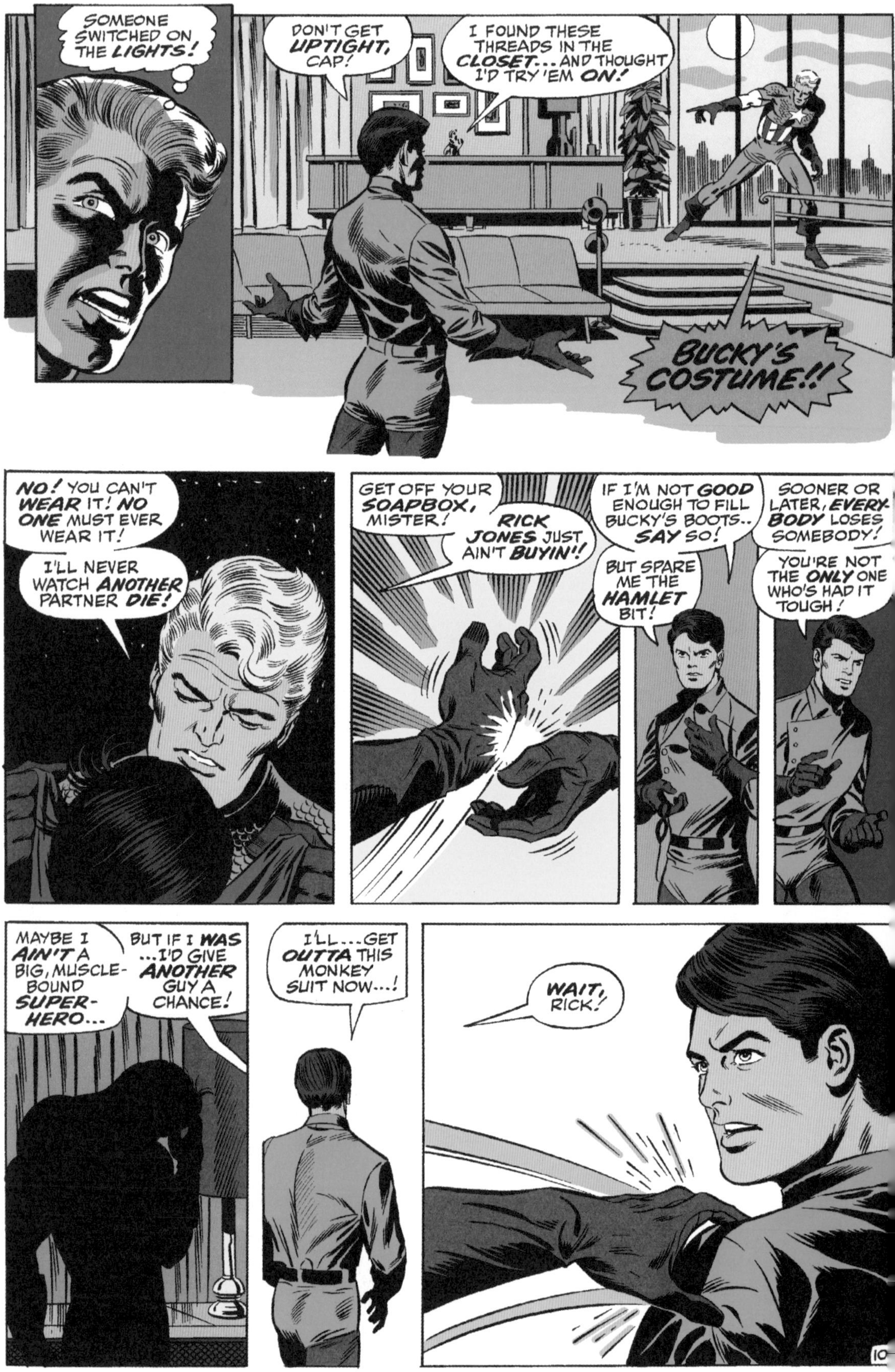

SOMEONE SWITCHED ON THE LIGHTS!
DON'T GET UPTIGHT, CAP!
I FOUND THESE THREADS IN THE CLOSET... AND THOUGHT I'D TRY 'EM ON!
BUCKY'S COSTUME!!
NO! YOU CAN'T WEAR IT! NO ONE MUST EVER WEAR IT!
I'LL NEVER WATCH ANOTHER PARTNER DIE!
GET OFF YOUR SOAPBOX, MISTER!
RICK JONES JUST AIN'T BUYIN'!
IF I'M NOT GOOD ENOUGH TO FILL BUCKY'S BOOTS.. SAY SO!
BUT SPARE ME THE HAMLET BIT!
SOONER OR LATER, EVERYBODY LOSES SOMEBODY!
YOU'RE NOT THE ONLY ONE WHO'S HAD IT TOUGH!
MAYBE I AIN'T A BIG, MUSCLE-BOUND SUPER-HERO...
BUT IF I WAS ...I'D GIVE ANOTHER GUY A CHANCE!
I'LL...GET OUTTA THIS MONKEY SUIT NOW...!
WAIT, RICK!
10

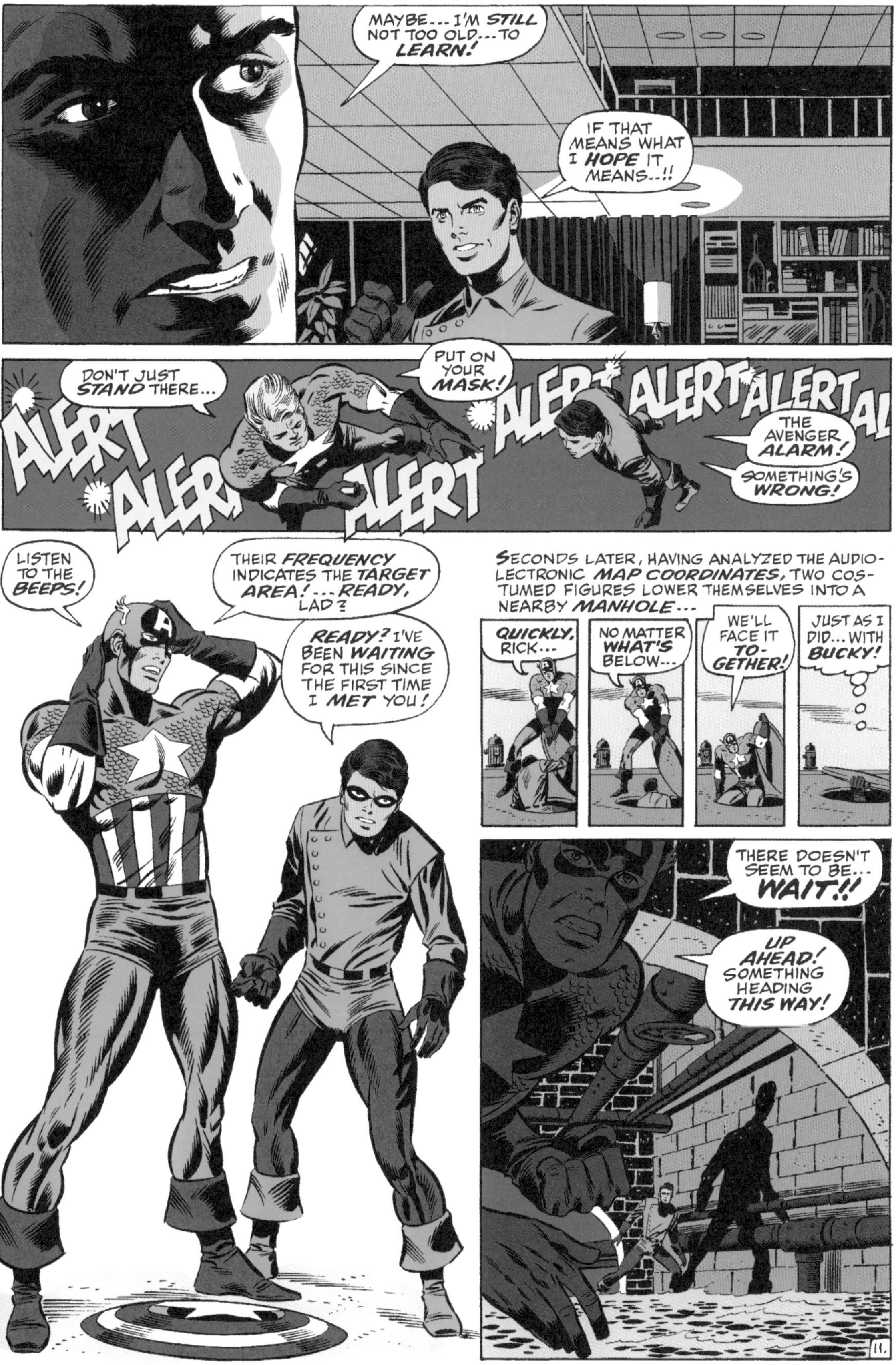

MAYBE... I'M STILL NOT TOO OLD... TO LEARN!
IF THAT MEANS WHAT I HOPE IT MEANS--!!
DON'T JUST STAND THERE...
PUT ON YOUR MASK!
ALERT ALERT ALERT ALERT ALERT ALERT
THE AVENGER ALARM!
SOMETHING'S WRONG!
LISTEN TO THE BEEPS!
THEIR FREQUENCY INDICATES THE TARGET AREA!... READY, LAD?
READY? I'VE BEEN WAITING FOR THIS SINCE THE FIRST TIME I MET YOU!
SECONDS LATER, HAVING ANALYZED THE AUDIO-LECTRONIC MAP COORDINATES, TWO COSTUMED FIGURES LOWER THEMSELVES INTO A NEARBY MANHOLE...
QUICKLY, RICK...
NO MATTER WHAT'S BELOW...
WE'LL FACE IT TO-GETHER!
JUST AS I DID... WITH BUCKY!
THERE DOESN'T SEEM TO BE... WAIT!!
UP AHEAD! SOMETHING HEADING THIS WAY!
11.

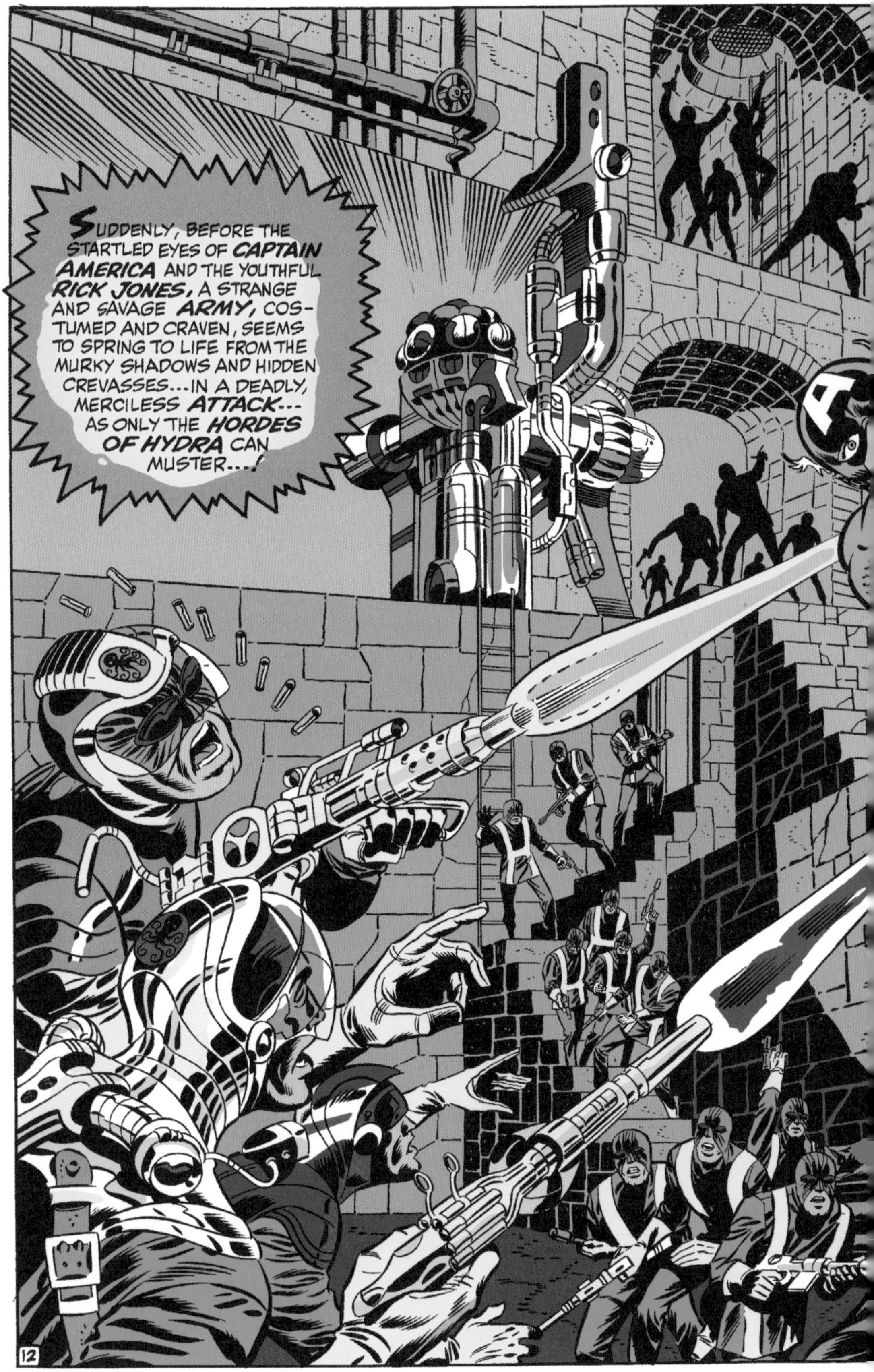
SUDDENLY, BEFORE THE STARTLED EYES OF CAPTAIN AMERICA AND THE YOUTHFUL RICK JONES, A STRANGE AND SAVAGE ARMY, COSTUMED AND CRAVEN, SEEMS TO SPRING TO LIFE FROM THE MURKY SHADOWS AND HIDDEN CREVASSES...IN A DEADLY, MERCILESS ATTACK... AS ONLY THE HORDES OF HYDRA CAN MUSTER...!
12

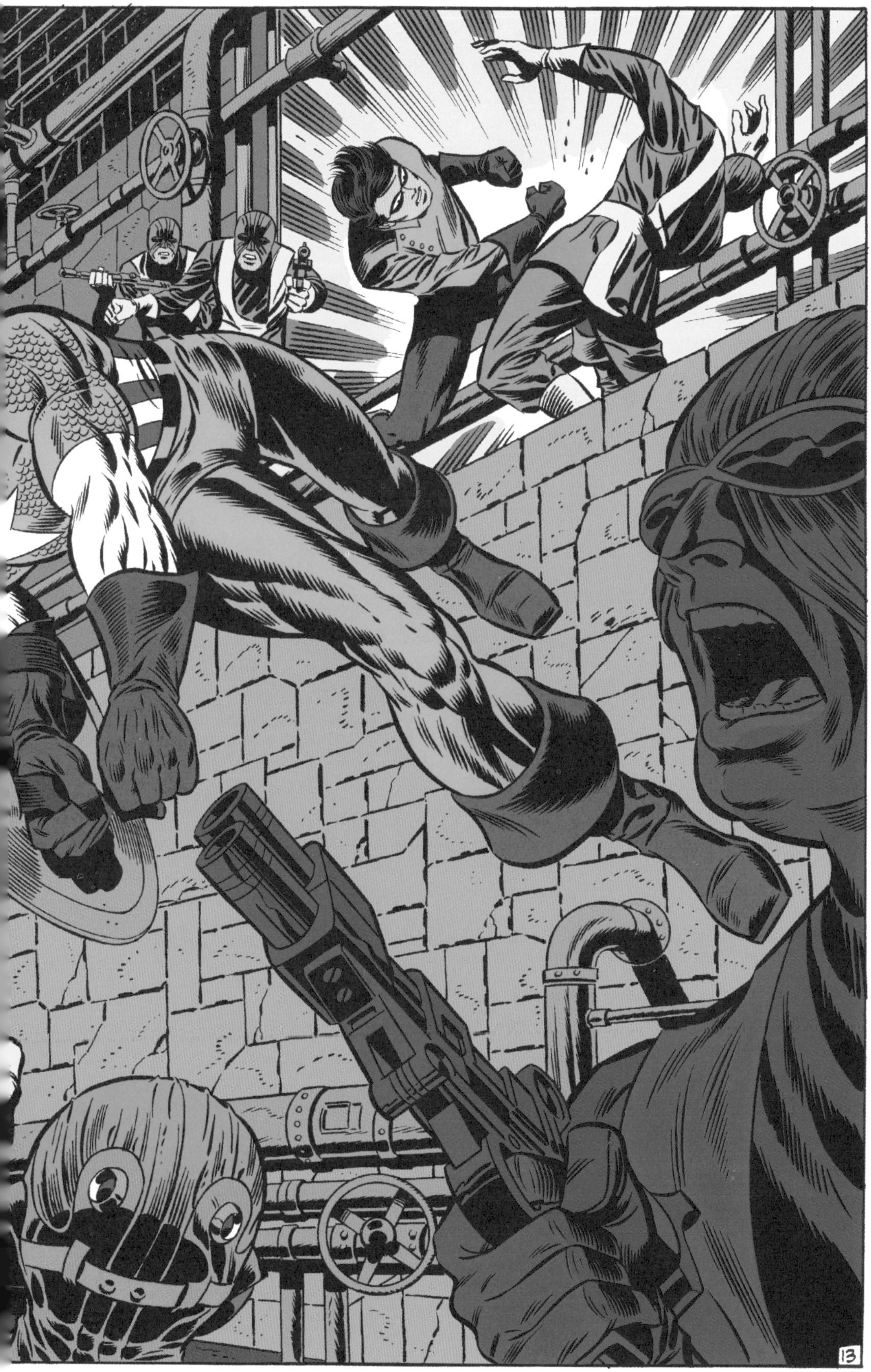
13

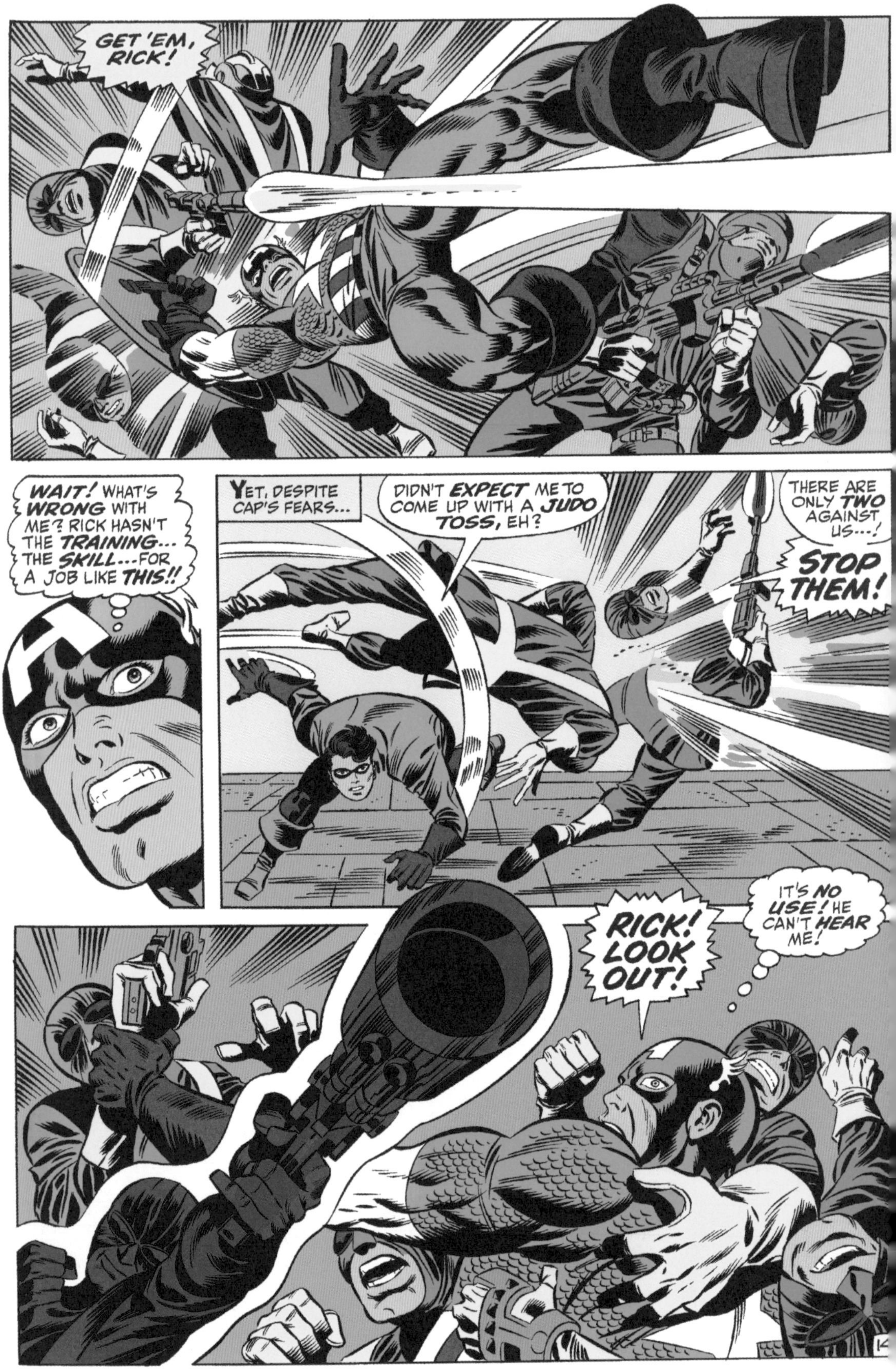
GET 'EM, RICK!
WAIT! WHAT'S WRONG WITH ME? RICK HASN'T THE TRAINING... THE SKILL...FOR A JOB LIKE THIS!!
YET, DESPITE CAP'S FEARS...
DIDN'T EXPECT ME TO COME UP WITH A JUDO TOSS, EH?
THERE ARE ONLY TWO AGAINST US...!
STOP THEM!
RICK! LOOK OUT!
IT'S NO USE! HE CAN'T HEAR ME!

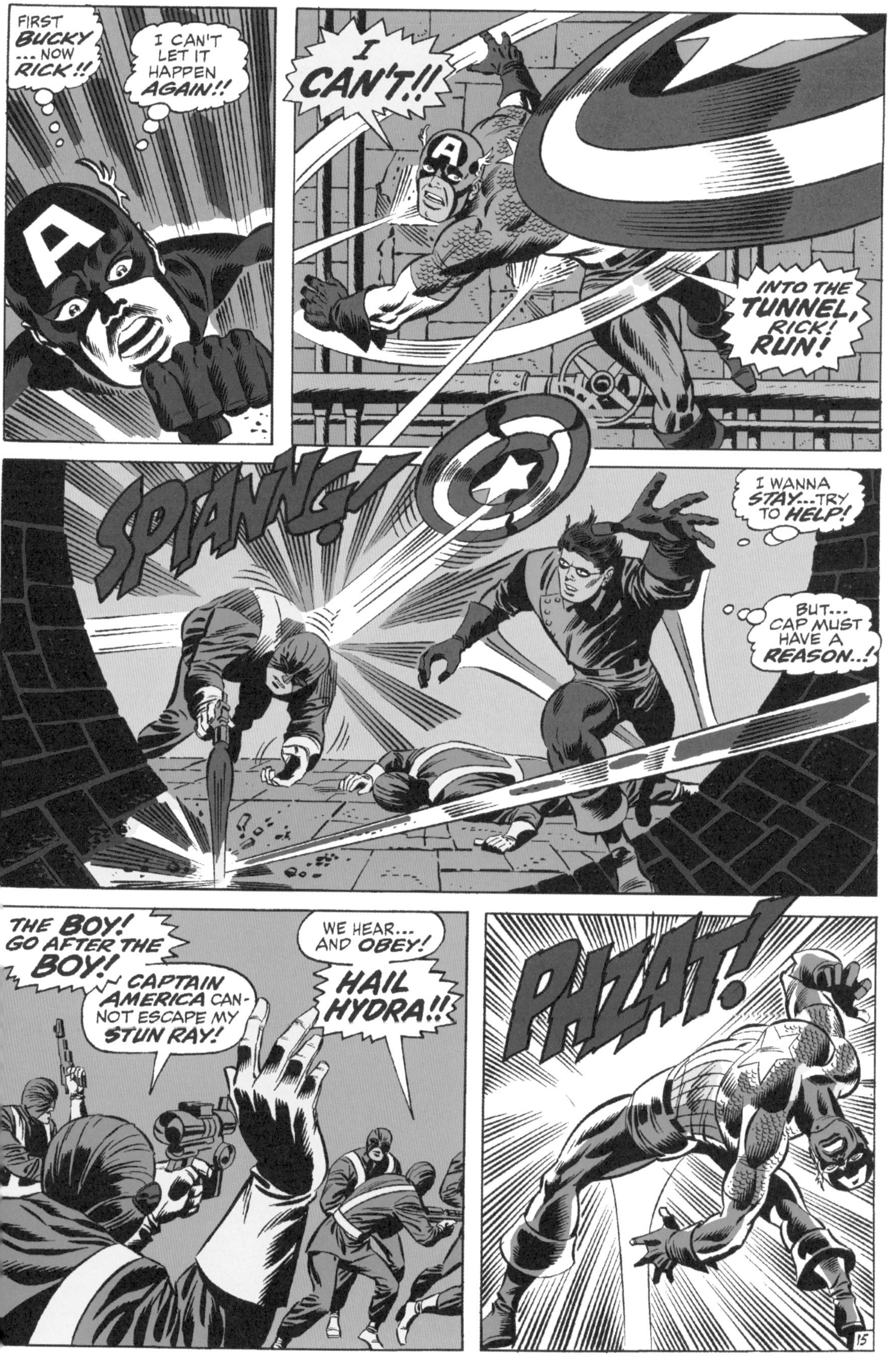

FIRST BUCKY ... NOW RICK!!
I CAN'T LET IT HAPPEN AGAIN!!
I CAN'T!!
INTO THE TUNNEL, RICK! RUN!
SPTANNG!
I WANNA STAY...TRY TO HELP!
BUT... CAP MUST HAVE A REASON..!
THE BOY! GO AFTER THE BOY!
CAPTAIN AMERICA CANNOT ESCAPE MY STUN RAY!
WE HEAR... AND OBEY!
HAIL HYDRA!!
PHZAT!
15

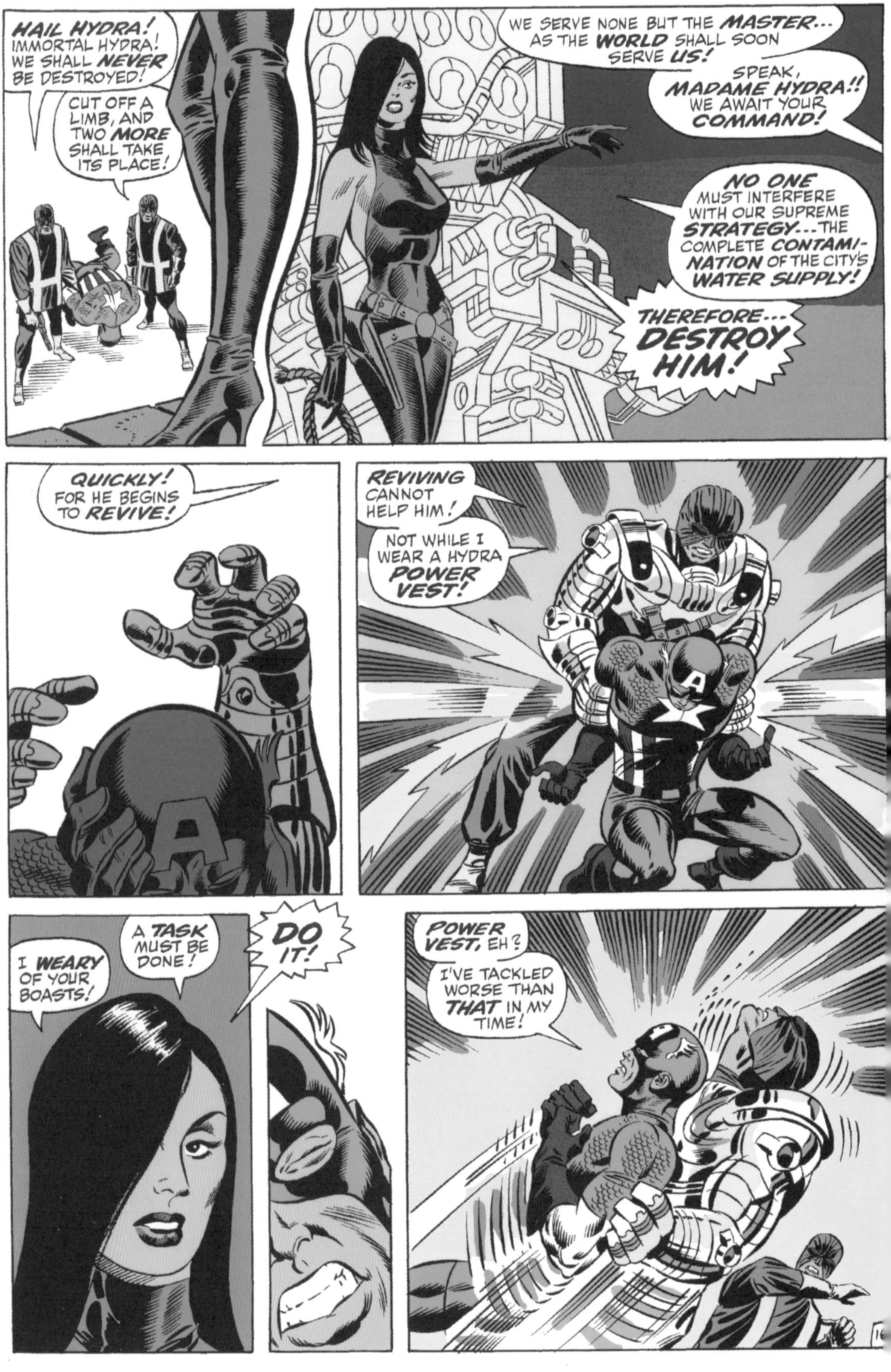
HAIL HYDRA! IMMORTAL HYDRA! WE SHALL NEVER BE DESTROYED!
CUT OFF A LIMB, AND TWO MORE SHALL TAKE ITS PLACE!
WE SERVE NONE BUT THE MASTER... AS THE WORLD SHALL SOON SERVE US!
SPEAK, MADAME HYDRA!! WE AWAIT YOUR COMMAND!
NO ONE MUST INTERFERE WITH OUR SUPREME STRATEGY... THE COMPLETE CONTAMI-NATION OF THE CITY'S WATER SUPPLY!
THEREFORE... DESTROY HIM!
QUICKLY! FOR HE BEGINS TO REVIVE!
REVIVING CANNOT HELP HIM!
NOT WHILE I WEAR A HYDRA POWER VEST!
I WEARY OF YOUR BOASTS!
A TASK MUST BE DONE!
DO IT!
POWER VEST, EH?
I'VE TACKLED WORSE THAN THAT IN MY TIME!

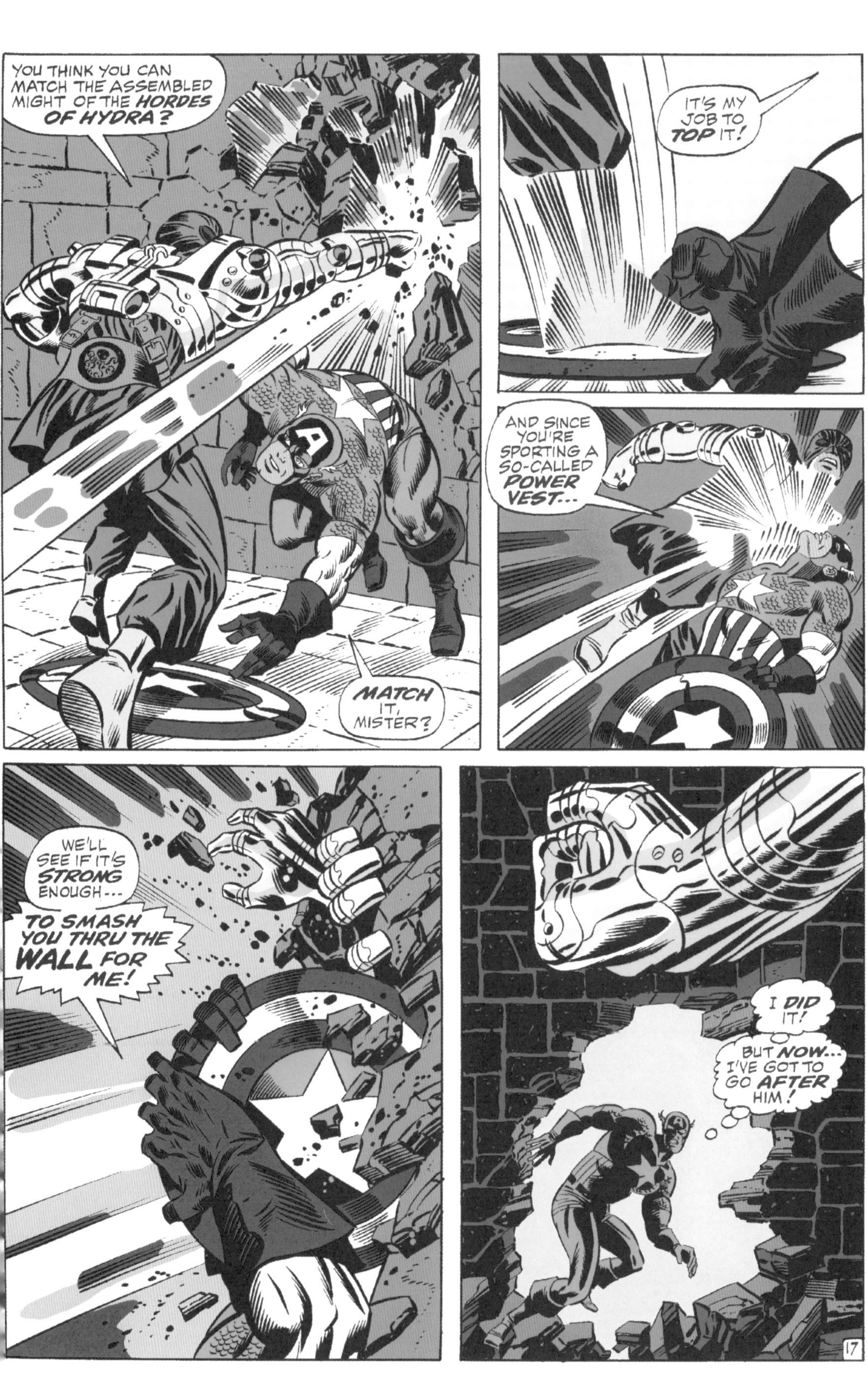
YOU THINK YOU CAN MATCH THE ASSEMBLED MIGHT OF THE HORDES OF HYDRA?
MATCH IT, MISTER?
IT'S MY JOB TO TOP IT!
AND SINCE YOU'RE SPORTING A SO-CALLED POWER VEST...
WE'LL SEE IF IT'S STRONG ENOUGH---
TO SMASH YOU THRU THE WALL FOR ME!
I DID IT!
BUT NOW... I'VE GOT TO GO AFTER HIM!
17

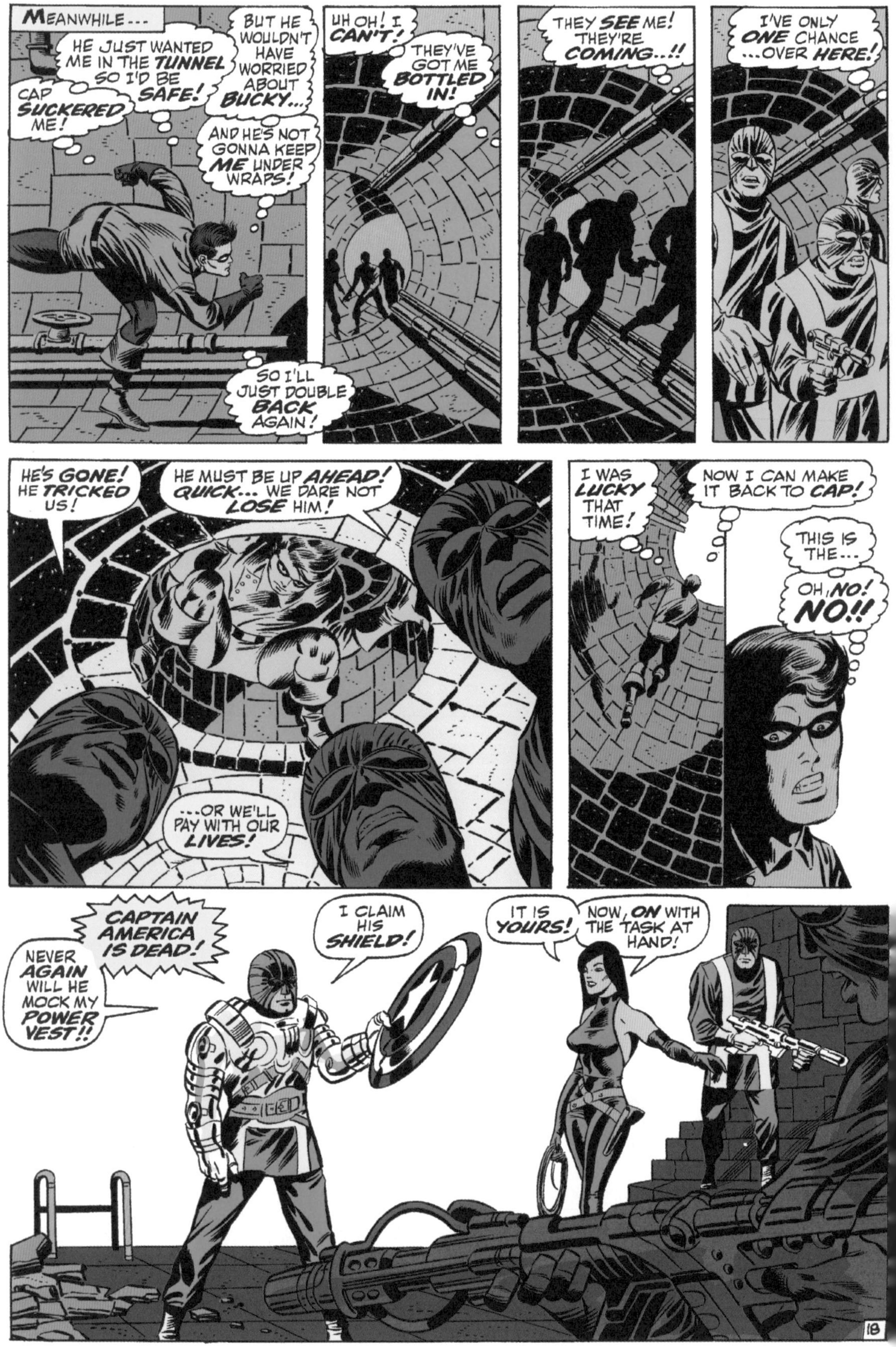
MEANWHILE...
CAP SUCKERED ME!
HE JUST WANTED ME IN THE TUNNEL SO I'D BE SAFE!
BUT HE WOULDN'T HAVE WORRIED ABOUT BUCKY...
AND HE'S NOT GONNA KEEP ME UNDER WRAPS!
SO I'LL JUST DOUBLE BACK AGAIN!
UH OH! I CAN'T!
THEY'VE GOT ME BOTTLED IN!
THEY SEE ME! THEY'RE COMING..!!
I'VE ONLY ONE CHANCE ...OVER HERE!
HE'S GONE! HE TRICKED US!
HE MUST BE UP AHEAD! QUICK... WE DARE NOT LOSE HIM!
...OR WE'LL PAY WITH OUR LIVES!
I WAS LUCKY THAT TIME!
NOW I CAN MAKE IT BACK TO CAP!
THIS IS THE...
OH, NO! NO!!
CAPTAIN AMERICA IS DEAD!
NEVER AGAIN WILL HE MOCK MY POWER VEST!!
I CLAIM HIS SHIELD!
IT IS YOURS!
NOW, ON WITH THE TASK AT HAND!
18

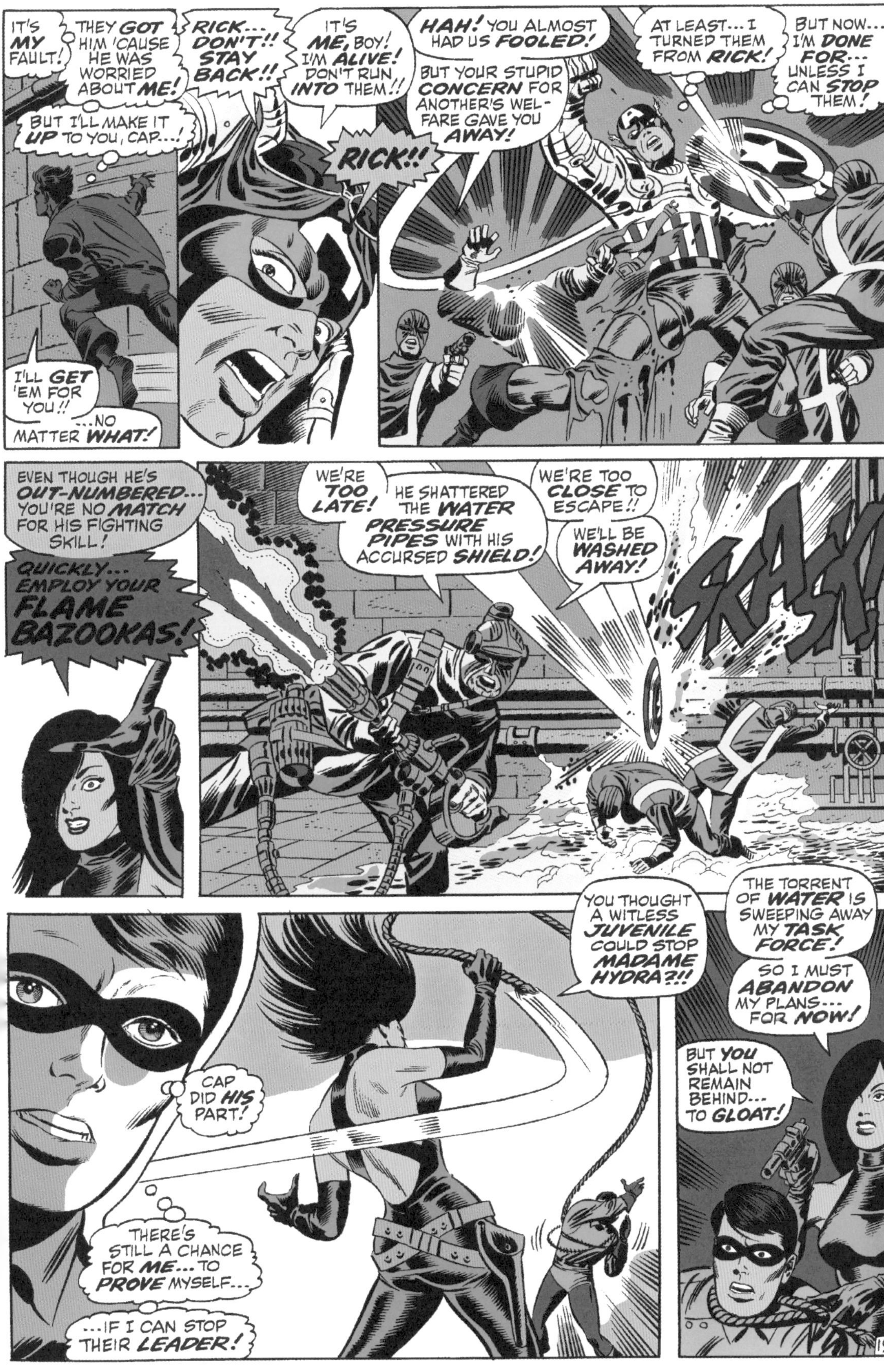
IT'S MY FAULT!
THEY GOT HIM 'CAUSE HE WAS WORRIED ABOUT ME!
BUT I'LL MAKE IT UP TO YOU, CAP...!
I'LL GET 'EM FOR YOU!!
...NO MATTER WHAT!
RICK... DON'T!! STAY BACK!!
IT'S ME, BOY! I'M ALIVE! DON'T RUN INTO THEM!!
RICK!!
HAH! YOU ALMOST HAD US FOOLED!
BUT YOUR STUPID CONCERN FOR ANOTHER'S WEL-FARE GAVE YOU AWAY!
AT LEAST... I TURNED THEM FROM RICK!
BUT NOW... I'M DONE FOR... UNLESS I CAN STOP THEM!
EVEN THOUGH HE'S OUT-NUMBERED... YOU'RE NO MATCH FOR HIS FIGHTING SKILL!
QUICKLY... EMPLOY YOUR FLAME BAZOOKAS!
WE'RE TOO LATE!
HE SHATTERED THE WATER PRESSURE PIPES WITH HIS ACCURSED SHIELD!
WE'RE TOO CLOSE TO ESCAPE!!
WE'LL BE WASHED AWAY!
SKASH!
CAP DID HIS PART!
THERE'S STILL A CHANCE FOR ME... TO PROVE MYSELF...
...IF I CAN STOP THEIR LEADER!
YOU THOUGHT A WITLESS JUVENILE COULD STOP MADAME HYDRA?!!
THE TORRENT OF WATER IS SWEEPING AWAY MY TASK FORCE!
SO I MUST ABANDON MY PLANS... FOR NOW!
BUT YOU SHALL NOT REMAIN BEHIND... TO GLOAT!
19.

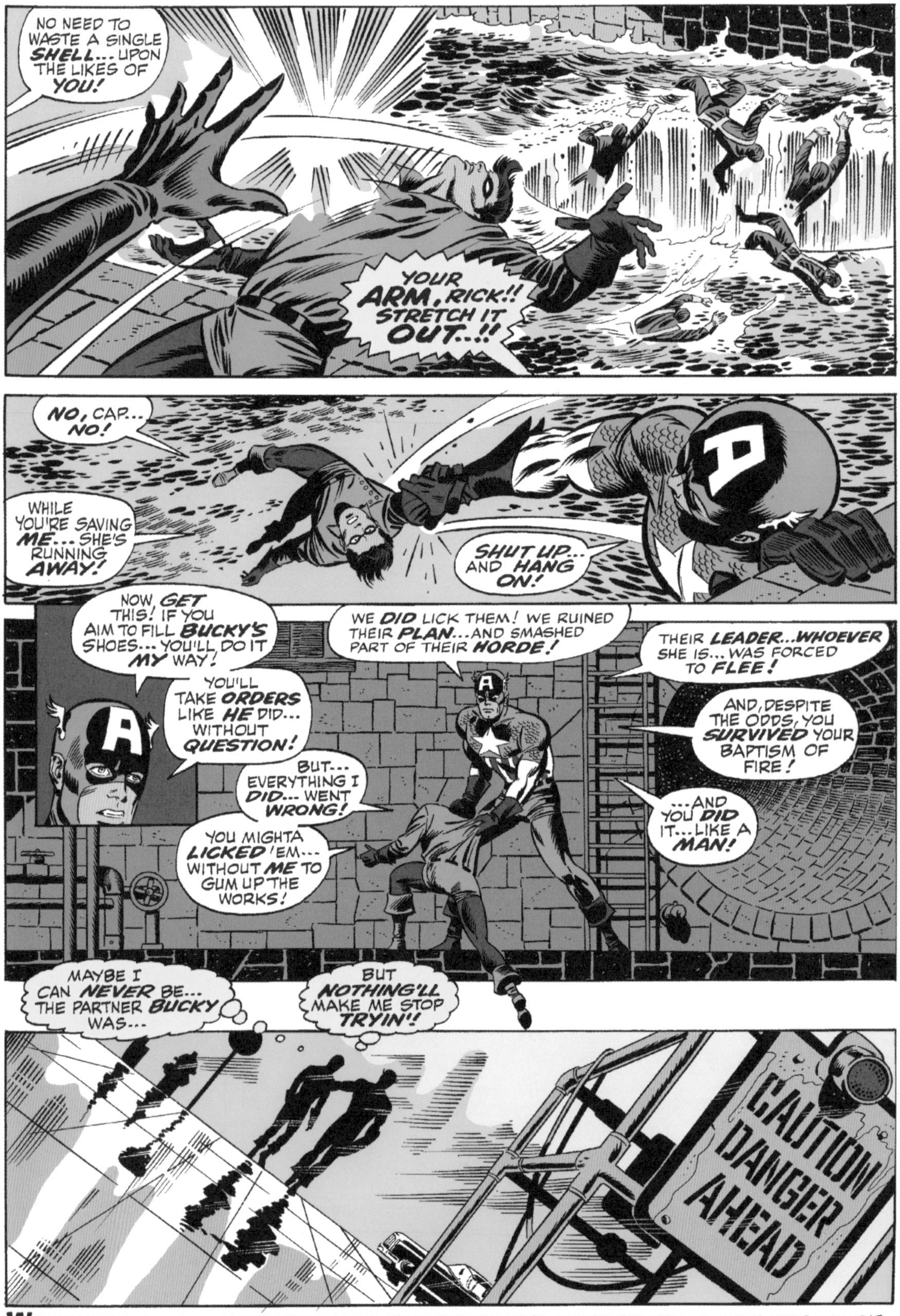
NO NEED TO WASTE A SINGLE SHELL... UPON THE LIKES OF YOU!
YOUR ARM, RICK!! STRETCH IT OUT..!!
NO, CAP... NO!
WHILE YOU'RE SAVING ME... SHE'S RUNNING AWAY!
SHUT UP... AND HANG ON!
NOW, GET THIS! IF YOU AIM TO FILL BUCKY'S SHOES... YOU'LL DO IT MY WAY!
YOU'LL TAKE ORDERS LIKE HE DID... WITHOUT QUESTION!
BUT... EVERYTHING I DID... WENT WRONG!
YOU MIGHTA LICKED 'EM... WITHOUT ME TO GUM UP THE WORKS!
WE DID LICK THEM! WE RUINED THEIR PLAN... AND SMASHED PART OF THEIR HORDE!
THEIR LEADER... WHOEVER SHE IS... WAS FORCED TO FLEE!
AND, DESPITE THE ODDS, YOU SURVIVED YOUR BAPTISM OF FIRE!
...AND YOU DID IT... LIKE A MAN!
MAYBE I CAN NEVER BE... THE PARTNER BUCKY WAS...
BUT NOTHING'LL MAKE ME STOP TRYIN'!
CAUTION DANGER AHEAD

WRAPPED IN A SILENCE, MORE MEANINGFUL THAN WORDS, TWO WEARY FIGURES SLOWLY MELT INTO THE RAINSWEPT SHADOWS OF THE GATHERING DAWN... AND WHO ARE WE TO SAY WHETHER A LEGEND HAS DIED... OR IS JUST A'BORNING?

SEND YOUR
LETTERS TO:

THE MARVEL
COMICS GROUP
SECOND FLOOR
625 MADISON AV.
NEW YORK 10022
N.Y.

Dear Stan,

The other day I was going over the last six CAPTAIN AMERICA mags and noticed two items. Stan, you assisted in producing the extraordinary plots and the majority of them (the mags) opened with action. "So," you may ask, "what does that prove?" Well, be patient! During my years as a Marvel Maniac someone told me that you were very fond of Shakespeare. As it happens, in most of Shakespeare's plays there was a quality of "enveloping action" which opened them. Now, here comes the question. Is it coincidence or not that this similarity occurred. If not, Stan, it's a brilliant idea . . . to combine some of Shakespeare's fabulous ideas, plots, and proverbs with your own enormous talent. Marvel Comics could become even greater than they already are if you continue to do this to a greater degree. On a closing note, I shall call forth some of Shakespeare's own words. "In my stars I am above thee, but be not afraid of greatness; some are born great, some achieve greatness, and some have greatness thrust upon them." Dang it, Stan, how'd you do it?   Robin Stover, P.O. Box 865
Dunedin, Florida 33528

Dear Stan,

After suffering through five incredibly mediocre issues of CAPTAIN AMERICA in a row, I was overjoyed to find that issue =106 was actually worth reading. Not for the story, which was as bad as the preceding five, or for the villain, who was downright lousy (and, Stan, how's about laying off lines like "I am the instrument which will destroy your nation and your liberty?" Let someone else edit the 'Golden Age' reprints for a while. They seem to be getting to you.), but for a nameless agent of S.H.I.E.L.D. and two brothers whose scruples left a bit to be desired. The supremely calm, non-cool-blowing S.H.I.E.L.D. agent was an excellent contrast to Cap, who of late seems to be very high-strung and unable to say anything without shouting half the words. He deserves a reappearance somewhere, be it in Cap or S.H.I.E.L.D. As for the two Lucas brothers, they were a refreshing change from the villains who go around robbing vending machines just to give the slugs to blind beggars. They were two very human human beings. Brother Cyril was the prime example of a man compromising his ideals for a dream. He was a human being whose love for his brother overrode everything else; who owned a quiet courage as depicted in the last panels of the story; who realized that he was violating his moral code and tried to rationalize by saying "it's just another movie." It is fortunate that you are a good writer, because story-savers such as these are few and far between.   Bruce Dravis, 9150 Plaza Park Dr.
Elk Grove, Calif. 95624

Dear Stan and Jack,

Out of the goodness of my heart (and the emptiness of my scrapbook) I'm writing this letter designed for the sole purpose of getting you off the hook. In issue #107 a certain somebody wrote about the nuclear tape on the back of Cap's neck. That person's first question was "Doesn't Cap wash his neck?" Cap definitely does, but at that time he was so busy trying to think about the Skull that he just couldn't. The person's second question was "Why didn't Cap feel the tape?" Cap did not feel it because obviously the tape had control over his mind. The tape caused slight numbness around the area on which it was located. His third and final question was, "Why didn't Sharon feel the tape while she was kissing him on the way back?" This question does not really need an answer because it is assumption, but nevertheless I'll give you an answer. Cap was so exhausted from the fight with the Red Skull that he just wasn't in the mood for kissing. There, all three questions have been satisfactorily answered courtesy of . . .   Eric Nash, 100 Bleecher St.
New York, New York 10022

Dear Stan and Jack,

I've got your latest CAPTAIN AMERICA mag and needless to say, it's GREAT! Now that I've got you Joes all confused about what ish I mean it's ish #106. Page 8 was the most magnificent piece of artistry I've ever seen. But, so much for this, and on to my topic. This deals with a certain paperback novel I just bought on none other than Captain America himself, in which he tangled forces with the notorious Red Skull in a caper called 'The Great Gold Steal.' Stan, your introduction put new hopes in my outlook on life. Captain America it seems originated as a symbol in W. W. II to give new hopes to the people of America. To me Cap is a sort of thing like . . . say . . . for you Yanks, Uncle Sam, but different, in that he represents all that is free and democratic, and is a symbol for all, not just Americans, but Canadians, British — the works! He is a man with the qualities of patriotism, love for freedom from oppression, love for a democratic society without malignant policies such as Communism. He is a man built on stern policies which must rid an already torn world of prejudice, crime, oppression, and much more. Captain America is a man created to do this if only by imprinting on the minds of the masses these ideals. Captain America is a man for all to rally behind and believe in, not just Americans but everybody who believes in such ideals.   Brian Clancey, 108 Cormorant Bay
Winnipeg 6, Manitoba, Canada

KNOW YE THESE, THE HALLOWED RANKS OF MARVELDOM:

R.F.O. (REAL FRANTIC ONE)—A BUYER OF AT LEAST 3 MARVEL MAGS A MONTH.

T.T.B. (TITANIC TRUE BELIEVER)—A DIVINELY-INSPIRED 'NO-PRIZE' WINNER.

Q.N.S. (QUITE 'NUFF SAYER)—A FORTUNATE FRANTIC ONE WHO'S HAD A LETTER PRINTED.

K.O.F. (KEEPER OF THE FLAME)—ONE WHO RECRUITS A NEWCOMER TO MARVEL'S ROLLICKIN' RANKS.

P.M.M. (PERMANENT MARVELITE MAXIMUS)—ANYONE POSSESSING ALL FOUR OF THE OTHER TITLES.

F.F.F. (FEARLESS FRONT FACER)—AN HONORARY TITLE BESTOWED FOR DEVOTION TO MARVEL ABOVE AND BEYOND THE CALL OF DUTY.

Dear Stan and Jack,

First, let me compliment you on your development of Captain America since the Avengers rescued him. At the start, he was truly a man from the past, with a terrible feeling of guilt about Bucky. Since that time he has made much progress in adjusting to the 1960's. First, he has just about gotten over Bucky's death. The feeling of guilt was overcome when Zemo was killed. Now, in AVENGERS #56 he has reassured himself that Bucky is really dead (thank goodness — I was always afraid you'd revive him). Second, he has managed to develop a present-day personal life. He has left the Avengers to fend for himself and has been able to spend at least part of his time as Steve Rogers. More important, he has found a present-day girl, thus driving a wedge between himself and still more sad memories of the past. There remains just one thing binding him to the past — the Red Skull. As a superhero of the 1960's, Cap should not have villains from the 1940's. The Red Skull could have become a modern villain, but he hasn't. He's still fighting for the Third Reich, something which vanished over 20 years ago. I don't feel that this is right. I think Cap should become completely free of the 1940's and he can't do that by battling the Red Skull. The Red Skull is one of your poorer villains, anyway. Any super-villain (or hero) has some unusual aspect which the reader must accept for the villain to be effective. Okay, the Skull is an evil genius, and as such he'd be an acceptable villain. But he isn't just that, he's also a man living in the past, fighting for something that's been over and done with these many long years. I find this difficult to accept. No, I'm not insisting you kill off the Skull. I think it'd be better if you did, but there are other possibilities. For example, you could have him be captured, and put in a mental institution for a *long* time. Or, you could have him start seeing a psychiatrist to help him get over his Nazi Germany obsession. There are all kinds of things you could do. But, I appeal to you, for Cap's sake, for the sake of your development of Cap's personality, for the sake of the general excellence of Marvel publications, do something about the Red Skull!!   Roger Vanous, RFO, 301 Waugh St. Columbia, Mo. 65201

Dear Stan and Jack,

I've seen, as others have, 'Nuff of Capt. America's incessant conservative speechmaking during the heat of battle. From my point of view CA belongs to the past in more ways than one. Stan, the day of the hero worship is gone. CA is the type of man who lives to fight for his personal brand of liberty. He believes just as the warmongers of the past wars and of today do. His roots belong in the past, not now. Doesn't CA realize that today the so-called patriotic fighter is gone? You guys know that Cap is a defender of the Establishment. The Captain does not reason. In #101, page 17, panel 6, and I quote, "And those who would grind us underfoot can never hope to keep us from reaching our eventual destiny!" Sure, I agree with this ideal, in the fact that tyrants are enemies to freedom, equality, and fraternity. But does he have to make it sound as if he and a few other glory mongers can decide what justice individuals may have or may not have? No! Today in America, there are many hawks who favor conservatism. Obviously, Cap is an upholder of this policy. In the above issue, page 18, panel 2, Cap says "It's you who have outgrown the dream — You who are blind to the promise of tomorrow!" Ha! Look who's talking. He's just as blind. There are many promising people who are expounding the cause of peace and liberty. This magazine does not fit in with today's society. Cap ought to know that someday the world will be built on a pinnacle of peace and freedom. Cap believes the same way, but must he show it through violence and heroics? Of course, without this element there would be no Captain America.

All I question is his reasoning, which is entirely out of date. This is a strong plea against war lovers and so-called patriots. One more thing. Get rid of that Living Legend of World War II deal. Who wants to be reminded of a shameful ideal? Aside from this, Cap is one of your best characters. It would fit the standards of today, though, if he were more liberal.   Albert Rodriquez, 214½ South Bjai St. Santa Paulo, Calif. 93060

Dear Stan and Jack,

CAPTAIN AMERICA #107 was very good. However, I hope you have ended his events concerning Bucky Barnes. I figured that Cap called Dr. Faustus' bluff when his "non-nightmare" pills were delivered. But when he took them and grew old overnight (Jack drew a wonderfully grotesque, ugly, old Captain America), that thought was quickly put out of my mind. So naturally the surprise was completely unexpected. There's one question, though. How come Cap couldn't sleep? He didn't know Faustus' complete plan. I hope someone writes to you and answers my question.
Kenwood Dennard, 334 E. 108th St. New York, New York 10029

Dear Stan, Roy and Company;

If I had any brains, I wouldn't stick my neck out like this but I might as well try to explain also why there are CAPTAIN AMERICA comics in the '50's while Cap and Bucky disappeared in 1945. You remember how on April 29th, while the battle of Berlin was raging, Captain America and the Red Skull were slugging it out in a bunker beneath the city, don't you? It was in SUSPENSE #72. Hitler committed suicide not far away. Well, after the Red Skull got buried, Cap and Bucky returned to England the next day, April 30th, 1945. This brings us to the current AVENGERS #56. They got back in time to catch Zemo stealing the drone plane. In case you're wondering about Zemo's reference to der Feuhrer, remember, Zemo probably didn't know that Hitler had committed suicide the day before. I need not bother repeating the whole story because it's all in AVENGERS #56. Anyway, Captain America and Bucky disappeared on April 30, 1945. Naturally, the whole free world was shocked to learn that its greatest defender was gone. As famous heroes, Cap and Bucky had already made the comic pages and magazines come alive with their exploits. Seeking to perpetuate the legend of Captain America, comic magazines published *fictional* instead of the real adventures of their hero. Thus, while Cap was floating in that glacier (which isn't so far-fetched if you consider how cold the North Atlantic is, even in April) comic about him continued into the 1950's. Eventually the public forgot about him and the mags were discontinued. And as we all know, the real Captain America made his reappearance 19 years later, in 1964. There you have it. I hope that clears up some of the confusion about Marvel's interpretation of Captain America and Cap's Golden Age tales of the '50's which appear in MARVEL SUPER-HEROES. Whew! That about finishes me! Keep up the great work, and may next year's AVENGERS SPECIAL surpass even this year's (which is doubtful)!
Joe Trainor, 9 Foley Street Attleboro, Mass. 02703

NEXT: THE DEATH OF STEVE ROGERS!

CAPTAIN AMERICA #111,
MARCH 1969,
"TOMORROW YOU LIVE,
TONIGHT I DIE!"

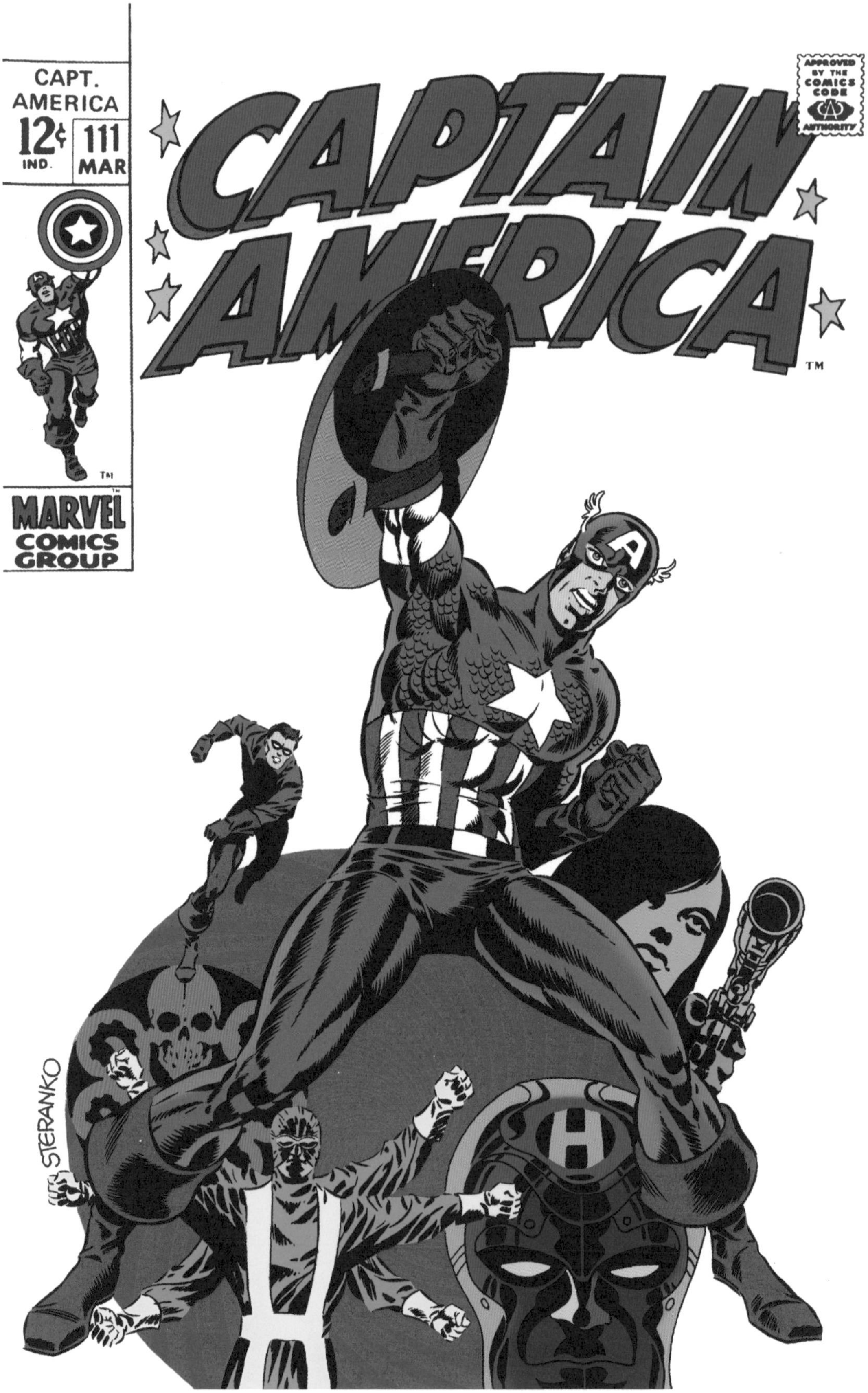
CAPT.
AMERICA
12¢
IND.
111
MAR
MARVEL
COMICS
GROUP
CAPTAIN
AMERICA
APPROVED
BY THE
COMICS
CODE
AUTHORITY
STERANKO

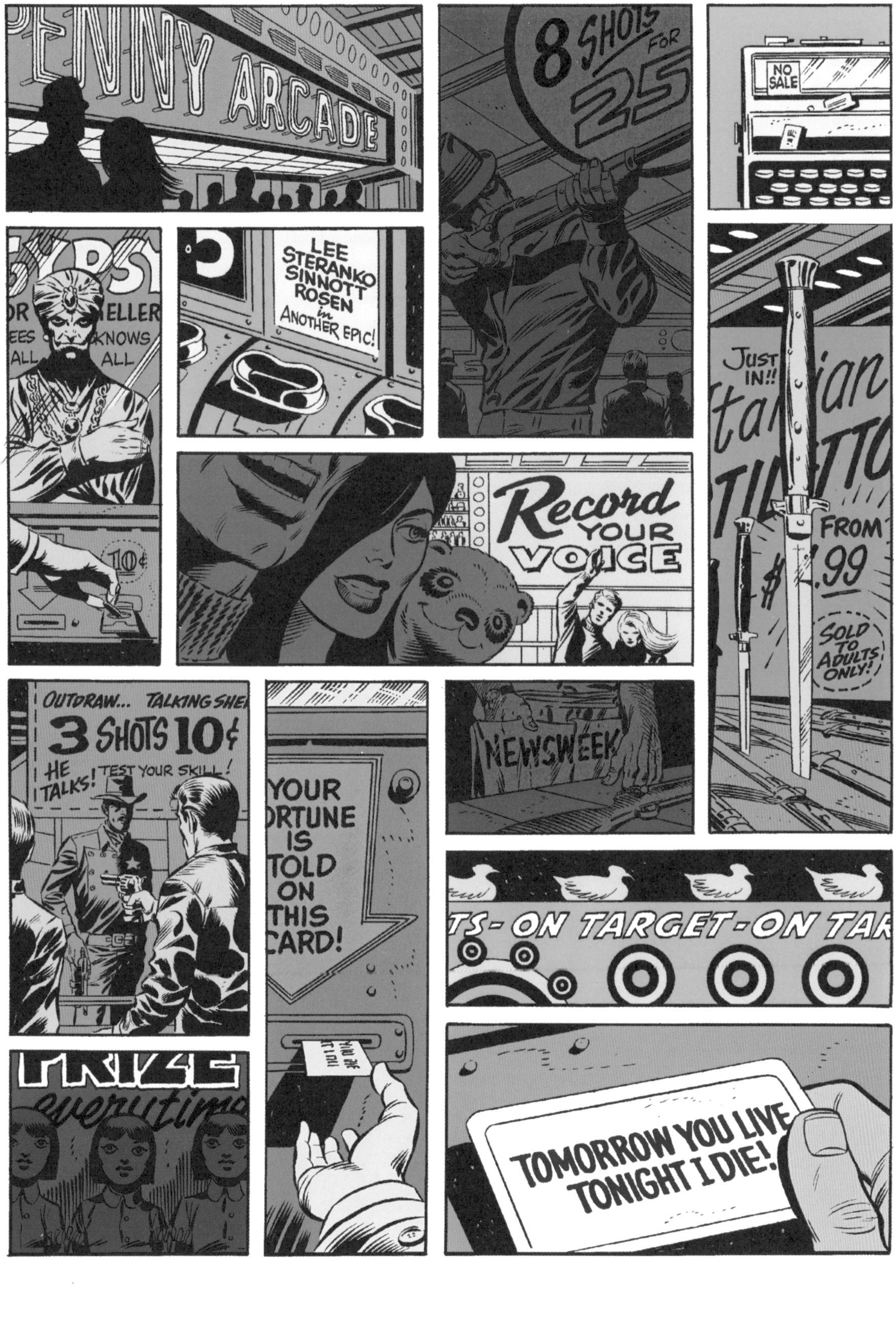
PENNY ARCADE
8 SHOTS FOR 25
NO SALE
ALL ALL
10¢
LEE STERANKO SINNOTT ROSEN in ANOTHER EPIC!
JUST IN!!
FROM
SOLD TO ADULTS ONLY!
Record YOUR VOICE
3 SHOTS 10¢
HE TALKS! TEST YOUR SKILL!
YOUR
IS
TOLD
ON
CARD!
NEWSWEEK
ON TARGET
TOMORROW YOU LIVE TONIGHT I DIE!

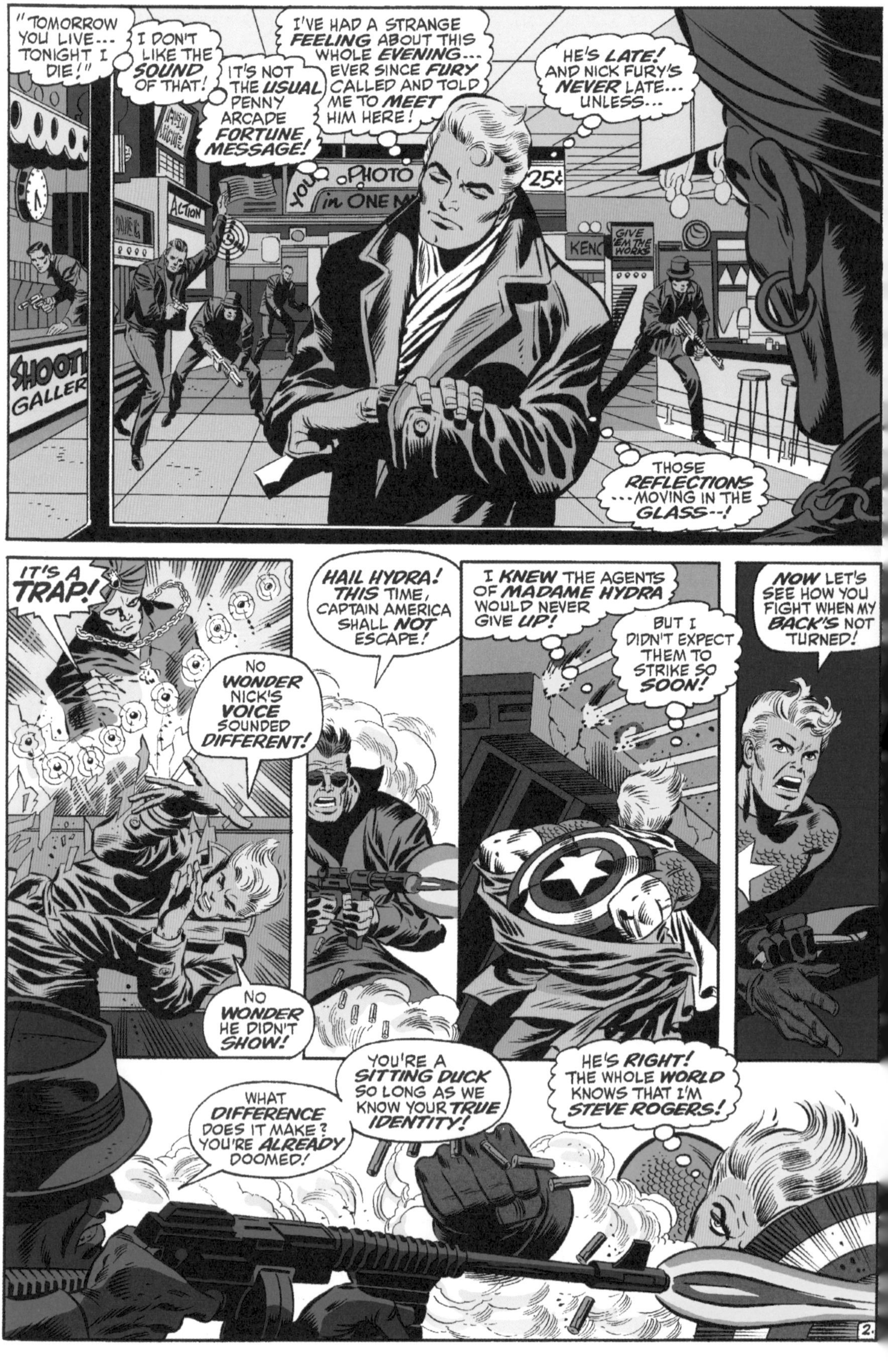
"TOMORROW YOU LIVE--- TONIGHT I DIE!"
I DON'T LIKE THE SOUND OF THAT!
IT'S NOT THE USUAL PENNY ARCADE FORTUNE MESSAGE!
I'VE HAD A STRANGE FEELING ABOUT THIS WHOLE EVENING... EVER SINCE FURY CALLED AND TOLD ME TO MEET HIM HERE!
HE'S LATE! AND NICK FURY'S NEVER LATE... UNLESS...
THOSE REFLECTIONS ---MOVING IN THE GLASS--!
IT'S A TRAP!
NO WONDER NICK'S VOICE SOUNDED DIFFERENT!
NO WONDER HE DIDN'T SHOW!
HAIL HYDRA! THIS TIME, CAPTAIN AMERICA SHALL NOT ESCAPE!
I KNEW THE AGENTS OF MADAME HYDRA WOULD NEVER GIVE UP!
BUT I DIDN'T EXPECT THEM TO STRIKE SO SOON!
NOW LET'S SEE HOW YOU FIGHT WHEN MY BACK'S NOT TURNED!
WHAT DIFFERENCE DOES IT MAKE? YOU'RE ALREADY DOOMED!
YOU'RE A SITTING DUCK SO LONG AS WE KNOW YOUR TRUE IDENTITY!
HE'S RIGHT! THE WHOLE WORLD KNOWS THAT I'M STEVE ROGERS!
2.

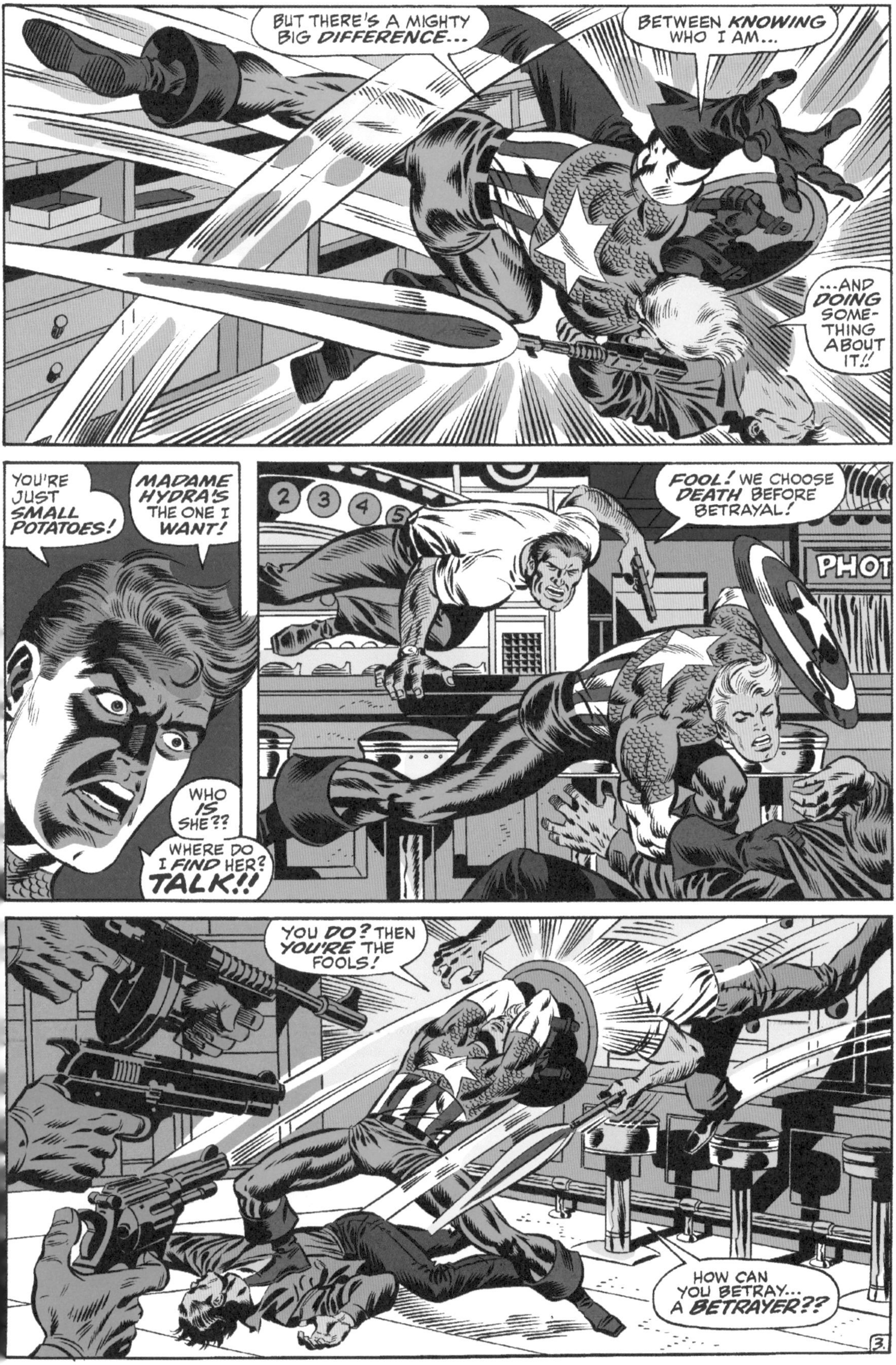
BUT THERE'S A MIGHTY BIG DIFFERENCE...
BETWEEN KNOWING WHO I AM...
...AND DOING SOMETHING ABOUT IT!!
YOU'RE JUST SMALL POTATOES!
MADAME HYDRA'S THE ONE I WANT!
WHO IS SHE??
WHERE DO I FIND HER? TALK!!
FOOL! WE CHOOSE DEATH BEFORE BETRAYAL!
PHOT
YOU DO? THEN YOU'RE THE FOOLS!
HOW CAN YOU BETRAY... A BETRAYER??
3.

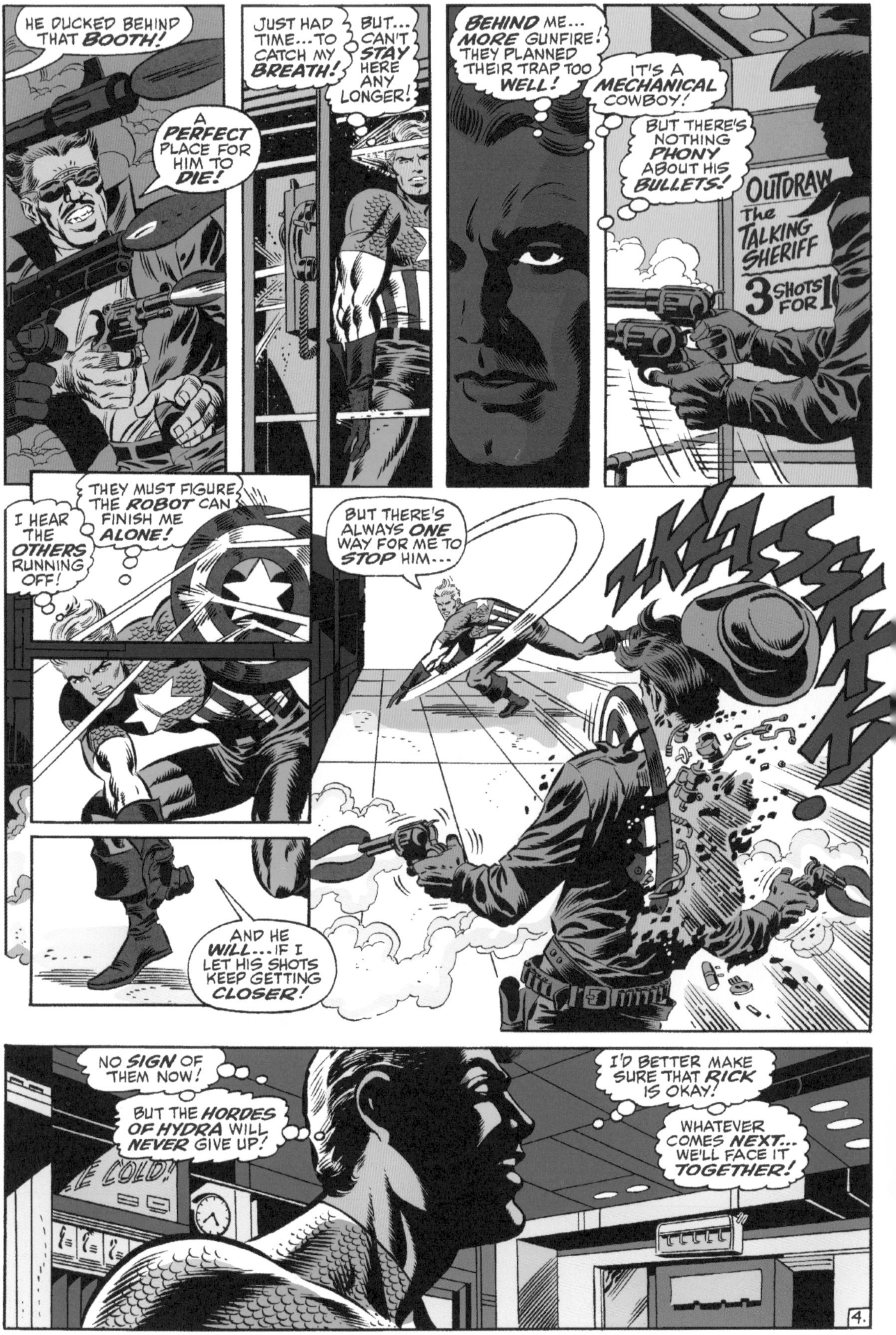

HE DUCKED BEHIND THAT **BOOTH!**
A **PERFECT** PLACE FOR HIM TO **DIE!**
JUST HAD TIME...TO CATCH MY **BREATH!**
BUT... CAN'T **STAY** HERE ANY LONGER!
BEHIND ME... **MORE** GUNFIRE! THEY PLANNED THEIR TRAP TOO **WELL!**
IT'S A **MECHANICAL** COWBOY!
BUT THERE'S NOTHING **PHONY** ABOUT HIS **BULLETS!**
OUTDRAW The TALKING SHERIFF
3 SHOTS FOR 1
I HEAR THE **OTHERS** RUNNING OFF!
THEY MUST FIGURE THE **ROBOT** CAN FINISH ME **ALONE!**
AND HE **WILL**...IF I LET HIS SHOTS KEEP GETTING **CLOSER!**
BUT THERE'S ALWAYS **ONE** WAY FOR ME TO **STOP** HIM...
NO **SIGN** OF THEM NOW!
BUT THE **HORDES OF HYDRA** WILL **NEVER** GIVE UP!
I'D BETTER MAKE SURE THAT **RICK** IS OKAY!
WHATEVER COMES **NEXT**... WE'LL FACE IT **TOGETHER!**
4.

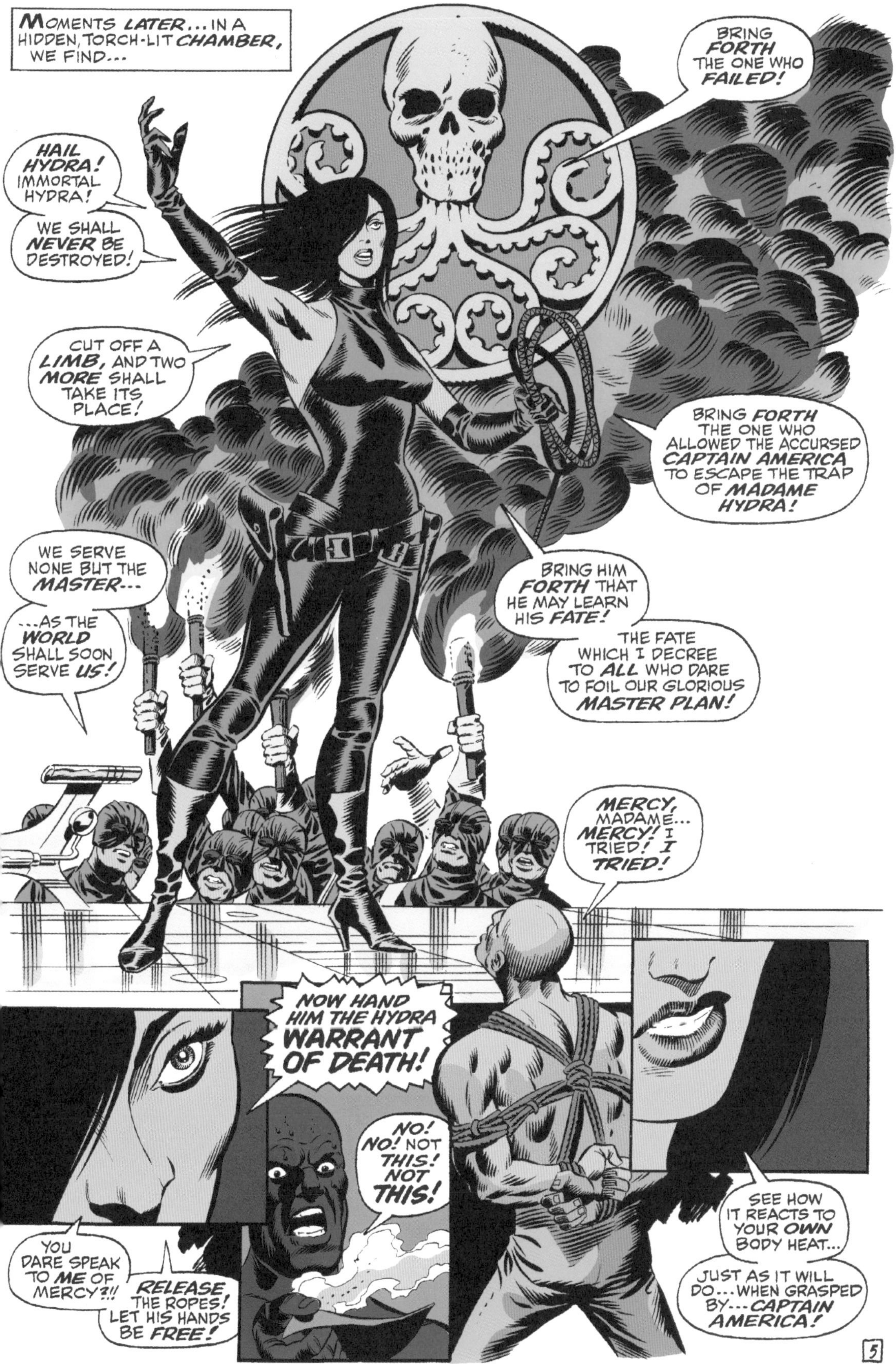
MOMENTS LATER... IN A HIDDEN, TORCH-LIT CHAMBER, WE FIND...
HAIL HYDRA! IMMORTAL HYDRA!
WE SHALL NEVER BE DESTROYED!
BRING FORTH THE ONE WHO FAILED!
CUT OFF A LIMB, AND TWO MORE SHALL TAKE ITS PLACE!
BRING FORTH THE ONE WHO ALLOWED THE ACCURSED CAPTAIN AMERICA TO ESCAPE THE TRAP OF MADAME HYDRA!
WE SERVE NONE BUT THE MASTER--
...AS THE WORLD SHALL SOON SERVE US!
BRING HIM FORTH THAT HE MAY LEARN HIS FATE!
THE FATE WHICH I DECREE TO ALL WHO DARE TO FOIL OUR GLORIOUS MASTER PLAN!
MERCY, MADAME... MERCY! I TRIED! I TRIED!
NOW HAND HIM THE HYDRA WARRANT OF DEATH!
YOU DARE SPEAK TO ME OF MERCY?!!
RELEASE THE ROPES! LET HIS HANDS BE FREE!
NO! NO! NOT THIS! NOT THIS!
SEE HOW IT REACTS TO YOUR OWN BODY HEAT...
JUST AS IT WILL DO... WHEN GRASPED BY... CAPTAIN AMERICA!
5

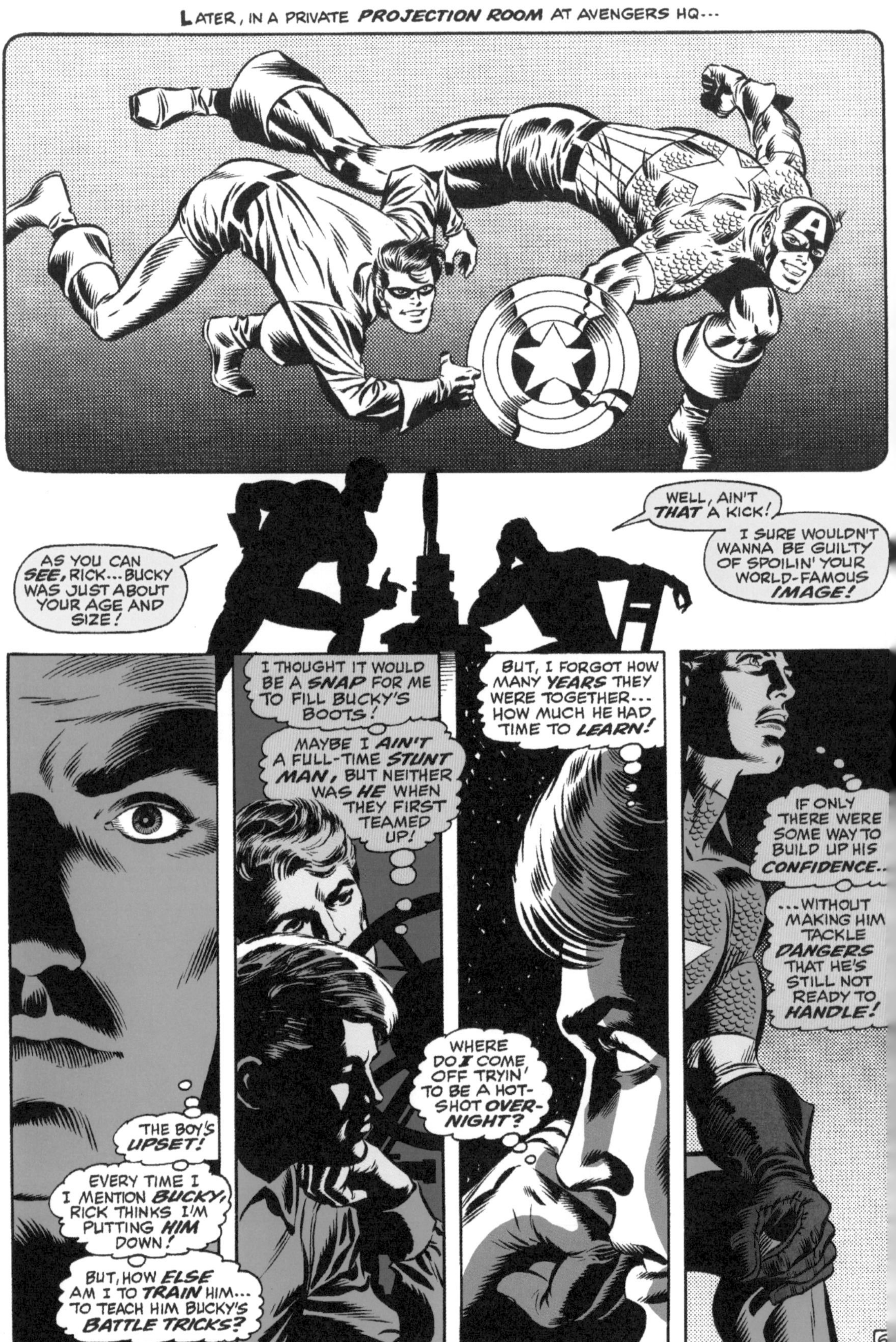
LATER, IN A PRIVATE PROJECTION ROOM AT AVENGERS HQ...
AS YOU CAN SEE, RICK... BUCKY WAS JUST ABOUT YOUR AGE AND SIZE!
WELL, AIN'T THAT A KICK!
I SURE WOULDN'T WANNA BE GUILTY OF SPOILIN' YOUR WORLD-FAMOUS IMAGE!
THE BOY'S UPSET!
EVERY TIME I I MENTION BUCKY, RICK THINKS I'M PUTTING HIM DOWN!
BUT, HOW ELSE AM I TO TRAIN HIM... TO TEACH HIM BUCKY'S BATTLE TRICKS?
I THOUGHT IT WOULD BE A SNAP FOR ME TO FILL BUCKY'S BOOTS!
MAYBE I AIN'T A FULL-TIME STUNT MAN, BUT NEITHER WAS HE WHEN THEY FIRST TEAMED UP!
BUT, I FORGOT HOW MANY YEARS THEY WERE TOGETHER... HOW MUCH HE HAD TIME TO LEARN!
WHERE DO I COME OFF TRYIN' TO BE A HOT-SHOT OVER-NIGHT?
IF ONLY THERE WERE SOME WAY TO BUILD UP HIS CONFIDENCE..
...WITHOUT MAKING HIM TACKLE DANGERS THAT HE'S STILL NOT READY TO HANDLE!
6

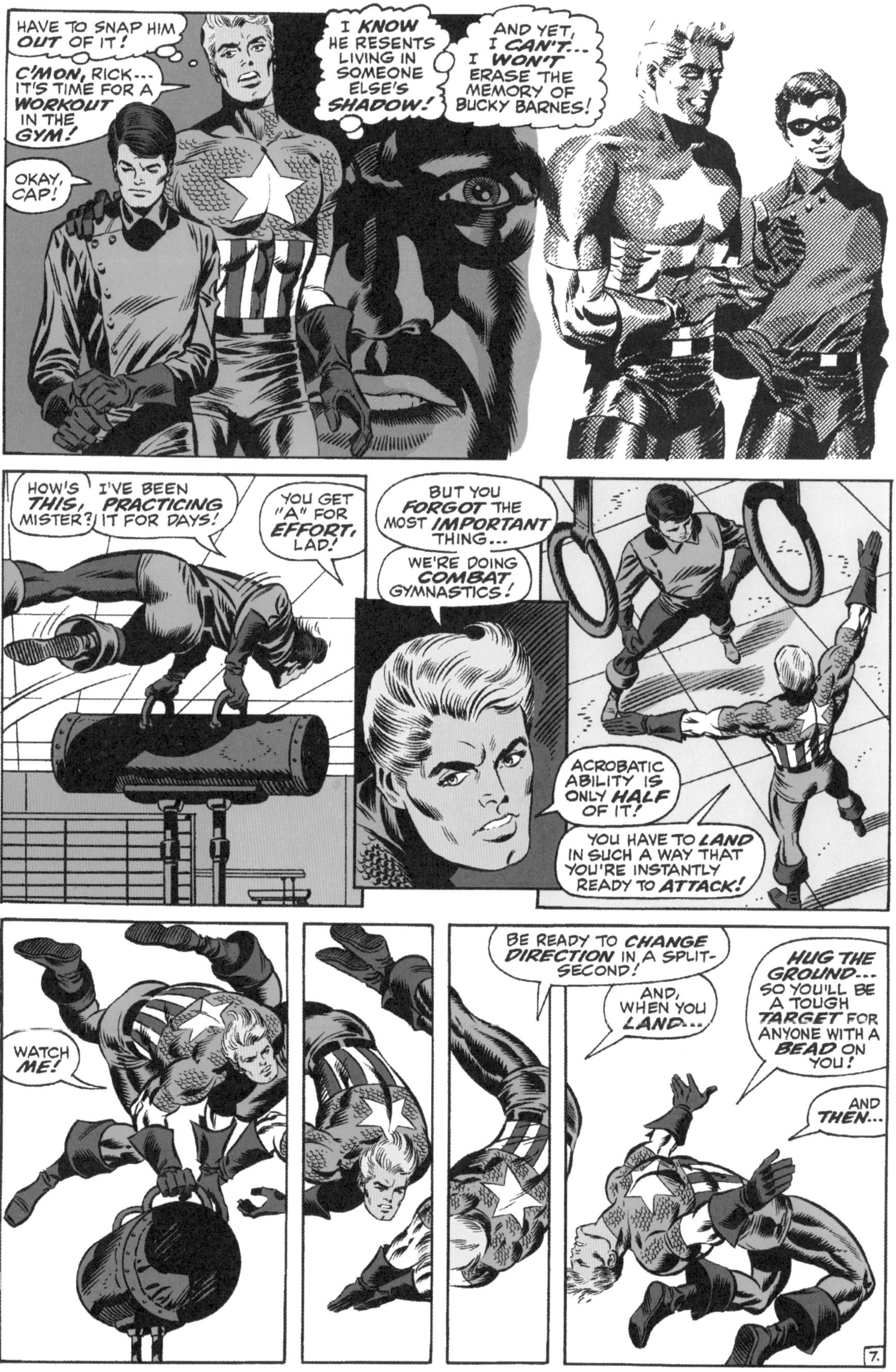
HAVE TO SNAP HIM OUT OF IT!
C'MON, RICK... IT'S TIME FOR A WORKOUT IN THE GYM!
OKAY, CAP!
I KNOW HE RESENTS LIVING IN SOMEONE ELSE'S SHADOW!
AND YET, I CAN'T... I WON'T ERASE THE MEMORY OF BUCKY BARNES!
HOW'S THIS, MISTER?
I'VE BEEN PRACTICING IT FOR DAYS!
YOU GET "A" FOR EFFORT, LAD!
BUT YOU FORGOT THE MOST IMPORTANT THING...
WE'RE DOING COMBAT GYMNASTICS!
ACROBATIC ABILITY IS ONLY HALF OF IT!
YOU HAVE TO LAND IN SUCH A WAY THAT YOU'RE INSTANTLY READY TO ATTACK!
WATCH ME!
BE READY TO CHANGE DIRECTION IN A SPLIT-SECOND!
AND, WHEN YOU LAND...
HUG THE GROUND... SO YOU'LL BE A TOUGH TARGET FOR ANYONE WITH A BEAD ON YOU!
AND THEN...
7.

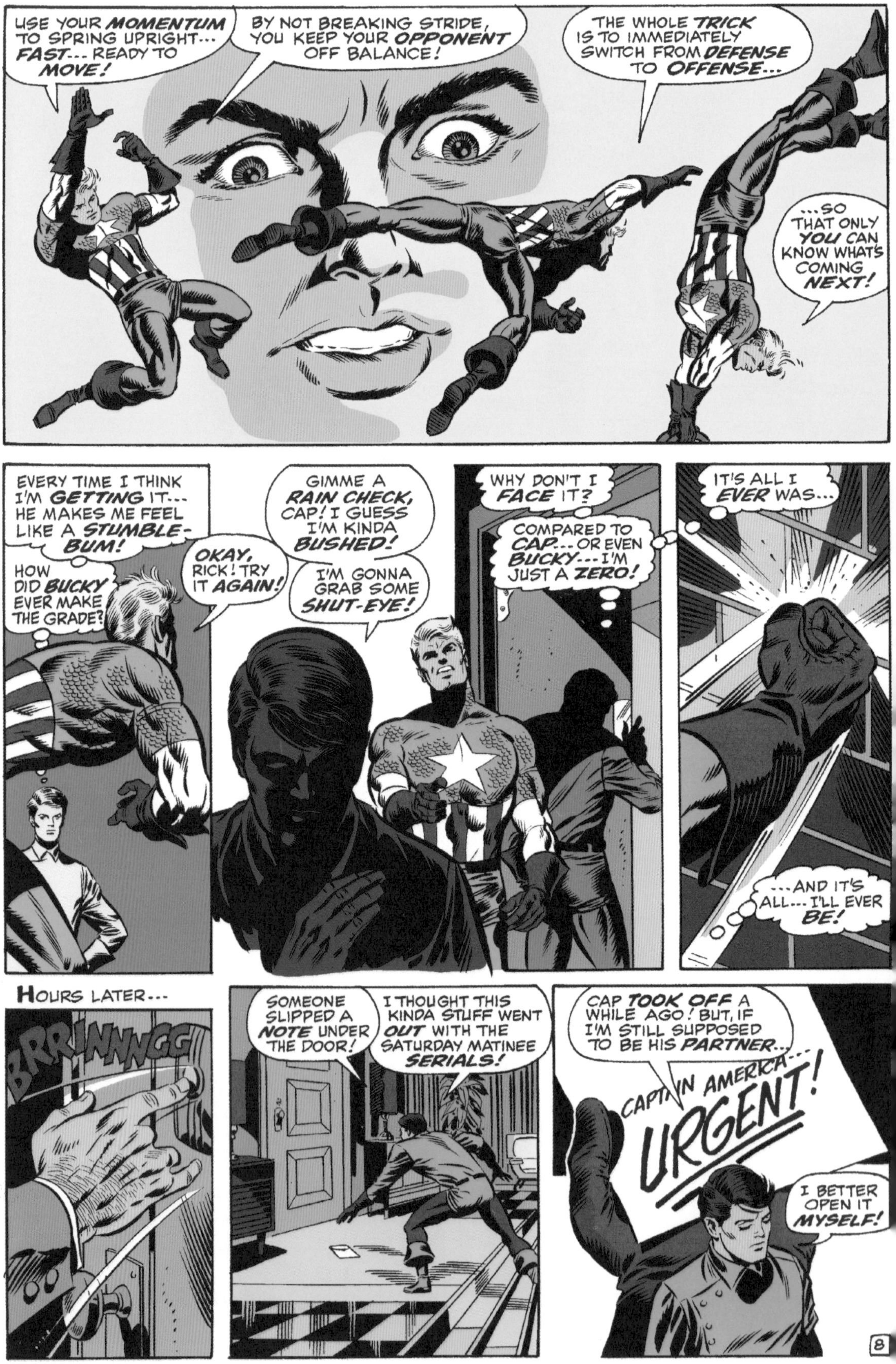
USE YOUR MOMENTUM TO SPRING UPRIGHT... FAST... READY TO MOVE!
BY NOT BREAKING STRIDE, YOU KEEP YOUR OPPONENT OFF BALANCE!
THE WHOLE TRICK IS TO IMMEDIATELY SWITCH FROM DEFENSE TO OFFENSE...
...SO THAT ONLY YOU CAN KNOW WHAT'S COMING NEXT!
EVERY TIME I THINK I'M GETTING IT... HE MAKES ME FEEL LIKE A STUMBLE-BUM!
HOW DID BUCKY EVER MAKE THE GRADE?
OKAY, RICK! TRY IT AGAIN!
GIMME A RAIN CHECK, CAP! I GUESS I'M KINDA BUSHED!
I'M GONNA GRAB SOME SHUT-EYE!
WHY DON'T I FACE IT?
COMPARED TO CAP... OR EVEN BUCKY... I'M JUST A ZERO!
IT'S ALL I EVER WAS...
...AND IT'S ALL... I'LL EVER BE!
HOURS LATER...
BRRINNNGG
SOMEONE SLIPPED A NOTE UNDER THE DOOR!
I THOUGHT THIS KINDA STUFF WENT OUT WITH THE SATURDAY MATINEE SERIALS!
CAP TOOK OFF A WHILE AGO! BUT, IF I'M STILL SUPPOSED TO BE HIS PARTNER...
CAPTAIN AMERICA... URGENT!
I BETTER OPEN IT MYSELF!
8

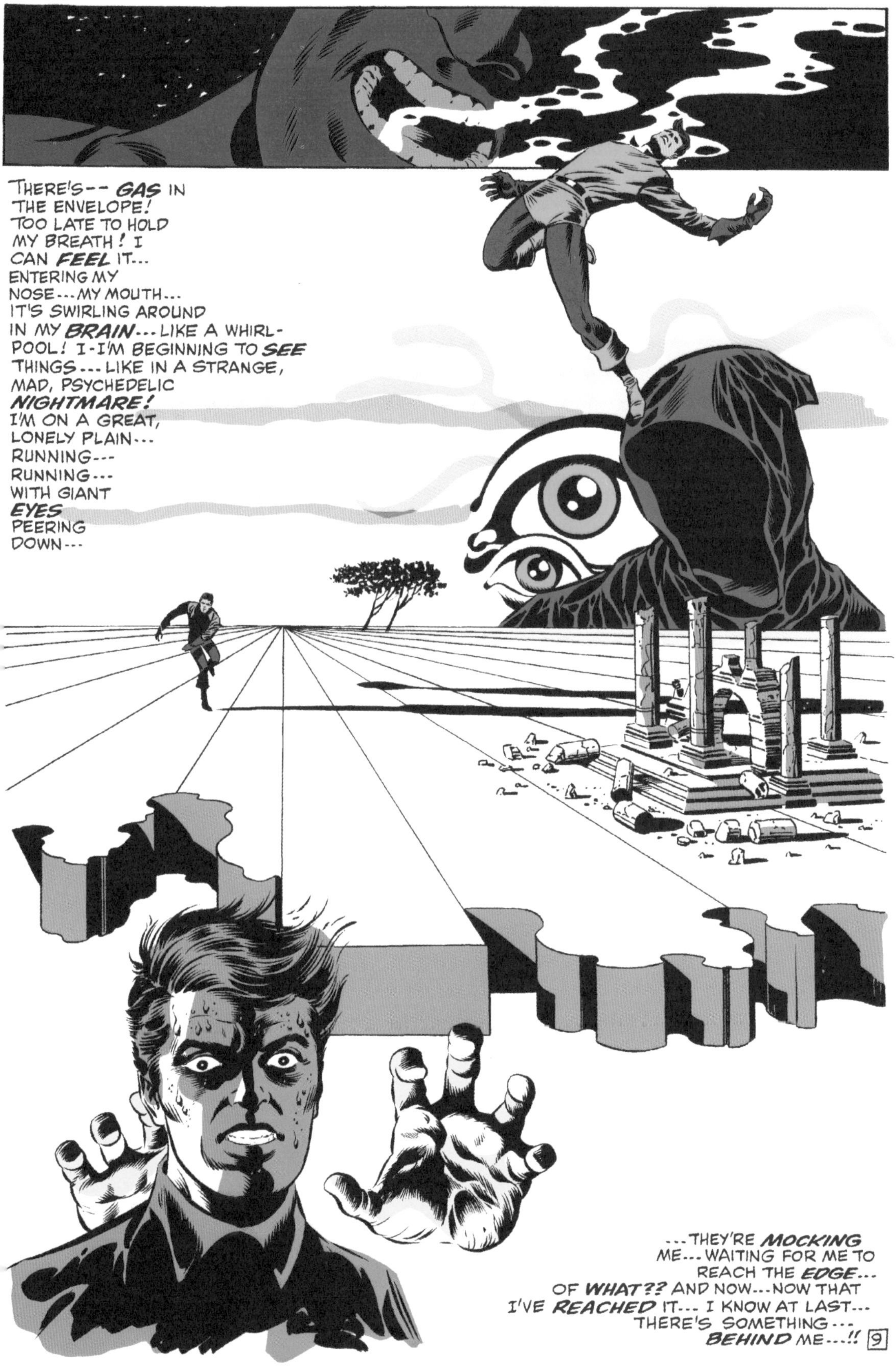
THERE'S-- GAS IN THE ENVELOPE! TOO LATE TO HOLD MY BREATH! I CAN FEEL IT... ENTERING MY NOSE---MY MOUTH... IT'S SWIRLING AROUND IN MY BRAIN--- LIKE A WHIRL-POOL! I-I'M BEGINNING TO SEE THINGS--- LIKE IN A STRANGE, MAD, PSYCHEDELIC NIGHTMARE! I'M ON A GREAT, LONELY PLAIN--- RUNNING--- RUNNING--- WITH GIANT EYES PEERING DOWN---
---THEY'RE MOCKING ME---WAITING FOR ME TO REACH THE EDGE--- OF WHAT?? AND NOW---NOW THAT I'VE REACHED IT--- I KNOW AT LAST--- THERE'S SOMETHING--- BEHIND ME---!!
9

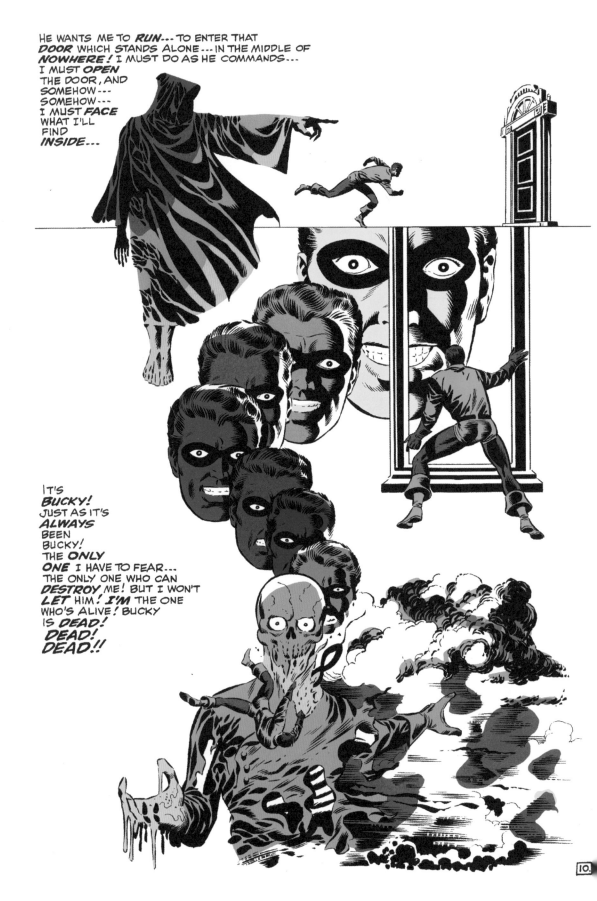

HE WANTS ME TO *RUN*--- TO ENTER THAT *DOOR* WHICH STANDS ALONE...IN THE MIDDLE OF *NOWHERE!* I MUST DO AS HE COMMANDS... I MUST *OPEN* THE DOOR, AND SOMEHOW--- SOMEHOW--- I MUST *FACE* WHAT I'LL FIND *INSIDE*...

IT'S *BUCKY!* JUST AS IT'S *ALWAYS* BEEN BUCKY! THE *ONLY* *ONE* I HAVE TO FEAR... THE ONLY ONE WHO CAN *DESTROY* ME! BUT I WON'T *LET* HIM! *I'M* THE ONE WHO'S ALIVE! BUCKY IS *DEAD!* *DEAD!* *DEAD!!*

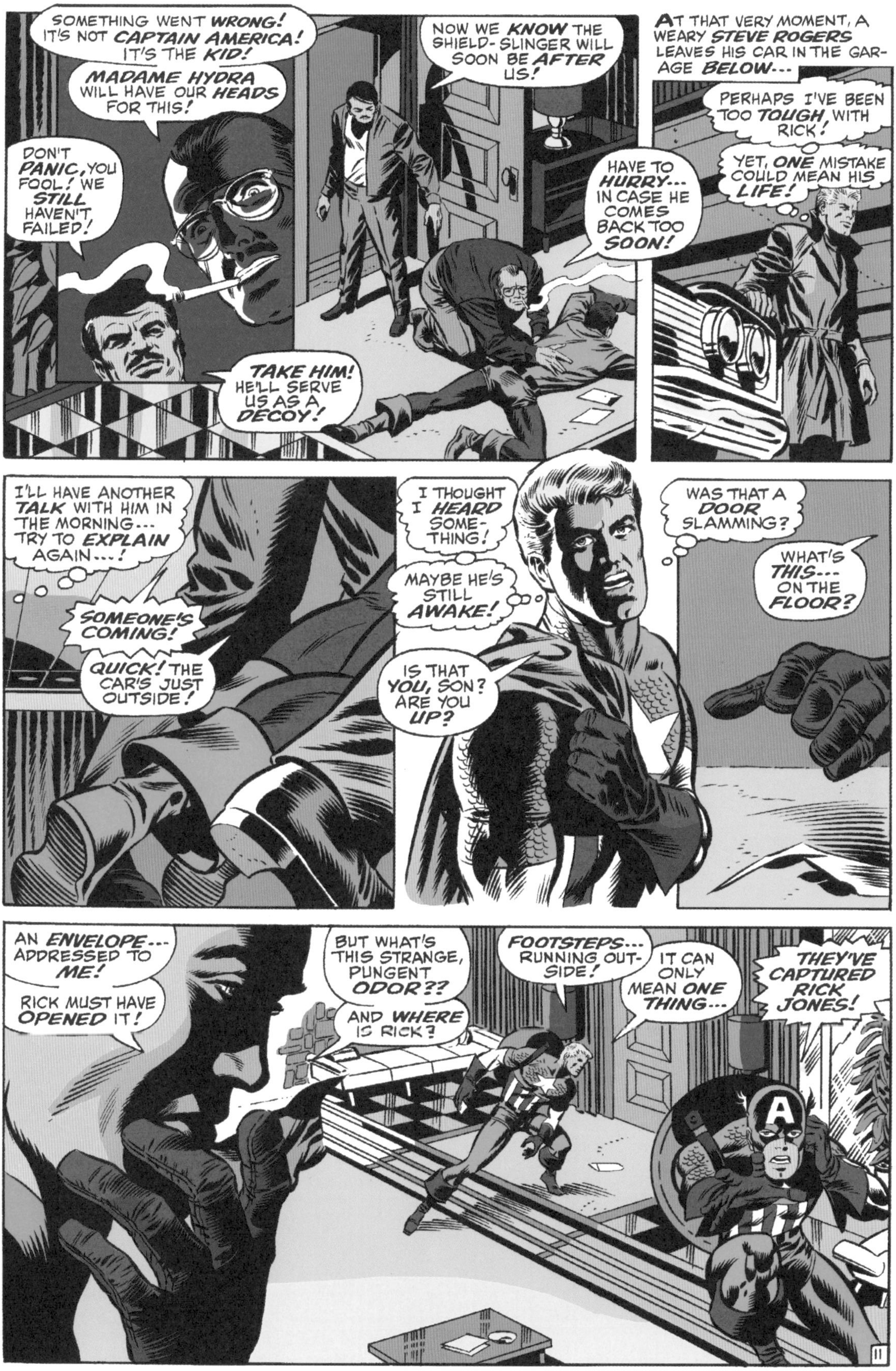
SOMETHING WENT WRONG! IT'S NOT CAPTAIN AMERICA! IT'S THE KID!
MADAME HYDRA WILL HAVE OUR HEADS FOR THIS!
DON'T PANIC, YOU FOOL! WE STILL HAVEN'T FAILED!
TAKE HIM! HE'LL SERVE US AS A DECOY!
NOW WE KNOW THE SHIELD-SLINGER WILL SOON BE AFTER US!
HAVE TO HURRY... IN CASE HE COMES BACK TOO SOON!
AT THAT VERY MOMENT, A WEARY STEVE ROGERS LEAVES HIS CAR IN THE GARAGE BELOW...
PERHAPS I'VE BEEN TOO TOUGH, WITH RICK!
YET, ONE MISTAKE COULD MEAN HIS LIFE!
I'LL HAVE ANOTHER TALK WITH HIM IN THE MORNING... TRY TO EXPLAIN AGAIN...!
SOMEONE'S COMING!
QUICK! THE CAR'S JUST OUTSIDE!
I THOUGHT I HEARD SOMETHING!
MAYBE HE'S STILL AWAKE!
IS THAT YOU, SON? ARE YOU UP?
WAS THAT A DOOR SLAMMING?
WHAT'S THIS... ON THE FLOOR?
AN ENVELOPE... ADDRESSED TO ME!
RICK MUST HAVE OPENED IT!
BUT WHAT'S THIS STRANGE, PUNGENT ODOR??
AND WHERE IS RICK?
FOOTSTEPS... RUNNING OUTSIDE!
IT CAN ONLY MEAN ONE THING...
THEY'VE CAPTURED RICK JONES!
11

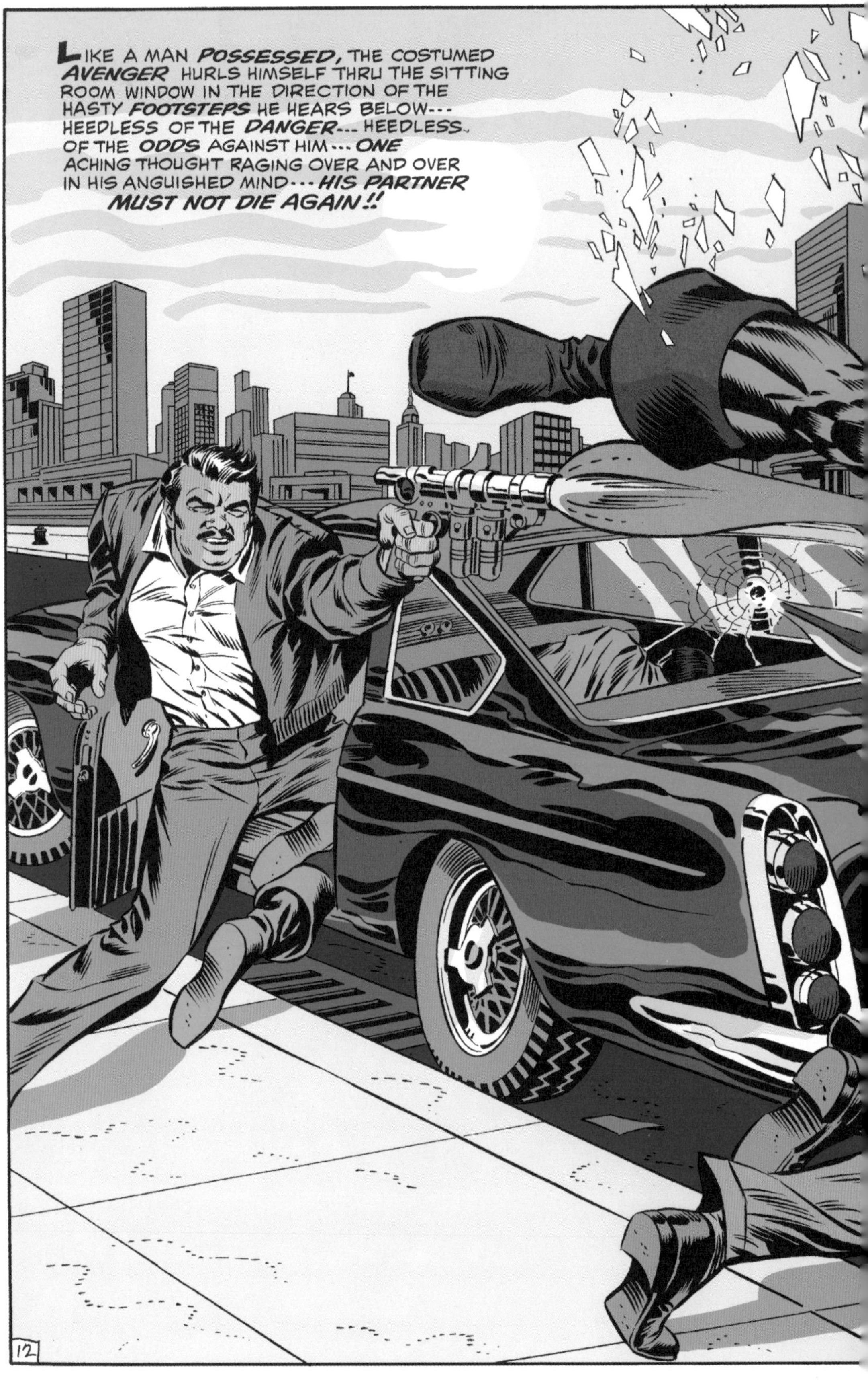
LIKE A MAN POSSESSED, THE COSTUMED AVENGER HURLS HIMSELF THRU THE SITTING ROOM WINDOW IN THE DIRECTION OF THE HASTY FOOTSTEPS HE HEARS BELOW--- HEEDLESS OF THE DANGER--- HEEDLESS OF THE ODDS AGAINST HIM--- ONE ACHING THOUGHT RAGING OVER AND OVER IN HIS ANGUISHED MIND--- HIS PARTNER MUST NOT DIE AGAIN!!
12

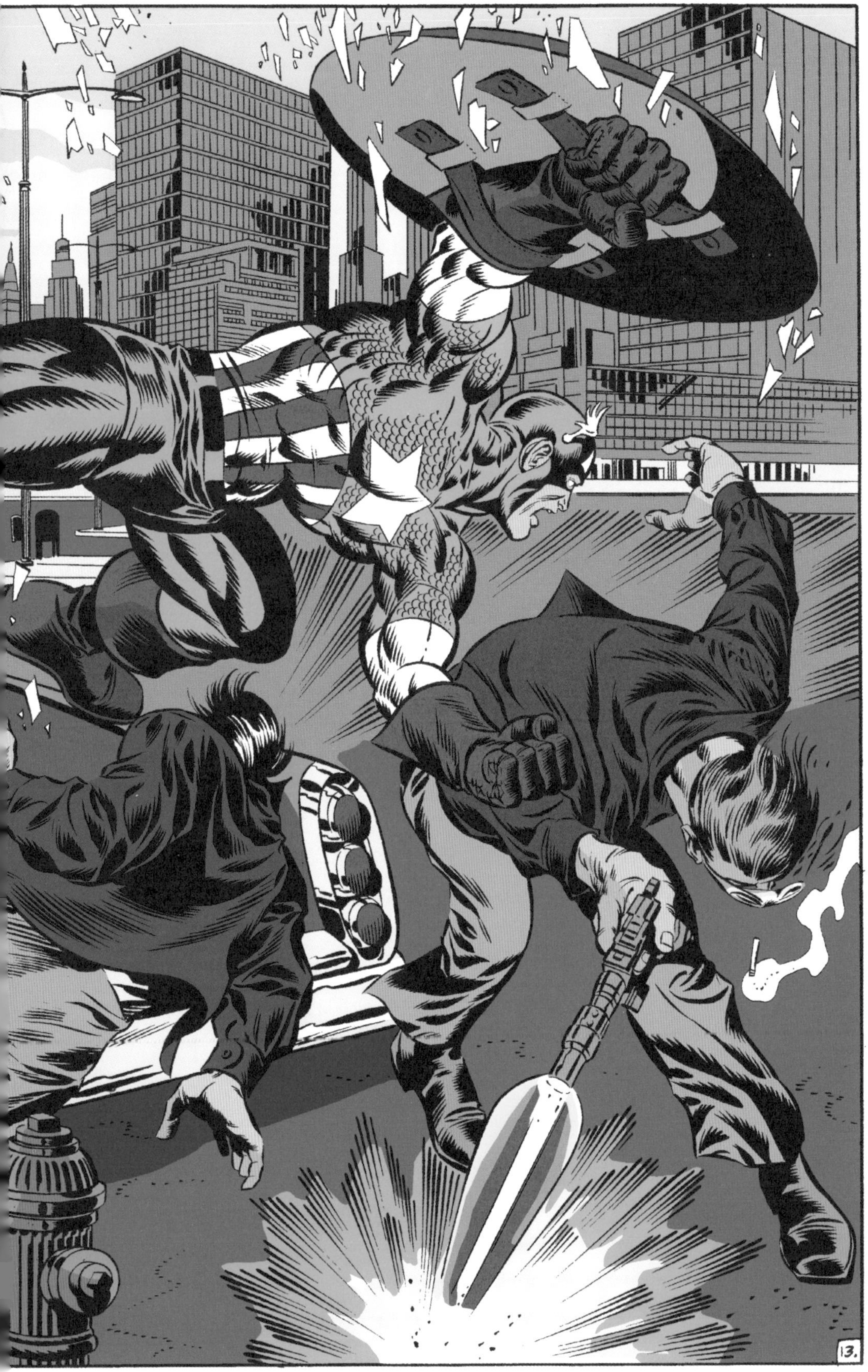
13.

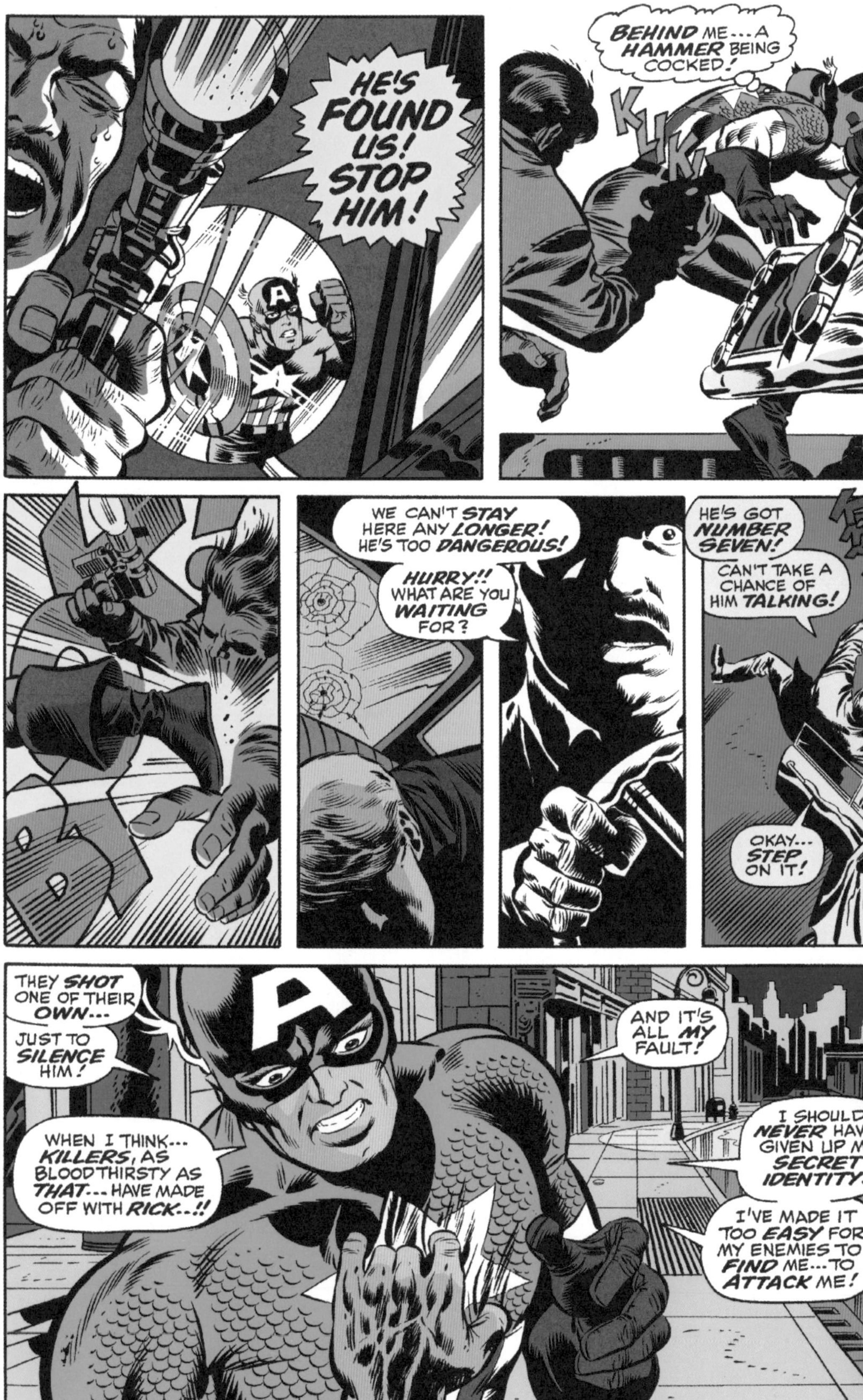
HE'S FOUND US! STOP HIM!
BEHIND ME... A HAMMER BEING COCKED!
KLIK
WE CAN'T STAY HERE ANY LONGER! HE'S TOO DANGEROUS!
HURRY!! WHAT ARE YOU WAITING FOR?
HE'S GOT NUMBER SEVEN!
CAN'T TAKE A CHANCE OF HIM TALKING!
KRAK!
OKAY... STEP ON IT!
THEY SHOT ONE OF THEIR OWN...
JUST TO SILENCE HIM!
WHEN I THINK... KILLERS, AS BLOODTHIRSTY AS THAT... HAVE MADE OFF WITH RICK..!!
AND IT'S ALL MY FAULT!
I SHOULD NEVER HAVE GIVEN UP MY SECRET IDENTITY!
I'VE MADE IT TOO EASY FOR MY ENEMIES TO FIND ME... TO ATTACK ME!
14

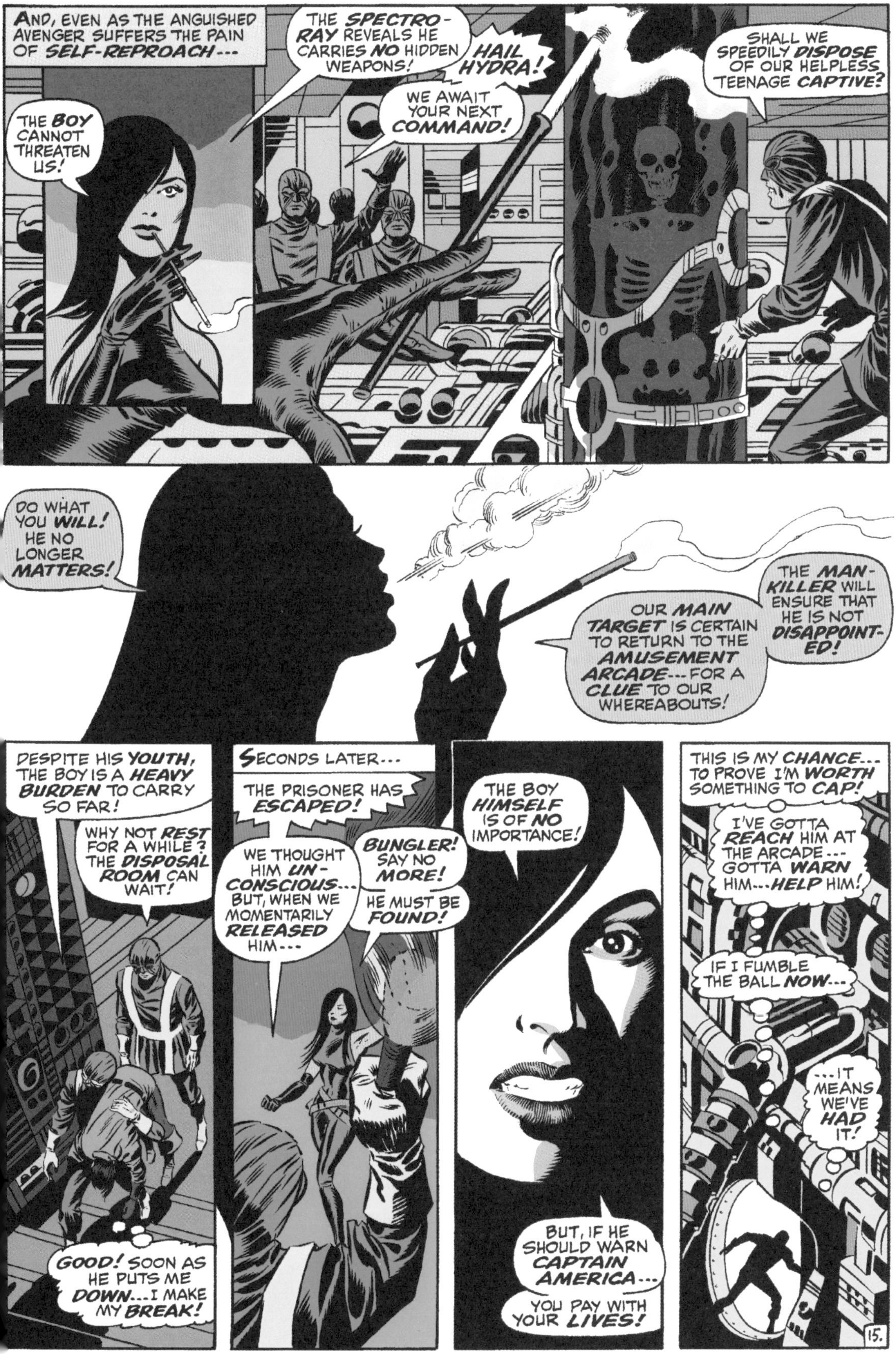
AND, EVEN AS THE ANGUISHED AVENGER SUFFERS THE PAIN OF SELF-REPROACH---
THE BOY CANNOT THREATEN US!
THE SPECTRO-RAY REVEALS HE CARRIES NO HIDDEN WEAPONS!
HAIL HYDRA!
WE AWAIT YOUR NEXT COMMAND!
SHALL WE SPEEDILY DISPOSE OF OUR HELPLESS TEENAGE CAPTIVE?
DO WHAT YOU WILL! HE NO LONGER MATTERS!
OUR MAIN TARGET IS CERTAIN TO RETURN TO THE AMUSEMENT ARCADE--- FOR A CLUE TO OUR WHEREABOUTS!
THE MAN-KILLER WILL ENSURE THAT HE IS NOT DISAPPOINT-ED!
DESPITE HIS YOUTH, THE BOY IS A HEAVY BURDEN TO CARRY SO FAR!
WHY NOT REST FOR A WHILE? THE DISPOSAL ROOM CAN WAIT!
GOOD! SOON AS HE PUTS ME DOWN...I MAKE MY BREAK!
SECONDS LATER---
THE PRISONER HAS ESCAPED!
WE THOUGHT HIM UN-CONSCIOUS... BUT, WHEN WE MOMENTARILY RELEASED HIM---
BUNGLER! SAY NO MORE!
HE MUST BE FOUND!
THE BOY HIMSELF IS OF NO IMPORTANCE!
BUT, IF HE SHOULD WARN CAPTAIN AMERICA...
YOU PAY WITH YOUR LIVES!
THIS IS MY CHANCE... TO PROVE I'M WORTH SOMETHING TO CAP!
I'VE GOTTA REACH HIM AT THE ARCADE--- GOTTA WARN HIM---HELP HIM!
IF I FUMBLE THE BALL NOW...
...IT MEANS WE'VE HAD IT!
15.

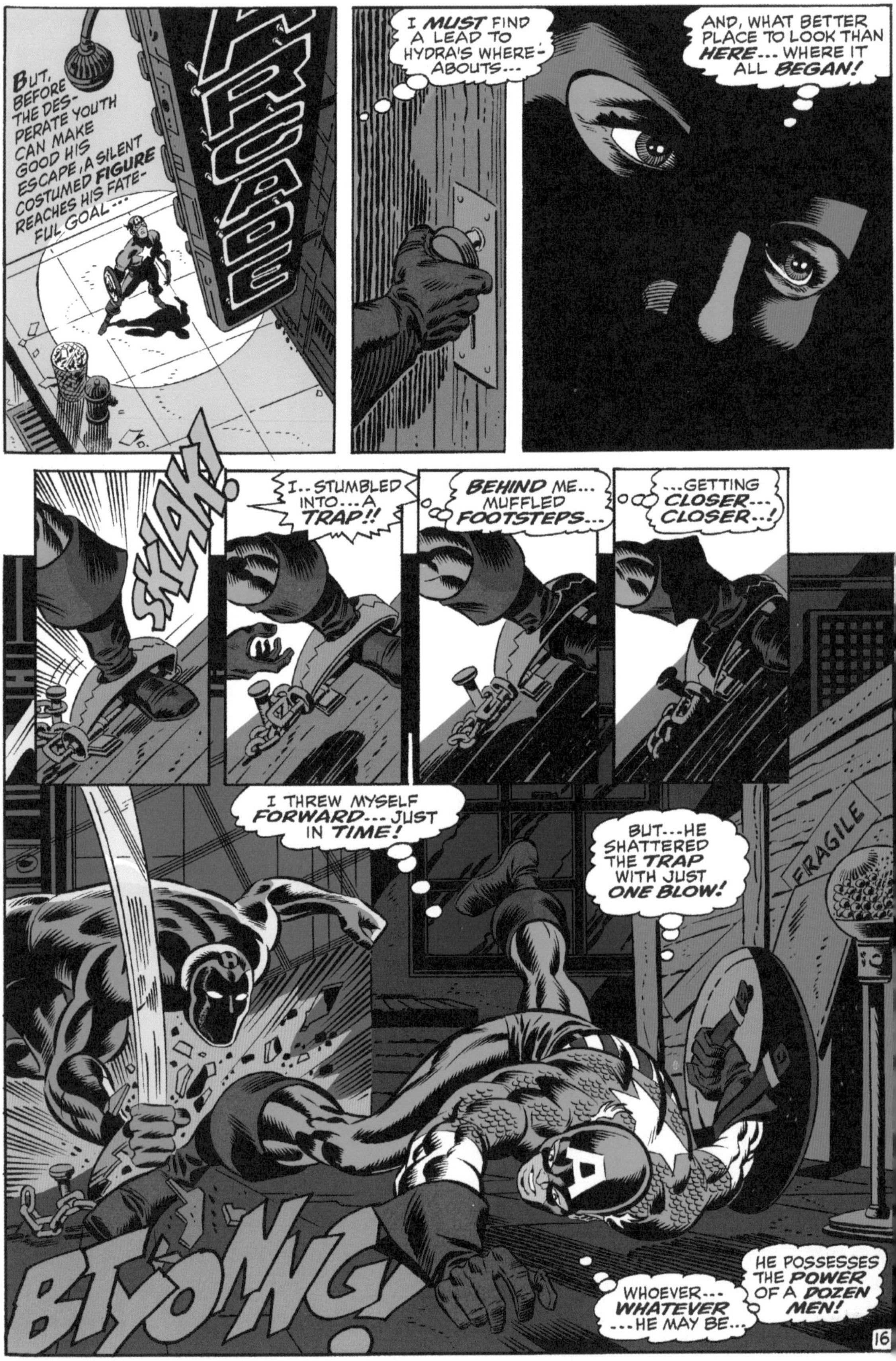

BUT, BEFORE THE DESPERATE YOUTH CAN MAKE GOOD HIS ESCAPE, A SILENT COSTUMED FIGURE REACHES HIS FATEFUL GOAL...
ARCADE
I MUST FIND A LEAD TO HYDRA'S WHEREABOUTS---
AND, WHAT BETTER PLACE TO LOOK THAN HERE--- WHERE IT ALL BEGAN!
SKLAK!
I.. STUMBLED INTO... A TRAP!!
BEHIND ME... MUFFLED FOOTSTEPS...
...GETTING CLOSER--- CLOSER--!
I THREW MYSELF FORWARD--- JUST IN TIME!
BUT---HE SHATTERED THE TRAP WITH JUST ONE BLOW!
FRAGILE
BTYONNG!
WHOEVER--- WHATEVER ---HE MAY BE...
HE POSSESSES THE POWER OF A DOZEN MEN!
16

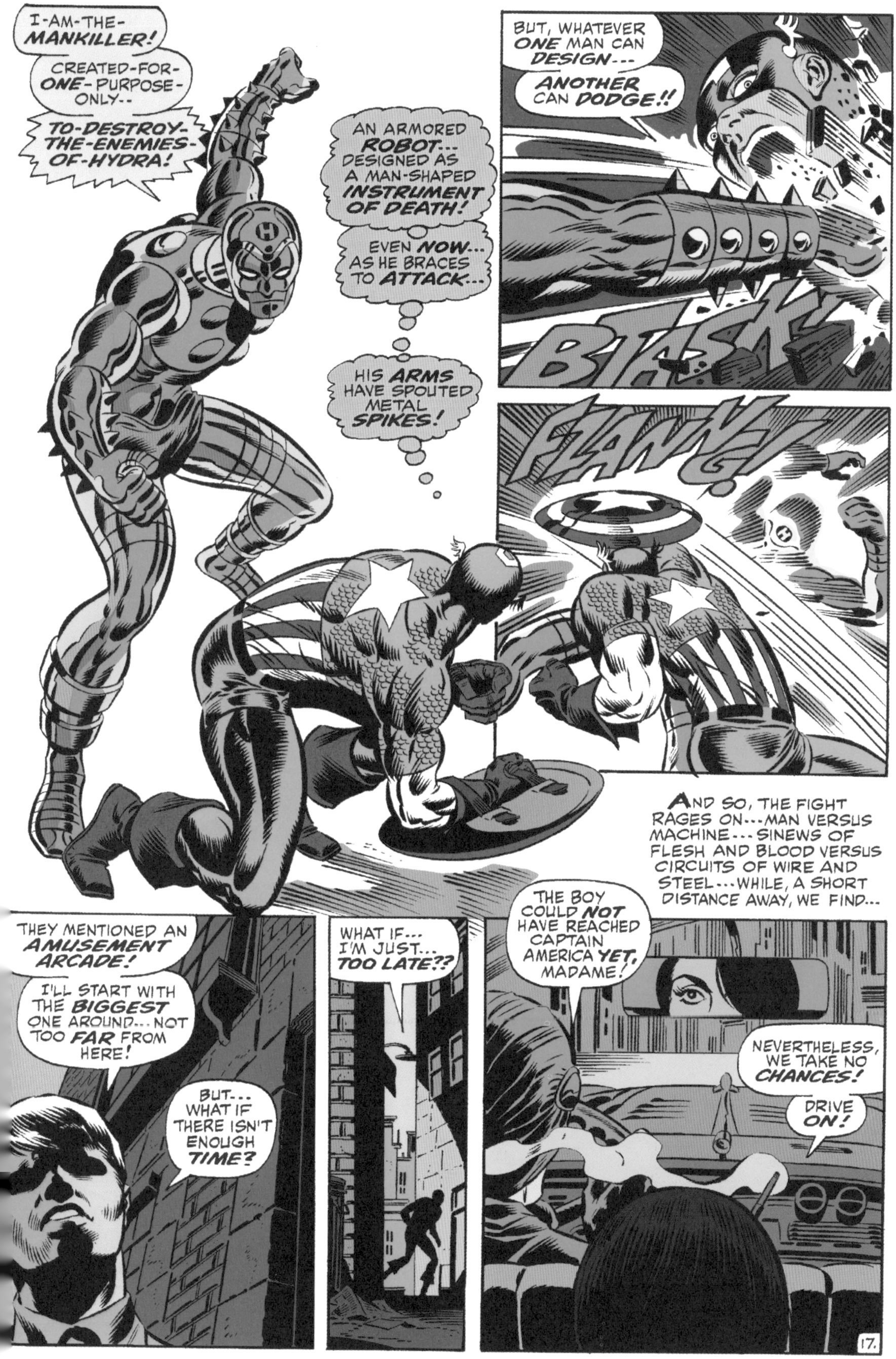
I-AM-THE-MANKILLER!
CREATED-FOR-ONE-PURPOSE-ONLY--
TO-DESTROY-THE-ENEMIES-OF-HYDRA!
AN ARMORED ROBOT... DESIGNED AS A MAN-SHAPED INSTRUMENT OF DEATH!
EVEN NOW... AS HE BRACES TO ATTACK...
HIS ARMS HAVE SPOUTED METAL SPIKES!
BUT, WHATEVER ONE MAN CAN DESIGN---
ANOTHER CAN DODGE!!
BTASK!
FZANNG!
AND SO, THE FIGHT RAGES ON---MAN VERSUS MACHINE---SINEWS OF FLESH AND BLOOD VERSUS CIRCUITS OF WIRE AND STEEL---WHILE, A SHORT DISTANCE AWAY, WE FIND...
THEY MENTIONED AN AMUSEMENT ARCADE!
I'LL START WITH THE BIGGEST ONE AROUND... NOT TOO FAR FROM HERE!
BUT... WHAT IF THERE ISN'T ENOUGH TIME?
WHAT IF... I'M JUST... TOO LATE??
THE BOY COULD NOT HAVE REACHED CAPTAIN AMERICA YET, MADAME!
NEVERTHELESS, WE TAKE NO CHANCES!
DRIVE ON!
17.

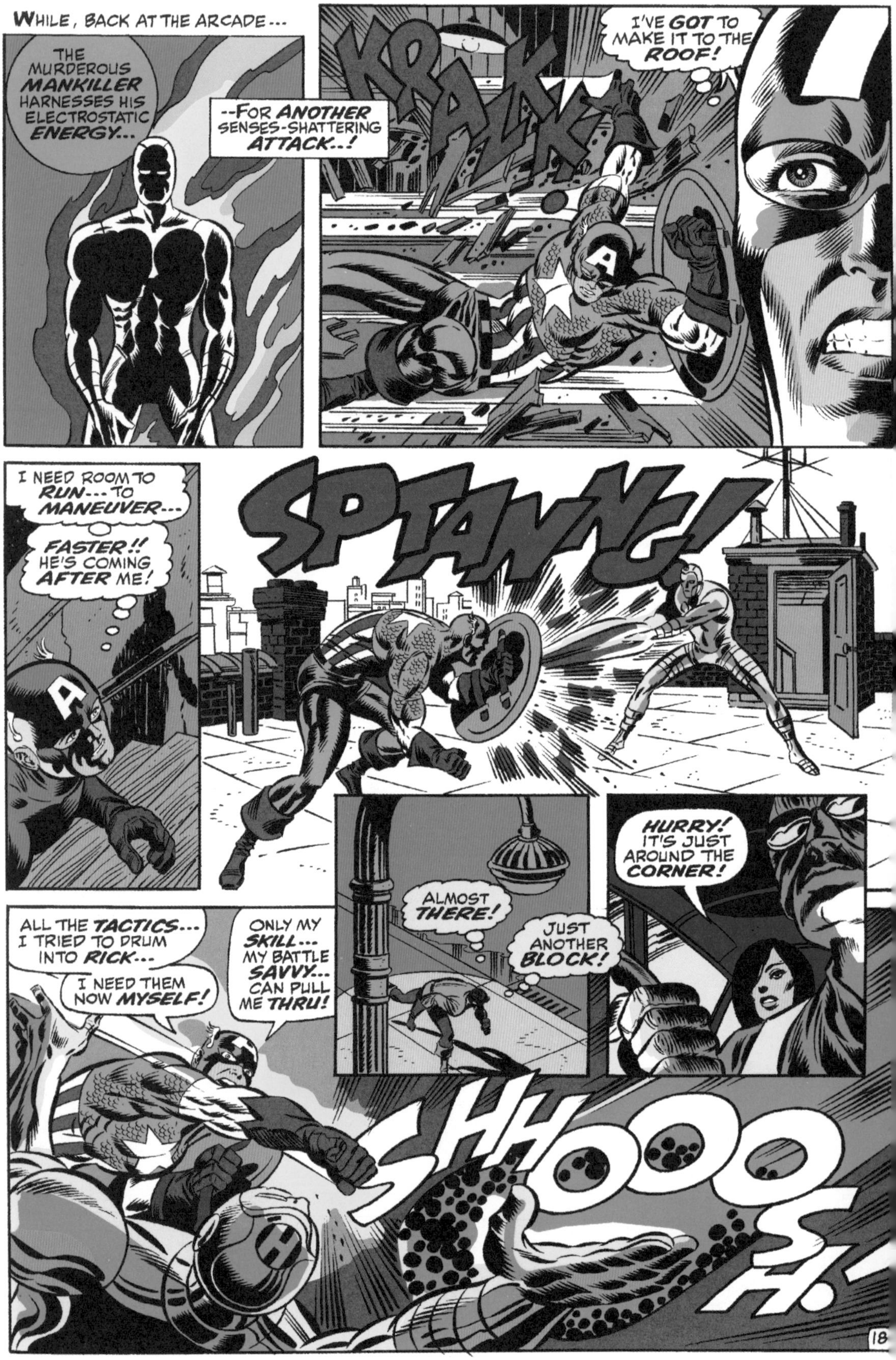
WHILE, BACK AT THE ARCADE...
THE MURDEROUS MANKILLER HARNESSES HIS ELECTROSTATIC ENERGY...
--FOR ANOTHER SENSES-SHATTERING ATTACK..!
KRAKK!
I'VE GOT TO MAKE IT TO THE ROOF!
I NEED ROOM TO RUN--- TO MANEUVER---
FASTER!! HE'S COMING AFTER ME!
SPTANNG!
ALMOST THERE!
JUST ANOTHER BLOCK!
HURRY! IT'S JUST AROUND THE CORNER!
ALL THE TACTICS... I TRIED TO DRUM INTO RICK...
I NEED THEM NOW MYSELF!
ONLY MY SKILL... MY BATTLE SAVVY... CAN PULL ME THRU!
SHHOOOSH!
18

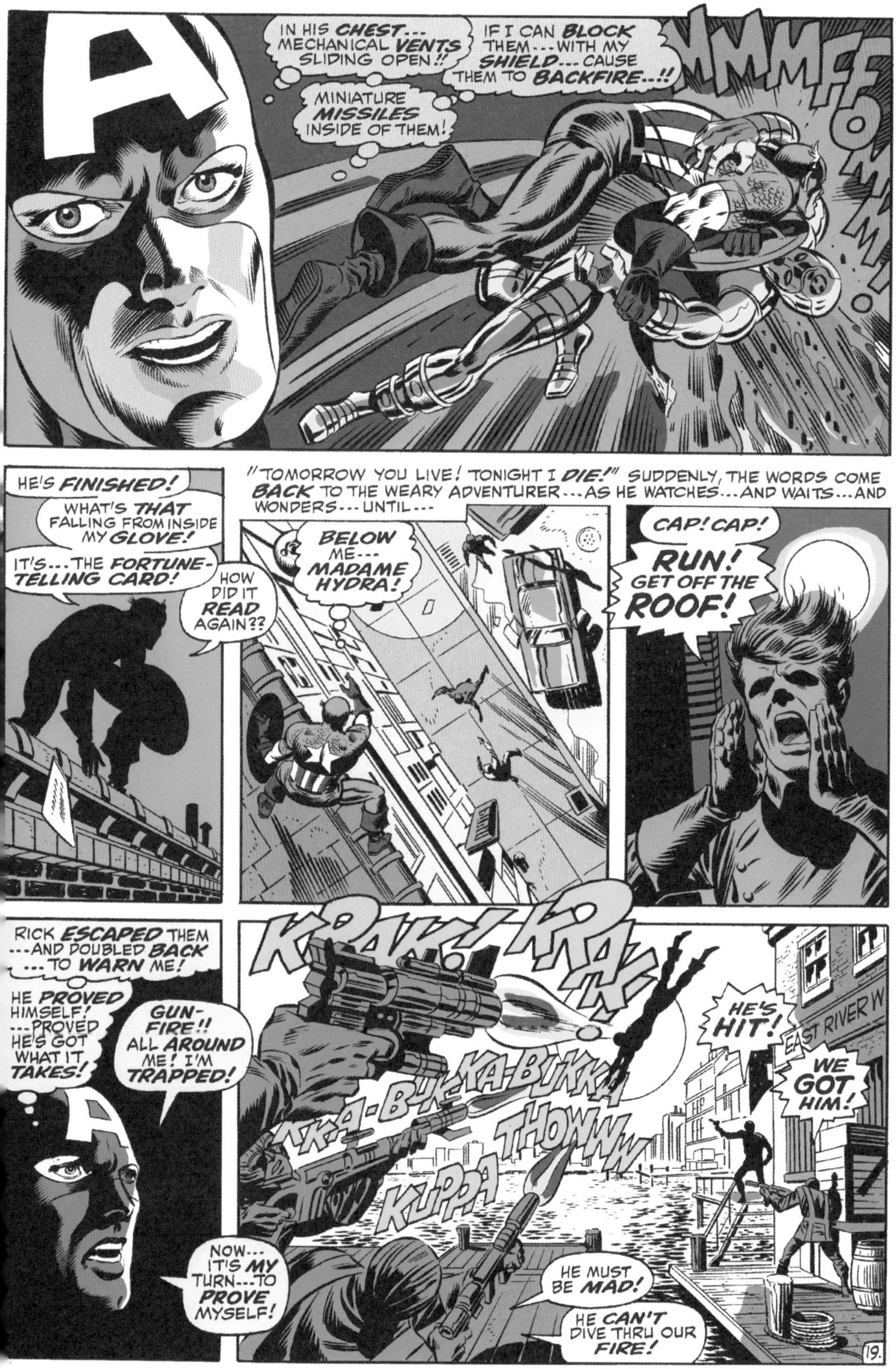

IN HIS CHEST... MECHANICAL VENTS SLIDING OPEN!!
MINIATURE MISSILES INSIDE OF THEM!
IF I CAN BLOCK THEM---WITH MY SHIELD--- CAUSE THEM TO BACKFIRE..!!
MMMFFOMM!
HE'S FINISHED!
WHAT'S THAT FALLING FROM INSIDE MY GLOVE!
IT'S--- THE FORTUNE-TELLING CARD!
HOW DID IT READ AGAIN??
"TOMORROW YOU LIVE! TONIGHT I DIE!" SUDDENLY, THE WORDS COME BACK TO THE WEARY ADVENTURER---AS HE WATCHES---AND WAITS---AND WONDERS---UNTIL---
BELOW ME--- MADAME HYDRA!
CAP! CAP!
RUN! GET OFF THE ROOF!
RICK ESCAPED THEM ---AND DOUBLED BACK ---TO WARN ME!
HE PROVED HIMSELF! ---PROVED HE'S GOT WHAT IT TAKES!
GUN-FIRE!! ALL AROUND ME! I'M TRAPPED!
NOW--- IT'S MY TURN---TO PROVE MYSELF!
KRAK! KRAK!
KKA-BUKKA-BUKKA
THOWW
KUPPA
HE'S HIT!
EAST RIVER W
WE GOT HIM!
HE MUST BE MAD!
HE CAN'T DIVE THRU OUR FIRE!
19.

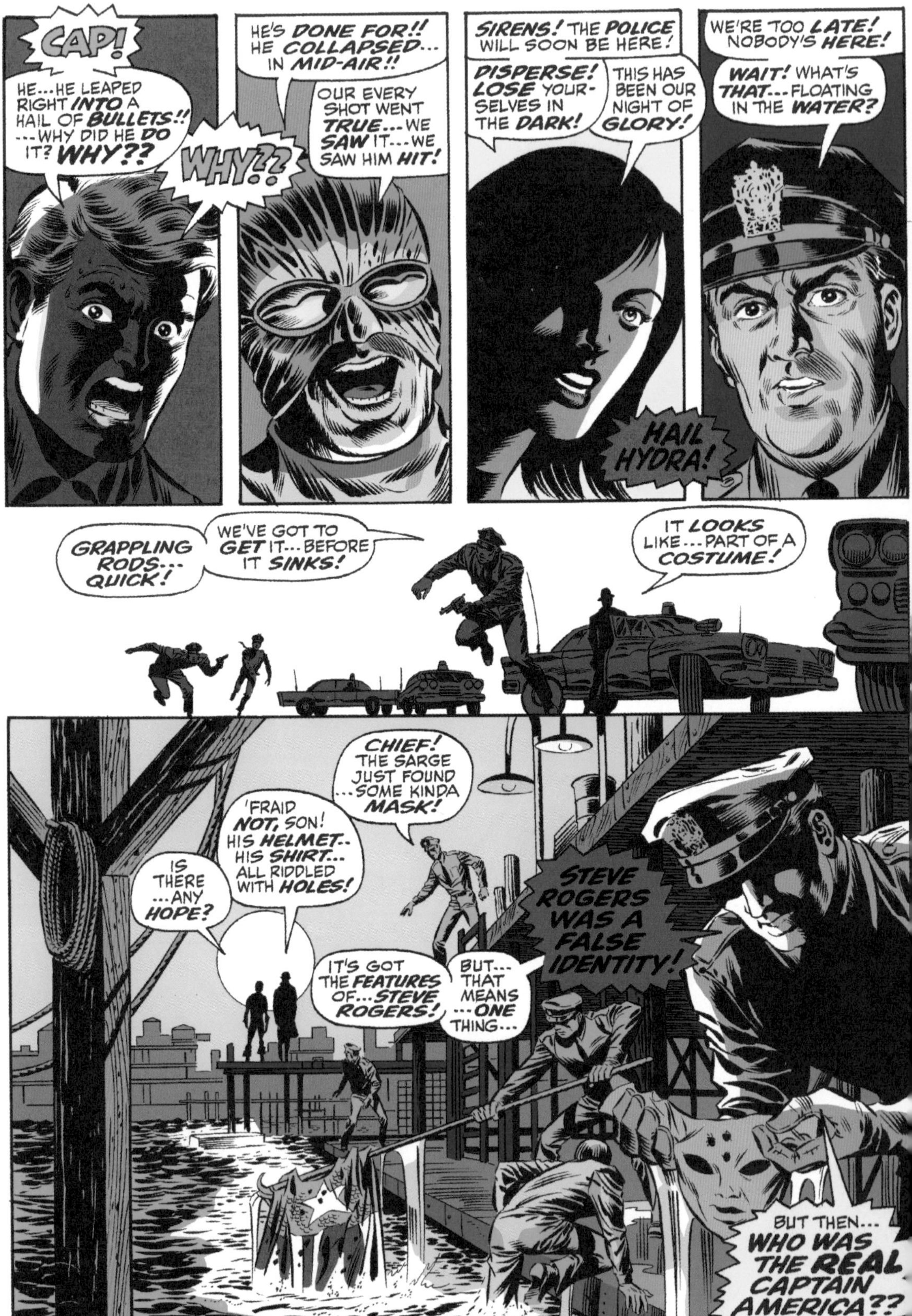
CAP!
HE...HE LEAPED RIGHT INTO A HAIL OF BULLETS!! ...WHY DID HE DO IT? WHY??
WHY??
HE'S DONE FOR!! HE COLLAPSED... IN MID-AIR!!
OUR EVERY SHOT WENT TRUE...WE SAW IT...WE SAW HIM HIT!
SIRENS! THE POLICE WILL SOON BE HERE!
DISPERSE! LOSE YOURSELVES IN THE DARK!
THIS HAS BEEN OUR NIGHT OF GLORY!
HAIL HYDRA!
WE'RE TOO LATE! NOBODY'S HERE!
WAIT! WHAT'S THAT...FLOATING IN THE WATER?
GRAPPLING RODS... QUICK!
WE'VE GOT TO GET IT...BEFORE IT SINKS!
IT LOOKS LIKE...PART OF A COSTUME!
IS THERE ...ANY HOPE?
'FRAID NOT, SON! HIS HELMET.. HIS SHIRT... ALL RIDDLED WITH HOLES!
CHIEF! THE SARGE JUST FOUND ...SOME KINDA MASK!
IT'S GOT THE FEATURES OF...STEVE ROGERS!
BUT... THAT MEANS ...ONE THING...
STEVE ROGERS WAS A FALSE IDENTITY!
BUT THEN... WHO WAS THE REAL CAPTAIN AMERICA??
PERHAPS WE WILL LEARN...NEXT ISSUE!
20

CAPTAIN AMERICA #113,

MAY 1969,

"THE STRANGE DEATH OF

CAPTAIN AMERICA!"

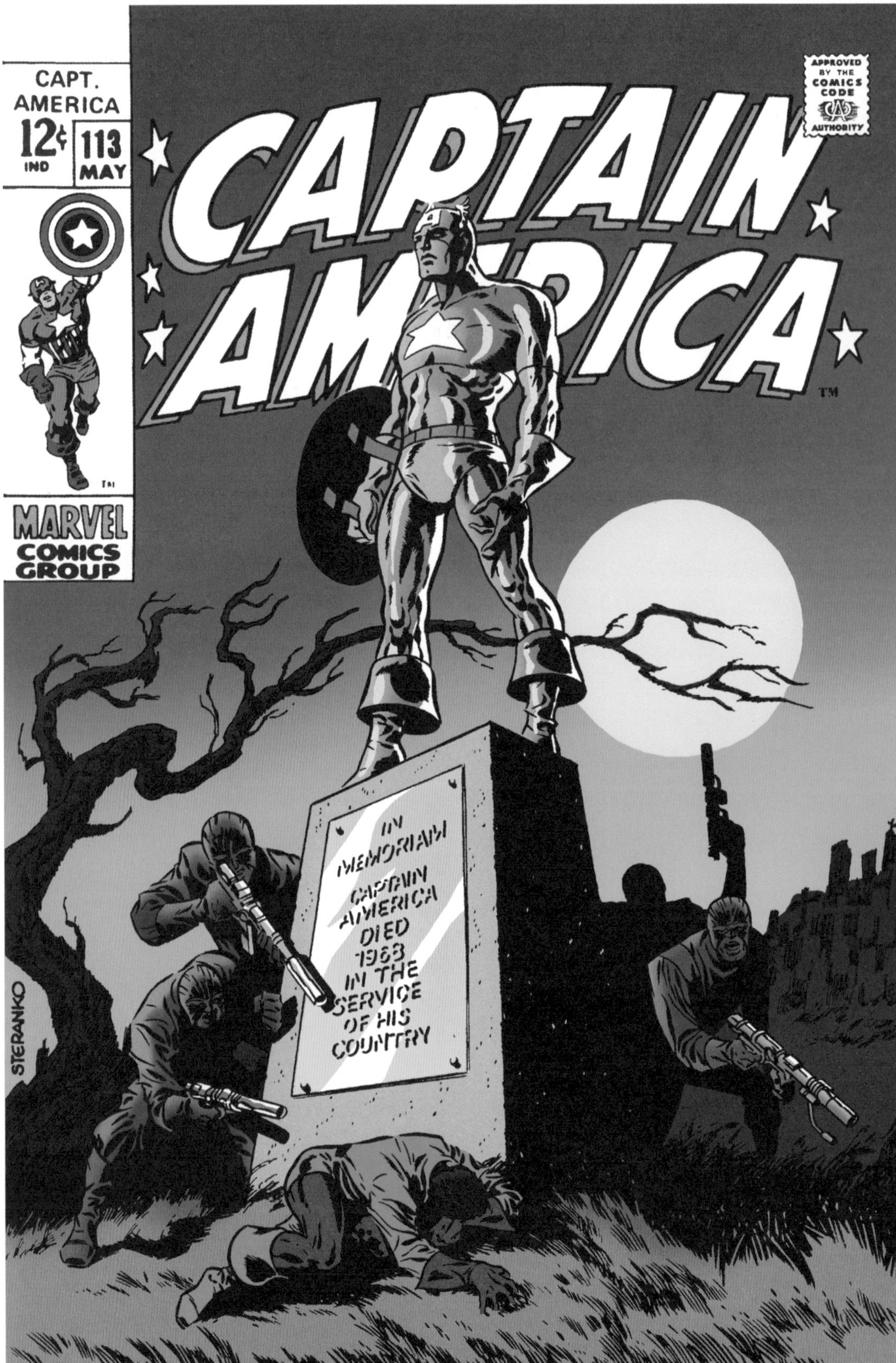
CAPT.
AMERICA
12¢
IND
113
MAY
APPROVED BY THE COMICS CODE AUTHORITY
CAPTAIN AMERICA
TM
MARVEL
COMICS
GROUP
IN MEMORIAM
CAPTAIN AMERICA
DIED
1968
IN THE SERVICE
OF HIS
COUNTRY
STERANKO

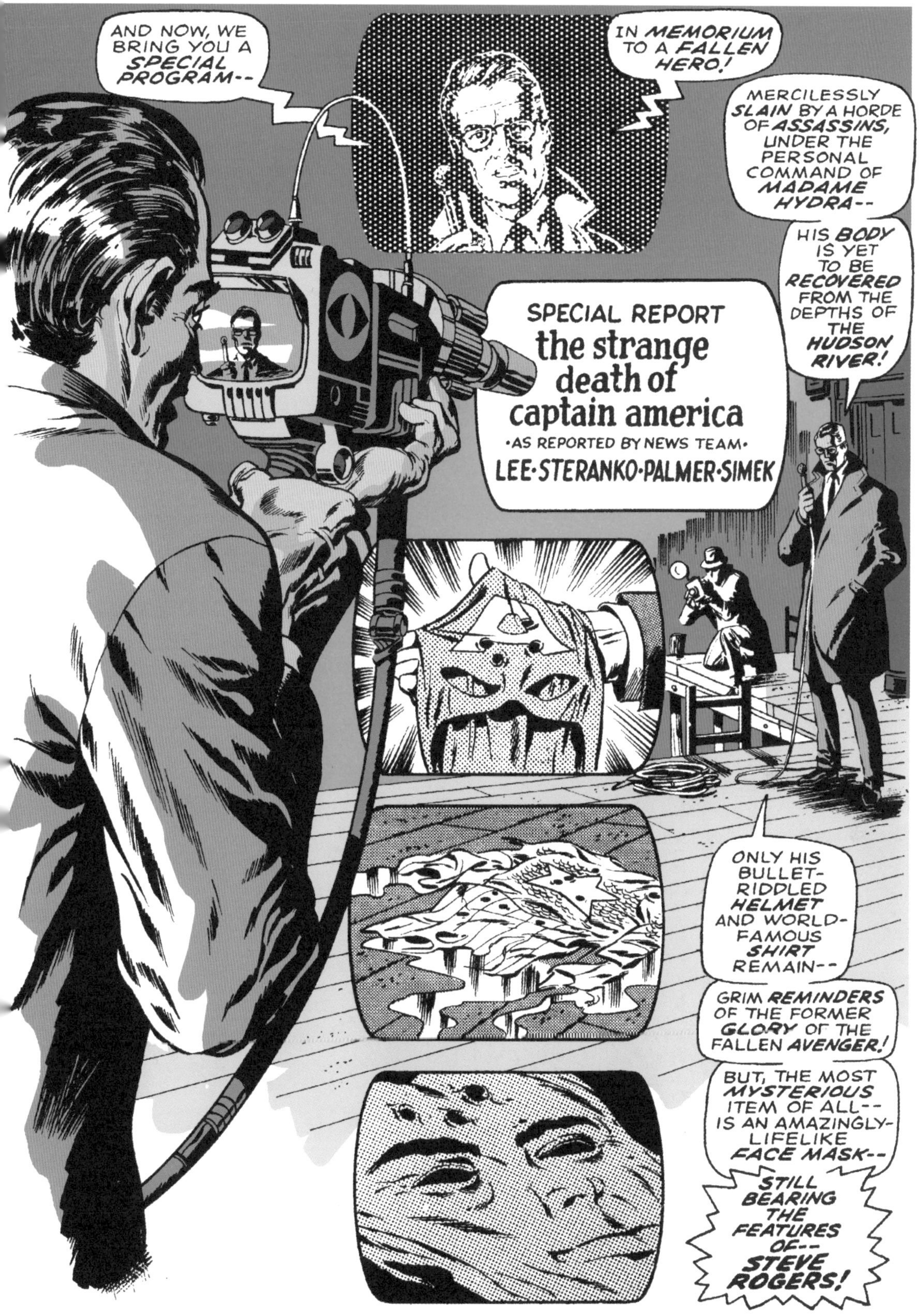
AND NOW, WE BRING YOU A SPECIAL PROGRAM--
IN MEMORIUM TO A FALLEN HERO!
MERCILESSLY SLAIN BY A HORDE OF ASSASSINS, UNDER THE PERSONAL COMMAND OF MADAME HYDRA--
HIS BODY IS YET TO BE RECOVERED FROM THE DEPTHS OF THE HUDSON RIVER!
SPECIAL REPORT
the strange death of captain america
•AS REPORTED BY NEWS TEAM•
LEE•STERANKO•PALMER•SIMEK
ONLY HIS BULLET-RIDDLED HELMET AND WORLD-FAMOUS SHIRT REMAIN--
GRIM REMINDERS OF THE FORMER GLORY OF THE FALLEN AVENGER!
BUT, THE MOST MYSTERIOUS ITEM OF ALL-- IS AN AMAZINGLY-LIFELIKE FACE MASK--
STILL BEARING THE FEATURES OF-- STEVE ROGERS!

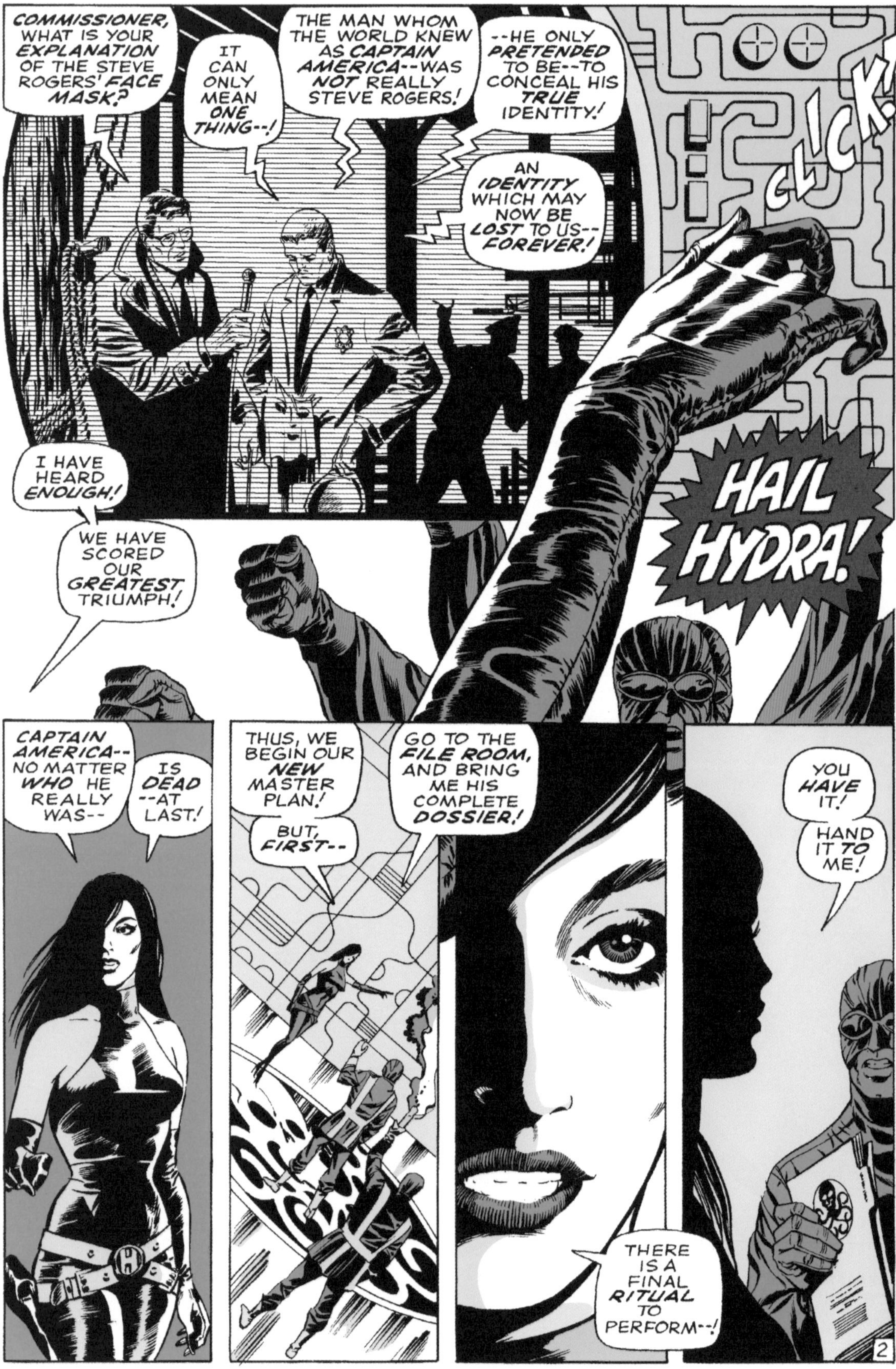
COMMISSIONER, WHAT IS YOUR EXPLANATION OF THE STEVE ROGERS' FACE MASK?
IT CAN ONLY MEAN ONE THING--!
THE MAN WHOM THE WORLD KNEW AS CAPTAIN AMERICA--WAS NOT REALLY STEVE ROGERS!
--HE ONLY PRETENDED TO BE--TO CONCEAL HIS TRUE IDENTITY!
AN IDENTITY WHICH MAY NOW BE LOST TO US--FOREVER!
CLICK!
I HAVE HEARD ENOUGH!
WE HAVE SCORED OUR GREATEST TRIUMPH!
HAIL HYDRA!
CAPTAIN AMERICA--NO MATTER WHO HE REALLY WAS--
IS DEAD--AT LAST!
THUS, WE BEGIN OUR NEW MASTER PLAN!
BUT, FIRST--
GO TO THE FILE ROOM, AND BRING ME HIS COMPLETE DOSSIER!
THERE IS A FINAL RITUAL TO PERFORM--!
YOU HAVE IT!
HAND IT TO ME!
2

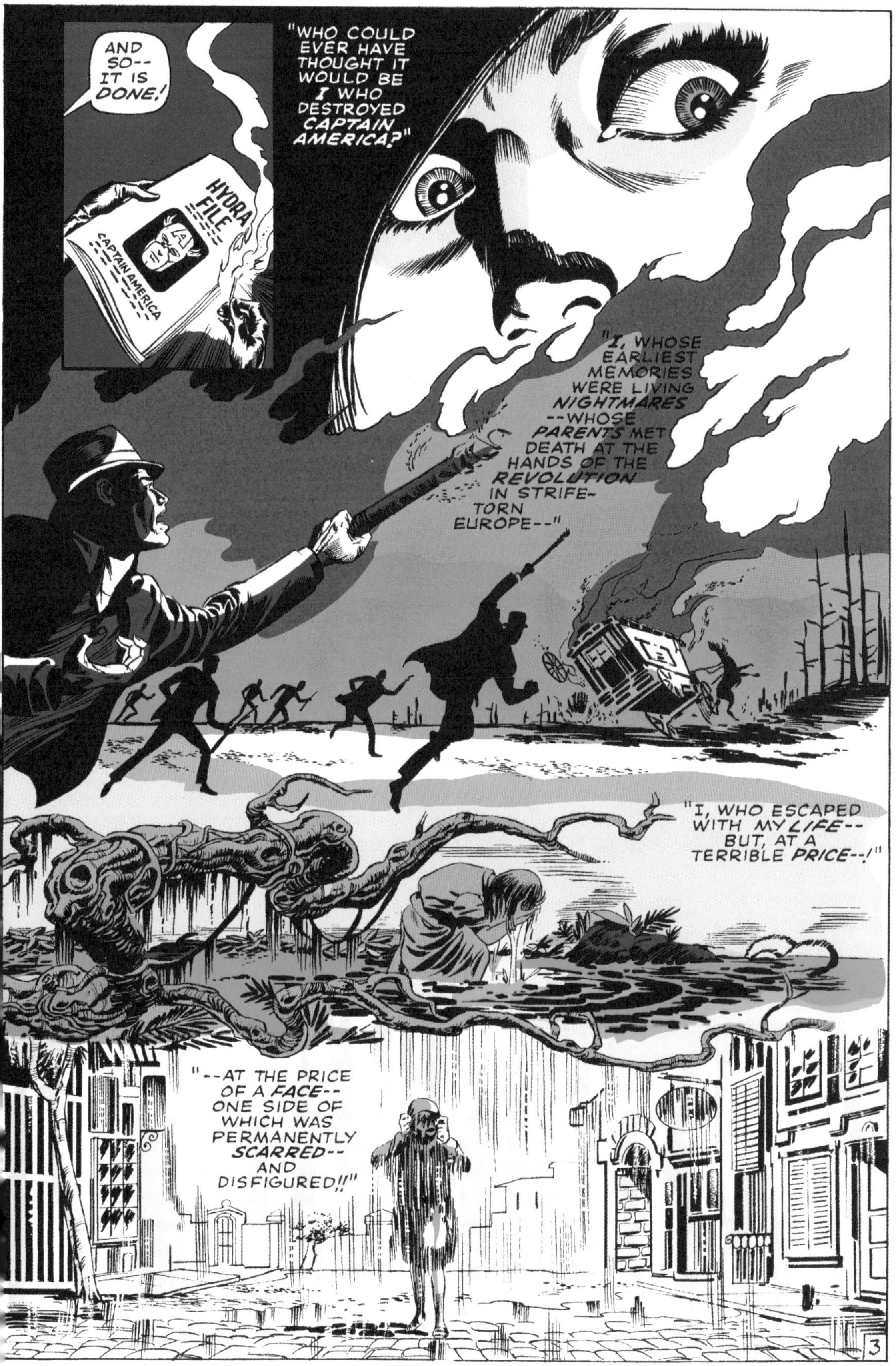
AND SO-- IT IS DONE!
"WHO COULD EVER HAVE THOUGHT IT WOULD BE I WHO DESTROYED CAPTAIN AMERICA?"
HYDRA FILE
CAPTAIN AMERICA
"I, WHOSE EARLIEST MEMORIES WERE LIVING NIGHTMARES --WHOSE PARENTS MET DEATH AT THE HANDS OF THE REVOLUTION IN STRIFE-TORN EUROPE--"
"I, WHO ESCAPED WITH MY LIFE-- BUT, AT A TERRIBLE PRICE--!"
"--AT THE PRICE OF A FACE-- ONE SIDE OF WHICH WAS PERMANENTLY SCARRED-- AND DISFIGURED!!"
3

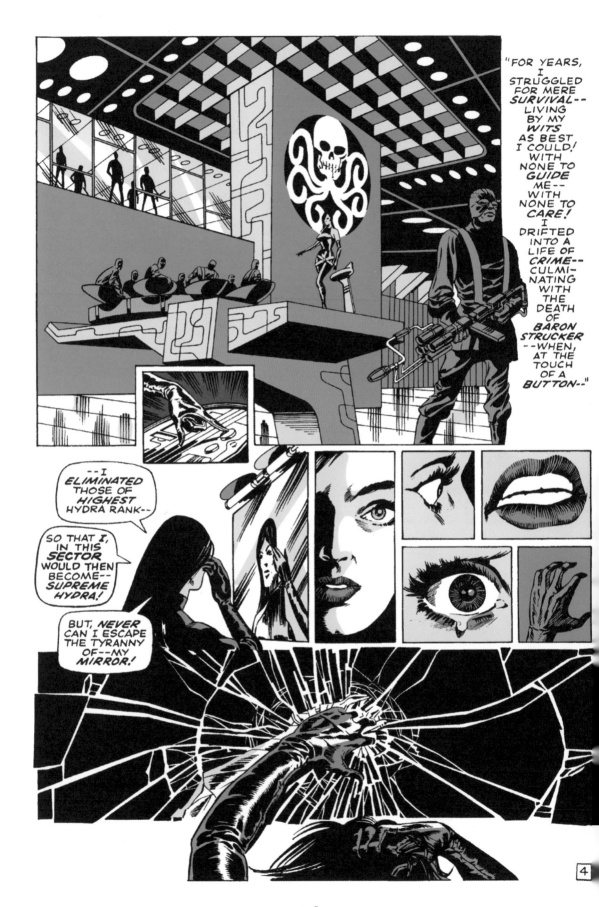

"FOR YEARS, I STRUGGLED FOR MERE *SURVIVAL*-- LIVING BY MY *WITS* AS BEST I COULD! WITH NONE TO *GUIDE* ME-- WITH NONE TO *CARE!* I DRIFTED INTO A LIFE OF *CRIME*-- CULMINATING WITH THE DEATH OF *BARON STRUCKER* --WHEN, AT THE TOUCH OF A *BUTTON*--"

--I *ELIMINATED* THOSE OF *HIGHEST* HYDRA RANK--

SO THAT *I*, IN THIS *SECTOR* WOULD THEN BECOME-- *SUPREME HYDRA!*

BUT, *NEVER* CAN I ESCAPE THE *TYRANNY* OF--MY *MIRROR!*

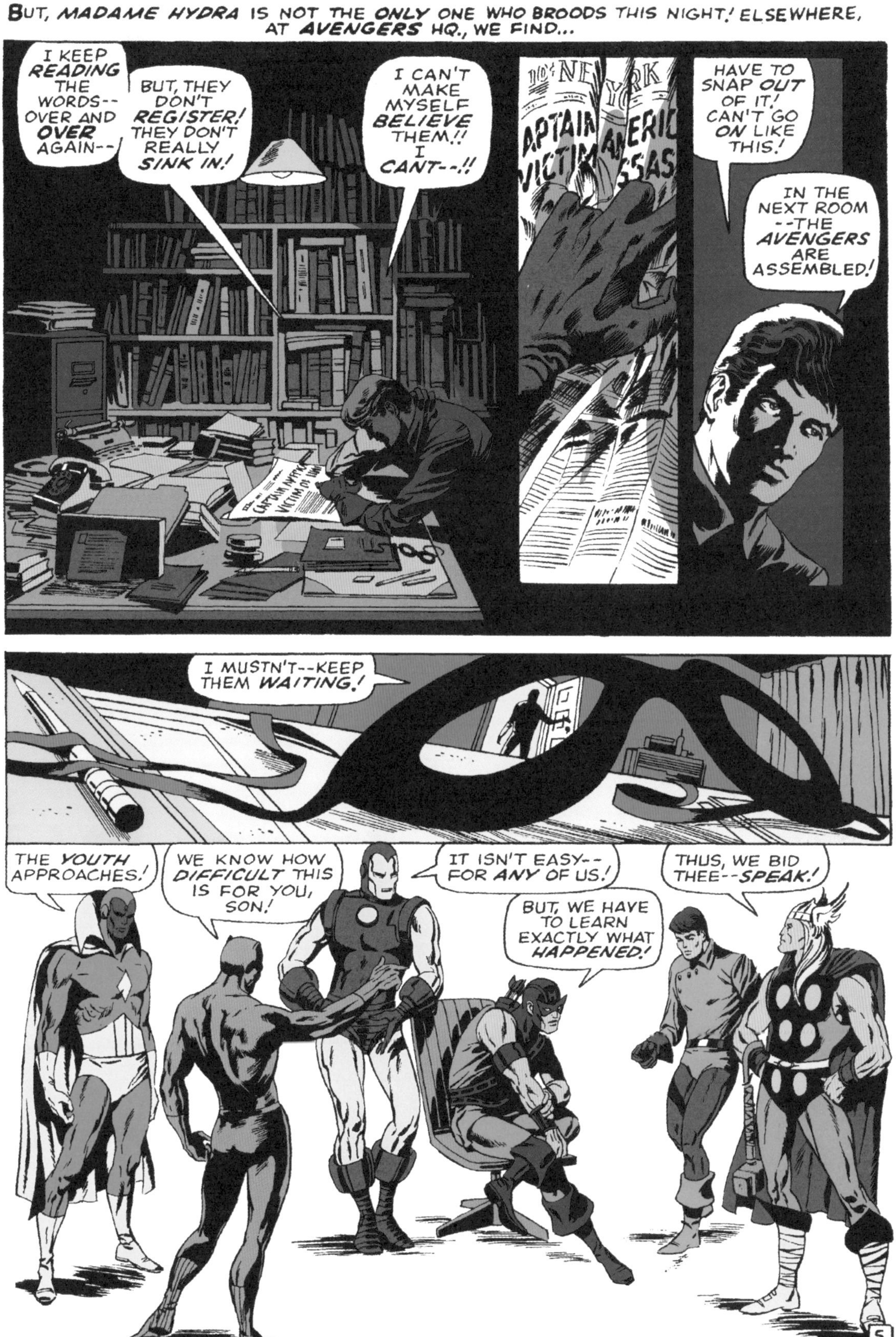

BUT, MADAME HYDRA IS NOT THE ONLY ONE WHO BROODS THIS NIGHT! ELSEWHERE, AT AVENGERS HQ., WE FIND...
I KEEP READING THE WORDS-- OVER AND OVER AGAIN--
BUT, THEY DON'T REGISTER! THEY DON'T REALLY SINK IN!
I CAN'T MAKE MYSELF BELIEVE THEM!! I CANT--!!
HAVE TO SNAP OUT OF IT! CAN'T GO ON LIKE THIS!
IN THE NEXT ROOM --THE AVENGERS ARE ASSEMBLED!
I MUSTN'T--KEEP THEM WAITING!
THE YOUTH APPROACHES!
WE KNOW HOW DIFFICULT THIS IS FOR YOU, SON!
IT ISN'T EASY-- FOR ANY OF US!
BUT, WE HAVE TO LEARN EXACTLY WHAT HAPPENED!
THUS, WE BID THEE--SPEAK!
5

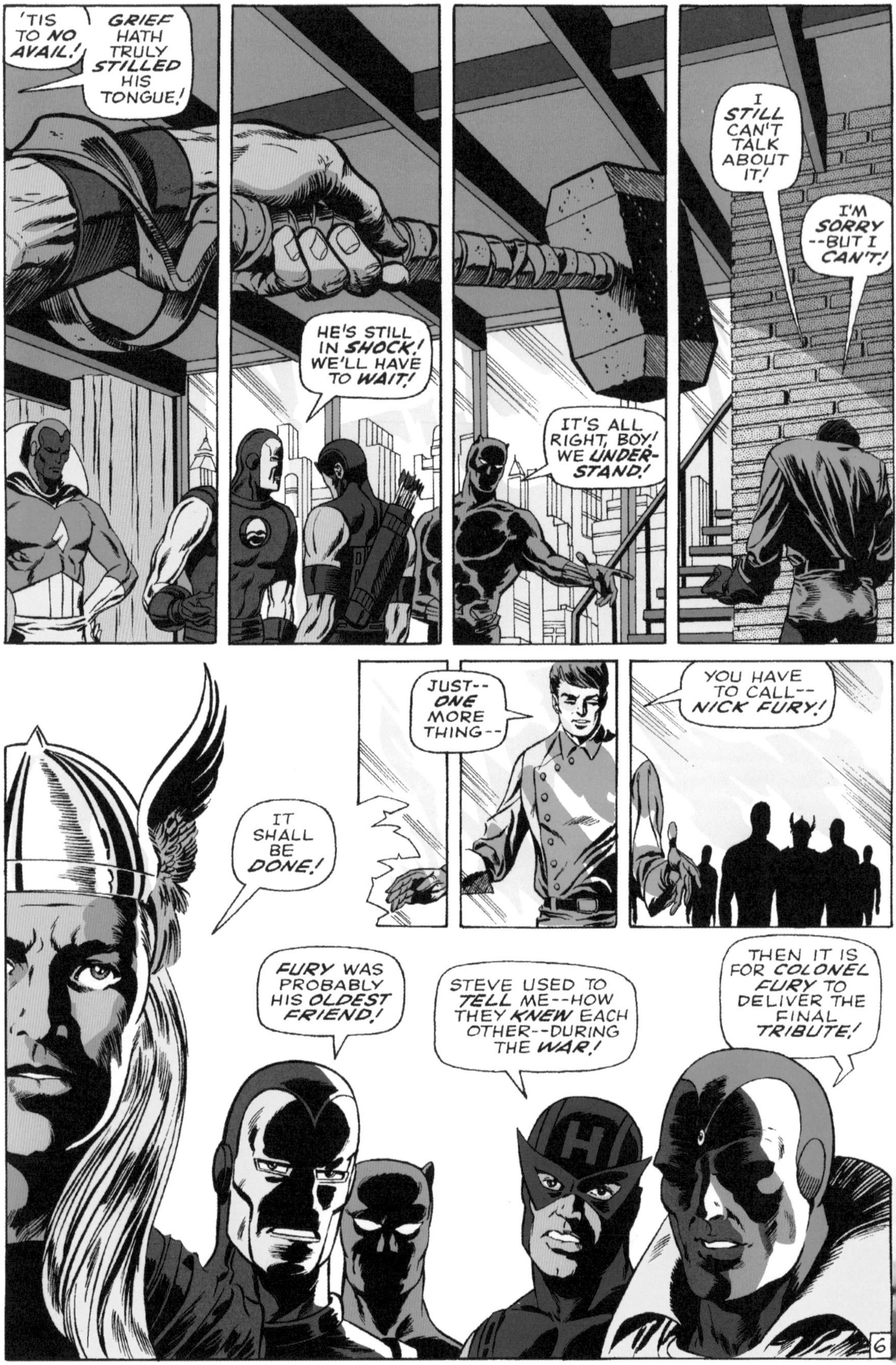
'TIS TO NO AVAIL!
GRIEF HATH TRULY STILLED HIS TONGUE!
HE'S STILL IN SHOCK! WE'LL HAVE TO WAIT!
IT'S ALL RIGHT, BOY! WE UNDERSTAND!
I STILL CAN'T TALK ABOUT IT!
I'M SORRY --BUT I CAN'T!
IT SHALL BE DONE!
JUST-- ONE MORE THING--
YOU HAVE TO CALL-- NICK FURY!
FURY WAS PROBABLY HIS OLDEST FRIEND!
STEVE USED TO TELL ME--HOW THEY KNEW EACH OTHER--DURING THE WAR!
THEN IT IS FOR COLONEL FURY TO DELIVER THE FINAL TRIBUTE!
6

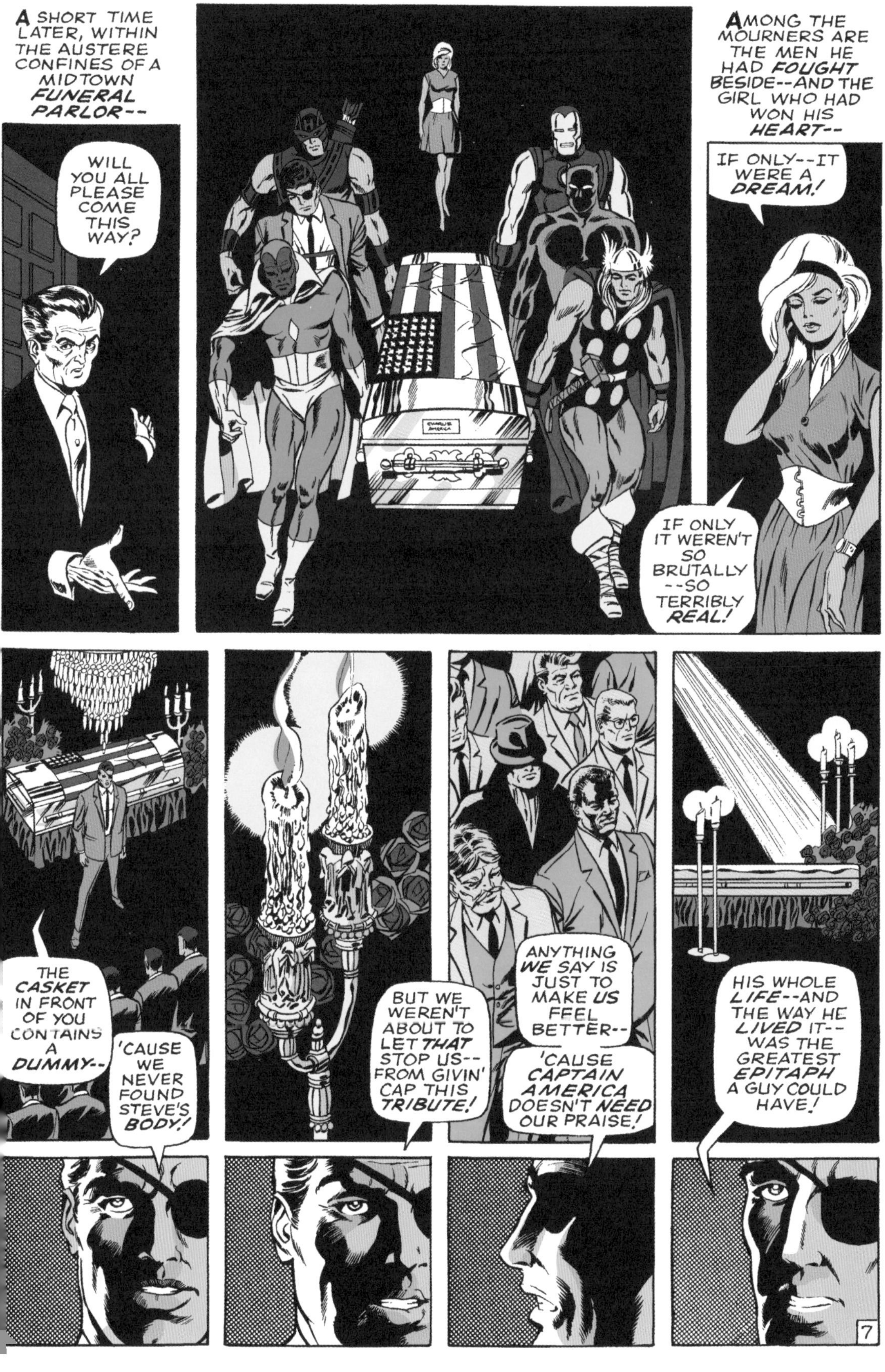
A SHORT TIME LATER, WITHIN THE AUSTERE CONFINES OF A MIDTOWN FUNERAL PARLOR--
WILL YOU ALL PLEASE COME THIS WAY?
AMONG THE MOURNERS ARE THE MEN HE HAD FOUGHT BESIDE--AND THE GIRL WHO HAD WON HIS HEART--
IF ONLY--IT WERE A DREAM!
IF ONLY IT WEREN'T SO BRUTALLY --SO TERRIBLY REAL!
THE CASKET IN FRONT OF YOU CONTAINS A DUMMY--
'CAUSE WE NEVER FOUND STEVE'S BODY!
BUT WE WEREN'T ABOUT TO LET THAT STOP US--FROM GIVIN' CAP THIS TRIBUTE!
ANYTHING WE SAY IS JUST TO MAKE US FEEL BETTER--
'CAUSE CAPTAIN AMERICA DOESN'T NEED OUR PRAISE!
HIS WHOLE LIFE--AND THE WAY HE LIVED IT--WAS THE GREATEST EPITAPH A GUY COULD HAVE!
7

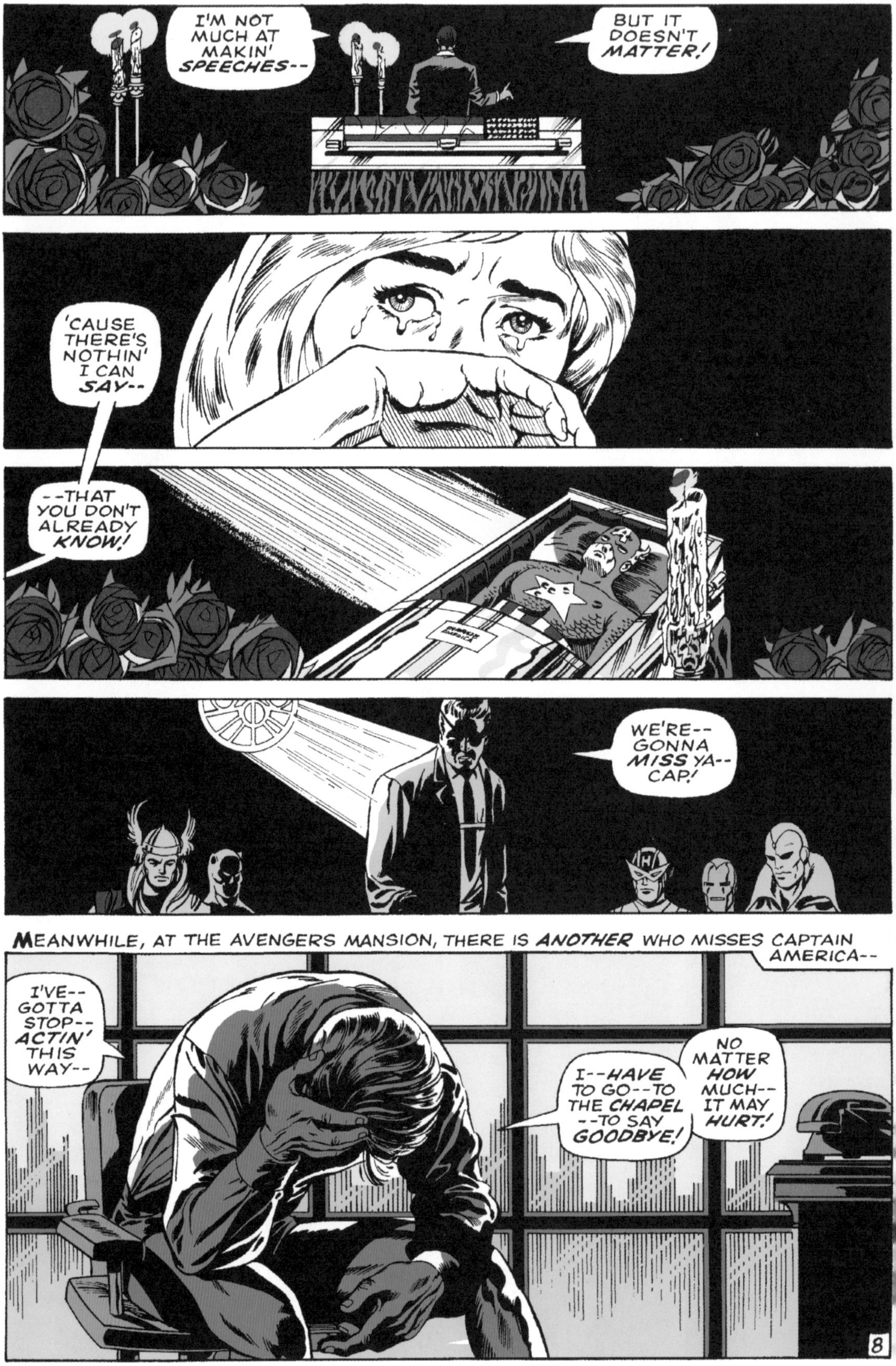
I'M NOT MUCH AT MAKIN' SPEECHES--
BUT IT DOESN'T MATTER!
'CAUSE THERE'S NOTHIN' I CAN SAY--
--THAT YOU DON'T ALREADY KNOW!
WE'RE-- GONNA MISS YA-- CAP!
MEANWHILE, AT THE AVENGERS MANSION, THERE IS ANOTHER WHO MISSES CAPTAIN AMERICA--
I'VE-- GOTTA STOP-- ACTIN' THIS WAY--
I--HAVE TO GO--TO THE CHAPEL --TO SAY GOODBYE!
NO MATTER HOW MUCH-- IT MAY HURT!
8

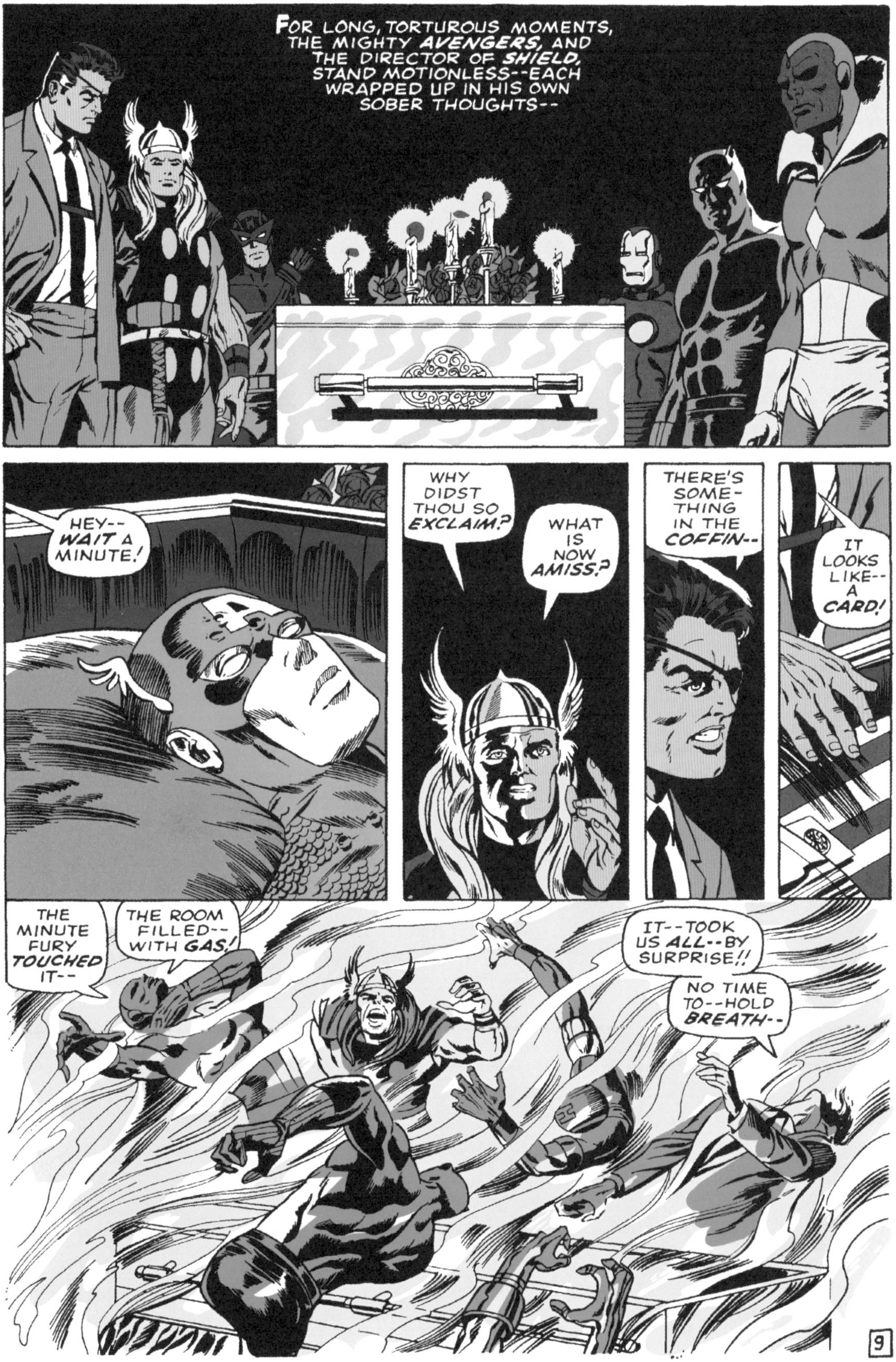
FOR LONG, TORTUROUS MOMENTS, THE MIGHTY AVENGERS, AND THE DIRECTOR OF SHIELD, STAND MOTIONLESS--EACH WRAPPED UP IN HIS OWN SOBER THOUGHTS--
HEY-- WAIT A MINUTE!
WHY DIDST THOU SO EXCLAIM?
WHAT IS NOW AMISS?
THERE'S SOME-THING IN THE COFFIN--
IT LOOKS LIKE-- A CARD!
THE MINUTE FURY TOUCHED IT--
THE ROOM FILLED-- WITH GAS!
IT--TOOK US ALL--BY SURPRISE!!
NO TIME TO--HOLD BREATH--
9

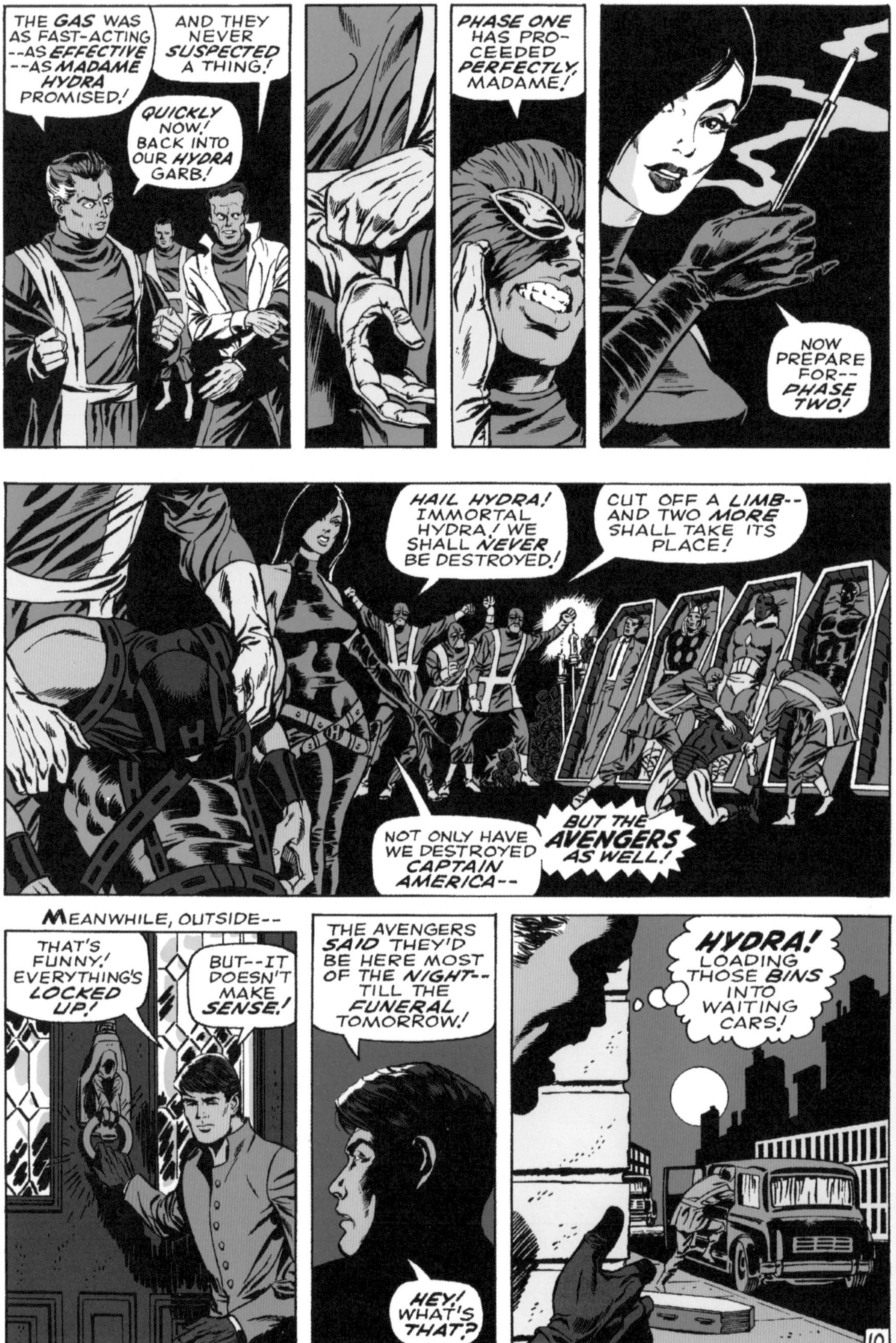
THE GAS WAS AS FAST-ACTING --AS EFFECTIVE --AS MADAME HYDRA PROMISED!
AND THEY NEVER SUSPECTED A THING!
QUICKLY NOW! BACK INTO OUR HYDRA GARB!
PHASE ONE HAS PRO-CEEDED PERFECTLY, MADAME!
NOW PREPARE FOR-- PHASE TWO!
HAIL HYDRA! IMMORTAL HYDRA! WE SHALL NEVER BE DESTROYED!
CUT OFF A LIMB-- AND TWO MORE SHALL TAKE ITS PLACE!
NOT ONLY HAVE WE DESTROYED CAPTAIN AMERICA--
BUT THE AVENGERS AS WELL!
MEANWHILE, OUTSIDE--
THAT'S FUNNY! EVERYTHING'S LOCKED UP!
BUT--IT DOESN'T MAKE SENSE!
THE AVENGERS SAID THEY'D BE HERE MOST OF THE NIGHT-- TILL THE FUNERAL TOMORROW!
HEY! WHAT'S THAT?
HYDRA! LOADING THOSE BINS INTO WAITING CARS!
10

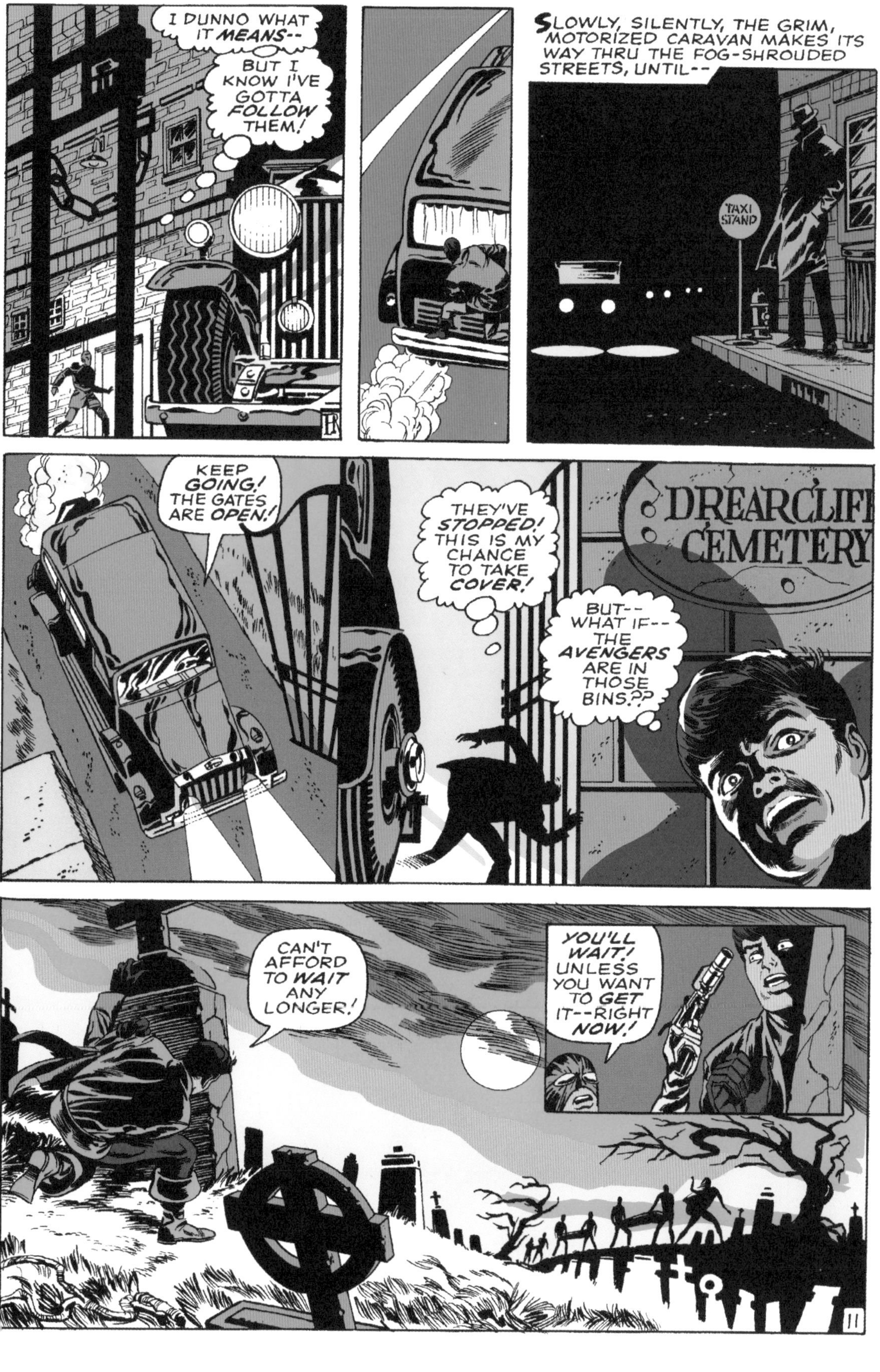
I DUNNO WHAT IT MEANS--
BUT I KNOW I'VE GOTTA FOLLOW THEM!
SLOWLY, SILENTLY, THE GRIM, MOTORIZED CARAVAN MAKES ITS WAY THRU THE FOG-SHROUDED STREETS, UNTIL--
TAXI STAND
KEEP GOING! THE GATES ARE OPEN!
THEY'VE STOPPED! THIS IS MY CHANCE TO TAKE COVER!
DREARCLIFF CEMETERY
BUT--WHAT IF--THE AVENGERS ARE IN THOSE BINS??
CAN'T AFFORD TO WAIT ANY LONGER!
YOU'LL WAIT! UNLESS YOU WANT TO GET IT--RIGHT NOW!
11

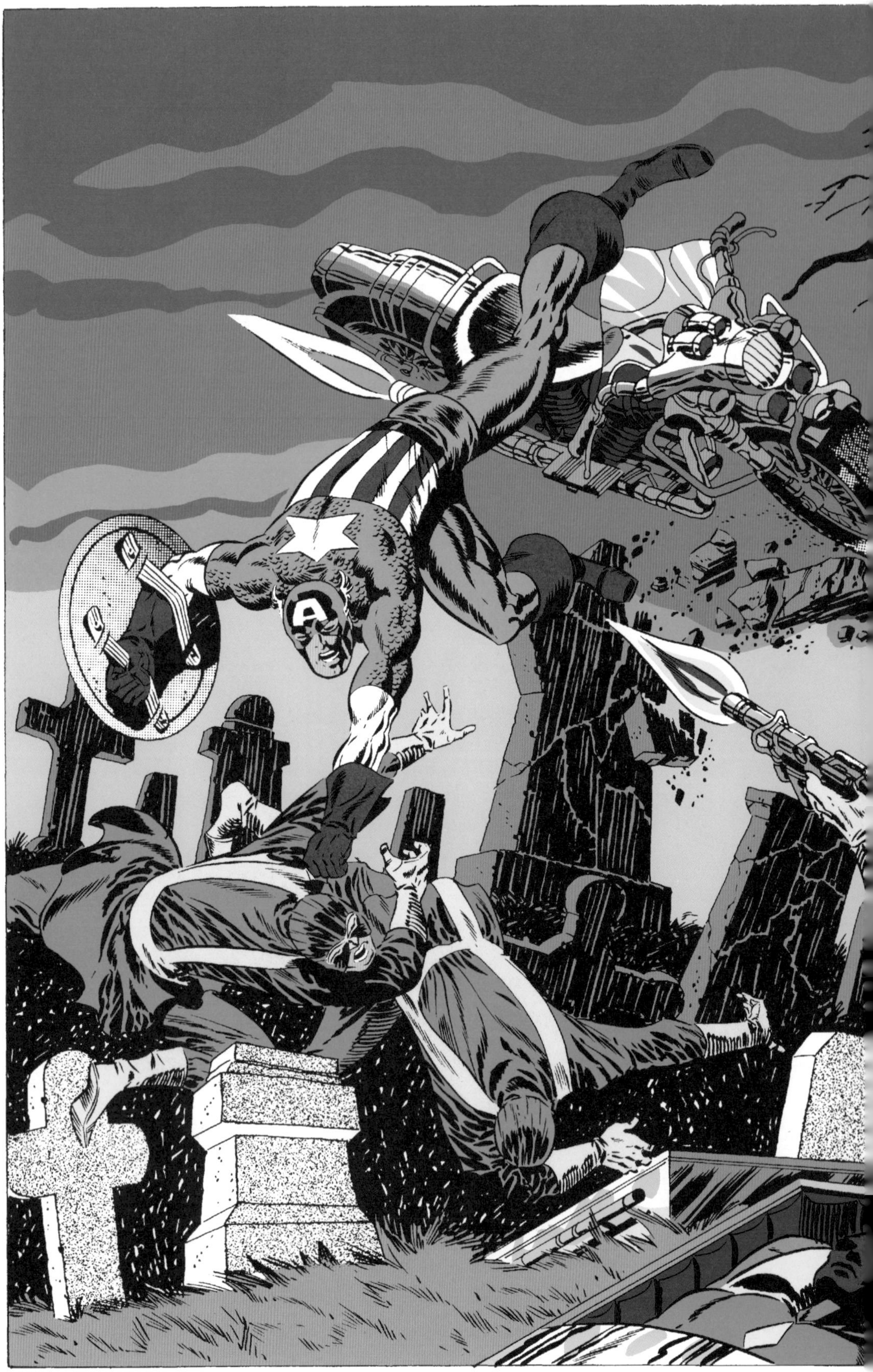

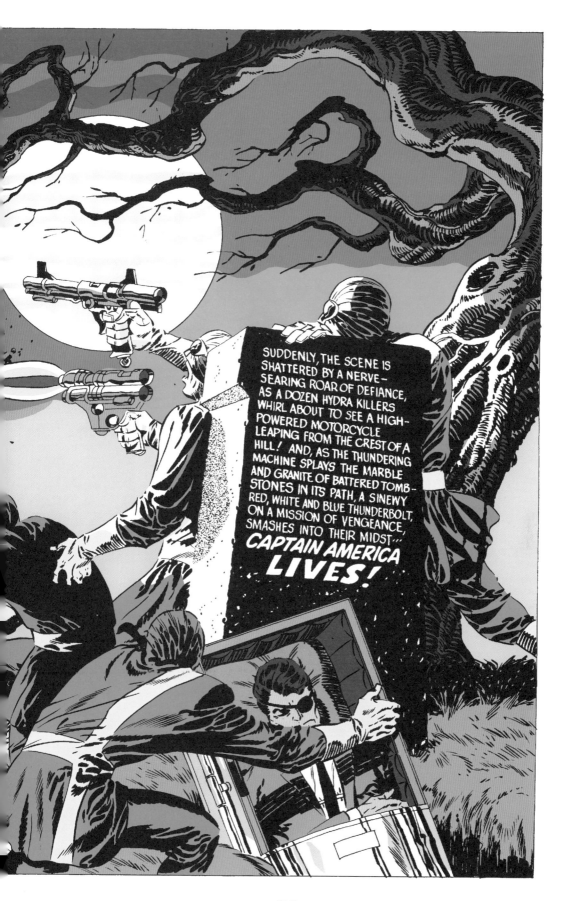

SUDDENLY, THE SCENE IS SHATTERED BY A NERVE-SEARING ROAR OF DEFIANCE, AS A DOZEN HYDRA KILLERS WHIRL ABOUT TO SEE A HIGH-POWERED MOTORCYCLE LEAPING FROM THE CREST OF A HILL! AND, AS THE THUNDERING MACHINE SPLAYS THE MARBLE AND GRANITE OF BATTERED TOMB-STONES IN ITS PATH, A SINEWY RED, WHITE AND BLUE THUNDERBOLT, ON A MISSION OF VENGEANCE, SMASHES INTO THEIR MIDST... **CAPTAIN AMERICA LIVES!**

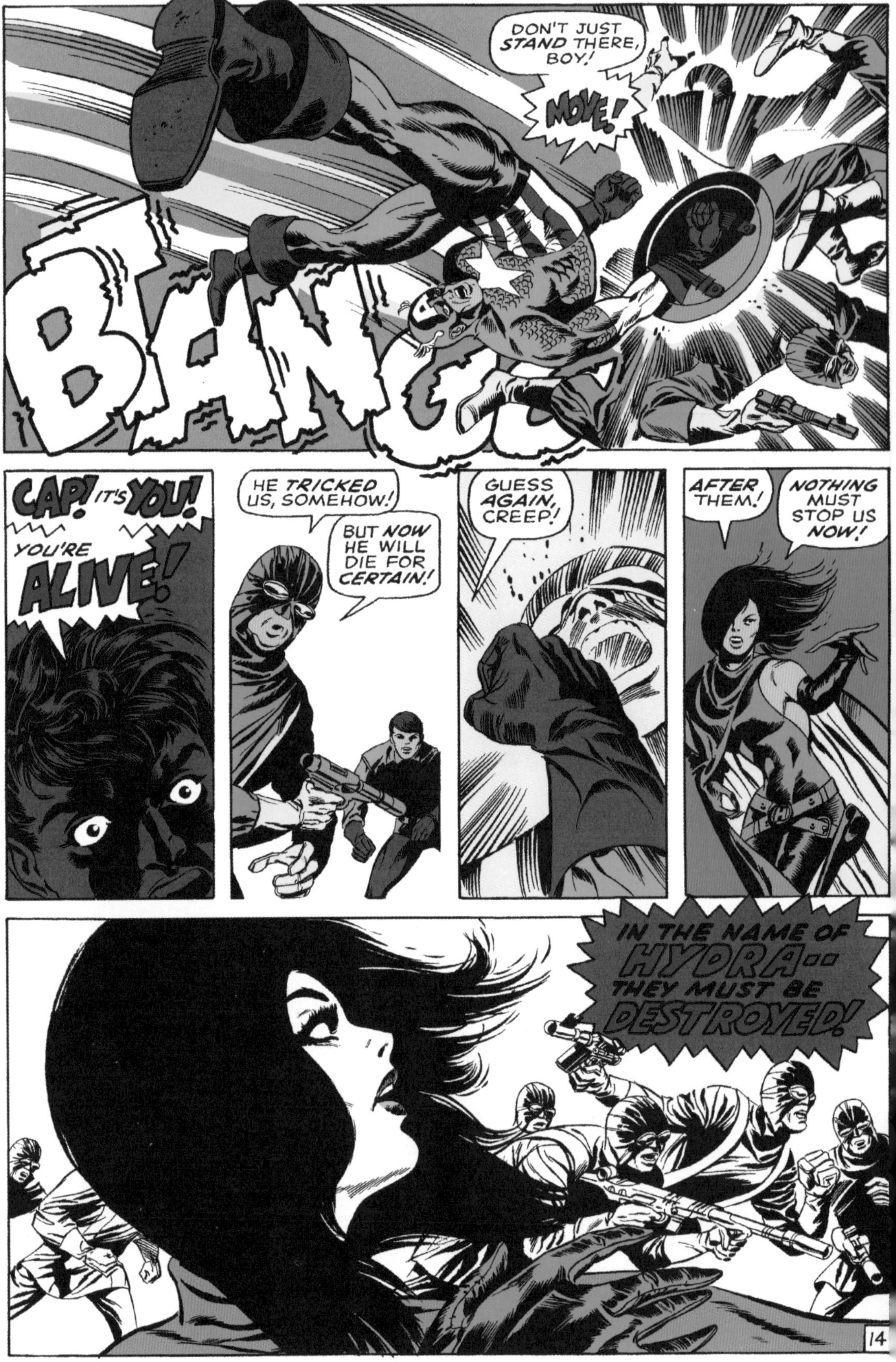
DON'T JUST STAND THERE, BOY!
MOVE!
BANG
CAP! IT'S YOU! YOU'RE ALIVE!
HE TRICKED US, SOMEHOW!
BUT NOW HE WILL DIE FOR CERTAIN!
GUESS AGAIN, CREEP!
AFTER THEM!
NOTHING MUST STOP US NOW!
IN THE NAME OF HYDRA.. THEY MUST BE DESTROYED!
14

A **MAN** CAN BE DESTROYED! A **TEAM**, OR AN **ARMY** CAN BE DESTROYED! BUT, HOW DO YOU DESTROY AN **IDEAL**--A **DREAM**? HOW DO YOU DESTROY A LIVING **SYMBOL**--OR HIS INDOMITABLE **WILL**--HIS UNQUENCHABLE **SPIRIT**? PERHAPS **THESE** ARE THE THOUGHTS WHICH THUNDER WITHIN THE MURDEROUS **MINDS** OF THOSE WHO HAVE CHOSEN THE WAY OF **HYDRA**--OF THOSE WHO FACE THE **FIGHTING FURY** OF FREEDOM'S MOST FEARLESS **CHAMPION**--THE GALLANT, RED-WHITE-AND-BLUE-GARBED FIGURE WHO HAS BEEN A TOWERING SOURCE OF **INSPIRATION** TO LIBERTY-LOVERS EVERYWHERE! HOW CAN THE FEARSOME FORCES OF **EVIL** EVER HOPE TO DESTROY THE UNCONQUERABLE *CAPTAIN AMERICA?*

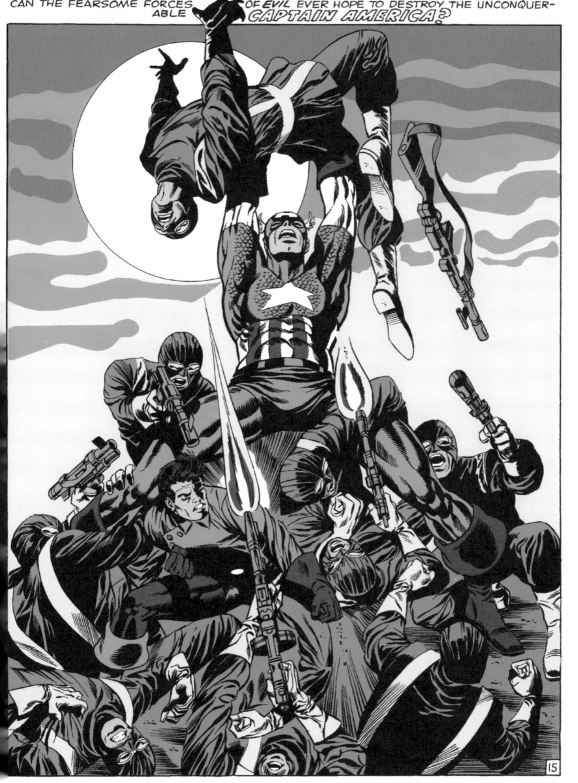

15

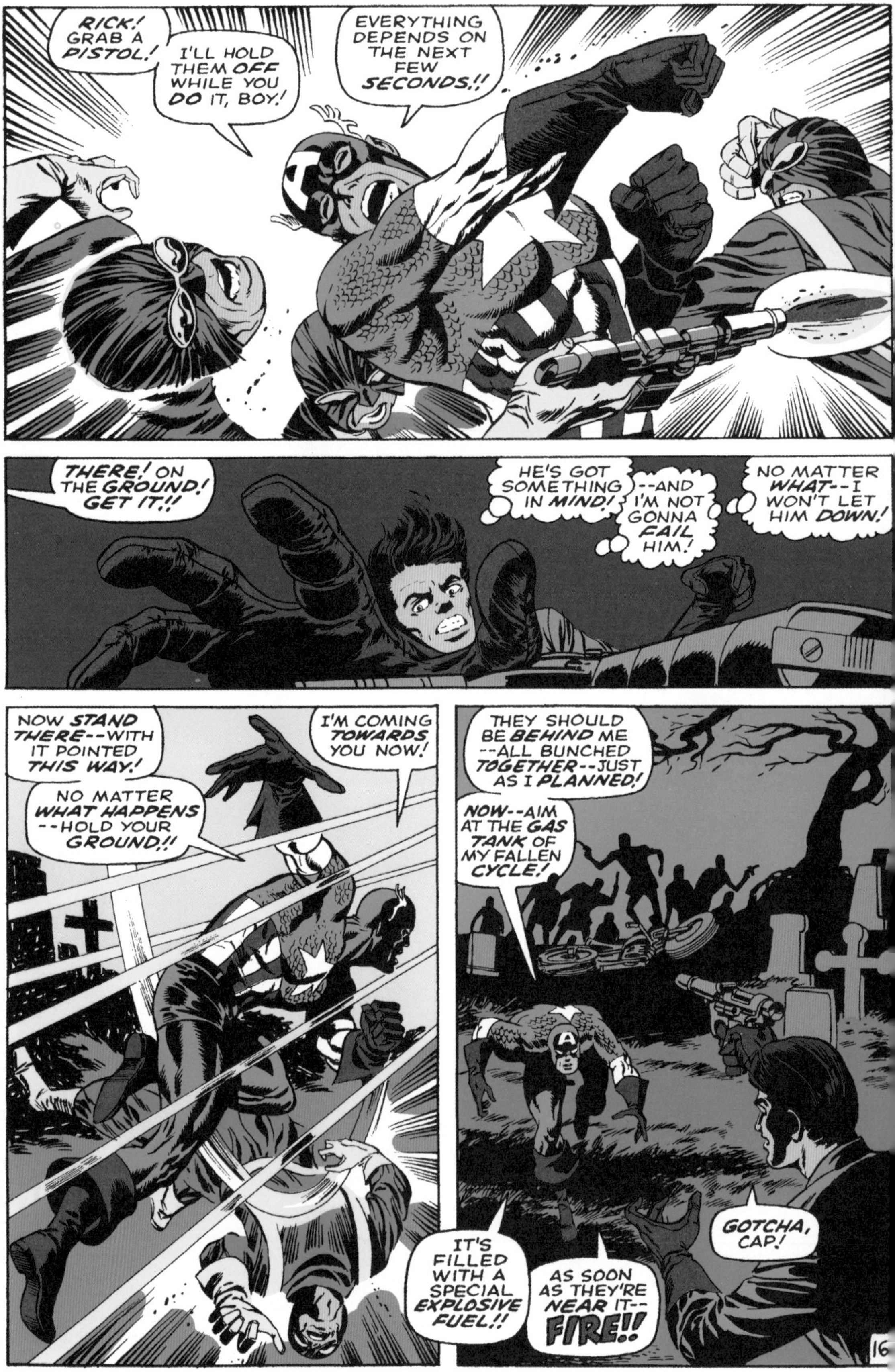
RICK! GRAB A PISTOL!
I'LL HOLD THEM OFF WHILE YOU DO IT, BOY!
EVERYTHING DEPENDS ON THE NEXT FEW SECONDS!!
THERE! ON THE GROUND! GET IT!!
HE'S GOT SOMETHING IN MIND!
--AND I'M NOT GONNA FAIL HIM!
NO MATTER WHAT--I WON'T LET HIM DOWN!
NOW STAND THERE--WITH IT POINTED THIS WAY!
NO MATTER WHAT HAPPENS--HOLD YOUR GROUND!!
I'M COMING TOWARDS YOU NOW!
THEY SHOULD BE BEHIND ME--ALL BUNCHED TOGETHER--JUST AS I PLANNED!
NOW--AIM AT THE GAS TANK OF MY FALLEN CYCLE!
IT'S FILLED WITH A SPECIAL EXPLOSIVE FUEL!!
AS SOON AS THEY'RE NEAR IT--FIRE!!
GOTCHA, CAP!
16

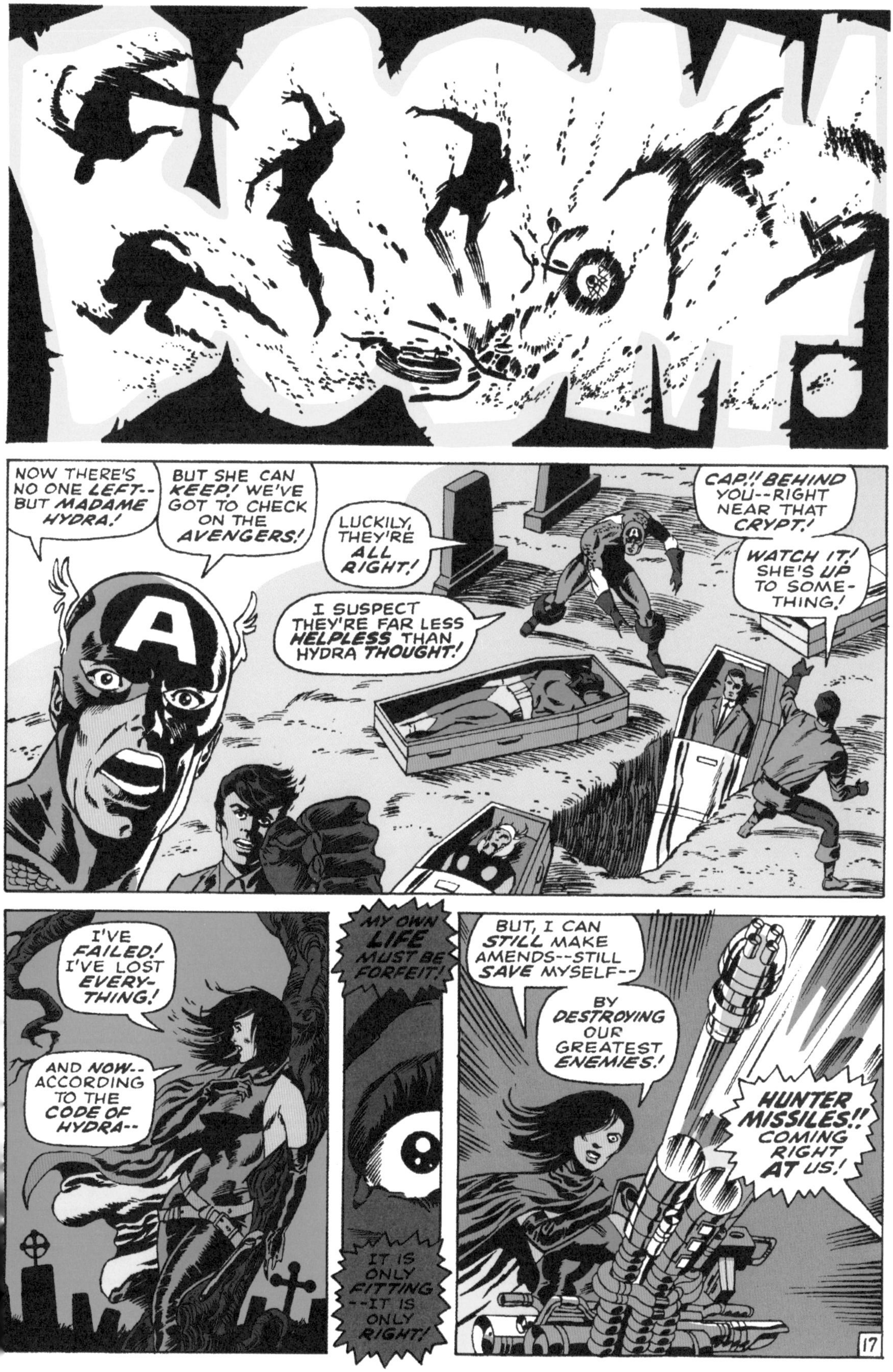

BOOOM!
NOW THERE'S NO ONE LEFT-- BUT MADAME HYDRA!
BUT SHE CAN KEEP! WE'VE GOT TO CHECK ON THE AVENGERS!
LUCKILY, THEY'RE ALL RIGHT!
I SUSPECT THEY'RE FAR LESS HELPLESS THAN HYDRA THOUGHT!
CAP!! BEHIND YOU--RIGHT NEAR THAT CRYPT!
WATCH IT! SHE'S UP TO SOME-THING!
I'VE FAILED! I'VE LOST EVERY-THING!
AND NOW-- ACCORDING TO THE CODE OF HYDRA--
MY OWN LIFE MUST BE FORFEIT!
IT IS ONLY FITTING --IT IS ONLY RIGHT!
BUT, I CAN STILL MAKE AMENDS--STILL SAVE MYSELF--
BY DESTROYING OUR GREATEST ENEMIES!
HUNTER MISSILES!! COMING RIGHT AT US!
17

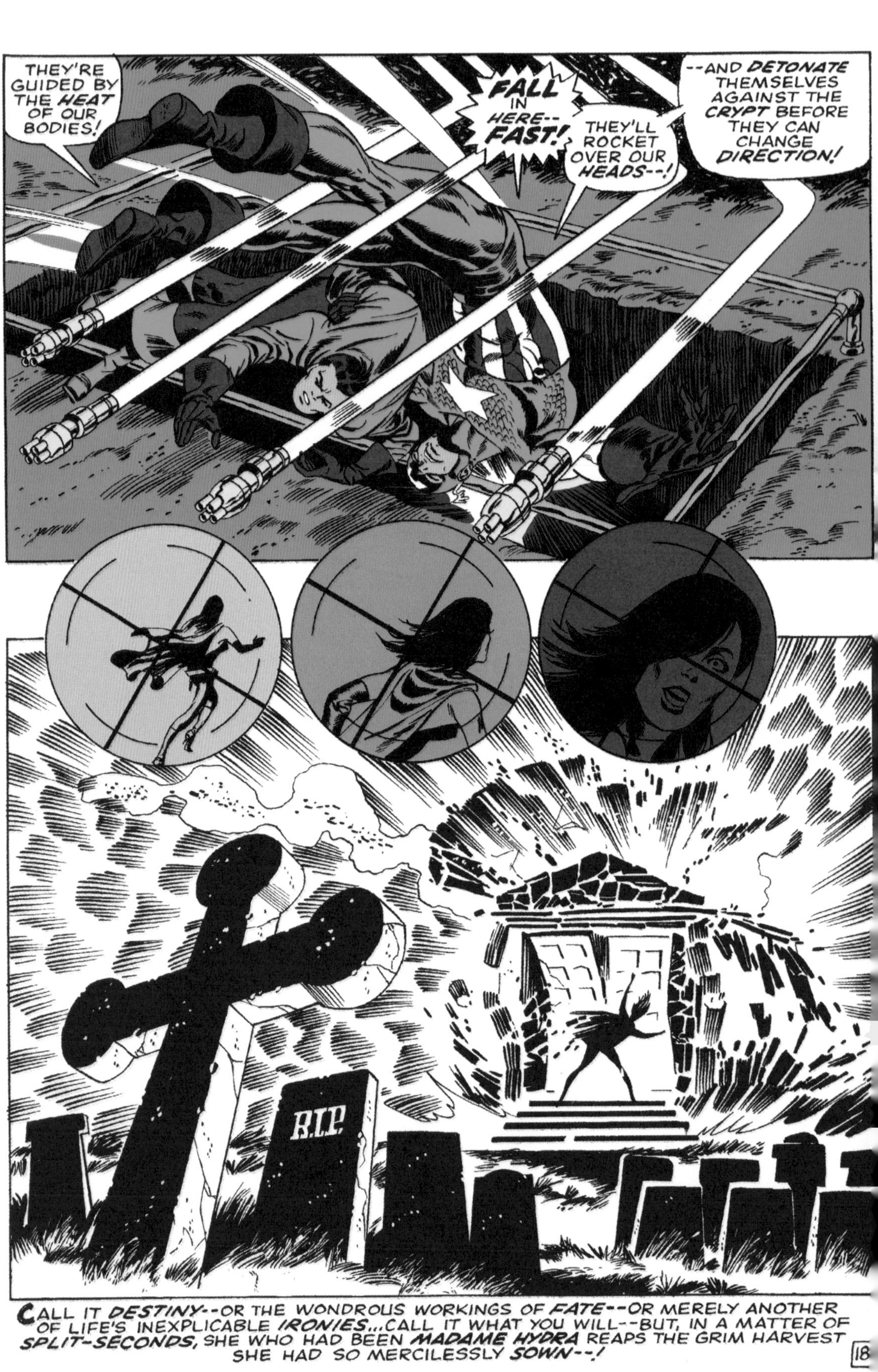
THEY'RE GUIDED BY THE HEAT OF OUR BODIES!
FALL IN HERE-- FAST!
THEY'LL ROCKET OVER OUR HEADS--!
--AND DETONATE THEMSELVES AGAINST THE CRYPT BEFORE THEY CAN CHANGE DIRECTION!
R.I.P.
CALL IT DESTINY--OR THE WONDROUS WORKINGS OF FATE--OR MERELY ANOTHER OF LIFE'S INEXPLICABLE IRONIES...CALL IT WHAT YOU WILL--BUT, IN A MATTER OF SPLIT-SECONDS, SHE WHO HAD BEEN MADAME HYDRA REAPS THE GRIM HARVEST SHE HAD SO MERCILESSLY SOWN--!
18

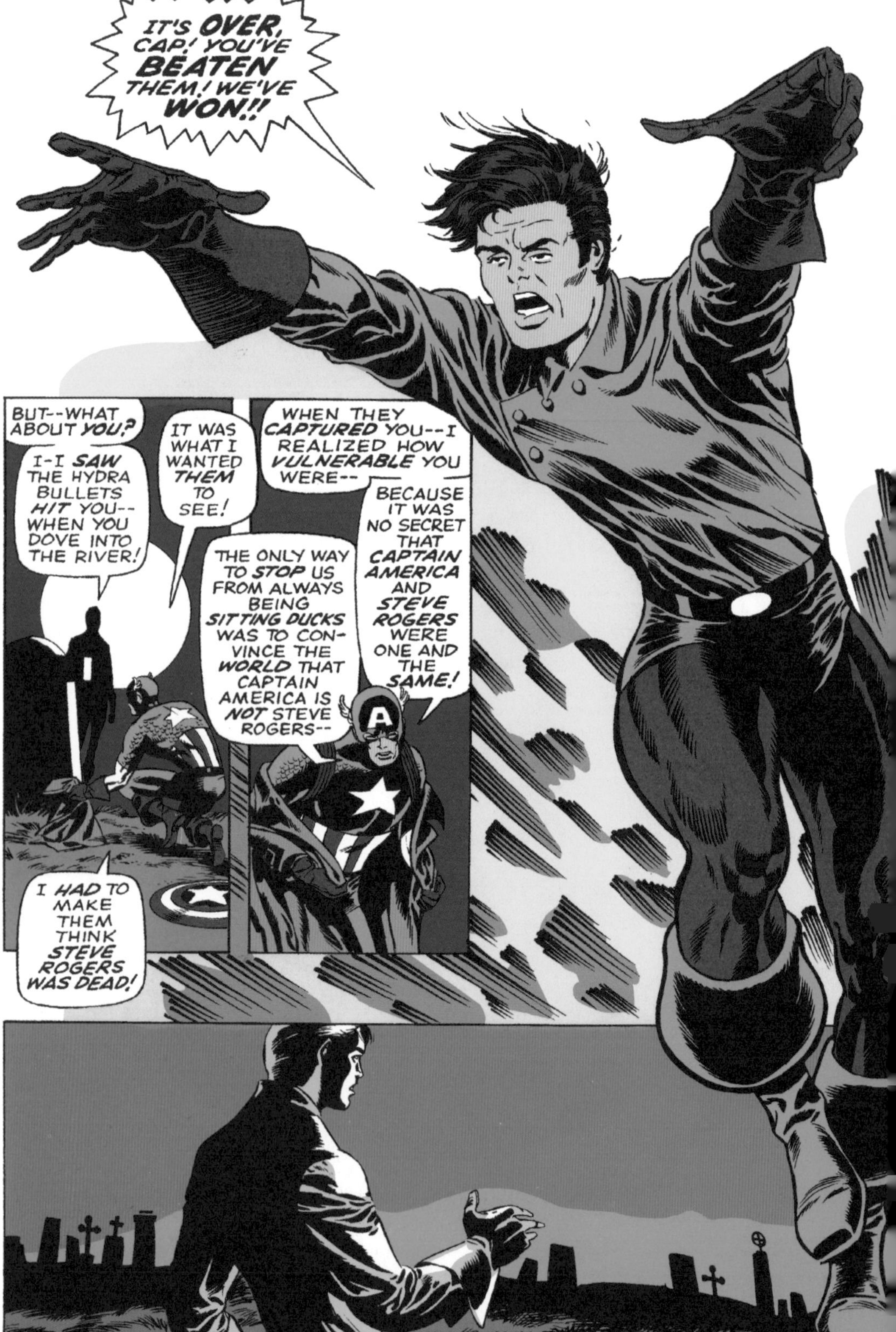
IT'S OVER, CAP! YOU'VE BEATEN THEM! WE'VE WON!!
BUT--WHAT ABOUT YOU?
I-I SAW THE HYDRA BULLETS HIT YOU--WHEN YOU DOVE INTO THE RIVER!
IT WAS WHAT I WANTED THEM TO SEE!
I HAD TO MAKE THEM THINK STEVE ROGERS WAS DEAD!
WHEN THEY CAPTURED YOU--I REALIZED HOW VULNERABLE YOU WERE--
BECAUSE IT WAS NO SECRET THAT CAPTAIN AMERICA AND STEVE ROGERS WERE ONE AND THE SAME!
THE ONLY WAY TO STOP US FROM ALWAYS BEING SITTING DUCKS WAS TO CONVINCE THE WORLD THAT CAPTAIN AMERICA IS NOT STEVE ROGERS--
19

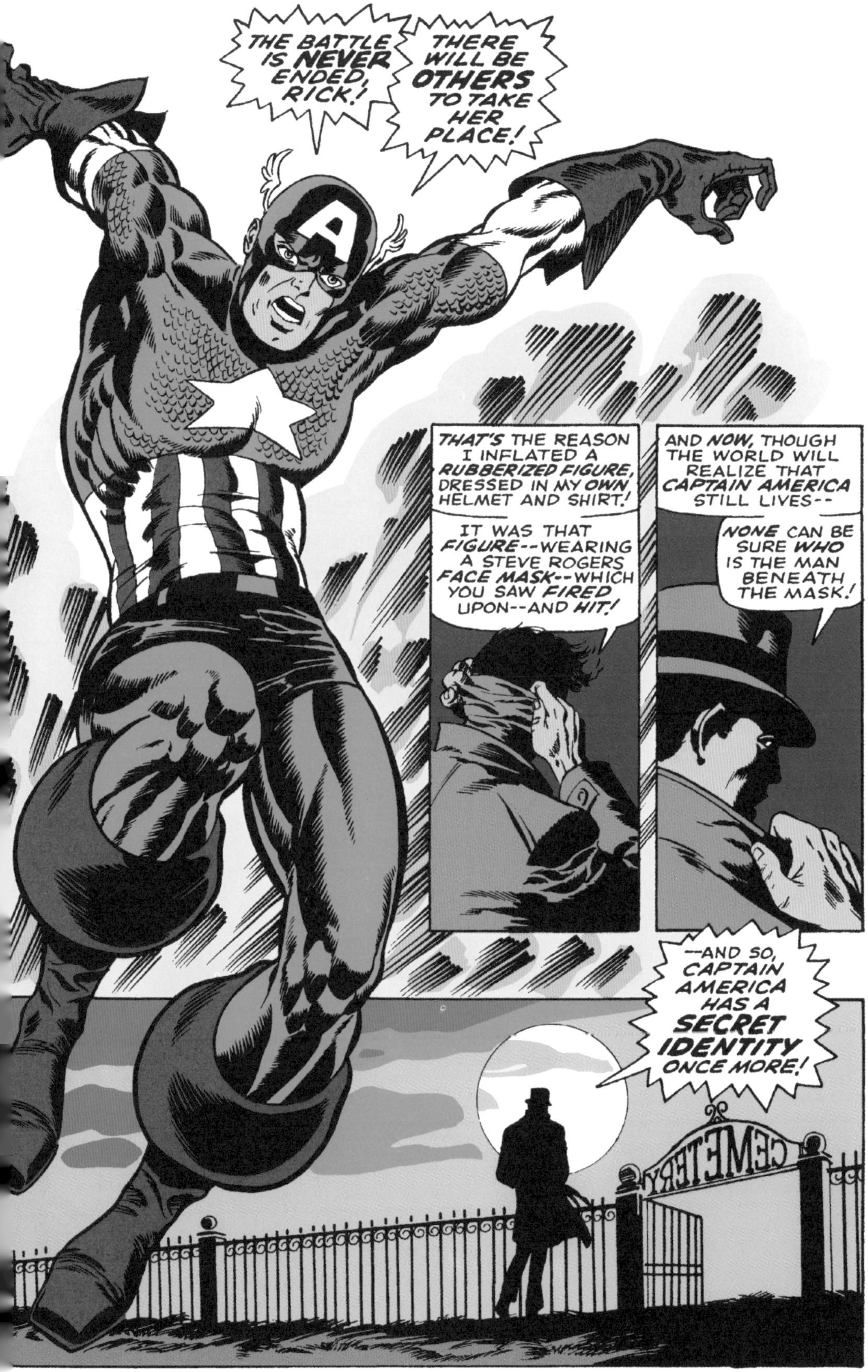
THE BATTLE IS NEVER ENDED, RICK!
THERE WILL BE OTHERS TO TAKE HER PLACE!
THAT'S THE REASON I INFLATED A RUBBERIZED FIGURE, DRESSED IN MY OWN HELMET AND SHIRT!
IT WAS THAT FIGURE--WEARING A STEVE ROGERS FACE MASK--WHICH YOU SAW FIRED UPON--AND HIT!
AND NOW, THOUGH THE WORLD WILL REALIZE THAT CAPTAIN AMERICA STILL LIVES--
NONE CAN BE SURE WHO IS THE MAN BENEATH THE MASK!
--AND SO, CAPTAIN AMERICA HAS A SECRET IDENTITY ONCE MORE!
CEMETERY

SEND YOUR LETTERS TO:

THE MARVEL COMICS GROUP SECOND FLOOR 625 MADISON AV. NEW YORK 10022 N. Y.

Dear Stan and Jack,

I, and a great many like me, have grown extremely weary of those who seem to feel qualified to be a final authority on what is true and what is not. I, therefore, would like to take exception to what Mr. Rodriquez said in CAPTAIN AMERICA #110, as his is one of the exceedingly few letters out of the many printed over the years that has succeeded in seriously arousing me. In Mr. Rodriquez's letter, he brandished phrases like "conservative", "hero worship", "personal brand of liberty", "so-called patriot", "establishment", etc., etc., ad infinitum, yet he makes no move to substantiate his claims. Further, he does not even attempt to explain why these qualities (that is, the qualities for which these phrases are used as synonyms) are faults. Instead, he seemingly expects all rational beings to automatically adhere to his brand of political philosophy and therefore agree to it. This, to me, is typical of those who do their thinking with slogans and it brings to mind those who use "bourgeois" and "imperialist" as synonyms for "democratic" and "American". Well, I reserve the right to disagree, as does Captain America; and under our present form of government, we may still do so — fortunately. Mr. Rodriquez states that Captain America is one of your best characters, aside from his ideals. The fallacy of this statement is that Captain America is the ideal — and his super-powers are strictly secondary. Captain America was born as a patriotic symbol (not "supernationalistic") during the dark days of World War II when men particularly needed their ideals to inspire them. Patriotism in the United States does not refer to that supernationalism which caused the old imperial nations to go to war over affairs of "grandeur". It refers, instead, to the belief that the principles of our democracy are worth going to war for — a belief that I share. Indeed, I believe that Stan also shares this belief, for he transferred it to Captain America, and I fear that Stan would be altogether too "conservative" for Mr. Rodriquez's tastes. To mold men's minds to a certain man's standard is an attempt to make flesh-and-blood robots (as some nations have tried), no matter how perfect the standard is supposed to be. When one begins to think his ideas are absolute truths, he stops reasoning and starts dictating. Therefore, I emphasize that the ideas I have set forth here are my opinion, no matter how deeply I believe them, and I recognize that other points of view are quite possible, and quite necessary in a free society. However, I also feel that Stan should have the right to state his opinion through Captain America. Perhaps the unhappy day shall dawn in this nation when "liberalism" reaches its absolute as "conservatism" did in Nazi Germany (when either reaches that point, they are no longer distinguishable). If so, I strongly suspect that Captain America, Stan, I, and many others will, as Churchill (another of those nasty conservatives) said, continue to resist because it is better to perish than to surrender to

such a foe. Is that "warmongering" and "stupid," Mr. Rodriquez? Is it irrational and terribly naive? Perhaps it's merely democracy's special form of madness. I wouldn't want to live in a nation where it didn't exist.

Joe Pearson, Farm 45 Rt. 2
Iowa Park, Texas 76367

Many thanks for that stirring soliloquy, Joe. The case of Cap's origin is a singular one . . . you are right in the fact that he was created as a symbol of liberty during the war. So the fact that his patriotic characteristics have lingered is not due to his capacity as a mouthpiece . . . but that these very traits are inherent in his character. It'd be rather pointless to build, say, a T V set that only receives sound . . . or an airplane that travels by road. By the same token, when you create a character like Cap . . . who is virtually a living symbol . . . then he has to eat, sleep and breathe his beliefs, whether they agree with the writer's or not! So there you have it. Characters are often used to reflect a writer's own opinions . . . but a guy like Cap would have to believe the things he does . . . otherwise why would he bother to go on fighting? And if he stopped fighting . . . you wouldn't have any stories to read, and there'd be an even bigger uproar! So you see, faithful ones, there is method if our Marvels seem madness!

Dear Stan and Jack,

CAPTAIN AMERICA is to my estimate the greatest comic magazine ever published. I am sure that I am very far from being alone in this line of thought. And your issue with the origin of Cap was no exception. But what I would really like to talk to you about is the question you raised at the end of the story "Shall Bucky Live?" YES!!! In the old days, as I look through my ancient collection, Bucky was part of the living force that drove Captain America's comics. They were a great team that fitted together perfectly. I believe that Captain America will be much greater if the original Bucky, just as he was, is fighting at his side! One of the great things about comics is that they can perform the impossible — such as bringing back someone who is supposedly dead for 20 years.

Lewis R. Valladares, 109-07 Francis-Lewis Blvd.
Queens Village, N.Y.

All that and more, Lewis, ol' buddy. Can you imagine anyone else making a nut who runs around in colorful long-johns and a crazy shield believable? Of course not . . . it takes a very special brand of lunacy, found only between these captivatin' covers. And if you think this ish was a blast . . . be here next month, believer . . . we dare you!

KNOW YE THESE, THE HALLOWED RANKS OF MARVELDOM:

R.F.O. (REAL FRANTIC ONE) — A BUYER OF AT LEAST 3 MARVEL MAGS A MONTH.

T.T.B. (TITANIC TRUE BELIEVER) — A DIVINELY-INSPIRED 'NO-PRIZE' WINNER.

Q.N.S. (QUITE 'NUFF SAYER) — A FORTUNATE FRANTIC ONE WHO'S HAD A LETTER PRINTED.

K.O.F. (KEEPER OF THE FLAME) — ONE WHO RECRUITS A NEWCOMER TO MARVEL'S ROLLICKIN' RANKS.

P.M.M. (PERMANENT MARVELITE MAXIMUS) — ANYONE POSSESSING ALL FOUR OF THE OTHER TITLES.

F.F.F. (FEARLESS FRONT FACER) — AN HONORARY TITLE BESTOWED FOR DEVOTION TO MARVEL ABOVE AND BEYOND THE CALL OF DUTY.

Dear Stan and Jim,

After reading CAPTAIN AMERICA #110, I write the following without hesitation. 1) Jim Steranko is the greatest artist in Marveldom or anywhere-else-dom. 2) The last few ishes of CAPTAIN AMERICA haven't been up to par. Cap's constant reminiscing about the war and Bucky have been uninteresting and certainly detract from the action Cap is capable of. 3) This is the most important. Get rid of Rick Jones!!!! Ship him back to the Hulk from whence he sprang or (better still) get rid of him altogether. And besides, Rick looks surprisingly like a partner in an unnamed mag of a (echh) competitor. Don't you remember what happened to the latter when they began giving every character an assistant? The assistants had assistants, then the assistants' assistants got super animals. Then everybody quit reading their mags. I implore you, nip this in the bud! Can you imagine Iron Man and Tin Boy, or the Silver Surfer and the Gold Skater? Of course not!
Russ Tulp, 433 Parkside Ave.
Buffalo, N.Y. 14216

You'd better believe it, Russ. You'll only find that kinda thing in the pages of NOT BRAND ECHH! Hey! Come to think of it . . . that's not a bad idea. We'll get the Rascally One to dream up a plot . . . Mirthful Marie can draw up the whole bit; it'll be a smash! Then we'll have a continued series . . . Son of the Sons of Satannish! Not forgetting Marvel Girl and the Marvelettes (a duo of caped aardvarks)! We can see it all now . . . Nick Fury and his sidekick, Irving Angry. Thor and Mini-Thor . . . sheeh! It's like a livin' nightmare!

Dear Stan and Jack,

Well, at long last you've done it! You've given Cap a partner to work with! What's more, his new partner is exactly whom we readers thought he would be: Rick Jones. Seems that Rick has always wanted to work with Cap ever since he "star-spangled avenger" made his reappearance years ago in THE AVENGERS. Now that Cap has a new partner, let it remain that way. Please? I know that many fans feel he should be a loner, but after reading the Golden Age adventures of the patriotic avenger, I truly feel that he should have Rick Jones as his partner.
John Stewart II, 1219 Nolan St.
San Antonio, Texas 78202

As we said before, John opinion is really divided so far as to whether Rick should stay or go. Personally, we're all for him . . . but you know how much weight that carries. Besides, we wouldn't want people to think we're trying to influence them in any way!

Dear Stan and Jim,

Cap has always been one of my favorite characters. Often this has been true more because of his symbolic representation of "all that is American" rather than the plots of the individual tales in which he has appeared. After the death of Zemo (AVENGERS #15) Cap's personal appeal — his individual character — declined through his long term as ramrod for the mighty assemblers. Then, beginning with his departure from the Avengers (AVENGERS #47) Cap's personality became, at least for me, much more interesting (in TALES OF SUSPENSE #95 and following into Cap's own mag.) I just received CAP #110 and was surprised to see Steranko doing the honors along with Joe Sinnott. I'm not too sure how I'm going to like the new "Bucky" (I didn't care for the old one) but, like Rick Jones said, "Sooner or later, everybody loses somebody," and that bit was getting old. One last comment: what's so bad about a guy being patriotic, Mr. Albert Rodriquez?
James Petty, 525 Lakeview St.
Pineville, La. 71360

'Fraid we can't answer that one . . . it wasn't meant for us, Jim! Don't hesitate to give us your opinion on the new Bucky, though (and that goes for you too, hallowed ones). We must admit, Cap's new partner kinda grabbed us, but from now on . . . it's up to you!

Dear Stan and Jim,

Jim Steranko is Captain America! Never have I ever seen Captain America drawn so magnificently, and this is including Jack Kirby. Perhaps I'm biting off a pretty big chunk in saying this, but that's how I feel. Jim Steranko adds a flair to Cap never seen before, and I hope he keeps it up! Then came the center spread — that brought back thoughts of the old days when Cap had these — and Steranko did it beautifully. Now, concerning Rick Jones taking over the honored place of Bucky. My first thoughts were against it, but I soon changed my train of thought into total agreement when I realized how perfect it will work out. You've got something big on your hands, and I only expect the best from you!
Craig Battmer, 1530 Upton Ave. No.
Minneapolis, Minn. 55411

We're inclined to agree with you about the Jaunty One's flair, Craig. And you' can bet we'll keep trying to give you our very best. Though the odds are often against us . . . through readers' blasts, through shot and shell of headline and deadline, comes our leader's undaunted cry: "Get tha Marvels to tha stands . . . or I'll clobber ya!"

Dear Stan and Jim,

I decided to let you know what I thought about CAPTAIN AMERICA #110. The story was good, but Rick Jones' presence sort of messed things up. Don't keep him as a regular, but perhaps as a guest star every 20 or so issues. I hope you'll move Jim back to his spot on S.H.I.E.L.D., and it was nice to see good ol' Hydra back in action in the traditional Steranko style. 'Til Cap's shield turns into a hash slicer, make mine Marvel!
Jeff King, 901 N. Stanley Ave.
Los Angeles, Calif. 90046

You shouldn't have said that, Jeff. With the changes that are going on around here, you can never be sure of anything! The introduction of Rick Jones has caused a lot of reaction already . . . but as usual you frantic ones seem to be so timid about voicing your opinions! (Yeah, about as timid as the Red Skull when he got his hands on the Cosmic Cube!)

NEXT> WHO IS CAPTAIN AMERICA?

APPENDIX ONE

"CAPTAIN AMERICA . . . COMMIE SMASHER!"

In 1953 publisher Martin Goodman asked his editor Stan Lee to bring back the Sub-Mariner, the Human Torch, and Captain America—all of whom had been out of print since the late 1940s. Goodman's precise reasons are unknown. He may have imagined that super heroes would be seen as more wholesome fare than crime and horror comics, the main targets of a rising tide of anti-comics sentiment among parents and teachers; or he may have been hoping to tempt a producer with the prospect of adapting one of these older properties for a television show, in imitation of DC's Superman. In any event, editor Stan Lee reintroduced all three characters in the anthology *Young Men* #24 (December 1953) before launching new solo titles for each hero in early 1954. Confusingly, the first issue of the relaunched solo Cap title was #76

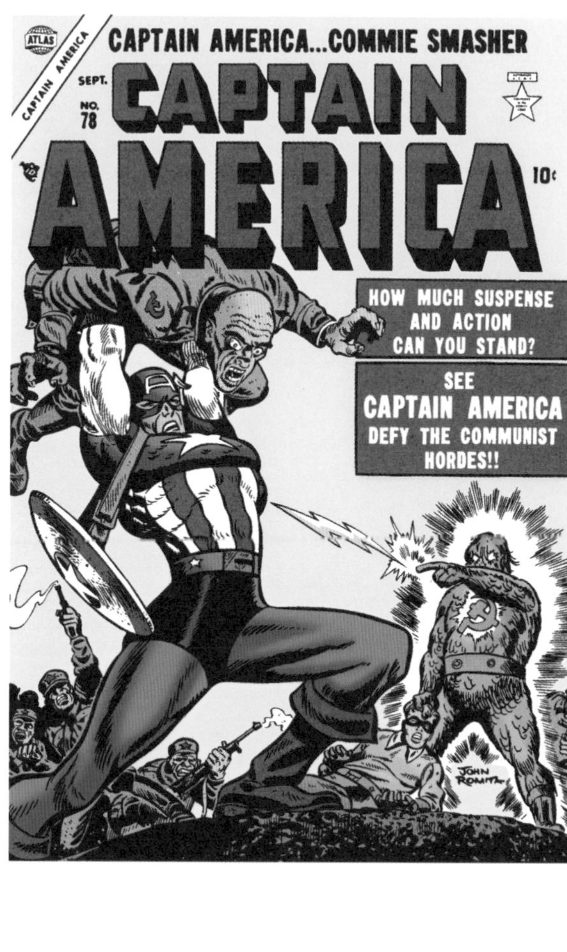
ATLAS
CAPTAIN AMERICA
CAPTAIN AMERICA...COMMIE SMASHER
SEPT.
NO. 78
CAPTAIN
AMERICA
10¢
HOW MUCH SUSPENSE
AND ACTION
CAN YOU STAND?
SEE
CAPTAIN AMERICA
DEFY THE COMMUNIST
HORDES!!
JOHN ROMITA

(following on from the numbering of the original Captain America Comics series, which had been discontinued in 1949).

For reasons discussed in the introduction to this volume, the revival was unsuccessful, and the new Captain America was canceled again after just three issues, with #78 (the cover of which is reproduced here). This time he would remain absent from the newsstands for almost a decade.

"CAPTAIN AMERICA LIVES AGAIN!"

By early 1964, the Marvel Revolution, as Stan Lee would later call it, was well underway. In less than two years, the core creative team—Lee; his brother, Larry Lieber; and artists Jack Kirby, Steve Ditko, and Don Heck—had brought several new super heroes into print, including the Fantastic Four, the Hulk, Spider-Man, Ant-Man and the Wasp, Iron Man, Thor, Doctor Strange, and the X-Men. They had also already reintroduced Namor the Sub-Mariner, one of Martin Goodman's most successful properties of the 1940s—an ambivalent character who combined innate nobility with hostility and arrogance, and who could play hero or villain on an as-needed basis.

At the time, Namor was the only character in the rapidly expanding Marvel Universe to have first emerged during the initial wave of 1940s comic book super heroes. (The Human Torch of the Fantastic Four shared his name and power-set with another 1940s hero, but he was otherwise entirely different: a literally "hot-headed" teenager rather than an android.) As such, Namor was a direct link connecting the Timely super hero comic books of the past with the Marvel Comics of the present. It therefore must have appealed to Lee and Kirby's sense of history to make Namor the unwitting agent of Captain America's revival in *The Avengers* #4 (March 1964). As can be seen in the short excerpt on the following pages, while traveling in the frozen North looking, Namor discovers a "petrified figure" within a block of ice—an object of veneration among the indigenous population. Namor reacts with rage, hurling the frozen figure into the ocean and then terrorizing the locals, for reasons that are marked as unclear even to Namor himself. ("Is this all my strength is good for?" he wonders, even as he lashes out.)

It's tempting to imagine that Lee and Kirby had slightly different interpretations of Namor's motivation in this moment. If we temporarily ignore the captions and read the images alone, we might note that Kirby depicts Namor entering the scene in the first panel with a regal, declarative bearing—as if to say, "Why worship an idol when you can worship me?" His hurling away of the frozen figure and subsequent display of destructive power could then be read as expressions of his wounded narcissism, entitlement, and hostility (all consistent with his character). However, Lee's dialogue and captions emphasize Namor's inner "turmoil"—even feelings of "shame" in the midst of his anger. But whatever forces drive the Sub-Mariner's actions, the important consequence is that the frozen figure ends up floating into warmer waters, where it is discovered, now free of ice, by the Avengers. (This is, of course, a credulity-stretching coincidence—although perhaps not so much of a reach as all that in the context of established comic book genre conventions of the period.) The Avengers recognize the costume the figure is wearing, and then, before their eyes, he returns to life—though not, at first, to the present. His first words are a twenty-year-old warning to his lost companion, Bucky. Thus, the scene captures in miniature the psychological drama that will mark the character for decades to come—the tension between the demands of the present and the unhealed wounds of the past.

The final tier of panels on page 5 displays Kirby's mastery of characterization through gesture and posture, as Steve Rogers comes to himself, dons his mask and shield, and then stands to attention before the gaze of the astonished Avengers. Decades later, this economical sequence remains poignant and powerful; still and always the brave soldier, Cap stands alone, as if reporting for duty once again, mere minutes after awakening from his decades-long sleep.

THE AVENGERS #4,

MARCH 1964

(EXCERPT)

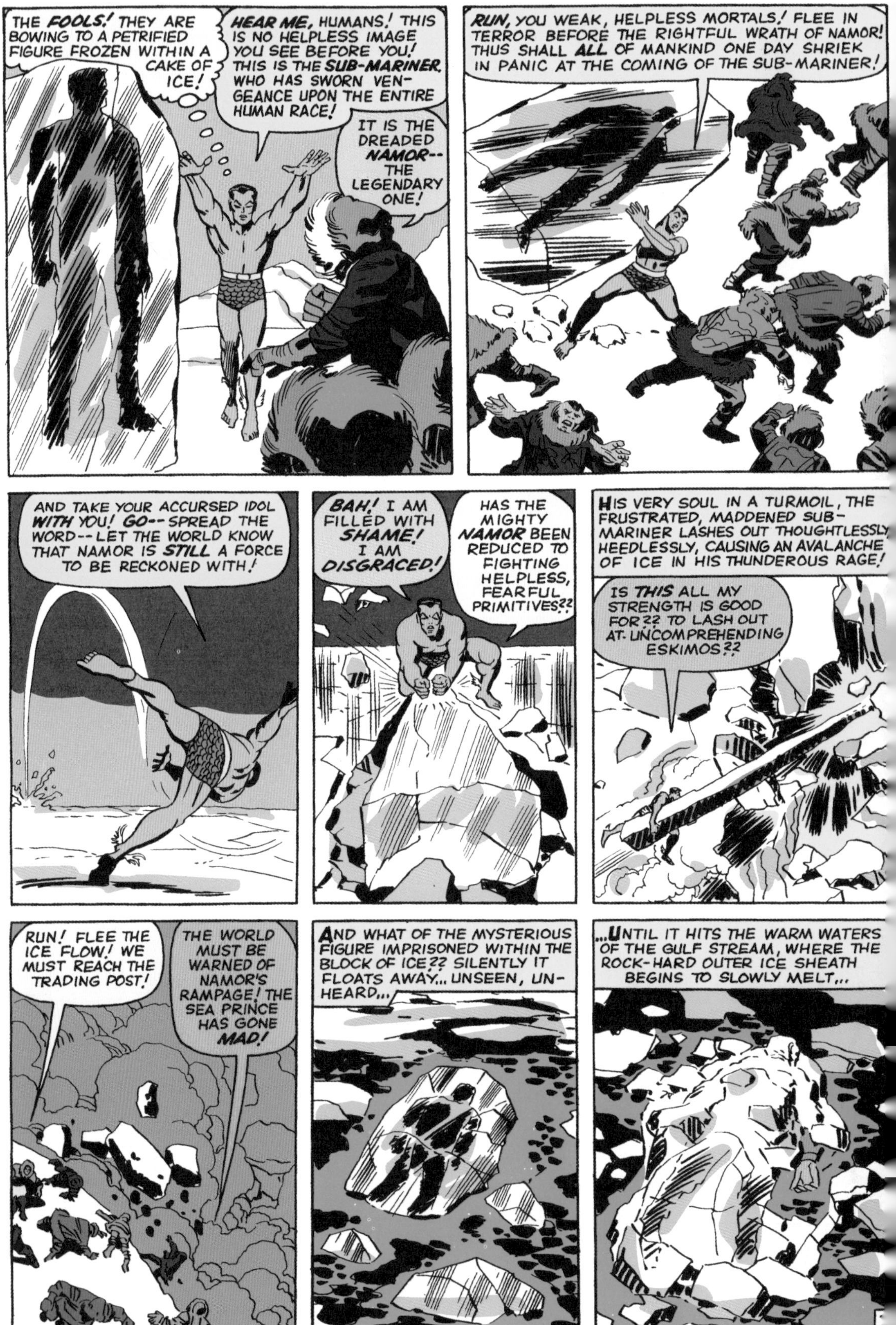
THE FOOLS! THEY ARE BOWING TO A PETRIFIED FIGURE FROZEN WITHIN A CAKE OF ICE!
HEAR ME, HUMANS! THIS IS NO HELPLESS IMAGE YOU SEE BEFORE YOU! THIS IS THE SUB-MARINER, WHO HAS SWORN VENGEANCE UPON THE ENTIRE HUMAN RACE!
IT IS THE DREADED NAMOR-- THE LEGENDARY ONE!
RUN, YOU WEAK, HELPLESS MORTALS! FLEE IN TERROR BEFORE THE RIGHTFUL WRATH OF NAMOR! THUS SHALL ALL OF MANKIND ONE DAY SHRIEK IN PANIC AT THE COMING OF THE SUB-MARINER!
AND TAKE YOUR ACCURSED IDOL WITH YOU! GO-- SPREAD THE WORD-- LET THE WORLD KNOW THAT NAMOR IS STILL A FORCE TO BE RECKONED WITH!
BAH! I AM FILLED WITH SHAME! I AM DISGRACED!
HAS THE MIGHTY NAMOR BEEN REDUCED TO FIGHTING HELPLESS, FEARFUL PRIMITIVES??
HIS VERY SOUL IN A TURMOIL, THE FRUSTRATED, MADDENED SUB-MARINER LASHES OUT THOUGHTLESSLY, HEEDLESSLY, CAUSING AN AVALANCHE OF ICE IN HIS THUNDEROUS RAGE!
IS THIS ALL MY STRENGTH IS GOOD FOR?? TO LASH OUT AT UNCOMPREHENDING ESKIMOS??
RUN! FLEE THE ICE FLOW! WE MUST REACH THE TRADING POST!
THE WORLD MUST BE WARNED OF NAMOR'S RAMPAGE! THE SEA PRINCE HAS GONE MAD!
AND WHAT OF THE MYSTERIOUS FIGURE IMPRISONED WITHIN THE BLOCK OF ICE?? SILENTLY IT FLOATS AWAY... UNSEEN, UNHEARD...
...UNTIL IT HITS THE WARM WATERS OF THE GULF STREAM, WHERE THE ROCK-HARD OUTER ICE SHEATH BEGINS TO SLOWLY MELT...

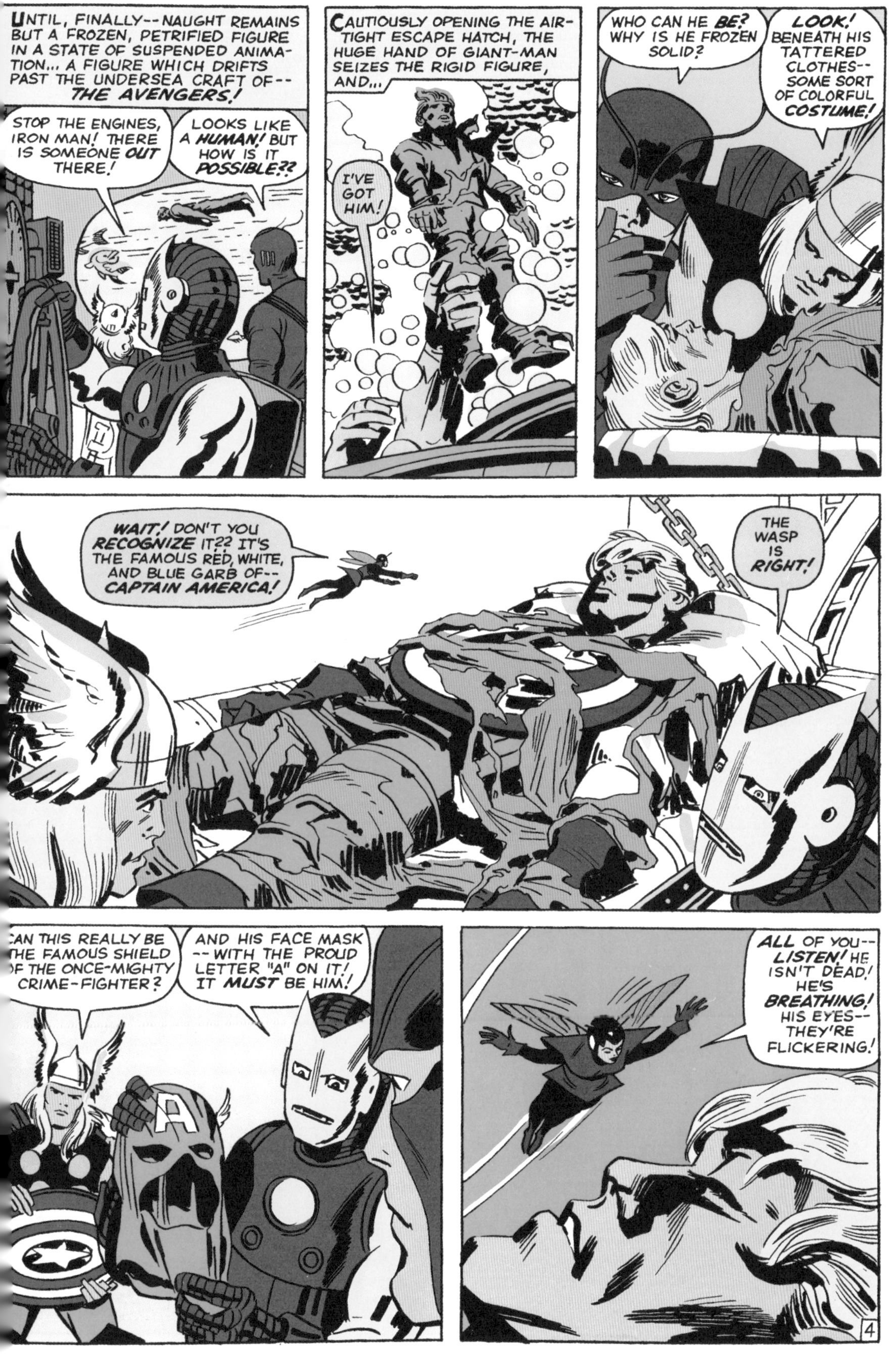
UNTIL, FINALLY--NAUGHT REMAINS BUT A FROZEN, PETRIFIED FIGURE IN A STATE OF SUSPENDED ANIMATION... A FIGURE WHICH DRIFTS PAST THE UNDERSEA CRAFT OF-- THE AVENGERS!
STOP THE ENGINES, IRON MAN! THERE IS SOMEONE OUT THERE!
LOOKS LIKE A HUMAN! BUT HOW IS IT POSSIBLE??
CAUTIOUSLY OPENING THE AIR-TIGHT ESCAPE HATCH, THE HUGE HAND OF GIANT-MAN SEIZES THE RIGID FIGURE, AND...
I'VE GOT HIM!
WHO CAN HE BE? WHY IS HE FROZEN SOLID?
LOOK! BENEATH HIS TATTERED CLOTHES-- SOME SORT OF COLORFUL COSTUME!
WAIT! DON'T YOU RECOGNIZE IT?? IT'S THE FAMOUS RED, WHITE, AND BLUE GARB OF-- CAPTAIN AMERICA!
THE WASP IS RIGHT!
CAN THIS REALLY BE THE FAMOUS SHIELD OF THE ONCE-MIGHTY CRIME-FIGHTER?
AND HIS FACE MASK --WITH THE PROUD LETTER "A" ON IT! IT MUST BE HIM!
ALL OF YOU-- LISTEN! HE ISN'T DEAD! HE'S BREATHING! HIS EYES-- THEY'RE FLICKERING!
4

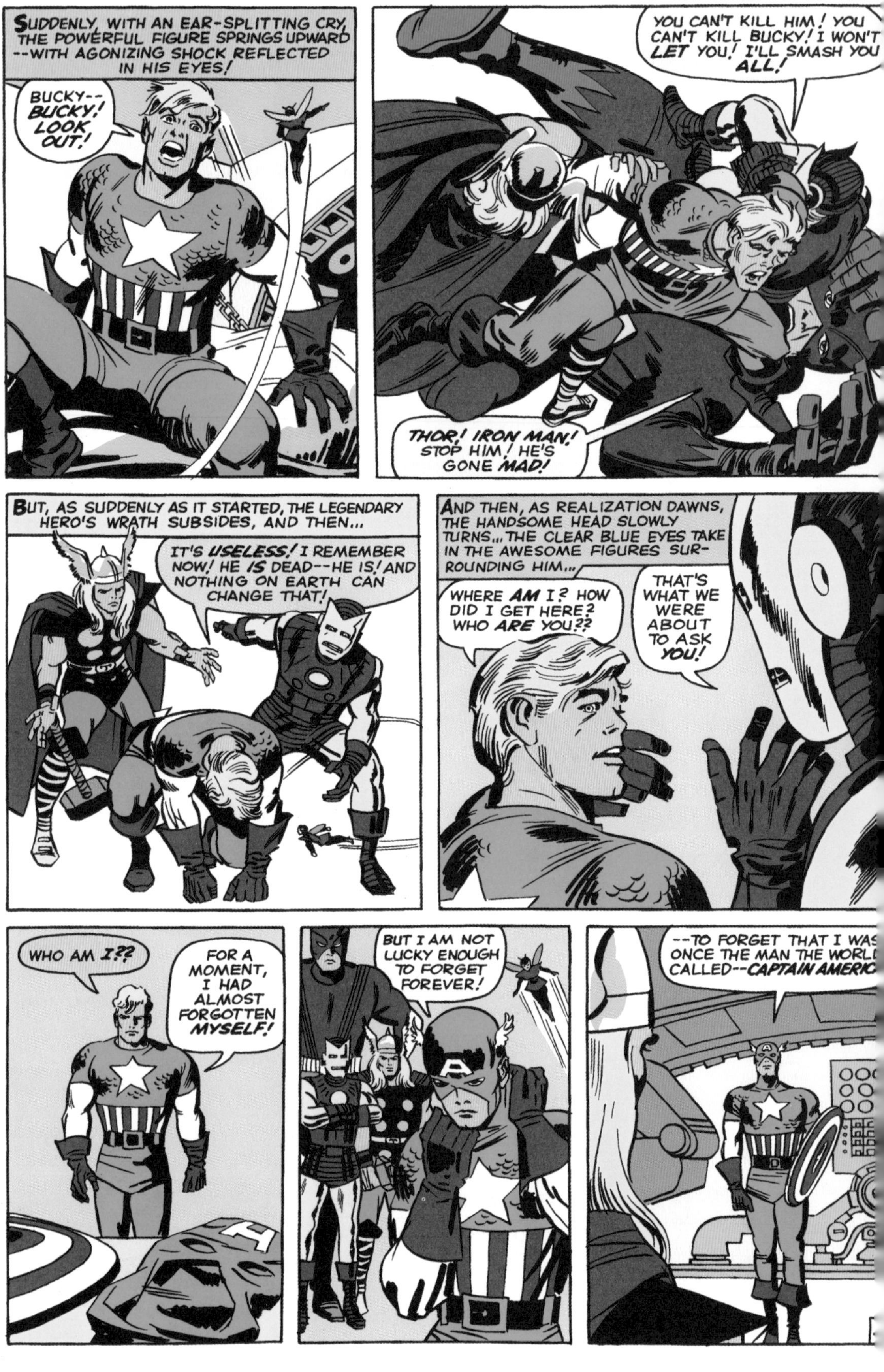
SUDDENLY, WITH AN EAR-SPLITTING CRY, THE POWERFUL FIGURE SPRINGS UPWARD --WITH AGONIZING SHOCK REFLECTED IN HIS EYES!
BUCKY-- BUCKY! LOOK OUT!
YOU CAN'T KILL HIM! YOU CAN'T KILL BUCKY! I WON'T LET YOU! I'LL SMASH YOU ALL!
THOR! IRON MAN! STOP HIM! HE'S GONE MAD!
BUT, AS SUDDENLY AS IT STARTED, THE LEGENDARY HERO'S WRATH SUBSIDES, AND THEN...
IT'S USELESS! I REMEMBER NOW! HE IS DEAD--HE IS! AND NOTHING ON EARTH CAN CHANGE THAT!
AND THEN, AS REALIZATION DAWNS, THE HANDSOME HEAD SLOWLY TURNS... THE CLEAR BLUE EYES TAKE IN THE AWESOME FIGURES SURROUNDING HIM...
WHERE AM I? HOW DID I GET HERE? WHO ARE YOU??
THAT'S WHAT WE WERE ABOUT TO ASK YOU!
WHO AM I??
FOR A MOMENT, I HAD ALMOST FORGOTTEN MYSELF!
BUT I AM NOT LUCKY ENOUGH TO FORGET FOREVER!
--TO FORGET THAT I WAS ONCE THE MAN THE WORL CALLED--CAPTAIN AMERIC

"AFTERWORD" BY JIM STERANKO

Jim Steranko spent a portion of his teens and early twenties working as a stage magician, and his later work as an artist for Marvel reflected some of that theatrical flamboyance. He published his first penciled stories with Harvey Comics in 1966, moving to Marvel shortly afterward to take over the Nick Fury strip from Jack Kirby. Steranko rapidly evolved as an artist, combining the spectacle and bombast of Jack Kirby with the narrative techniques of Bernie Krigstein (best known for his work at EC Comics in the 1950s) and adding new design elements derived from contemporary advertising and music culture, such as the psychedelic rock posters of the period. Steranko followed his acclaimed run on Fury with very brief stints on the X-Men and Captain America, but would largely leave comics behind in the 1970s to pursue work as a cover painter for genre paperbacks. Steranko's total comic book output is therefore quite slender, but the impact of his work was immediate and immense. Today his legacy is less a matter of direct stylistic influence—though that can certainly be seen in the 1970s work of artists such as Billy Graham and Paul Gulacy—and more a function of his willingness to look beyond the world of comics for effects and techniques, thereby expanding the visual horizons of the super hero genre.

This text first appeared in Marvel's collectible hardcover *Captain America Omnibus, Volume One* (2011). It provides a rare insight into a comic book artist's process, revealing a deep investment in the representation of symbolic action through repeated motifs and visual metaphor.

A F T E R W O R D
B Y   J I M   S T E R A N K O

To the youth of 1941, two wars were being fought simultaneously: one that had taken their fathers and brothers across the ocean, and the other, in the pages of their comicbooks. One spoke their language and helped clarify the rapacity of the other.

They knew the Aryan bloodtide had terrorized Austria, Czechoslovakia, Poland, Norway, Denmark, France, Romania, Hungary, Russia, and England, and that Hitler had ordered the annihilation of the Jews. The USA had allied with France and England against the invading Axis of Germany, Italy, and Japan, both sides mobilizing their forces for warfare like none other in human history.

Against the backdrop of world conflict, a brace of young Manhattan artists saw the war effort as a catalyst for a new kind of hero, one who would take America's red, white, and blue banner into battle against the bloody fascist regime to score victory for the Yanks. Jack Kirby and Joe Simon pitched the concept to publisher Martin Goodman, who immediately recognized its potential and sanctioned a solo book for the untested super-patriot.

All three, of course, were searching for the Holy Grail of Comicbooks: a character to compete with Superman and Batman. So, a year before President FDR officially declared war, three energetic Jews armed with 42nd Street moxie launched their personal crusade against the Nazi juggernaut. The first issue's incendiary cover dramatized the rationale for their hero's existence: he was the mythic materialization of the nationalistic ideal: the fighting Spirit of America!

Unlike other characters that were here because their rocket landed on Earth or they were hit by a lightning bolt, the Sentinel of Liberty was spawned from raw newsreel footage and real front-page headlines— and he gave American kids their own reasons to relate to the conflagration of WW2. Soon, the book's circulation matched, perhaps eclipsed that of any other comics of the period.

In the first volume of **THE HISTORY OF COMICS**, I explored the phenomena: "Those who were critical of his two-dimensional character failed to grasp the true implication of his being. Steve Rogers never existed, except perhaps as an abstract device for the convenience of storytelling. Captain America was not the embodiment of human characteristics, but *a pure idea*. He was not a man, but all men; not a being, but a cumulative entity that symbolized the inner reality of man. He was the American Truth."

When the war ended in 1945, however, the concept of super-patriotism became an anachronism—and sales began to diminish. Sentimentality kept the series alive as Cap swapped his khakis for civilian garb— and Steve Rogers became a teacher at Lee High School. By late 1949, Cap had vanished, an artifact of an era past. The Heroic Age was over. *Sic transit gloria mundi.*

Captain America was gone, but not forgotten during the next fifteen years, except for a brief, undistinguished 1954 revival that pitted him against the metaphysics of Communism. It was not until a decade later that he was inexorably revived in **AVENGERS** 4. Lee and Kirby were also back, and their collaboration on Cap capers in forty issues of **TALES OF SUSPENSE** were experiments which mixed and matched themes, co-stars, and villains, to find an adequate formula for the character in a modern, non-war environment.

Then, it was official! Issue 100 revealed Cap had been a human ice cube since WW2, and thrust him into a Three Musketeers gig with the Black Panther and Agent 13. We got the works: the enemy squad of superior numbers, the raving mastermind, and the invincible juggernaut—all mandatory elements in the new Captain America equation, a mix of WW2 kibbles with contemporary bits.

Subsequent issues repeated it with kaleidoscopic variations, which, while honorable, never quite hit the conceptual bull's-eye. For all his patriotic power, Captain America was a hero *without a cause,* even though the tales never let us forget his legend: repeating the Bucky Barnes crisis, the Red Skull revivals, and origin story reboots.

There were, however, other problems. Cap had been stripped of his magic. When I took over the series with issue 110, the formula that had made him a cultural icon had been deconstructed. I opted to reestablish it.

I had just abandoned **S.H.I.E.L.D.** because Stan slipped a stray issue into my long-running series, thinking it would relieve some deadline pressure (although I was never late with any book). I felt it destroyed my carefully-established continuity. So, when he asked where I'd like to be, I told him, and he made my wish come true.

The first order of business was reinstating Cap's secret identity because, for no apparent reason, Marvel had unmasked him in issues 105-107, alerting the world that he was something less than the quintessential symbol of patriotism, that he was only a man. The universal mystique once surrounding him—providing a reason to wear the cowl—was corrupted, thrusting him into an even shallower position.

The threadbare aspect of *Bucky guilt* also needed resolution. So, I planned a three-issue origin to establish a contemporary sidekick for Cap in a contemporary world. The Nazi theme was another cliché that desperately needed updating, and I recruited Hydra's global terrorists, which I'd groomed in **S.H.I.E.L.D.** Nazis were yesterday's villains. Hydra was about tomorrow!

I had transformed **S.H.I.E.L.D.** through massive alterations and storytelling innovations, but could I make lightning strike twice? I needed a provocative, powerhouse concept around which to rebuild the series iconic architecture—and found it, an idea that would send a tremor through the comics' world: *The Death of Captain America!*

I'd essentially learned to draw from the comics, but my narrative approach derived from film. The *Zap Art* style I'd created for Nick Fury was inappropriate for comics' uberpatriot. He required an approach more expressive and sophisticated, more worthy of his historic eminence.

Most artists use their standard, one-size-fits-all approach on every assignment, but I had another idea for Captain America: *to construct the series using the same techniques that Hollywood directors used for their films*: tight answering shots, integrated pan and tracking sequences, cinematic lighting, and reaction inserts. I felt Cap should have his own unique look in the Marvel Universe—and here's how I did it:

Page One of issue 110 opens with an evocative *Cinematic Entrance,* a solitary figure moving through a city of shadows and fog, coming to rest before a poster of his alter ego, a metaphor that visually dramatizes *his inner conflict,* one that pits the patriotic colossus against his human persona—and demands to know which one is *more* real: the man in the mask *or the man under it!* His state of mind is underscored symbolically by the urban decay surrounding him.

Page Two continues the confrontation in a riveting, symmetrical shot, the eyes of one almost hypnotically holding the other in thrall: the macrocosm and the microcosm! A poetic beat, then the introspection shifts with a progressive zoom to a close-up of the man's eye, wide with anxiety, to an Objective Shot of what he is witnessing–a second entrance! Steve Rogers now becomes the subordinate figure, dominated by the brute force of the menacing, green hands.

Page Three's establishment shot pulls back to reveal the Hulk (withholding facial information to *increase* suspense). Three insert panels move the story ahead to set up the explosive third entrance (tilt shot suggesting a violent invasion) of Captain America. (The three-page sequence is carefully choreographed to create a series of rising and falling dramatic actions that build tension.)

Page Four: Shock close-up of the Hulk (on turning the page) is answered by a Subjective Shot (Hulk's viewpoint) of Army ordnance and personnel. The vertical panel below suggests a perilous height (drawing reader's eye upward); the cannon shot blasts downward (drawing reader's eye with it). Hulk caroms across panel (shifting the reader's eye to next page). Note how the panel compositions keep moving the eye smoothly from one to another, enhancing the narrative thrust of the story.

Page Five cuts to another character (fourth entrance) and the reason the sequence was created: to introduce Rick Jones into the plot. Because in the Western world we read left to right, my panel designs almost always move in a left-to-right direction, increasing the *velocity of the pacing.* I also use graphic devices to pull the eye to the tier below, such as the angle of the fire escape and the vertical window frame in the top tier, and cropping Cap's foot in the middle tier. The large, angled head in the bottom tier also helps readers move smoothly to that area. Notice how I returned to the hand motif to bring the Hulk back into the action.

Page Six begins the interplay between the three characters. Note how sparingly the *Subjective Shot* (a character's viewpoint) occurs—primarily panel four, as the Hulk would see it (hands again). (Subjective shots are like punctuation and should be used only to make a special point. Non-character views are called *Objective Shots*, which comprise most sequences.)

Page Seven's opening panel features an interesting tri-level effect, focusing from Cap to Rick to the Hulk. The shot creates the illusion of *deep space,* and is followed by more insert panels, repeating the theme of the eyes in close-up. The repetition of themes and narrative techniques helps unify stories. For example, three panels in the center tier repeat the *Zoom Effect* from page two, except in reverse. Note that the shots on facing pages are never monotonous or confusing. None, however, are so offbeat that they have a jarring quality, but just flow naturally from one action to another. The page ends with a jolt, making readers turn the page—which is basic Storytelling 101.

Page Eight climaxes the sequence with the Hulk literally leaping out of the panel. (Note how the wide horizontal gutter serves two purposes: ending the scene and keeping the Hulk from touching the next, visually separating Rick from the green behemoth, a *dramatic point* underscored in Rogers' dialogue in the final panel.)

Page Nine begins with a *Cinematic Pan* across a stationary background (like a full-panel establishing shot) as the protagonist moves through it in four equal beats. I revealed Cap's emotional isolation visually by reducing his size (top tier), showing him in silhouette (center), and finally dwarfing him against the negative space of the cityscape—and smaller still in the next panel. The final shot is another page-turning hook.

Page Ten repeats the insert-panel effect. Despite its dense emotional content, the page has an uncluttered quality, achieved by opening the bottom of the establishing shot and using no background color in the final two panels. I also repeated the "hands" motif again.

Page Eleven gets busier with information as the new team is formed (a kind of origin for Rick Jones, with both characters masked and overlapping to visually express their unity). The four stationary panels hold cinematically on the duo as they provide the movement, while the camera then drops below street level into the underground storm drain (another deep-space composition to create a hush of page-turning suspense).

That silence is detonated on Page Twelve-Thirteen, which affirms an aspect of my Narrative Philosophy: *always expect the unexpected!* The scene—and the set-up before it—is a classic example of falling and rising action, a dramatic device as old as Greek tragedy and as effective in comics as it is in music, theatre, literary works, and film.

Page Fourteen continues the battle with panel compositions that move the reader's eye around the page with storytelling logic. Notice how the close-up in the second panel relieves the action for a beat—and simultaneously sets up the next shot, a narrative device used six times throughout the story. The bottom tier exploited a new innovation I call a *Cutout Insert,* which was a solution for the presentation of *two actions happening simultaneously.*

Page Fifteen extends the action. Note how little of the background is depicted during the entire fight sequence; I was counting on the previous double-page to continue informing the reader where the scene takes place.

Page Sixteen begins with a variation of the *Cutout Insert,* which is used again three pages later. The hands theme reoccurs heavily on this and the following page. (FYI: one of my girlfriends was the model for Madame Hydra.)

Page Seventeen features larger panels, which increases the story's pace and the impact of the content. I placed an emphasis on Cap's shield because it's his only weapon and should be utilized as often as possible.

Page Eighteen cuts away from the hero to give Rick some story time in a sequence told completely through imagery, as in a *silent movie*—and paid off with a revealing low-angle shot. The scene not only shows Rick's competence, but sets up the next plot development—with a twist. The future is grimly foreshadowed with the line: "Captain America is dead!"

Page Nineteen is a wave of compressed information (although the twelve balloons Stan shoehorned into the top tier may have been a slight matter of overkill), all stated cleanly, without confusion. The Comics Code changed Madame Hydra's whip to a rope, but at least they let her keep the black-leather catsuit. The page ends with a hook.

Page Twenty resolves the action with a lightning, two-panel climax and wraps up loose ends with an insert and a long shot. (Note a repeat of my wide-gutter device to indicate the scene is over.) However, to bookend the story's opening, I tagged on a poetic coda, tilting the shot to foreshadow unsettling times to come—and soon, if you believe the ironic message of the street sign the pair just passed. Can you almost hear the end-title theme as the scene fades to black?

The same cinematic techniques and devices were used for the complete three-part *Death of Captain America.* So, for brevity, I'll just cover the highlights and innovations of the other issues here.

An experimental page kicks off the next chapter, with twelve panels happening almost simultaneously (it's incidental in what order they are read) because I wanted to *surround the reader* with the flash of neon, the sound of gunshots, and the clutter of gaudy arcade signage. (FYI, that's the switchblade—it opened to 13"—I purchased as a kid at just such a 42nd Street arcade.) The story's title appears on a fortune-teller's card from Steve Rogers' viewpoint. Every panel is subjective because I wanted the reader to experience what he sees, hears, and feels.

The *Triple-Stacked Inserts* on Page Four were an interesting touch (like a downward pan that was a new narrative device for comics) that should have had balloons in equal beats; instead of two balloons in the first insert and none in the second, destroying the aspect of uniform eye movement.

Stan also overruled my concept for Page Five. It was created to read *clockwise,* which meant the bottom tier would read right to left, instead of left-to-right. Stan felt it would confuse readers, and rewrote the bottom tier to be read conventionally, which creates confusion regarding the victim's hands being free, then bound for no reason.

Page Seven has two attempts to portray continuous time, rather than time chopped into panels. The first simply overlaps images, but cinematically visualizes the emotional close-up in deep shadow to reveal a change in the character, one that evinces the past (here shown in B&W tone to distinguish it from reality, somewhat similar to the handling of the B&W movie-screen image on the previous page).

The *Strobe Effect* at the bottom was adapted from a **S.H.I.E.L.D.** innovation and fits well here by transforming a common action into an intriguing visual passage that continues to the following page with a variation, one that might qualify cinematically as a *Double Exposure.* (As a high-school athlete, the flying rings and parallel bars were my specialty and served as an inspiration for the scene.) Note the two similar hand movements in subsequent panels; in filmic terms the device is called a *Lightning Match Cut.* The final panel is another pass at portraying time simultaneously.

The two-page surreal dream sequence that follows was influenced by Alfred Hitchcock's **SPELLBOUND,** a film that had a profound impact on me as a kid. I felt that such fine-art movements such as expressionism, surrealism, and op-art would translate well into the comicbook medium, and employed them numerous times in my Marvel work.

A comment on the double-page spread: I was feeling confident about my vision of Cap by this point (although the first issue was not yet published) and when I hit this double, decided to make the character a living powerhouse, like not even Kirby had done previously. How? By layering muscle atop muscle—realistic, yet of ultrahuman proportions. A new dimension of super heroics was established, not just for Cap, but the entire field. Months later, the mail drawer was choked with envelopes—confirmation that the MMM (major muscle mass) Theory would make waves for generations to come.

The mini-series peaked in *The Strange Death of Captain America* with an on-site news broadcast summing up the action and the TV screen-panels segueing smoothly into Hydra headquarters, the fire-and-water ordeal of the deadly dominatrix, and her self-loathing, mirror-shattering rant.

I used the same epic double-page device in all three issues, but making certain they fell at exactly the right place was no accident in plotting. (The third issue's centerspread, was penciled, inked, lettered, and colored by me, which was another Marvel first.)

One of my favorite panels symbolically shows Rick Jones psychologically ensnared *within the eyehole* of his discarded mask (you can take the mask away from the boy, but not the boy away from the mask). A few others include the stained-glass-window page design, the A (for America) combat page, and the climax showing Cap exiting the cemetery, a visual metaphor for him leaving his "death" behind and starting a new life.

A new chapter in his saga was established. Cap's identity was a secret again. He had a bona fide sidekick and a modern, non-Nazi cause to battle. My mission was completed.

It was a defining moment in my career because Captain America was—and always will be—my favorite comicbook character. His colors, his stars and stripes, his wings (symbolic of the American eagle) had always inspired a patriotic celebration within my childhood spirit and extended into my adult life. For a moment in eternity, I became Captain America—and it doesn't get any better than that.

2010

Suggestions for Further Reading

CAPTAIN AMERICA COLLECTIONS

There are literally dozens of Captain America collections drawing upon decades of material—this is a mere sample of potential highlights for readers who might want to read more.

Joe Simon, Jack Kirby, et al., *Golden Age Captain America Omnibus, Volume 1*, 2014
    Collects the first twelve issues of the 1941 series in a deluxe hardcover.

Stan Lee, John Romita Sr., et al., *Marvel Masterworks: Atlas Era Heroes, Volume 2*, 2008
    This anthology includes all of Captain America's solo comics from 1950s, alongside similar anti-communist-themed stories featuring the Sub-Mariner and the original Human Torch.

Stan Lee, Jack Kirby, et al., *Penguin Classics Marvel Collection: The Avengers*, 2021
    Includes Cap's first adventures with the Avengers following his successful revival in 1964 as a hero-out-of-time.

Steve Englehart, Sal Buscema, et al., *Captain America and the Falcon: Secret Empire*, 2011
    Cap responds to the national scandal of Watergate and Nixon's abuse of power in this collection of material from the 1970s.

Mark Gruenwald et al., *Captain America: The Captain*, 2011
In the 1980s, Mark Gruenwald embarked on a lengthy exploration of Cap's struggle to represent the ideals of an increasingly divided nation—culminating in this narrative in which Steve Rogers is replaced by John Walker.

Robert Morales and Kyle Baker, *Truth: Red, White & Black*, 2004
One of the most powerful explorations of racial injustice ever published in a mainstream super hero title, this remarkable work explores the history behind the experiments that led to Captain America's creation.

Mark Millar and Bryan Hitch, *The Ultimates: Ultimate Collection*, 2010
The origin story of the Avengers, reimagined for the twenty-first century; this series had a significant shaping influence on the modern Marvel Cinematic Universe (MCU).

Ed Brubaker, Steve Epting, et al., *Captain America, Volume 1: Winter Soldier Ultimate Collection*, 2010
Starting in 2004, Ed Brubaker's lengthy run on Captain America remains the most important twenty-first-century take on character. Particularly notable for the return of Bucky as the "Winter Soldier."

Mark Waid and Jorge Molina, *Captain America: Man Out of Time*, 2011
A well-written update of the story of Cap's return—now after almost a half century spent in suspended animation.

Nick Spencer, Daniel Acuña, et al., *Captain America: Sam Wilson—The Complete Collection, Volumes One and Two*, 2021
Sam Wilson takes over the rank and shield from Steve Rogers in a politically intelligent and allegorically rich contemporary series.

RESOURCES FOR STUDENTS AND SCHOLARS

Barbara Brownie and Danny Graydon, *The Superhero Costume: Identity and Disguise in Fact and Fiction*, 2016
  A succinct but theoretically astute account of the social and symbolic significance of super hero costume design.

Brannon Costello, "Southern Super-Patriots and United States Nationalism: Race, Region, and Nation in *Captain America*," in Brannon Costello and Qiana J. Whitted (eds.), *Comics and the U.S. South*, 2012, pp. 62–87
  An important analysis of the John Walker storyline from Mark Gruenwald's 1980s *Captain America* run.

Jason Dittmer, *Captain America and the Nationalist Superhero*, 2013
  A jargon-heavy but often thoughtful sociological reading of Captain America as a nationalist symbol.

Danny Fingeroth, *A Marvelous Life: The Amazing Story of Stan Lee*, 2019
  An evenhanded narrative of Lee's life and career.

Conseula Francis, "American Truths: Blackness and the American Superhero," in Frances Gateward and John Jennings (eds.), *The Blacker the Ink: Constructions of Black Identity in Comics and Sequential Art*, 2015, pp. 137–51
  A careful reading of Morales and Baker's *Truth: Red, White & Black*.

Ramzi Fawaz, *The New Mutants: Superheroes and the Radical Imagination of American Comics*, 2016
  Contains (among many interesting chapters) several valuable pages of analysis on Cap in the early 1970s.

Charles Hatfield and Ben Saunders, *Comic Book Apocalypse: The Graphic Worlds of Jack Kirby*, 2015
  Includes several insightful essays on Kirby, including a reading of

his work on Captain America through the lens of his personal wartime experiences, by the novelist Glen David Gold.

Sean Howe, *Marvel Comics: The Untold Story*, 2012
   A detailed history of the company.

Shawna Kidman, *Comic Books Incorporated: How the Business of Comics Became the Business of Hollywood*, 2019
   Essential reading for anyone hoping to understand the larger media context of Marvel's growth.

Christopher Murray, *Champions of the Oppressed: Superhero Comics, Popular Culture, and Propaganda in America During World War II*, 2011
   A detailed historicist analysis of World War II–era super heroes, including Captain America.

Joe Simon and Jim Simon, *The Comic Book Makers*, 2003
   An important and informative memoir by the co-creator of Captain America.

J. Richard Stevens, *Captain America, Masculinity, and Violence: The Evolution of a National Icon*, 2018
   A well-written and thoroughly researched survey; essential reading for any serious Cap scholar.

Robert G. Weiner (ed.), *Captain America and the Struggle of the Superhero*, 2009
   A wide-ranging collection of essays, with an excellent preface by John Shelton Lawrence.

Matt Yockey (ed.), *Make Ours Marvel: Media Convergence and a Comics Universe*, 2017
   A state-of-the-art academic collection on a variety of Marvel-related topics.

Notes

SERIES INTRODUCTION

1. Variations on this phrase greet the reader at the head of several Superman stories in the late 1930s. See Jerry Siegel, ed., *The Superman Chronicles, Volume 1* (DC Comics, 2006).
2. Mike Benton, *Superhero Comics of the Golden Age: The Illustrated History* (Taylor, 1992), 65.
3. See Jean-Paul Gabilliet, *Of Comics and Men: A Cultural History of American Comics*, trans. Bart Beaty and Nick Nguyen (University Press of Mississippi, 2010), pages 3–28 for the economic history of the early American comic book industry.
4. Ian Gordon, *Comic Books and Consumer Culture, 1890–1945* (Smithsonian Institution Press, 1998), 135–51.
5. Gabilliet, 34.
6. See Benton, 57–62. It should be noted that the Green Arrow and Aquaman also clung to life as backup features, and that Superman still enjoyed respectable sales—boosted by the success of *The Adventures of Superman* television show. Plastic Man was canceled, however, when Quality Comics folded in 1956.
7. *Mad*—one of the most original and influential comic books of the 1950s—featured an acclaimed Superman parody by Harvey Kurtzman and Wallace Wood entitled "Superduperman" in #4 (1953); it was followed by "Bat Boy and Rubin" in *Mad* #8 (1953) and "Woman Wonder" in *Mad* #10 (1954).
8. For a detailed account of these failed revivals, see Bill Schelly, *American Comic Book Chronicles: The 1950s* (TwoMorrows, 2013), 95–102. For a cultural history of the moral panic over comics, see David Hadju, *The Ten-Cent Plague: The Great Comic-Book Scare and How It Changed America* (Farrar, Straus and Giroux, 2008).
9. The company also introduced the Martian Manhunter as a backup strip in the pages of *Detective Comics* in 1955. Although notable as DC's first

new super-powered character in years, the Manhunter made no discernible difference to sales, and his impact upon fandom—and the larger super hero genre—does not compare with that of the Flash's revival.

10. In the 1940s, Goodman's comic book company was generally known as Timely. Betweeen 1951 and 1957, it was called Atlas. It had no single name between 1958 and 1961.

11. Goodman was one of the publishers who attempted to revive the genre in 1954, but he swiftly abandoned super heroes again when sales proved weak.

12. See *Penguin Classics Marvel Collection: The Fantastic Four* for a detailed discussion of Lee and Kirby's groundbreaking work on this series.

13. This achievement is even more impressive if we consider that Lee, Lieber, and Kirby also launched a Western title—The Rawhide Kid, in August 1960, which they continued to work on—as well as on a solo Human Torch strip for the pages of Strange Tales. In addition, Lee was also continuously working on Marvel's girl-oriented books, such as Millie the Model (with artist Stan Goldberg) and Patsy and Hedy (with artist Al Hartley). Although inevitably overshadowed today by Marvel's super heroes, the company continued to produce numerous titles in other genres under Lee's general editorship during these early years.

14. This phrase served as the headline for one of the first pieces of significant media coverage of the company—an article by Nat Freedland that appeared in the *New York Herald Tribune Sunday Magazine*, January 9, 1966.

15. Stan Lee, speaking at the 1975 San Diego Comic-Con, as cited in John Morrow, ed., *Kirby and Lee: Stuf' Said!: The Complex Genesis of the Marvel Universe, in Its Creators' Own Words* (TwoMorrows, 2018), 119–120. As Jean-Paul Gabilliet notes, Lee always spoke as if he "invented this method of work, but [Will] Eisner had already been practicing it in his studio at the end of the 1930s." See Gabilliet, 127.

16. For a brilliant discussion of authorship, ownership, and the comic book industry, see Shawna Kidman, *Comic Books Incorporated: How the Business of Comics Became the Business of Hollywood* (University of California Press, 2019), 91–135.

VOLUME INTRODUCTION

1. Among them we can number the African American Sam Wilson, the Latinx Roberta Mendez, and the biracial Danielle Cage—daughter of Jessica Jones and Luke Cage. Also noteworthy is Isaiah Bradley, the first African American to bear the shield, according to Robert Morales and

Kyle Baker in *Truth: Red, White & Black* (2003), one of the bravest treatments of racial injustice in the history of the super hero genre.

2. John Walker became Captain America for an extended run starting with issue #333 (September 1987); writer Mark Gruenwald used the character to explore the persistence of post–Civil War tensions between the US North and South. For an analysis of this era of the comic book, see Brannon Costello, "Southern Super-Patriots and United States Nationalism: Race, Region, and Nation in *Captain America*," in Brannon Costello and Qiana J. Whitted, eds., *Comics and the U.S. South* (University Press of Mississippi, 2012), 62–87. Sam Wilson's progressive values have been a feature of his character since the 1970s, when he was depicted as an inner-city social worker in his civilian identity; Wilson became Captain America in 2015 as part of a storyline by Nick Spencer and Daniel Acuña that explicitly addresses the question of whether Cap could (or should) be "above" politics.

3. *Captain America Comics* #1 bears a cover date of March 1941. During this period, however, cover dates functioned as guides for retailers as to when to return unsold books. Since publishers wanted their titles available as long as possible, these dates were standardly set about three months ahead, meaning that *Captain America Comics* #1 would have been on the stands by December 1940—so Simon and Kirby must have first come up with the concept in the late fall of that same year.

4. Joe Simon and Jim Simon, *The Comic Book Makers* (Vanguard, 2003), 42.

5. The Shield wore a star-spangled costume with a heraldic shield emblem on his chest; apparently, MLJ publisher John Goldwater thought Captain America bore too much of a similarity to his property, and the design of Cap's shield was changed (from heraldic to a round shape) to placate him—although it soon became apparent that it was more serviceable as a Frisbee-like weapon that way. See Simon and Simon, *Comic Book Makers*, 52.

6. Prior to his appearance on the cover of *Captain America Comics* #1, Hitler had appeared inside only a handful of American comics—one being an early Simon and Kirby story from *Daring Mystery Comics* #6 (September 1940). Even here his identity is thinly disguised by the name "Hiller."

7. See Simon and Simon, *Comic Book Makers*, 45.

8. According to Simon, "Sales were close to the million mark, and that was monthly," making *Captain America Comics* one of the biggest-selling titles in the business. See Simon, quoted in Les Daniels, *Marvel: Five Fabulous Decades of the World's Greatest Comics* (Abrams/Marvel, 1991), 37.

9. See Simon and Simon, *Comic Book Makers*, 40–47, and also Joe Simon's later memoir, *My Life in Comics* (Titan, 2011), 80–93, for a detailed account of Simon's working relationship with Kirby.

10. Simon and Simon, *Comic Book Makers*, 46.

11. Simon and Simon, *Comic Book Makers*, 46.

12. For more information on the possible reasons for the dispute, see Daniels, *Marvel*, 49, and also Simon and Simon, *Comic Book Makers*, 52–53.

13. At first Goodman assigned the role to his brother Abe, but within a few short weeks the job had fallen to Lee. See Danny Fingeroth, *A Marvelous Life: The Amazing Story of Stan Lee* (St. Martin's, 2019), 28.

14. J. Richard Stevens, *Captain America, Masculinity, and Violence: The Evolution of a National Icon* (Syracuse University Press, 2018), 59. Stevens's book-length study should be considered essential reading for anyone interested in learning more about the full range of Cap's comic book adventures.

15. The thinking behind this ill-fated relaunch is unknown, but it's likely that Goodman hoped to turn these properties into TV shows, in imitation of DC's Superman. Years later, Bill Everett, creator of the Sub-Mariner, said he was briefly consulted in 1954 about a Sub-Mariner TV show potentially starring Richard Egan. Obviously, these plans came to nothing, but the possibility would explain why the Sub-Mariner revival lasted a few months longer than Cap's. The relevant interview with Everett can be found in *Alter Ego* # 46 (March 2005), 5–35.

16. Roy Thomas and Jim Amash, *John Romita . . . and All That Jazz* (Two-Morrows, 2007), 70.

17. Bradford Wright, *Comic Book Nation: The Transformation of Youth Culture in America* (Johns Hopkins University Press, 2001), 123.

18. See Gabilliet, *Of Comics and Men*, 41–55, and Kidman, *Comic Books Incorporated*, 46–90, for detailed discussions of this period.

19. *Strange Tales* #114 (November 1963), 18.

20. William Burnside was first introduced as a retroactive explanation for the "Commie Smasher" era in *Captain America* #153 (September 1972) by writer Steve Englehart and artists Sal Buscema and Jim Mooney.

21. Stan Lee and Jack Kirby, *The Avengers* #4 (March 1964), 10.

22. See Ed Brubaker and Steve Epting, *Captain America* #1 (January 2005).

23. Lee and Kirby, *Avengers* #4, 11.

24. See Glen David Gold, "The Red Sheet," in Charles Hatfield and Ben Saunders, eds., *Comic Book Apocalypse: The Graphic Worlds of Jack Kirby* (IDW, 2015), for a thoughtful discussion of Cap's symptoms of PTSD and their relationship to Kirby's own traumatic war experiences.

25. For more on this topic, see Stevens, *Captain America, Masculinity, and Violence*, especially 88–97; for further meditations on the ways Captain America comics have reflected US national and foreign policy at different times, see Robert G. Weiner, ed., *Captain America and the Struggle of the Superhero* (McFarland, 2009), and Jason Dittmer, *Captain America and the Nationalist Superhero* (Temple University Press, 2013).

26. *Captain America* #114 (June 1969), by Lee, John Romita Sr., and Sal Buscema, opens with the hero wandering the streets of Manhattan wondering what to do with his life; the Falcon displaces Rick Jones's Bucky in *Captain America* #117 (September 1969), by Lee, Gene Colan, and Joe Sinnott.

27. Rodriquez initiated a debate about Cap's role as a patriotic symbol that persisted for six years in the letters page of the comic book (and that continues to reverberate in contemporary academic studies). For a brief but useful account of the "patriotism controversy," see Stevens, *Captain America, Masculinity, and Violence*, 92–94.

28. Interested readers should consult the "Suggestions for Further Reading" at the end of this volume for examples.

OLD FOES RETURN: *TALES OF SUSPENSE* #96–99, *CAPTAIN AMERICA* #100–109

1. See Ronin Ro, *Tales to Astonish: Jack Kirby, Stan Lee, and the American Comic Book Revolution* (Bloomsbury, 2004), 118–34 *et passim*.